A CONSUMPTION-SAVINGS MODEL AND ITS APPLICATIONS

CONTRIBUTIONS
TO
ECONOMIC ANALYSIS

79

Honorary Editor

J. TINBERGEN

Editors

D. W. JORGENSON

J. WAELBROECK

NORTH-HOLLAND PUBLISHING COMPANY – AMSTERDAM · LONDON

AMERICAN ELSEVIER PUBLISHING COMPANY, INC. – NEW YORK

A CONSUMPTION-SAVINGS MODEL AND ITS APPLICATIONS

W. H. SOMERMEYER and R. BANNINK

Econometric Institute,
Netherlands School of Economics,
Rotterdam

Catholic School
of Economics,
Tilburg

1973

NORTH-HOLLAND PUBLISHING COMPANY – AMSTERDAM · LONDON

AMERICAN ELSEVIER PUBLISHING COMPANY, INC. – NEW YORK

Library of Congress Catalog Card Number: 72-79734

ISBN North-Holland for this series 0 7204 3100 x
ISBN North-Holland for this volume 0 7204 3179 4
ISBN American Elsevier for this volume 0 444 10490 9

Publishers:

NORTH-HOLLAND PUBLISHING COMPANY – AMSTERDAM
NORTH-HOLLAND PUBLISHING COMPANY, LTD. – LONDON

Sole distributors for the U.S.A. and Canada:
AMERICAN ELSEVIER PUBLISHING COMPANY, INC.
52 VANDERBILT AVENUE, NEW YORK, N.Y. 10017

PRINTED IN GERMANY

INTRODUCTION TO THE SERIES

This series consists of a number of hitherto unpublished studies, which are introduced by the editors in the belief that they represent fresh contributions to economic science.

The term economic analysis as used in the title of the series has been adopted because it covers both the activities of the theoretical economist and the research worker.

Although the analytical methods used by the various contributors are not the same, they are nevertheless conditioned by the common origin of their studies, namely theoretical problems encountered in practical research. Since for this reason, business cycle research and national accounting, research work on behalf of economic policy, and problems of planning are the main sources of the subjects dealt with, they necessarily determine the manner of approach adopted by the authors. Their methods tend to be 'practical' in the sense of not being too far remote from application to actual economic conditions. In addition they are quantitative rather than qualitative.

It is the hope of the editors that the publication of these studies will help to stimulate the exchange of scientific information and to reinforce international cooperation in the field of economics.

THE EDITORS

CONTENTS

Chapter 3 Micro-theory of optimal allocation of consumption and savings over time based on an additive-separable utility function

Chapter 4 A micro-savings model based on an addi-log utility function

Chapter 5 Macro-savings theory

EMPIRICAL PART

Chapter 6 Application of the micro-savings function to survey data

ACKNOWLEDGEMENTS

Many people contributed to this book; only a few are mentioned here.

In particular, we wish to thank Dr. A.L. Hempenius of the Econometric Institute (Rotterdam) and Professor Dr. W. Krelle of the University of Bonn (Germany) for the valuable proposals they made at an earlier stage of the analysis. Dr. Hempenius first intimated that the way in which consumer demand theory was developed by Slutsky might as well be applied to savings theory. In his comments on a paper by the first author and Van de Rotte – essentially the present chapter 5 –, Professor Krelle suggested that the simple savings model presented therein might be generalized, by allowing for intertemporal want-dependence and uncertainty. These hints resulted in chapters 2 and 3 of the present volume.

Mr. A. Langhout of the Econometric Institute critically examined an earlier version of these chapters, and contributed the derivation of a number of the more complicated formulae. Mr. K. van de Rotte, formerly at the Econometric Institute, co-operated with the first author in the preparation of chapter 7, in attempts to adopt a simultaneous equations approach and in initiating calculations on the impact of credit restrictions on the optimal savings plan (Appendix A to chapter 4). Dr. Y.P. Gupta,momentarily on the staff of the Indian Agricultural Research Institute, New Delhi, gave the authors valuable advice on possibilities of applying analysis of variance.

The data for this analysis was kindly provided and suited to our needs by the Netherlands Central Bureau of Statistics. In particular, we are indebted to to Dr. J.B.D. Derksen, heading the Bureau of Statistical Analysis, for supervising the statistical operations, to Mr. J.W.W.A. Wit, Chief of the Central Data Processing Division, for supervising the programming and electronic processing of the data, and to Mr. E. Jager for his assistance in preparing the input and compiling the output.

We also appreciate the permission given by the Netherlands Central Bureau of Statistics and W. de Haan N.V. to make use of our article on 'urgency to consume' in: Statistische en econometrische onderzoekingen no. 7, issued by the former and published by the latter; in a modified and extended version, it is reproduced in chapter 6.

Valuable assistance was rendered by Mr. F. A. Palm and Mr. L. Hordijk of the Econometric Institute, in particular by programming the computations needed for chapters 6 and 8 on the Institute's IBM 1130, and by reading the proofs.

The first author's wife, Mrs. W. L. A. Somermeyer-McLeod, patiently undertook to compose the Indexes.

We were lucky to find Mr. S. J. Ahern, Lecturer in English at the Technical University of Delft, willing to improve our English.

Last but not least, we highly value the excellent typing job performed by the first author's former secretary, Mrs. M. F. F. van Delft-Slingerland.

To all of them we express our gratitude.

W. H. Somermeyer

R. Bannink

June 1972

GENERAL PART

PRELIMINARIES

Genesis of the book

Work on the present volume started about twelve years ago. At that time, the authors were impressed by the potentialities of Modigliani and Brumberg's theory, featuring the impact of life expectancy on savings behaviour. They were interested in applying that theory to data to be collected in a savings survey planned by their (former) employer, the Netherlands Central Bureau of Statistics.

For that purpose, the first author started by stripping that theory of its over-simplifications, a phenomenon all too common in economics. The resulting generalized version of the Modigliani–Brumberg's savings theory was published (in Dutch) in the Bureau's quarterly 'Statistische en econometrische onderzoekingen' (Statistical and Econometric Studies) in 1960; essentially the same model appears in chapter 4 below, albeit adorned by a number of extensions and refinements.

Next, the questionnaire of the 1960 savings survey of the Netherlands as well as the processing of its outcome had to be adapted in order to enable an econometric analysis to be carried out on the basis of that amplified theory; thus, the authors took up the trend set by Klein c.s. with respect to the Consumer Finance Surveys of the Federal Reserve system at the Michigan Survey Research Center and expressed in their 'Contributions of Survey Methods to Economics'. The authors are to a certain extent content but not entirely satisfied with the concessions made by the Central Bureau of Statistics in order to meet their desiderata as far as possible without jeopardizing the hazardous venture. The three publications in which the Bureau tabulated the results of the survey in 1962 and 1963 testified to its success; the outcome of the econometric analysis which the authors carried out on the basis of individual data appeared (again in Dutch) in issue no. 7 of 'Statistische en econometrische onderzoekingen' in 1966; in essence, chapter 6 presents an anglicized and slightly modified version of that study.

From the original micro-model, the authors derived a macro savings function for a time-series analysis of aggregate savings in the Netherlands. The result, achieved with the co-operation of Mr. K. van de Rotte, was laid down in Report 6912 of the Econometric Institute, Rotterdam; extended and modified versions of its theoretical and empirical parts became chapters 5 and 7, respectively, of the present book.

In his comments on that paper, presented at the European Meeting of the Econometric Society, Brussels 1969, Professor Krelle of Bonn University questioned the realism of the model in that it precludes between-period complementarity of consumption and disregards uncertainty.

This much appreciated criticism brought about an extensive generalization of the theory of savings by the first author, skilfully assisted by Mr. A.Langhout; the results are shown in chapters 2 and 3 below, as preliminary to the more specific model presented in chapter 4. The upshot is a savings theory modelled in a manner resembling Slutsky's consumer demand theory, by interpreting discount factors as indicators of prices of 'saving'.

Furthermore, in their micro-model the present authors went deeper into the impact of biological factors on the individual's savings behaviour, as stressed by Modigliani and Brumberg; its macro-analogon is the impact of demographic factors on aggregate savings, in continuation of a study by Eizenga [1960], also included in the 'Contributions to Economic Analysis' series of the North-Holland Publishing Company, Amsterdam.

In order to stimulate research on the relationships between demography and economics, the first author contributed a paper entitled 'Demographic effects on savings' to the Latin-American Regional Population Conference, held in Mexico, 1970; in essence, it became chapter 8 of the present book.

This program maps out the field to be covered below. An introductory chapter explains in what respects the theory and its applications to be set forth in this volume are related to earlier studies and in what other respects they differ.

Since empirical research should rest on a well-developed theory, a theoretical part (chapters 2 through 5) precedes the empirical part (chapters 6 through 8). Since macro-models should be derived from micro-models by aggregation, micro-analysis precedes macro-analysis in both parts. Thus, chapter 5 derives a macro-theory of savings on the basis of the special micro-theory set forth in chapter 4. A macro time-series analysis in chapter 7 follows on a micro cross-section analysis in chapter 6. Chapter 8 starts by examining

Plan of the book

In brief this book has the following aims:	to be achieved by means of:	in chapters	
I. to contribute towards the unity of (economic) science, mutual consistency and completeness of economic relationships	(a) constructing a general savings theory allowing special theories to fit in;	2 + 3	
	(b) shaping it like Slutsky's consumer demand theory, and in particular:		
	(c) rehabilitating the role of the rate of interest in savings behaviour, as well as:	2 through 7	
	(d) deriving a macro-savings function from a micro-model by aggregation:	5	
II. to narrow the gap between theory and empirical analysis		micro	macro
	(a) adapting theory to available data;	6	7
	(b) adapting data to theoretical requirements	4	5
III. to bring out the importance of biological factors	(a) cross-section analysis of individual data;	6	
	(b) simulating effects of extending life expectancy;	8	
and of corresponding demographic factors	(c) time-series analysis of aggregate data;	7	
	(d) simulating effects of varying a population's age distribution	8	

the impact of biological characteristics on personal savings and ends with a study of demographic characteristics on aggregate savings by nations.

The relationships derived in chapter 2 are based on utility functions unspecified with regard to their form, apart from the signs of the partial derivatives. In chapter 3 the utility functions are specified as additive separable, i.e. either completely or pairwise additive.

The theory developed in chapter 4 is based on a particular kind of additive-separable utility function, viz. the log-linear one.

With respect to the contents of the models, chapters 2 and 3 develop alternatives in addition to a basic model; in corresponding sections of these chapters final personal wealth, hours of work, price levels of consumption and of assets, as well as consumption by others, enter the utility function alongside the usual per-period consumption; survival rates are included and the rate of interest is made variable in the constraining lifetime budget equations. The impact of uncertainty on optimal savings decisions is studied briefly. The final section of chapter 3 presents a continuous savings model as an extreme consequence of additive-separability of the utility function.

All those alternatives were inspired by other economists and examined with respect to their theoretical and practical implications. Since they were found wanting with respect to applicability, they were dropped from chapter 4 onwards.

In both the theoretical and the empirical part, effects of changes in the independent variables on savings are stressed. In the theoretical chapters 2 through 5, those variables are mainly of an economic nature: initially available or finally desired personal wealth, expected income and rate of interest, or parameters of the expected future time-paths of the latter two factors. In the macro-analysis of chapter 7 too, the same three variables (personal wealth, income and rate of interest) play a key role; here, they are specified with respect to time.

In chapters 6 and 8, however, personal characteristics or demographic factors predominate, i.e. after elimination of the three economic variables combined into 'financial resources'.

The empirical studies presented in chapters 6 through 8 relate to the post-war Netherlands, i.e. chapters 6 and 7 exclusively, and chapter 8 partly.

The Netherlands were chosen because of the nationality of the authors, the knowledge they acquired of the statistical data in their country of origin, and the ready availability and reasonable reliability of such figures. In chapter 8, Mexico was adopted as a 'counterpart' because of the immediate purpose for which the study was made (a Conference on Latin-American population problems), and because Mexico and the Netherlands show interesting similarities as well as dissimilarities when compared with each other and within the regions in which they are embedded, respectively. On the one hand, Mexico shows a higher death rate, a higher birth rate and a lower level of welfare compared with the Netherlands; on the other hand, the Mexican population is not over-fertile, fairly longevous and rather prosperous according to Latin-American standards, whereas the Netherlands, besides showing longevity, had the highest birth rate and (therefore?) the lowest level of per capita income in Western Europe.

The analyses presented here are, of course, far from complete: while occasionally the shortcomings and gaps will be shown in the context in which they appear, the last chapter (9) reviews what may be done in the way of improvements, in the light of what has already been achieved.

In order to avoid misunderstanding or disappointment: the present volume does *not* deal with collectivistic theories of (national) optimal savings, such as those initially devised by Ramsey[1]; neither do we consider savings behaviour of Governments or (corporate) enterprise: essentially, our theoretical and empirical analyses are confined to the private sector of the economy, for reasons disclosed in chapter 7.

Moreover, private savings are considered in their entirety, instead of by components, such as life insurance (cf. Kreinin c.s. [1957]), or purposes; the reason for such a comprehensive treatment is revealed in section 6.1.4.

Finally, we like to point out that our analyses aim at theoretical elaboration rather than at statistical sophistication (which is often hardly worthwhile, in view of deficiencies of the data if not of the theory).

Requirements for reading and directions to the reader

The latter restriction means that as far as econometrics is concerned, acquaintance with single-equation estimation techniques suffices for understanding the empirical analyses in chapters 6 and 7, while it is not necessary for comprehending chapter 8. Apart from high-school algebra, grasping the theoretical part requires knowledge of no more than the principles of economics

---

[1] Ideally, such theories result in optimum savings models derived for entire nations (or other macro-units) by maximization of a social welfare function subject to constraints (among which one or more production functions are ever-present). No Government – irrespective of its nature, i.e. authoritarian or democratic – that might consider drawing up a social welfare function can derive it unambiguously from the utility or preference functions of the individuals constituting the collectivity to which it allegedly pertains. Consequently, the socially optimal savings functions need not, and generally will not, coincide with the sums of the individually optimal savings functions. A similar distinction applies to the theory of production, showing that optimal behaviour of firms merging into a monopoly tends to deviate from the sum of optimal behaviour by the individual firms separately (but interdependently), even if the utility functions of all are the same, viz. profit functions. Readers interested in collectivistic theory of optimum savings are referred to (inter alia) the pioneering efforts of Ramsey [1928], the hitherto most sophisticated studies by Inagaki [1969, 1970] and the review article by Koopmans [1967].

and the essentials of calculus and matrix operations. Moreover, the main derivations and their results are presented in scalar notation as well.

The reader who is merely (or mainly) interested in results may skip sections 2.4 through 2.10 and 3.1.2 through 3.4, if only provisionally; since the theory is not repeated in the applied part, the reader is advised, however, to study at least chapters 4 and 5; preferably, the reader should begin with the underlying general theory set forth in sections 2.1 through 2.3 and continue with section 3.1, as stepping-stones to the specific savings theory of chapter 4.

CHAPTER 1

STUDIES IN SAVINGS – PAST AND PRESENT

1.1. Theory versus empirical research

In economic science, theorists and empirical research workers are often on strained relations with each other[1]. On the one hand, theory is often not operational and specific enough to serve as a basis for empirical analysis, i.e. theory without (the possibility of) measurement. On the other hand, empirical studies usually lack a sound theoretical basis.

The latter circumstance is, of course, due – at least partly – to the former one. An additional reason is that economic theorists and empirical research workers or econometricians frequently are of different types, with different backgrounds, interests and points of view.

Theorists tend to look down upon the humdrum of economic reality[2]; or, they consider application of the theories they developed not worth their while, in view of the insufficiency of the observations (in both a qualitative and a quantitative sense). The empirists may agree with the latter contention; however, they are inclined to draw quite another conclusion, viz. that just because of the deficiencies of the statistical data, theoretical sophistication is a dispensable luxury. Furthermore, econometricians tend to stress improvements in estimation methods even when applied to a model that is incorrectly specified, with variables that are inaccurately measured.

In particular, the foregoing applies to the analysis of savings, or its complement: total consumption. One of the reasons is that saving – like its counterpart investment – is even more future-oriented than most other economic behaviour. This means that savings are pre-eminently determined by expecta-

---

[1] Even if they happen to coincide bodily (since schizoid tendencies are not at all uncommon in this field).

[2] This attitude was clearly shown at a recent meeting of the Econometric Society; at the end of his speech in praise of the newly elected President, the past-President quipped: 'He even dabbled in empirical research, but nobody can be perfect.'

tions – about future income, future rates of interest, and future conditions of life in addition to current ones. Such expectations are difficult – albeit not impossible[3] – to measure. Therefore, expectations, playing a key rôle in the theory of savings, are often ignored in pertinent empirical studies; at best, they are taken account of implicitly, by means of make-shift variables, relating to the past rather than to the future. If such substitute variables would be worth consideration at all, they would be based upon, or at least presuppose a theory on generation of expectations, by way of extrapolation of past developments.

These comments on the prevailing situation in savings research hold for macro-functions even more than for the corresponding micro-functions (numerically specified in both cases). One may object to the run-of-the-mill macro-theory precisely on the grounds that it is not derived from micro-theory by aggregation.

In the present study, an attempt is made to remedy at least some of the deficiencies of savings research mentioned above. Primarily, the authors try to bridge the gap between theory and empirical research in the field of savings and consumption; for that purpose, they worked from both sides, viz. by developing an operational theory and by processing observations to which the theory could be linked. Furthermore, they provided for two levels (a lower micro-level and an upper macro-level, resting on the lower one), along which the traffic from theory to fact and back to theory can be directed.

Evidently, these attempts are not entirely novel, but lean heavily on past performances, which are both theoretical and empirical.

Sections 1.2 and 1.3 below provide a brief review of what is valuable for our purpose in earlier developments of theory and in cumulated experience gained by empirical studies on savings, respectively.

---

[3] Expectations may be – and sometimes are – asked for in surveys, viz. about variables that are not considered as instrumental by the interviewers (cf. Morgan [1954], Katona [1960]). Official statistical services, however, are generally reluctant to incorporate into surveys questions of fancy rather than of fact, for fear of jeopardizing the whole enterprise (e.g. by stirring up artificial emotions among meddling members of Parliament or other busy-bodies).

1.2. Progress in operationally significant savings theory

For many decades, savings research has been lagging behind consumer demand analysis, theoretically as well as empirically. In a sense, this may seem strange, considering that savings and consumption are each others' complements; pertinent information may even be derived from the same statistical sources, viz. household expenditure surveys. A partial explanation of this paradox may be that age-old registrations of market transactions with respect to prices paid and quantities marketed stimulated demand analysis from Gregory King's days onwards, whereas savings research did not receive a comparable impetus. Only recently, economic theory took account of what has been recognized for centuries in financial circles, viz. that (money) savings, like commodities, have a price, i.e. the discount rate. The latter acknowledgement enabled the transposition of Slutsky's consumer demand theory into savings theory (cf. chapters 2 and 3 below).

Another reason for the lack of interest in savings or dissavings may have been the not uncommon view that such dealings are virtually reserved for the happy few, i.e. those whose income allows them to save, or whose personal wealth permits them to dissave. Curiously enough, the very same considerations explain why (aggregate) consumption functions became so popular in the Keynesian repertory, from the mid-thirties onwards: the mere fact that income and total consumption, on either a macro- or a micro-level, are generally of the same order of magnitude ensures success in regressing consumption on income. Even though regressing *savings* on income yields exactly the same estimates of marginal propensities to consume, lower coefficients of correlation do result, due to the unreliability and erratic nature of observed savings, in addition to obvious shortcomings of the theory, implied rather than explicated.

Therefore, application of a more sophisticated theory seems fully justified, even for practical purposes.

For such a theory, the foundations were laid by Ricci [1926] and Fisher [1930]; a few years later, a more refined version was elaborated by Von Stackelberg [1939]. In all these theories and subsequent ones of the same kind, the (income-receiving) individuals supposedly allocate their expenditures over time in such a way as to maximize the satisfaction to be drawn from it, given their income expectations. Still, these theories have been restricted in the sense that they deal with only two periods at a time. Fortunately, however, they are generalized easily – at least analytically – by sub-division of the two periods or by extension of the planning horizon by including a larger number of periods[4].

The unit periods may even be reduced and their number may be increased unlimitedly until finally a continuous savings- or consumption-model emerges, with a finite or an infinite planning horizon.

Obviously, models with infinite planning horizons hardly bear any relationship to actual life (which is patently finite); but also models with finite horizons may be unrealistic.

Even fairly realistic models may be inoperational. In particular, this applies to the continuous models, since the variables entering them are not registered continuously – unlike some physical quantities such as voltage, amperage, or steam pressure in power generating plants – but at best are measured or estimated for discrete periods or at discrete points of time. In a sense, this is a pity, because by their very elegance and simplicity, continuous models are pre-eminently suited to the derivation of a number of 'meaningful theorems', which may be tested empirically, at least in a qualitative way. Therefore, a number of important studies dealt with continuous models, and sometimes even with infinite horizon[5]! In particular, they examine problems of uncertainty, of lifetime and other expectations (cf. Yaari [1964, 1965], Hakansson [1969], Srinivasan and Levhari [1969], Hahn [1970], and Sandmo [1970]). In the same tradition, the present study too paid homage to continuous models – as evidenced by section 3.2.

Nevertheless, the main emphasis will be on operational models, with discrete time periods as a prerequisite for applicability to empirical data. In this

---

4 On the other hand, I. Fisher offered more than a mere savings theory: by introducing 'income transformation' curves (or functions) in addition to consumption utility ditto, he attempted to outline a theory in which rates of discount (represented by the slopes of lines tangent to both curves at the same point) would be determined in a 'market' for the supply of and demand for savings.

5 Apart from lack of realism, models with infinite horizon run the risk that the utility function $u = \int_0^\infty f\{c(t)\}\,dt$, with the rate of consumption $c(t)$ a function of time and f a monotonically increasing function of c, may become infinite. Inclusion of a (subjective) discounting factor exp $\{-\varrho(t)\}$ in the integrand – may be considered as a measure to keep the integral finite, although it may be neither sufficient nor necessary. Even models with finite horizon – such as the one dealt with by Yaari [1964] – sometimes feature such subjective discount factors in the utility function; since they are merely confusing by redundance, they are also dispensable.

Consequently, boundedness assumptions have to be specified, whether or not discounting is subsumed in the utility function, as is done, e.g. by Arrow and Kurz [1969].

sense, Modigliani and Brumberg's [1955] multi-period life-cycle savings model, should be considered as an earnest attempt at bridging the gap between theory and empirical research. Interpreting the planning period as the individual's life-expectancy, and pointing out its impact on savings, both directly and indirectly through lifetime income appears to be their most valuable contribution to economic theory.

In their zeal to facilitate and further the application of their theory, however, they unfortunately introduced a number of unwarranted as well as unnecessary (over-) simplifications. In particular, they assumed that:

(a) the 'urgency to consume' would remain constant over time (hence the nick-name: 'bachelor's theory'),
(b) expected future income would not change over time,
(c) both initial and intended final personal wealth could be disregarded, and
(d) the rate of interest would be zero.

Therefore, the theory discards the possibility of studying a number of interesting and unsolved problems, dealt with only superficially in empirical research; viz. how savings are affected by (anticipated) changes in needs, in personal wealth, in income, and in the rate of interest. Since substitution effects and "wealth accumulation" effects of changes in the rate of interest generally counteract each other, the rash conclusion was drawn that savings would be independent of the rate of interest. Empirical studies appeared to confirm it; actually, however, they were inconclusive, because of the theoretically inappropriate way in which they took account of the rate of interest.

In order to overcome the limitations enumerated under (a) through (d) above, the Modigliani–Brumberg theory was generalized by Somermeyer [1960]. This version was based on the hypothesis that income recipients maximize a multi-period utility function[6] of consumer expenditures subject to a lifetime budget constraint; no a priori restrictions are imposed on prospective time shapes of future income, and the "urgency to consume", personal wealth (both initial and final) and interest rates are accepted at face value. Accordingly, this model has also been adopted in the present study, as the main basis for the subsequent empirical studies described in chapters 6

[6] In 1958, Samuelson introduced a utility function of consumption in three periods – generally unequal, since the last period would be for 'resting', against the former two periods for working; it was exemplified by the log-additive specification also adopted by the present authors. Later on, Ophir [1961] made Samuelson's three-period utility function still more general by incorporating survival rates and time-preference factors in its coefficients.

through 8. The model in question is based on a fairly special – although apparently plausible and common (viz. log-additive) – type of utility function. Its main advantage is that it allows rather specific conclusions to be drawn. On the other hand, one might well doubt its universal validity. Construction of a more general model is possible, but limits the attainability of sufficiently specific ends.

One way of solving this dilemma is to examine the extent to which the conclusions based on the special model remain valid if the latter is generalized in various directions. The present study, however, follows the opposite route, viz. by starting off with more general versions of the model (in chapter 2), and making it successively more specific (in chapters 3 and 4); at the same time, generalized versions of the consumption-savings model incorporate varying additional sets of variables, suggested by a number of authors but left out of the more simple special model.

In recent years, economists became aware that decisions with respect to savings and consumption may take account of other considerations as well. Inter alia, allocation of time to work, study or leisure has been incorporated in savings-consumption models developed by Pfouts [1960], Ghez [1970], Gronau [1970] and Lee-Gramm [1970]; the latter three even relate to different members of the same household simultaneously. Ben-Porath [1970] extends his model to the number of children wanted in relation to consumption required by a couple. Somermeyer [1968] linked the choice of residence to interregional differences in cost of living within the framework of a savings model with discount rates including prospective changes in consumer price levels.

Neither this brief review on contributions to savings analyses, nor the ones to follow in sections 1.3 and 1.4 on empirical (cross-section and time-series) additions to savings analysis even pretend to be complete or do justice to the work performed in this field. In particular, we leave aside all theories developed and results obtained by empirical analysis relating to the consumption of specific goods and services, hence to total consumer expenditure and to savings as well; these studies frequently take care of factors not accounted for in the more global ones on total consumption or savings. The sole purpose of the tour d'horizon of the present chapter is to connect the analyses carried out by the present authors (and presented in the following chapters) with theoretical or empirical studies made by others.

1.3. Regress in empirically applied savings theory

1.3.1. CLEARING THE GROUND

Notwithstanding the strained relations between theorists and empiricists in savings research, mentioned in section 1.1, the latter category *did* contribute to economics – as justly claimed by the title of a compilatory publication in this field ('Contributions of Survey Methods to Economics', ed. L.R. Klein [1954]). This holds for cross-section analyses to a higher degree than for time-series analyses – especially since the macro-models adopted in the latter are seldom derived from micro-models used in the former type of research.

In time-series analysis, one has to make do with whatever information is available in the form of statistical series bearing on savings and constructed for general purposes rather than for specific savings research. On the other hand, cross-section data are usually derived from (sample) surveys that may – and anyhow should – take account of savings theory. In general, at least some, if only embryonal theory is habitually incorporated in such surveys, viz. in the questionnaires asking for information about factors that might affect savings according to theory and/or previous results of savings analyses.

Usually, however, data obtained in this way is far from complete, in particular with respect to (long-term) expectations about the future course of income and family living conditions – even though they are assigned an important rôle in savings behaviour[7].

As a consequence, even special savings surveys restrict us in the application of a full-fledged savings theory. Consequently, most econometricians content themselves with short-cut, make-shift models – as already noted in section 1.1. Apparently, they despair of obtaining any further knowledge about the motivation of savings behaviour.

Therefore, the simplifications Modigliani and Brumberg [1955] imposed on the application-oriented version of their model, referred to in section 1.2, as well as the essentially similar model adopted by Ando and Modigliani [1963], may be interpreted as symptoms of such an agnostic belief and defaitistic attitude.

---

7 The main reason for this lack of information provided by savings surveys has already been mentioned in footnote 3 to this chapter.

Likewise, Milton Friedman's "permanent income" hypothesis should be exposed as an attempt to evade the issue of how to evaluate expectations. True, his circumscription (rather than definition) of permanent income *hints* at the individual's earning capacity[8], even though for that purpose it lacks two essential elements, viz. survival rates and discount rates, as well as less essential ones, such as property. True, he (alternatively or equivalently?) likens permanent income to the 'expected' value of a probability distribution (l.c., p. 26), but he omits to define the nature of both the analogy and the distribution.

Moreover, he apparently cannot make up his mind as to whether these two fictional components are additive or multiplicative[9].

He is ready to admit that his permanent income cannot be measured, and that in the most general form the permanent income hypothesis is empty, 'in the same sense that no empirical data can contradict it' (l.c., p. 26).

However, by specifying zero correlations between the permanent and transitory components (not only of income, but of consumption as well), in addition to zero correlation between both transitory components[10], he contends that it may be contradicted by observed data. Of course, these restrictions cannot separate the permanent from the transitory components, but at most their effects[11].

Therefore, Friedman suggests that 'the precise line to be drawn between permanent and transitory components is best left to be determined by the

---

[8] 'The permanent component is to be interpreted as reflecting the effect of those factors that the unit regards as determining its capital value of wealth: the non-human wealth it owns; the personal attributes of the earners in the unit, such as their training, ability, personality; the attributes of the economic activity of the earners, such as the occupation followed, the location of the economic activity, and so on' (Friedman [1957] p. 21).

This selected list of factors might be interpreted as the determinants of the individual's expected future course of income; for evaluating the present value of this stream (in Friedman's terminology: capital value or wealth), however, at least life expectancy and rates of discounting should be known (not to mention initial personal wealth).

[9] As specified by his equations (3.1) and (3.1′) respectively. The latter construction would, of course, preclude negative or even zero transitory (not to mention: permanent) income components. Anyhow, it is at variance with Friedman's earlier admissions of positive, zero or negative mean transitory income components (l.c., p. 22), especially if logarithms are taken, as in (3.1′).

[10] This is in the best tradition of established economic theory, abounding with artefacts such as 'normal', 'natural', 'equilibrium', 'short-run', 'long-run', etc.

[11] Originally, the device was developed by Frisch [1934] – not acknowledged by Friedman – for separating effects of systematic factors from those of errors.

data themselves, to be whatever seems to correspond to consumer behaviour' (l.c., p. 23). Apparently, this amounts to equaling permanent income to mean actual income over a number of past years.

Thus, the future is substituted by the past – a procedure that would be justified only if expectations are rooted unalterably in the past[12].

On the credit side, Friedman's consumption function has some commendable properties, viz. proportionality, with a factor depending, inter alia, on the consumer's taste[13].

Still, this does not compensate sufficiently for the lack of a firm theoretical basis, despite Friedman's allegation to the contrary[14].

1.3.2. CROSS-SECTION ANALYSIS

Friedman indulged in both cross-section and time-series analysis, in order to glorify his own permanent income hypothesis. Others more modestly stuck to one of the two.

Cross-section analysis is often a mere by-product of the tabulation of savings survey data; only too rarely is it premeditated, in the sense that the plan of the analyses preceded the survey and co-determined its contents. Prior to this joint effort by Klein c.s. [1954] more limited or partial studies relating to

---

[12] The trouble, of course, is the lack of a dependable theory for the generation of expectations in the absence of pertinent reliable data. Psychological theory makes default, whereas economic theory rarely passes the stage of naive extrapolation. The most thorough analyses of expectations have been carried out by Theil c.s. [1961] and Jochems [1962] on the basis of Business Test data, while the psychologistic school of Katona c.s. [1960] also contributed towards a better insight into causes as well as results of expectations. With respect to prices, both the generation and realization (= quality) of expectations has been studied by Lange and Kaptein [1958].

[13] In passing, we note that the other variables on which – according to Friedman – the proportionality would depend are misplaced: rate(s) of interest and preferences for consumption versus addition to wealth should instead be incorporated in the capital value alias permanent income variable.

[14] 'The permanent income hypothesis follows directly from the accepted pure theory of consumer behaviour...' (l.c., p. 6). It is true that Chapter II presents a simple (two-period) version of that theory, while Chapter III discusses the permanent income hypothesis, but it does not result from the 'pure theory'. He simply *could* not do it, since a hypothesis can *never* follow from a theory, but *is* a (partial) theory. In Friedman's catechism, the permanent income hypothesis *supersedes* the pure theory, which is subsequently dropped like a hot potato.

the U.S.A. were performed by both the same and other econometricians; among these, especially Brady and Friedman [1946, 1947], Katona [1949], Klein [1951], and Klein and Morgan [1951] are worth mentioning.

It was succeeded by many other analyses, also based on consumer finance or savings surveys for various countries, and running along essentially the same lines. Notable examples are presented by Watts [1958] for the U.S.A., M.R. Fischer [1956] and Lydall [1953] for the United Kingdom, Tabard [1960] for France, Pezek [1963] for Czechoslovakia and Thore [1959] for Sweden. Since we shall revert to these studies when comparing results obtained by us with those procured by others, we confine ourselves at this stage to pointing out the main characteristics of such studies.

With regard to their contents, variables adduced to explain savings differentials between individuals are income, personal wealth and personal characteristics.

Occasionally, expectations are brought into the picture, albeit of a qualitative nature only, i.e. by a mere distinction between increase, (approximate) constancy and decrease, without quantification. Such expectations are generally restricted to income, but may be extended to prices. Generally savings are assumed to be higher according as current income is higher, and according as income is expected to decrease rather than increase in the near future. On the other hand, lagged income is sometimes introduced in addition to current income. Such a treatment may be based on supposed delays in savings behaviour and/or on extrapolation of expectations from past developments.

More often, however, cross-section analyses abstain from introducing lagged variables. First, the surveys on which such analyses are based rarely ask for data relating to moments or time-intervals expired before the beginning of the reference period; most likely, the rate of response and the quality of the answers would be insufficient, while they would not raise enough interest to justify the effort. This may be due, at least partly, to the fact that cross-section analyses cannot well discriminate between lags, because of a high degree of parallelism between movements of individual variables (such as income), let alone common ones (such as prices or rates of interest).

Personal wealth – if entering the savings equation at all – nearly always relates to the beginning of the reference period shared by all individuals observed; this means an average lag of one-half period (or six months). Instead of total personal wealth, however, often but a part of it, viz. liquid assets, is included in the savings function. Such a procedure is sometimes defended on the grounds that 'fixed' personal wealth would not affect savings; an alternative or additional argument can be that liquid assets is the only personal wealth component known (with sufficient accuracy)[15].

In one model (Klein [1954] Ch. V.) debt is taken account of separately instead of being subsumed among personal wealth as a whole; possibly different rates of interest applying to positive and negative personal wealth components may be a reason for such a discriminatory treatment. Almost unanimously, wealth is assumed to reduce a person's propensity to save, just as debt is assumed to raise it – the more so according as the values of these factors are higher.

Personal characteristics included in savings functions may relate to age, family size, education and occupation. In general, such characteristics apply to the head of the household, to the exclusion of its other members; moreover, the former is usually supposed to be a male.

On the other hand, the economic variables, such as savings and income, are regularly attributed to the household as a whole rather than to its income-earning members separately. However, such an approach becomes less and less realistic according as the authority of the pater familias is on the wane, by being passed on to his wife and/or divided among other members of the household[16]. Renting or owning one's living quarters is subsumed under the same heading.

Naturally, most of these characteristics are of an attributive rather than of a distributive nature. This means that the separate or joint effects of these factors on savings can be incorporated in the model by means of dummy variables (for each of the alternatives). Even in the case where the variable can be expressed in a quantitative way, representation by a set of dummies may be preferable; this applies in particular if the effects of these factors on the variable to be explained are not necessarily monotonic, let alone linear. Effects of age (whether or not combined with other factors, such as size of the household) are a case in point. Several of the studies referred to above adopted the dummy-variable approach[17]; in view of the large number of observations covered, they could afford the price to be paid for such a ven-

---

[15] The two arguments may, of course, be related in the sense that liquid assets is often the only personal wealth component asked for in the savings survey, viz. if its organizers opine that other personal wealth components are irrelevant in that context.

[16] For relationships between savings behaviour of different members of the household, cf. sections 6.5.3 and 6.6.6.

[17] E.g. Klein [1954] and Watts [1958]; M. R. Fisher [1956], however, adopted a parabolic function in order to cover a possible non-monotonic partial relationship between savings and age.

ture, viz. the large number of explanatory variables to be adduced. This consequence was accepted most generously by Watts [1958], who handled 568 explanatory variables (mostly dummies) simultaneously. It induced others to keep at a minimum the numbers of interactions distinguished.

By the introduction of dummy variables for the representation of main effects as well as interactions, some but not all of the problems of specifying the form of the relationships may be solved. Anyhow, specification of the savings function in terms of the quantitative variables remains a life-sized problem; in view of the generally larger coefficients of variation of the variables (such as income and personal wealth), the specification problem is of even greater importance in cross-section studies than in time-series analyses.

Unfortunately, however, precious little attention has been paid to this question; as far as the scanty information provided on this issue allowed us to conclude, most of the numerically specified savings functions were the result of a process of trial and error, starting from a basically additive-linear, hence disjoint causal pattern. Notwithstanding a few favourable exceptions, apparently most of the attempts at covering non-linearities by means of (e.g.) quadratic terms and reciprocals of variables carried more weight than theoretical considerations. Below, we shall argue that especially personal characteristics, such as age, sex, status in and composition of household, affect savings not independently, but through the discounted flow of income and the intended change in personal wealth, as summarized in one variable named (initial) financial resources.

1.3.3. TIME-SERIES ANALYSIS

The latter consideration leads us to the contributions of time-series analyses to savings research. On the one hand, time-series analyses may bring to the fore factors that show hardly any variation between the units dealt with by cross-section analyses (relating to the same point or period of time), or that vary over time for the same units in almost the same degree. In particular, this applies to the rate of interest[18]. Unfortunately, however, only a minority of

[18] One should, however, realize that even in (synchronous) cross-section analysis rates of interest may vary between the observed units. First, rates of interest that individuals may receive on assets and will have to pay on loans depend, inter alia, on the size of the assets or loans, terms of notice, and the nature and value of the collateral they can provide. Moreover, in the material to be described in chapter 6, we can distinguish between those who participate in bonus savings plans (and receive more than the normal interest) and those who do not do so (and receive normal interest only).

the time-series analyses took account of effects of the rate of interest on savings, at any rate in the studies published[19]. This may be due, at least partly, to assigning a negligible rôle to the rate of interest as a savings-determining factor; such an attitude might even be rationalized by the argumentation that the supposedly counteracting substitution and wealth accumulation components of the rate of interest effect cancel each other almost completely. In addition, empirical results – which contradict each other occasionally – seem to support such an assumption.

On the other hand, lack of evidence on the direction (let alone the degree) in which the rate of interest acts on savings, may be due to misspecification of the manner in which that factor used to be included in the savings function, i.e. in a generally additive-linear way.

On the contrary, we show (in chapters 4 and 5) that savings are affected by rates of interest through products with income and personal wealth. In this respect, the rate of interest resembles the biological factors referred to in section 1.3.2.

Due to their trend-like movements, however, the latter factors cannot be incorporated successfully in time-series analysis; in addition, their effects are blurred by aggregation in the usual macro-economic kind of time-series.

Because of difficulties in measuring aggregate personal wealth statistically, this kind of variable appears less frequently in time-series analyses than in cross-section analyses. On the other hand, both kinds of analyses have in common that whenever wealth is included as an explanatory variable, it is usually represented by deposits or some such (liquid) part of it, rather than in toto.

Contrariwise, price variables crop up fairly frequently in time-series analyses. Since expected rather than current or past development of prices helps in shaping the time-pattern of savings, the index-number of consumer prices is sometimes replaced or accompanied by its rate of change. In the statistical representation of these as well as other variables, usually (distributed) time-lags are involved. In general, time-series analyses appear to cherish effects from the past rather than from the present (let alone the future) on current consumption or savings. The underlying reasoning appears to be of a psycho-

---

[19] In particular, we mention Tinbergen and Van der Meer [1937], and Radice [1939]. Occasionally, one or more interest rates appear in savings equations or equations for total consumer expenditures belonging to systems of equations for describing, forecasting and/or planning (short-term) fluctuations of the main variables for national economies; cf. the annual model for the Netherlands drawn up by Verdoorn c.s. [1970].

logical nature: difficulties of adjustment to new situations (in the short run), or yearning after a possibly more blissful past (in the long run). Especially the latter consideration induced Duesenberry [1967] to drag into the model the highest level of income ever reached, as a variable that might help to explain fluctuations in aggregate savings, as well as the apparent lack of a trend in the average rate of savings.

Since different people may experience peaks in income at different points of time – notwithstanding synchronizing forces – such a top-level variable would not have much effect left in macro-analyses. In addition to the alleged psychological justification of the introduction of lags, juggling with retardations has the obvious advantage of raising coefficients of correlation; this holds good in particular if lagged consumption is adduced to help explain fluctuations (cf. e.g. Ball and Drake [1964]). As a rule such a procedure promises success because of the generally 'sluggish' nature of the consumption series. On the other hand, we have to admit that the latter phenomenon may be due, at least partly, to hysteresis in consumer behaviour.

The micro-models developed in chapters 2 through 4 do not exclude the contingency of such delayed reactions, since their parameter(s) may depend on past experiences of the individuals with respect to income, consumption, etc.

In the derivation of the macro-model by aggregation of the micro-functions, however, such possible links with the past were disregarded; they did not seem to be sufficiently well-founded from either a theoretical or an empirical point of view.

In time-series macro-analyses, linearity of the relationships is the rule, even more so than in cross-section micro-analyses. Still, non-linearities in the micro-functions carry over to the macro-relationships, at least in principle.

---

[20] For example: in the case where total consumption C_i would be a quadratic function of income Y_i of individuals, i.e.

$$C_i = a_0 + a_1 Y_i + a_2 Y_i^2,$$

the corresponding macro-consumption function is:

$$C = \sum_{i=1}^{I} C_i = Ia_0 + a_1 Y + a_2 I^{-1} Y^2 (1 + v_Y^2),$$

with the coefficient of variation $v_Y = \text{var } Y_i/\bar{Y}$ as a measure of income inequality. Of course, such a consumption function is non-sensical, since it implies that for Y increasing indefinitely, C tends to minus infinity if $a_2 < 0$, and C/Y (and a fortiori C) tends to plus infinity if $a_2 > 0$.

If non-linearity is assumed in the partial relationships between individual savings or consumption on the one hand and income on the other hand, its effect in the corresponding macro-functions is sometimes taken care of by means of an indicator for the inequality of the distribution of personal income (cf. Staehle [1937]). As shown by de Wolff [1939], such a procedure is correct under fairly restrictive conditions only. On the other hand, splitting total income by source (wages and salaries versus other income)[20] in the savings- and consumption functions is still fashionable (cf. Verdoorn c.s. [1970]).

---

20 On p. 22.

THEORETICAL PART

CHAPTER 2

A GENERAL MICRO-THEORY OF OPTIMAL ALLOCATION OF CONSUMPTION AND SAVINGS OVER TIME

2.1. Alternative approaches to savings theory

2.1.1. SAVINGS AS RESOURCE ALLOCATION 'SUI GENERIS'?

In the analysis of savings behaviour, two main lines of thought might be followed, viz.:

(1) treatment of savings like any other way of 'spending' money, and
(2) treatment of savings in a way essentially different from that applied to expenditures on consumer goods and services proper.

Two arguments may be advanced in favour of the former approach. First, treating savings (e.g. in the form of buying bonds) just like any other item of spending money is *simpler* than treating savings as different from consumer goods and services. Second, the distinction between savings and consumption is often unclear in practice. In particular, purchases of durable consumer goods imply consumption in the current period for only a fraction of the price paid (i.e. depreciation), whereas for the rest they represent 'investment' (i.e. a form of savings); on the other hand, depreciation of durable consumer goods should be entered into the individual's or household's profit and loss account. However, estimation of depreciation, especially on inventories of durable goods, appears to be difficult; often the statistical basis, i.e. information about such stocks, distinguished by vintage, is lacking or deficient. Consequently, the pertinent estimates of savings are generally subject to fairly large margins of error.

Evidently, these two arguments in favour of procedure (1) are of a practical rather than of a theoretical nature. This explains why such an approach is adopted more often in empirical work than in theoretical analysis. According as more and better information becomes available, the second argument in favour of the former approach loses its apparent cogency. For this reason too, approach (1) is adopted less frequently in more recent studies compared with older ones, albeit with occasional revivals (cf. e.g. Bodkin [1970]).

Theoretically, strong arguments support the second approach. The main difference is that savings may be negative (i.e. dissavings) as well as positive (or zero, as a borderline case); on the other hand, consumption is always positive. Consequently, demand functions, which would not permit negative values of demand or consumption, would be inappropriate for describing savings (including *dis*savings) behaviour[1]. Secondly, savings differ from consumption items proper in the sense that one cannot attach 'prices' to savings (let alone dissavings) in precisely the same manner and with the same meaning as attributed to consumer goods and services.

The latter argument may be countered, however, since the reciprocal of the discount factor, i.e. $(1 + r_\tau)^{-1}$, with r_τ = rate of interest per unit of time in period τ, might be considered and used as an indicator of the "price" of savings (i.e. apart from an arbitrary multiplier). The underlying reasoning is that an assumed rise of r_τ would decrease the savings price $(1 + r_\tau)^{-1}$, thus favouring savings and disfavouring dissavings compared with consumption. In this way, substitution effects can be brought out. On the one hand, such a "solution" might seem to be rather artificial and somewhat arbitrary, due to the dependence of r_τ – with dimension: reciprocal of time – on the unit of time chosen. On the other hand, this might be avoided by proposing alternatively the reciprocal of the "continuous" discount rate $\exp(-\varrho\tau)$ as the price of savings. Consequently, this analogy between savings and the allocation of consumer expenditure seems strong enough to serve as a starting point for the savings theory developed below.

The objection that (dis)savings differ from consumption in time perspective, however, cannot be overcome as easily. True, this difference is one of degree rather than of essence. Still, it cannot reasonably be denied that as a rule savings decisions are made with respect to long periods ahead, whereas purchases of consumer items are usually planned for periods of (say) one year or shorter. In this respect, durable consumer goods take up an intermediate position; however – as observed before –, purchases of durable consumer goods represent savings as well as consumption of the services of such goods.

Consequently, *consumer* behaviour in a narrow sense (i.e. of allocating total consumer expenditures per unit of time to all budget items distinguished)

[1] Excepting, perhaps, Stone's [1954] system of linear expenditure functions.

might be considered 'in the long run' or 'in the short run', but savings behaviour should *always* be analyzed in long-term perspective.

The distinction between the long-term and the short-term view of allocation of consumer expenditures gives rise to a subsequent alternative in the second approach, viz.:

2.1.2. SINGLE-STAGE OR MULTI-STAGE ALLOCATION OF CONSUMER EXPENDITURES AND SAVINGS

Taking for granted the special nature of savings, the latter result from the consumer's optimalization process residually, i.e. as positive or negative differences between income and total consumption per period.

Still, the consumer may allocate his lifetime financial resources–to be defined in section 2.5–either at one stage or at two or more stages, i.e. by either:

(2a) allocating (or re-allocating) lifetime resources to all items of consumption to each future period, leaving savings (or dissavings) as the (positive or negative) differences between (expected or planned) total income and total consumer expenditure in each period,

or as:

(2b) allocating lifetime resources in (at least) two stages, viz.:
primarily: to each prospective period's total consumption and (dis)savings, and
secondarily: sub-allocating the total amount earmarked for consumption in each period to the various consumer goods and services available on the market (perhaps in more than one stage).

From a formal point of view, alternative (2a) might seem attractive because of its simultaneous treatment of all consumer decisions, including savings. On the other hand, precisely the latter characteristic of that approach, i.e. detailed planning of all expenditures item by item till the end of life, may strike us as too "far-fetched". The second alternative, i.e. a global long-term planning (of total consumer expenditures and savings as each others' complements), and subsequent short-term planning (for allocating total expenditures per period to budget items) looks more realistic; moreover, it is easier to handle, hence "operational". For these reasons, the savings theory to be derived and applied below relates to the first stage of the approach mentioned under (2b). Nevertheless, alternative (2a) appears to be of sufficient theoretical interest to justify a summary exposition in Appendix A to this chapter, especially since this kind of procedure has been given an impetus by recent studies (cf. Lluch [1970] a.o.).

2.2. *Theoretical frame-work of multi-stage resource allocation*

In the established theory of consumption, utility u is assumed to be an amorphous function of the quantities $q_1, \ldots, q_M$ of all commodities (including services) m (= 1, ..., M) consumed during a certain period:

$$u = u(q_1, \ldots, q_M). \tag{2.2.1}$$

Strotz [1957] considered, however, the possibility (and its consequences) that the M commodities might be arranged into a categorical system of subsets l (= 1, ..., L) with numbers of commodities M_l, hence satisfying:

$$\sum_{l=1}^{L} M_l = M; \tag{2.2.2}$$

consequently, u can be written as a function of functions v_l:

$$u = u\,[v_1(q_{11}, \ldots, q_{1M_1}), \ldots, v_L(q_{L1}, \ldots, q_{LM_L})]. \tag{2.2.3}$$

In principle, the notion of a utility tree as expressed by (2.2.3) may be generalized by assuming that in *their* turn one or more of the sub-functions v_l could be expressed in terms of sub-sub-functions w_{ln_l}:

$$v_l = v_l\,\{w_{l1}(q_{l11}, \ldots, q_{l1M_{l1}}), \ldots, w_{lN_l}(q_{lN_l1}, \ldots, q_{lN_lM_{lN_l}})\}, \tag{2.2.4}$$

with

$$\sum_{n_l=1}^{N_l} M_{ln_l} = M_l. \tag{2.2.5}$$

Such sub-ramifications of the utility tree appear to be useful in the analysis of the allocation of consumer expenditure to the various budget items. Within the context of savings theory, however, we shall confine ourselves to one ramification only.

By considering u as the utility to be derived from lifetime consumption of amounts q_{lm_l} of commodities m_l (= 1, ..., M_l) in each of the periods l (= 1, ..., L) into which the individual's (remaining) lifetime L may be divided, the v_l are assumed to be functions of the q_{lm_l} in such a way that together they constitute 'real' consumption in period l:

$$v_l = v_l(q_{l1}, \ldots, q_{lM_l}) = v_l\,(\sum_{m_l=1}^{M_l} p_m q_{lm_l}) = v_l(C_l), \tag{2.2.6}$$

with p_m representing prices of the consumer goods and services identified by m, i.e. independent of l, but in need of further specification (e.g. as prices prevailing for $l = 1$); the last two members of (2.2.6) imply the definition of C_l as (real) expenditure per period l:

$$C_l = \sum_{m_l=1}^{M_l} p_m q_{lm_l}. \tag{2.2.7}$$

Thus, by means of (2.2.6), (2.2.3) may be simplified into:

$$\begin{aligned} u &= u\,[v_1(C_1), \ldots, v_L(C_L)] \\ &= \omega\,(C_1, \ldots, C_L), \end{aligned} \tag{2.2.8}$$

with ω a function comprising the composite functions in the second member.

2.3. *Optimum allocation of savings over time: a theme with variations*

All theories to be discussed below have a common basis, viz. maximization of a lifetime utility function of (at least) consumption over time – such as (2.2.8) – subject to a lifetime budget constraint. These versions, however, differ with respect to contents and form of the utility functions, and the nature of the variables entering the model.

As in other theoretical problems, the economist is faced with a dilemma. He may aspire to formulate a theory as general as possible, with universal validity as his reward; the drawback of such an approach, however, is the meagerness of the conclusions to be drawn as well as the difficulty or impossibility of application to real world phenomena.

A more specific model enables the formulation of stronger and more detailed implications; on the other hand, the latter usually depend on the particular specifications adopted. In practice, one has to strike the happy mean.

Chapters 2, 3 and 4 examine the extent to which the conclusions depend on the degree of detail and restrictiveness of the specifications imposed on the model.

First, a basic consumption and savings model is derived in section 2.4. This model is called 'basic', since it includes but the most essential variables, assuming invariance or irrelevance of other factors.

Subsequent sections deal with a number of extensions and modifications. For convenience's sake, however, these variations are introduced separately rather than jointly.

In the first place, other variables beside consumption in prospective time periods may be incorporated in the utility function. The implications of the suggestion made by Friedman [1957, Ch. 1] that utility may also depend on the final amount of personal wealth, are worked out in section 2.5; it means that in the budget equation too, final personal wealth should be considered as a variable – to be optimized together with the other variables – instead of as 'given'.

Such an approach may be useful in case the planning period would fall short of the expected lifetime; in the latter case, "final" personal wealth would be a "carry-over" variable, representing the future beyond the planning horizon.

Especially in view of the latter contingency, the marginal utility of final personal wealth is assumed to be positive, like the marginal utility of consumption.

Secondly, utility may be considered to depend not only on consumption, but also on the efforts required for earning the future income, necessary – in conjunction with a change in personal wealth – for financing future consumption. As (rough) indicators of such efforts, amounts of time to be spent on work (including studying), are incorporated in the utility function. Apparently, we are justified in assuming that the marginal utility of work (for the individual's feeling of well-being, in contradistinction to his earning capacity) is negative (at least above a minimum number of hours of work).

Such an extended model is presented in section 2.6. It may also serve as a multi-period generalization of Henderson and Quandt's single-period 'income versus leisure' theory [1958, ch. 2.5]. Of course, the model must be supplemented by a set of income generating functions, linking income to past and present time spent on work. We suppose that all first-order partial derivatives of income with respect to hours worked are non-negative.

One of the assumptions underlying the basic model is the fixed nature of the planning period. In the case where this time-span is identified with the individual's remaining lifetime, its entire probability distribution instead of its expected value only may be taken into account – as is done in section 2.7. It means that:

(a) for each *type* of variable (consumption, etc.) its number is extended to the number of unit periods comprised within the *maximum* life-span, and

(b) survival rates are introduced into the lifetime budget equation, as a modest step towards making the model stochastic (cf. also Yaari [1965]).

Another way of enhancing the flexibility of the model is to assume that individuals look upon interest rates and/or price levels of consumption and of assets as variable instead of constant (in the future).

Therefore, in section 2.8 variables interest rates take the place of fixed interest rates, and prospective consumer price levels and asset price levels enter the budget equation; in the utility function, moreover, nominal consumption is replaced by real consumption. Considering the interest rate as varying over time enables us to study incidental and temporary changes in the discount rates – as compared with permanent changes – on the prospective time-pattern of consumption. Effects of prospective changes in consumer price levels and asset price levels on consumption are similar to those of rates of interest, as has been explained by the first author in the context of timing and directing the individual's migration (Somermeyer [1967]).

Changes in consumer price levels and in asset price levels may be considered as purely exogenous from the individual's point of view, since he cannot influence them noticeably. Rates of interest, for converting future to present values, however, may depend on the individual's current life expectancy, as well as on his or her personal wealth in the future.

For an individual 'playing against nature' (= death), the value of one dollar he may expect to obtain *for himself* after one unit period equals $s_l\,(1 + r_l)$ if he postpones spending that dollar by one unit period – with s_l and r_l denoting the survival rate of a person and his interest rate in period l, respectively. Consequently, for inducing a person to save rather than to consume, at least:

$$s_l\,(1 + r_l) > 1 \tag{2.3.1}$$

should hold good.

This means that the individual's discount factor $1 + r_l$ has a lower limit, which is higher according as his survival rate is lower, i.e. generally according as he (or she) is older and consequently has a lower life expectancy.

The rate of interest an individual may expect to receive is generally higher according as his (positive) personal wealth is larger (cf. e.g. table 19 of Somermeyer's monograph [1965] on 'income inequality'). On the other hand, the rate of interest an individual has to pay on loans is more onerous according as his personal wealth is smaller, or his debt is heavier.

Therefore, we may assume:

$$r_\tau = r(K_{\tau-1}), \tag{2.3.2}$$

with

$$K_\tau \frac{\mathrm{d}r}{\mathrm{d}K_{\tau-1}} > 0;$$

since the time pattern of K_τ is fixed by the time patterns of income, consumption *and* the rate of interest, (2.3.2) implies the endogeneity of r_τ. Section 2.8 traces the implications of exogenous changes and of endogenous changes in r_τ separately.

The consumption-savings models dealt with in sections 2.4 through 2.8 and 2.10 are deterministic. In recent years, however, increasing attention has been paid to the impact of uncertainty on individual (optimal) time-patterns of savings and consumption (cf. e.g. Yaari [1965]). Consequently section 2.9 examines the impact of the stochastic nature of income expectations on the optimal time pattern of consumption; viz. according to the hypothesis that the utility of the time-pattern of consumption depends not only on consumption itself, but also on deviations of consumption from its optimal value in case income would assume its expected value, i.e. would be non-stochastic. Since the form of the utility function is left unspecified, no analytical solution for optimal consumption and savings could be derived.

Still, *some* conclusions may be reached regarding the impact of changes in the 'data' on the optimum values of consumption in future periods of time. The notion of what is 'given', however, varies between the different versions of the model, as shown in table 2.1 below.

Initial personal wealth is always 'known'; desired final personal wealth too is considered as given, except in the case – dealth with in section 2.5 – where it is incorporated in the utility function.

Expectations about the future time-paths of income, rates of interest and price levels are also regarded as 'data', with assumed invariance over prospective time as a particular case.

In the impact or sensitivity analysis changes in parameters take the place of changes in the variables. In addition, variables may be functions of other variables beside time. This applies to the situation dealt with in section 2.6, where income is assumed to depend on the amount of time (to be) worked per period, which variable is introduced into the utility function. It also holds good in the case where the rate of interest in any period depends on personal wealth at the beginning of the same period (section 2.8.3.2).

For all these versions of savings theory, the relationships resemble those of the traditional theory of consumer demand.

TABLE 2.1.

Survey of the models of sections 2.4 through 3.7

I. General quasi-static discontinuous models	Section							
	2.4	2.5	2.6	2.7	2.8.1	2.8.2	2.9	2.10
	Basic model	Variable final wealth	Working hours incorporated	Survival rates inc.	Variable interest rates and price levels		Uncertainty inc.	Intra-group effects inc.
1. *Other main characteristics*								
1.1. Deterministic (D) or stochastic (S)	D	D	D	D	D	D	S	D
1.2. Individualistic (I) or sociometric (soc)	I	I	I	I	I	I	I	soc
1.3. *Time span:* life expectancy (*L*) or max. lifetime (*M*) for unit periods *l*	*L*	*L*	*L*	*M*	*L*	*L*	*L*	*M*
2. *Contents*								
2.1. *Utility function* arguments	C_l	C_l, K_L	C_l, W_l	C_l	c_l	C_l	$\{\bar{C}_l$; $C_l - \bar{C}_l$	${}_iC_l$; ${}_1C_1 \dots {}_IC_1$
2.2. *Budget-equation* variables	C_l	C_l, K_L	C_l, Y_l	C_l	c_l	C_l, r_l	C_l	${}_iC_l$
data	Y_l, r; K_0, K_L	Y_l, r; K_0	K_0, K_L, r	Y_l, r; K_0, K_L; s_l	y_l, r_l; K_0, K_L; p_l; a_l	Y_l; K_0, K_L	prob (Y'); K_0, K_L, r	${}_iY_l$; ${}_1Y_1 \dots {}_IY_1$; ${}_is', {}_ir'$
2.3. *Supplementary relationships* parameters			$Y_l = Y_l(W_1 \dots W_l)$; $\zeta_{l1} \dots \zeta_{lZ_l}$			$r_l = r(K_{l-1})$; $\vartheta_1 \dots \vartheta_K$		

Table 2.1 (cont.)

II. Special discontinuous models, with additive-separable utility functions	Section									
	3.1		3.2		3.3		3.4	3.5		3.6
	3.1.1	3.1.2	3.2.1	3.2.2	3.3.2	3.3.3		3.5.2	3.5.3	
	Basic model		Variable final wealth		Working hours incorporated		Variable etc.	Uncertainty incorporated		Intragroup effects
3. *Forms*										
3.1. *Utility function* Completely (CAS) or pairwise additive-separable, with pairs (PAS)	CAS		CAS		CAS		CAS	CAS		CAS
		C_l, C_{l-1}		C_l, K_L		C_l, W_l			$\{\bar{C}_l, C_l - \bar{C}_l$	
3.2. *Supplementary functions*					$Y = U \cdot W$			prob. (Y') symmetric normal		$i'g_i$ const.

III. Continuous model, with separable utility function	Section 3.7	
	3.7.1–3.7.3	3.7.4
	Completely additive-separable utility	Pairwise additive-separable function
2. *Contents*		
2.1. *Utility function* arguments	$C(\tau)$	$C(\tau), \dot{C}(\tau)$
2.2. *Budget equation*		
variables	$C(\tau)$	
data	$Y(\tau), K_F, K_0, \varrho$, or $\varrho(\tau)$	
parameters	η, ξ	

Explanation of symbols

$_{(i)}C_l$ consumption by individuals i (= 1, ..., I) in periods l (= 1, ..., L)
$C_l^{(*)}$ (optimal*) consumption in l in case of absence of uncertainty
$C(\tau)$ rate of flow of consumption at point of time τ ($\bar{C}_\tau$ certainty-equivalent ditto)
c_l 'real' consumption in l
$\dot{C}(\tau)$ rate of change in the rate of flow of consumption at τ
W_l hours to be worked in l
$_{(i)}Y_l$ income (excluding interest on savings or dissavings originating after the beginning of period 1 expected or planned for period l by i)
K_0, K_L or K_F initial and desired final personal wealth, respectively
r_l rate of interest per unit period l
r rate of interest per unit period, equal for all l
$\varrho(\tau)$ continuous rate of interest at time τ
ϱ continuous rate of interest, equal for $0 \leq \tau \leq L$
a_l relative change in the asset price level between the beginning and the end of period l
p_l relative change in the average consumer price level between periods $l-1$ and l
s_l probability of surviving from the beginning of period 1 till the end of period l
prob (Y') = prob ($Y_1, \ldots, Y_L$) probability density function of the stochastic variables $Y_1, \ldots, Y_L$

The reason is the correspondence

between

(a) discount factors	and	prices,
(b) consumption per (future) period	and	consumption per budget item
in savings theory	and	in demand theory

respectively.

Thus, savings theory, like consumer-demand theory, has its 'Slutsky conditions' for utility maximization subject to a budget constraint. On the one hand, such a theoretical unification of related parts of economic science may be gratifying. On the other hand, the conclusions to be drawn with respect to effects of changing 'data' on the (optimal) time pattern of consumption are somewhat meagre, unless the utility function is further specified.

For that reason, restrictions on the form of the utility function are imposed in chapter 3. Alternatively, the basic utility function is assumed to be completely additive-separable and pairwise additive-separable. According to these specifications, subsections 3.1 through 3.6 of chapter 3 deal with the model versions presented in a more general way in sections 2.4 through 2.10 respectively.

The first choice is made because the utility function adopted for the specific savings model derived by Somermeyer [1960] and applied by Bannink [1966] represents a particular (addi-log) type of additive-separability.

Moreover, it enables the development of a continuous version of the consumption and savings model as presented in section 3.7; this removes the theoretically unsatisfactory and inelegant manner of treating interest receipts and payments with lags depending on arbitrarily chosen units of time and it obviates the need of expressing life expectancy by an integer. Moreover, the continuous treatment of optimal saving problems fits in with recent studies in this field by Yaari [1964] a.o.

In the same section (subsection 3.7.4), the model is further dynamized by introducing rates of change of consumption into the utility function, in addition to the rate of flow of consumption itself.

In the discrete versions of the model the expectations relate to (future) unit periods of time; therefore the implications of changes in the expected values of variables for *any or all* such periods on consumption may be studied. In the continuous version of the model, however, we cannot but examine effects of changes of one or more *parameters* in the time-functions of the variables.

Complete additive-separability of the utility function might be considered as too restrictive, since it implies intertemporal independence of consumption. For this reason, pair-wise additive separability of the utility function – allowing for dependence of consumption between successive periods, or between different types of variables (such as consumption and working hours) – is examined alternatively.

All models mentioned so far assume that individuals plan and act in isolation. Duesenberry a.o., however, introduce the notion that individuals' consumption behaviour may be affected by their surroundings, e.g. in the way of 'keeping up with the Joneses' (Duesenberry [1967]).

Negative marginal utility of other people's consumption may reflect 'jealousy'. Sections 2.10 and 3.5 present versions of the basic model taking account of the impact of intra-group relationships between individuals on their consumption and savings behaviour; these also imply 'guestimates' by individuals regarding the way and degree others would change their consumption in response to possible variations in their own consumption.

The latter, 'sociometric' type of model, however, is so complex that it does not seem worthwhile to proceed any further along this arduous road towards more 'realism'. On the contrary, it might be preferable to return to simpler versions of the model, as suggested in the last section of chapter 3.

General note: All functions are supposed to be at least twice differentiable (in order to enable the formulation of the first-order and second-order maximum conditions in the traditional manner).

Furthermore, the utility functions are assumed to be neither linear nor convertible into a linear form (lest the first-order conditions become insolvable).

Finally, boundary solutions of the optimum problems are precluded a priori (lest the solution of the first-order conditions becomes ineffective).

2.4. Basic model

2.4.1. UTILITY FUNCTION AND LIFETIME BUDGET EQUATION

The main assumption underlying this basic model is that individuals maximize the utility of their consumption C_l in prospective periods $l\,(=1,\ldots,L)$[2] subject to a lifetime budget constraint; here, L is interpreted as the life expectancy[3] of the individual at the moment it 'plans' its time-pattern of (future) consumption and savings[4]. Therefore, the utility function may be expressed by:

$$\omega = \omega\,(C_1, \ldots, C_L) = \omega(C') \quad \text{(in vector notation)}, \qquad (2.4.1.1)$$

with $\partial\omega/\partial C_l > 0$ for $l = 1, \ldots, L$.

The lifetime budget constraint is an identity, expressing the difference between desired 'final' personal wealth K_L of the individual (i.e. at the expected end of his life) and his 'initial' personal wealth K_0 (at the planning point of

---

[2] These periods are supposed to be of equal lengths.

[3] Depending on age, sex, occupation, living conditions and possible other characteristics of the individuals, and assumed to be an integer in the unit periods of time chosen.

[4] There may be (and generally will be) many, or even infinitely many 'planning' moments. The 'planning', however, may be (and generally will be) less deliberate or conscious than the word suggests.

time) in terms of cumulated savings S_l ($l = 1, \ldots, L$):

$$K_L - K_0 = \sum_{l=1}^{L} S_l . \tag{2.4.1.2}$$

In their turn, savings (or dissavings) effectuated in any period (l) equal the difference in personal wealth between the end and the beginning of the period (i.e. K_l and K_{l-1} respectively), as well as the difference between income Y_l^+ and consumption C_l in the same period:

$$S_l = K_l - K_{l-1} = Y_l^+ - C_l \quad \text{for } l = 1, \ldots, L. \tag{2.4.1.3}$$

Y_l^+ includes interest on savings (or dissavings) accumulated since the beginning of the planning period, in addition to income Y_l excluding this component. Since the time-pattern of savings in the planning period is as yet unknown – but to be determined by the model –, those two components should be distinguished for the latter purpose, i.e. by rewriting (2.4.1.3) as:

$$K_l - K_{l-1} = r\,(K_{l-1} - K_0) + (Y_l - C_l) \quad \text{for } l = 1, \ldots, L; \tag{2.4.1.4}$$

with r as the rate of interest[5] and assuming that interest on (dis-) savings in any period $l-1$ is due at the end of the next period (l) only[6].

By repeated application of (2.4.1.4) to $l = 1, 2, \ldots, \tau$, we find as the solution of this first-order linear difference equation in K_l:

$$K_\tau = K_0 + \sum_{l=1}^{\tau} (Y_l - C_l)\,(1 + r)^{\tau - l} \quad \text{for } \tau = 1, \ldots, L; \tag{2.4.1.5}$$

---

5 Here we assume that r is considered a constant for the entire planning period; in section 2.8, however, the prospective rate of interest is allowed to change.

6 Implying (dis-) savings to be 'timed' at the end of each period; otherwise the formulae for the accumulation of personal wealth would have to be modified in a manner depending on the time distribution of savings within the unit periods. In the case of uniform distribution of savings, for instance, the formula would become:

$$K_l - K_{l-1} = r\,(K_{l-1} - K_0) + (1 + \tfrac{1}{2}r)\,(Y_l - C_l), \tag{2.4.1.4$^\text{m}$}$$

resulting in a correspondingly modified life-time budget equation, viz.:

$$K_L - K_0 \approx \sum_{l=1}^{L} (Y_l - C_l)\,(1 + r)^{L-l+1/2}. \tag{2.4.1.6$^\text{m}$}$$

This arbitrariness in timing interest receipts or payments disappears in the continuous version of the model developed in section 3.7.

in particular for $\tau = L$:

$$\Delta K = K_L - K_0 = \sum_{l=1}^{L} (Y_l - C_l)(1 + r)^{L-l}$$

$$= (Y - C)' d \tag{2.4.1.6}$$

with

$$(Y - C)' = \{Y_1 - C_1 \cdots Y_L - C_L\}$$

and

$$d' = \{(1 + r)^{L-1} \cdots \underset{(=1)}{(1 + r)^{L-L}}\}.$$

Since C' is a positive vector, K should satisfy

$$\Delta K < Y'd. \tag{2.4.1.7}$$

Equation (2.4.1.6) is referred to as the 'lifetime' budget equation; K_L as well as K_0 and $Y_1, \ldots, Y_L$ are assumed to be known, whereas $C_1, \ldots, C_L$ are the unknowns. The latter have to be solved from:

2.4.2. OPTIMUM CONDITIONS

The optimum conditions for allocating consumption and savings over (future) time are the first-order conditions of maximizing the utility function (2.4.1.1) subject to the lifetime budget constraint (2.4.1.6):

$$\frac{\partial \omega}{\partial C_\tau} = \lambda (1 + r)^{L-\tau} \quad \text{for } \tau = 1, \ldots, L, \tag{2.4.2.1}$$

with λ a positive Lagrangean multiplier, or

$$\omega_C = \lambda \cdot d \quad \text{(in vector notation)}, \tag{2.4.2.1'}$$

with

$$\omega_C' = \left\{\frac{\partial \omega}{\partial C_1} \cdots \frac{\partial \omega}{\partial C_L}\right\}.$$

Equations (2.4.2.1) and (2.4.1.6) are equal in number to the $L + 1$ variables $C_1, \ldots, C_L$ and λ – a necessary but not a sufficient condition for solving the latter unknowns.

Premultiplying (2.4.2.1') by C' and making use of (2.4.1.6), we obtain:

$$C'\omega_C = \lambda \cdot C'd = \lambda R_L, \tag{2.4.2.2}$$

with

$$R_L = Y'd - \Delta K \tag{2.4.2.3}$$

representing resources for financing lifetime consumption valuated at the end of the planning period L.

Hence,

$$\lambda = R_L^{-1} \cdot C'\omega_C, \tag{2.4.2.4}$$

provided (2.4.1.7) is satisfied, i.e. $R_L > 0$.

Substitution of (2.4.2.4) into (2.4.2.1′) yields:

$$\omega_C = R_L^{-1} \cdot C'\omega_C \cdot d. \tag{2.4.2.5}$$

From the L equations comprised by (2.4.2.5), the L unknown $C_1, \ldots, C_L$ may be solved, at least in principle[7]. Of these – possibly multiple – solutions only those are relevant that yield a positive C-vector (say C^*) and ensure a maximum value of ω.

In order to derive the second-order conditions for ω attaining a proper maximum, at values of $\{(C^*)', \lambda^*\}$ satisfying (2.4.2.1) and (2.4.1.6), we expand $\omega(C')$ in terms of $\Delta C = C - C^*$, as follows:

$$\omega(C') = \omega^* + (\Delta C)' \, \omega_C^* + \tfrac{1}{2}(\Delta C)' \, \Omega_{CC}^*(\Delta C) \tag{2.4.2.6}$$

$$+ \text{ terms with elements of } \Delta C \text{ of third and higher degree,}$$

---

[7] For instance, see the derivation of consumption functions (4.1.3.2) in chapter 4. Sometimes, however, it is simpler to retain λ for the time being. As an example, we specify a quadratic utility function:

$$\omega = C'a + \tfrac{1}{2}C'AC, \tag{I}$$

a being a vector of length L, and A being a square, non-singular and negative-definite matrix of order L. Maximization of (I) subject to:

$$C'd = R_L \tag{II}$$

requires:

$$a + AC = \lambda d. \tag{III}$$

Pre-multiplication of both members of (III) by A^{-1} yields:

$$C = A^{-1} [-a + \lambda d], \tag{IV}$$

and pre-multiplication of both members of (IV) by d' enables use to solve λ as:

$$\lambda = (d'A^{-1}d)^{-1} (R_L + d'A^{-1}a). \tag{V}$$

Substitution of (V) into (IV) finally results in

$$C = -A^{-1} [a - (d'A^{-1}d)^{-1} (R_L + d'A^{-1}a) \, d]. \tag{VI}$$

with * denoting the values of the scalar, vectors and matrices for $C = C^*$ and $\Omega_{CC} = [\partial^2\omega/\partial C_l\, \partial C_{l'}]$ the Hessian matrix of ω for $l, l' = 1, \ldots, L$.

In order that $\omega(C') < \omega^*$ for $(\Delta C) \to \{0 \cdots 0\}$, the third term at the right-hand side of (2.4.2.6) should satisfy:

$$(\Delta C)'\, \Omega^*_{CC} \Delta C < 0 \tag{2.4.2.7}$$

with the second term vanishing:

$$\Delta C)'\, \omega^*_C = \lambda\, (\Delta C)'\, d = 0 \quad \text{according to (2.4.2.1) and (2.4.1.6.),} \tag{2.4.2.8}$$

and the sum of the higher-order terms converging towards zero; or:

$$\{(\Delta C)' \quad 1\} \begin{bmatrix} \Omega^*_{CC} & \omega^*_C \\ (\omega^*_C)' & 0 \end{bmatrix} \begin{bmatrix} \Delta C \\ 1 \end{bmatrix} < 0; \tag{2.4.2.9}$$

or, by virtue of (2.4.2.1′):

$$\{(\Delta C)' \quad 1\} \begin{bmatrix} \Omega^*_{CC} & d \\ d' & 0 \end{bmatrix} \begin{bmatrix} \Delta C \\ 1 \end{bmatrix} < 0 \tag{2.4.2.10}$$

for vectors ΔC with arbitrarily small elements, satisfying $(\Delta C)'d = 0$.

Evidently, for satisfying (2.4.2.7), (2.4.2.9) or (2.4.2.10) subject to (2.4.2.8):

$$\Omega^*_{CC} \quad \text{negative-definite} \tag{2.4.2.11}$$

(and a fortiori Ω_{CC} negative-definite for positive but otherwise arbitrary vectors C) is a sufficient but not a necessary condition[8].

The bordered Hessians

$$\begin{bmatrix} \Omega^*_{CC} & \omega^*_C \\ (\omega^*_C)' & 0 \end{bmatrix} \quad \text{and} \quad \begin{bmatrix} \Omega^*_{CC} & d \\ d' & 0 \end{bmatrix}$$

cannot be definite at all.

For ω convex, ω^* is not only a relative (constrained) maximum, but the global maximum as well.

For particular specifications, single analytical feasible solutions for the C-vector may be found (cf. chapter 4 and footnote 7 to the present chapter); they result in values of C_l depending on the values of the 'data':

$$C_l = C_l\,(Y_1, \ldots, Y_L, r, \Delta K). \tag{2.4.2.12}$$

---

[8] As an example, take $L = 2$, $\Delta C_1 = 1$ and $\Delta C_2 = -0.909$ with $r = 0.10$ and $\Omega_{CC} = \begin{bmatrix} -1 & 2 \\ 2 & -1 \end{bmatrix}$ indefinite, satisfying (2.4.2.7), (2.4.2.9) or (2.4.2.10) subject to (2.4.2.8).

Alternatively, the optimization problem can be solved by expressing one of the C_l in terms of the $L-1$ other $C_{l'}$ ($l' \neq l$) by means of (2.4.1.6), yielding for instance:

$$C_L = R_L - \sum_{l=1}^{L-1} C_l (1 + r)^{L-l}, \tag{2.4.2.13}$$

and substituting it into (2.1.1), with the result:

$$\omega = \omega_{-L} (C_1, \ldots, C_{L-1}). \tag{2.4.2.14}$$

Then, the first-order conditions for maximum ω would become

$$\frac{\partial \omega_{-L}}{\partial C_l} = 0 \quad \text{for} \quad l = 1, \ldots, L - 1, \tag{2.4.2.15}$$

and the second-order condition:

$$\Omega_{-L} = \left[\frac{\partial^2 \omega_{-L}}{\partial C_l \cdot \partial C_{l'}} \right], \tag{2.4.2.16}$$

i.e. the reduced Hessian of order $L-1$, negative-definite for values of $C_l^*, C_{l'}^*$ ($l, l' = 1, \ldots, L$) satisfying (2.4.2.15).

The same vector C^* would, of course, be obtained as according to the equivalent multiplier method outlined above.

The advantage of the substitution method is its simplicity; this applies to both the first-order conditions (smaller number of equations to be solved, viz. $L-1$, against L or $L+1$ according to the multiplier method) and the second-order condition (negative definiteness of the reduced Hessian as not merely a sufficient but also a necessary condition for arriving at a local utility maximum). Its disadvantage is the asymmetrical treatment of the C_l it requires and the ensueing inelegance of further analytical derivations. Since the latter deficiencies are absent from the multiplier-procedure, treating all C_l alike, the latter method is the only one adopted below.

The vector of optimal savings $S_1^* \cdots S_L^*$ corresponding to the vector of optimal consumption $C_1^* \cdots C_L^*$ may be calculated as:

$$\left.\begin{aligned} S_1^* &= Y_1 - C_1^* \\ &\vdots \\ S_l^* &= Y_l - C_l^* + r \sum_{\tau=1}^{l-1} (Y_\tau^+ - C_\tau^*) \quad \text{for } l = 2, \ldots, L. \end{aligned}\right\} \tag{2.4.2.17}$$

These values satisfy the identity:

$$K_L - K_0 = \sum_{l=1}^{L} S_l^*. \tag{2.4.2.18}$$

2.4.3. EFFECTS OF VARYING THE 'DATA' ON THE OPTIMAL TIME-PATTERN OF CONSUMPTION

In the basic model, three or four kinds of 'data' may be varied, i.e.

(a) income expectations Y_l,

(b) the rate of interest r, and either

(c1) the desired change in personal wealth (ΔK)

or

(c2) initial and desired final personal wealth (K_0 and K_L) separately.

Expressions for the effects of each of these variations may be obtained by partial differentiation of either (2.4.2.12) or the first-order optimum conditions (2.4.2.1) and the lifetime budget equation (2.4.1.6) with respect to those data. As a result, we obtain:

$$\frac{\partial}{\partial Y_k}\left(\frac{\partial \omega}{\partial C_\tau}\right) = \sum_{l=1}^{L} \frac{\partial^2 \omega}{\partial C_\tau \cdot \partial C_l} \cdot \frac{\partial C_l}{\partial Y_k} = \frac{\partial \lambda}{\partial Y_k} \cdot (1 + r)^{L-\tau} \qquad (2.4.3.1)$$

and

$$0 = (1 + r)^{L-k} - \sum_{l=1}^{L} \frac{\partial C_l}{\partial Y_k} (1 + r)^{L-l} \qquad (2.4.3.2)$$

for varying Y_k $(k = 1, \ldots, L)$,

$$\frac{\partial}{\partial r}\left(\frac{\partial \omega}{\partial C_\tau}\right) = \sum_{l=1}^{L} \frac{\partial^2 \omega}{\partial C_\tau \cdot \partial C_l} \cdot \frac{\partial C_l}{\partial r} = \frac{\partial \lambda}{\partial r} (1 + r)^{L-\tau} + \lambda (L - \tau)(1 + r)^{L-\tau-1} \qquad (2.4.3.3)$$

and

$$0 = -\sum_{l=1}^{L} \frac{\partial C_l}{\partial r} (1 + r)^{L-l} + \sum_{l=1}^{L} (Y_l - C_l)(L - l)(1 + r)^{L-l-1} \qquad (2.4.3.4)$$

for varying r,

$$\frac{\partial}{\partial(\Delta K)}\left(\frac{\partial \omega}{\partial C_\tau}\right) = \sum_{l=1}^{L} \frac{\partial^2 \omega}{\partial C_\tau \cdot \partial C_l} \frac{\partial C_l}{\partial (\Delta K)} = \frac{\partial \lambda}{\partial (\Delta K)} \cdot (1 + r)^{L-\tau} \qquad (2.4.3.5)$$

and

$$1 = -\sum_{l=1}^{L} \frac{\partial C_l}{\partial (\Delta K)} (1 + r)^{L-l} \qquad (2.4.3.6)$$

for varying ΔK and $\tau = 1, \ldots, L$.

In matrix notation, eqs. (2.4.3.1) through (2.4.3.6) may be combined as follows:

$$\begin{bmatrix} \Omega & \dot{d} \\ \dot{d}' & 0 \end{bmatrix} \begin{bmatrix} C_Y & C_r & C_{\Delta K} \\ -\lambda'_Y & -\lambda_r & -\lambda_{\Delta K} \end{bmatrix} = \begin{bmatrix} 0 & \lambda(1+r)^{-1}\dot{d}L_- & 0 \\ \dot{d}' & (1+r)^{-1}(Y' - C')\dot{d}L_- & -1 \end{bmatrix} \tag{2.4.3.7}$$

with

$$C_Y = \left[\frac{\partial C_\tau}{\partial Y_k}\right] \quad \text{a matrix of order } L \times L$$

$$\left.\begin{aligned} C'_r &= \left\{\frac{\partial C_1}{\partial r} \cdots \frac{\partial C_L}{\partial r}\right\} \\ C'_{\Delta K} &= \left\{\frac{\partial C_1}{\partial(\Delta K)} \cdots \frac{\partial C_L}{\partial(\Delta K)}\right\} \\ \lambda'_Y &= \frac{\partial \lambda}{\partial Y_1} \cdots \frac{\partial \lambda}{\partial Y_L} \end{aligned}\right\} \quad \text{row vectors of lengths } L$$

$$\left.\begin{aligned} \lambda_r &= \frac{\partial \lambda}{\partial r} \\ \lambda_{\Delta K} &= \frac{\partial \lambda}{\partial(\Delta K)} \end{aligned}\right\} \quad \text{scalars}$$

$\dot{d}$ = a diagonal matrix of order L, with $d_1 \cdots d_L$ on the main diagonal

$$L'_- = \{(L-1) \cdots (L-L)\} \quad \text{a row vector of length } L;$$
$$(= 0)$$

consequently, the matrix in the right-hand member of (2.4.3.7) has an $L \times L$ "0"-sub-matrix at its North-Western corner, and an $L \times 1$ '0'-vector at its North-Eastern corner. Naturally, at the right-hand member of (2.4.3.7) C' assumes its optimal value for Y, r and ΔK being given intially; Ω is evaluated accordingly.

The second matrix at the left-hand side of (2.4.3.7) is the matrix of the unknown effects of variations in the $\{Y', r, \Delta K\}$ vector on the $\left[\begin{smallmatrix} C \\ \lambda \end{smallmatrix}\right]$ vector. These effects may be written explicitly by pre-multiplying both members of

(2.4.3.7) by:

$$\begin{bmatrix} \Omega & d \\ d' & 0 \end{bmatrix}^{-1} = (d'\Omega^{-1}d)^{-1} \begin{bmatrix} (d'\Omega^{-1}d)\,\Omega^{-1} - (\Omega^{-1}d)(\Omega^{-1}d)' & \Omega^{-1}d \\ (\Omega^{-1}d)' & -1 \end{bmatrix}, \tag{2.4.3.8}$$

assuming Ω to be non-singular[9].

Making use of (2.4.3.8), we derive from (2.4.3.7):

$$C_Y = (d'\Omega^{-1}d)^{-1}\,\Omega^{-1}dd' \;(= -C_{\Delta K}d'), \tag{2.4.3.9}$$

$$C_r = \lambda(1+r)^{-1}\,[\Omega^{-1} - (d'\Omega^{-1}d)^{-1}(\Omega^{-1}d)(\Omega^{-1}d)']\,\dot{d}L- \\ + (1+r)^{-1}(d'\Omega^{-1}d)^{-1}(\Omega^{-1}d)(Y' - C')\,\dot{d}L-, \tag{2.4.3.10}$$

and

$$C_{\Delta K} = -(d'\Omega^{-1}d)^{-1}\,\Omega^{-1}d. \tag{2.4.3.11}$$

Since d' is a positive vector, (2.4.3.2) implies that for any $k\,(= 1, \ldots, L)$ the weighted mean of the $\partial C_l/\partial Y_k$, with the $(1+r)^{l-1}$ as weights, is positive, i.e. that the $\partial C_l/\partial Y_k$ are positive *on the average*.

Multiplication of both members of (2.4.3.2) by $(1+r)^{k-l}$ results in:

$$\sum_{l=1}^{L}(1+r)^{k-l}\,\frac{\partial C_l}{\partial Y_k} = 1. \tag{2.4.3.12}$$

Since $(1+r)^{h-l} < (1+r)^{k-l}$ for $h < k$:

$$\frac{\partial C_l}{\partial Y_k} < \frac{\partial C_l}{\partial Y_h} \quad \text{for} \quad h < k \textit{ on the average.} \tag{2.4.3.13}$$

The meaning of (2.4.3.13) is that the effect of an expected change in income for any period k on consumption in any period l will generally be smaller according as k belongs to a more remote future, irrespective of whether $k \gtreqless l$, i.e. whether the period k of variation in C_l precedes, coincides with or comes after the period of variation in Y_k.

According to (2.4.3.10), the effects of a variation in the rate of interest on the (optimal) time-pattern of consumption are more difficult to evaluate than either the income effects or the desired change-in-personal-wealth effects.

---

[9] If Ω is negative-definite, (2.4.3.8) implies that the bordered Hessian cannot be negative definite, because at least the element at the south-east corner of its inverse is positive, $d'\Omega^{-1}d$ being negative.

The reason is that according to (2.4.3.10) the interest-effects C_r may be decomposed into a substitution effect:

$$(C_r)_{\mathrm{I}} = \lambda (1 + r)^{-1} [\Omega^{-1} - (d'\Omega^{-1}d)^{-1} (\Omega^{-1}d) (\Omega^{-1}d)'] \dot{d}L- \qquad (2.4.3.14)$$

and a 'wealth accumulation' effect:

$$\begin{aligned}(C_r)_{\mathrm{II}} &= (1 + r)^{-1} (d'\Omega^{-1}d)^{-1} \Omega^{-1}d (Y' - C') \dot{d}L- \\ &= (1 + r)^{-1} (d'\Omega^{-1}d)^{-1} \Omega^{-1}dd'\dot{L}-. (Y - C) \\ &= (1 + r)^{-1} C_Y (\dot{Y} - \dot{C}) L- \\ &= -(\Delta K)_r\, C_{\Delta K},^{9a} \quad \text{by means of (2.4.3.9) and (2.4.3.11),}\end{aligned} \qquad (2.4.3.15)$$

with $(\Delta K)_r = \partial(\Delta K)/\partial r = (1 + r)^{-1} d'(\dot{Y} - \dot{C}) L-$, i.e. the effect which a change in r would have on ΔK, given the vectors Y and C.

The matrix within square brackets at the right-hand side of (2.4.3.14) may be identified with the symmetric Slutsky-matrix

$$\Xi = \Omega^{-1} - (d'\Omega^{-1}d)^{-1} (\Omega^{-1}d) (\Omega^{-1}d)', \qquad (2.4.3.16)$$

which plays an important rôle in traditional demand theory. The elements of d, i.e. $(1 + r)^{L-\tau}$ for $\tau = 1, \ldots, L$, may be interpreted as ratios of the 'prices' of consumption in period τ, to the 'price' of saving – till the end of period L; obviously, these prices decrease with increasing τ, i.e. according as consumption relates to a more remote future. This means that (2.4.3.14) expresses the shifts in consumption between different periods due to changes in the prices of their complements, i.e. savings – apart from effects on wealth accumulation as represented by (2.4.3.15).

The Slutsky matrix is singular, since

$$d'\Xi \equiv 0 \equiv d'(C_r)_{\mathrm{I}}. \qquad (2.4.3.17)$$

This means that on the average the substitution effect of the rate of interest is zero, when weighted by the elements of d.

The latter property implies that unless all elements of Ξ are zero (an idea to be discarded forthwith), at least one element of $(C_r)_{\mathrm{I}}$ is positive and at least one other element is negative. For $\Omega^{(*)}$ negative-definite, Ξ is negative

[9a] Mr. J. van Driel of the Econometric Institute, Rotterdam, kindly provided the authors with both the derivation and interpretation of this elucidating expression.

semi-definite[10]. This means that the elements on the main diagonal of Ξ are non-positive (and generally negative).

On the other hand, the off-diagonal elements may be positive, negative or zero, indicating substitutability, complementarity and indifference between consumption in different periods, respectively. This bears an obvious analogy to traditional demand theory, relating to consumption of different goods and services in the same period. Without a more precise specification of the utility function (cf. chapter 3) no further conclusions can be drawn about the signs of the substitution effects of the rate of interest on prospective consumption.

The wealth accumulation effects of the rate of interest may also vary, depending upon the signs of the elements of the C_Y-matrix and of the $(Y-C)$-vector. According to (2.4.3.9), in C_Y positive elements at least dominate over negative ones (if the latter are present at all). Hence, the elements of $(C_r)_{\text{II}}$ will generally be positive or negative depending on whether positive or negative values of 'net' savings $Y_\tau - C_\tau$ – weighted by $L-\tau$ – dominate; obviously, earlier periods carry more weight than later ones.

These alternatives will come out most clearly where strong wealth *acc*umulation or strong wealth *de*cumulation is aimed at; i.e. as expressed by large positive or negative values of $K_L - K_0$.

The reason is that hoarders, in order to attain a predetermined positive level of wealth accumulation may save less, and may consume more according as higher rates of interest contribute larger interest receipts (per dollar saved); conversely, wealth decumulation takes place more rapidly, by larger amounts of interest payments foregone, so that spendthrifts have to cut down on consumption if interest rates go up.

As appears from a comparison of (2.4.3.11) with (2.4.3.9) and (2.4.3.10), the change-in-personal-wealth effect is simpler than either the income effect or the interest effect. For similar reasons as mentioned with respect to the signs of the elements of C_Y, positive elements $C_{\Delta K}$ will dominate in (2.4.3.11).

The interpretation of the second component of the interest effect on (optimal) consumption is shown most clearly by the last member of (2.4.3.15): it features this component $(C_r)_{\text{II}}$ as the change-in-personal wealth effect on

---

[10] Proof: For Ω negative-definite, a matrix of real elements P exists such that $\Omega^{-1} = -PP'$; hence

$$(x'x)\cdot z'\Xi z = -x'x\cdot y'y + x'y\cdot y'x = -\tfrac{1}{2}\,\text{tr}(xy' - yx')^2$$

(inequality of Cauchy-Schwarz) if $x' = d'P$, $y' = z'P$.

consumption $C_{\Delta K}$ multiplied by minus the ceteris paribus effect of a change in the rate of interest on change in personal wealth $(\Delta K)_r$. Hence, the signs of the elements of $(C_r)_{\text{II}}$ depend on both the sign of $(\Delta K)_r$ and the signs of the elements of $C_{\Delta K}$. As expressed by the definition of $(\Delta K)_r$ under (2.4.3.15), its sign depends on the signs and magnitudes of the elements of the vector $(Y - C)$, as well as on their distribution over future time. That means that less initial personal wealth K_0 (given K_L) as well as higher aspirations with respect to final personal wealth K_L (given K_0) will reduce consumption as a rule; obviously, this agrees with common sense considerations.

2.4.4. INVARIANCE OF THE RESULTS AGAINST ARBITRARY MONOTONICALLY INCREASING TRANSFORMATION OF THE UTILITY FUNCTION

Suppose that the utility function (2.4.1.1) is replaced by:

$$\varphi = f(\omega) \tag{2.4.4.1}$$

with f a function satisfying:

$$\frac{\mathrm{d}f}{\mathrm{d}\omega} = f_\omega > 0. \tag{2.4.4.2}$$

Then, first-order conditions (2.4.2.1) pass into:

$$\varphi_C = \mu d \quad \text{with} \quad \varphi'_C = \left\{\frac{\partial \varphi}{\partial C_1} \cdots \frac{\partial \varphi}{\partial C_L}\right\}, \tag{2.4.4.3}$$

and μ a new Lagrangean multiplier.

By (2.4.4.1):

$$\varphi_C = f_\omega \omega_C. \tag{2.4.4.4}$$

If also

$$\mu = f_\omega \lambda, \tag{2.4.4.5}$$

2.4.4.3) is equivalent to (2.4.2.1).

Furthermore, (2.4.4.4) implies:

$$\Phi = f_\omega \Omega + f_{\omega\omega} \omega_C \omega'_C, \tag{2.4.4.6}$$

with $\Phi = [\partial^2 \varphi / \partial C_l \, \partial C_{l'}]$.

Because of (2.4.4.6), the second-order conditions (2.4.2.6) become:

$$\{(\Delta C)' \ \ 1\}\begin{bmatrix}\Phi & d\\ d' & 0\end{bmatrix}\begin{bmatrix}\Delta C\\ 1\end{bmatrix} = f_\omega (\Delta C)' \Omega (\Delta C) + 2 f_{\omega\omega} \{(\Delta C)' \omega_C\} \{(\Delta C)' \omega_C\}'$$

$$= f_\omega (\Delta C)' \Omega (\Delta C) \quad \text{for } \Delta C \to 0 \qquad \text{(cf. (2.4.2.8))}$$

$$< 0^{11} \qquad (2.4.4.7)$$

because of (2.4.4.2) and (2.4.2.7).

Hence, also the second-order conditions for a constrained utility maximum are invariant against a – monotonically increasing, but otherwise arbitrary – transformation of ω.

In addition:

$$\mu_Y = f_\omega \lambda_Y + \lambda f_{\omega\omega} C_Y' \omega_C, \qquad (2.4.4.8)$$

$$\mu_r = f_\omega \lambda_r + \lambda f_{\omega\omega} \omega_C' C_r, \qquad (2.4.4.9)$$

and

$$\mu_{\Delta K} = f_\omega \lambda_{\Delta K} + \lambda f_{\omega\omega} \omega_C' C_{\Delta K} \qquad (2.4.4.10)$$

follow from (2.4.4.5).

By application of the transformation function (2.4.4.1), eqs. (2.4.3.7) pass into:

$$\begin{bmatrix}\Phi & d\\ d' & 0\end{bmatrix}\begin{bmatrix}C_Y & C_r & C_{\Delta K}\\ -\mu_Y' & -\mu_r & -\mu_{\Delta K}\end{bmatrix} = \begin{bmatrix}0 & \mu (1+r)^{-1} \cdot \dot{d}L- & 0\\ d' & (1+r)^{-1} \cdot (Y' - C')\, \dot{d}L- & -1\end{bmatrix}. \qquad (2.4.4.11)$$

After substitution of (2.4.4.6) and (2.4.4.8) through (2.4.4.10) into (2.4.4.11), it appears that (2.4.4.11) is equivalent to (2.4.3.7), since the first

---

[11] Again, Φ negative-definite is a sufficient but not a necessary condition for satisfying this kind of inequality. The non-necessity of such a property is evident in view of the fact that (negative-) definiteness of a Hessian is not invariant against an arbitrary monotonically increasing transformation (as is proved in this sub-section for all meaningful deterministic theorems), but only against a convex monotonically increasing transformation of the utility function. The latter restriction follows from (2.4.4.6), implying:

$$z'\Phi z = f_\omega \cdot z'\Omega z + f_{\omega\omega} (z'\omega_C)(z'\omega_C)' \qquad (2.4.4.6a)$$

with z an arbitrary vector of length L; ensuring $z'\Phi z < 0$ for $z'\Omega z < 0$ requires $f_\omega \geq 0$ and $f_{\omega\omega} \leq 0$, with the latter two equality signs not holding simultaneously.

3 L of the eqs. (2.4.4.11) may be written as:

$$\begin{aligned} \Phi C_Y - d\mu'_Y &= f_\omega\,[\Omega C_Y - d\lambda'_Y] + f_{\omega\omega}\,[\omega_C \omega'_C C_Y - \lambda\, d\omega'_C\, C_Y] \\ &= f_\omega\,[\Omega C_Y - d\lambda'_Y] + 0 \quad \text{(by virtue of (2.4.2.1'))} \\ &= 0 \text{ (by virtue of (2.4.3.7))}, \end{aligned} \tag{2.4.4.12}$$

and

$$\begin{aligned} \Phi C_x - d\mu'_x &= f_\omega\,[\Omega C_x - d\lambda'_x] + f_{\omega\omega}\,[\omega_C \omega'_C C_x - \lambda d\omega'_C C_x] \\ &= f_\omega\,[\Omega C_x - d\lambda'_x] + 0 \\ &= \begin{cases} f_\omega \lambda\,(1+r)^{-1} \cdot \dot{d}L - & \text{for } x = r \\ 0 & \text{for } x = \Delta K. \end{cases} \end{aligned} \tag{2.4.4.13}$$

The last 3 equations of (2.4.4.11), starting with d', are the same as those of (2.4.3.7) but for the change of λ into $\mu = f_\omega \lambda$, as also evidenced by (2.4.4.13) for $x = r$.

Consequently, the 'effects' formulae are invariant against any monotonically increasing transformation of the utility function. This holds good also for the other deterministic versions of the model, to be dealt with in sections 2.5 through 2.10.

Under conditions of uncertainty, however, the effects formulae remain invariant only if a *linear* (increasing) transformation is applied to the utility function.

2.5. *Model with desired final personal wealth incorporated in the utility function*

2.5.1. UTILITY FUNCTION

The utility function now becomes:

$$\omega = \omega\,(C_1, \ldots, C_L, K_L). \tag{2.5.1.1}$$

Presumably, the advocates of incorporating final personal wealth in the utility function assume that:

$$\partial\omega / \partial K_L > 0, \tag{2.5.1.2}$$

at least for K_L not exceeding a certain upper limit.

This positive appreciation of K_L may be ascribed to its nature of a 'carry-over' variable. This holds good in particular if L runs short of the expected lifetime, so that K_L has to provide against a rainy day, beyond the planning horizon (cf. also section 2.9.4). It may apply, however, even if L equals expected lifetime, because of the uncertainty inherent to actual lifetime. Moreover, K_L may serve as a provision for the surviving spouse or relatives. Belief in re-incarnation or other forms of life after death may strengthen that bequest motive. Belief in possible revival due to hoped-for progress in medical science and technique may assign to K_L the role of cost for tiding over in deep-freeze the interval between death and anticipated time of resuscitation (cf. Ettinger [1963]). In an even more literal sense, the ancient Greeks provided the dead with a small coin for paying the ferryman carrying them over the Styx in order to reach the Elysean fields.

The lifetime budget equation remains the same (i.e. (2.4.1.6)), albeit that K_L is re-interpreted as a variable (instead of as a constant).

2.5.2. OPTIMUM CONDITIONS

The first-order conditions for maximizing (2.5.1.1) subject to (2.4.1.6) now become:

$$\begin{bmatrix} \omega_C \\ \omega_{K_L} \end{bmatrix} = \lambda \begin{bmatrix} d \\ 1 \end{bmatrix}, \tag{2.5.2.1}$$

with $\omega_{K_L} = \partial\omega/\partial K_L$, and λ a (positive) Lagrangean multiplier.

Here too, equation (2.4.2.5) applies; the only difference is that in the present section financial resources R_L are not given, but depend on the unknown K_L according to $R_L = Y'd + K_0 - K_L$. Therefore, we may use the system of L equations:

$$\omega_C = [Y'd + K_0 - K_L]^{-1} \cdot C'\omega_C \cdot d, \tag{2.5.2.2}$$

in order to express all $C_1, \ldots, C_L$ in terms of K_L and the data; next, these expressions may be substituted into:

$$\omega_{K_L} = \lambda = [Y'd + K_0 - K_L]^{-1} \, C'\omega_C, \tag{2.5.2.3}$$

in order to solve ω_{K_L}.

Of the (possibly multiple) solutions only those are worth further consideration that yield a positive C-vector and a real K_L-value, and meet the second-order conditions for ω reaching a maximum:

$$\{(\Delta C)' \quad \Delta K_L \quad 1\} \begin{bmatrix} \Omega^*_{CC} & \omega^*_{CK_L} & \omega^*_C \\ (\omega^*_{CK_L})' & \omega^*_{K_L K_L} & \omega^*_{K_L} \\ (\omega^*_C)' & (\omega^*_{K_L})' & 0 \end{bmatrix} \begin{bmatrix} \Delta C \\ \Delta K_L \\ 0 \end{bmatrix} < 0, \tag{2.5.2.4}$$

or

$$\{(\Delta C)' \quad \Delta K_L \quad 1\} \begin{bmatrix} \Omega^*_{CC} & \omega^*_{CK_L} & d \\ (\omega^*_{CK_L})' & \omega^*_{K_L K_L} & 1 \\ d' & 1 & 0 \end{bmatrix} \begin{bmatrix} \Delta C \\ \Delta K_L \\ 1 \end{bmatrix} < 0, \tag{2.5.2.5}$$

(in view of (2.5.2.1)) with

$$\omega'_{CK_L} = \left\{ \frac{\partial^2 \omega}{\partial C_1 \, \partial K_L} \cdots \frac{\partial^2 \omega}{\partial C_L \, \partial K_L} \right\} \quad \text{a } 1 \times L \text{ vector,}$$

$$\omega_{K_L K_L} = (\partial^2 \omega / \partial K_L^2) \quad \text{a scalar,}$$

and asterisks denoting valuation at values of C_l and K_L satisfying (2.5.2.1), for vectors $\{(\Delta C)' \quad \Delta K_L\}$ with arbitrarily small elements satisfying:

$$\Delta K_L = -(\Delta C)' \, d. \tag{2.5.2.6}$$

Equations (2.5.2.1), $L+1$ in number, in addition to (2.4.1.6), permit solving the optimum values of the unknown C_l^*, K_L and λ, provided supplementary conditions, similar to those mentioned in section 2.4.2, are satisfied.

Again, the optimum values of prospective savings S_l^* may be computed according to (2.4.2.17).

2.5.3. EFFECTS OF VARYING THE 'DATA' ON THE OPTIMAL TIME-PATTERN OF CONSUMPTION

As in section 2.4.3, the effects of varying Y_l $(l = 1, \ldots, L)$, r and K_0 on the optimal values of C_l and K_L may be found by differentiating the first-order conditions (2.5.2.1) and the lifetime budget equation (2.4.1.6) partially with respect to the first three types of 'data'.

As a result, we obtain:

$$\begin{bmatrix} \Omega_{CC'} & \omega_{CK_L} & d \\ \omega'_{CK_L} & \omega_{K_LK_L} & 1 \\ d' & 1 & 0 \end{bmatrix} \begin{bmatrix} C_Y & C_r & C_{K_0} \\ (K_L)'_Y & (K_L)_r & (K_L)_{K_0} \\ -\lambda'_Y & -\lambda_r & -\lambda_{K_0} \end{bmatrix}$$

$$= \begin{bmatrix} 0 & \lambda(1+r)^{-1}\, \dot{d}L- & 0 \\ 0 & 0 & 0 \\ d' & (1+r)^{-1}(Y'-C')\,\dot{d}L- & 1 \end{bmatrix}, \tag{2.5.3.1}$$

again evaluated at the 'optimum' values of the variables. By striking out the $(K+1)$th rows of the matrices in (2.5.3.1) and dropping the $(K+1)$th column of the first matrix as well, eqs. (2.4.3.7) of the preceding section are regained.

In order to solve (2.5.3.1) for the 'effects', represented by C_Y, C_r, C_{K_0}, $(K_L)_Y$, $(K_L)_r$ and $(K_L)_{K_0}$, we pre-multiply both members of (2.5.3.1) by:

$$\begin{bmatrix} \Omega_{CC} & \omega_{CK_L} & d \\ \omega'_{CK_L} & \omega_{K_LK_L} & 1 \\ d' & 1 & 0 \end{bmatrix}^{-1} = s_0^{-1} \begin{bmatrix} M & v & w \\ v' & s_1 & s_2 \\ w' & s_2 & s_3 \end{bmatrix} \tag{2.5.3.2}$$

with

$$\begin{cases} s_0 = (d'\Omega_{CC}^{-1}d)(\omega_{K_LK_L} - \omega'_{CK_L}\Omega_{CC}^{-1}\omega_{CK_L}) + (1-\omega'_{CK_L}\Omega_{CC}^{-1}d)^2 = -s_1s_3 + s_2^2, \\ M = s_0\Omega_{CC}^{-1} + (d'\Omega_{CC}^{-1}d)(\Omega_{CC}^{-1}\omega_{CK_L})(\Omega_{CC}^{-1}\omega_{CK_L})' \\ \quad + (1-\omega'_{CK_L}\Omega_{CC}^{-1}d)\,\Omega_{CC}^{-1}(\omega_{CK_L}d' + d\omega'_{CK_L})\,\Omega_{CC}^{-1} \\ \quad - (\omega_{K_LK_L} - \omega'_{CK_L}\Omega_{CC}^{-1}\omega_{CK_L})(\Omega_{CC}^{-1}d)(\Omega_{CC}^{-1}d)', \\ v = -\Omega_{CC}^{-1}\,[(d'\Omega_{CC}^{-1}d)\,\omega_{CK_L} + (1-\omega'_{CK_L}\Omega_{CC}^{-1}d)\,d], \\ w = -\Omega_{CC}^{-1}\,[(1-\omega'_{CK_L}\Omega_{CC}^{-1}d)\,\omega_{CK_L} - (\omega_{K_LK_L} - \omega'_{CK_L}\Omega_{CC}^{-1}\omega_{CK_L})\,d], \\ s_1 = d'\Omega_{CC}^{-1}d, \\ s_2 = 1 - \omega'_{CK_L}\Omega_{CC}^{-1}d, \\ s_3 = -(\omega_{K_LK_L} - \omega'_{CK_L}\Omega_{CC}^{-1}\omega_{CK_L}). \end{cases}$$

(2.5.3.3)

Thus, we arrive at the following expressions for the "effects":

$$C_Y = s_0^{-1} w d'$$
$$= -s_0^{-1} \Omega_{CC}^{-1} [(1 - \omega'_{CK_L} \Omega_{CC}^{-1} d) \omega_{CK_L} - (\omega_{K_L K_L} - \omega'_{CK_L} \Omega_{CC}^{-1} \omega_{CK_L}) d] d', \tag{2.5.3.4}$$

$$\begin{aligned} C_r &= s_0^{-1} (1+r)^{-1} [\lambda M + w (Y' - C')] \dot{d}L- \\ &= s_0^{-1} (1+r)^{-1} [\lambda \{s_0 \Omega_{CC}^{-1} + (d'\Omega_{CC}^{-1} d)(\Omega_{CC}^{-1} \omega_{CK_L})(\Omega_{CC}^{-1} \omega_{CK_L})' \\ &+ (1 - \omega'_{CK_L} \Omega_{CC}^{-1} d) \Omega_{CC}^{-1} (\omega_{CK_L} d' + d\omega'_{CK_L}) \Omega_{CC}^{-1} \\ &- (\omega_{K_L K_L} - \omega'_{CK_L} \Omega_{CC}^{-1} \omega_{CK_L})(\Omega_{CC}^{-1} d)(\Omega_{CC}^{-1} d)'\} \\ &- \Omega_{CC}^{-1} \{(1 - \omega'_{CK_L} \Omega_{CC}^{-1} d) \omega_{CK_L} - (\omega_{K_L K_L} - \omega'_{CK_L} \Omega_{CC}^{-1} \omega_{CK_L}) d\} \\ &\times (Y' - C')] \dot{d}L-, \end{aligned} \tag{2.5.3.5}$$

$$\begin{aligned} C_{K_0} &= s_0^{-1} w = -s_0^{-1} \Omega_{CC}^{-1} [(1 - \omega'_{CK_L} \Omega_{CC}^{-1} d) \omega_{CK_L} \\ &- (\omega_{K_L K_L} - \omega'_{CK_L} \Omega_{CC}^{-1} \omega_{CK_L}) d], \end{aligned} \tag{2.5.3.6}$$

$$(K_L)_Y = s_0^{-1} s_2 d' = s_0^{-1} (1 - \omega'_{CK_L} \Omega_{CC}^{-1} d) d', \tag{2.5.3.7}$$

$$\begin{aligned} (K_L)_r &= s_0^{-1} (1+r)^{-1} [\lambda v' + s_2 (Y' - C')] \dot{d}L- \\ &= -s_0^{-1} (1+r)^{-1} [\lambda \{(d'\Omega_{CC}^{-1} d)(\Omega_{CC}^{-1} \omega_{CK_L})' + (1 - \omega'_{CK_L} \Omega_{CC}^{-1} d) \\ &\times (\Omega_{CC}^{-1} d)'\} - (1 - \omega'_{CK_L} \Omega_{CC}^{-1} d)(Y' - C')] \dot{d}L-, \end{aligned} \tag{2.5.3.8}$$

$$(K_L)_{K_0} = s_0^{-1} s_2 = s_0^{-1} (1 - \omega'_{CK_L} \Omega_{CC}^{-1} d). \tag{2.5.3.9}$$

Assuming that Ω_{CC}^{-1} is negative-definite, with a view to satisfying the second-order condition (2.5.2.5) for a (constrained) maximum of ω, we conclude:

$$s_1 < 0. \tag{2.5.3.10}$$

For the same reason, we state:

$$\omega_{K_L K_L} < 0, \tag{2.5.3.11}$$

to be interpreted as diminishing marginal utility of desired final personal wealth. Thus, the sign of s_3 will depend on whether the interaction term $-\omega'_{CK_L} \Omega_{CC}^{-1} \omega_{CK_L}$ – positive for Ω_{CC} negative-definite – does or does not overcompensate $\omega_{K_L K_L}$. In the latter case, i.e. with relatively weak interaction between consumption and final personal wealth:

$$s_3 > 0. \tag{2.5.3.12}$$

Then, a fortiori:

$$s_0 > 0, \tag{2.5.3.13}$$

for which (2.5.3.12) is a sufficient but not a necessary condition according to (2.5.3.3) and (2.5.3.10); and also:

$$s_2 > 0. \tag{2.5.3.14}$$

According to (2.5.3.4), C_Y may be split into two parts, viz.:

$$(C_Y)_{\text{I}} = -s_0^{-1} s_2 \Omega_{CC}^{-1} \omega_{CK_L} d' \tag{2.5.3.15}$$

and

$$(C_Y)_{\text{II}} = -s_0^{-1} s_3 \Omega_{CC}^{-1} dd'. \tag{2.5.3.16}$$

The first part may be called the 'interaction' component of the income effect; it can be positive or negative, depending, inter alia, on the signs of the elements of the interaction vector ω_{CK_L}. For $\omega_{CK_L} \equiv 0$, the income effect reduces to (2.5.3.16), representing the income effect proper (cf. section 3.2.2.). Most likely, positive elements will dominate in $(C_Y)_{\text{I}}$, as well as in $(C_Y)_{\text{II}}$, by virtue of (2.5.3.12) through (2.5.3.14). Even if negative elements prevail in $(C_Y)_{\text{I}}$, they would probably be overruled by corresponding positive elements in $(C_Y)_{\text{II}}$; i.e. the vector w in (2.5.3.4) will predominantly consist of positive elements.

Consequently, under those circumstances our conclusions about the income effect are the same, whether or not desired final personal wealth is incorporated in the utility function.

As in section 2.4.3, interest effects (2.5.3.5) may be split into a part with λ and a part without λ, i.e.:

$$\begin{aligned}(C_r)_{\text{I}} = \lambda s_0^{-1} (1+r)^{-1} [s_0 \Omega_{CC}^{-1} &+ (d'\Omega_{CC}^{-1} d)(\Omega_{CC}^{-1} \omega_{CK_L})(\Omega_{CC}^{-1} \omega_{CK_L})' \\ &+ (1 - \omega'_{CK_L} \Omega_{CC}^{-1} d) \Omega_{CC}^{-1} (\omega_{CK_L} d' + d\omega'_{CK_L}) \Omega_{CC}^{-1} \\ &- (\omega_{K_L K_L} - \omega'_{CK_L} \Omega_{CC}^{-1} \omega_{CK_L})(\Omega_{CC}^{-1} d)(\Omega_{CC}^{-1} d)'] \dot{d}L- \end{aligned} \tag{2.5.3.17}$$

and

$$(C_r)_{\text{II}} = s_0^{-1} (1+r)^{-1} w (Y - C)' \dot{d}L-. \tag{2.5.3.18}$$

If, as in the discussion on the signs of the elements of C_Y, positive elements in w will dominate over negative ones (if present at all), possibly negative wealth accumulation effects of interest will be due to C_τ exceeding Y_τ, especially for lower values of τ (in view of elements of $L-$ decreasing with increasing τ).

In contradistinction to $(C_r)_{\mathrm{I}}$ in (2.4.3.14), $(C_r)_{\mathrm{I}}$ in (2.5.3.17) cannot be identified with a mere substitution effect of the rate of interest on consumption; on the other hand, it may be written as the sum of one real substitution term (Ia), one quasi-substitution term (Ib) and one non-substitution term (Ic), as follows:

$$(C_r)_{\mathrm{I}} = -\lambda(1+r)^{-1} s_0^{-1} s_1 s_3 [\Omega_{CC}^{-1} - (d'\Omega_{CC}^{-1}d)^{-1}(\Omega_{CC}^{-1}d)(\Omega_{CC}^{-1}d)'] \dot{d}L- \qquad \text{(Ia)}$$

$$- \lambda(1+r)^{-1} s_0^{-1} s_1 (\omega'_{CK_L}\Omega_{CC}^{-1}\omega_{CK_L}) \times$$

$$\times [\Omega_{CC}^{-1} - (\omega'_{CK_L}\Omega_{CC}^{-1}\omega_{CK_L})^{-1}(\Omega_{CC}^{-1}\omega_{CK_L})(\Omega_{CC}^{-1}\omega_{CK_L})'] \dot{d}L- \qquad \text{(Ib)}$$

$$+ \lambda(1+r)^{-1} s_0^{-1} [\{s_2^2 + s_1(\omega_{CK_L}\Omega_{CC}^{-1}\omega_{CK_L})\} I$$

$$+ s_2\Omega_{CC}^{-1}(\omega_{CK_L}d' + d\omega'_{CK_L})] \Omega_{CC}^{-1}\dot{d}L-. \qquad \text{(Ic)} \qquad (2.5.3.19)$$

Of these three terms, (Ia) agrees with the substitution sub-effect of section 2.4.3, even as regards the signs of its elements; the factor $-s_0^{-1}s_1s_3$, by which (Ia) differs from the right-hand expression in (2.4.3.14), is positive.

Term (Ib) resembles a substitution effect by the structure of its expression between [ ]: this expression is symmetric, negative semi-definite and singular, since it vanishes when pre- or post-multiplied by ω'_{CK_L} or ω_{CK_L}, respectively. It may be looked upon as a quasi-substitution effect when the elements of ω_{CK_L} are considered as 'prices' of the interaction between prospective consumption and final personal wealth.

Most likely, the majority of the elements in the matrix [ ] of (Ic) will be positive, i.e. unless interaction effects represented by ω_{CK_L} would be strongly negative. Since negative elements will dominate in the vector $\Omega_{CC}^{-1}\dot{d}L-$, this non-substitution effect will be mainly negative.

Consequently, we draw the tentative conclusion that the elements of $(C_r)_{\mathrm{I}}$ in (2.5.3.17) tend to be smaller (algebraically) than the corresponding elements of $(C_r)_{\mathrm{I}}$ in (2.4.3.14).

Predominance of positive elements in w, together with (2.5.3.10), imply that in (2.5.3.6):

$$C_{K_0} > 0 \quad \text{in general.} \qquad (2.5.3.20)$$

Obviously, a higher amount of initial personal wealth permits consumption to be more generous in future.

Furthermore, (2.5.3.13) and (2.5.3.14) imply for (2.5.3.7) and (2.5.3.9) respectively:

$$(K_L)_Y, (K_L)_{K_0} > 0. \qquad (2.5.3.21)$$

According to (2.5.3.8), $(K_L)_r$ may be split into:

$$\{(K_L)_r\}_{\text{I}} = \lambda s_0^{-1} (1 + r)^{-1} v' \dot{d}L- \tag{2.5.3.22}$$

and

$$\{(K_L)_r\}_{\text{II}} = s_0^{-1} s_2 (1 + r)^{-1} (Y' - C') \dot{d}L-. \tag{2.5.3.23}$$

Predominance of positive elements in the vector v seems reasonable for the same or similar reasons as those advanced for prevalence of positive elements over negative ones in the w-vector. Thus, 'substitution' effects of the rate of interest on desired final personal wealth according to (2.5.3.22) will be mainly positive.

Again, the 'wealth accumulation' effect (2.5.3.23) depends on the signs of $Y_\tau - C_\tau$ to a degree decreasing with τ.

2.6. Model with working hours incorporated in the utility function

2.6.1. UTILITY FUNCTION AND INCOME-GENERATING FUNCTIONS

In this case the utility function becomes:

$$\begin{aligned} \omega &= \omega (C_1, \ldots, C_L, W_1, \ldots, W_L) \\ &= \omega (C', W') \quad \text{in vector notation,} \end{aligned} \tag{2.6.1.1}$$

with $C' \geq 0$, $W' \geq 0$ (non-negative consumption and work) and the additional specification $\partial\omega/\partial W_l < 0$ for $l = 1, \ldots, L$, expressing 'disutility of labour' W_l, at least for W_l exceeding a certain minimum level.

Furthermore, we assume that (labour) income in any prospective period l depends upon the number of hours worked in the same period as well as in previous periods (in order to take account of possible cumulative effects of working – and especially studying – on income):

$$Y_l = Y_l (W_1, \ldots, W_l) \quad \text{for } l = 1, \ldots, L \tag{2.6.1.2}$$

$$\text{with} \quad \partial Y_l/\partial W_\tau \begin{cases} > 0 & \text{for } \tau \leq l,^{12} \\ = 0 & \text{for } \tau > l. \end{cases}$$

The lifetime budget restriction remains (2.4.1.6).

---

12 This assumption need not be universally true: for instance, extremely long hours of work in any period τ may impair a person's physical and/or mental health to such an extent that in a later period l he will earn less than he would have done if he had taken it easier; this would mean a negative value of $\partial Y_l/\partial W_\tau$. In particular, working oneself to the bone may cause (or at least increase the probability of) an accident or heart failure such as to reduce one's income afterwards, or maybe even end one's life.

2.6.2. OPTIMUM CONDITIONS

The conditions for maximizing (2.6.1.1) subject to (2.6.1.2) and (2.4.1.6) are tantamount to maximizing:

$$z = \omega - \lambda \left[K_L - K_0 - \sum_{l=1}^{L} \{Y_l (W_1, \ldots, W_l) - C_l\} (1 + r)^{L-l}\right] \qquad (2.6.2.1)$$

with λ a (positive) Lagrangean multiplier, i.e. after substitution of (2.6.1.2) into (2.4.1.6)[13].

In matrix notation, the first-order conditions for maximizing (2.6.2.1) are:

$$\frac{\partial z}{\partial C} = \omega_C - \lambda d = 0 \qquad (2.6.2.2)$$

and

$$\frac{\partial z}{\partial W} = \omega_W + \lambda Y'_W d = 0, \qquad (2.6.2.3)$$

with $\omega'_W = \{\partial\omega/\partial W_1 \cdots \partial\omega/\partial W_L\}$ a vector of length L and

$$Y_W = \begin{bmatrix} \frac{\partial Y_1}{\partial W_1} & 0 \cdots\cdots 0 \\ \vdots \ \ \ddots & \vdots \\ & 0 \\ \frac{\partial Y_L}{\partial W_1} \ \cdots & \frac{\partial Y_L}{\partial W_L} \end{bmatrix}$$ a lower triangular matrix.

Equations (2.6.2.2) and (2.6.2.3) may be combined into:

$$\begin{bmatrix} \omega_C \\ \omega_W \end{bmatrix} = \lambda \begin{bmatrix} I \\ -Y'_W \end{bmatrix} d. \qquad (2.6.2.4)$$

---

[13] Alternatively, we could have tried to 'invert' the income generating equations (2.6.1.2) into 'working time requirement' equations:

$$W_l = W_l (Y_1, \ldots, Y_l) \quad \text{for} \quad l = 1, \ldots, L \qquad (2.6.1.2\text{a})$$

and substitute the latter into (2.6.1.1), resulting in:

$$\omega = \varphi\, (C_1 \ldots C_L, Y_1 \ldots Y_L); \qquad (2.6.1.1\text{a})$$

thus the W_l – instead of the Y_l – are eliminated.

Conditions (2.6.2.4) represent $2L$ equations, enabling us to solve the $2L$ unknown 'optimal' C_t and W_t and the unknown λ if (2.4.1.6) is added to this system, and provided the other conditions for obtaining a (constrained) utility maximum are met as well. The corresponding 'optimal' Y_t^* could be obtained by substituting W_t^* for W_t in (2.6.1.2).

The second-order conditions for C^* and W^* satisfying (2.6.2.4) are:

$$\{(\Delta C)' \quad (\Delta W)' \quad 1\} \begin{bmatrix} \Omega_{CC}^* & \Omega_{CW}^* & \omega_C^* \\ \Omega_{CW}^* & \Omega_{WW}^* + \lambda Y'_{WW} D & \omega_W^* \\ (\omega_C^*)' & (\omega_W^*)' & 0 \end{bmatrix} \begin{bmatrix} \Delta C \\ \Delta W \\ 1 \end{bmatrix} < 0 \qquad (2.6.2.5)$$

or

$$\{(\Delta C)' \quad (\Delta W)' \quad 1\} \begin{bmatrix} \Omega_{CC}^* & \Omega_{CW}^* & d \\ (\Omega_{CW}^*)' & \Omega_{WW}^* + \lambda Y'_{WW} D & -(Y_W^*)' d \\ d' & -d' Y_W^* & 0 \end{bmatrix} \begin{bmatrix} \Delta C \\ \Delta W \\ 1 \end{bmatrix} < 0, \qquad (2.6.2.6)$$

with

$$\Omega_{CW} = \Omega'_{WC} = \left[\frac{\partial^2 \omega}{\partial C_t \, \partial W_{t'}}\right], \qquad D = \begin{bmatrix} d & & & \\ & d & & 0 \\ & & \ddots & \\ 0 & & & d \end{bmatrix} \text{ an } L^2 \times L \text{ matrix,}$$

$$\Omega_{WW} = \left[\frac{\partial^2 \omega}{\partial W_t \, \partial W_{t'}}\right] \qquad \text{and} \quad Y'_{WW} = \left[\frac{\partial^2 Y_\tau}{\partial W_t \, \partial W_{t'}}\right] \text{ an } L \times L^2 \text{ matrix}$$

and asterisks denoting evaluation of the vectors and matrices for C^* and W^* satisfying (2.6.2.4), for vectors ΔC and ΔW with arbitrarily small elements such that:

$$[(\Delta C)' - (\Delta W)' (Y_W^*)'] \, d = 0. \qquad (2.6.2.7)$$

2.6.3. EFFECTS OF VARYING THE 'DATA' ON THE OPTIMAL TIME-PATTERNS OF CONSUMPTION AND OF WORKING HOURS

In sections 2.4 and 2.5, prospective incomes were considered as 'data'. In the present case, however, incomes – like working hours and consumption – per period are considered as variables. Instead, we may hypothetically vary the way in which incomes are linked to working hours according to (2.6.1.2), by changing the values of the parameters in these relationships. For studying the resulting effects on the optimal vector $(C^{*\prime} W^{*\prime} Y^{*\prime})$, we rewrite (2.6.1.2) as:

$$Y_l = Y_l\,(W_1, \ldots, W_l;\, \zeta_{l1}, \ldots, \zeta_l Z_l) \quad \text{for } l = 1, \ldots, L, \qquad (2.6.3.1)$$

ζ_{lm} $(m = 1, \ldots, Z_l)$ being the parameters of the lth equation.

All parameters together may be represented by the parameter vector

$$\zeta' = \{\zeta_{11} \cdots \zeta_{1Z_1} \cdots \zeta_{L1} \cdots \zeta_{LZ_L}\} = \{\zeta_1 \cdots \zeta_Z\}$$

after re-numbering the parameters such that $Z = \sum_{l=1}^{L} Z_l$.

Then, the effects of varying ζ on the optimal values of C, W (and hence of Y) may be derived from:

$$\begin{bmatrix} \Omega_{CC} & \Omega_{CW} & d \\ \Omega_{WC} & \Omega_{WW} & -Y'_W d \\ d' & -d'Y_W & 0 \end{bmatrix} \begin{bmatrix} C_\zeta \\ W_\zeta \\ -\lambda'_\zeta \end{bmatrix} = \begin{bmatrix} 0 \\ -\lambda\,[Y'_{W\zeta} D_{(Z)} + Y'_{WW} D W_\zeta] \\ d' Y_\zeta \end{bmatrix},$$

or, by shifting $\lambda Y'_{WW} D W_\zeta$ to the left-hand side of the equality sign:

$$\begin{bmatrix} \Omega_{CC} & \Omega_{CW} & d \\ \Omega_{WC} & \Omega_{WW} + \lambda Y'_{WW} D & -Y'_W d \\ d' & -d'Y_W & 0 \end{bmatrix} \begin{bmatrix} C_\zeta \\ W_\zeta \\ -\lambda'_\zeta \end{bmatrix} = \begin{bmatrix} 0 \\ -\lambda Y'_{W\zeta} D_{(Z)} \\ d' Y_\zeta \end{bmatrix}$$

with

$$\left.\begin{aligned} C_\zeta &= \left[\frac{\partial C_l}{\partial \zeta_z}\right] \\ W_\zeta &= \left[\frac{\partial W_l}{\partial \zeta_z}\right] \\ Y_\zeta &= \left[\frac{\partial Y_l}{\partial \zeta_z}\right] \end{aligned}\right\} \text{ matrices of order } L \times Z$$

$$D_{(Z)} = \begin{bmatrix} d & & & 0 \\ & d & & \\ & & \ddots & \\ 0 & & & d \end{bmatrix} \quad \text{an } LZ \times Z \text{ matrix}$$

$$Y'_{W\zeta} = \left[\frac{\partial^2 Y_\tau}{\partial W_l \cdot \partial \zeta_z}\right] \quad \text{an } L \times LZ \text{ matrix}$$

and

$$\lambda' = \left\{\frac{\partial\lambda}{\partial\zeta_1} \cdots \frac{\partial\lambda}{\partial\zeta_Z}\right\} \quad \text{an } 1 \times Z \text{ vector.}$$

Similarly, the effects of changes in r and in ΔK on the optimal values of C and W may be arrived at. All effects together are ruled by:

$$\begin{bmatrix} \Omega_{CC} & \Omega_{CW} & d \\ \Omega_{WC} & \Omega_{WW} + \lambda Y'_{WW} D & -Y'_W \cdot d \\ d' & -d' Y_W & 0 \end{bmatrix} \begin{bmatrix} C_\zeta & C_r & C_{\Delta K} \\ W_\zeta & W_r & W_{\Delta K} \\ -\lambda'_\zeta & -\lambda_r & -\lambda_{\Delta K} \end{bmatrix}$$

$$= \begin{bmatrix} 0 & \lambda(1+r)^{-1} \dot{d}L- & 0 \\ -\lambda Y'_{W\zeta} D_{(Z)} & -\lambda(1+r)^{-1} Y'_W \dot{d}L- & 0 \\ d' Y_\zeta & (1+r)^{-1}(Y' - C')\dot{d}L- & -1 \end{bmatrix}, \qquad (2.6.3.2)$$

$$\begin{bmatrix} \Omega_{CC} & \Omega_{CW} & d \\ \Omega'_{CW} & \Omega_{WW} + \lambda Y'_{WW} D & -Y'_W \cdot d \\ d' & -d' Y_W & 0 \end{bmatrix}^{-1} = \begin{bmatrix} M_{CC} & M_{CW} & m_C \\ M'_{CW} & M_{WW} & m_W \\ m'_C & m'_W & n \end{bmatrix} \qquad (2.6.3.3)$$

with

$$\left.\begin{aligned} M_{CC} &= \Omega_{CC}^{-1}\,[I - (d'\Omega_{CC}^{-1}d)^{-1}\,\{1 - d'U_*TU'_*d\}\,dd'\Omega_{CC}^{-1}] \\ &\quad + (d'\Omega_{CC}^{-1}d)\,\Omega_{CC}^{-1}\Omega_{CW}T\Omega_{WC}\Omega_{CC}^{-1} \\ &\quad - \Omega_{CC}^{-1}\,[\Omega_{CW}TU'_* \cdot dd' + dd'U_*T\Omega_{WC}]\,\Omega_{CC}^{-1}, \\ M_{CW} &= \Omega_{CC}^{-1}dd'U_*T - (d'\Omega_{CC}^{-1}d)\,\Omega_{CC}^{-1}\Omega_{CW}T, \\ M_{WW} &= (d'\Omega_{CC}^{-1}d)\,T, \\ m_C &= +(d'\Omega_{CC}^{-1}d)^{-1}\,\{1 - d'U_*TU'_*d\}\,\Omega_{CC}^{-1}d + \Omega_{CC}^{-1}\Omega_{CW}TU'_*d, \\ m_W &= -TU'_*d, \\ n &= -(d'\Omega_{CC}^{-1}d)^{-1}\,\{1 - d'U_*TU'_*d\}, \\ U_* &= Y_W + \Omega_{CC}^{-1}\Omega_{CW}, \\ T &= [(d'\Omega_{CC}^{-1}d)\,(\Omega_{WW} + \lambda Y'_{WW}D - \Omega_{WC}\Omega_{CC}^{-1}\Omega_{CW}) \\ &\quad + U'_*dd'U_*]^{-1}. \end{aligned}\right\}$$

(2.6.3.4)

The 'effects' result from substitution of (2.6.3.4) into the following 6 sets of equations:

$$C_\zeta = -\lambda M_{CW} Y'_{W\zeta} D_{(Z)} + m_C \cdot d' Y_\zeta, \tag{2.6.3.5}$$

$$C_r = (1 + r)^{-1} [\lambda (M_{CC} - M_{CW} Y'_W) + m_C (Y' - C')] \dot{d}L-, \tag{2.6.3.6}$$

$$C_{\Delta K} = -m_C, \tag{2.6.3.7}$$

$$W_\zeta = -\lambda M_{WW} Y'_{W\zeta} D_{(Z)} + m_W d' Y_\zeta, \tag{2.6.3.8}$$

$$W_r = (1 + r)^{-1} [\lambda (M'_{CW} - M_{WW} Y'_W) + m_W (Y' - C')] \dot{d}L-, \tag{2.6.3.9}$$

$$W_{\Delta K} = -m_W. \tag{2.6.3.10}$$

In view of the complexity of the relationships we cannot draw any conclusions about signs of the effects unless the utility function (2.6.1.1) is specified in a more precise way (cf. section 3.3).

2.7. Model with survival rates incorporated in the lifetime budget equation

Incorporating survival rates in the model implies extension of the planning horizon beyond life expectancy. For the utility function, this merely means replacing the number (L) of arguments C_l by M, i.e. the *maximum* prospective lifetime (expressed in an assumedly integer number of unit periods):

$$\omega = \omega (C_1, \ldots, C_M). \tag{2.7.1}$$

In the lifetime budget equation, desired final personal wealth no longer refers to a particular point of time, hence K_L is replaced by K_F.[14] Change in personal wealth during the (remaining) lifetime of the individual equals the *expected* value of savings over that time, with s_l = probabilities of surviving l years as weights:

$$K_F - K_0 = \sum_{l=1}^{M} (Y_l - C_l)\, s_l\, (1 + r)^{M-l}$$

$$= (Y' - C')\, \mathring{s} d_+ \quad \text{(in vector-notation)}, \tag{2.7.2}$$

with

$$d'_+ = \{(1 + r)^{M-1} \cdots \underset{(=1)}{(1 + r)^{M-M}}\}$$

[14] Assuming that the value of K_F is independent of the moment of death.

and

$$\dot{s} = \begin{bmatrix} s_1 & & 0 \\ & \ddots & \\ 0 & & s_M \end{bmatrix}.$$

By defining:

$$d_x = \dot{s} d_+ \tag{2.7.3}$$

as the vector of compound interest rates corrected for mortality risk and substituting (2.7.3) into (2.7.2), we formally reduce this model with survival rates to the basic model. Nevertheless, it may be interesting to study the effects of changes in survival rates on the optimal time pattern of consumption and savings. One should realize, however, that survival rates pertaining to different future periods are not independent of each other, but satisfy:

$$1 \geq s_{l-1} > s_l \geq 0 \quad \text{for } l = 1, \ldots, M. \tag{2.7.4}$$

Hence, the more appropriate question to ask is how variations in the shape of the survival probability function, as represented by changes in its parameters, would affect savings allocation over time. Such a question, however, can better be answered in the context of the continuous version of the model, to be dealt with in section 3.7.

The differences in time patterns of optimal consumption and savings as implied by the present model compared with the basic model can be evaluated only on the basis of a more specific utility function.

2.8. *Model with varying prospective rates of interest, consumer price levels and asset price levels*

2.8.1. UTILITY FUNCTION AND LIFETIME BUDGET EQUATION

2.8.1.1. Exogenous prospective rates of interest and price levels. In the case where changes in future consumer price levels are foreseen, an explicit distinction should be made between nominal consumption C_l (featuring in the budget equation) and real consumption c_l for periods l (= 1, ..., L) as the arguments of the utility function:

$$\begin{aligned} \omega &= \omega\,(c_1, \ldots, c_L) \\ &= \omega(c') \quad \text{(in vector notation).} \end{aligned} \tag{2.8.1.1.1}$$

Nominal and real consumption are linked by:

$$C_l = c_l P_l = c_l \prod_{\tau=2}^{l} (1 + p_\tau) = c_l (1 + p_{l+1})^{-1} \prod_{\tau=1}^{l} (1 + p_{\tau+1}), \qquad (2.8.1.1.2)$$

with P_l = the average prospective consumer price level in period l compared with the base period 1 (implying $P_1 \equiv 1$ and $C_1 \equiv c_1$)
and $p_\tau = (P_\tau - P_{\tau-1})/P_{\tau-1}$ = the relative change in the average consumer price level between periods $\tau - 1$ and τ.

Likewise,

$$Y_l = y_l P_l = y_l (1 + p_{l+1})^{-1} \prod_{\tau=1}^{l} (1 + p_{\tau+1}), \qquad (2.8.1.1.3)$$

with y_l = real income foreseen for period $l\,(= 1, \ldots L)$, with period 1 as the basis.

Taking account of possible changes in levels of prices of assets in which initial personal wealth and later savings are invested means that in the budget equation K_0 should be replaced by:

$$K_0 A_L = K_0 (1 + a_{L+1})^{-1} \prod_{\tau=l}^{L} (1 + a_{\tau+1})$$

and $Y_l - C_l$ should be replaced by

$$(Y_l - C_l)\, A_L/A_l = (Y_l - C_l)(1 + a_{L+1})^{-1} \prod_{\tau=l}^{L} (1 + a_{\tau+1})$$

with A_l = the prospective asset price level at the end of period l compared with the beginning of period 1 (implying $A_0 \equiv 1$)
and $a_\tau = (A_\tau - A_{\tau-1})/A_{\tau-1}$
= the relative change in the asset price level between the ends of periods $\tau - 1$ and τ.

Finally, if varying rates of interest r_l instead of a uniform rate of interest r are foreseen for periods $l = 1, \ldots, L$, the discount factors $(1 + r)^{L-l}$ in the budget equation should be replaced by:

$$(1 + r_{L+1})^{-1} \prod_{\tau=l}^{L} (1 + r_{\tau+1}).^{15}$$

---

[15] With $r_{\tau+1}$ instead of r_τ, since assumedly (dis-) savings begin to bear interest only at the end of the period preceding the one in which they originate.

Therefore, the lifetime budget equation becomes:

$$K_L = K_0 (1 + a_{L+1})^{-1} \prod_{l=1}^{L} (1 + a_{l+1}) \tag{2.8.1.1.4}$$

$$+ \sum_{l=1}^{L} (y_l - c_l)(1 + p_{L+1})(1 + a_{L+1})^{-1} (1 + r_{L+1})^{-1} \cdot \prod_{\tau=l}^{L} (1 + p_{\tau+1})^{-1}$$

$$\times (1 + a_{\tau+1})(1 + r_{\tau+1}) = K_0 A_L + (y' - c')f \quad \text{(in vector notation)},$$

with $f' = \{f_1 \cdots f_l \cdots f_L\}$

and $f_l = (1 + p_{L+1})(1 + a_{L+1})^{-1} (1 + r_{L+1})^{-1}$

$$\times \prod_{\tau=l}^{L} (1 + p_{\tau+1})^{-1} (1 + a_{\tau+1})(1 + r_{\tau+1})$$

as the generalized discount factors[16], including prospective changes in consumer and asset price levels, in addition to prospective rates of interest; for $p_l, a_l, r_l \ll 1, f_l$ may be approximated by:

$$f_l \approx (1 + r_{L+1} + a_{L+1} - p_{L+1})^{-1} \prod_{\tau=l}^{L} (1 + r_{\tau+1} + a_{\tau+1} - p_{\tau+1}) \tag{2.8.1.1.5}$$

with $r_{\tau+1} + a_{\tau+1} - p_{\tau+1}$ as 'generalized' rates of interest.

Thus, consumption and savings theory may deal with prospective changes in consumer price levels and in asset price levels in ways similar to or in combination with interest rates, acting in the opposite direction and in the same direction, respectively.

2.8.1.2. Endogenous prospective rates of interest and constant prospective price levels. So far, possibly varying rates of interest r_l were treated as purely exogenous variables. According to the considerations of section 2.3, however, rates of interest r_τ are likely to depend upon the individual's wealth $K_{\tau-1}$ at the beginning of periods τ (= 1, ..., L).

If r_τ changes merely according to $K_{\tau-1}$, we may write:

$$r_\tau = r(K_{\tau-1}) \quad \text{for } \tau = 1, \ldots, L \tag{2.8.1.2.1}$$

with $K_\tau(\mathrm{d}r/\mathrm{d}K_\tau) > 0$.

---

[16] The concept of 'generalized' rates of interest is closely related to I. Fisher's [1930] concept of real rates of interest, defined as $r_l - p_l$ in our notation.

In their turn, however, the K_τ depend upon the $r_{\tau'}$ ($\tau' = 1, \ldots, \tau$) according to the identity:

$$K_\tau = K_0 + (1 + r_{\tau+1})^{-1} \cdot \sum_{l=1}^{\tau} (Y_l - C_l) \prod_{\tau'=l}^{\tau} (1 + r_{\tau'+1}) \quad \text{for } \tau = 1, \ldots, L. \tag{2.8.1.2.2}$$

Substitution of (2.8.1.2.2) into (2.8.1.2.1) results in a system of L eqs. for the L unknown r_τ. From these equations, the r_τ may be 'solved' in principle, i.e. expressed in terms of K_0 and the $(Y_l - C_l)$ for $l = 1, \ldots, \tau - 1$:

$$r_\tau = r_\tau (K_0, Y_1 - C_1, \ldots, Y_{\tau-1} - C_{\tau-1}) \quad \text{for } \tau = 1, \ldots, L. \tag{2.8.1.2.3}$$

The lifetime budget equation – (2.8.1.2.2) for $\tau = L$ – now becomes:

$$K_L = K_0 + (1 + r_{L+1})^{-1} \sum_{l=1}^{L} (Y_l - C_l) \times \prod_{\tau=l}^{L} \{1 + r_{\tau+1} (K_0, Y_1 - C_1, \ldots, Y_\tau - C_\tau)\}. \tag{2.8.1.2.4}$$

2.8.2. OPTIMUM CONDITIONS

2.8.2.1. Exogenous prospective rates of interest and price levels. The conditions for maximizing the utility function (2.4.1.1) subject to the budget constraint (2.8.1.1.4) are analogous to those stated in section 2.4.2, i.e.:

$$\frac{\partial \omega}{\partial c_\tau} = \lambda f_\tau \tag{2.8.2.1.1}$$

or

$$\omega_c = \lambda f, \tag{2.8.2.1.1'}$$

with $\omega_c' = \left\{ \dfrac{\partial \omega}{\partial c_1}, \ldots, \dfrac{\partial \omega}{\partial c_L} \right\}$

and $f' = \{f_1, \ldots, f_L\}$.

The second-order conditions are:

$$\{\Delta c \quad 1\} \begin{bmatrix} \Omega_{cc}^* & \omega_c^* \\ (\omega_c^*)' & 0 \end{bmatrix} \begin{bmatrix} \Delta c \\ 1 \end{bmatrix} < 0; \tag{2.8.2.1.2}$$

i.e. like (2.4.2.10), with C replaced by c, and Δc satisfying $(\Delta c)' f = 0$.

Equations (2.8.2.1.1), in addition to (2.8.1.1.4), provide the necessary conditions for solving the unknown c_l ($l = 1, \ldots, L$) and λ in terms of y', f' and ΔK.

The corresponding optimal savings $S_1, \ldots, S_L$ may be calculated as:

$$\left.\begin{aligned} S_1^* &= Y_1 - C_1^* = y_1 - c_1^* \\ &\vdots \\ S_l^* &= (y_l - c_l^*) P_l + P_l r_{l-1} \sum_{\tau=1}^{l-1} (y_\tau^+ - c_\tau^*), \end{aligned}\right\} \qquad (2.8.2.1.3)$$

i.e. stepwise, in a manner similar to (2.4.2.17).

2.8.2.2. Endogenous prospective rates of interest and constant prospective price levels. The first-order conditions for maximizing the utility function:

$$\omega = \omega(C') \qquad (2.8.2.2.1)$$

subject to the budget equation:

$$K_L - K_0 = f'(Y - C) \qquad (2.8.2.2.2)$$

are

$$\omega_C = \lambda \left[f + F'_{Y-C} (Y - C)\right] \qquad (2.8.2.2.3)$$

where λ is a Lagrangean multiplier, while the r_τ in the elements of f' are difined by (2.0.1.2.3.) and

$$F'_{Y-C} = \begin{bmatrix} \dfrac{\partial f_1}{\partial (Y_1 - C_1)} & \cdots & \dfrac{\partial f_{L-1}}{\partial (Y_1 - C_1)} & 0 \\ \vdots & & \vdots & \vdots \\ \dfrac{\partial f_1}{\partial (Y_{L-1} - C_{L-1})} & \cdots & \dfrac{\partial f_{L-1}}{\partial (Y_{L-1} - C_{L-1})} & 0 \\ 0 & \cdots\cdots & 0 & 0 \end{bmatrix}$$

with

$$\frac{\partial f_l}{\partial (Y_\tau - C_\tau)} = (1 + r_{L+1})^{-1} \left\{ \sum_{\tau'=\max(\tau, l)}^{L} (1 + r_{\tau'+1})^{-1} \frac{\partial r_{\tau'+1}}{\partial (Y_\tau - C_\tau)} \right\} \times \prod_{\tau'=l}^{L} (1 + r_{\tau'+1});$$

or l and/or τ equaling L, $\partial f_l / \partial (Y_\tau - C_\tau) = 0$.

The second-order condition for a constrained maximum of ω is:

$$\{(\Delta C)' \quad 1\} \begin{bmatrix} \Omega + \lambda\,(F_{Y-C} + F'_{Y-C,Y-C}\,\Delta + F'_{Y-C}) & f + F'_{Y-C}\,(Y - C) \\ f' + (Y - C)'\,F_{Y-C} & 0 \end{bmatrix}$$

$$\times \begin{bmatrix} \Delta C \\ 1 \end{bmatrix} < 0 \qquad (2.8.2.2.4)$$

provided ΔC satisfies

$$\{f' + (Y - C)'\,F_{Y-C}\}\,\Delta C = 0, \qquad (2.8.2.2.5)$$

as implied by (2.8.2.2.2), with

$$F'_{Y-C,Y-C} = \left[\frac{\partial^2 f_l}{\partial\,(Y_\tau - C_\tau)\cdot\partial\,(Y_{\tau'} - C_{\tau'})}\right]$$

an $L \times L^2$ matrix, and

$\Delta' =$

$$\begin{bmatrix} Y_1 - C_1 \cdots Y_L - C_L & & & 0 \\ & Y_1 - C_1 \cdots Y_L - C_L & & \\ & & \ddots & \\ 0 & & & Y_1 - C_1 \cdots Y_L - C_L \end{bmatrix}$$

an $L \times L^2$ matrix.

2.8.3. EFFECTS OF VARYING THE 'DATA' ON THE OPTIMAL TIME-PATTERN OF CONSUMPTION

2.8.3.1. Exogenous prospective rates of interest and price levels. The effects of varying y_l, r_l and K_L on c_l^* may be expressed in a way resembling (2.4.3.7) for the effects of varying Y_l, r and ΔK (or K_L), viz. by:

$$\begin{bmatrix} \Omega_{cc} & f \\ f' & 0 \end{bmatrix} \begin{bmatrix} c_y & c_r & c_{K_L} \\ -\lambda'_y & -\lambda'_r & -\lambda_{K_L} \end{bmatrix} = \begin{bmatrix} 0 & \lambda F R^{-1} & 0 \\ f' & (y' - c')\,F R^{-1} & -1 \end{bmatrix}, \qquad (2.8.3.1.1)$$

with

$$c_y = [\partial c_\tau / \partial y_l] \quad \text{and} \quad c_r = [\partial c_\tau / \partial r_l]$$

matrices of orders $L \times L$,

$$\left.\begin{aligned} C'_{K_L} &= \left\{\frac{\partial C_1}{\partial K_L} \cdots \frac{\partial C_L}{\partial K_L}\right\} \\ \lambda'_y &= \left\{\frac{\partial \lambda}{\partial y_1} \cdots \frac{\partial \lambda}{\partial y_L}\right\} \\ \lambda'_r &= \left\{\frac{\partial \lambda}{\partial r_1} \cdots \frac{\partial \lambda}{\partial r_L}\right\} \end{aligned}\right\} \text{ row vectors of lengths } L,$$

$$\lambda_{K_L} = \partial\lambda/\partial K_L \quad \text{a scalar},$$

$$F = \begin{bmatrix} 0 & f_1 & f_2 & \cdots & f_{L-1} \\ 0 & 0 & f_2 & \cdots & f_{L-1} \\ \vdots & & \ddots & \ddots & \vdots \\ \vdots & & & 0 & f_{L-1} \\ 0 & \cdots & \cdots & 0 & 0 \end{bmatrix} \quad \text{and} \quad R^{-1} = \begin{bmatrix} f_1 f_0^{-1} & & & 0 \\ & f_2 f_1^{-1} & & \\ & & \ddots & \\ 0 & & & f_L f_{L-1}^{-1} \end{bmatrix}$$

$L \times L$ matrices with $f_l f_{l-1}^{-1} = (1 + p_l)(1 + a_l)^{-1}(1 + r_l)^{-1}$.

The formulae for the 'effects' implied by (2.8.3.1.1) are:

$$c_y = (f'\Omega_{cc}^{-1}f)^{-1}\,\Omega_{cc}^{-1}ff', \tag{2.8.3.1.2}$$

$$c_r = c_a = -c_p = \lambda\,[\Omega_{cc}^{-1} - (f'\Omega_{cc}^{-1}f)^{-1}(\Omega_{cc}f)(\Omega_{cc}f)']\,FR^{-1}$$
$$+ (f'\Omega_{cc}^{-1}f)^{-1}(\Omega_{cc}^{-1}f)(\Omega_{cc}^{-1}f)'(Y - C)'\,FR^{-1} \tag{2.8.3.1.3}$$

$$C_{K_L} = -C_{K_0} = C_{\Delta K} = -(f'\Omega_{cc}^{-1}f)^{-1}\,\Omega_{cc}^{-1}f. \tag{2.8.3.1.4}$$

According to (2.8.3.1.2) and (2.8.3.1.4), effects of changes in income and in (change in) personal wealth are expressed by essentially the same formulae as those derived for the basic model, viz. (2.4.3.9) and (2.4.3.11), respectively – except that f takes the place of d, and Ω_{cc} is substituted for Ω.

As in the case of one uniform rate of interest for all prospective periods, the first term in the last member of (2.8.3.1.2) represents the substitution effect, whereas the last term represents the wealth accumulation effect.

Still, the most conspicuous difference between the present model and the basic one concerns effects of rate of interest on real income. In particular, the upper triangular and diagonal structures of F and R^{-1} respectively imply that FR^{-1} too is upper-triangular. This means that effects of changes in the rate of interest anticipated for any period τ tend to increase in an absolute sense according as they relate to consumption in a more remote future; i.e. seeing that f_l, as the continuous products of terms generally exceeding 1 (if $r_l + a_l - p_l > 0$) tend to be larger according as l is higher.

According to (2.8.3.1.3), effects of varying rates of change in asset price levels and in consumer price levels will affect consumption in exactly the same way and in an opposite but otherwise equal way and degree respectively.

2.8.3.2. Endogenous prospective rates of interest and constant prospective price levels. By differentiating (2.8.2.1.1′) and (2.8.1.2.4) partially with respect to the Y-vector and the K_0-scalar, we find relationships for the effects of changes in these variables on C_Y. Since, however, r_τ is now endogenous, differentiation of the first-order conditions with respect to r_τ itself has to be replaced by differentiation with respect to parameters $\vartheta' = \vartheta_1, \ldots, \vartheta_G$ assumed to rule the dependence of r_τ on K_0 and the $Y_l - C_l$. As a result we find:

$$\left[\begin{array}{c|c} \Omega + \lambda\,(F_{Y-C} + F'_{Y-C,Y-C}\,\Delta + F'_{Y-C}) & f + F'_{Y-C}\,(Y - C) \\ f' + (Y - C)'\,F_{Y-C} & 0 \end{array}\right] \left[\begin{array}{ccc} C_Y & C_\vartheta & C_{K_0} \\ -\lambda'_Y & -\lambda'_\vartheta & -\lambda_{K_0} \end{array}\right]$$
$$= \left[\begin{array}{c|c|c} \lambda\,[F_{Y-C} + F'_{Y-C,Y-C}\,\Delta + F'_{Y-C}] & \lambda\,[F'_\vartheta + F'_{Y-C,\vartheta}(Y - C)] & \lambda\,[f'_{K_0} + F'_{Y-C,K_0}(Y - C)] \\ f' + (Y - C)'\,F_{Y-C} & (Y - C)'\,F'_\vartheta & 1 + (Y - C)'\,F_{K_0} \end{array}\right] \tag{2.8.3.2.1}$$

or

$$C_Y = \lambda M\,[F_{Y-C} + F'_{Y-C,Y-C}\,\Delta + F'_{Y-C}] + m\,[f' + (Y - C)'\,F_{Y-C}] \tag{2.8.3.2.2}$$

$$C_\vartheta = \lambda M\,[F'_\vartheta + F'_{Y-C,\vartheta}\,(Y - C)] + m\,(Y - C)'\,F_\vartheta \tag{2.8.3.2.3}$$

$$C_{K_0} = \lambda M\,[f'_{K_0} + F'_{Y-C,K_0}\,(Y - C)] + m\,\{1 + (Y - C)'\,F_{K_0}\}, \tag{2.8.3.2.4}$$

with

$$C_\vartheta = [\partial C_l/\partial\vartheta_g] \quad \text{an } L \times G \text{ matrix,}$$
$$\lambda'_\vartheta = \{\partial\lambda/\partial\vartheta_1, \ldots, \partial\lambda/\partial\vartheta_G\} \quad \text{a } 1 \times G \text{ vector}$$
$$F_\vartheta = [\partial f_l/\partial\vartheta_g] \quad \text{an } L \times G \text{ matrix}$$
$$F'_{Y-C,\vartheta} = [(\partial^2 f_l)/(\partial\,(Y_\tau - C_\tau)\cdot\partial\vartheta_g)] \quad \text{an } L \times LG \text{ matrix,}$$
$$M = N^{-1} - (n'N^{-1}n)^{-1}\,(N^{-1}n)\,(N^{-1}n)'$$
$$m = (n'N^{-1}n)^{-1}\cdot(N^{-1}n)$$

and

$$N = \Omega + \lambda\,[F_{Y-C} + F'_{Y-C,Y-C}\,\Delta + F'_{Y-C}]$$

$$n = f + F'_{Y-C}\,(Y - C)$$

appearing in the first (partitioned) matrix

$$\begin{bmatrix} N & n \\ n' & 0 \end{bmatrix} \text{ of (2.8.3.2.1).}$$

Conclusions about the effects shown by (2.8.3.2.2) through (2.8.3.2.4) have to await more detailed specification.

2.9. *Basic model incorporating uncertainty*

2.9.1. BUDGET EQUATION AND UTILITY FUNCTION

Outwardly, the lifetime budget equation is the same as (2.4.1.6) in the basic model, i.e.:

$$\Delta K = \sum_{l=1}^{L} (Y_l - C_l)\,(1 + r)^{L-l} \tag{2.9.1.1}$$

$$= (Y - C)'d \quad \text{in vector notation.}$$

The intrinsic difference between (2.9.1.1) and (2.4.1.6), however, is that in the latter the vector Y' is assumed to be known, whereas in (2.9.1.1) it is stochastic, with a given joint probability density function prob $(Y_1 \cdots Y_L)$, satisfying

$$\underbrace{\int_{-\infty}^{\infty} \cdots \int_{-\infty}^{\infty}}_{L} \text{prob}\,(Y_1 \cdots Y_L)\,\mathrm{d}Y_1 \cdots \mathrm{d}Y_L \equiv 1 \tag{2.9.1.2}$$

and yielding expected values:

$$EY_l = \underbrace{\int_{-\infty}^{\infty} \cdots \int_{-\infty}^{\infty}}_{L} Y_l \cdot \text{prob}\,(Y_1 \cdots Y_L)\,\mathrm{d}Y_1 \cdots \mathrm{d}Y_l \cdots dY_L \text{ for } l = 1, \ldots, L. \tag{2.9.1.3}$$

In the utility function, uncertainty due to Y_l possibly differing from $\mathrm{E}Y_l$ is taken care of by including differences $C_l - \bar{C}_l$ between future consumption C_l for Y_l stochastic and ditto $\bar{C}_l$ if $Y_l \equiv \mathrm{E}Y_l$, in addition to $\bar{C}_l$ on their own:

$$\omega = \omega\,(\bar{C}_1 \cdots \bar{C}_L;\, C_1 - \bar{C}_1 \cdots C_L - \bar{C}_L)$$

$$= \omega\,\{(\bar{C})', (C - \bar{C})'\} \quad \text{in vector notation,} \tag{2.9.1.4}$$

with $\partial\omega/\partial\bar{C}_l > \partial\omega/\partial(C_l - \bar{C}_l) > 0$ for $l = 1, \ldots, L$; it means that an uncertain increase in consumption is valued positively, albeit less than an equal certainty-equivalent increase in consumption.

2.9.2. OPTIMUM CONDITIONS

The problem facing the individual under uncertainty is to maximize the *expected* value of ω subject to (2.9.1.1) holding for all possible Y-vectors. This amounts to maximizing:

$$\begin{aligned} z &= \mathrm{E}\omega\,\{\bar{C}', (C - \bar{C})'\} + \lambda\,\{(Y - C)'\,d - \Delta K\} \\ &= \mathrm{E}\omega\,\{\bar{C}', (C - \bar{C})'\} \\ &\quad + \lambda\,[\{(Y - \mathrm{E}Y)' - (C - \bar{C})' + (\mathrm{E}Y - \bar{C})'\}\,d - \Delta K], \end{aligned} \tag{2.9.2.1}$$

with

$$\mathrm{E}\omega = \int_{-\infty}^{\infty} \omega\,\{\bar{C}', (C - \bar{C})'\}\,\mathrm{prob}\,(Y_1 \cdots Y_L) \cdot \mathrm{d}Y_1 \cdots \mathrm{d}Y_L,$$

and λ a Lagrangean multiplier.

The first-order conditions for maximizing z are:

$$\partial z/\partial\bar{C} = (\mathrm{E}\omega)_{\bar{C}} - \lambda d = 0 \tag{2.9.2.2}$$

and

$$\partial z/\partial\,(C - \bar{C}) = (\mathrm{E}\omega)_{C-\bar{C}} - \lambda d = 0 \tag{2.9.2.3}$$

with

$$(\mathrm{E}\omega)'_{\bar{C}} = \left\{\frac{\partial \mathrm{E}\omega}{\partial\bar{C}_1} \cdots \frac{\partial \mathrm{E}\omega}{\partial\bar{C}_L}\right\}$$

and

$$\frac{\partial \mathrm{E}\omega}{\partial\bar{C}_\tau} = \int_{-\infty}^{\infty} \cdots \int_{-\infty}^{\infty} \frac{\partial\omega}{\partial\bar{C}_\tau}\ \mathrm{prob}\,(Y')\,\mathrm{d}Y_1 \cdots \mathrm{d}Y_L,$$

and likewise $(\mathrm{E}\omega)'_{C-\bar{C}}$ if $\bar{C}$ is replaced by $C - \bar{C}$.

The $2L$ equations (2.9.2.2), together with (2.9.1.1), should yield the $2L$ unknown $\bar{C}$ and $C - \bar{C}$ (or $\bar{C}$ and C) in terms of r, ΔK and the parameters of the probability distribution of Y' (among which, e.g. their means and (co-) variances).

The trouble with (2.9.2.2), however, is that one needs knowledge concerning the partial relationships between the $\bar{C}_\tau$ and C_τ on the one hand and those parameters on the other hand in order to evaluate $(\mathrm{E}\omega)_{\bar{C}}$ and $(\mathrm{E}\omega)_{C-\bar{C}}$. This dependence should be such that all $2L$ L-tuple integrals show the same dependence on those parameters – apart from discount factors.

In order to break through this vicious circle, one could start with a particular kind of relationship, say for $\bar{C}$ in terms of r, ΔK and $\mathrm{E}Y$, such that at any rate equations (2.9.2.2) would be satisfied, at least approximately. If $(E\omega)_{\bar{C}}$ is independent of C, $\bar{C}$ may be expressed in those terms such that (2.9.2.2) would be satisfied exactly. Then $\lambda = (ER)^{-1}(C'\omega_{\bar{C}})$ too would be a function of only the means of the probability density function, in addition to ΔK and r. Thus, $C - \bar{C}$ might be a function of ΔK, r and EY as well as higher moments of that density function, e.g. of (co-) variances $E(y - Ey)(y - Ey)'$, with parameters such as to 'neutralize' those of the probability density function – meaning that the L-tuple integration should yield $(ER)^{-1} d\bar{C}'\omega_{\bar{C}}$.

As mentioned near the end of section 2.4.4 above, the results of the analysis dealt with in the present section are invariant only against linear increasing transformation of the utility function. The reason is that such invariance can be ensured merely in the case where the expectation of a function of stochastic variables is identically equal to the function of the expectations of the variables; this requires that that function is linear.

The second-order condition ensuring that $\bar{C}^*$ and C^* satisfying (2.9.2.3) yield a maximum value of z is:

$$\{(\Delta\bar{C})' \quad \Delta(C-\bar{C})' \quad 1\} \begin{bmatrix} \underline{E\Omega}^*_{\bar{C}\bar{C}} & \underline{E\Omega}^*_{\bar{C},C-\bar{C}} & d \\ \underline{E\Omega}^*_{C-\bar{C},\bar{C}} & \underline{E\Omega}^*_{C-\bar{C},C-\bar{C}} & d \\ d' & d' & 0 \end{bmatrix} \begin{bmatrix} \Delta\bar{C} \\ \Delta(C-\bar{C}) \\ 1 \end{bmatrix}$$

$$= \{(\Delta\bar{C})' \quad (\Delta C)' \quad 1\}$$

$$\times \begin{bmatrix} \underline{E\Omega}^*_{\bar{C}\bar{C}} - 2\underline{E\Omega}^*_{\bar{C},C-\bar{C}} + \underline{E\Omega}^*_{C-\bar{C},C-\bar{C}} & \underline{E\Omega}^*_{\bar{C},C-\bar{C}} - \underline{E\Omega}^*_{C-\bar{C},C-\bar{C}} & d \\ \underline{E\Omega}^*_{C-\bar{C},\bar{C}} - \underline{E\Omega}^*_{C-\bar{C},C-\bar{C}} & \underline{E\Omega}^*_{C-\bar{C},C-\bar{C}} & d \\ d' & d' & 0 \end{bmatrix}$$

$$\times \begin{bmatrix} \Delta\bar{C} \\ \Delta C \\ 1 \end{bmatrix} < 0 \tag{2.9.2.4}$$

with

$$\underline{E\Omega}^*_{\bar{C}\bar{C}} = \left[\frac{\partial E\omega}{\partial\bar{C}_\tau \partial\bar{C}_{\tau'}}\right]^*, \quad \underline{E\Omega}^*_{\bar{C},C-\bar{C}} = \left[\frac{\partial E\omega}{\partial\bar{C}_\tau \cdot \partial(C_{\tau'} - \bar{C}_{\tau'})}\right]^* = \underline{E\Omega}^*_{C-\bar{C},\bar{C}}$$

and

$$\underline{E\Omega}^*_{C-\bar{C},C-\bar{C}} = \left[\frac{\partial E\omega}{\partial(C_\tau - \bar{C}_\tau)\,\partial(C_{\tau'} - \bar{C}_{\tau'})}\right],$$

while $(\Delta\bar{C})'d = (\Delta C)'d = 0$.

The underlining of $\underline{\mathrm{E}\omega}$ in $\underline{\mathrm{E}\omega}^{*}_{\bar{C}\bar{C}}$ etc. should make clear that the elements of these matrices are second-order derivatives of the expected value of ω, and not the expected values of the second-order derivatives of ω.

Therefore, the positive values $\bar{C}^*$ of $\bar{C}$ and C^* of C, satisfying (2.9.2.2), (2.9.2.3), (2.9.1.1) and (2.9.2.4) while yielding the highest value of $\mathrm{E}\omega$ will represent the solution of the optimization problem.

The interesting question of the signs of the elements of $C_l - \bar{C}_l$ cannot be answered until further specification of the utility function in section 3.5.

2.9.3. EFFECTS OF VARYING THE 'DATA' ON THE OPTIMAL TIME-PATTERN OF CONSUMPTION

Since the probability density function of the Y's is given, we may study the effects of varying its parameters. For a number of the more common probability density functions, like the (log-) normal ones, at least some of their parameters coincide with moments, in particular means (the $\mathrm{E}Y_l$) and (co-) variances.

The effects of varying r and ΔK on (future) consumption may be obtained and expressed in a way resembling (2.4.3.7). For evaluating effects of changing parameters $\{\mathrm{par}_1 \cdots \mathrm{par}_K\}$ of the probability density function, however, we keep in mind that the latter is implicit in $\mathrm{E}\omega^*$, in the following way:

$$\mathrm{E}\omega^* = \int_{-\infty}^{\infty} \cdots \int_{-\infty}^{\infty} \omega^* \,\mathrm{prob}\,(Y')\,\mathrm{d}Y_1 \cdots \mathrm{d}Y_L. \qquad (2.9.3.1)$$

Therefore, taking all the effects together, we may write:

$$\begin{bmatrix} \underline{\mathrm{E}\Omega}^{*}_{\bar{C}\bar{C}} & \underline{\mathrm{E}\Omega}^{*}_{\bar{C},C-\bar{C}} & d \\ \underline{\mathrm{E}\Omega}^{*}_{C-\bar{C},\bar{C}} & \underline{\mathrm{E}\Omega}^{*}_{C-\bar{C},C-\bar{C}} & d \\ d' & d' & 0 \end{bmatrix}$$

$$\times \begin{bmatrix} \bar{C}_{\mathrm{E}Y} & \bar{C}_{\mathrm{par}} & \bar{C}_r & \bar{C}_{\Delta K} \\ (C-\bar{C})_{\mathrm{E}Y} & (C-\bar{C})_{\mathrm{par}} & (C-\bar{C})_r & (C-\bar{C})_{\Delta K} \\ -\lambda'_{\mathrm{E}Y} & -\lambda'_{\mathrm{par}} & -\lambda'_r & -\lambda'_{\Delta K} \end{bmatrix}$$

$$= \begin{bmatrix} -\underline{\mathrm{E}\Omega}^{*}_{\bar{C},\mathrm{E}Y} & -\underline{\mathrm{E}\Omega}^{*}_{\bar{C},\mathrm{par}} & \lambda\,(1+r)^{-1}\dot{d}L- & 0 \\ -\underline{\mathrm{E}\Omega}^{*}_{C-\bar{C},\mathrm{E}Y} & -\underline{\mathrm{E}\Omega}^{*}_{C-\bar{C},\mathrm{par}} & \lambda\,(1+r)^{-1}\dot{d}L- & 0 \\ d' & d' & (1+r)^{-1}\,(\mathrm{E}Y-\bar{C})'\dot{d}L- & -1 \end{bmatrix}, \qquad (2.9.3.2)$$

with

$$\left.\begin{aligned} \bar{C}_{\text{par}} &= \left[\frac{\partial C_{\tau'}}{\partial \, \text{par}_{\varkappa}}\right] \\ (C - \bar{C})_{\text{par}} &= \left[\frac{\partial\,(C_{\tau'} - \bar{C}_{\tau'})}{\partial \, \text{par}_{\varkappa}}\right] \\ \underline{\text{E}\Omega}_{\bar{C},\text{par}} &= \left[\frac{\partial^2 \text{E}\omega}{\partial C_{\tau} \cdot \partial \, \text{par}_{\varkappa}}\right] \end{aligned}\right\} \quad L \times K \text{ matices}$$

$$\lambda'_{\text{par}} = \left\{\frac{\partial \lambda}{\partial \, \text{par}_1} \cdots \frac{\partial \lambda}{\partial \, \text{par}_K}\right\} \quad \text{a } 1 \times K \text{ vector, etcetera,}$$

and * denoting valuation at the optimum values of the instrument variables[17].

From (2.9.3.2), the 'effects' may be solved by premultiplying its members by:

$$\begin{bmatrix} \underline{\text{E}\Omega}^*_{\bar{C}\bar{C}} & \underline{\text{E}\Omega}^*_{\bar{C},C-\bar{C}} & d \\ \underline{\text{E}\Omega}^*_{\bar{C}-C,\bar{C}} & \underline{\text{E}\Omega}^*_{C-\bar{C},C-\bar{C}} & d \\ d' & d' & 0 \end{bmatrix}^{-1} = \begin{bmatrix} M_{11} & M_{12} & v_1 \\ M_{21} & M_{22} & v_2 \\ v'_1 & v'_2 & s \end{bmatrix} \tag{2.9.3.3}$$

with the M's: $L \times L$ matrices
with the v's: $L \times 1$ vectors
and s: a scalar, such that:

$$\begin{bmatrix} M_{11} & M_{12} \\ M_{21} & M_{22} \end{bmatrix} = \begin{bmatrix} \Omega^{11} & \Omega^{12} \\ \Omega^{21} & \Omega^{22} \end{bmatrix} + s \begin{bmatrix} \Omega^{11} & \Omega^{12} \\ \Omega^{21} & \Omega^{22} \end{bmatrix} \cdot \begin{bmatrix} dd' & dd' \\ dd' & dd' \end{bmatrix} \begin{bmatrix} \Omega^{11} & \Omega^{12} \\ \Omega^{21} & \Omega^{22} \end{bmatrix}, \tag{2.9.3.4}$$

$$\begin{bmatrix} v_1 \\ v_2 \end{bmatrix} = -s \begin{bmatrix} \Omega^{11} & \Omega^{12} \\ \Omega^{21} & \Omega^{22} \end{bmatrix} d, \tag{2.9.3.5}$$

and

$$s = -\{d' (\Omega^{11} + 2\Omega^{12} + \Omega^{22})\, d\}^{-1} > 0 \tag{2.9.3.6}$$

with

$$\left.\begin{aligned} \Omega^{11} &= [\underline{\text{E}\Omega}_{\bar{C}\bar{C}} - \underline{\text{E}\Omega}_{\bar{C},C-\bar{C}} \cdot \underline{\text{E}\Omega}^{-1}_{C-\bar{C},C-\bar{C}} \cdot \underline{\text{E}\Omega}_{C-\bar{C},\bar{C}}]^{-1} \\ \Omega^{12} &= (\Omega^{21})' = [\underline{\text{E}\Omega}_{C-\bar{C},\bar{C}} - \underline{\text{E}\Omega}_{C-\bar{C},C-\bar{C}} \cdot \underline{\text{E}\Omega}^{-1}_{\bar{C},C-\bar{C}} \cdot \underline{\text{E}\Omega}_{\bar{C}\bar{C}}]^{-1} \\ \Omega^{22} &= [\underline{\text{E}\Omega}_{C-\bar{C},C-\bar{C}} - \underline{\text{E}\Omega}_{C-\bar{C},\bar{C}} \cdot \underline{\text{E}\Omega}^{-1}_{\bar{C},\bar{C}} \cdot \underline{\text{E}\Omega}_{\bar{C},C-\bar{C}}]^{-1} \end{aligned}\right\} \tag{2.9.3.7}$$

---

[17] To be omitted hereafter, for simplicity's sake.

Thus, by means of (2.9.3.2) through (2.9.3.8) the following expressions are obtained for the 'effects':

$$\bar{C}_{EY} = -M_{11}\underline{E\Omega_{\bar{C},EY}} - M_{12}\underline{E\Omega_{C-\bar{C},EY}} + v_1 d' \tag{2.9.3.8}$$

$$(C - \bar{C})_{EY} = -M_{21}\underline{E\Omega_{\bar{C},EY}} - M_{22}\underline{E\Omega_{C-\bar{C},EY}} + v_2 d' \tag{2.9.3.9}$$

$$\bar{C}_{par} = -M_{11}\underline{E\Omega_{\bar{C},par}} - M_{12}\underline{E\Omega_{C-\bar{C},par}} + v_1 d' \tag{2.9.3.10}$$

$$(C - \bar{C})_{par} = -M_{21}\underline{E\Omega_{\bar{C},par}} - M_{22}\underline{E\Omega_{C-\bar{C},par}} + v_2 d' \tag{2.9.3.11}$$

$$\bar{C}_r = (1 + r)^{-1} [\lambda (M_{11} + M_{12}) + v_1 (EY - \bar{C})'] \dot{d}L- \tag{2.9.3.12}$$

$$(C - \bar{C})_r = (1 + r)^{-1} [\lambda (M_{21} + M_{22}) + v_2 (Y - C)'] \dot{d}L- \tag{2.9.3.13}$$

$$\bar{C}_{\Delta K} = -v_1 \tag{2.9.3.14}$$

$$(C - \bar{C})_{\Delta K} = -v_2 . \tag{2.9.3.15}$$

By adding (2.9.3.9) to (2.9.3.8), (2.9.3.11) to (2.9.3.10), (2.9.3.13) to (2.9.3.12) and (2.9.3.15) to (2.9.3.14), we may obtain the expressions for C_{EY}, C_{par}, C_r and $C_{\Delta K}$ respectively. In order to draw definite conclusions about at least the signs of these effects, however, the utility function has to be made more specific, as has been done in section 3.5.

2.9.4. ALTERNATIVES

Chance deviations of the prospective time pattern of income from its expected time pattern may also affect a consumer's *default risk*, i.e. the probability that at any future point of time his or her personal wealth will fall below a certain value, possibly negative, considered as a minimum *a priori*. This minimum value, however, may vary, for instance with increasing age of the person in question. Moreover, in his utility function the individual may attach different importance to default risk (of the same probability) at different points of time. This suggests introducing the probability of personal wealth falling below pre-determined minimum values for (the beginnings or the ends of) all unit periods within the planning horizon into the utility function; i.e. in addition to the 'certainty-equivalent' amounts of consumption $\bar{C}_t$, and supplementing or replacing the 'uncertainty' deviations $C_t - \bar{C}_t$.

Introducing probabilities into the utility function, however, gives rise to complications that do not seem worth the trouble, (inter alia) in view of the arbitrariness of the choice of the minimum personal wealth levels. Instead, it would be simpler, and also more realistic, to include prospective personal wealth (at the beginning of each unit period within the time horizon) among the arguments of the utility function as a generalization of model 2.5:

$$\omega = \omega(C_1, \ldots, C_L, K_1, \ldots, K_L)$$
$$= \omega(C', K') \quad \text{in vector notation} \tag{2.9.4.1}$$

with $\partial\omega/\partial C_l, \partial\omega/\partial K_l > 0$ for $l = 1, \ldots, L$.

The K-variables are linked to the C-variables by the budget identities (2.4.1.4); the latter may be rewritten in matrix notation as:

$$K = \underline{D}'(Y - C) + K_0\iota \tag{2.9.4.2}$$

with

$$K' = \{K_L \cdots K_1\},$$

$$(Y - C)' = \{(Y_1 - C_1) \cdots (Y_L - C_L)\}$$

and

$$\underline{D}' = \begin{bmatrix} d_1 & 0 & \cdots & 0 \\ d_1 & d_2 & \ddots & \vdots \\ \vdots & \vdots & \ddots & 0 \\ d_1 & d_2 & \cdots & d_L \end{bmatrix}$$

with $d_l = (1 + r)^{L-l}$, as in the basic model (cf. (2.4.1.6)).

Again, we maximize $E\omega$ instead of ω, with a probability distribution of Y as introduced in section 2.9.1, and subject to (2.9.4.2). This amounts to maximization of:

$$z = E\omega - \lambda'[K - \underline{D}'(Y - C) - K_0\iota] \tag{2.9.4.3}$$

with

$$\lambda' = \{\lambda_1 \cdots \lambda_L\} \quad \text{a vector of Lagrangean multipliers.}$$

Maximization of z requires:

$$\begin{bmatrix} E\omega_C \\ E\omega_K \end{bmatrix} = \begin{bmatrix} \underline{D} \\ I \end{bmatrix} \cdot \lambda \tag{2.9.4.4}$$

(2.9.4.4) and (2.9.4.2) together represent $3L$ equations, from which the unknowns are to be solved, viz. $C_1 \cdots C_L$, $K_1 \cdots K_L$ and $\lambda_1 \cdots \lambda_L$.

In order that solutions C^*, K^* (and λ^*) yield a proper maximum ω^* of ω,

$$\{(\Delta C)' \quad (\Delta K)' \quad 1\} \begin{bmatrix} \underline{E\Omega}^*_{CC} & \underline{E\Omega}^*_{CK} & \underline{D} \\ \underline{E\Omega}^*_{KC} & \underline{E\Omega}^*_{KK} & I \\ \underline{D}' & I & 0 \end{bmatrix} \begin{bmatrix} \Delta C \\ \Delta K \\ 1 \end{bmatrix} < 0 \qquad (2.9.4.5)$$

with

$$\left.\begin{aligned} \underline{E\Omega}_{CK} &= \left[\frac{\partial^2 E\omega}{\partial C_l\, \partial K_{l'}}\right] = \underline{E\Omega}'_{KC} \\ \underline{E\Omega}_{KK} &= \left[\frac{\partial^2 E\omega}{\partial K_l\, \partial K_{l'}}\right] \end{aligned}\right\} \text{matrices of order } L \times L \text{ for } l, l' = 1, \ldots, L$$

and

$$(\Delta K)' = \{(K_1 - K_1^*) \cdots (K_L - K_L^*)\}$$

subject to:

$$\Delta K = -\underline{D}'\,\Delta C. \qquad (2.9.4.6)$$

Substitution of (2.9.4.6) into (2.9.4.5) reduces the latter condition to:

$$\underline{E\Omega}^*_{CC} - \underline{E\Omega}^*_{CK}\underline{D} - \underline{D}'\underline{E\Omega}^*_{KC} + \underline{D}'\underline{E\Omega}^*_{KK} \cdot \underline{D} \text{ negative-definite.} \qquad (2.9.4.7)$$

Effects of variations in EY, in parameters of the probability distribution function of Y, in r and in K_0 on C and Y are ruled by:

$$\begin{bmatrix} \underline{E\Omega}_{CC} & \underline{E\Omega}_{CK} & \underline{D} \\ \underline{E\Omega}_{KC} & \underline{E\Omega}_{KK} & I \\ \underline{D}' & I & 0 \end{bmatrix} \begin{bmatrix} C_{EY} & C_{par} & C_r & C_{K_0} \\ K_{EY} & K_{par} & K_r & (K)_{K_0} \\ -[\Lambda_{EY}] & -[\Lambda_{par}] & -\lambda_r & -\lambda_{K_0} \end{bmatrix}$$

$$= \begin{bmatrix} -\underline{E\Omega}_{C,EY} & -\underline{E\Omega}_{C,par} & (1+r)^{-1} \cdot \Lambda_* \underline{D}' \cdot L - & 0 \\ -\underline{E\Omega}_{K,EY} & -\underline{E\Omega}_{K,par} & 0 & 0 \\ \underline{D} & 0 & (1+r)^{-1} \cdot \underline{D}'(\dot{Y} - \dot{C})L - & \iota \end{bmatrix}; \qquad (2.9.4.8)$$

$$\Lambda_* = \begin{bmatrix} \lambda_1 & & 0 \\ & \ddots & \\ 0 & & \lambda_L \end{bmatrix},$$

ι' a summation vector.

Again, these effects may be expressed explicitly by premultiplying both members of (2.9.4.8) by:

$$\begin{bmatrix} \underline{E\Omega}_{CC} & \underline{E\Omega}_{CK} & \underline{D} \\ \underline{E\Omega}_{KC} & \underline{E\Omega}_{KK} & I \\ \underline{D}' & I & 0 \end{bmatrix}^{-1} = \begin{bmatrix} P_{11} & P_{12} & P_{13} \\ P_{21} & P_{22} & P_{23} \\ P_{31} & P_{32} & P_{33} \end{bmatrix} \tag{2.9.4.9}$$

with all sub-matrices of order $L \times L$, and

$$\left.\begin{aligned} P_{11} &= [\underline{E\Omega}_{CC} - \underline{E\Omega}_{CK} \cdot \underline{D}' - \underline{D} \cdot \underline{E\Omega}_{KC} + \underline{D}' \cdot \underline{E\Omega}_{KK} \cdot \underline{D}]^{-1} \\ P_{21} &= P'_{12} = P_{11}\underline{D} \\ P_{31} &= P'_{13} = [\underline{E\Omega}_{KK}\underline{D}' - \underline{E\Omega}_{KC}]\, P_{11} \\ P_{22} &= \underline{D}'P_{11}\underline{D} \\ P_{32} &= P'_{23} = I + [\underline{E\Omega}_{KC} - \underline{E\Omega}_{KK} \cdot \underline{D}']\, P_{11}\underline{D} \\ P_{33} &= [\underline{E\Omega}_{KC} - \underline{E\Omega}_{KK}\underline{D}'] \cdot P_{11}\, [\underline{E\Omega}_{CK} - \underline{D}\underline{E\Omega}_{KK}] - \underline{E\Omega}_{KK}. \end{aligned}\right\} \tag{2.9.4.10}$$

Thus we obtain:

$$C_{EY} = -P_{11}\underline{E\Omega}_{C,EY} - P_{12}\underline{E\Omega}_{K,EY} + P_{13}\underline{D}' \tag{2.9.4.11}$$

$$K_{EY} = -P_{21}\underline{E\Omega}_{C,EY} - P_{22}\underline{E\Omega}_{K,EY} + P_{23}\underline{D}' \tag{2.9.4.12}$$

$$C_{\text{par}} = -P_{11}\underline{E\Omega}_{C,\text{par}} - P_{12}\underline{E\Omega}_{K,\text{par}} \tag{2.9.4.13}$$

$$K_{\text{par}} = -P_{21}\underline{E\Omega}_{C,\text{par}} - P_{22}\underline{E\Omega}_{K,\text{par}} \tag{2.9.4.14}$$

$$C_r = (1 + r)^{-1}\, [P_{11}\Lambda_* \underline{D}' + P_{13}\underline{D}'\, (\dot{Y} - \dot{C})]\, L- \tag{2.9.4.15}$$

$$K_r = (1 + r)^{-1}\, [P_{21}\Lambda_* \underline{D}' + P_{23}\underline{D}'\, (\dot{Y} - \dot{C})]\, L- \tag{2.9.4.16}$$

$$C_{K_0} = P_{13}\iota \tag{2.9.4.17}$$

$$K_{K_0} = P_{23}\iota. \tag{2.9.4.18}$$

In this case too, we have to await a further specification of ω in section 3.5, before we shall be able to draw conclusions about the signs of these effects.

2.10. Sociometric version of the model with survival rates incorporated

2.10.1. UTILITY FUNCTION AND BUDGET EQUATION

The models of consumption and savings dealt with above are all of the individualistic type. This implies a limitation, which may be removed by including consumption by others in the utility function, for instance, as follows:

$$_i\omega = {_i\omega} \, ({_iC_2} \cdots {_iC_L}, {_1C_1} \cdots {_IC_1}) \tag{2.10.1.1}$$

with

$$\frac{\partial_i \omega}{\partial_i C_l} > 0 \quad \text{for } i = 1, \dots, I; \; l = 1, \dots, L$$

and

$$\frac{\partial_i \omega}{\partial_{i'} C_1} < 0 \quad \text{for } i'(\neq i) = 1, \dots, I.$$

The latter inequality is meant as an indication of 'jealousy'. Therefore, we consider utility functions for *sets* of individuals – interdependent with respect to their consumption.

First, this requires attaching subscripts i to functions and their parameters as well as to variables; life expectancies ${_iL}$ figure among the latter. In order to get rid of the mathematically awkward inequality of the number of arguments between the ${_i\omega}$ for different i, the device introduced in section 2.7 may be adopted here, i.e. extending ${_iL}$ to M = the maximum lifetime for all decision-making individuals within the set $\{1, \dots, I\}$.[18]

Thus,

$$\begin{aligned} {_i\omega} &= {_i\omega} \, ({_iC_2}, \dots, {_iC_M}, {_1C_1}, \dots, {_IC_1}) \\ &= {_i\omega} \, ({_iC'}, C'_1) \quad \text{replaces (2.10.1.1) in vector notation.} \end{aligned} \tag{2.10.1.2}$$

In (2.10.1.2), as in (2.10.1.1), the assumed dependence of consumers on

---

[18] The set $\{1, \dots, I\}$ consists of individuals whose consumption pattern (over time) depend, inter alia, on consumption by others *within this set*, and vice versa. In addition, an individual's consumption pattern may also depend on consumption by people outside that set; if this dependence, however, is not reciprocated, it need not be taken into account *explicitly* in the context of the present model: consumption by those 'outsiders' may be considered as given, while it may affect parameters of the 'insiders' utility function. Typically, such sets of individuals coincide with the 'small groups' in sociometry.

each other is restricted to *current* consumption, for theoretical as well as for practical reasons. While an individual's feeling of well-being may be influenced by his or her neighbours' or relatives' *contemporary* consumption, it seems too far-fetched to assume that it will also be affected by their prospective consumption in later periods.

Again, the individuals are supposed to maximize their utility subject to lifetime budget constraints:

$$\Delta_i K = \sum_{l=1}^{{}_iL} ({}_iY_l - {}_iC_l)(1 + {}_ir)^{{}_iL-l}. \tag{2.10.1.3}$$

Here too, variations in the number of terms may be removed by extending ${}_iL$ to M. As set forth in section 2.7, however, this requires the introduction of survival rates ${}_is_l$ into the budget equation:

$$\Delta_i K = \sum_{l=1}^{M} ({}_iY_l - {}_iC_l)\, {}_is_l\, (1 + {}_ir)^{M-l} = ({}_iY. - {}_iC.)'\, {}_i\underline{d} \quad \text{(in vector notation)} \tag{2.10.1.4}$$

with

$$({}_iY. - {}_iC.)' = \{({}_iY_1 - {}_iC_1) \cdots ({}_iY_M - {}_iC_M)\}$$

and

$${}_i\underline{d} = \{{}_is_1\,(1 + {}_ir)^{M-1} \cdots \underset{(=1)}{{}_is_M\,(1 + {}_ir)^{\overset{(=0)}{M-M}}}\}$$

being $1 \times M$ vectors for $i = 1, \ldots, I$.

2.10.2. OPTIMUM CONDITIONS

The first-order conditions for maximizing (2.10.1.2) subject to (2.10.1.4) are:

$$\frac{\partial_i\omega}{\partial_i C_1} + \sum_{i' \neq i} \frac{\partial_i\omega}{\partial_{i'} C_1} \cdot \frac{\partial_{i'} C_1}{\partial_i C_1} = \sum_{i'=1}^{I} \frac{\partial_i\omega}{\partial_{i'} C_1} \cdot \frac{\partial_{i'} C_1}{\partial_i C_1}$$

$$= {}_i\lambda \cdot {}_is_1\,(1 + {}_ir)^{M-1} = {}_i\lambda \cdot {}_i\underline{d}_1 \tag{2.10.2.1 a}$$

$$\frac{\partial_i\omega}{\partial_i C_l} = {}_i\lambda \cdot {}_is_l\,(1 + {}_ir)^{M-l} = {}_i\lambda \cdot {}_i\underline{d}_l \quad \text{for} \quad i = 1, \ldots, I;\ l = 2, \ldots, M, \tag{2.10.2.1 b}$$

with $\partial_{i'} C_1 / \partial_i C_1$ denoting Frisch' 'conjectural variations', i.e. the reaction of current consumption by i' on a unit change in current consumption by i for $i' \neq i$, and $\partial_i C_1 / \partial_{i'} C_1 \overset{\text{def}}{=} 1$.

In matrix notation, (2.10.2.1 a) and (2.10.2.1 b) may be combined into

$$ {}_i\mathsf{T} \cdot {}_i g. = {}_i\lambda \cdot {}_i\underline{d}., \qquad (2.10.2.2) $$

with

$$ {}_i\mathsf{T} = \begin{bmatrix} \dfrac{\partial_i \omega}{\partial_1 C_1} & \cdots & \dfrac{\partial_i \omega}{\partial_i C_1} & \cdots & \dfrac{\partial_i \omega}{\partial_I C_1} \\ \cdots & & \cdots & & \cdots \\ 0 \cdots 0 & & \dfrac{\partial_i \omega}{\partial_i C_2} & & 0 \cdots 0 \\ \vdots \quad \vdots & & \vdots & & \vdots \quad \vdots \\ 0 \cdots 0 & & \dfrac{\partial_i \omega}{\partial_i C_M} & & 0 \cdots 0 \end{bmatrix} $$

i.e. $M \times I$ matrices, with the first row and the i's column with generally non-zero elements and zeroes everywhere else,

and

$$ {}_i g'. = \left\{ \frac{\hat{\partial}_1 C_1}{\hat{\partial}_i C_1} \cdots \frac{\partial_i C_1}{\partial_i C_1} \cdots \frac{\hat{\partial}_I C_1}{\hat{\partial}_i C_1} \right\} \quad \text{a } 1 \times I \quad \text{vector} $$

for $i = 1, \ldots, I$.

For all individuals together, the first-order conditions may be expressed by:

$$.\mathsf{T}. \times .g. = .\underline{D} \cdot .\lambda, \qquad (2.10.2.3) $$

with

$$.\mathsf{T} = \begin{bmatrix} {}_1\mathsf{T} & & 0 \\ & \ddots & \\ 0 & & {}_I\mathsf{T} \end{bmatrix} \quad \text{an } IM \times I^2 \text{ matrix} $$

$$ .g'. = \{{}_1 g'. \cdots {}_I g'.\} \quad \text{a } 1 \times I^2 \text{ vector,} $$

$$.\underline{D} = \begin{bmatrix} {}_1\underline{d} & & 0 \\ & \ddots & \\ 0 & & {}_I\underline{d} \end{bmatrix} \quad \text{an } IM \times I \text{ matrix,} $$

and

$$.\lambda' = \{{}_1\lambda \cdots {}_I\lambda\} \quad \text{a } 1 \times I \text{ vector.} $$

One should notice that the 'conjectural variations' $\hat{\partial}_i C_1 / \hat{\partial}_{i'} C_1$ cannot be 'solved' from the equations (2.10.2.1), (2.10.2.2) or (2.10.2.3), but should be *known* beforehand, i.e. either as functions of the IM variables ${}_i C_l$ or as constants.

The latter alternative may be considered as a particular case of the former one; identically zero values for those 'reaction coefficients' would be a super-special case of constancy.

In any case, the *IM* values ${}_iC_l$, together with the *I* values ${}_i\lambda$, could be solved – at least in principle – from either of the equivalent systems (2.10.2.1), (2.10.2.2) or (2.10.2.3), together with the *I* lifetime budget equations (2.10.1.4), provided the $\hat{\partial}_i C_1/\hat{\partial}_{i'} C_1$ would be known, either as fully specified functions (including the values of its parameters) or as constants.

The $\hat{\partial}_i C_1/\hat{\partial}_{i'} C_1$ may be mutually consistent or not. In the latter case, these quasi-parameters may assume any value independent of each other, according to the whims of the consumers-savers; in the former case, the reversal test

$$\frac{\hat{\partial}_i C_1}{\hat{\partial}_{i'} C_1} \cdot \frac{\hat{\partial}_{i'} C_1}{\hat{\partial}_i C_1} = 1, \tag{2.10.2.4}$$

and the triangularity test

$$\frac{\hat{\partial}_i C_1}{\hat{\partial}_{i'} C_1} = \frac{\hat{\partial}_i C_1}{\hat{\partial}_{i''} C_1} \cdot \frac{\hat{\partial}_{i''} C_1}{\hat{\partial}_{i'} C_1} \tag{2.10.2.5}$$

should hold for any pair (i, i') and any triplet (i, i', i''), respectively.

Therefore, a sub-set of $I - 1$ such "conjectural variations" would enable us to calculate of the rest of them. Otherwise, the $I(I-1)$ functions or constants $\hat{\partial}_i C_1/\hat{\partial}_{i'} C_1$ would have to be specified for all i, i' $(= 1, \ldots, I;\ i \neq i')$ independently.

In order that a solution vector, say ${}_iC^*$ for any i, would result in a (constrained) utility maximum:

$$\{(\Delta_i C_{(-1)})' \quad \Delta_i C_1 \quad 1\} \cdot {}_iH^* \cdot \begin{bmatrix} \Delta_i C_{(-1)} \\ \Delta_i C_1 \\ 1 \end{bmatrix}' < 0 \tag{2.10.2.6}$$

should hold good for $i = 1, \ldots, I$, if

$$\begin{aligned} {}_iH^* &= \begin{bmatrix} {}_iH^*_{11} & {}_iH^*_{12} & {}_i\underline{d}_{(-1)} \\ {}_iH^*_{21} & {}_iH^*_{22} & {}_i\underline{d}_1 \cdot e_i \\ {}_i\underline{d}'_{(-1)} & {}_i\underline{d}_1 \cdot e'_i & 0 \end{bmatrix} \\ &= \begin{bmatrix} {}_i\Omega^*_{ii(-1,-1)} & {}_i\Omega^*_{i.(-1,1)} + (.G^*_{ii(-1,1)})'\,({}_i\dot{\omega})_{.C_1} & {}_i\underline{d}_{(-1)} \\ {}_i\Omega^*_{.i(1,-1)} + ({}_i\dot{\omega})_{.C_1} \cdot .G^*_{ii(1,-1)} & {}_i\Omega^*_{..(1,1)} + ({}_i\dot{\omega})_{.C_1} \cdot .G^*_{i.(1,1)} & {}_i\underline{d}_1 \cdot e_i \\ {}_i\underline{d}'_{(-1)} & {}_i\underline{d}_1 \cdot e'_i & 0 \end{bmatrix} \end{aligned} \tag{2.10.2.7}$$

with

$$(\Delta_i C._{(-1)})' = \{({}_iC_2 - {}_iC_2^*) \cdots ({}_iC_M - {}_iC_M^*)\} \quad \text{a } 1 \times (M-1) \text{ vector}$$

$${}_i\Omega_{ii(-1,-1)} = \left[\frac{\partial_i^2 \omega}{\partial_i C_l \cdot \partial_i C_{l'}}\right] \quad \text{a matrix of order } (M-1) \times (M-1)$$

$${}_i\Omega_{i.(-1,1)} = {}_i\Omega'_{.i(1,-1)} = \left[\frac{\partial_i^2 \omega}{\partial_i C_l \cdot \partial_{i'} C_1}\right] \quad \text{a matrix of order } (M-1) \times I$$

$${}_i\Omega_{..(1,1)} = \left[\frac{\partial_i^2 \omega}{\partial_{i'} C_1 \cdot \partial_{i''} C_1}\right] \quad \text{a matrix of order } I \times I$$

$${}_iG_{ii(-1,1)} = \left[\frac{\partial_{i'}^2 C_1}{\partial_i C_1 \cdot \partial_i C_{l'}}\right] = .G'_{ii(1,-1)} \quad \text{an } I \times (M-1) \text{ matrix}$$

$$.G_{i.(1,1)} = .G_{.i(1,1)} = \left[\frac{\partial_{i'}^2 C_1}{\partial_i C_1 \cdot \partial_{i''} C_1}\right] \quad \text{an } I \times I \text{ matrix}$$

$${}_i\underline{d}_{(-1)} = \{{}_i\underline{d}_2 \cdots {}_i\underline{d}_M\} \quad \text{a } 1 \times (M-1) \text{ vector}$$

e_i' = a unit vector of length M, with 1 at the ith spot and zero everywhere else, and

$$({}_i\dot{\omega})._{C_1} = \begin{bmatrix} \dfrac{\partial_i \omega}{\partial_1 C_1} & & 0 \\ & \ddots & \\ 0 & & \dfrac{\partial_i \omega}{\partial_I C_1} \end{bmatrix}$$

provided

$$(\Delta_i C_{(-1)})' \cdot {}_i\underline{d}_{(-1)} + (\Delta_i C_1) \cdot {}_i\underline{d}_1 = 0. \tag{2.10.2.8}$$

If also

$$\Delta_{i'} C_1 = \frac{\partial_{i'} C_1}{\partial_i C_1} \cdot \Delta_i C_1 \tag{2.10.2.9}$$

would hold good for all i, i' (= 1, ..., I) simultaneously, i.e. if the consistency conditions (2.10.2.4) and (2.10.2.5) would apply, then (2.10.2.6) might be condensed into:

$$\{(\Delta_i C_{(-1)})' \quad \Delta_i C_1 \quad 1\}\ {}_iH^{**} \begin{bmatrix} \Delta_i C_{(-1)} \\ \Delta_i C_1 \\ 1 \end{bmatrix} < 0 \text{ for } i = 1, \ldots, I \tag{2.10.2.10}$$

if

$$
{}_iH^{**} = \underbrace{\begin{bmatrix} {}_iH^{**}_{11} & {}_iH^{**}_{12} & {}_i\underline{d}_{(-1)} \\ {}_iH^{**}_{21} & {}_iH^{**}_{22} & {}_i\underline{d}_1 \\ {}_i\underline{d}'_{(-1)} & {}_i\underline{d}_1 & 0 \end{bmatrix}}_{\substack{M-1 \quad 1 \quad 1 \\ \text{columns}}} \left.\begin{matrix} M-1 \\ 1 \\ 1 \end{matrix}\right\} \text{rows} \qquad \text{for each } i, \tag{2.10.2.11}
$$

with

$$
\begin{aligned}
{}_iH^{**}_{11} &= {}_i\Omega^*_{ii(-1,-1)} \\
{}_iH^{**}_{12} &= ({}_iH^{**}_{21})' = [{}_i.\Omega^*_{i(-1,1)} + (.G^*_{ii(-1,1)})'\,({}_i\dot{\omega}).{}_{c_1}]\,{}_ig. \\
{}_iH^{**}_{22} &= {}_ig'\,[{}_i\Omega^*_{..(1,1)} + ({}_i\dot{\omega}).{}_{c_1} \cdot .G^*_{i.(1,1)}]\,{}_ig_{.}.
\end{aligned}
$$

2.10.3. EFFECTS OF VARYING THE 'DATA' ON THE OPTIMAL TIME-PATTERN OF CONSUMPTION

For each individual, income expectations, rates of interest, and intended change in personal wealth of either himself or of others (within the set $\{1, \ldots, I\}$) are assumed to be given; i.e.

$$
.Y'_. = \{{}_1Y_1 \cdots {}_1Y_M \cdots {}_IY_1 \cdots {}_IY_M\} \quad \text{a } 1 \times IM \text{ vector}
$$

$$
\left.\begin{aligned} .r' &= \{{}_1r \cdots {}_Ir\} \\ (\Delta_. K)' &= \{\Delta_1 K \cdots \Delta_I K\} \end{aligned}\right\} \quad 1 \times I \text{ vectors.}
$$

The effects of varying this data on consumption result from differentiation of the first-order conditions (2.10.2.1) or (2.10.2.2) and of the budget equation (2.10.1.4) with respect to the data:

$$
\begin{bmatrix} {}_iH^*_{11} & {}_iH^*_{12} & {}_i\underline{d}_{(-1)} \\ {}_iH^*_{21} & {}_iH^*_{22} & {}_i\underline{d}_1 \cdot e_i \\ {}_i\underline{d}'_{(-1)} & {}_i\underline{d}_1 \cdot e'_i & 0 \end{bmatrix}
\begin{bmatrix} ({}_iC_{(-1)}).{}_{Y.} & ({}_iC_{(-1)}).{}_r & ({}_iC_{(-1)})_{\Delta.K} \\ {}_i(.C_1).{}_{Y.} & {}_i(.C_1).{}_r & {}_i(.C_1)_{\Delta.K} \\ -({}_i\lambda).{}_{Y.} & -({}_i\lambda)\,.{}_r & -({}_i\lambda)_{\Delta.K} \end{bmatrix}
$$

$$
= \begin{bmatrix} 0 & {}_i\lambda \cdot (1 + {}_ir)^{-1} \cdot {}_i\underline{\dot{d}}_{(-1)} \cdot M^-_{(-1)} \cdot e'_i & 0 \\ 0 & {}_i\lambda \cdot (1 + {}_ir)^{-1} \cdot {}_i\underline{d}_1 \cdot (M-1) \cdot e_i \cdot e'_i & 0 \\ {}_i\underline{d}' \cdot E'_i & (1 + {}_ir)^{-1}\,({}_iY'_. - {}_iC'_.)\,{}_i\underline{\dot{d}} \cdot M^- \cdot e'_i & -e'_i \end{bmatrix}
$$

$$
\text{for } i = 1, \ldots, I; \tag{2.10.3.1}
$$

the sub-matrices within the second matrix of (2.10.3.1) result from differentiation of the elements of the column vectors ${}_iC_{(-1)}$ and ${}_i(.C_1)$, of lengths $M-1$ and I respectively, and of the scalar ${}_i\lambda$, with respect to the row vectors $.Y'_.$, $.r'$ and $(\Delta .K)'$ of lengths IM, I and I respectively, where

$$ {}_iC'_{(-1)} = \{{}_iC_2 \cdots {}_iC_M\} $$

$$ {}_i(.C_1) = \{{}_{(i)1}C_1 \cdots {}_{(i)I}C_1\}, $$

with the pre-subscript (i) denoting consideration from i's point of view; furthermore:

$$ {}_i\underline{d}_{(-1)} = \begin{bmatrix} {}_i\underline{d}_2 & & 0 \\ & \ddots & \\ 0 & & {}_i\underline{d}_M \end{bmatrix} \quad \text{an } (M-1)\times(M-1) \text{ diagonal matrix} $$

$$ M^{-\prime}_{(-1)} = \{(M-2)\cdots(M-M)\} \quad \text{a } 1\times(M-1) \text{ vector} $$

$$ E'_i = \begin{bmatrix} e'_i & & & 0 \\ & e'_i & & \\ & & \ddots & \\ 0 & & & e'_i \end{bmatrix} \quad \text{an } M\times IM \text{ matrix.} $$

In order to make the (second) 'effects' matrix in (2.10.3.1) explicit, both members of this set of equations have to be premultiplied by the inverse of the first matrix, i.e. by

$$ {}_iH^{-1} = \begin{bmatrix} {}_iM_{11} & {}_iM_{12} & {}_im_1 \\ {}_iM_{21} & {}_iM_{22} & {}_im_2 \\ {}_im'_1 & {}_im'_2 & {}_in \end{bmatrix}, \tag{2.10.3.2} $$

provided ${}_iH$ is non-singular (asterisks deleted for simplicity's sake).

Therefore, (2.10.3.1) and (2.10.3.2) imply:

$$ ({}_iC_{(-1)})_{.Y.} = {}_im_1 \cdot {}_id' \cdot E'_i \tag{2.10.3.3} $$

$$ {}_i(.C_1)_{.Y.} = {}_im_2 \cdot {}_id' \cdot E'_i \tag{2.10.3.4} $$

$$({}_iC_{(-1)})_{.r} = (1 + {}_ir)^{-1} [{}_i\lambda \{{}_iM_{11} \cdot {}_i\underline{d}_{(-1)} \cdot M^-_{(-1)} + {}_i\underline{d}_1 \cdot (M-1)\, {}_iM_{12} \cdot e_i\} + ({}_iY'_. - {}_iC'_.) \cdot {}_i\underline{d} \cdot M^- \cdot {}_im_1]\, e'_i \tag{2.10.3.5}$$

$$_i(.C_1)_{.r} = (1 + {}_ir)^{-1} [{}_i\lambda \{{}_iM_{21} \cdot {}_i\underline{d}_{(-1)} M_{(-1)} + {}_i\underline{d}_1 \cdot (M-1) \cdot {}_iM_{22} \cdot e_i\} + ({}_iY'_. - {}_iC'_.) \cdot {}_i\underline{d} \cdot M^- \cdot {}_im_2]\, e'_i \tag{2.10.3.6}$$

$$({}_iC_{(-1)})_{\Delta.K} = -{}_im_1 \cdot e'_i \tag{2.10.3.7}$$

$$_i(.C_1)_{\Delta.K} = -{}_im_2 \cdot e'_i. \tag{2.10.3.8}$$

Due to the structure of E'_i and e'_i in (2.10.3.3) through (2.10.3.8) these equations imply zero effects with respect to changes in ${}_{i'}Y_l$, ${}_{i'}r$ and $\Delta_{i'}K$ unless $i' = i$. This means that even in this sociometric version of the model consumption (present or future) is *not* affected by changes in other people's data, except current consumption in the opinion of the latter (i.e. the imaginary reactions denoted by $_i({}_{i'}C_1)_{{}_iY_l}$, $_i({}_{i'}C_1)_{{}_ir}$ and $_i({}_{i'}C_1)_{\Delta_i K}$); the latter kind of reactions, however, is restricted to changes in data relating to the person evaluating other people's reactions. Consequently, contradictions between different people's opinions about other (or the same) people's reactions are excluded. Therefore, (2.10.3.1) may be reduced by attaching subscripts i to the data, i.e. by replacing $_.Y_.$, $_.r$ and $\Delta_.K$ in the second matrix by ${}_iY_.$, ${}_ir$ and Δ_iK respectively, and by deleting E'_i and e'_i in the third matrix. Accordingly, the effects equations (2.10.3.3) through (2.10.3.8) are reduced to:

$$({}_iC_{(-1)})_{{}_iY.} = {}_im_1 \cdot {}_i\underline{d}' \tag{2.10.3.9}$$

$$_i(.C_1)_{{}_iY.} = {}_im_2 \cdot {}_i\underline{d}' \tag{2.10.3.10}$$

$$({}_iC_{(-1)})_{{}_ir} = (1 + {}_ir)^{-1} [{}_i\lambda \{{}_iM_{11} \cdot {}_i\underline{d}_{(-1)} \cdot M^-_{(-1)} + {}_i\underline{d}_1 (M-1) \cdot {}_iM_{12} \cdot e_i\} + {}_im_1 ({}_iY'_. - {}_iC'_.) \cdot {}_i\underline{d} \cdot M^-] \tag{2.10.3.11}$$

$$_i(.C_1)_{{}_ir} = (1 + {}_ir)^{-1} [{}_i\lambda \{{}_iM_{21} \cdot {}_i\underline{d}_{(-1)} \cdot M^-_{(-1)} + {}_i\underline{d}_1 \cdot (M-1) \cdot {}_iM_{22} \cdot e_i\} + {}_im_2 ({}_iY'_. - {}_iC'_.) \cdot {}_i\underline{d} \cdot M^-] \tag{2.10.3.12}$$

$$({}_iC_{(-1)})_{\Delta_iK} = -{}_im_1 \tag{2.10.3.13}$$

$$_i(.C_1)_{\Delta_iK} = -{}_im_2. \tag{2.10.3.14}$$

In the case where the conjectural variations $\partial_{i'}C_1/\partial_i C_1$ satisfy the consistency conditions (2.10.2.4) and (2.10.2.5), the effects equations may be expressed by means of (2.10.2.11); as before, only those effects on anyone's consumption are considered that result from changes in the same person's data, since all effects of changes in other people's data are zero. Therefore, the effects equations may be written as:

$$\begin{bmatrix} {}_iH_{11}^{**} & {}_iH_{12}^{**} & {}_i\underline{d}_{(-1)} \\ {}_iH_{21}^{**} & {}_iH_{22}^{**} & {}_i\underline{d}_1 \\ {}_i\underline{d}'_{(-1)} & {}_i\underline{d}_1 & 0 \end{bmatrix} \begin{bmatrix} ({}_iC_{(-1)})_{iY_.} & ({}_iC_{(-1)})_{ir} & ({}_iC_{(-1)})_{\Delta_i K} \\ ({}_iC_1)_{iY_.} & ({}_iC_1)_{ir} & ({}_iC_1)_{\Delta_i K} \\ -({}_i\lambda)_{iY_.} & -({}_i\lambda)_{ir} & -({}_i\lambda)_{\Delta_i K} \end{bmatrix}$$

$$= \begin{bmatrix} 0 & {}_i\lambda \cdot (1 + {}_ir)^{-1} \cdot {}_i\dot{\underline{d}}_{(-1)} M^-_{(-1)} & 0 \\ 0 & {}_i\lambda \cdot (1 + {}_ir)^{-1} \cdot {}_i\underline{d}_1 \, (M - 1) & 0 \\ {}_i\underline{d} & (1 + {}_ir)^{-1} \, ({}_iY'_. - {}_iC'_.) \cdot {}_i\dot{\underline{d}} M^- & 1 \end{bmatrix}, \qquad (2.10.3.15)$$

for $i = 1, \ldots, I$.

The differences between (2.10.3.1) and (2.10.3.15) are in essence differences in order between the corresponding matrices, viz.:

(a) the second rows and columns of sub-matrices in (2.10.3.2) are row- and column-vectors respectively, instead of $I \times (M - 1)$ and $(M - 1) \times I$ matrices in (2.10.2.7);

(b) accordingly, the second row of sub-matrices in the second member of (2.10.3.15) consists of row vectors, instead of $I \times (M - 1)$ matrices in the second member of (2.10.3.1).

According to (2.10.3.15), the imaginary effects of changes in anyone's data on other people's current consumption disappeared from the scene.

Thus, by re-arrangement of rows and columns, the system of equations (2.10.3.15) may be further condensed into:

$$\begin{bmatrix} {}_iH_* & {}_i\underline{d} \\ {}_i\underline{d}' & 0 \end{bmatrix} \begin{bmatrix} ({}_iC_.)_{Y_.} & ({}_iC_.)_{r} & ({}_iC_.)_{\Delta . K} \\ -({}_i\lambda)_{Y_.} & -({}_i\lambda)_{r} & -({}_i\lambda)_{\Delta . K} \end{bmatrix}$$

$$= \begin{bmatrix} 0 & {}_i\lambda. \, (1 + {}_ir)^{-1} \cdot {}_i\dot{\underline{d}} \cdot M^- & 0 \\ {}_i\underline{d} & (1 + {}_ir)^{-1} \, ({}_iY_. - {}_iC') \cdot {}_i\underline{d} \cdot M^- & -1 \end{bmatrix}, \qquad (2.10.3.16)$$

with

$$ {}_iH_* = \begin{bmatrix} {}_iH^{**}_{22} & {}_iH^{**}_{12} \\ {}_iH^{**}_{21} & {}_iH^{**}_{11} \end{bmatrix} \quad M \times M \text{ matrices, for each } i, $$

with

$$ {}_iH^{**}_{12} = ({}_iH^{**}_{21})' \quad (M-1) \times 1 \text{ vectors} $$

and

$$ {}_iH^{**}_{11} \quad \text{scalars.} $$

For the 'solution' of (2.10.3.16), we find:

$$ ({}_iC_.)_{{}_iY_.} = ({}_i\underline{d}' \cdot {}_iH_*^{-1} \cdot {}_i\underline{d})^{-1} \cdot {}_iH_*^{-1} \cdot {}_i\underline{d} \cdot {}_i\underline{d}', \qquad (2.10.3.17) $$

$$ ({}_iC_.)_{{}_ir} = (1 + {}_ir)^{-1} [{}_i\lambda \{{}_iH_*^{-1} - ({}_i\underline{d}' \cdot {}_iH_*^{-1} \cdot {}_i\underline{d})^{-1} \cdot ({}_iH_*^{-1} \cdot {}_i\underline{d})({}_iH_*^{-1} \cdot \underline{d}_i)'\} $$
$$ + ({}_i\underline{d}' \cdot {}_iH_*^{-1} \cdot {}_i\underline{d})^{-1} ({}_iH_*^{-1} \cdot {}_i\underline{d})({}_iY'_. - {}_iC'_.)] \, {}_i\dot{\underline{d}} \cdot M^-, \qquad (2.10.3.18) $$

$$ ({}_iC_.)_{\Delta_i K} = -({}_i\underline{d}' \cdot {}_iH_*^{-1} \cdot {}_i\underline{d})^{-1} \cdot {}_iH_*^{-1} \cdot {}_i\underline{d}, \qquad (2.10.3.19) $$

provided the matrix inversions are not precluded by singularity.

Formally, these three sets of equations are analogous to (2.10.3.9) through (2.10.3.11) for the basic model. Again, the interest effects (2.10.3.18) may be split into substitution effects and wealth accumulation effects, with and without multipliers ${}_i\lambda$ respectively; the first average out to zero when weighted by the elements of the discount vector ${}_i\underline{d}$, while the wealth accumulation effects too may be positive or negative.

Materially, however, there is a difference in the sense that in the sociometric model inter-individual demonstration effects on people's consumption as well as individuals' reactions to other people's changes in consumption are incorporated through the matrices ${}_iH_*$.

Those demonstration effects would have an impact on people's consumption patterns even in the case where the conjectural variations are zero.

On the other hand, conjectural variations would *not* affect *changes* in consumer behaviour following changes in data if those variations are constant; in that case the G-matrices entering the H-matrix would become zero (cf. section 3.6.2). Still, the optimal consumption vectors themselves would depend on the conjectural variations even if constant.

All these observations apply equally well to the effects represented by equations (2.10.3.3) through (2.10.3.8) in case mutual consistency of the conjectural variations is not assumed. Therefore, inter-individual consumer relationships affect reactions of consumption patterns to changes in data *in*directly, but not directly.

More definite conclusions about these effects in a sociometric context can be drawn only after further specification and simplification of the model with respect to the utility function and the conjectural variations, as shown in section 3.6.

APPENDIX A TO CHAPTER 2

SINGLE-STAGE INTERTEMPORAL ALLOCATION OF FINANCIAL RESOURCE TO CONSUMER BUDGET ITEMS, RESIDUAL DETERMINATION OF SAVINGS, AND EVALUATION OF DEMAND

In section 2.1.2, a theory of two-stage allocation of lifetime resources (2a) has been opted for. Consumption and Savings would be determined at the first stage, such as to maximize a lifetime utility function of total consumption in all prospective periods subject to a lifetime budget constraint; allocation of the total amount earmarked for consumption in the current period to budget items would be left to the second stage.

According to the alternative approach, consumption expenditures on each item, in each prospective period, would be determined (but possibly revised later on) in such a way as to maximize the utility of those expenditures in– all prospective periods, again subject to a lifetime budget constraint. Thus, savings per period would come out as differences between (prospective) income and the total amou ntspent onall expenditure items for the same period.

This may be shown as follows. Suppose that the consumer maximizes a utility function:

$$\omega = \omega(q'), \tag{2A.1}$$

with $q' = \{q_{11}, \ldots, q_{K1}, \ldots, q_{1L}, \ldots, q_{KL}\}$, the vector of quantities q_{kl} to be consumed of budget items $k\,(= 1, \ldots, K)$ in periods $l\,(= 1, \ldots, L)$, subject to the budget constraint:

$$q'p_x = R_L, \tag{2A.2}$$

with $p_x = \dot{d}_x p$ such that

$$\dot{d}_x = \begin{bmatrix} \dot{d}_{1x} & & & 0 \\ & \dot{d}_{2x} & & \\ & & \ddots & \\ 0 & & & \dot{d}_{Lx} \end{bmatrix} \quad \text{a diagonal matrix of order } KL,$$

comprising $\dot{d}_{lx} = d_l I_K$ as diagonal sub-matrices of order K, relating to discount factor $d_l = (1 + r)^{L-l}$, $p' = \{p_{11}, \ldots, p_{K1}, \ldots, p_{1L}, \ldots, p_{KL}\}$ the vector of prices p_{kl} of items k to be consumed in periods l, and $R_L = -\Delta K + Y'd$ the financial resources discounted till the end of period L, as defined by (2.4.2.3).

In this way, the problem is formally reduced to that dealt with in section 2.4, if C' is replaced by q', and d by p_x. Therefore, the first-order conditions for this optimalization problem are:

$$\omega_q = \lambda \cdot p_x, \tag{2A.3}$$

with $\omega_q = \partial\omega/\partial q$ (a $KL \times 1$ vector), and the second-order conditions for a constrained maximum are:

$$[(\Delta q)' \quad 1] \begin{bmatrix} \Omega_{qq} & p_x \\ p_x' & 0 \end{bmatrix} \begin{bmatrix} \Delta q \\ 1 \end{bmatrix} < 0 \tag{2A.4}$$

provided

$$(\Delta q)' p_x = 0, \tag{2A.5}$$

with $\Delta q = q - q^*$, and q^* the optimum values of q, satisfying (2A.3).

These optimum values depend on the data:

$$q^* = q^* (\Delta K, r, Y', p') = q^* (R_L^+, r, p').^1 \tag{2A.6}$$

Then, the present value of total consumption in each period could be written as:

$$C_l^* = \sum_{k=1}^{K} p_{kl}^x q_{kl}^*, \tag{2A.7}$$

---

1 For example, this set of demand functions might assume the form of a temporally extended, i.e. lifetime budget allocation model, such as:

$$q_{kl} = \frac{c_{kl} (p_{kl} d_l / R_L^+)^{\alpha_{kl} - 1}}{\sum_{k'=1}^{K} \sum_{l'=1}^{L} c_{k'l'} (p_{k'l'} d_{l'} / R_L^+)^{\alpha_{k'l'}}}, \tag{2A.6ex}$$

satisfying the additivity requirement:

$$\sum_{k=1}^{K} \sum_{l=1}^{L} q_{kl} p_{kl} d_l = R_L^+ \overset{\text{def}}{=} R_L + \Delta K,$$

as well as zero-homogeneity with respect to p_{kl} and R_L, and the Slutsky symmetry conditions (cf. eq. (2.6.3.20)), all implied by the constrained utility maximization. For further details, cf. e.g. Somermeyer c.s. [1962].

with $p^x_{kl} = p_{kl}(1 + r)^{1-l}$ = discounted expected future price of k in period l, and personal wealth at the end of period could be expressed by:

$$K_l = K_0 + \sum_{l'=1}^{l} (Y^*_{l'} - C^*_{l'}) = K_0 + \sum_{l'=1}^{l} Y^*_{l'} - \sum_{k=1}^{K}\sum_{l=1}^{L} p^x_{kl} q^*_{kl} \qquad (2A.8)$$

with $Y^*_{l'} = Y_l (1 + r)^{1-l'}$.

Hence, savings in any period l would equal:

$$S_l = Y_l - C_l + r(K_l - K_0)$$
$$= Y_l - \sum_{k=1}^{K} p^x_{kl} q^*_{kl} + r \sum_{l'=1}^{l} (Y^*_{l'} - \sum_{k=1}^{K} p^x_{kl} q^*_{kl}). \qquad (2A.9)$$

In this way, prospective savings for any future (or current) period l would be determined residually, as a result of optimal, one-stage allocation of lifetime resources to expenditures on all budget items in all future periods till the expected end of life.

For evaluating the effects of hypothetical changes in the data of q^*, i.e. for gaining insight into demand functions (2A.6), we differentiate both the first-order conditions (2A.3) and the lifetime budget constraint partially with respect to the data, resulting in:

$$\begin{bmatrix} \Omega_{qq} & p_x \\ p'_x & 0 \end{bmatrix} \begin{bmatrix} q_Y & q_p & q_r & q_{\Delta K} \\ -\lambda'_Y & -\lambda'_p & -\lambda_r & -\lambda_{\Delta K} \end{bmatrix}$$
$$= \begin{bmatrix} 0 & -\lambda d_x & \lambda(1 + r)^{-1} \dot{p} \dot{d}_x L^-_x & 0 \\ p'_x & -q' & (1 + r)^{-1} \cdot (Y - C)'_x \dot{p} \dot{d}_x L^-_x & -1 \end{bmatrix}, \qquad (2A.10)$$

with

$$\Omega_{qq} = \left[\frac{\partial^2 \omega}{\partial q_{kl} \cdot \partial q_{k'l}}\right]$$ a Hessian matrix of order KL $(k, k' = 1, \ldots, K;\ l, l' = 1, \ldots, L)$,

$$q_Y = \left[\frac{\partial q_{kl}}{\partial Y_{l'}}\right]$$ an income effect matrix of order $KL \times L$,

$$q_p = \left[\frac{\partial q_{kl}}{\partial p_{k'l'}}\right]$$ a price effect matrix of order $KL \times KL$,

$$q'_r = \left\{\frac{\partial q_{11}}{\partial r} \cdots \frac{\partial q_{KL}}{\partial r}\right\}$$ a $1 \times KL$ vector of interest effects,

$$q'_{\Delta K} = \left\{\frac{\partial q_{11}}{\partial \Delta K} \cdots \frac{\partial q_{KL}}{\partial r}\right\}$$ a $1 \times KL$ vector of change-in-wealth effects,

$$\lambda'_Y = \left\{\frac{\partial\lambda}{\partial Y_1} \cdots \frac{\partial\lambda}{\partial Y_L}\right\} \quad \text{a } 1 \times L \text{ vector,}$$

$$\lambda'_p = \left\{\frac{\partial\lambda}{\partial p_{11}} \cdots \frac{\partial\lambda}{\partial p_{KL}}\right\} \quad \text{a } 1 \times KL \text{ vector,}$$

$$\lambda_r = \partial\lambda/\partial r \quad \text{and} \quad \lambda_{\Delta K} = \partial\lambda/\partial\Delta K \quad \text{scalars,}$$

$$(Y - C)'_x = \{\underbrace{(Y_1 - C_1) \cdots (Y_1 - C_1)}_{K \text{ times}} \cdots \underbrace{(Y_L - C_L) \cdots (Y_L - C_L)}_{K \text{ times}}\}$$

and

$$L'_x = \{\underbrace{(L - 1) \cdots (L - 1)}_{K \text{ times}} \cdots \underbrace{(L - L) \cdots (L - L)}_{K \text{ times}}\}$$

$1 \times KL$ vectors

and

$\dot{p}$ = the $KL \times KL$ diagonal matrix with $p_{11}, \ldots, p_{KL}$ as its main diagonal elements.

The set of equations (2A.7) resembles (2.4.3.7), except for the additional price effects[2] and the slight change in sub-matrices (1.3) and (2.3), corresponding to the interest rate effects. The reason for the latter differences is that the same discount factors relate to sub-sets pertaining to K consecutive elements for each of the L successive periods.

Premultiplication of (2A.7) by the inverse of the first (bordered Hessian) matrix of (2A.7) yields explicit 'effects' formulae resembling those dealt with in chapters 2 and 3.

Ultimately, however, we are not interested in the effects of the data on the quantities of separate items to be consumed, but on total consumption per period. The latter are related to the former by means of the transformation matrix:

$$P = \begin{bmatrix} p_{11} \cdots p_{K1} & & & 0 \\ & p_{12} \cdots p_{K2} & & \\ & & \ddots & \\ 0 & & & p_{1L} \cdots p_{KL} \end{bmatrix} \qquad (2A.11)$$

of order $L \times KL$,

[2] Cf. Barten [1966] and Theil [1967].

yielding

$$C_z = P \cdot q_z \quad \text{for } z = Y, p, r \text{ and } \Delta K. \tag{2A.12}$$

Unless the detailed ω-function (2A.1) and the global ω-function (2.4.1.1) are specified – in mutually corresponding forms – no conclusions can be drawn about differences in effects resulting from those two specifications of the model.

Despite its methodological appeal of comprehensiveness, this line of reasoning has not been pursued: as intimated in section 2.1.2, the operational and empirical significance of such an approach is questionable.

CHAPTER 3

MICRO-THEORY OF OPTIMAL ALLOCATION OF CONSUMPTION AND SAVINGS OVER TIME BASED ON AN ADDITIVE-SEPARABLE UTILITY FUNCTION

3.1. Basic model

3.1.1. COMPLETELY SEPARABLE UTILITY FUNCTION (CAS)

The basic utility function (2.4.1.1) is completely additive separable in the case where it may be written[1] as:

$$\omega = \sum_{l=1}^{L} \alpha_l(C_l) = \alpha_.(C_.)\,\iota_L \quad \text{in vector notation,} \qquad (3.1.1.1)$$

with $\{\alpha_.(C_.)\} = \{\alpha_1(C_1) \cdots \alpha_L(C_L)\} > 0$ a positive row vector of functions of single arguments only, and $\iota_L' = \{1 \cdots 1\}$ likewise a vector of length L.

By virtue of (3.1.1.1):

$$\omega_C = \alpha_C, \quad \text{with} \quad \alpha_C' = \left\{\frac{\partial\alpha_1(C_1)}{\partial C_L} \cdots \frac{\partial\alpha_L(C_L)}{\partial C_L}\right\} > 0 \quad \text{a positive vector of marginal utilities,} \qquad (3.1.1.2)$$

and

$$\Omega = \begin{bmatrix} \alpha_{C_1C_1} & & 0 \\ & \ddots & \\ 0 & & \alpha_{C_LC_L} \end{bmatrix} \quad \text{a diagonal matrix} \qquad (3.1.1.3)$$

with $\alpha_{C_lC_l} = \partial^2\alpha_l(C_l)/\partial C_l^2$ for $l = 1, \ldots, L$.

The optimum conditions (2.4.2.4) now become (in scalar notation):

$$\alpha_{C_\tau} = R_L^{-1}\,(1 + r)^{L-\tau}\,(\sum_{l=1}^{L} C_l\alpha_{C_l}) \quad \text{for } \tau = 1, \ldots, L, \qquad (3.1.1.4)$$

---

[1] Possibly after some monotonically increasing transformation (cf. section 2.4.4).

implying

$$\alpha_{C_\tau}/\alpha_{C_1} = (1 + r)^{1-\tau}. \quad (3.1.1.5)$$

Since α_{C_τ} is a function of C_τ alone, C_τ might be expressed in terms of C_1 and r for $\tau = 2, \ldots, L$:

$$C_\tau = f_\tau(C_1, r) \quad \text{for } \tau = 2, \ldots, L \quad (3.1.1.6)$$

and $f_1(C_1, r) = C_1$.

C_1 might be solved from

$$\sum_{\tau=1}^{L} f_\tau(C_1, r)(1 + r)^{L-\tau} = R_L, \quad (3.1.1.7)$$

at least in principle. Substitution of the resulting expression for C_1 in terms of r and R_L (itself a function of r, as well as of ΔK and the vector Y) into (3.1.1.6) yields expressions for C_τ in the same variables. If, moreover,

$$a_l \overset{\text{def}}{=} \alpha_{C_l C_l} < 0 \quad \text{for values } C_l^* \text{ of } C_l \quad (3.1.1.8)$$

satisfying the first-order conditions for maximizing ω, the pertinent second-order conditions too are met, in the sense that it ensures negative-definiteness. Since d is a positive vector, (3.1.1.3) and (3.1.1.8) also ensure:

$$(\Omega^{-1}d)' = \{a_1^{-1}d_1 \cdots a_L^{-1}d_L\} < 0, \quad (3.1.1.9)$$

i.e. a negative vector.

Therefore, according to (2.4.3.9):

$$C_Y = (\sum_{\tau=1}^{L} a_\tau^{-1}d_\tau^2)^{-1}\,[a_l^{-1}d_l d_{l'}] > 0, \quad (3.1.1.10)$$

i.e. a matrix with all elements ($l, l' = 1, \ldots, L$ for $\partial C_l/\partial Y_{l'}$) positive, and according to (2.3.11):

$$C_{\Delta K} = -(\sum_{\tau=1}^{L} a_\tau^{-1}d_\tau^2)^{-1}\,\{a_l^{-1}d_l\}' < 0, \quad (3.1.1.11)$$

i.e. a vector with all elements ($l = 1, \ldots, L$) for $\partial C_l/\partial(\Delta K)$ negative.

In view of (3.1.1.10)

$$0 < \frac{\partial C_l}{\partial Y_{l'}}, \quad \text{and} \quad \frac{\partial C_l}{\partial Y_l} < 1 \quad \text{for} \quad l, l' = 1, \ldots, L \quad (3.1.1.12)$$

Furthermore, (3.1.1.10) suggests that $\partial C_l/\partial Y_{l'}$ tends to decline according as $l + l'$ is larger. Finally, (3.1.1.10) implies:

$$\frac{\partial C_l}{\partial Y_{l'}} \Big/ \frac{\partial C_l}{\partial Y_{l''}} = (1+r)^{l''-l'}, \quad \text{i.e. independent of } l \text{ and,}$$

$$\gtreqless 1 \text{ according as } l'' \gtreqless l'; \tag{3.1.1.13}$$

this means that effects of changes in income $Y_{l'}$ on consumption C_l decrease in proportion to the discount factor according as the income-change-period l' moves farther into the future.

The 'substitution' and 'wealth accumulation' components of interest effects on consumption, represented by (2.4.3.14) and (2.4.3.15), boil down to:

$$\left\{\frac{\partial C_l}{\partial r}\right\}_{\text{I}} = \lambda\,(1+r)^{-1}\,(\sum_{\tau=1}^{L} a_\tau^{-1} \cdot d_\tau^2)^{-1}\, a_l^{-1} d_l \cdot \sum_{\tau=1}^{L} a_\tau^{-1}\,(\tau - l)\, d_\tau^2 \tag{3.1.1.14}$$

and

$$\left\{\frac{\partial C_l}{\partial r}\right\}_{\text{II}} = (1+r)^{-1}\,(\sum_{\tau=1}^{L} a_\tau^{-1} d_\tau^2)^{-1}\, a_l^{-1} d_l \sum_{\tau=1}^{L} (Y_\tau - C_\tau)\,(L-\tau)\, d_\tau \tag{3.1.1.15}$$

$$\text{for } l = 1, \ldots, L.$$

The Slutsky matrix Ξ, defined in (2.4.3.16), consists of all-negative elements:

$$a_l^{-1}\,\{1 - (\sum_{\tau=1}^{L} a_\tau^{-1} d_\tau^2)^{-1}\}\, a_l^{-1} d_l^2 \quad \text{on the main diagonal}$$

and of all-positive elements:

$$-(\sum_{\tau=1}^{L} a_\tau^{-1} d_\tau^2)^{-1}\,(a_l a_{l'})^{-1}\, d_l d_{l'} \quad \text{off the main diagonal, for } l, l' = 1, \ldots, L.$$

The latter means that between consumption in different periods complementarity is excluded and substitutability is ensured by complete additive separability of the utility function.

In (3.1.1.14):

$$\left\{\frac{\partial C_l}{\partial r}\right\}_{\text{I}} \gtreqless 0 \quad \text{according as} \quad \sum_{\tau=1}^{L} a_\tau^{-1}\,(\tau - l)\, d_\tau^2 \gtreqless 0. \tag{3.1.1.16}$$

Since $\alpha_l < 0$, evidently negative signs of these partial effects will prevail for small l, and positive signs will prevail for large l; near-zero effects will be found between values of l, $l + 1$ which are higher according as a_l is smaller and d_l is larger.

According to (3.1.1.15), wealth accumulation effects have the same sign for all $l = 1, \ldots, L$, i.e. the sign of $\sum_{\tau=1}^{L} (Y_\tau - C_\tau)(L - \tau) d_\tau$. Since in (3.1.1.15) for $l = 1, \ldots, L$, $\{\partial C_l / \partial r\}_{\text{II}}$ is proportional to $a_l^{-1} d_l$ as its only variable and specific part, and since d_l decreases with increasing l, these component-effects likewise tend to weaken according as they relate to a more remote future.

3.1.2. PAIRWISE SEPARABLE UTILITY FUNCTION (PAS)

Pairwise separability of the utility function means that it may be written as:

$$\omega = \sum_{l=1}^{L} \sum_{l'=1}^{L} a_{ll'} (C_l, C_{l'}) = \iota_L' A (C_., C_.) \iota_L \text{ in vector notation,} \qquad (3.1.2.1)$$

with

$$A (C_., C_.) = \begin{bmatrix} a_{11} (C_1, C_1) & a_{12} (C_1, C_2) \cdots a_{1L} (C_1, C_L) \\ a_{21} (C_2, C_1) & a_{22} (C_2, C_2) \cdots a_{2L} (C_2, C_L) \\ \vdots & \vdots \quad \ddots \quad \vdots \\ a_{L1} (C_L, C_1) & a_{L2} (C_L, C_2) \cdots a_{LL} (C_L, C_L) \end{bmatrix}$$

a matrix of functions each of which depends on one or two variables, i.e. on and off the main diagonal, respectively. In this manner, possible interaction (substitutability or complementarity) between the consumption variables in the utility function is retained.

Since (3.1.2.1.) states that ω is the sum of all elements of $A (C_., C_.)$, this matrix may be replaced by an (upper or lower) triangular matrix, with the same diagonal elements and $a_{ll'} (C_l, C_{l'}) + a_{l'l} (C_{l'}, C_l)$ as the off-diagonal elements (for $l, l' = 1, \ldots, L$ and $l \neq l'$).

On the one hand, (3.1.2.1) may be generalized into a sum of functions of n-tuples of variables ($n = 3, 4$, etc.):

$$\omega = \sum_{l(1)=1}^{L} \cdots \sum_{l(n)=1}^{L} a_{l(1)\ldots l(n)} (C_{l(1)} \cdots C_{l(n)}) \quad \text{for } n < L. \qquad (3.1.2.2)$$

On the other hand, (3.1.2.1) may be further particularized by requiring that:

$$a_{ll'}(C_l, C_{l'}) = 0 \tag{3.1.2.3}$$

unless either $l' = l$ or $l' = l + 1$,[2] for $l = 1, \dots, L$; and $l' = 1, \dots, L - 1$, respectively. This means that intertemporal interaction of consumption would be taken into account *between successive periods only* ('chain-linking'). It implies that $A(C_., C_.)$ would become band-diagonal; i.e. it would consist of zeroes except on the main diagonal and on the upper parallel adjoining the main diagonal.

Therefore, (3.1.2.1) could be reduced to:

$$\omega = \{\alpha_.(C_.)\}\,\iota_L + \{a(C_., C_{.+})\}\,\iota_{L-1} \tag{3.1.2.4}$$

with (again)

$$\{\alpha_.(C_.)\} = \{\alpha_1(C_1) \cdots \alpha_L(C_L)\},$$

where

$$\alpha_l(C_l) = a_{ll}(C_l, C_l) \quad \text{for } l = 1, \dots, L,$$

and

$$\{a(C_., C_{.+})\} = \{a_1(C_1, C_2) \cdots a_{L-1}(C_{L-1}, C_L)\},$$

where

$$a_l(C_l, C_{l+1}) = a_{l,l+1}(C_l, C_{l+1}).$$

Defining $\Delta C_{l+1} = C_{l+1} - C_l$, we may rewrite $a_l(C_l, C_{l+1})$ as $a_l(C_l, C_l + \Delta C_{l+1}) = a_l^+(C_l, \Delta C_{l+1})$. Therefore, (3.1.2.4) may be reformulated by:

$$\omega = \sum_{l=1}^{L-1} \{\alpha_l(C_l) + a_l(C_l, C_{l+1} - C_l)\} + \alpha_L(C_L)$$

$$= \alpha_.^*(C_., \Delta C_{.+})\,\iota_L, \quad \text{in vector notation} \tag{3.1.2.5}$$

with

$$\{\alpha_.^*(C_., \Delta C_{.+})\} = \{\alpha_1(C_1) + a_1^+(C_1, \Delta C_2) \vdots \cdots \vdots \alpha_{L-1}(C_{L-1}) + a_{L-1}^+(C_{L-1}, \Delta C_L) \vdots \alpha_L(C_L)\}.$$

The latter expression facilitates the transition from the discrete models of sections 2.4 through 2.9 and 3.1 through 3.6 to the dynamized continuous model of section 3.7.4.

---

[2] Equivalent to (3.1.2.3) are the assumptions that $a_{ll'}(C_l, C_{l'}) = 0$ unless either $l' = l$ or $l' = l - 1$, or unless either $l' = l$ or $l' = l \pm 1$.

For the marginal utilities, (3.1.2.4) implies:

$$\frac{\partial\omega}{\partial C_\tau} = \frac{\partial a_{\tau-1}(C_{\tau-1}, C_\tau)}{\partial C_\tau}\delta_{\tau>1} + \frac{\partial \alpha_\tau(C_\tau)}{\partial C_\tau} + \frac{\partial a_\tau(C_\tau, C_{\tau+1})}{\partial C_\tau}\delta_{\tau<L}$$

$$\text{for} \quad \tau = 1, \ldots, L \qquad (3.1.2.6)$$

and $\delta_{\tau>1}$ and $\delta_{\tau<L}$ 0 or 1 according as

$$\tau = 1 \quad \text{or} \quad \tau > 1$$

and

$$\tau = L \quad \text{or} \quad \tau < L, \quad \text{respectively.}$$

In this case, solution of the optimum conditions is less simple than in the case of CAS. By virtue of (3.1.2.6), these conditions can now be written as:

$$\left.\begin{aligned}
\frac{\partial\omega}{\partial C_2}\bigg/\frac{\partial\omega}{\partial C_1} &= \varphi_2(C_1, C_2, C_3)/\varphi_1(C_1, C_2) = 1 + r \\
\frac{\partial\omega}{\partial C_3}\bigg/\frac{\partial\omega}{\partial C_2} &= \varphi_3(C_2, C_3, C_4)/\varphi_2(C_1, C_2, C_3) = 1 + r \\
&\vdots \\
\frac{\partial\omega}{\partial C_{L-1}}\bigg/\frac{\partial\omega}{\partial C_{L-2}} &= \varphi_{L-1}(C_{L-2}, C_{L-1}, C_L)/\varphi_{L-2}(C_{L-3}, C_{L-2}, C_{L-1}) \\
&= 1 + r \\
\frac{\partial\omega}{\partial C_L}\bigg/\frac{\partial\omega}{\partial C_{L-1}} &= \varphi_L(C_{L-1}, C_L)/\varphi_{L-1}(C_{L-2}, C_{L-1}, C_L) = 1 + r
\end{aligned}\right\} \qquad (3.1.2.7)$$

yielding:

$$\left.\begin{aligned}
C_3 &= \varphi_{12}(C_1, C_2, r) \\
C_4 &= \varphi_{23}(C_1, C_2, C_3, r) = \varphi_{1|3}(C_1, C_2, r) \\
C_5 &= \varphi_{34}(C_2, C_3, C_4, r) = \varphi_{1|4}(C_1, C_2, r) \\
&\vdots \\
C_{L-1} &= \varphi_{L-3,L-2}(C_{L-4}, C_{L-3}, C_{L-2}, r) = \varphi_{1|L-2}(C_1, C_2, r) \\
C_L &= \varphi_{L-2,L-1}(C_{L-3}, C_{L-2}, C_{L-1}, r) = \varphi_{1|L-1}(C_1, C_2, r) \\
C_L &= \varphi_{L-1,L}(C_{L-2}, C_{L-1}, C_L, r) = \varphi_{1|L}(C_1, C_2, r)
\end{aligned}\right\} \qquad (3.1.2.8)$$

with $\varphi_{1|\tau}$ for $\tau = 3, \ldots, L$ being obtained after successive substitution of the expressions for $C_{\tau-1}$ ($\tau > 1$) and $C_{\tau-2}$ ($\tau > 2$) in terms of C_1, C_2 and r.

From the last two equations of (3.1.2.8), C_1 and C_2, hence also $C_3, \ldots, C_{L-1}$, might be solved in terms of C_L:

$$C_\tau = \Psi_\tau(C_L, r) \quad \text{for} \quad \tau = 1, \ldots, L-1, \tag{3.1.2.9}$$

and $\Psi_L(C_L, r) = C_L$, with C_L to be determined by:

$$\sum_{\tau=1}^{L} (1+r)^{L-\tau} \Psi_\tau(C_L, r) = \sum_{\tau=1}^{L} Y_\tau (1+r)^{L-\tau} + K_L - K_0 . \tag{3.1.2.10}$$

On the basis of (3.1.2.6), we find that the Hessian

$$\Omega = \begin{bmatrix} \omega_{11} & \omega_{12} & 0 & \cdots & 0 \\ \omega_{21} & \omega_{22} & \ddots & \ddots & \vdots \\ 0 & \ddots & \ddots & \ddots & 0 \\ \vdots & \ddots & \ddots & \ddots & \omega_{L-1,L} \\ 0 & \cdots & 0 & \omega_{L,L-1} & \omega_{LL} \end{bmatrix} \tag{3.1.2.11}$$

is band-diagonal,

with

$$\left.\begin{aligned} \omega_{\tau-1,\tau} &= \frac{\partial^2 a_{\tau-1}(C_{\tau-1}, C_\tau)}{\partial C_{\tau-1} \cdot \partial C_\tau} \cdot \delta_{\tau>1} \\ \omega_{\tau\tau} &= \frac{\partial^2 a_{\tau-1}(C_{\tau-1}, C_\tau)}{\partial C_\tau^2} \cdot \delta_{\tau>1} + \frac{d^2 \alpha_\tau(C_\tau)}{dC_\tau^2} + \frac{\partial^2 a_\tau(C_\tau, C_{\tau+1})}{\partial C_\tau^2} \cdot \delta_{\tau<L} \end{aligned}\right\} \tag{3.1.2.12}$$

and

$$\omega_{\tau\tau'} = 0 \quad \text{for} \quad |\tau - \tau'| > 1 .$$

In order that Ω be negative-definite, the determinants

$$\omega_{11}, \quad \begin{vmatrix} \omega_{11} & \omega_{12} \\ \omega_{21} & \omega_{22} \end{vmatrix}, \quad \begin{vmatrix} \omega_{11} & \omega_{21} & 0 \\ \omega_{21} & \omega_{22} & \omega_{23} \\ 0 & \omega_{23} & \omega_{33} \end{vmatrix}, \quad \text{etc.}$$

must alternate in sign, starting with $\omega_{11} < 0$.

The general expression for the determinant of Ω of order L is:

$$|\Omega| = (\prod_{l=1}^{L} \omega_{ll}) \{1 + \sum_{i=1}^{(L-\delta)/2} (-1)^i \times$$

$$\times \sum_{l_1=1}^{L+1-2i} \sum_{l_2=l_1+2}^{L+1-2(i-1)} \cdots \sum_{l_i=l_{i-1}+2}^{L-1} \prod_{j=1}^{i} \omega_{l_j l_j+1}^2 (\omega_{l_j l_j} \cdot \omega_{l_j+1, l_j+1})^{-1}\},$$

which should be (3.1.2.13)

$$> 0 \quad \text{for } L = \text{even} \quad \text{and} \quad \delta = 0$$

$$< 0 \quad \text{for } L = \text{odd} \quad \text{and} \quad \delta = 1.$$

A sufficient (but not necessary) condition for sign alternation of those determinants of successive orders is:

$$\omega_{ll} < 0 \quad \text{for } l = 1, \ldots, L \tag{3.1.2.14a}$$

and

$$\tfrac{1}{2}(L-\delta) | \sum_{l_1=1}^{L+1-2i} \sum_{l_2=l_1+2}^{L+1-2(i-1)} \cdots \sum_{l_i=l_{i-1}+2}^{L-1} \prod_{j=1}^{i} \omega_{l_j, l_j+1}^2 (\omega_{l_j l_j} \cdot \omega_{l_j+1, l_j+1})^{-1} | < 1$$

$$\text{for} \quad i = 1, \ldots, \tfrac{1}{2}(L+\delta). \tag{3.1.2.14b}$$

Condition (3.1.2.14a) ensures alternation in sign of $\prod_{l=1}^{L} \omega_{ll}$ for successive values of L, while (3.1.2.14b) ensures that in (3.1.2.13) $\{ \quad \} > 0$.

In turn:

$$\omega_{l_j, l_j+1}^2 < 2(L-\delta)^{-1} (L-1)^{-1} \omega_{l_j l_j} \cdot \omega_{l_j+1, l_j+1} \tag{3.1.2.14c}$$

is a sufficient but not a necessary condition for satisfying (3.1.2.14b).

Conditions (3.1.2.14c) mean that in an absolute sense the off-diagonal elements of Ω should be small compared with the diagonal elements, the more so according as L is larger.

The elements $\omega^{\tau\tau'}$ of Ω^{-1} are:

$$\omega^{\tau\tau'} = |\Omega|^{-1} |\Omega_{1,\tau-1}| \cdot |\Omega_{\tau'+1,L}| \cdot \omega_{\tau',\tau'+1}^{-1} \prod_{l=\tau}^{\tau'} \omega_{l,l+1},$$

$$\text{for} \quad \tau' \geq \tau = 1, \ldots, L \tag{3.1.2.15}$$

with $|\Omega_{1,\tau-1}|$ and $|\Omega_{\tau'+1,L}|$ the determinants of the matrices Ω with rows and columns τ through L, and rows and columns 1 through τ' struck out respectively, and $|\Omega_{1,0}| \stackrel{\text{def}}{=} 1$ and $|\Omega_{L+1,L}| \stackrel{\text{def}}{=} 1$.

The inequality under (3.1.2.13) implies:

$$\omega^{\tau\tau'} < 0 \quad \text{for } \tau, \tau' = 1, \ldots, L \tag{3.1.2.16}$$

in the case where $\omega_{l,l+1} > 0$ for $l = 1, \ldots, L-1$, and

$$\omega^{\tau\tau'} < 0 \text{ or } > 0 \quad \text{for } \tau', \tau = 1, \ldots, L \tag{3.1.2.17}$$

according as $|\tau' - \tau|$ non-odd or odd respectively in case $\omega_{k,k+1} > 0$ for $k = 1, \ldots, L-1$.

Finally, (3.1.2.15) and (3.1.2.13) imply:

$$\omega^{\tau\tau'}/\omega^{\tau\tau} = \{\quad\}_{\tau'+1,L} \cdot \{\quad\}_{\tau+1,L}^{-1} \cdot (\omega_{\tau',\tau'+1}/\omega_{\tau\tau})^{-1} \prod_{l=\tau}^{\tau'} (\omega_{l,l+1}/\omega_{ll}), \tag{3.1.2.18}$$

with $\{\quad\}_{\tau'+1,L}$ equaling the corresponding expression in (3.1.2.13) with $i = 1$ replaced by $i = \tau' + 1$.

Assuming that (3.1.2.14c) is satisfied,

$$\lim_{L\to\infty} \{\quad\}_{\tau+1,L} = 1 \quad \text{for fixed } \tau. \tag{3.1.2.19}$$

This means that for large L and $|\tau' - \tau| \ll L$, (3.1.2.18) may be approximated by:

$$|\omega^{\tau\tau'}/\omega^{\tau\tau}| \approx (L-1)^{|\tau-\tau'|+1} \, |\omega_{\tau,\tau+1}^2/(\omega_{\tau'\tau'} \cdot \omega_{\tau+1,\tau+1})| \tag{3.1.2.20}$$

if $|\tau' - \tau|$ and/or L sufficiently large,

i.e. that on each row of Ω^{-1} its elements tend to decrease according as they become farther removed from the main diagonal (at least, within certain limits).

In the case where (3.1.2.16) applies:

$$\Omega^{-1}d < 0, \tag{3.1.2.21}$$

i.e. a vector with all elements negative. In the case where (3.1.2.17) and (3.1.2.20) hold good, at least the first element of $\Omega^{-1}d$ would be negative; one may even expect the second, third, etc. of not (much) more than the first half of the elements of $\Omega^{-1}d$ to be negative, whereas the remaining elements of this vector would be positive. In particular, this is of importance with respect to income effects. Therefore, if (3.1.2.21) – equivalent to the *in*equality (3.1.1.9) – will be satisfied, inequalities (3.1.1.10) and (3.1.1.11) would likewise apply in those particular cases of pairwise additive separability of the utility function. If, however, (3.1.2.13) holds good in conjunction with (3.1.2.20), positive elements of C_Y may be expected to dominate in its upper rows, whereas negative elements will probably be more frequent in its lower rows. Anyhow, there will be overall dominance of positive elements.

For $C_{\Delta K}$ the opposite is true, in the sense that its anterior elements tend to be negative, with a more generous sprinkling of positive elements in the posterior part of this vector. Still, here an overall dominance of negative elements will prevail.

Pairwise additive separability, even in the particular versions represented by (3.1.2.16) or by (3.1.2.17) in conjunction with (3.1.2.20) allows for complementarity (beside substitutability) between consumption in different periods – adjacent as well as non-adjacent ones. This would be represented by negative (beside positive) off-diagonal elements in the Slutsky matrix Ξ.

3.2. Model with desired final personal wealth incorporated in the utility function

3.2.1. COMPLETELY SEPARABLE UTILITY FUNCTION (CAS)

For the model of section 2.5, complete additive separability of the utility function may be expressed by:

$$\omega = \{\alpha_{.}(C_{.})\}\, \iota_L + \gamma(K_L) \tag{3.2.1.1}$$

with $\gamma(K_L)$ a function of K_L.

The vector of marginal utilities corresponding to (3.2.1.1) is

$$\{\omega_C, \omega_{K_L}\} = \{\alpha_C \quad \gamma_{K_L}\} > 0 \tag{3.2.1.2}$$

with $\gamma_{K_L} = \mathrm{d}\gamma/\mathrm{d}K_L$.

The optimum conditions with respect to $C_1, \ldots, C_L$ are now the same as those expressed by (3.1.1.4) for the basic model, with *formally* the same results as in (3.1.1.6) and (3.1.1.7). Then – after normalization of ω – the vector ω_C will be known, enabling the solution of the optimal K_L from

$$\gamma_{K_L} = R_L^{-1}\,(C'\omega_C). \tag{3.2.1.3}$$

The Hessian corresponding to (3.2.1.2) is:

$$\Omega = \left[\begin{array}{ccc|c} \alpha_{C_1C_1} & & 0 & 0 \\ & \ddots & & \vdots \\ 0 & & \alpha_{C_LC_L} & 0 \\ \hline 0 & \cdots & 0 & \gamma_{K_LK_L} \end{array}\right] \quad \text{a diagonal matrix of order } L+1, \tag{3.2.1.4}$$

with $\gamma_{K_LK_L} = \mathrm{d}^2\gamma/\mathrm{d}K_L^2$.

Because of the diagonality of Ω and since

$$\omega_{CK_L} = 0, \tag{3.2.1.5}$$

as implied by (3.2.1.1), the sub-matrices of Ω^{-1} as expressed by (2.5.3.3) are simplified to:

$$\left.\begin{aligned}
s_0 &= (d'\Omega_{CC}^{-1}d)\,\omega_{K_LK_L} + 1 > 0\\
M &= \omega_{K_LK_L}(d'\Omega_{CC}^{-1}d)\,[\Omega_{CC}^{-1} - (d'\Omega_{CC}^{-1}d)^{-1}(\Omega_{CC}^{-1}d)(\Omega_{CC}^{-1}d)'] + \Omega_{CC}^{-1}\\
v &= -\Omega_{CC}^{-1}d > 0\\
w &= \omega_{K_LK_L}\Omega_{CC}^{-1}d > 0\\
s_1 &= d'\Omega_{CC}^{-1}d < 0\\
s_2 &= 1\\
s_3 &= -\omega_{K_LK_L} > 0.
\end{aligned}\right\} \tag{3.2.1.6}$$

Consequently, the 'effects' equations (2.5.3.4) through (2.5.3.9) are reduced to:

$$C_Y = \{\omega_{K_LK_L}^{-1} + d'\Omega_{CC}^{-1}d\}^{-1}\cdot\Omega_{CC}^{-1}\cdot dd' \tag{3.2.1.7}$$

$$\begin{aligned}C_r = (1+r)^{-1}\,[\lambda\,\{&\Omega_{CC}^{-1} - (d'\Omega_{CC}^{-1}d)^{-1}(\Omega_{CC}^{-1}d)(\Omega_{CC}^{-1}d)'\\
&+ (1 + (d'\Omega_{CC}^{-1}d)\,\omega_{K_LK_L})^{-1}(\Omega_{CC}^{-1}d)(\Omega_{CC}^{-1}d)'\}\\
&- \omega_{K_LK_L}(d'\Omega_{CC}^{-1}d)^{-1}\,\Omega_{CC}^{-1}d\,(Y - C)']\,\dot{d}L-\end{aligned} \tag{3.2.1.8}$$

$$C_{K_0} = \{\omega_{K_LK_L}^{-1} + d'\Omega_{CC}^{-1}d\}^{-1}\,\Omega_{CC}^{-1}d > 0 \tag{3.2.1.9}$$

$$d' > (K_L)_Y = \{1 + (d'\Omega_{CC}^{-1}d)\,\omega_{K_LK_L}\}^{-1}\,d' > 0 \tag{3.2.1.10}$$

$$\begin{aligned}(K_L)_r = \{&1 + (d'\Omega_{CC}^{-1}d)\,\omega_{K_LK_L}\}^{-1}(1+r)^{-1}\\
&\times[-\lambda d'\Omega_{CC}^{-1} + (Y - C)']\,\dot{d}L-\end{aligned} \tag{3.2.1.11}$$

$$1 > (K_L)_{K_0} = \{1 + (d'\Omega_{CC}^{-1}d)\,\omega_{K_LK_L}\}^{-1}. \tag{3.2.1.12}$$

Effect equations (3.2.1.7) through (3.2.1.9), ruling C_Y, C_r and C_{K_0}, have much in common with the corresponding equations (2.4.3.9) through (2.4.3.11) for the basic model.

Apart from the conversion of $C_{\Delta K}$ in (2.4.3.11) into $-C_{K_0}$ in (3.2.1.9), Ω^{-1} is replaced by Ω_{CC}^{-1} and $\omega_{K_LK_L}$ ($\neq 0$) is inserted in the latter equations; in particular, $(d'\Omega^{-1}d)^{-1}$ is replaced by $\{1 + (d'\Omega^{-1}d)\,\omega_{K_LK_L}\}^{-1} < 1$.

Of the two parts, $(C_Y)_{\mathrm{I}}$ and $(C_Y)_{\mathrm{II}}$ into which C_Y was decomposed according to (2.5.3.15) and (2.5.3.16) respectively, the first one, due to possible interaction between prospective consumption and desired final personal wealth, drops out, while the latter one, representing the income effect proper, remains. This latter matrix – like C_Y in (3.1.1.10) – consists of positive elements only, since both $\omega_{K_L K_L}$ and $d'\Omega_{CC}^{-1}d$ are negative. For the same reason, C_{K_0} in (3.2.1.9) is a positive vector, comparable with $-C_{\Delta K}$ according to (3.1.1.11).

Of the three parts into which $(C_r)_{\mathrm{I}}$ was divided according to (2.5.3.19), the quasi-substitution term (Ib) vanishes, while (Ic) is simplified considerably:

$$(C_r)_{\mathrm{I}} = \lambda (1+r)^{-1} \{\Omega_{CC}^{-1} - (d'\Omega^{-1}d)^{-1} (\Omega_{CC}^{-1}d)(\Omega^{-1}d)'\} \dot{d}L- \qquad \text{(Ia)}$$

$$+ \lambda (1+r)^{-1} \{1 + (d'\Omega_{CC}^{-1}d)\, \omega_{K_L K_L}\}^{-1} \Omega_{CC}^{-1} \dot{d}L-. \qquad \text{(Ic)}$$

(3.2.1.13)

Now, we may conclude that *all* elements of the non-substitution matrix (Ic) are negative, i.e. not only the (weighted) majority of them, as mentioned for the more general case dealt with in section 2.5.3.

About $(K_L)_Y$ and $(K_L)_{K_0}$, i.e. the income and initial personal wealth effects on desired final personal wealth, a more specific conclusion may be drawn than has been done already in section 2.5.3 [cf. (2.5.3.21)], viz. that the effects of changes in *discounted* Y and K_0 are transmitted to K_L at a reduced degree. Compared with (2.5.3.22), (3.2.1.11) permits the more specific conclusion that all elements of $\{(K_L)_r\}_{\mathrm{I}}$ are positive. Evidently, raising the rate of interest increases final personal wealth without requiring (extra) economizing on consumption.

3.2.2. PAIRWISE SEPARABLE UTILITY FUNCTION (PAS)

For this (as well as for other) extended versions of the basic model, pairwise additive separability (PAS) of the utility function will be applied to *different kinds* of synchronous variables entering that function, instead of to differently timed variables of the same kind (as in section 3.1.2). In particular, we assume the following type of utility function:

$$\omega = \{\alpha_{.}(C_{.})\}\, \iota_L + \gamma(K_L) + \{g_{.}(C_{.}, K_L)\}\, \iota_L \quad \text{in vector notation,} \qquad (3.2.2.1)$$

with

$$\{g(C_{.}, K_L)\} = \{g_1(C_1, K_L) \cdots g_L(C_L, K_L)\}.$$

The vector of marginal utilities corresponding to (3.2.2.1) is:

$$\{\omega'_c \quad \omega_{K_L}\} = \{a_1(C_1) + g_1(C_1, K_L) \cdots a_L(C_L) + g_L(C_L, K_L) \\ \vdots\, \gamma_{K_L}(K_L) \,\vdots\, g'_{K_L}(C'_., K_L)\, \iota_L\} \quad (3.2.2.2)$$

with

$$a_l = \frac{\partial \alpha_l(C_l)}{\partial C_l}, \quad g_{ll} = \frac{\partial g_l(C_l, K_l)}{\partial C_l} \quad \text{for } l = 1, \ldots, L$$

and

$$g'_{.K_L}(C'_., K_L) = \left\{\frac{\partial g_1(C_1, K_L)}{\partial K_L} \cdots \frac{\partial g_L(C_L, K_L)}{\partial K_L}\right\}.$$

These assumptions do not enable us to simplify visibly the 'effects' formulae (2.5.3.4) through (2.5.3.9). Nevertheless, they reinforce the tentative statements made in (2.5.3.10)ff. about the elements of Ω^{-1} expressed by (2.5.3.3) on that basis, and strengthen the conclusions drawn about the effects dealt with in (2.5.3.14) through (2.5.3.21).

The optimum conditions now become (in scalar notation):

$$\frac{\partial \omega}{\partial C_\tau} = a_\tau(C_\tau) + g_{\tau\tau}(C_\tau, K_L) = \lambda (1 + r)^{L-\tau} \quad (3.2.2.3)$$

for $\tau = 1, \ldots, L$,

and

$$\frac{\partial \omega}{\partial K_L} = \gamma_{K_L} + \sum_{l=1}^{L} g_{lk_l}(C_1, \ldots, C_L, K_L) = \lambda. \quad (3.2.2.4)$$

From (3.2.2.3) we may derive:

$$C_\tau = h_\tau(K_L, r, \lambda). \quad (3.2.2.5)$$

Substitution of (3.2.2.5) into (3.2.2.4) yields:

$$\lambda = \lambda(K_L, r), \quad (3.2.2.6)$$

and substitution of (3.2.2.6) into (3.2.2.5) results in:

$$C_\tau = k_\tau(K_L, r). \quad (3.2.2.7)$$

Substitution of (3.2.2.7) into:

$$\sum_{\tau=1}^{L} C_\tau (1 + r)^{L-\tau} = R_L \quad (3.2.2.8)$$

will produce K_L in terms of r and R_L, and substitution of the expression for K_L into (3.2.2.3) will produce C_τ in the same terms.

3.3. *Model with working hours incorporated in the utility function*

3.3.1. LINEAR INCOME-GENERATING FUNCTIONS

The general income-generating functions (2.6.1.2) might be approximated linearly, i.e. by:

$$Y = \underline{Y} \cdot \iota_L + UW, \qquad (3.3.1.1)$$

with $\underline{Y}$ a scalar, representing 'basic income' (but possibly negative), and

$$U = \begin{bmatrix} u_{11} & 0 \cdots\cdots 0 \\ u_{21} & u_{22} & \vdots \\ \vdots & \ddots & 0 \\ u_{L1} & \cdots\cdots & u_{LL} \end{bmatrix} \quad \text{a lower triangular matrix of order } L \times L, \qquad (3.3.1.2)$$

with elements $u_{ll'}$ ($l' \leq l = 1, \ldots, L$) representing marginal rates of remunerating in period l hours (to be) worked in period l'. Usually, these constants will be positive, excepting the case envisaged in footnote 12 of chapter 2.[3]

Thus, $\underline{Y}$ and $u_{ll'}$ may be identified with parameters ζ_{lm_l} ($l = 1, \ldots, L$; $m_l = m_1, \ldots, m_L$) introduced in section 2.6.3, while

$$Y_W = U \qquad (3.3.1.3)$$

and

$$Y_{WW} = 0. \qquad (3.3.1.4)$$

3.3.2. COMPLETELY SEPARABLE UTILITY FUNCTION (CAS)

For the model of section 2.6 complete additive separability of the utility function may be expressed by:

$$\begin{aligned} \omega &= \sum_{l=1}^{L} \alpha_l(C_l) + \sum_{l=1}^{L} \beta_l(W_l) \\ &= \{\alpha_.(C_.)\}\, \iota_L + \{\beta_.(W_.)\}\, \iota_L \quad \text{in vector notation,} \end{aligned} \qquad (3.3.2.1)$$

with $\{\beta_.(W_.)\} = \{\beta_1(W_1) \ldots \beta_L(W_L)\}$ – like $\{\alpha_.(C_.)\}$ – a vector of functions of single arguments only.

[3] In the latter case, however, the linearity of the relationships between the elements of Y and those of W, as expressed by (3.3.1.1), would break down.

The vector of marginal utilities corresponding to (3.3.2.1) is:

$$\{\omega_C' \quad \omega_W'\} = \{\alpha_C' \quad \beta_W'\} \quad \text{of length } 2L, \tag{3.3.2.2}$$

with $\beta_W'' = \{\mathrm{d}\beta_1(W_1)/\mathrm{d}W_1 \ldots \mathrm{d}\beta_L(W_L)/\mathrm{d}W_L\} < 0$, i.e. a sub-vector with negative elements only.

The first-order conditions may be solved, first by extricating the optimal C-vector from:

$$\alpha_C = R_L^{-1}(C'\alpha_C)\,d, \tag{3.3.2.3}$$

and substituting the resulting C into:

$$\beta_W = -R_L^{-1}(C'\alpha_C)\,U'd \tag{3.3.2.4}$$

for obtaining the optimal W-vector.

The Hessian corresponding to (3.3.2.1) is:

$$\Omega = \begin{bmatrix} \Omega_{CC} & 0 \\ 0 & \Omega_{WW} \end{bmatrix}, \tag{3.3.2.5}$$

a diagonal matrix of order $2L$, with

$$\Omega_{WW} = \begin{bmatrix} \dfrac{\mathrm{d}^2\beta_1}{\mathrm{d}W_1^2} & & 0 \\ & \ddots & \\ 0 & & \dfrac{\mathrm{d}^2\beta_L}{\mathrm{d}W_L^2} \end{bmatrix}.$$

By means of (3.3.1.4) and (3.3.2.5), expressions (2.6.3.4) are simplified to:

$$\left.\begin{aligned} M_{CC} &= \Omega_{CC}^{-1}[I + ndd'\Omega_{CC}^{-1}] \\ M_{CW} &= -n\Omega_{CC}^{-1}dd'U\Omega_{WW}^{-1} \\ M_{WW} &= \Omega_{WW}^{-1}[I + nU'dd'U\Omega_{WW}^{-1}] \\ m_C &= -n\Omega_{CC}^{-1}d \\ m_W &= n\Omega_{WW}^{-1}U'd \\ n &= -(d'\Omega_{CC}^{-1}d + d'U\Omega_{WW}^{-1}U'd)^{-1} \end{aligned}\right\} \tag{3.3.2.6}$$

Thus, the relationships for the effects become:

$$C_{u'} = -\lambda M_{CW} D_* + m_C d' W_* \tag{3.3.2.7}$$

$$C_r = (1 + r)^{-1} [\lambda (M_{CC} - M_{CW} U') + m_C (Y' - C')] \dot{d}L- \tag{3.3.2.8}$$

$$C_{\Delta K} = -m_C \tag{3.3.2.9}$$

$$W_{u'} = -\lambda M_{WW} D_* + m_W d' W_* \tag{3.3.2.10}$$

$$W_r = (1 + r)^{-1} [\lambda (M_{WC} - M_{WW} U') + m_W (Y' - C')] \dot{d}L- \tag{3.3.2.11}$$

$$W_{\Delta K} = -m_W, \tag{3.3.2.12}$$

with

$$D_* = \begin{bmatrix} d_1 \cdots d_L & & & & & 0 \\ & d_2 \cdots d_L & & & & \\ & & d_3 \cdots d_L & & & \\ & & & \ddots & & \\ & 0 & & & & \\ & & & & d_{L-1} & d_L \end{bmatrix}$$

and

$$W_* = \begin{bmatrix} W_1 & & & & & & 0 \\ & W_1 & W_2 & & & & \\ & & & W_1 & W_2 & W_3 & \\ & & & & & \ddots & \\ & 0 & & & & & \\ & & & & & & W_1 \cdots W_L \end{bmatrix}$$

$L \times \{\frac{1}{2}L\,(L + 1)\}$ matrices

Assuming Ω_{CC} and Ω_{WW} to be negative definite – so that second-order conditions for maximum ω are satisfied – we may conclude from (3.3.2.6):

$$n > 0 \tag{3.3.2.13}$$

$$M_{CW} < 0 \tag{3.3.2.14}$$

$$m_C, -m_W > 0, \tag{3.3.2.15}$$

i.e. vectors consisting of positive elements only; hence:

$$W_{\Delta K} > 0 > C_{\Delta K}, \tag{3.3.2.16}$$

i.e. longer hours will have to be worked and a smaller quantity will have to be consumed in any future period according as a lower value of personal wealth is started with and/or a higher value of final personal wealth is aspired at. These conclusions seem to be corroborated by common sense.

According to (3.3.2.7), $C_{u'}$ is the sum of:

$$(C_{u'})_{\mathrm{I}} = -\lambda M_{CW} D_* > 0 \tag{3.3.2.17}$$

and

$$(C_{u'})_{\mathrm{II}} = m_C d' W_* > 0. \tag{3.3.2.18}$$

In view of their genesis, these components may be identified respectively with 'hours of work' and 'income' sub-effects of increasing marginal rates of remuneration on consumption, without attaching too much weight to these labels. The important thing is that:

$$C_{u'} = (C_{u'})_{\mathrm{I}} + (C_{u'})_{\mathrm{II}} > 0, \tag{3.3.2.19}$$

i.e. matrices with positive elements only. This means that an increase in any marginal rate of remuneration will boost consumption in any (future) period.

The effects of varying these rates on working hours themselves, however, are less simple and straightforward. According to (3.3.2.10) in conjunction with (3.3.2.6), $W_{u'}$, like $C_{u'}$ may be split into two additive components, viz.:

$$(W_{u'})_{\mathrm{I}} = -\lambda \left[\Omega_{WW}^{-1} - (d'\Omega_{CC}^{-1} d + d'U\Omega_{WW}^{-1}U'd)^{-1} \cdot (\Omega_{WW}^{-1}U'd)(\Omega_{WW}^{-1}U'd)'\right] D_* \tag{3.3.2.20}$$

and

$$(W_{u'})_{\mathrm{II}} = -(d'\Omega_{CC}^{-1} d + d'U\Omega_{WW}^{-1}U'd)^{-1} (\Omega_{WW}^{-1}U'd) d' W_*. \tag{3.3.2.21}$$

The latter component may again be considered as an income sub-effect. In contradistinction to $(C_{u'})_{\mathrm{II}}$, however, $(W_{u'})_{\mathrm{II}}$ represents a matrix with *negative* elements only:

$$(W_{u'})_{\mathrm{II}} < 0. \tag{3.3.2.22}$$

Clearly, this reflects the possibility of earning the same income with less work in case (marginal) rates of remuneration are increased.

The first component may be further decomposed, viz. into:

$$(W_{u'})_{\mathrm{Ia}} = -\lambda \left[\Omega_{WW}^{-1} - (d'U\Omega_{WW}^{-1}U'd)^{-1} (\Omega_{WW}^{-1}U'd)(\Omega_{WW}^{-1}U'd)'\right] D_* \tag{3.3.2.23}$$

and

$$(W_{u'})_{\mathrm{Ib}} = -\lambda \cdot \frac{d'\Omega_{CC}^{-1}d}{d'\Omega_{CC}^{-1}d + d'U\Omega_{WW}^{-1}U'd} (d'U\Omega_{WW}^{-1}U'd)^{-1}$$

$$\times (\Omega_{WW}^{-1}U'd)(\Omega_{WW}^{-1}U'd)' D_{*}. \tag{3.3.2.24}$$

Component $(W_{u'})_{\mathrm{Ia}}$ represents the substitution effect proper; $(W_{u'})_{\mathrm{Ib}}$ may be conceived of as the effect of increasing marginal rates of remuneration with a view to allowing an expansion of consumption.

This interpretation of $(W_{u'})_{\mathrm{Ia}}$ is in formal agreement with the substitution components of interest effects, expressed by essentially the same 'Slutsky' matrices (between square brackets in (3.3.2.23)). This also implies (weighted) zero means of these effects, with $d'U$ as the weight vector.

Since Ω_{WW}^{-1} is diagonal and negative-definite, $-(d'U\Omega_{WW}^{-1}U'd)^{-1}(\Omega_{WW}^{-1}U'd) \cdot$ $\cdot(\Omega_{WW}^{-1}U'd)' > 0$, i.e. a matrix with positive elements only; moreover, since their sum is negative semi-definite,

$$\left(\frac{\partial W_l}{\partial u_{ll}}\right)_{\mathrm{Ia}} \geq 0 \tag{3.3.2.25}$$

and

$$\left(\frac{\partial W_l}{\partial u_{l''l'}}\right)_{\mathrm{Ia}} \leq 0 \quad \text{for} \quad l, l', l'' = 1, \ldots, L \tag{3.3.2.26}$$

such that $l' \leq l''$ and excluding that three l, l', l'' coincide.

This means that working hours are positively affected by increases in marginal rates of remuneration in the same period for income in the same period, but negatively by marginal rates of remuneration for hours worked in other periods (with a view to labour income to be earned at another time).

Clearly, (3.3.2.24) implies:

$$(W_{u'})_{\mathrm{Ib}} > 0. \tag{3.3.2.27}$$

Hence, in $(W_{u'})_{\mathrm{I}}$, positive elements dominate over negative ones. In view of (3.3.2.22), however, no such conclusion may be drawn for $W_{u'}$ as a whole: increasing marginal rates of remuneration may have negative as well as positive effects on hours to be worked, precluding any a priori conclusions about preponderance of either positive or negative signs.

From the effects of interest on consumption and working hours, as represented by (3.3.2.8) and (3.3.2.11), again wealth accumulation components may be split off:

$$(C_r)_{\mathrm{II}} = (1 + r)^{-1} m_C (Y' - C') \dot{d}L - \tag{3.3.2.28}$$

and

$$(W_r)_{II} = (1 + r)^{-1} \, m_W \, (Y' - C') \, \dot{d}L - . \tag{3.3.2.29}$$

The remainder components, viz.:

$$(C_r)_I = \lambda \, (1 + r)^{-1} \, (M_{CC} - M_{CW} U') \, \dot{d}L - \tag{3.3.2.30}$$

and

$$(W_r)_I = \lambda \, (1 + r)^{-1} \, (M_{WC} - M_{WW} U') \, \dot{d}L - \tag{3.3.2.31}$$

may again be considered as substitution effects, since:

$$(M_{CC} - M_{CW} U') \, d = (M_{WC} - M_{WW} U') \, d = 0 \tag{3.3.2.32}$$

by virtue of (2.6.3.4).

Hence:

$$(C_r)_I^* \stackrel{\text{def}}{=} \lambda \, (1 + r)^{-1} \, (M_{CC} - M_{CW} U') \, d = 0 \tag{3.3.2.33}$$

and

$$(W_r)_I^* \stackrel{\text{def}}{=} \lambda \, (1 + r)^{-1} \, (M_{WC} - M_{WW} U') \, d = 0, \tag{3.3.2.34}$$

i.e. the substitution effects would be zero if the 'weight' vector $\{d_1 \, (L - 1) \; d_2 \, (L - 2) \cdots d_{L-1} \; 0\}$ in (3.3.2.30) and (3.3.2.31) is replaced by the weight vector $\{d_1 \; d_2 \cdots d_{L-1} \; d_L\}$; i.e. like $(C_r)_I$ in (2.4.3.8) if there too the vector $\dot{d}L-$ would be replaced by $\dot{d}\iota = d$, resulting in $(C_r)_I^* = 0$.

3.3.3. PAIRWISE SEPARABLE UTILITY FUNCTION (PAS)

In the model with working hours incorporated in the utility function, the *pair*-wise separability (PAS) is restricted to *pairs* of synchronized variables of *different* kinds, viz. consumption and working hours:

$$\begin{aligned} \omega &= \sum_{l=1}^{L} \alpha_l(C_l) + \sum_{l=1}^{L} \beta_l(W_l) + \sum_{l=1}^{L} \gamma_l \, (C_l, W_l) \\ &= \{\alpha_.(C_.) + \beta_.(W_.) + \gamma_. \, (C_., W_.)\} \, \iota_L \quad \text{in vector notation,} \end{aligned} \tag{3.3.3.1}$$

with

$$\begin{aligned} \{\alpha_.(C_.)\} &= \{\alpha_1(C_1) \cdots \alpha_L(C_L)\} \\ \{\beta_.(W_.)\} &= \{\beta_1(W_1) \cdots \beta_L(W_L)\} \\ \{\gamma_. \, (C_., W_.)\} &= \{\gamma_1 \, (C_1, W_1) \cdots \gamma_L \, (C_L, W_L)\}. \end{aligned}$$

Thus, possible 'interactions' between variables of the same kind, but relating to different periods of time – as considered in section 3.1.2 – are disregarded here.

Consequently, the vector of marginal utilities becomes:

$$\{\omega_C \quad \omega_W\} = \{\alpha_C + \gamma_C \quad \beta_W + \gamma_W\}, \tag{3.3.3.2}$$

with

$$\{\alpha_C + \gamma_C\} = \left\{\frac{\mathrm{d}\alpha_1(C_1)}{\mathrm{d}C_1} + \frac{\partial\gamma_1(C_1, W_1)}{\partial C_1} \cdots \frac{\mathrm{d}\alpha_L(C_L)}{\mathrm{d}C_L} + \frac{\partial\gamma_L(C_L, W_L)}{\partial C_L}\right\}$$

and

$$\{\beta_W + \gamma_W\} = \left\{\frac{\mathrm{d}\beta_1(W_1)}{\mathrm{d}W_1} + \frac{\partial\gamma_1(C_1, W_1)}{\partial W_1} \cdots \frac{\mathrm{d}\beta_L(W_L)}{\mathrm{d}W_L} + \frac{\partial\gamma_L(C_L, W_L)}{\partial W_L}\right\}.$$

At this stage, no restrictions are imposed on the signs of $\partial\gamma_l/\partial C_l$ and $\partial\gamma_l/\partial W_l$ for $l = 1, \ldots, L$.

The first-order conditions pass into:

$$\frac{\partial\omega}{\partial C_\tau} = \alpha_{C_\tau}(C_\tau) + \gamma_{C_\tau}(C_\tau, W_\tau) = \lambda(1 + r)^{L-\tau} \tag{3.3.3.3}$$

and

$$\frac{\partial\omega}{\partial W_\tau} = \beta_{W_\tau}(W_\tau) + \gamma_{W_\tau}(C_\tau, W_\tau) = \lambda \sum_{\tau'=1}^{\tau} u_{\tau'\tau}(1 + r)^{L-\tau'} \tag{3.3.3.4}$$

$$\text{for} \quad \tau = 1, \ldots, L.$$

From (3.3.3.4) we derive:

$$W_\tau = w_\tau(C_\tau, r, \lambda), \tag{3.3.3.5}$$

yielding

$$C_\tau = c_\tau(r, \lambda) \tag{3.3.3.6}$$

after substitution of (3.3.3.5) into (3.3.3.3).

Next, we insert (3.3.3.6) into:

$$\sum_{\tau=1}^{L} C_\tau(1 + r)^{L-\tau} = R_L, \tag{3.3.3.7}$$

in order to obtain:

$$\lambda = \lambda(r, R_L). \tag{3.3.3.8}$$

Substitution of (3.3.3.8) into (3.3.3.6) produces:

$$C_\tau = C_\tau(r, R_L), \tag{3.3.3.9}$$

and finally

$$W_\tau = W_\tau(r, R_L). \tag{3.3.3.10}$$

In the Hessian

$$\Omega = \begin{bmatrix} \Omega_{CC} & \Omega_{CW} \\ \Omega_{WC} & \Omega_{WW} \end{bmatrix}, \tag{3.3.3.11}$$

all sub-matrices Ω_{CC}, Ω_{WW} and $\Omega_{CW} = \Omega'_{WC}$ are diagonal; in particular:

$$\Omega_{CW} = \begin{bmatrix} \frac{\partial^2 \gamma_1}{\partial C_1 \, \partial W_1} & & 0 \\ & \ddots & \\ 0 & & \frac{\partial^2 \gamma_L}{\partial C_L \, \partial W_L} \end{bmatrix}. \tag{3.3.3.12}$$

As in the case of complete separability of the utility function, the 'effects' equations are again represented by (3.3.2.7) through (3.3.2.12). In view of the non-nullity of Ω_{CW}, however, the simplified expressions in (3.3.2.4) for the sub-matrices of the inverse of the bordered Hessian Ω no longer apply: this means that we have to revert to the general expressions (2.6.3.4).

At least some of the conclusions drawn in section 3.3.2, however, may still apply in the present case. This is true, in particular if all elements on the main diagonal of Ω_{CW} (and of Ω_{WC}) are negative.

In this case, the matrices U_* defined in (2.6.3.4) consist of non-negative elements only, like U. The expression for T in (2.6.3.4) is simplified, because the term $\lambda Y_{WW} D$ drops out by virtue of (3.3.1.4). The expressions for M_{CC}, M_{CW} and m_C in (2.6.3.4) have one or two terms more than those in (3.3.2.6). The supplementary terms constituting M_{CC} in (2.6.3.4) – on the second and third line – are negative-definite and positive-definite, respectively, provided that T remains positive-definite; the latter will be the case if

$$\begin{bmatrix} \Omega_{CC} & \Omega_{CW} \\ \Omega_{WC} & \Omega_{WW} \end{bmatrix} \text{ is negative-definite,}$$

sufficient but not necessary for satisfying the second-order conditions (2.6.2.5).

M_{CW} includes a diagonal matrix $(d'\Omega_{CC}^{-1} d)^{-1} \, \Omega_{CC}^{-1} \Omega_{CW} T$ with all elements non-negative. In the additional term $\Omega_{CC}^{-1} \Omega_{CW} T U'_* d$ for m_C positive elements will probably dominate.

These changes do not affect the effects formulae (3.3.2.7) through (3.3.2.12), applying as well to the present case of a pairwise additive-separable utility function, provided U is replaced by U_*.

In the case of a PAS utility function, the elements of $W_{\Delta K}$ are presumed to be positive *as a rule*, whereas in the case of a CAS utility function they appear to be *always* positive [cf. (3.3.2.16)]. In general, the additional term in the expression for m_C only adds to the *uncertainty* of the signs of the elements of $C_{\Delta K}$. As a result of that addition, these elements may differ in sign, while their chances of being positive are enhanced.

With respect to effects of varying marginal rates of remuneration on working hours (incorporated in $W_{u'}$) no essential differences can be observed between the cases of pairwise and complete separability of the utility function.

Contrariwise, the statements made in section 3.3.2 with respect to the impact of remuneration on consumption ($C_{u'}$) no longer hold good, since the elements of $(C_{u'})_{\text{I}}$ need not be positive, even in general.

Effects of interest rates on consumption and working hours (C_r and W_r) may still be split into pairs of components. The interpretation of these components as 'substitution' and 'wealth accumulation' effects, however, does not make much sense anymore. The obvious reason is the 'interaction' of consumption and working hours in the utility function. Hence, no such properties as (3.3.2.17), (3.3.2.25) and (3.3.2.27) apply to $(C_{u'})_{\text{I}}$ and $(W_{u'})_{\text{I}}$, at least not for these partial effects separately.

Evidently, pairwise additive-separability of the utility function severely limits the range of conclusions to be drawn about the 'effects', and makes them less definite.

3.4. *Model with varying prospective rates of interest and price levels*

Throughout this section, prospective rates of interest and price levels are assumed to be exogenous. For further simplification, the discussion will be restricted to the case of a completely separable utility function.

Thus, the only difference between the model of this section and that of section 3.1 is that the discount vector d is replaced by f, and that the vectors C and Y for nominal consumption and income are replaced by their 'real' counterparts c and y, as in section 2.8.3. Here, we shall make use of the diagonal matrix expression (3.1.1.3) for Ω if ω is completely additive-separable. As a consequence, principally the same considerations and conclusions as mentioned in section 3.1 apply to the effects of varying y and ΔK on c in the present case. The only notable difference in 'effects' relates to the impact of varying (quasi-) rates of interest (i.e. $r_l + a_l - p_l$) on consumption.

For Ω specified by (3.1.1.3), the typical elements of the effect matrices represented by the two terms in the last member of (2.8.3.1.3) become:

$$\left(\frac{\partial c_l}{\partial r_k}\right)_{\mathrm{I}} = \lambda a_l^{-1} f_l^{-1} (1 + r_k)^{-1} \{\delta_{k>l} - (\sum_{\tau=1}^{L} f_\tau^2 a_\tau^{-1})^{-1} (\sum_{\tau=1}^{k-1} f_\tau^2 a_\tau^{-1})\, \delta_{k>1}\}, \tag{3.4.1}$$

with $\delta_{k>l} = 1$ if $k > 1$, and $= 0$ otherwise; likewise, $\delta_{k>1} = 1$ and 0 for $k > 1$ and $= 1$, respectively, and

$$\left(\frac{\partial c_l}{\partial r_k}\right)_{\mathrm{II}} = a_l^{-1} f_l^{-1} (1 + r_k)^{-1} (\sum_{\tau=1}^{L} f_\tau^2 a_\tau^{-1})^{-1} \{\sum_{\tau=1}^{k-1} (y_\tau - c_\tau) f_\tau\}\, \delta_{k>1}; \tag{3.4.2}$$

(3.4.1) and (3.4.2) represent the substitution component and the wealth accumulation component, respectively.

Equations (3.4.1) imply:

$$\left(\frac{\partial c_l}{\partial r_k}\right)_{\mathrm{I}} \begin{cases} > 0 & \text{for} \quad k > l \\ < 0 & \text{for} \quad k \leq l. \end{cases} \tag{3.4.3}$$

This means that an isolated variation in an interest rate, for a single period k only, will tend to change later consumption in the same direction, and preceding or simultaneous consumption in the opposite direction – *as far as the substitution effect is concerned*: by an incidental increase in r_k, relative prices of savings are raised in later periods and reduced in periods preceding k or coinciding with k. In other words, an increase in the rate of interest expected for any period k will induce people to save beforehand in order to benefit from the interest payments thus increased doubly.

Furthermore, (3.4.1) suggests that the substitution component of the interest effect tends to decrease algebraically ('fades away') according as k moves away from l towards L or towards 1.

According to (3.4.2), the sign of the wealth accumulation component equals the sign of $\sum_{\tau=1}^{k-1} (y_\tau - c_\tau) f_\tau$, i.e. savings or dissavings accumulated and put on interest from period 1 through $k - 1$.

3.5. *Model incorporating uncertainty*

3.5.1. JOINT PROBABILITY DISTRIBUTION OF PROSPECTIVE INCOMES

In section 2.9.1 the joint probability distribution density of the prospective incomes Y_l ($l = 1, \ldots, L$) was introduced as an essential element of a stochastic version of the basic consumption-savings model.

Here, we impose symmetry on the density function, viz.:

$$\text{prob}\,(Y_1 - \text{E}Y_1 \cdots Y_l - \text{E}Y_l \cdots Y_L - \text{E}Y_L)$$
$$= \text{prob}\,(Y_1 - \text{E}Y_1 \cdots \text{E}Y_l - Y_l \cdots Y_L - \text{E}Y_L), \qquad (3.5.1.1)$$

i.e. invariance against change of sign of one, more or all $Y_l - \text{E}Y_l$ for $l = 1, \ldots, L$.

As a particular case of such a density function, we may consider the normal one, i.e.:

$$\text{prob}\,(Y') = \{(2\pi)^L\,|M|\}^{-1/2} \cdot \exp\left[-\tfrac{1}{2}\,(Y - \text{E}Y)'\,M^{-1}\,(Y - \text{E}Y)\right], \qquad (3.5.1.2)$$

with $M = \text{E}\,(Y - \text{E}Y)\,(Y - \text{E}Y)'$ the covariance matrix of Y, and $|M|$ its determinant value.

Another – additional or alternative – assumption to be made with respect to such density functions is multiplicative separability; i.e.:

$$\text{prob}\,(Y_1 \cdots Y_L) = \prod_{l=1}^{L} \text{prob}\,(Y_l); \qquad (3.5.1.3)$$

this means that the $Y_1 \cdots Y_L$ would be distributed independently.

3.5.2. COMPLETELY SEPARABLE UTILITY FUNCTION (CAS)

In this case, the utility function (2.9.1.4) becomes:

$$\omega = \{\alpha_{.}(\bar{C}_{.})\}\,\iota_L + \{\varepsilon_{.}\,(C - \bar{C})\}\,\iota_L, \qquad (3.5.2.1)$$

with

$$\{\varepsilon_{.}\,(C - \bar{C})\} = \{\varepsilon_1\,(C_1 - \bar{C}_1) \cdots \varepsilon_L\,(C_L - \bar{C}_L)\},$$

and its expected value:

$$\text{E}\omega = \sum_{l=1}^{L} \alpha_l(\bar{C}_l) + \sum_{l=1}^{L} \int_{-\infty}^{\infty} \cdots \int_{-\infty}^{\infty} \varepsilon_l\,(C_l - \bar{C}_l)\,\text{prob}\,(Y')\,\text{d}Y_1 \cdots \text{d}Y_L, \qquad (3.5.2.2)$$

since $\bar{C}_l$, hence $\alpha_l(\bar{C}_l)$, are non-stochastic (by definition).

In the case where (3.5.1.3) holds good, (3.5.2.2) can be simplified to

$$\mathrm{E}\omega = \sum_{l=1}^{L} [\alpha_l(C_l) + \int_{-\infty}^{\infty} \varepsilon_l\,(C_l - \bar{C}_l)\,\mathrm{prob}\,(Y_l)\,\mathrm{d}Y_l]. \qquad (3.5.2.3)$$

In the particular case where ε_l are odd functions of their arguments, i.e.:

$$\varepsilon_l\,(C_l - \bar{C}_l) \equiv -\varepsilon_l\,(\bar{C}_l - C_l), \qquad (3.5.2.4)$$

and (3.5.1.1) applies, the second term at the right-hand side of (3.5.2.2) would vanish, and certainty-equivalence would prevail. This means that the expected optimal consumption and savings plan would coincide with the one resulting from conditional maximization of a utility function such as (3.1.1.1) if prospective incomes are replaced by their expected values; in other words: as if uncertainty would be absent.

If the second term at the right-hand side of (3.5.2.2) does not vanish, however, we find:

$$\frac{\partial \mathrm{E}\omega}{\partial \bar{C}_t} = \frac{\mathrm{d}\alpha_t\,(\bar{C}_t)}{\mathrm{d}\bar{C}_t} = \lambda d_t \qquad (3.5.2.5)$$

and

$$\frac{\partial \mathrm{E}\omega}{\partial\,(C_t - \bar{C}_t)} = \int_{-\infty}^{\infty} \cdots \int_{-\infty}^{\infty} \frac{\mathrm{d}\varepsilon_t}{\mathrm{d}\,(C_t - \bar{C}_t)}\,\mathrm{prob}\,(Y')\,\mathrm{d}Y_1 \cdots \mathrm{d}Y_L = \lambda d_t$$

$$\text{for} \quad t = 1, \ldots, L. \qquad (3.5.2.6$$

The special case ($(\mathrm{E}\omega)_{\bar{C}}$ being independent of C) referred to in section 2.9 is represented by (3.5.2.5) in a particularly simple way; therefore, the solution outlined in section 2.9.2 may be applied here a fortiori.

The Hessians become:

$$\mathrm{E}\Omega = \begin{bmatrix} \Omega_{\bar{C}\bar{C}} & 0 \\ 0 & \underline{\mathrm{E}\Omega}_{C-\bar{C},C-\bar{C}} \end{bmatrix}, \qquad (3.5.2.7)$$

with

$$\Omega_{\bar{C}\bar{C}} = \underline{\mathrm{E}\Omega}_{\bar{C}\bar{C}} = \begin{bmatrix} \frac{\partial^2\alpha_1}{\partial\bar{C}_1^2} & & 0 \\ & \ddots & \\ 0 & & \frac{\partial^2\alpha_L}{\partial\bar{C}_L^2} \end{bmatrix}$$

and

$$\underline{\mathrm{E}\Omega}_{C-\bar{C},C-\bar{C}} = \begin{bmatrix} \dfrac{\partial^2 \mathrm{E}\varepsilon_1}{\partial\,(C_1 - \bar{C}_1)^2} & & 0 \\ & \ddots & \\ 0 & & \dfrac{\partial^2 \mathrm{E}\varepsilon_L}{\partial\,(C_L - \bar{C}_L)^2} \end{bmatrix}$$

as diagonal matrices, and

$$\frac{\partial^2 \mathrm{E}\varepsilon_l}{\partial\,(C_l - \bar{C}_l)^2} = \int_{-\infty}^{\infty} \cdots \int_{-\infty}^{\infty} \frac{\partial^2 \varepsilon_l}{\partial\,(C_l - \bar{C}_l)^2}\, \mathrm{prob}\,(Y')\,\mathrm{d}Y_1 \cdots \mathrm{d}Y_L.$$

In the particular case that all ε_l would be quadratic in their arguments, $\underline{\mathrm{E}\Omega}_{C-\bar{C},C-\bar{C}}$ would become a null-matrix. Consequently, certainty equivalence[4] in Theil's sense would arise (cf. Theil [1961]).

For the sub-matrices, vectors and scalars in the inverse of the bordered Hessian in (2.9.3.3), we would find:

$$\left.\begin{aligned} M_{11} &= \underline{\mathrm{E}\Omega}_{\bar{C}\bar{C}}^{-1} - (d'\underline{\mathrm{E}\Omega}_{\bar{C}\bar{C}}^{-1}d)^{-1} \cdot (\underline{\mathrm{E}\Omega}_{\bar{C}\bar{C}}^{-1}d)\,(\underline{\mathrm{E}\Omega}_{\bar{C}\bar{C}}^{-1}d)' \\ M_{12} &= M'_{21} = 0 \\ M_{22} &= \underline{\mathrm{E}\Omega}_{C-\bar{C},C-\bar{C}}^{-1} - (d'\underline{\mathrm{E}\Omega}_{C-\bar{C},C-\bar{C}}^{-1}d)^{-1}(\underline{\mathrm{E}\Omega}_{C-\bar{C},C-\bar{C}}^{-1}d)(\underline{\mathrm{E}\Omega}_{C-\bar{C},C-\bar{C}}^{-1}d)' \\ v_1 &= \{d'\,(\underline{\mathrm{E}\Omega}_{\bar{C}\bar{C}}^{-1} + \underline{\mathrm{E}\Omega}_{C-\bar{C},C-\bar{C}}^{-1})\,d\}^{-1} \cdot \underline{\mathrm{E}\Omega}_{\bar{C}\bar{C}} \cdot d \\ v_2 &= \{d'\,(\underline{\mathrm{E}\Omega}_{\bar{C}\bar{C}}^{-1} + \underline{\mathrm{E}\Omega}_{C-\bar{C},C-\bar{C}}^{-1})\,d\}^{-1} \cdot \underline{\mathrm{E}\Omega}_{C-\bar{C},C-\bar{C}}^{-1}\,d \\ s &= -\{d'\,(\underline{\mathrm{E}\Omega}_{\bar{C}\bar{C}}^{-1} + \underline{\mathrm{E}\Omega}_{C-\bar{C},C-\bar{C}}^{-1})\,d\}^{-1}. \end{aligned}\right\} \tag{3.5.2.8}$$

These expressions represent simplifications of the more general expressions (2.9.3.4) through (2.9.3.6) for the case $\underline{\mathrm{E}\Omega}_{C-\bar{C},\bar{C}} = 0$; they have the following properties:

$$M_{11}, M_{22}\text{: negative semi-definite matrices} \tag{3.5.2.9}$$

$$v_1, v_2 > 0\text{: positive vectors} \tag{3.5.2.10}$$

$$s < 0\text{: negative scalar.} \tag{3.5.2.11}$$

[4] One should note, however, that for such 'certainty equivalence', conditions (3.5.1.1) and (3.5.2.4) are sufficient but not necessary.

Separability of the utility function (3.5.2.1) ensures:

$$\underline{\mathrm{E}\Omega}_{\bar{C},\mathrm{EY}} = 0 \tag{3.5.2.12}$$

$$\underline{\mathrm{E}\Omega}_{\bar{C},\mathrm{par}} = 0. \tag{3.5.2.13}$$

Therefore, according to (3.5.2.12), (3.5.2.13) and (3.5.2.8), the 'effects' equations (2.9.3.8) through (2.9.3.15) are simplified to:

$$\bar{C}_{\mathrm{EY}} = v_1 d' \tag{3.5.2.14}$$

$$(C - \bar{C})_{\mathrm{EY}} = -M_{22}\underline{\mathrm{E}\Omega}_{C-\bar{C},\mathrm{EY}} \tag{3.5.2.15}$$

$$\bar{C}_{\mathrm{par}} = 0 \tag{3.5.2.16}$$

$$(C - \bar{C})_{\mathrm{par}} = -M_{22}\underline{\mathrm{E}\Omega}_{C-\bar{C},\mathrm{par}} + v_2 d' \tag{3.5.2.17}$$

$$\bar{C}_r = (1 + r)^{-1} [\lambda M_{11} + v_1 (\mathrm{E}Y - \bar{C})'] \dot{d}L- \tag{3.5.2.18}$$

$$(C - \bar{C})_r = (1 + r)^{-1} [\lambda M_{22} + v_2 (\mathrm{E}Y - \bar{C})'] \dot{d}L- \tag{3.5.2.19}$$

$$\bar{C}_{\Delta K} = -v_1 \tag{3.5.2.20}$$

$$(C - \bar{C})_{\Delta K} = -v_2. \tag{3.5.2.21}$$

This leaves $\underline{\mathrm{E}\Omega}_{C-\bar{C},\mathrm{EY}}$ and $\underline{\mathrm{E}\Omega}_{C-\bar{C},\mathrm{par}}$ to be evaluated.

In case the Y's would be distributed independently, in accordance with (3.5.1.3):

$$\underline{\mathrm{E}\Omega}_{C-\bar{C},\mathrm{EY}} = \left[\frac{\partial^2 \mathrm{E}\varepsilon_l}{\partial (C_l - \bar{C}_l) \cdot \partial \mathrm{E}Y_k}\right] \tag{3.5.2.22}$$

with

$$\frac{\partial^2 \mathrm{E}\varepsilon_l}{\partial (C_l - \bar{C}_l) \cdot \partial \mathrm{E}Y_k} = \delta_{kl} \int_{-\infty}^{\infty} \frac{\mathrm{d}\varepsilon_l}{\mathrm{d}(C_l - \bar{C}_l)} \frac{\partial \operatorname{prob} Y_l}{\partial \mathrm{E}Y_l} \mathrm{d}Y_l$$

$$\text{for} \quad l, k = 1, \ldots, L \quad \text{and} \quad \delta_{kl} = \begin{cases} 1 & \text{for} \quad k = 1 \\ 0 & \text{for} \quad k \neq l; \end{cases}$$

$$\underline{\mathrm{E}\Omega}_{C-\bar{C},\mathrm{par}} = \left[\frac{\partial^2 \mathrm{E}\varepsilon_l}{\partial (C_l - \bar{C}_l) \cdot \partial \, \mathrm{par}_\varkappa}\right] \tag{3.5.2.23}$$

with

$$\frac{\partial^2 \mathrm{E}\varepsilon_l}{\partial (C_l - \bar{C}_l) \cdot \partial \, \mathrm{par}_\varkappa} = \int_{-\infty}^{\infty} \frac{\mathrm{d}\varepsilon_l}{\mathrm{d}(C_l - \bar{C}_l)} \frac{\partial \, \mathrm{prob} \, Y_l}{\partial \, \mathrm{par}_\varkappa} \, \mathrm{d}Y_l .$$

According to (3.5.2.22), $\underline{\mathrm{E}\Omega}_{C-\bar{C},\mathrm{E}Y}$ is square and diagonal, with elements on the main diagonal that may be positive, zero or negative. On the other hand, the matrix $\underline{\mathrm{E}\Omega}_{C-\bar{C},\mathrm{par}}$, of order $L \times K$, is generally non-square, but may show zeroes, viz. in places where $\mathrm{par}_\varkappa$ would not affect prob Y_l.

In the case where the Y's are distributed normally (but not necessarily independently), we find:

$$\underline{\mathrm{E}\Omega}_{C-\bar{C},\mathrm{E}Y} = \int_{-\infty}^{\infty} \cdots \int_{-\infty}^{\infty} \varepsilon_{C-\bar{C}} (Y - \mathrm{E}Y)' \, M^{-1} \, \mathrm{prob}\,(Y') \, \mathrm{d}Y_1 \cdots \mathrm{d}Y_L , \tag{3.5.2.24}$$

with the latter expression representing an $L \times L$ matrix of L-tuple integrals.

In case the Y's are distributed normally *and independently*, i.e. if (3.5.1.2) and (3.5.1.3) hold simultaneously, the M^{-1} matrix is diagonal, with variances $\mathrm{E}\,(Y_l - \mathrm{E}Y_l)^2$ for $l = 1, \ldots, L$ on its main diagonal. Then the integrands of the elements on the main diagonal of $\underline{\mathrm{E}\Omega}_{C-\bar{C},\mathrm{E}Y}$ are $\varepsilon_{C_l - \bar{C}_l} (Y_l - \mathrm{E}Y_l) \, \sigma_l^{-2}$ prob (Y_l), i.e. positive or negative according as $Y_l > \mathrm{E}Y_l$ or $Y_l < \mathrm{E}Y_l$ respectively. This suggests that in an absolute sense, these elements are likely to be small. Anyhow, the elements of $(C - \bar{C})_{\mathrm{E}Y}$ will be positive on the average, since $d'M_{22} = 0$, so that:

$$d'\,(C - \bar{C})_{\mathrm{E}Y} = 0; \tag{3.5.2.25}$$

moreover:

$$\bar{C}_{\mathrm{E}Y} > 0; \tag{3.5.2.26}$$

hence, both together:

$$d'C_{\mathrm{E}Y} > 0; \tag{3.5.2.27}$$

i.e., effects of expected income on 'normal' future consumption are always *positive*, and ditto on prospective income are *predominantly* positive. This means that what is certain under certainty, i.e. $C_Y > 0$, is highly likely under uncertainty.

Sometimes, 'par' may be identified with variances, in the case where the latter are parameters of a distribution function, such as the normal one.

In particular, if the Y's are distributed normally and independently, the

$L \times L$ matrix $\underline{\mathrm{E}\Omega}_{C-\bar{C},\mathrm{var}}$ has as elements:

$$\frac{\partial^2 \mathrm{E}\omega}{\partial (C_l - \bar{C}_l) \cdot \partial \sigma_k^2} =$$

$$-\tfrac{1}{2}\sigma_k^{-1} \int_{-\infty}^{\infty} \frac{\mathrm{d}\varepsilon_l}{\mathrm{d}(C_l - \bar{C}_l)} \cdot \mathrm{prob}(Y_l) \cdot \mathrm{d}Y_l$$

$$+ \delta_{kl}\sigma_k^{-2} \int_{-\infty}^{\infty} \frac{\mathrm{d}\varepsilon_l}{\mathrm{d}(C_l - \bar{C}_l)} (Y_l - \mathrm{E}Y_l)^2 \, \mathrm{prob}(Y_l) \cdot \mathrm{d}Y_l, \qquad (3.5.2.28)$$

with

$$\delta_{kl} = \begin{cases} 1 & \text{for} \quad k = l \\ 0 & \text{for} \quad k \neq l. \end{cases}$$

Thus, the off-diagonal elements of $\underline{\mathrm{E}\Omega}_{C-\bar{C},\mathrm{par}}$ are all negative, whereas the diagonal elements may be positive or negative, according as the second term or the first term in the second member of (3.5.2.28) dominates.

Furthermore,

$$\bar{C}_{\Delta K} < 0, \qquad (3.5.2.29)$$

$$(C - \bar{C})_{\Delta K} < 0, \qquad (3.5.2.30)$$

hence

$$C_{\Delta K} < 0, \qquad (3.5.2.31)$$

in perfect agreement with our findings in the case of certainty.

Analogously, both $\bar{C}_r$ and $(C - \bar{C})_r$ may be decomposed into substitution effects of the rate of interest on certainty-equivalent consumption and on consumption deviations in case of uncertainty.

As a result we obtain:

$$(C_r)_{\mathrm{I}} = \lambda (1 + r)^{-1} [M_{11} + M_{22}] \dot{d}L- \qquad (3.5.2.32)$$

and

$$(C_r)_{\mathrm{II}} = (1 + r)^{-1} (v_1 + v_2) (\mathrm{E}Y - \bar{C})' \dot{d}L- \qquad (3.5.2.33)$$

for the substitution and the wealth accumulation components respectively.

Again, the former are zero on the average, since

$$\lambda^{-1} d' (M_{11} + M_{22}) = d'(C_r)_{\mathrm{I}} = 0. \qquad (3.5.2.34)$$

Summarizing, we find that at least as regards signs, the effects in the case of uncertainty do not differ essentially from those in the case of certainty.

3.6. *Sociometric version of the model*

3.6.1. CONSTANT 'CONJECTURAL VARIATIONS'

Throughout section 3.6 we assume: constancy of the 'conjectural variations' introduced in section 2.10:

$$\frac{\partial_{i'}C_1}{\partial_i C_1} = {}_{i'}g_i \geq 0 \quad \text{for} \quad (i, i' = 1, \ldots, I); \tag{3.6.1.1}$$

hence, the ${}_{i'}g_i$ are termed 'reaction coefficients'.

In the special case of mutual consistency of the conjectural variations according to (2.10.2.4) and (2.10.2.5):

$${}_{i'}g_i = {}_ig_{i'}^{-1} \tag{3.6.1.2}$$

and

$${}_ig_{i'} = {}_ig_{i''} \cdot {}_{i''}g_{i'}. \tag{3.6.1.3}$$

Invariance of the ${}_{i'}g_i$ implies:

$$G_{ii(-1,-1)} = 0 \tag{3.6.1.4}$$

and

$$.G_{i.(1,1)} = 0, \tag{3.6.1.5}$$

hence simplifies the bordered Hessian ${}_iH^*$ in (2.10.2.7).

3.6.2. COMPLETELY SEPARABLE UTILITY FUNCTION (CAS)

Complete additive separability of the utility functions (2.10.1.1) results in:

$${}_i\omega = \sum_{l=2}^{M} {}_i\alpha_{il}({}_iC_l) + \sum_{i'=1}^{I} {}_i\alpha_{i'1}({}_{i'}C_1) \quad \text{for} \quad i = 1, \ldots, I, \tag{3.6.2.1}$$

with

$$\left.\begin{aligned} &\frac{\partial_i\alpha_{il}}{\partial_i C_l} > 0 &(3.6.2.2)\\ &\frac{\partial_i^2\alpha_{il}}{\partial_i C_l^2} < 0 &(3.6.2.3)\end{aligned}\right\} \quad \text{for} \quad i = 1, \ldots, I;\ l = 1, \ldots, M$$

and

$$\frac{\partial_i \alpha_{i'1}}{\partial_{i'} C_1} < 0 \quad \text{for} \quad i, i' = 1, \ldots, I \ (i \neq i'). \tag{3.6.2.4}$$

Thus, in the first-order conditions (2.10.2.1) for maximizing $_i\omega$ subject to the budget constraints:

$$\frac{\partial_i \omega}{\partial_i C_l} = \frac{\partial_i \alpha_{il}}{\partial_i C_l} \quad \text{for} \quad i = 1, \ldots, I; \ l = 1, \ldots, M \tag{3.6.2.5}$$

$$\frac{\partial_i \omega}{\partial_{i'} C_1} = \frac{\partial_i \alpha_{i'1}}{\partial_{i'} C_1} \quad \text{for} \quad i, i' = 1, \ldots, I. \tag{3.6.2.6}$$

Equations (3.6.2.5) and (3.6.2.6) ensure that the optimal values of $_iC_l$ ($l = 1, \ldots, L$) may be approximated for each i ($= 1, \ldots, I$) separately; the optimal values of $_{i'}C_1$ in the opinion of i ($i \neq i'$) may be disregarded, since these are either redundant or inconsistent with the $_{i'}C_1^*$ according to individuals i' themselves (cf. section 2.10.2).

Furthermore:

$$_iH = \begin{bmatrix} _iA_{i(-1)} & 0 & _i\underline{d}_{(-1)} \\ 0 & _iA_{.1} & _i\underline{d}_1 \cdot {_ie} \\ _i\underline{d}'_{(-1)} & _i\underline{d}_1 \cdot {_ie'} & 0 \end{bmatrix}, \tag{3.6.2.7}$$

with

$$_iA_{i(-1)} = \begin{bmatrix} \frac{\partial_i^2 \alpha_{i2}}{\partial_1 C_2} & & 0 \\ & \ddots & \\ 0 & & \frac{\partial_i^2 \alpha_{iM}}{\partial_i C_M^2} \end{bmatrix} \quad \text{and} \quad _iA_{.1} = \begin{bmatrix} \frac{\partial_i^2 \alpha_{11}}{\partial_i C_1^2} & & 0 \\ & \ddots & \\ 0 & & \frac{\partial_i^2 \alpha_{I1}}{\partial_I C_1^2} \end{bmatrix}$$

diagonal matrices of orders $M - 1$ and I respectively.

On the analogy of (3.3.2.6), we find

$$(_iH)^{-1} = \begin{bmatrix} _iM_{11} & _iM_{12} & _im_1 \\ _iM_{21} & _iM_{22} & _im_2 \\ _im'_1 & _im'_2 & _in \end{bmatrix}, \tag{3.6.2.8}$$

with sub-matrices corresponding to those of ${}_iH$ in (3.6.2.8), equaling:

$$\left.\begin{aligned}
{}_iM_{11} &= {}_iA^{-1}_{i(-1)}\,[I + {}_in\cdot{}_i\underline{d}_{(-1)}\cdot{}_id'_{(-1)}\cdot{}_iA^{-1}_{i(-1)}] \quad \text{negative-definite}\\
{}_iM_{12} &= {}_i\underline{d}_1\cdot{}_in\cdot{}_iA^{-1}_{i(-1)}\cdot{}_i\underline{d}_{(-1)}\cdot e'_i\cdot{}_iA^{-1}_{.1} > 0\\
{}_iM_{22} &= {}_iA^{-1}_{.1}\,[I + {}_i\underline{d}_1\cdot{}_in\cdot e_i\cdot e'_i\cdot{}_iA^{-1}_{.1}] \quad \text{negative-definite}\\
{}_im_1 &= -{}_in\cdot{}_iA^{-1}_{i(-1)}\cdot{}_i\underline{d}_{(-1)} > 0\\
{}_im_2 &= -{}_i\underline{d}_1\cdot{}_in\cdot{}_iA^{-1}_{.1} > 0\\
{}_in &= -({}_i\underline{d}'_{(-1)}\cdot{}_iA^{-1}_{i(-1)}\cdot{}_i\underline{d}_{(-1)} + {}_i\underline{d}^2_1\cdot e'_i\cdot{}_iA^{-1}_{i1}\cdot e_i)^{-1} > 0.
\end{aligned}\right\} \tag{3.6.2.9}$$

Substitution of these expressions into (2.10.3.9) through (2.10.3.14) yields the following 'effects' equations:

$$({}_iC_{(-1)})_{{}_iY_.} = -{}_in\cdot{}_iA^{-1}_{i(-1)}\cdot{}_i\underline{d}_{(-1)}\cdot{}_i\underline{d}' = ({}_iC_{(-1)})_{\Delta_iK}\cdot{}_i\underline{d}' > 0 \tag{3.6.2.10}$$

$${}_i(.C_1)_{{}_iY_.} = -{}_i\underline{d}_1\cdot{}_in\cdot{}_iA^{-1}_{.1}\cdot{}_i\underline{d}' = {}_i(.C_1)_{\Delta_iK}\cdot{}_i\underline{d}' > 0 \tag{3.6.2.11}$$

$$\begin{aligned}
({}_iC_{(-1)})_{{}_ir} &=\\
&{}_i\lambda\,(1+{}_ir)^{-1}\cdot{}_iA^{-1}_{i(-1)}\cdot[I + {}_in\cdot{}_i\underline{d}_{(-1)}\cdot{}_id'_{(-1)}\cdot{}_iA^{-1}_{i(-1)}]\,{}_id_{(-1)}\cdot M^-_{(-1)}\\
&+ {}_i\lambda\,(1+{}_ir)^{-1}\cdot{}_i\underline{d}^2_1\cdot{}_in\cdot(M-1)\cdot{}_iA^{-1}_{i(-1)}\cdot{}_i\underline{d}_{(-1)}\cdot e'_i\cdot{}_iA^{-1}_{.1}\cdot e_i\\
&- (1+{}_ir)^{-1}\cdot{}_in\cdot{}_iA^{-1}_{i(-1)}\cdot{}_i\underline{d}_{(-1)}\cdot({}_iY'_. - {}_iC'_.)\cdot{}_i\underline{d}\cdot M^-
\end{aligned} \tag{3.6.2.12}$$

$$\begin{aligned}
{}_i(.C_1)_{{}_ir} &= {}_i\lambda\,(1+{}_ir)^{-1}\cdot{}_i\underline{d}_1\cdot{}_in\cdot{}_iA^{-1}_{.1}\cdot e_i\cdot{}_i\underline{d}'_{(-1)}\cdot{}_iA^{-1}_{i(-1)}\cdot{}_i\underline{d}_{(-1)}\cdot M^-_{(-1)}\\
&+ {}_i\lambda\,(1+{}_ir)^{-1}\cdot{}_i\underline{d}_1\cdot(M-1)\cdot{}_iA^{-1}_{.1}\,[I + {}_i\underline{d}_1\cdot{}_in\cdot e_i\cdot e'_i\cdot{}_iA^{-1}_{.1}]\,e_i\\
&- (1+{}_ir)^{-1}\cdot{}_i\underline{d}_1\cdot{}_in\cdot{}_iA^{-1}_{.1}\cdot({}_iY'_. - {}_iC'_.)\cdot{}_i\underline{d}\cdot M^-
\end{aligned} \tag{3.6.2.13}$$

$$({}_iC_{(-1)})_{\Delta_iK} = {}_in\cdot{}_iA^{-1}_{i(-1)}\cdot{}_i\underline{d}_{(-1)} < 0 \tag{3.6.2.14}$$

$${}_i(.C_1)_{\Delta_iK} = {}_i\underline{d}_1\cdot{}_in\cdot{}_iA^{-1}_{.1} < 0. \tag{3.6.2.15}$$

In this special case, the nature of the ${}_iA^{-1}_{i.}$ and ${}_iA^{-1}_{.1}$ matrices – i.e. diagonal with all-negative elements on the main diagonal – and the non-negativeness of the (other) vectors and scalars involved, yield positive matrices and negative vectors for the effects expressed by (3.6.2.10) and (3.6.2.11), and by (3.6.2.14) and (3.6.2.15), respectively. Evidently, increases in current or expected future income affect consumption in any period in a positive sense;

the same applies to current consumption of other people as viewed by the person whose income is assumed to change.

On the other hand, intended increase in wealth accumulation (or decrease of wealth decumulation) obviously has a depressing effect on current as well as on future consumption by the same person and anticipated current consumption by others.

The positiveness of $({}_iC.)_{{}_iY.}$ according to (3.6.2.10/11) and the negativeness of $({}_iC.)_{\Delta_i K}$ according to (3.6.2.14/15) correspond to $C_Y > 0$ and $C_{\Delta K} > 0$ for the basic model, by virtue of (3.1.1.10) and (3.1.1.11), respectively.

As before, the effects of the interest rate on consumption may be split into substitution effects and wealth accumulation effects, i.e. the first two terms and the third one respectively of (3.6.2.12) and (3.6.2.13). The expressions for the substitution parts (with the ${}_i\lambda$) resemble those found for the model incorporating working hours according to (3.3.2.30) – after substitution of the expressions for M_{CC} and M_{CW}.

Even an analogon to (3.3.2.33) for zero substitution effects obtained after reweighting', arises in the present context. First, we notice that

$$ {}_iM_{11} \cdot {}_i\underline{d}_{(-1)} + {}_i\underline{d}_1 \cdot {}_iM_{12} \cdot e_i = 0, \tag{3.6.2.16} $$

corresponding to (3.3.2.32) for the model incorporating working hours. This implies that if in the 'substitution' part of $({}_iC_{(-1)})_{{}_ir}$, i.e. in

$$ [({}_iC_{(-1)})_{{}_ir}]_{\text{I}} = {}_i\lambda \cdot (1 + {}_ir)^{-1} \{{}_iM_{11} \cdot {}_i\underline{d}_{(-1)} \cdot M^{-}_{(-1)} + {}_i\underline{d}_1 (M-1) \cdot {}_iM_{12} \cdot e_i\} \tag{3.6.2.17} $$

the weight vector $\{{}_i\underline{d}_2\,(M-2),\ {}_i\underline{d}_3\,(M-3) \cdots {}_i\underline{d}_M,\ 0,\ {}_i\underline{d}_1\,(M-1)\}$ is replaced by $\{{}_i\underline{d}_2, {}_i\underline{d}_3 \cdots {}_i\underline{d}_M, 0, {}_i\underline{d}_1\}$, the substitution effects would average out to zero, i.e.:

$$ [({}_iC_{(-1)})_{{}_ir}]_{\text{I}*} = {}_i\lambda\,(1 + {}_ir)^{-1} \{{}_iM_{11} \cdot {}_i\underline{d}_{(-1)} + {}_i\underline{d}_1 \cdot {}_iM_{12} \cdot e_i\} = 0. \tag{3.6.2.18} $$

Similarly, we find:

$$ [{}_i(.C_1)_{{}_ir}]_{\text{I}*} = {}_i\lambda\,(1 + {}_ir)^{-1} \cdot \{{}_iM_{21} \cdot {}_i\underline{d}_{(-1)} + {}_i\underline{d}_1 \cdot {}_iM_{22} \cdot e_i\} = 0 \tag{3.6.2.19} $$

with respect to substitution effects of changes in the rate of interest on current consumption as anticipated by *i* for himself as well as for others.

As before, these substitution effects may be positive or negative depending on the relative strengths of the negative elements of ${}_iM_{11} \cdot {}_i\underline{d}_{(-1)} \cdot M^{-}_{(-1)}$ and ${}_i\underline{d}_1 \cdot (M-1)\,{}_iM_{22} \cdot e_i$ on the one hand, and the positive elements of ${}_i\underline{d}_1 \cdot {}_iM_{12} \cdot e_i$ and $(M-1) \cdot {}_iM_{21} \cdot {}_i\underline{d}_{(-1)}$ on the other hand.

In the case where the reaction coefficients ${}_{i'}g_i$ would be mutually consistent according to (3.6.1.2) and (3.6.1.3), ${}_iH^*$ in (2.10.3.16) become:

$$
{}_iA_{i.} = \begin{bmatrix} \frac{\partial_i^2 \alpha_{i1}}{\partial_i C_1^2} & & & 0 \\ & \frac{\partial_i^2 \alpha_{i2}}{\partial_i C_2^2} & & \\ & & \ddots & \\ 0 & & & \frac{\partial_i^2 \alpha_{iM}}{\partial_i C_M^2} \end{bmatrix} \quad \text{diagonal } M \times M \text{ matrices.} \tag{3.6.2.20}
$$

Therefore, the ${}_iH_*^{-1}$ in (2.10.3.17) through (2.10.3.19) may be replaced by ${}_iA_{i.}^{-1}$, resulting in:

$$({}_iC.)_{{}_iY.} > 0 \tag{3.6.2.21}$$

and

$$({}_iC.)_{\Delta_i K} < 0. \tag{3.6.2.22}$$

3.7. *Continuous versions of the basic model*

3.7.1. UTILITY FUNCTION AND BUDGET EQUATION

As a limiting case of the completely additive-separable utility function (3.1.1.1), we find:

$$
\begin{aligned}
\omega &= \lim_{\substack{\Delta_n l \to 0 \\ N \to \infty}} \sum_{n=1}^{N} \left(\frac{\alpha_{\Delta_n l}(C_{\Delta_n l})}{\Delta_n l} \right) \cdot \Delta_n l \\
&\qquad \text{with } \sum_{n=1}^{N} \Delta_n l = L \quad \text{(remaining constant)} \\
&= \int_0^L \varphi\,\{C(\tau)\} \cdot d\tau \\
&\qquad \text{with } \varphi\,\{C(\tau)\} = \lim_{\Delta_n l \to 0} \frac{\alpha_{\Delta_n l}(C_{\Delta_n l})}{\Delta_n l} \\
&\qquad \text{and } C(\tau) = \lim_{\Delta_n l \to 0} \frac{C_{\Delta_n l}}{\Delta_n l}
\end{aligned} \tag{3.7.1.1}
$$

as the flow rate of consumption at point of time τ.

On the analogy of the *discrete* completely additive-separable utility function, we assume:

$$\varphi\{C(\tau)\} > 0 \quad \text{for } 0 \leq \tau \leq L. \tag{3.7.1.2}$$

Similarly, a continuous version of the lifetime budget equation appears to be a limiting case of the discrete budget equation (2.4.1.7), viz.:

$$\Delta K = K_L - K_0 = \lim_{\substack{\Delta_n l \to 0 \\ N \to \infty}} \sum_{n=1}^{N} \left\{ \frac{Y_{\Delta_n l}}{\Delta_n l} - \frac{C_{\Delta_n l}}{\Delta_n l} \right\} \{1 + r_{\Delta_n l}\}^{N-n}$$

$$\text{with} \quad \sum_{n=1}^{N} \Delta_n l = L \quad \text{(remaining constant)}$$

$$= \int_0^L \{Y(\tau) - C(\tau)\} \exp\{(L - \tau)\varrho\}\, d\tau$$

$$\text{with} \quad Y(\tau) = \lim_{\Delta_n l \to 0} \frac{Y_{\Delta_n l}}{\Delta_n l} \tag{3.7.1.3}$$

as the flow rate of income at point of time τ,[5]

$$\varrho = \lim_{\Delta_n l \to 0} \frac{r_{\Delta_n l}}{\Delta_n l}$$

as the continuous rate of interest, hence

$$\exp(-\varrho\tau) = \lim_{\substack{\Delta_n l \to 0 \\ n \to \infty}} \{1 + r_{\Delta_n l}\}^{-n} \quad \text{with } n \cdot \Delta_n l = \tau\,.$$

As before, L is the individual's life expectancy at the beginning of his planning period, but it need not be an integer anymore.

In the case where the planning period extends over the maximum lifetime M of the individual, however, the budget equation should be modified to

$$\Delta K = K(F) - K(0) = \int_0^M \{Y(\tau) - C(\tau)\}\, s(\tau) \exp\{(M - \tau)\varrho\}\, d\tau, \tag{3.7.1.4}$$

with $s(\tau)$ rates of survival over periods of length τ $(0 \leq \tau \leq M)$.

In the utility function (3.7.1.1) replacement of L by M suffices for representing – together with (3.7.1.4) – a continuous version of the model presented in section 2.7.

---

[5] As in the discrete case: exclusive of interest receipts or payments on savings or dissavings accruing from the beginning of the planning period onwards.

Finally, modifications suggested in section 2.8 might be passed on to a continuous model by assuming ϱ to depend on time, i.e. by substituting $\varrho(\tau)$ for ϱ. Rates of change in levels of consumer prices and/or asset prices might also be incorporated in ϱ as indicated by (2.8.1.1.5) – provided τ becomes an argument of functions instead of a subscript attached to variables. Moreover, inclusion of prospective changes in consumer prices requires replacement of nominal rates of income and consumption $Y(\tau)$ and $C(\tau)$ by real rates $y(\tau)$ and $c(\tau)$; taking account of changes in asset price levels would necessitate replacement of $K(0)$ by $K(0) \cdot A(L)$.

For brevity's sake, however, possible prospective changes in price levels are disregarded forthwith; neither do we consider possible dependence of $\varrho(\tau)$ on $K(\tau)$. Therefore, the following analysis will be restricted to consequences of (exogenous) prospective changes in the rate of interest.

3.7.2. OPTIMUM CONDITIONS

Maximizing (3.7.1.1) subject to (3.7.1.3) amounts to maximizing:

$$z = \omega + \lambda\,[-\Delta K + \int_0^L \{Y(\tau) - C(\tau)\} \exp\{(L-\tau)\varrho\}\, d\tau]$$

$$= \int_0^L [\varphi\{C(\tau)\} + \lambda\{Y(\tau) - C(\tau)\} \exp\{(L-\tau)\varrho\} - \lambda L^{-1}\Delta K]\, d\tau, \tag{3.7.2.1}$$

with λ a Lagrangean multiplier.

Maximization of (3.7.2.1) requires compliance with the Euler conditions:

$$\frac{\partial[\;\;]}{\partial C(\tau)} = \frac{\partial\varphi\{C(\tau)\}}{\partial C(\tau)} - \lambda \exp\{(L-\tau)\varrho\} = 0 \tag{3.7.2.2}$$

and

$$\frac{\partial^2[\;\;]}{\partial C^2(\tau)} = \frac{\partial^2\varphi\{C(\tau)\}}{\partial C^2(\tau)} < 0 \tag{3.7.2.3}$$

for $0 \le \tau \le L$ (both conditions)

with [ ] denoting the integrand in the last member of (3.7.2.1).

Evidently, (3.7.2.2) implies:

$$\varphi_C(\tau) = \varphi_C(0) \exp(-\varrho\tau) \tag{3.7.2.4}$$

if $\varphi_C(\tau) = \partial\varphi\{C(\tau)\}/\partial C(\tau)$.

By substituting (3.7.1.3) into (3.7.2.2) we get:

$$R_L = \int_0^L C(\tau) \exp\{(L-\tau)\varrho\}\, d\tau = \lambda^{-1} \int_0^L C(\tau)\, \varphi_C(\tau)\, d\tau \quad (3.7.2.5)$$

with

$$R_L \overset{\text{def}}{=} \int_0^L Y(\tau) \exp\{(L-\tau)\varrho\}\, d\tau,$$

or

$$\lambda = R_L^{-1} \int_0^L C(\tau)\, \varphi_C(\tau)\, d\tau. \quad (3.7.2.6)$$

Substitution of (3.7.2.5) into (3.7.2.2) finally results in:

$$\varphi_C(\tau) = R_L^{-1} \exp\{(L-\tau)\varrho\} \int_0^L C(\tau')\, \varphi_C(\tau')\, d\tau'; \quad (3.7.2.7)$$

from the latter equation, $C(\tau)$ can be solved provided the function $\varphi\{C(\tau)\}$ is known[6].

Considering ϱ as a function of τ would merely require ϱ to be replaced by $\varrho(\tau)$ in (3.7.2.1) and (3.7.2.2).

If the 'maximum lifetime' version is opted for, i.e. if (3.7.1.1) is maximized subject to (3.7.1.4), condition (3.7.2.2) becomes:

$$\frac{\partial[\ ]}{\partial C(\tau)} = \frac{\partial \varphi\{C(\tau)\}}{\partial C(\tau)} - \lambda s(\tau) \exp\{(M-\tau)\varrho\} = 0 \quad (3.7.2.8)$$

$$\text{for} \quad 0 \leq \tau \leq M,$$

while the second-order condition remains the same (at least formally).

3.7.3. EFFECTS OF VARYING THE 'DATA' ON THE OPTIMAL TIME-PATTERN OF CONSUMPTION

3.7.3.1. *Changes in personal wealth, time-patterns of income and the rate of interest.* In order to find the effects of varying the rate of interest ϱ and the intended change in personal wealth ΔK, we follow the same procedure as adopted before, i.e. differentiate the first-order conditions (3.7.2.2) and the side condition (3.7.1.3) partially with respect to ϱ and ΔK, respectively; thus,

[6] One such particular specification is shown in section 4.3.5.

we get:

$$\frac{\partial^2 \varphi\{C(\tau)\}}{\partial C(\tau)\,\partial \varrho} = \frac{\partial^2 \varphi\{C(\tau)\}}{\partial C^2(\tau)} \cdot \frac{\partial C(\tau)}{\partial \varrho} = \left\{\lambda(L-\tau) + \frac{\partial \lambda}{\partial \varrho}\right\} \exp\{(L-\tau)\varrho\} \tag{3.7.3.1.1}$$

for $0 \leq \tau \leq L$

$$0 = \int_0^L \left[\{Y(\tau) - C(\tau)\}(L-\tau) - \frac{\partial C(\tau)}{\partial \varrho}\right] \exp\{(L-\tau)\varrho\}\, \mathrm{d}\tau \tag{3.7.3.1.2}$$

$$\frac{\partial^2 \varphi\{C(\tau)\}}{\partial C(\tau) \cdot \partial(\Delta K)} = \frac{\partial^2 \varphi\{C(\tau)\}}{\partial C^2(\tau)} \cdot \frac{\partial C(\tau)}{\partial(\Delta K)} = \frac{\partial \lambda}{\partial \Delta K} \exp\{(L-\tau)\varrho\} \tag{3.7.3.1.3}$$

for $0 \leq \tau \leq L$

$$1 = -\int_0^L \frac{\partial C(\tau)}{\partial(\Delta K)} \exp\{(L-\tau)\varrho\}\, \mathrm{d}\tau. \tag{3.7.3.1.4}$$

By putting $\tau = L$, we obtain from (3.7.3.1.1)

$$\varphi_{CC}(L)\, C_\varrho(L) = \lambda_\varrho, \tag{3.7.3.1.5}$$

and from (3.7.3.1.3):

$$\varphi_{CC}(L)\, C_{\Delta K}(L) = \lambda_{\Delta K}, \tag{3.7.3.1.6}$$

with $\varphi_{CC}(\tau) = \partial^2 \varphi\{C(\tau)\}/\partial C^2(\tau)$,

$$C_\varrho(\tau) = \partial C(\tau)/\partial \varrho, \quad C_{\Delta K}(\tau) = \partial C(\tau)/\partial(\Delta K),$$

$$\lambda_\varrho = \frac{\partial \lambda}{\partial \varrho}, \quad \lambda_{\Delta K} = \frac{\partial \lambda}{\partial(\Delta K)}.$$

Substitution of (3.7.3.1.5) and (3.7.3.1.6) into (3.7.3.1.1) and (3.7.3.1.3) for λ_ϱ and $\lambda_{\Delta K}$ respectively yields:

$$C_\varrho(\tau) = \varphi_{CC}^{-1}(\tau)\{\lambda(L-\tau) + \varphi_{CC}(L)\, C_\varrho(L)\}\, \delta(\tau) \tag{3.7.3.1.7}$$

and

$$C_{\Delta K}(\tau) = \varphi_{CC}^{-1}(\tau)\, \varphi_{CC}(L)\, C_{\Delta K}(L)\, \delta(\tau), \tag{3.7.3.1.8}$$

with

$$\delta(\tau) = \exp\{(L-\tau)\varrho\} \quad (\text{hence } \delta(L) = 1).$$

Substitution of (3.7.3.1.7) and (3.7.3.1.8) into (3.7.3.1.2) and (3.7.3.1.4), respectively, produces:

$$\varphi_{CC}(L) \cdot C_\varrho(L) = \bar{\varphi} \int_0^L \{Y(\tau) - C(\tau) - \lambda \varphi_{CC}^{-1}(\tau)\, \delta(\tau)\}(L-\tau)\, \delta(\tau)\, \mathrm{d}\tau \tag{3.7.3.1.9}$$

and

$$\varphi_{CC}(L) \cdot C_{\Delta K}(L) = -\bar{\varphi} = -\left[\int_0^L \varphi_{CC}^{-1}(\tau)\, \delta^2(\tau)\, d\tau\right]^{-1} > 0. \tag{3.7.3.1.10}$$

If ϱ is a function of time instead of a constant, we may examine the effects of varying the vector par_ϱ of *parameters* of that function. Therefore:

$$\varphi_{CC}(\tau)\, C_{\mathrm{par}_\varrho}(\tau) = \{\lambda\,(L-\tau)\,\varrho_{\mathrm{par}_\varrho}(\tau) + \lambda_{\mathrm{par}_\varrho}\}\, \delta(\tau) \tag{3.7.3.1.11}$$

and

$$0 = \int_0^L [\{Y(\tau) - C(\tau)\}\,(L-\tau)\,\varrho_{\mathrm{par}_\varrho}(\tau) - C_{\mathrm{par}_\varrho}(\tau)]\,\delta(\tau)\, d\tau, \tag{3.7.3.1.12}$$

with $C_{\mathrm{par}_\varrho}(\tau)$, $\lambda_{\mathrm{par}_\varrho}$ and $\varrho_{\mathrm{par}_\varrho}$ vectors of derivatives of $C(\tau)$, λ and ϱ with respect to the parameters of ϱ; hence, both (3.7.3.1.11) and (3.7.3.1.12) represent numbers of equations equal to the number of parameters of $\varrho(\tau)$.

Solving $C_{\mathrm{par}_\varrho}(\tau)$ from (3.7.3.1.11) and (3.7.3.1.12) in a way similar to that expressed by (3.7.3.1.5), (3.7.3.1.7) and (3.7.3.1.9) we now obtain:

$$C_{\mathrm{par}_\varrho}(\tau) = \varphi_{CC}^{-1}(\tau)\,\{\lambda\,(L-\tau)\,\varrho_{\mathrm{par}_\varrho}(\tau) + \varphi_{CC}(L)\, C_{\mathrm{par}_\varrho}(L)\}\,\delta(\tau), \tag{3.7.3.1.13}$$

with

$$\varphi_{CC}(L)\, C_{\mathrm{par}_\varrho}(L) = -\bar{\varphi}\int_0^L \{Y(\tau) - C(\tau) - \lambda\varphi_{CC}^{-1}(\tau) \times \varrho_{\mathrm{par}_\varrho}(\tau)\,\delta(\tau)\,(L-\tau)\}\,\delta(\tau)\, d\tau. \tag{3.7.3.1.14}$$

Similarly, when varying the vector par_Y of parameters of $Y(\tau)$, we find:

$$\varphi_{CC}(\tau)\, C_{\mathrm{par}_Y}(\tau) = \lambda_{\mathrm{par}_Y}\, \delta(\tau) \tag{3.7.3.1.15}$$

and

$$0 = \int_0^L \{Y_{\mathrm{par}_Y}(\tau) - C_{\mathrm{par}_Y}(\tau)\}\,\delta(\tau)\, d\tau, \tag{3.7.3.1.16}$$

representing a number of equations equaling twice the number of parameters distinguished.

The solution of (3.7.3.1.15) and (3.7.3.1.16) is

$$C_{\mathrm{par}_Y}(\tau) = \varphi_{CC}^{-1}(\tau) \cdot \varphi_{CC}(L)\, C_{\mathrm{par}_Y}(L)\,\delta(\tau), \tag{3.7.3.1.17}$$

with

$$\varphi_{CC}(L) \cdot C_{\mathrm{par}_Y}(L) = \bar{\varphi}\int_0^L Y_{\mathrm{par}_Y}(\tau)\,\delta(\tau)\, d\tau. \tag{3.7.3.1.18}$$

From the preceding 'effects' equations, the following conclusion may be drawn. According to (3.7.3.1.9), the effect of varying the rate of interest on the consumption vector may be split into a 'substitution' component:

$$\{C_\varrho(\tau)\}_{\mathrm{I}} = \lambda\varphi_{CC}^{-1}(\tau)\left[(L-\tau) - \bar{\varphi}\int_0^L \varphi_{CC}^{-1}(\tau')\cdot(L-\tau')\,\delta^2(\tau')\,\mathrm{d}\tau'\right]\delta(\tau) \tag{3.7.3.1.19}$$

and a 'wealth accumulation' component:

$$\{C_\varrho(\tau)\}_{\mathrm{II}} = \varphi_{CC}^{-1}(\tau)\,\bar{\varphi}\left[\int_0^L \{Y(\tau') - C(\tau')\}\,(L-\tau')\,\delta^2(\tau')\,\mathrm{d}\tau'\right]\delta(\tau) \tag{3.7.3.1.20}$$

[cf. (2.4.3.14) and (2.4.3.15) for the discrete basic model].

If both members of (3.7.3.1.19) are multiplied by $\delta(\tau)$, and subsequently integrated from $\tau = 0$ to $\tau = L$, we find:

$$\int_0^L \{C_\varrho(\tau)\}_{\mathrm{I}}\,\delta(\tau)\,\mathrm{d}\tau = 0, \tag{3.7.3.1.21}$$

i.e. the analogon of (2.4.3.17) for the discrete model. Again, it means that the substitution component of interest effects on consumption is zero on the average if discount rates are used as weights.

Since the second term within square brackets at the right-hand side of (3.7.3.1.19) is independent of τ, the substitution effect will become (more) positive according as the future period τ is farther removed from the present. Furthermore, differentiation of both members of (3.7.3.1.19) with respect to ϱ shows that for small τ an increase in ϱ will lower $\{C_\varrho(\tau)\}_{\mathrm{I}}$ (algebraically), whereas it will raise this substitution effect for larger τ (near L).

The same conclusion may be drawn from (3.7.3.1.13) for variable ϱ, with the substitution component:

$$\{C_{\mathrm{par}_\varrho}(\tau)\}_{\mathrm{I}} = \lambda\varphi_{CC}^{-1}(\tau)\times$$

$$\times\left[(L-\tau)\,\varrho_{\mathrm{par}_\varrho}(\tau) - \bar{\varphi}\int_0^L \varphi_{CC}^{-1}(\tau')\,(L-\tau')\,\varrho_{\mathrm{par}_\varrho}(\tau')\,\delta^2(\tau')\,\mathrm{d}\tau'\right]\delta(\tau). \tag{3.7.3.1.22}$$

For (3.7.3.1.22), we find:

$$\int_0^L \{C_{\mathrm{par}_\varrho}(\tau)\}_{\mathrm{I}}\,\delta(\tau)\,\mathrm{d}\tau = 0, \tag{3.7.3.1.23}$$

like (3.7.3.1.21) for (3.7.3.1.19).

For a parameter of $\varrho(\tau)$ which may be identified with either the level or the rate of change of $\varrho(\tau)$ – at least in the short run – i.e. $\varrho_{\text{par}_\varrho} > 0$, the first (negative) term within square brackets at the right-hand side of (3.7.3.1.22) will dominate over the latter (positive) term for small τ, whereas it will be the other way round for large τ.[7]

The wealth accumulation (or decumulation) component of the interest effect will be positive or negative according as positive or negative values of $Y(\tau) - C(\tau)$, i.e. 'savings' or 'dissavings' – without interest on intra-planning period savings or dissavings, and weighted by $(L - \tau)\,\delta(\tau)$ – dominate in the integral at the right-hand side of (3.7.3.1.20). These effects have the same sign at all points of time within the planning period; with increasing τ, however, they decrease in an absolute sense.

According to (3.7.3.1.8) and (3.7.3.1.10), and in agreement with common sense considerations, an increase in the intended change in personal wealth will have a depressing effect on consumption; this effect will be less pronounced according as the future is farther removed from the present.

Equations (3.7.3.1.17) and (3.7.3.1.18) imply that consumption at any time within the planning period will react positively to changes in those parameters of the time-function $Y(\tau)$ that may be identified with either the level or the rate of change of prospective income; again, these reactions will be stronger in the short run than in the long run.

3.7.3.2. *Changes in life expectancy and in the time pattern of survival rates.* In the case of (small) changes in life-expectancy, we first assume that the utility density function $\varphi\{(\tau)\}$ decreases in the same ratio for all $0 \leq \tau \leq L$, i.e. inversely proportional to L according to the transformation:

$$\underline{\varphi}\,\{C(\tau)\} \stackrel{\text{def}}{=} L\varphi\,\{C(\tau)\}; \qquad (3.7.3.2.1)$$

this means that the parameters of the function $\underline{\varphi}$ are invariant with respect to L. Accordingly, the utility function (3.7.1.1) is replaced by:

$$\omega = L^{-1} \int_0^L \underline{\varphi}\,\{C(\tau)\}\,\mathrm{d}\tau. \qquad (3.7.3.2.2)$$

Furthermore, we assume that desired final personal wealth K_L is indepen-

[7] Already in 1939, J. R. Hicks drew attention to this 'tilting' effect of changes in the rate of interest.

dent of L, and that $Y(\tau)$ remains the same within the *original* time interval $0 \leq \tau \leq L$.

Thus, maximization of (3.7.3.2.2) subject to (3.7.1.3) requires:

$$\frac{\partial \underline{\varphi} \{C(\tau)\}}{\partial C(\tau)} = \lambda L \exp \{(L - \tau) \varrho\} \tag{3.7.3.2.3}$$

as the first-order condition, and (3.7.2.3) as the second-order condition.

For evaluating the effect of a change in L on the optimum time path of consumption, we differentiate (3.7.3.2.3) and (3.7.1.3) partially with respect to L; i.e.:

$$\frac{\partial^2 \underline{\varphi} \{C(\tau)\}}{\partial C(\tau) \partial L} = \underline{\varphi}_{CC}(\tau) C_L(\tau) = \{\lambda (1 + L\varrho) + \lambda_L\} \exp \{(L - \tau) \varrho\}, \tag{3.7.3.2.4}$$

with $C_L(\tau) = \partial C(\tau)/\partial L$ and $\lambda_L = \partial\lambda/\partial L$,

and

$$0 = \{Y(L) - C(L)\} + \int_0^L [\varrho \{Y(\tau) - C(\tau)\} - C_L(\tau)] \delta(\tau) d\tau, \tag{3.7.3.2.5}$$

with the solution:

$$C_L(\tau) = \underline{\varphi}_{CC}^{-1}(\tau) \underline{\varphi}_{CC}(L) C_L(L) \delta(\tau) \tag{3.7.3.2.6}$$

and

$$\underline{\varphi}_{CC}(L) C_L(L) = \bar{\varphi} [\varrho\Delta K + \{Y(L) - C(L)\}]. \tag{3.7.3.2.7}$$

Thus, the sign of $C_L(\tau)$ – which is the same within the entire time span $0 \leq \tau \leq L$ – equals the sign of $\varrho\Delta K + \{Y(L) - C(L)\}$. Clearly, the latter expression, hence $C_L(\tau)$, is positive for lifetime 'hoarders' (ΔK and $\{Y(L) - C(L)\}$ positive, or at least $\varrho\Delta K > \{C(L) - Y(L)\}$), and negative for lifetime 'spenders' (ΔK and $\{Y(L) - C(L)\}$ negative, or at least $\varrho\Delta K < \{C(L) - Y(L)\}$).

In the case where the 'survival rate' model replaces the 'life-expectancy' model, the first-order conditions for maximizing ω subject to (3.7.1.4) are expressed by (3.7.2.4). Changes in parameters par_s of the survival rate function $s(\tau)$ of time can be traced by differentiating (3.7.2.8) and (3.7.1.4) partially with respect to par_s; i.e.:

$$\frac{\partial^2 \varphi \{C(\tau)\}}{\partial C(\tau) \partial \text{par}_s} = \varphi_{CC}(\tau) C_{\text{par}_s}(\tau) = \{\lambda \cdot s_{\text{par}_s}(\tau) + \lambda_{\text{par}_s}\} \delta(\tau) \tag{3.7.3.2.8}$$

and

$$0 = -\int_0^M \{C_{\text{par}_s}(\tau) \cdot s(\tau) + C(\tau) \cdot s_{\text{par}_s}(\tau)\} \exp\{(M-\tau)\varrho\}\, \mathrm{d}\tau \qquad (3.7.3.2.9)$$

with the solution:

$$C_{\text{par}_s}(\tau) = \varphi_{CC}^{-1}(\tau)\, \varphi_{CC}(M)\, C_{\text{par}_s}(M) \cdot \delta(\tau) \qquad (3.7.3.2.10)$$

and

$$\varphi_{CC}(M)\, C_{\text{par}_s}(M) = -\bar{\varphi} \int_0^M C(\tau)\, s_{\text{par}_s}(\tau)\, \delta(\tau)\, \mathrm{d}\tau. \qquad (3.7.3.2.11)$$

Hence, for survival-raising par_s, $\varphi_{CC}(M) \cdot C_{\text{par}_s}(M) > 0$ and $C_{\text{par}_s}(\tau) < 0$ will hold good.

The latter result is to be expected under the assumption made before: $Y(\tau)$ is unaffected by rising survival rates. If, however, the flow rates of income would go up the effects of increasing longevity on future consumption might as well be positive.

3.7.4. DYNAMIC EXTENSION

As a limiting case of the pairwise additive separable utility function (3.1.2.5) we find:

$$\omega = \lim_{\substack{\Delta_n l \to 0 \\ N \to \infty}} \sum_{n=1}^{N} \frac{\alpha_{\Delta_n l}(C_{\Delta_n l}, \Delta C_{\Delta_n l})}{\Delta_n l} \cdot \Delta_n l$$

$$\text{with} \quad \sum_{n=1}^{N} \Delta_n l = L \quad \text{(remaining constant)}$$

$$= \int_0^L \varphi\,\{C(\tau), \dot{C}(\tau)\}\, \mathrm{d}\tau \qquad (3.7.4.1)$$

with $\dot{C}(\tau) = \partial C(\tau)/\mathrm{d}\tau$ and $\partial\varphi/\partial\dot{C}(\tau) > 0$ for $0 \leq \tau \leq L$.

Maximization of (3.7.4.1) subject to the (unaltered) budget equation (3.7.1.3) means maximization of z in (3.7.2.1), with $\varphi\,\{C(\tau)\}$ replaced by $\varphi\,\{C(\tau), \dot{C}(\tau)\}$.

As shown in Appendix A to this chapter, the first-order Euler condition for maximizing the last member of (3.7.2.1) thus modified is:

$$\frac{\partial[\ ]}{\partial C(\tau)} = \frac{\mathrm{d}}{\mathrm{d}\tau}\left\{\frac{\partial[\ ]}{\partial \dot{C}(\tau)}\right\} \qquad (3.7.4.2)$$

with [ ] the integrand in question; or:

$$\frac{\partial\varphi\,\{C(\tau),\dot{C}(\tau)\}}{\partial C(\tau)} - \lambda \exp\{(L-\tau)\varrho\} = \frac{\mathrm{d}}{\mathrm{d}\tau}\left[\frac{\partial\varphi\,\{C(\tau),\dot{C}(\tau)\}}{\partial\dot{C}(\tau)}\right] \qquad (3.7.4.3)$$

for $0 \le \tau \le L$.

The second-order condition for maximum z is:

$$\dot{}\varphi_{..}(\tau) = \varphi_{CC}(\tau) - \tfrac{1}{2}\{3\dot{\varphi}_{C\dot{C}}(\tau) - \ddot{\varphi}_{\dot{C}\dot{C}}(\tau)\} < 0, \qquad (3.7.4.4)$$

with

$$\varphi_{CC}(\tau) = \frac{\partial^2\varphi}{\partial C^2(\tau)}, \quad \dot{\varphi}_{C\dot{C}}(\tau) = \frac{\mathrm{d}}{\mathrm{d}\tau}\left[\frac{\partial^2\varphi}{\partial C(\tau)\,\partial\dot{C}(\tau)}\right] = \dot{\varphi}_{\dot{C}C}(\tau),$$

and

$$\ddot{\varphi}_{\dot{C}\dot{C}}(\tau) = \frac{\mathrm{d}^2}{\mathrm{d}\tau^2}\left[\frac{\partial^2\varphi}{\partial^2\dot{C}(\tau)}\right].$$

Given $C(\tau)$ at any point of time τ_0, (3.7.4.3) implies an (optimal) time path of $C(\tau)$.

An analytical solution, however, is generally impossible, i.e. unless φ assumes a very special form.

For assessing effects of variations in change in personal wealth, in the rate of interest, or in parameters of the rate of interest or of expected income as functions of time, we may apply the same method as adopted in section 3.7.3. Even the formulae are alike, except that $\varphi_{CC}(\tau)$ is replaced by $\dot{}\varphi_{..}$, as shown by equation (3A.2.6) in appendix A to this chapter.

E.g., (3.7.3.1.7) becomes:

$$C_\varrho(\tau) = \dot{}\varphi_{..}^{-1}(\tau)\,\{\lambda\,(L-\tau) + \dot{}\varphi_{..}(L)\,C_\varrho(L)\}\,\delta(\tau), \qquad (3.7.4.5)$$

with:

$$\dot{}\varphi_{..}(L)\cdot C_\varrho(L) = \dot{}\bar{\varphi}\int_0^L \{Y(\tau) - C(\tau) - \lambda\dot{}\varphi_{..}^{-1}(\tau)\,\delta(\tau)\}\,(L-\tau)\,\delta(\tau)\,\mathrm{d}\tau \qquad (3.7.4.6)$$

and

$$\dot{}\bar{\varphi} = \left[\int_0^L \dot{}\varphi_{..}^{-1}(\tau)\,\delta^2(\tau)\,\mathrm{d}\tau\right]^{-1}. \qquad (3.7.4.7)$$

Such a modification does not change the qualitative conclusions drawn in section 3.3, since $\dot{}\varphi_{..}(\tau)$ – like $\varphi_{CC}(\tau)$ before – must be negative, according to (3.7.4.4), in order to satisfy the second-order condition for a (constrained) utility maximum.

3.8. Recapitulation

3.8.1. GENERAL

In chapter 2, and sections 3.1 through 3.7 of the present chapter, a number of models have been considered as possible versions of a general consumption- and savings-theory; although still other versions, as well as joint versions, are conceivable, the ones considered above will suffice for the time being. Lest the wood cannot be seen for the trees, the similarities and dissimilarities between these versions will be briefly reviewed below.

As mentioned above, the more specific models dealt with in the present chapter – of a discrete and a continuous nature respectively – permit more definite conclusions than the more general models treated in sections 2.4 through 2.10 of the previous chapter; the reason is the diagonal and scalar nature of the Hessian of the utility functions in these particular cases, respectively. Furthermore, the amplification of the models by incorporation of new elements in the utility function generally obscures the implications of these models; this applies to the inclusion of final personal wealth (section 2.5), of working hours (section 2.6), of uncertainty (section 2.9) and of consumption by others (section 2.10). On the other hand, varying interest rates over future time as well as introducing price levels for assets and consumer goods (section 2.8) does not affect the essential properties of the model as regards effects of changing 'data' on consumption – except, of course, where interest rates are concerned; the same applies if life expectancy is replaced by survival rates. (seetion 2.7).

These implications will come out in the review of income effects (section 3.8.3), interest effects (section 3.8.4), personal wealth effects (section 3.8.5) and life-expectancy effects (section 3.8.6). First, however, we shall take a brief look at:

3.8.2. OPTIMUM CONDITIONS

Since the number of equations always equals the number of unknowns to be solved, the first-order conditions for optimal allocation of lifetime resources to consumption and (dis-)savings over time will generally allow for at least one solution; this applied to all versions. On the other hand, the solution(s) need not (all) be feasible, in the sense that all instrument variables assume real and relevant values (in particular, that consumption – and also working hours – where considered – be positive).

In the case of at least one feasible solution, only those satisfying the second-order conditions for a *local* maximum are acceptable. If more than one solution meets both the first-order and the second-order conditions, the chosen solution will be the one that yields the highest value of the utility function, i.e. the global maximum.

Uniqueness of the solution will be ensured only in the case where convexity is imposed on the utility function with respect to all those of its arguments that represent instrumental variables. This convexity condition is satisfied by the addi-log linear utility functions, underlying the special savings models derived by Somermeyer [1960] and applied by Bannink [1966] in the more general versions discussed; in the present chapter, however, that particular condition has not been imposed. Still, this can be done fairly easily, at least in the case of complete additive-separability of the utility function, viz. by assuming that all its additive component functions are monotonically increasing.

Nor is it hard to satisfy the second-order conditions, i.e. negative definiteness of the Hessian of the utility function for values of the variables meeting the first-order conditions. In the case of complete additive-separability of the utility function, decreasing marginal utilities of its arguments, at least for solution vectors ensuring stationarity, suffice. The variables involved are consumption (per period, or the rate of consumption per unit of time) in all versions, as well as final personal wealth (section 3.2), hours worked (section 3.3), and current-period consumption by others (section 3.6) – the latter two having 'disutility' in common – in particular versions.

It would be enticing to examine the effects of introducing variables other than the ever-present consumption into the utility function on the optimum consumption- and savings plan; this amounts to evaluating the effects of varying those additional variables from initial zero-values upwards. The very generality of the utility functions posited, however, precludes such a comparative study, even in the case of their complete additive separability; i.e. unless they would be specified still further.

On the other hand, we may (and did) consider effects of varying data on consumption as well as other instrumental variables around the latters' initial *optimal* values.

3.8.3. INCOME EFFECTS

3.8.3.1. *Income effects on consumption.* As a rule, prospective changes in income affect future consumption in the same direction. This rule applies without exception in the case of complete additive separability (CAS) of the utility function: then, an anticipated increase of income in any period boosts consumption in all future periods (cf. (3.1.1.10)). This case includes its continuous counterpart, in the sense that foreseen positive changes in either the level or the rate of change of future income will raise future consumption throughout the planning period (cf. (3.7.3.1.7)).

This theorem may be extended to the case of pairwise additive separability (PAS) of the utility function (in terms of consumption per future period), provided all non-zero elements of the Hessian are negative (a sufficient but not a necessary condition). Here too, a continuous analogon holds: for the dynamic extension of the continuous utility function, raising levels or rates of growth of future income favour future consumption, provided an additional condition is satisfied by second-order derivatives of the utility function with respect to the rate of consumption and its rate of change.

Effects of increases in expected income (in any future period) on consumption (in the same or any other period ahead) always remain positive, even if final personal wealth enters the utility function, provided the latter is CAS in all its arguments (cf. (3.2.1.7)). In the case of PAS, i.e. allowing for possible interaction between consumption with respect to utility, positiveness of income effects on consumption will still be the rule, but there may be exceptions (cf. the end of section 3.2.2).

In the case where working hours are incorporated in the utility function, CAS ensures that increases in marginal rates of remuneration anticipated for any future period will raise consumption in all periods (cf. (3.3.2.19)).

In case of PAS, allowing for possible interaction between working hours and consumption with respect to utility, such interaction may give rise to occasional negative remuneration effects on consumption; nevertheless, positiveness of such effects will prevail (cf. the end of section 3.3.3).

In the case of uncertainty, i.e. if the utility function includes both 'certainty-equivalent' consumption and possible deviation from its certainty-equivalent values, anticipated increases in the expected value of future income for any period will still raise certainty-equivalent consumption in all future periods – again provided the utility function is CAS (cf. (3.5.2.26)).

Since the effects of such changes on deviations of consumption from their certainty equivalent values will average out to zero if weighted by discount factors (cf. (3.5.2.25)), the income effects on *uncertain* future consumption will also be positive in general.

Finally, the positiveness of income effects on future consumption continues to prevail without exception even if 'consumption by others' is introduced in anyone's CAS utility function (cf. (3.6.2.21)).

In the case where CAS is dropped as a condition to be imposed on utility functions, positiveness of income effects on future consumption is no longer ensured, although it still remains the rule. According to the basic model set forth in section 2.4, effects of an increase in income anticipated for any future period on consumption in all future periods are positive on the average if weighted by discount rates (cf. (2.4.3.12)).

In the case where final personal wealth is included in the utility function, dominance of positive income effects on future consumption is nothing more than a likely presumption (cf. (2.5.3.15/16)).

In the case where hours of work are introduced into the utility function, even plausibility arguments about the signs of effects of increasing rates of remuneration on future consumption may be in default unless that function is specified in more detail (section 2.6).

The same inconclusiveness prevails in the case where uncertainty or sociometric factors are subsumed in the utility function without further specification (sections 2.9 and 2.10 respectively).

Due to the reducing effect of discount factors, the magnitude of income effects tends to decrease (in an absolute sense) according as the time interval between the change in income and the time of consumption is larger algebraically, i.e. according as the former is lagging farther behind the latter, or according as the latter is less far ahead of the former.

In the case of CAS, the marginal rates of consumption in any period with respect to income in the same period lie between 0 and 1 (cf. (3.1.1.12)).

3.8.3.2. *Income effects on other arguments of the utility function.* An increase in income anticipated for any period will raise final personal wealth, if the latter is included as a variable in the utility function (cf. (2.5.3.21)); this holds good irrespective of separability or non-separability of that function.

On the other hand, definite conclusions about the signs of income effects on optimal hours of work cannot be drawn even in case of a CAS utility function. The reason is that, in general, negative income sub-effects of increases of marginal rates of remuneration on working hours are partly counteracted and partly reinforced by substitution sub-effects in the same period and in other periods respectively (cf. (3.3.2.20) through (3.3.2.24)).

Effects of increases in anyone's income foreseen for any period on other people's future consumption are intractable unless the utility function incorporating the consumption by neighbours, etc. is specified further. In the case of CAS, we conclude that such effects are positive, but only according to the views of people expecting a change in their own future income (cf. (3.6.2.10/11) and (3.6.2.21)).

3.8.4. EFFECTS OF INTEREST RATES

3.8.4.1. *General.* In all cases we find that the effects of the rate of interest on consumption as well as on final personal wealth and hours of work (if included in the utility function) may be split into (at least) two components, viz. substitution sub-effects and wealth accumulation (or decumulation) sub-effects. Both these components may be negative as well as positive, independent of each other. The signs and sizes of the latter are related to the signs and sizes of intended wealth accumulation or -decumulation (i.e. with $\Delta K > 0$ or < 0 respectively). The substitution sub-effects, however, result from relative changes in the ratios of 'prices' of savings in different periods – reflected by discount factors, and affected by changes in interest rate(s); their signs depend, inter alia, on the kind of relationship between consumption in different periods with respect to utility (i.e. substitutability, independence or complementarity).

Changes in interest rates work out differently, of course, according as they relate to all future periods alike (in the case where a uniform rate of interest is assumed) or to a single future period (in the case where a variable rate of interest is assumed); in the latter case, effects of variations in rates of change in asset price levels and in consumer price levels may be subsumed among effects of changes in interest rates proper.

Last but not least, the effects differ according to the nature of the variables affected (consumption, final personal wealth, working hours).

3.8.4.2. Effects of changing a uniform rate of interest. The basic model (section 2.4) implies that substitution sub-effects average out to zero when weighted by discount rates (cf. (2.4.3.17)). Among the wealth accumulation sub-effects positive or negative elements will dominate according as the intended wealth accumulation is significantly positive or negative respectively.

Introduction of final personal wealth into the utility function tends to reduce the (algebraical) values of the substitution sub-effects (cf. (2.5.3.19)). This conclusion is reinforced in the case of CAS-specification of the utility function (cf. (3.2.1.13)).

Inclusion of either working hours or uncertainty in the model (sections 2.6 and 2.9 respectively) draws a smoke-screen over the effects of the rate of interest. Fortunately, however, this is lifted – at least partly – by CAS specification of that function. The substitution sub-effects of the interest rate on both consumption and working hours cancel out if weighted by the discount factors (cf. (3.3.2.33/34)).

Again, the wealth accumulation sub-effects are positive for lifetime "hoarders" and negative for lifetime "spenders"; the reverse is true for these component effects on working hours (cf. (3.3.2.28) and (3.3.2.29), respectively).

The sociometric version of the model – with or without CAS-specification of the utility function – shows expressions for the interest rate effects that are formally the same as those featured by the basic model (cf. (2.10.3.5/6)).

In the case of CAS-specification of the utility function in the basic model, we conclude that the substitution components of the interest rate in the near future and in the remote future are negative and positive respectively; moreover, these effects tend to be smaller in an absolute sense according as they relate to later periods (cf. (3.1.1.16)). M.m. the same conclusions apply to the continuous model of section 3.7 (cf. (3.7.3.1.19) through (3.7.3.1.21)).

In general, the effects of interest rates on final personal wealth (if included in the utility function) are too complicated to allow for definite conclusions. CAS-specification of this function, however, implies that the substitution sub-effects of increases in the interest rate on final personal wealth are always positive (cf. (3.2.1.11)).

Effects of interest rates on (optimum) hours of work are generally opposed to those on (optimum) consumption, although they are represented by similar expressions (cf. e.g. (3.3.2.28) through (3.3.2.34)).

3.8.4.3. *Effects of single-period changes in variable rates of interest.* The effects of changes in the rate of interest relating to a future period k on consumption in period l are similar to those of changes in a uniform rate of interest over the whole planning period. The difference, however, is that in the former case only that part of the terms constituting the effects in the latter case play a role that precede the period k; in other words, incidental changes in interest rates have but a restricted effect on consumption compared with overall changes in a uniform rate of interest (cf. (2.8.3.1.3)). This applies at least to the case in which (variable) rates of interest relating to future periods are considered as exogenous (data).

In the case of a CAS utility function, the substitution sub-effects of increasing the rate of interest raise consumption in periods $k > l$, i.e. from the period for which an increase in the rate of interest was anticipated onwards, and lower consumption in the same and preceding periods (cf. (3.4.3)).

Effects of changes in asset price levels and in consumer price levels on consumption are numerically equal to effects of changes in interest rates for corresponding periods, with the same and opposite sign, respectively.

In the continuous model, increases in the level or the rate of change in the rate of interest as a function of (future) time result in substitution and personal-wealth effects that resemble those derived for the basic discrete model.

3.8.5. CHANGE-IN-PERSONAL-WEALTH EFFECTS

Change-in-personal-wealth effects resemble income effects in the sense that more definite conclusions may be drawn about these two types of effects than about interest effects, and even more so.

Where both final and initial personal wealth are 'data', the final personal wealth effects equal the effects of intended change in personal wealth (over the expected lifetime), while they are equal but opposite to the initial personal wealth (IPW) effects.

According to the basic model, IPW-effects on consumption are *generally* positive, since their sum weighted by discount factors equals 1 (cf. (2.4.3.6)). In the case of a CAS utility function, *all* IPW-effects on consumption are positive (cf. (3.1.1.11)). Both conclusions remain valid after inclusion of final personal wealth in the utility function (cf. (2.5.3.20) and (3.2.1.9) respectively).

No specific conclusions about IPW-effects may be drawn if working hours (section 2.6), uncertainty (section 2.9), or other people's current consumption (section 2.10) are incorporated in the utility function unless the latter is specified further. In the case of CAS, we find that IPW-effects on consumption remain positive even if those additional variables are introduced into the utility function (cf. (3.3.2.16), (3.5.2.29) through (3.5.2.31), and (3.6.2.14/15) and (3.6.2.22), respectively).

Moreover, CAS ensures positive IPW-effects on final personal wealth and negative IPW-effects on working hours, in the case where these variables are included in the utility function (cf. (3.2.1.9) and (3.3.2.12), respectively, combined with (3.3.2.15)). In other words, initial affluence of individuals appears to promote their natural laziness. Contrariwise, a possible desire to leave their nearest and dearest well-off induces the testator to work harder.

In the continuous model, initial personal wealth raises the rates of consumption over the entire planning period (cf. (3.7.1.3.8) and (3.7.1.3.10)).

3.8.6. EFFECTS OF SURVIVAL RATES AND OF LIFE EXPECTANCY

Increases in the level of survival rates tend to raise or lower rates of consumption over the entire planning horizon according as the individuals concerned are lifetime 'hoarders' or 'spenders' respectively (cf. (3.7.3.2.10/11)); accordingly, increases in life-expectancy – as an integral of survival rates over time – have similar effects on the level of consumption (cf. (3.7.3.2.6\7)).

APPENDIX A TO CHAPTER 3

DERIVATION OF EULER CONDITIONS FOR INTEGRAL CONSTRAINED UTILITY MAXIMA AND OF EFFECTS FORMULAE[1]

3 A.1. *Euler conditions*

The problem is to find the condition for a (local) maximum of:

$$\omega = \int_0^L \varphi \{C(\tau), \dot{C}(\tau)\} \, d\tau \tag{3A.1.1}$$

subject to:

$$\int_0^L C(\tau) \, \delta(\tau) \, d\tau = \int_0^L Y(\tau) \, \delta(\tau) \, d\tau + K_0 - K_L = R_L, \tag{3A.1.2}$$

by an appropriate choice of the function $C(\tau)$ for τ between 0 and L, with given values of $C(\tau)$ and $\dot{C}(\tau) = dC(\tau)/d\tau$ at $\tau = 0$ and $\tau = L$, and a given function φ. This problem amounts to finding the maximum of:

$$z = \omega + \lambda \left(R_L - \int_0^L C(\tau) \, \delta(\tau) \, d\tau \right), \tag{3A.1.3}$$

with λ a Lagrangean multiplier.

Assume the *form* of the function $C(\tau)$ to be given, with parameters $\alpha' = \{\alpha_1 \cdots \alpha_T\}$ whose values are still to be fixed, i.e.

$$C(\tau) = C_* (\alpha', \tau). \tag{3A.1.4}$$

Then, in vector notation, the first-order condition for maximum z may be written as

$$z_\alpha = \int_0^L [\varphi_C C_\alpha + \varphi_{\dot{C}} \dot{C}_\alpha] \, d\tau - \lambda \int_0^L C_\alpha(\tau) \, \delta(\tau) \, d\tau = 0, \tag{3A.1.5}$$

[1] Cf. section 3.7.3.

with

$$z'_\alpha = \left\{\frac{\partial z}{\partial \alpha_1} \cdots \frac{\partial z}{\partial \alpha_T}\right\},$$

$$\overset{(.)}{C}_\alpha = \left\{\frac{\partial \overset{(.)}{C}(\tau)}{\partial \alpha_1} \cdots \frac{\partial \overset{(.)}{C}(\tau)}{\partial \alpha_T}\right\}, \quad \text{vectors of length } T, \text{ and}$$

$$\varphi_C = \frac{\partial \varphi}{\partial C(\tau)}, \quad \varphi_{\dot{C}} = \frac{\partial \varphi}{\partial \dot{C}(\tau)} \quad \text{scalars.}$$

Since:

$$\int_0^L \varphi_{\dot{C}} \dot{C}_\alpha \, d\tau = \varphi_{\dot{C}} C_\alpha \Big]_0^L - \int_0^L \dot{\varphi}_{\dot{C}} C_\alpha \, d\tau, \quad \text{with } \dot{\varphi}_{\dot{C}} = \frac{d}{d\tau}\left\{\frac{\partial \varphi}{\partial \dot{C}(\tau)}\right\}, \tag{3A.1.6}$$

(3A.1.5) becomes:

$$z_\alpha = \int_0^L [\varphi_C - \dot{\varphi}_{\dot{C}} - \lambda\delta]\, C_\alpha \, d\tau + \varphi_{\dot{C}} C_\alpha \Big]_0^I$$

$$= 0 \text{ irrespective of } C_\alpha \text{ as a function of } \tau, \text{ if:} \tag{3A.1.7}$$

$$\psi(C, \dot{C}) \overset{\text{def}}{=} \varphi_C - \varphi_{\dot{C}} = \lambda\delta,^2 \tag{3A.1.8}$$

and

$$\varphi_{\dot{C}}(0) = \varphi_{\dot{C}}(L) = 0. \tag{3A.1.9}$$

In order to ensure that z reaches a maximum for the vector α^* satisfying (3A.1.5) or (3A.1.7), we assume that the Hessian matrix:

$$Z_{\alpha\alpha'} = \left[\frac{\partial^2 z}{\partial \alpha \cdot \partial \alpha'}\right] \quad \text{of order } T \text{ is negative-definite.} \tag{3A.1.10}$$

From (3A.1.5) we derive:

$$Z_{\alpha\alpha'} = \int_0^L [\psi_C C_\alpha C'_\alpha + \psi_{\dot{C}} C_\alpha \dot{C}'_\alpha]\, d\tau + \int_0^L (\psi - \lambda\delta)\, C_{\alpha\alpha'}\, d\tau$$

$$= \int_0^L [\psi_C C_\alpha C'_\alpha + \psi_{\dot{C}} C \dot{C}'_\alpha]\, d\tau, \tag{3A.1.11}$$

(with $\psi_C = \partial\psi/\partial C(\tau)$ and $\psi_{\dot{C}} = \partial\psi/\partial \dot{C}(\tau)$

[2] For brevity's sake, time-arguments τ ($0 \leq \tau \leq L$) have been deleted.

since the second term at the right-hand side of (3A.1.11) vanishes for ψ satisfying (3A.1.8).

If we add to $Z_{\alpha\alpha'}$ its transpose $Z'_{\alpha\alpha'}$, we get:

$$Z_{\alpha\alpha'} + Z'_{\alpha\alpha'} = \int_0^L [2\psi_C C_\alpha C'_\alpha + \psi_{\dot{C}} (C_\alpha \dot{C}'_\alpha + \dot{C}_\alpha C'_\alpha)]\, \mathrm{d}\tau. \tag{3A.1.12}$$

Since:

$$\int_0^L \psi_{\dot{C}} (C_\alpha \dot{C}'_\alpha + \dot{C}_\alpha C'_\alpha)\, \mathrm{d}\tau = \psi_{\dot{C}} C_\alpha C'_\alpha \Big]_0^L - \int_0^L \dot{\psi}_{\dot{C}} C_\alpha C'_\alpha\, \mathrm{d}\tau, \tag{3A.1.13}$$

(3A.1.12) becomes:

$$Z_{\alpha\alpha'} + Z'_{\alpha\alpha'} = \int_0^L (2\psi_C - \dot{\psi}_{\dot{C}})\, C_\alpha C'_\alpha\, \mathrm{d}\tau + \psi_{\dot{C}} C_\alpha C'_\alpha \Big]_0^L. \tag{3A.1.14}$$

Negative-definiteness of $Z_{\alpha\alpha'} + Z'_{\alpha\alpha'}$ – or equivalently, of $Z_{\alpha\alpha'}$ – requires:

$$\cdot\varphi_{\cdot\cdot} \stackrel{\text{def}}{=} \psi_C - \tfrac{1}{2}\dot{\psi}_{\dot{C}} = \varphi_{CC} - \tfrac{1}{2}(3\dot{\varphi}_{C\dot{C}} - \ddot{\varphi}_{\dot{C}\dot{C}}) < 0, \tag{3A.1.15}$$

$$\text{with} \quad \dot{\varphi}_{C\dot{C}} = \frac{\mathrm{d}}{\mathrm{d}\tau}\left(\frac{\partial^2\varphi}{\partial C(\tau)\,\partial\dot{C}(\tau)}\right) \quad \text{and} \quad \ddot{\varphi}_{\dot{C}\dot{C}} = \frac{\mathrm{d}^2}{\mathrm{d}\tau^2}\left(\frac{\partial^2\varphi}{\partial\dot{C}^2(\tau)}\right),$$

and

$$\psi_{\dot{C}}(0) = \psi_{\dot{C}}(L) = 0 \quad \text{for } 0 \leq \tau \leq L; \tag{3A.1.16}$$

the latter condition is necessary (as well as sufficient) if no restrictions are imposed on either $C_\alpha(0)$ or $C_\alpha(L)$.

In the particular case where $\varphi\,\{C(\tau), \dot{C}(\tau)\}$ collapses into $\varphi\,\{C(\tau)\}$, the first-order condition for a maximum is simplified to:

$$\varphi_C(\tau) = \lambda\delta(\tau) \quad \text{for } 0 \leq \tau < L, \tag{3A.1.7'}$$

while its second-order condition is reduced to:

$$\varphi_{CC}(\tau) < 0 \quad \text{for } 0 \leq \tau \leq L. \tag{3A.1.15'}$$

3A.2. *Effects formulae*

In order to evaluate the effects of varying a vector or scalar x (say, ϱ or ΔK) on C, we differentiate (3A.1.7) partially with respect to x. As a result, we get:

$$Z_{x\alpha'} = \int_0^L [\psi_C C_x + \psi_{\dot{C}} \dot{C}_x - \delta\lambda_x - \lambda\delta_x]\, C'_\alpha\, \mathrm{d}\tau + \int_0^L \{\psi(C, \dot{C}) - \lambda\delta\}\, C_{x\alpha'}\, \mathrm{d}\tau. \tag{3A.2.1}$$

In order to get rid of $\dot{C}_x$ in (3 A.2.1) we proceed in a way similar to that leading from (3 A.1.11) to (3 A.1.14), viz. by means of the transpose $Z_{\alpha x'}$ of $Z_{x\alpha'}$. Differentiating (3 A.1.3) partially with respect to x, we find

$$z_x = \int_0^L [\varphi_C C_x + \varphi_{\dot{C}} \dot{C}_x - \lambda\delta C_x - C(\delta\lambda_x + \lambda\delta_x)]\,\mathrm{d}\tau,$$

$$= \int_0^L [(\psi_C - \lambda\delta)\, C_x - C(\delta\lambda_x + \lambda\delta_x)\,\mathrm{d}\tau, \tag{3 A.2.2}$$

on the analogy of (3 A.1.6) through (3 A.1.9), if the vector α is replaced by the vector x.

Differentiating (3 A.2.2) with respect to α, we find:

$$Z_{\alpha x'} = \int_0^L [(\psi_C C_\alpha + \psi_{\dot{C}} \dot{C}_\alpha)\, C'_x - \delta C_\alpha \lambda'_x - \lambda C_\alpha \delta'_x]\,\mathrm{d}\tau$$

$$+ \underset{(=0)}{\int_0^L (\psi_C - \lambda\delta)\, C_{\alpha x'}\,\mathrm{d}\tau}, \tag{3 A.2.3}$$

implying for its transpose

$$Z_{x\alpha'} = \int_0^L [\psi_C C_x C'_\alpha + \psi_{\dot{C}} C_x \dot{C}'_\alpha - (\delta\lambda_x + \lambda\delta_x)\, C'_\alpha]\,\mathrm{d}\tau, \tag{3 A.2.4}$$

since the second term in the second member of (3 A.2.3) vanishes by virtue of (3 A.1.8). Taking the unweighted average of (3 A.2.1) and (3 A.2.4) we obtain, on the analogy of (3A.1.12) through (3A.1.14), and by means of (3A,1.16):

$$Z_{x\alpha'} = \int_0^L [\dot{\varphi}_{..} C_x - \delta\lambda_x - \lambda\delta_x]\, C'_\alpha\,\mathrm{d}\tau = 0. \tag{3 A.2.5}$$

In order to ensure that $Z_{x\alpha'}$ vanishes irrespective of how C_α might turn out, the integrand in the right-hand member of (3A.2.5) should vanish. Hence,

$$\dot{\varphi}_{..} C_x - \delta\lambda_x = \lambda\delta_x \tag{3 A.2.6}$$

represents the general 'effects' formula for this kind of consumption and savings model; $\delta_x = 0$ unless $x = \varrho$, in which case $\delta_\varrho = (L - \tau)\,\delta$.

CHAPTER 4

A MICRO-SAVINGS MODEL BASED ON AN ADDI-LOG UTILITY FUNCTION

4.1. Derivation of the model

4.1.1. ASSUMPTIONS

The common assumptions underlying all versions of savings theory – dealt with in the present chapter as well as in the previous ones – is that individuals wish to maximize the utility of their consumption in future periods or points of time subject to a lifetime budget constraint.

The assumedly known elements ('data') of such a savings plan are at least:

(a) life expectancy L;

(b) the expected future incomes $Y_1, \ldots, Y_L$ (excluding interest on (dis)-savings originating after the initial date of the savings plan);

(c) the way in which utility ω depends upon the (as yet unknown) levels of consumption $C_1, \ldots, C_L$;

(d) initial personal wealth K_0 as well as desired personal wealth K_L to be left at the expected end of life;

(e) the rate of interest r at which future values (of income, consumption, and personal wealth) are discounted.

In particular, the utility function ω, mentioned under (c), has to be specified completely with respect to contents and form, in order to derive an empirically meaningful savings model, even at the cost of relinquishing its universal validity.

On the other hand, the values of the parameters need not be specified beforehand; on the contrary, they should be estimated on the basis of empirical data, within limits imposed by theory.

In the present section we confine ourselves to the 'basic' model, first presented in section 2.4, for simplicity's sake; in section 4.3 we shall deal summarily with alternative versions, most of which are outlined in chapters 2 and 3 above.

4.1.2. SPECIFICATION

The completely additive-separable utility function (3.1.1.1) introduced in chapter 3 provides a suitable starting point for a full specification of the utility function. One of its simplest versions results from positing:

$$\alpha_l(C_l) = \alpha_l \ln C_l, \tag{4.1.2.1}$$

yielding

$$\omega = \sum_{l=1}^{L} \alpha_l \ln C_l = \alpha' \ln C, \tag{4.1.2.2}$$

with

$$(\ln C)' = \{\ln C_1 \cdots \ln C_L\}$$

and

$$\alpha' = \{\alpha_1 \cdots \alpha_L\},$$

subject to

$$\alpha' \iota = 1,^1 \tag{4.1.2.3}$$

ι being a summation vector of length L.

Furthermore, we require

$$C > 0 \tag{4.1.2.4}$$

and

$$\alpha \geq 0, \tag{4.1.2.5}$$

meaning that C should be a positive vector (hence $\ln C$ a vector of real values), and that α should be a vector of non-negative elements.

In addition to simplicity, specifications (4.1.2.1) and (4.1.2.2), in conjunction with conditions (4.1.2.3) through (4.1.2.5), imply:

$$\omega_C = \dot{C}^{-1}\alpha \tag{4.1.2.6}$$

$$\text{with} \quad \dot{C}^{-1} = \begin{bmatrix} C_1^{-1} & & 0 \\ & \ddots & \\ 0 & & C_L^{-1} \end{bmatrix}$$

---

[1] In contradistinction to (4.1.2.4) and (4.1.2.5), requirement (4.1.2.3) is not essential, in view of the invariance of the results against monotonically or a fortiori linear increasing transformation of the utility function under deterministic and stochastic conditions respectively (cf. sections 2.4.4 and 2.9); the main purpose of (4.1.2.3) is to ensure the utmost simplicity, while a subsidiary objective is to facilitate the interpretation of the α_l (vide infra).

and

$$\Omega = \dot{C}^{-2}\dot{\alpha} = \begin{bmatrix} -\alpha_1 C_1^{-2} & & 0 \\ & \ddots & \\ 0 & & -\alpha_L C_L^{-2} \end{bmatrix}. \tag{4.1.2.7}$$

The meaning of (4.1.2.6) and (4.1.2.7) is that the marginal utility of consumption in any period is positive, independent of the consumption in any other period, while it decreases with increasing consumption in the same period. The latter two properties are not invariant against *arbitrary* monotonically increasing transformations of ω;[2] still, they have the advantage of simplifying the derivation and appealing to intuition. Moreover, utility functions such as (4.1.2.2) are already accepted in economic literature (cf. e.g. Modigliani and Brumberg [1955]).

In addition to simplicity and tractability, the addi-log linearity enables interpretation of its parameters α_l as indicators of the relative 'urgency to consume' in periods l. Such an interpretation is supported by the consideration that the effect of consumption C_l in any (current or future) period l on the lifetime utility ω is larger or smaller according as the corresponding α_l is larger or smaller. This relative 'urgency to consume' with respect to any future period, depends, inter alia, on the time-patterns of family conditions (for instance, first an increase and later on a decrease in the size of the family, expressed in equivalent adult units), as envisaged by the person planning his or her savings behaviour. Evidently, the expected time-pattern of the α's generally varies according to the individual involved. Anyhow, such an interpretation of the parameters of the utility function adds to its plausibility.

Apparently, the life expectancy and the units of time in which it is expressed determine the level of his or her α's, since

$$\bar{\alpha} = L^{-1} \sum_{l=1}^{L} \alpha_l = L^{-1} \tag{4.1.2.8}$$

holds good for their mean $\bar{\alpha}$; L, in turn depends, inter alia, on the individual's age and sex.

Especially the latter factors, in addition to the family dynamics mentioned above, infer that the savings theory fitting into this conceptual framework

[2] On the other hand, diagonality of the Hessian is preserved if ω is subjected to a linear transformation, while the negativity of the elements on the main diagonal is maintained under a weaker condition, viz. that the transformation function $f(\omega)$ must increase with and be concave in ω ($f_\omega > 0, f_{\omega\omega} < 0$).

relates to individual persons rather than to families or households. Naturally, this affects the application of savings theory to empirical data, as is shown in chapter 6.

The decisive argument in favour of the specification adopted, however, is the set of attractive properties of the savings- and consumption-functions it entails (cf. section 4.2).

The lifetime budget equation remains specified according to (2.4.1.6).

4.1.3. OPTIMIZATION AND OUTCOME

With ω specified by (4.1.2.2), equations (2.4.2.1), representing the first-order conditions for a utility maximum subject to the budget constraint, become:

$$\dot{C}^{-1}\alpha = R_L^{-1}d \tag{4.1.3.1}$$

(since by virtue of (4.1.2.6), $\omega_C'C = C'\omega_C = \iota'\alpha = 1$).

Pre-multiplication of both members of (4.1.3.1) by $R_L\dot{d}^{-1}\dot{C}$ results in:

$$C = R_L\dot{d}^{-1}\alpha = \dot{R}\alpha, \tag{4.1.3.2}$$

with

$$\dot{R} = \begin{bmatrix} R_1 & & 0 \\ & \ddots & \\ 0 & & R_L \end{bmatrix}$$

and

$$R_\tau = R_L \cdot d_\tau^{-1} \quad \text{for } \tau = 1, \dots, L;$$

or, in scalar notation:

$$C_\tau = \alpha_\tau R_\tau = \alpha_\tau \left[(K_0 - K_L)(1 + r)^{\tau - L} + \sum_{l=1}^{L} Y_l (1 + r)^{\tau - l}\right] \tag{4.1.3.3}$$

$$\text{for } \tau = 1, \dots L;$$

this means that prospective consumption in any period τ is a fraction α_τ (representing the prospective urgency to consume in that period) of lifetime resources discounted to the beginning of period τ.

In particular, we get:

$$\begin{aligned} C_1 &= \alpha_1 R_1 \\ &= \alpha_1 \left[(K_0 - K_L)(1 + r)^{1-L} + \sum_{l=1}^{L} Y_l (1 + r)^{1-l}\right], \\ &= \alpha_1 Y_1 + \alpha_1 \left[(K_0 - K_L)(1 + r)^{1-L} + \sum_{l=2}^{L} Y_l (1 + r)^{1-l}\right], \end{aligned} \tag{4.1.3.4}$$

for the current period $\tau = 1$; the latter is the most important one from a practical point of view, and virtually the only one to which empirical analysis can be and is applied.

R_1 denotes the present value of the financial resources (coming) at the disposal of the consumer. Likewise, we find for current savings:

$$S_1 = Y_1 - C_1$$
$$= (1 - \alpha_1) Y_1 - \alpha_1 [(K_0 - K_L)(1 + r)^{1-L} + \sum_{l=2}^{L} Y_l (1 + r)^{1-l}]. \quad (4.1.3.5)$$

The expression for prospective savings S_τ in any (future) period τ is somewhat more complicated. According to the definitional equation:

$$S_\tau = Y_\tau^+ - C_\tau = Y_\tau + r(K_{\tau-1} - K_0) - C_\tau; \quad (4.1.3.6)$$

total income Y_τ^+ includes income $r(K_{\tau-1} - K_0)$ on savings accumulated (or decumulated) from the beginning of period 1 through the end of period $\tau - 1$ – in addition to Y_τ, which excludes these subsequent interest receipts or payments.

Substitution of (4.1.3.6) into (2.4.1.5) yields:

$$K_\tau - K_0 = \sum_{l=1}^{\tau} Y_l (1 + r)^{\tau-l} - \hat{\alpha}_\tau R_\tau, \quad (4.1.3.7)$$

with $\hat{\alpha}_\tau = \sum_{l=1}^{\tau} \alpha_l$ for $\tau = 1, \ldots, L$.

Substitution of (4.1.3.7) and (4.1.3.4) into (4.1.3.6) results in:

$$S_\tau = Y_\tau - \alpha_\tau R_\tau + r(\sum_{l=1}^{\tau-1} Y_l (1 + r)^{\tau-l-1} - \hat{\alpha}_{\tau-1} R_{\tau-1}) \delta_{\tau>1}. \quad (4.1.3.8)$$

The consumption and savings functions (4.1.3.3) through (4.1.3.5), as well as (4.1.3.8), satisfy the requirement of dimensional homogeneity stressed by (a.o.) de Jong [1967].

As money flows per unit of time, C, S and Y have the dimension $[\mathrm{M}] \cdot [\mathrm{T}]^{-1}$, with M denoting money and T denoting length of time. Because of summation over time, the present value of the expected future income flow has dimension [M], just as the change in personal wealth. Hence, total resources R also have dimension [M], and consequently α has dimension $[\mathrm{T}]^{-1}$. This also follows from (4.1.2.3), implying that the sum of α's over time has dimension one. Accordingly, the α's are proportional to the unit of time chosen.

The dimensional soundness of the consumption and savings functions derived bolsters our confidence in the appropriateness of our specifications.

DIAGRAM 4.1.
Savings in relation to psychological, biological and economic factors

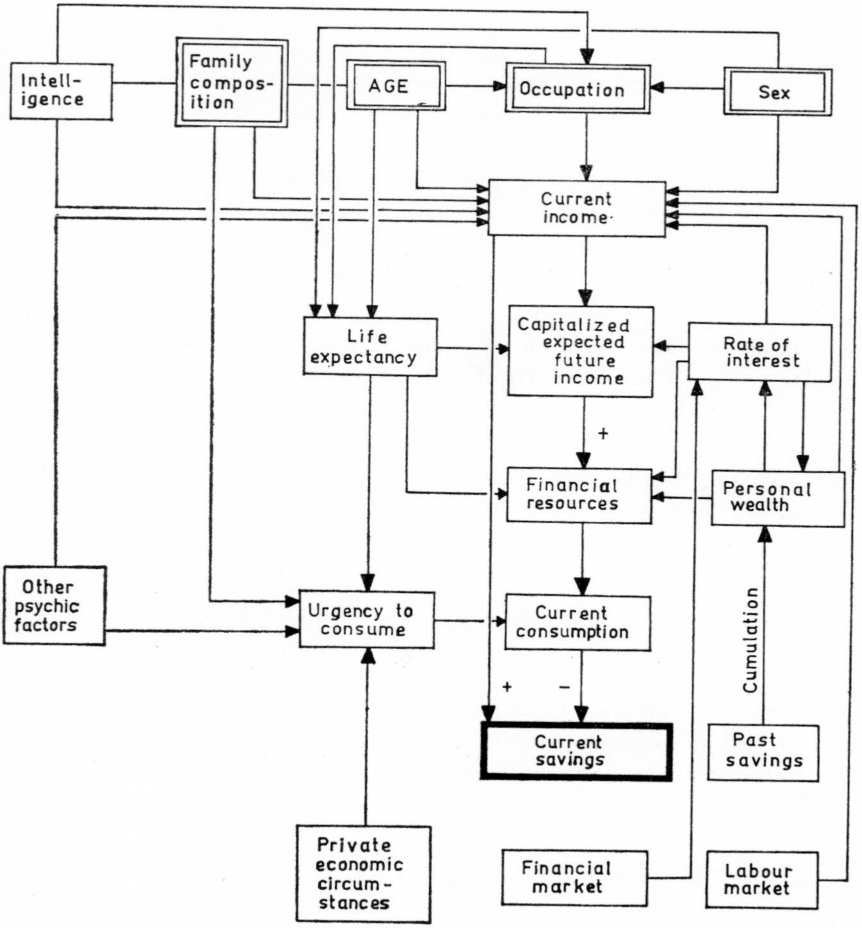

Thanks to Ω being negative definite, as shown by (4.1.2.7), equations (4.1.3.2) through (4.1.3.5) and (4.1.3.8) meet the second-order conditions for a constrained utility maximum. In view of the convexity of ω in terms of its arguments, the local maximum ensured by the first-order and second-order optimum conditions guarantees a global maximum as well.

In conclusion, the derivation of the micro-savings model is re-enacted in diagram 4.2.

4.2. Interpretation of the model

4.2.1. GENERAL PROPERTIES AND FRAMEWORK OF THE MODEL

The consumption and savings functions derived in the preceding section are linear and homogeneous in current and prospective future income as well as in initial and desired final personal wealth; on the other hand, savings and consumption depend upon the rate(s) of interest in an essentially non-linear way.

All these functions feature but one 'parameter', viz. the α_τ – and in particular the α_1 for consumption and savings in the current period $\tau = 1$; however, it still depends on personal characteristics of the consumers.

Diagram 4.1 shows how the 'hard core' of economic variables at the right-hand side is bordered (or fenced-in) by the basically responsible psychological and biological factors in the first column and in the first row, respectively. This means that the savings and consumption functions are more complicated than might be gathered from a glimpse at the deceptively simple-looking expressions such as (4.1.3.3.).

Disentangling the intricacies of individual savings behaviour is the main objective of the empirical analysis described in chapter 6.

4.2.2. SIGNS AND LEVELS OF CONSUMPTION AND SAVINGS

Naturally and logically consumption should always be positive, as required by (4.1.2.4). A *necessary* condition for it has already been expressed by (2.4.1.7), which may be rewritten as:

$$Y'd - \Delta K = R_L > 0. \qquad (4.2.2.1)$$

In view of (4.1.3.2) and (4.1.2.5), (4.2.2.1) also proves to be a *sufficient* condition for optimal $C = C^* > 0$, i.e. positiveness of C_l^* in any (future) period $l\,(=1, \ldots, L)$.

The first and the second term between brackets in the third member of (4.1.3.3) represent the income and wealth components, respectively, of R_τ.

Theoretically, both components of R_L may be negative: entrepreneurs may suffer or expect to suffer losses, resulting in negative values of Y_τ. Still, a negative present value of the entire expected future stream of incomes seems highly unlikely.

On the other hand, a positive value of the intended change in personal

DIAGRAM 4.2.

Derivation of the micro-savings model

Possible future expenditures $C_1, \ldots, C_L$

Utility function (non-specified) $\omega = \omega(C_1, \ldots, C_L)$

Expected income (except from future savings) $Y_1, \ldots, Y_L$

'Want' coefficients $\alpha_1, \ldots, \alpha_L$

Utility function (specified) $\omega = \sum_{l=1}^{L} \alpha_l \ln C_l$ maximized subject

desired K_L final wealth $=$ given K_0 initial wealth budget equation $+ \sum_{l=1}^{L} (Y_l - C_l)(1 + r)^{L-l}$ capitalized cumulated savings

Expected rate of interest r

Optimal (future) consumer expenditures
$$C_t = \alpha_t \left[(K_0 - K_L)(1 + r)^{t-L} + \sum_{l=1}^{L} Y_l (1 + r)^{t-l} \right]$$

Optimal current savings
$$S_1 = Y_1 - C_1 = (1 - \alpha_1) Y_1 - \alpha_1 \left[(K_0 - K_L)(1 + r)^{1-L} + \sum_{l=2}^{L} Y_l (1 + r)^{1-l} \right]$$

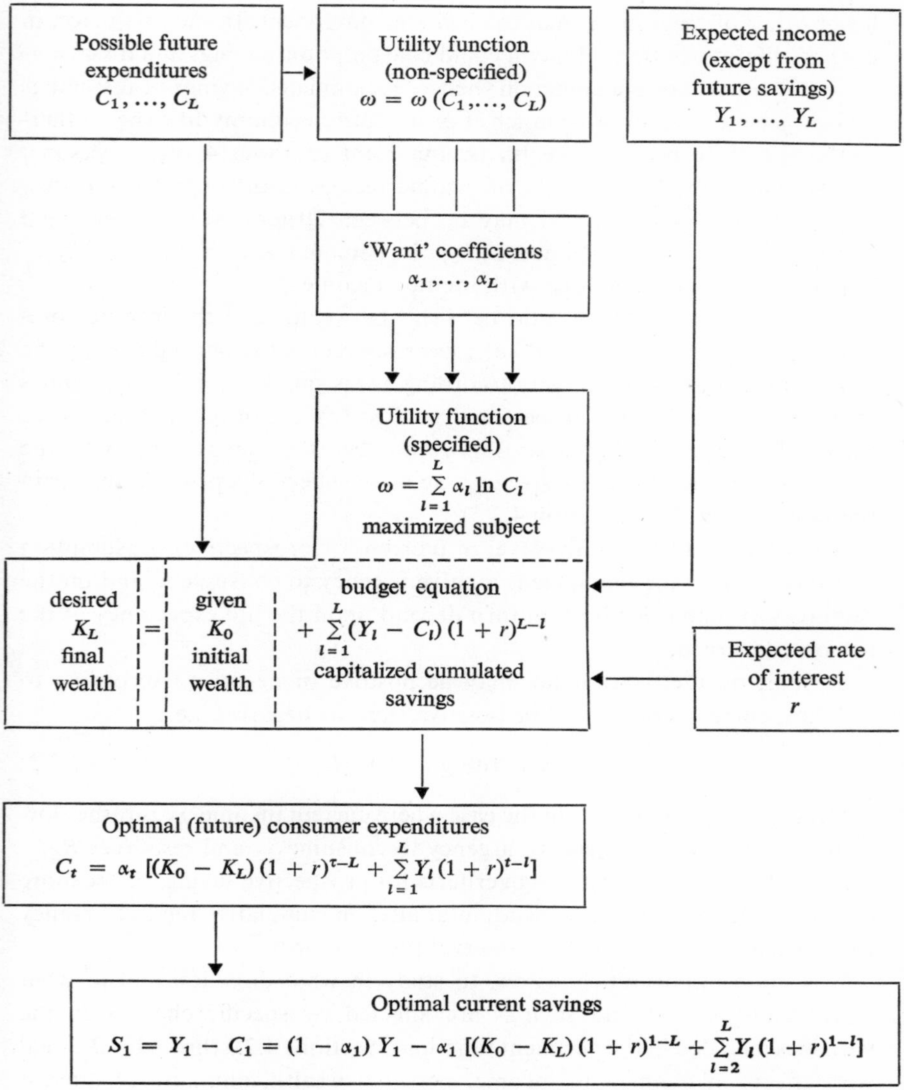

wealth $K_L - K_0$ is quite plausible, especially in the case where K_0 is negative, and the person in debt would feel that he could not sustain, let alone increase his indebtedness till the end of his life.

Apart from sign, however, the wealth component will generally be of a lower order of magnitude than the income component. In the first place, in people's lifetime pattern of income and consumption, savings and dissavings are but a temporary phenomenon; hence, accumulated savings or dissavings do not generally amount to much. For an entire economy like the Netherlands, aggregate personal wealth is equivalent to about 4 years' personal income. Since for the majority of income recipients the expected life-span extends beyond 4 years, and may lie between 20 and 30 years, personal wealth, and a fortiori intended *change* in personal wealth, is generally of minor importance, compared with lifetime income.

In the second place, the ratio between the wealth and the income components of the present value R_1 of total resources is further reduced by the discount factor, which is larger (according as l is smaller) for future incomes than for intended change in personal wealth – except in the final period L. This difference in quantitative importance between the two parts of the 'resources' appears to be decisive in gauging the effect of a possible change in the rate of interest (cf. section 4.2.5).

According to (4.1.3.3), the level of (current or prospective) consumption depends both on the (envisaged) relative urgency to consume α_τ and on the resources available R_τ; both in turn depend upon the life expectancy of the person concerned.

Savings, on the other hand, may be positive or negative. According to (4.1.3.5), current savings will be positive, zero or negative, i.e.:

$$S_1 \gtreqless 0 \quad \text{according as} \quad Y_1/R_1 \gtreqless \alpha_1 . \tag{4.2.2.2}$$

Hence, *dis*savings appear in the case where current income Y_1 is rather low compared with current relative urgency to consume α_1 and resources R_1.

According to (4.1.3.8), the sign criteria for prospective savings S_τ are more complicated, because they depend, inter alia, on cumulative relative urgency to consume $\hat{\alpha}_{\tau-1}$ over the time interval preceding period τ.

It is more important, however, to study in what direction and to what extent consumption and savings are affected by specific changes in the variables included in the pertinent functions. Sections 4.2.3 through 4.2.5 deal with effects of changes in income, personal wealth, and rate of interest respectively.

4.2.3. EFFECTS OF CHANGES IN INCOME

From (4.1.3.3) we derive:

$$\frac{\partial C_\tau}{\partial Y_{\tau'}} = \alpha_\tau (1 + r)^{\tau - \tau'},^{3} \text{ for } \tau, \tau' = 1, \ldots, L$$

$$\gtreqless \alpha_\tau \text{ according as } \tau \gtreqless \tau', \text{ but always} > 0. \quad (4.2.3.1)$$

Hence, differences in effect of specific changes in income envisaged for later or earlier periods appear in the discount factor $(1 + r)^{\tau - \tau'}$ only, and not through the relative urgency to consume: the latter is confined to the period τ for which the sensitivity of consumption C_τ with respect to changes in the data is studied.

For the current period in particular, we obtain:

$$\frac{\partial C_1}{\partial Y_{\tau'}} = \alpha_1 (1 + r)^{1 - \tau'} \leq \alpha_1 \quad \text{for } \tau' = 1, \ldots, L. \qquad (4.2.3.2)$$

Consequently, effects of expected income on current consumption are smaller according as the period for which the change in income is envisaged is farther ahead in time. Therefore, current consumption is affected most by a change in current income:

$$\partial C_1 / \partial Y_1 = \alpha_1 . \qquad (4.2.3.3)$$

This equation might be considered as expressing the marginal propensity to consume. This would agree completely with the psycho-physiological interpretation of α_1 presented in section 4.1.2. Numerically, however, such a concept of 'marginal propensity to consume' appears to differ widely from its Keynesian namesake, with a psychological connotation. The latter is claimed – on empirical, albeit dubious grounds – to lie somewhere between $\frac{1}{2}$ and 1 in general. Allegedly it depends, inter alia, on the occupational status of the person concerned; specifically, the employees' marginal propensity to consume would be nearer to the upper limit (1), while that of the entrepreneur would be nearer to the lower limit (of about $\frac{1}{2}$).

On the other hand, the value of α_1 will generally be much smaller (than $\frac{1}{2}$). If the relative urgency to consume in the current period (α_1) does not deviate

---

[3] This formula may also be obtained from (3.1.1.10), since $\sum_{\tau=1}^{L} \alpha_{\tau\tau}^{-1} d_\tau^2 = R_L^{-2}$ and $\alpha_{ll}^{-1} d_l d_{l'} = \alpha_l R_L^2 (1 + r)^{l - l'}$. Similarly, the formulae for the other effects may be derived from those obtained in section 3.1.1, considering, inter alia, that $C_\tau d_\tau = \alpha_\tau R_L$ and $\lambda = R_L^{-1}$. The method adopted in the main text is, however, simpler.

much from its average value ($\bar{\alpha}$) over the entire remaining life-span (L), its order of magnitude will be L^{-1}. Unless people's age (in developed countries) exceeds (say) 65 years, L will be at least 10 years, hence L^{-1} – and similarly α_1 – is less than 0.1. Moreover – as observed in section 4.1.3 – the level of the α's (including α_1) is inversely proportional to the unit of measurement chosen for the unit periods. In the extreme, continuous case, the rate of flow of consumption $C(\tau)$ at any point of time τ will not at all be affected by a change, however great, in the rate of flow of income at any (whether the same or another) point of time (cf. section 4.3.5).

The main reason for the wide divergence between the theoretical and the empirical values of the marginal propensity to consume, as noted above, is the following: what is usually called the marginal propensity to consume does not measure the purely direct effect of an *isolated* change in current income on current consumption, but a joint *direct and indirect* effect of such a change; this means that it includes effects of changes in prospective future income *induced* by a change in current income.

Most empirical studies – with the notable exception of the micro-analysis presented in chapter 6 – do not distinguish between such direct and indirect effects of a change in current income; presumably, it was found impossible to do so. The only known attempt to discriminate between both types of effects is due to Friedman [1957], distinguishing between 'permanent' and 'transitory' income.

Mathematically speaking, the difference between the marginal propensity to consume as defined by (4.2.3.3) and the Keynesian homonymous concept is that the former represents a *partial* derivative and the latter a *total* derivative. The two concepts are mutually related by:

$$\frac{\mathrm{d}C_1}{\mathrm{d}Y_1} = \frac{\partial C_1}{\partial Y_1} + \sum_{l=2}^{L} \frac{\partial C_1}{\partial Y_l} \cdot \frac{\mathrm{d}Y_l}{\mathrm{d}Y_1}, \tag{4.2.3.4}$$

In general, the income-expectation reaction-intensities $\mathrm{d}Y_l/\mathrm{d}Y_1$ are assumed to be positive. Suppose – merely for the sake of argument – that the 'elasticities of expectation'[4] of Y_l with respect to Y_1 are the same for all $l > 1$, i.e. that:

$$\frac{\mathrm{d}Y_l}{\mathrm{d}Y_1} = \varepsilon \frac{Y_l}{Y_1}, \tag{4.2.3.5}$$

[4] This concept has been introduced in a somewhat different context (i.e. with respect to prices) by J.R. Hicks [1939].

with ε a positive constant; then (4.2.3.4) would change into:

$$\frac{dC_1}{dY_1} = \alpha_1 \left[1 + \varepsilon \sum_{l=2}^{L} (1 + r)^{1-l} (Y_l/Y_1)\right]. \tag{4.2.3.6}$$

In the empirical analysis presented in chapter 6, the summation term in (4.2.3.6) – somewhat modified by means of survival rates, as explained in section 4.3.3 – has been called the 'capitalization factor'. Its value, depending upon life-expectancy, the lifetime pattern of prospective income and the rate of interest, has been computed for Dutch income recipients of various ages and occupations, and for both sexes, at a rate of interest of 4.08 per cent per annum, prevailing in the Netherlands during the reference year 1960.

For gainfully occupied people aged 35 and 55 years these factors range around 20 and 10 respectively, with fairly small differences between occupations and between the sexes. With life expectancies at those ages of about 41 and 24 years, the values of α_1 are around 0.024 and 0.042 respectively. Hence, according to (4.2.3.6), dC_1/dY_1 would become 0.024 $(1 + 19\varepsilon)$ for people aged 35 years, and about 0.042 $(1 + 9\varepsilon)$ for people aged 55 years. Consequently, in order to yield values dC_1/dY_1 of 0.55 and 0.95, i.e. near the lower and upper limits above, ε must assume the following values for these two ages:

TABLE 4.1.

Values of ε for selected ages and corresponding to selected values of dC_1/dY_1

$\frac{dC_1}{dY_1}$	ε age in years 35	45
0.55	1.2	1.3
0.95	2.0	2.4

These values of ε, all exceeding 1, do not look plausible: one would expect a certain relative change in current income to effect a less than proportional rather than a more than proportional change in prospective future income, as implied by $\varepsilon > 1$.[5] Part of these anomalies may be due to underestimation

[5] In the same sense, Hicks [1939, p. 205] suggests that 0 and 1 are the extreme values of the elasticities of expectation (ε). Also Friedman's [1957] distinction between 'permanent' and 'transitory' income likewise presupposes a value of $\varepsilon < 1$.

of α_1 at ages 35 and 55 by equating it to L^{-1}, since at those ages people may feel that the requirements consumption imposes on their financial resources tends to be less severe in the future than in the present.

Moreover, an increase or decrease in current income may have an effect in the same direction, not only on expected future income, but also on intended change in personal wealth $(K_0 - K_L)$. This means that a term:

$$+ \frac{\partial C_1}{\partial (K_0 - K_L)} \cdot \frac{\mathrm{d}(K_0 - K_L)}{\mathrm{d}Y_1} = \alpha_1 (1 + r)^{1-L} \frac{\mathrm{d}(K_0 - K_L)}{\mathrm{d}Y_1}$$

should be added to the second member of (4.2.3.4). It is questionable, however, whether $K_0 - K_L$ is affected at all by a change in Y_1, and if so, why the effect would be positive rather than negative. Moreover, the effect would probably be small anyhow, in view of the low value of $\alpha_1(1 + r)^{1-L}$, especially for large L.

We conclude that the gap between the empirical and the theoretical propensities to consume may be explained partly, but – to all appearances – not completely. Still, this should not surprise us, in view of the insufficient theoretical foundation of most empirical consumption functions for which marginal propensities are estimated.

For reactions of current savings on changes in current or prospective income we find:

$$\partial S_1 / \partial Y_1 = 1 - \alpha_1 > 0, \tag{4.2.3.7}$$

and

$$\partial S_1 / \partial Y_\tau = -\alpha_1 (1 + r)^{1-\tau} < 0 \quad \text{for } \tau = 2, \ldots, L. \tag{4.2.3.8}$$

The latter result agrees with common sense (the better one's income prospects, the less the need to save or the more justification to dissave in the present).

By combining (4.2.3.1) with (4.2.3.7) and (4.2.3.8), we get the identities:

$$\frac{\partial C_1}{\partial Y_\tau} + \frac{\partial S_1}{\partial Y_\tau} = \delta_{1\tau} \quad \text{for } \tau = 1, \ldots, L \quad \text{with } \delta_{1\tau} = \begin{cases} 1 & \text{for } \tau = 1 \\ 0 & \text{for } \tau > 1. \end{cases} \tag{4.2.3.9}$$

In words: the derivatives of current consumption and of current savings with respect to income in the same period τ are each others' complements, with respect to 1 and to 0, according as $\tau = 1$ or >1. This appears to hold good for the total derivatives (marginal propensities to consume and to save) as well as for the partial ones. In the latter sense, because of (4.2.3.9), the marginal propensity to save is as near to 1 as the marginal propensity to consume is near to 0; for the 'total' marginal propensities, however, it is just the other way round. In principle, the 'total' marginal propensity to save dS_1/dY_1 might even be negative, viz. whenever dC_1/dY_1 exceeds 1. According to (4.2.3.6), the latter contingency could formally be brought about by a sufficiently (albeit unrealistically) high value of ε. In the particular case where $\varepsilon = 1$, $dC_1/dY_1 > 1$ could be due to a relatively high value of α_1, i.e. exceeding L^{-1}; for $\alpha_1 = L^{-1}$ and $\varepsilon = 1$, however, dC_1/dY_1 could surpass 1 only if the average lifetime growth rate of Y_t exceeds r, in order to overcompensate the reducing effect of the discount factor $(1 + r)^{1-t}$. Consequently, we may conclude that a 'total' marginal propensity to consume larger than 1, and concomitantly a negative 'total' marginal propensity to save, are rare.

4.2.4. EFFECTS OF CHANGES IN PERSONAL WEALTH

From (4.1.3.4) and (4.1.3.5) we derive:

$$\frac{\partial C_1}{\partial (K_0 - K_L)} = - \frac{\partial S_1}{\partial (K_0 - K_L)} = \alpha_1 (1 + r)^{1-L}. \qquad (4.2.4.1)$$

Hence, current consumption is larger and current savings are smaller according as initial personal wealth is more substantial; and the other way round with respect to desired final personal wealth. These conclusions fall in line with common sense: the larger the cushion of initial personal wealth to fall back upon in hard times, the less need there is to save; a similar argument applies if a *lower* target of final personal wealth is aimed at.

By comparing (4.2.4.1) with (4.2.3.2), we conclude that the effect of varying intended net change in personal wealth over the individual's lifetime on consumption is never larger and generally (except for $\tau = L$) smaller than the effect of an equal change in income, since the respective discount factors satisfy:

$$(1 + r)^{1-L} < (1 + r)^{1-\tau} \qquad (4.2.4.2)$$

for $\tau = 2, \ldots, L - 1$, and positive r.

4.2.5. EFFECTS OF CHANGES IN THE RATE OF INTEREST

From (4.1.3.3) we derive:

$$\frac{\partial C_\tau}{\partial r} = -\alpha_\tau (L - \tau)(K_0 - K_L)(1 + r)^{\tau-L-1}$$
$$- \alpha_\tau \sum_{l=1}^{L} (l - \tau) Y_l (1 + r)^{\tau-l-1}. \qquad (4.2.5.1)$$

This partial derivative may be positive, zero or negative, since both terms may be positive or negative independently. The first (change-in-wealth) term is negative or positive according as $K_0 > K_L$ or $K_0 < K_L$ $(\tau < L)$, and zero if $K_0 = K_L$ and/or $\tau = L$; the last (income flow) term is positive or negative according as

$$\sum_{l=1}^{\tau-1} (\tau - l) Y_l (1 + r)^{\tau-l-1} > \quad \text{or} \quad < \sum_{l=\tau+1}^{L} (l - \tau) Y_l (1 + r)^{\tau-l-1}.$$

On the basis of the addi-log utility function (4.1.2.2) the substitution component (3.1.1.14) of the interest effect becomes:

$$\left(\frac{\partial C_\tau}{\partial r}\right)_{\mathrm{I}} = \alpha_\tau (1 + r)^{L-\tau-1} R_L \sum_{l=1}^{L} \alpha_l (l - \tau); \qquad (4.2.5.2)$$

$$\lesseqqgtr 0 \text{ according as } \sum_{l=1}^{L} \alpha_l l \lesseqqgtr 1;$$

the wealth accumulation (or decumulation) component passes into:

$$\left(\frac{\partial C_\tau}{\partial r}\right)_{\mathrm{II}} = \alpha_\tau (1 + r)^{L-\tau-1} \sum_{l=1}^{L} (\alpha_l R_L - Y_l l) d_l$$

$$\lesseqqgtr 0 \text{ according as } R_L \lesseqqgtr \sum_{l=1}^{L} Y_l l d_l / (\sum_{l=1}^{L} \alpha_l d_l). \qquad (4.2.5.3)$$

Anyhow, for $\tau = 1$, the last (income flow) term in the second member of (4.2.5.1) will always be negative, and the first term will have the same (positive or negative) sign as $K_L - K_0$ (or be zero if $K_0 = K_L$):

$$\frac{\partial C_1}{\partial r} = -\frac{\partial S_1}{\partial r} = -\alpha_1 (L - 1)(K_0 - K_L)(1 + r)^{-L}$$
$$-\alpha_1 \sum_{l=2}^{L} (l - 1) Y_l (1 + r)^{-l}. \qquad (4.2.5.4)$$

The sum of the capital-change and the income-flow effects, represented by those two terms – both multiplied by minus α_1 – may be positive, zero or negative, i.e.:

$$\frac{\partial S_1}{\partial r} \gtreqless 0, \quad \text{according as} \quad K_0 \gtreqless K_L - (L-1)^{-1} \sum_{l=2}^{L} (l-1)\, Y_l\, (1+r)^{L-l}. \tag{4.2.5.5}$$

Since the last summation term is always positive, $\partial S_1/\partial r$ will be positive anyhow (and $\partial C_1/\partial r$ will be negative accordingly) for $K_0 > K_L$ – a sufficient, but not a necessary condition.

On the other hand, in order that $\partial S_1/\partial r$ be positive (and $\partial C_1/\partial r$ be negative), K_L should exceed K_0 by the life expectancy times the average of the prospective incomes accruing by compound interest at the rate of r till the end of period L and weighted by the fractions of time $(l-1)/(L-1)$ left after the first period has expired. The latter contingency seems rather unlikely; consequently, we may expect that in general an overall rise in the rate of interest favours current savings, i.e. discourages consumption.

4.3. *Modifications of the model*

4.3.1. SYNOPSIS

The consumption and savings functions derived in section 4.1 may be modified, and especially refined, in various respects, alternatively or cumulatively, along the lines indicated in sections 2.5 through 2.10 and sections 3.2.through 3.7. Here, we confine ourselves to the simpler variations on the main theme.

First, the basic utility function is generalized by taking account of possible non-zero minimum consumption levels (section 4.3.2).

Second, survival rates are incorporated in the summands of the expression for the present value of the lifetime expected income stream instead of life expectancy in the upper limit of the summation – with a corresponding change in the meaning of desired final personal wealth (section 4.3.3).

Third, the rate of interest is allowed to vary over the (current or prospective) periods; in the same context, prospective changes in levels of consumer and/or asset prices are introduced into the lifetime budget equation, hence in the consumption and savings functions (section 4.3.4).

Finally, continuous variables take the place of discontinuous ones, with consequences for the form of the functions in which they appear (section 4.3.5).

The operational significance of these alternatives is reviewed in section 4.3.6.

4.3.2. CONSUMPTION MINIMA

The simple utility functions (4.1.1.2) can be generalized into:

$$\omega = \alpha' \ln (C - \underline{C}) = \alpha' \ln C_{-}, \text{[6]} \tag{4.3.2.1}$$

with

$\underline{C}' = \{\underline{C}_1 \cdots \underline{C}_L\}$ a vector of non-negative (minimum) subsistence consumption levels $\underline{C}_l$ envisaged for periods 1 through L,

so that $C_{-} = C - \underline{C}$ represents a non-negative vector of 'excess' consumption; again, α satisfies (4.1.2.3).

Accordingly, the budget constraint (2.4.1.6) may be rewritten as:

$$\Delta K = (Y_{-} - C_{-})' d, \tag{4.3.2.2}$$

with

$$Y_{-} = Y - \underline{C}.$$

Thus, the problem of maximizing (4.3.2.1) subject to (4.3.2.2) is formally reduced to maximizing (4.1.2.2) subject to (2.4.1.6), resulting in:

$$C_{-} = \dot{R}_{-}\alpha, \tag{4.3.2.3}$$

with $\dot{R}_{-}$ a diagonal matrix with elements

$$(R_{-})_{\tau} = \{ - \Delta K + (Y - \underline{C})'\} d_{\tau} = (C'_{-} d) d_{\tau}$$

the 'supernumerary' financial resources for financing 'excess' consumption C_{-}.

---

[6] The scalar antilog counterpart of (4.3.2.1) is:

$$\text{antilog}\, \omega = \prod_{l=1}^{L} (C_l - \underline{C}_l)^{\alpha_l}$$

which is analogous to the generalization by Tinbergen [1942] of the Cobb-Douglas production function (with C_l and $\underline{C}_l$ representing quantities of factors of production l consumed and minimally required, respectively), and antilog ω the amount of product thereby generated, i.e. a Stone-type model (cf. footnote 1 on page 28).

In scalar notation, (4.3.2.3) is expressed by:

$$C_\tau = \underline{C}_\tau + \alpha_\tau [(K_0 - K_L)(1+r)^{\tau-L} + \sum_{l=1}^{L} (Y_l - \underline{C}_l)(1+r)^{\tau-l}]$$

$$= \{(1-\alpha_\tau)\underline{C}_\tau - \alpha_\tau \sum_{l \neq \tau} \underline{C}_l (1+r)^{\tau-l}\}$$

$$+ \alpha_\tau [(K_0 - K_L)(1+r)^{\tau-L} + \sum_{l=1}^{L} Y_l (1+r)^{\tau-l}], \tag{4.3.2.4}$$

corresponding to (4.1.3.3), based on the simpler utility function (4.1.2.2).

According to (4.3.2.4), prospective consumption C_τ is again a linear function of the wealth variables K_0 and K_L and the income variables Y_l; due to the threshold values $\underline{C}_l(\underline{C}_\tau)$, however, that function is no longer homogeneous. The difference between C_τ according to (4.3.2.4) and according to (4.1.3.3) equals the term between curled brackets in the third member of (4.3.2.4); hence, this difference is positive, zero or negative according as

$$C_\tau \gtreqless \frac{\alpha_\tau}{1-\alpha_\tau} \sum_{l \neq \tau}^{L} \underline{C}_l (1+r)^{\tau-l}.$$

In view of the fact that $(1+r)^{\tau-l} \gtreqless 1$ according as $\tau \gtreqless l$, positiveness of the 'constant term' represented by $\{\quad\}$ will tend to prevail for small τ, and negativeness for large τ.

The formulae for income effects (C_Y) and (change of) wealth effects ($C_{(\Delta)K}$) remain the same as those shown by (4.2.3.1) through (4.2.3.3) and (4.2.4.1), respectively. In order to present the interest effects, however, we have to replace Y_l in (4.2.5.1) by $Y_l - \underline{C}_l$; consequently, the present model, with threshold levels of consumption will yield negative values for the interest effects on savings more readily than the former one.

4.3.3. SURVIVAL RATES INSTEAD OF LIFE EXPECTANCY

For the utility function, replacement of life expectancy by survival rates means a mere extension of its number of arguments from L to M (maximum lifetime):

$$\omega = \sum_{l=1}^{M} \tilde{\alpha}_l \ln C_l, \quad \text{with} \sum_{l=1}^{M} \tilde{\alpha}_l = 1. \tag{4.3.3.1}$$

Maximization of (4.3.3.1) subject to the lifetime budget equation (2.4.1.5) yields:

$$C_\tau = \tilde{\alpha}_\tau \cdot \tilde{R}_\tau, \tag{4.3.3.2}$$

with

$$\tilde{R}_\tau = (K_0 - K_F)(1 + r)^{\tau - M} + \sum_{l=1}^{M} Y_l s_l (1 + r)^{\tau - l} \quad \text{for } \tau = 1, \ldots, M$$

and s_l (again) the probability of surviving at least l units of time.

The effects formulae stated in sections 4.2.3 through 4.2.5 also apply to the model (4.3.3.2) – provided K_F is substituted for K_L, L is replaced by M and $(1 + r)^{\tau - l}$ is multiplied by s_l.

4.3.4. MODEL WITH VARYING RATES OF INTEREST

The model with survival rates mentioned above may also be interpreted as a model with varying rates of interest.

More explicitly, varying prospective rates of interest, in addition to varying prospective levels of consumer prices and of asset prices, have been dealt with in sections 2.8 and 3.4 above. In the present section, the model is particularized further by maximization of:

$$\omega = \sum_{l=1}^{L} \alpha_l \ln c_l \tag{4.3.4.1}$$

subject to the lifetime budget equation (2.8.1.1.4), with consumption c_l and income y_l per period l couched in 'real' terms. As a result, we get:

$$\begin{aligned} c_\tau &= \alpha_\tau f_\tau^{-1} [(K_0 A_L - K_L) + \sum_{l=1}^{L} y_l f_l] \\ &= \alpha_\tau [(K_0 A_L - K_L)(1 + \tilde{r}_{L+1}) \prod_{\tau'=\tau}^{L} (1 + \tilde{r}_{\tau'+1})^{-1} \\ &\quad + \sum_{l=1}^{\tau-1} y_l \prod_{\tau'=l}^{\tau-1} (1 + \tilde{r}_{\tau'+1})^{-1} \delta_{\tau>1} + Y_\tau \\ &\quad + \sum_{l=\tau+1}^{L} y_l \prod_{\tau'=\tau}^{l-1} (1 + \tilde{r}_{\tau'+1}) \delta_{\tau<L}] \end{aligned} \tag{4.3.4.2}$$

with

$$f_\tau = (1 + \tilde{r}_{L+1})^{-1} \prod_{\tau'=\tau}^{L} (1 + \tilde{r}_{\tau'+1})$$

where

$$1 + \tilde{r}_{\tau+1} \stackrel{\text{def}}{=} (1 + r_{\tau+1})(1 + a_{\tau+1})(1 - p_{\tau+1})^{-1},$$

the 'adjusted' discount factor incorporating changes in asset price and consumer price levels, and

$$A_L = (1 + a_{L+1})^{-1} \prod_{\tau=1}^{L} (1 + a_{\tau+1})$$

the final-period index-number of asset prices.

For the current period $\tau = 1$, (4.3.4.2) becomes more simply:

$$c_1 = \alpha_1 [(K_0 A_L - K_L)(1 + \tilde{r}_{L+1}) \prod_{\tau=1}^{L} (1 + \tilde{r}_{\tau+1})^{-1} + \sum_{l=1}^{L} y_l (1 + \tilde{r}_{l+1}) \prod_{\tau=1}^{l} (1 + \tilde{r}_{\tau+1})^{-1}]. \qquad (4.3.4.3)$$

For the effects of varying the data, we find:

$$\frac{\partial c_\tau}{\partial y_{\tau'}} = \alpha_\tau f_\tau^{-1} f_{\tau'} \quad (\tau, \tau' = 1, \ldots, L), \qquad (4.3.4.4)$$

$$\frac{\partial c_\tau}{\partial K_0} = \alpha_\tau f_\tau^{-1} A_L \quad (\tau = 1, \ldots, L), \qquad (4.3.4.5)$$

and

$$\frac{\partial c_\tau}{\partial r_{\tau'}} = -\alpha_\tau f_\tau^{-1} (1 + r_{\tau'})^{-1} [\{(K_0 A_L - K_L) + \sum_{l=1}^{L} y_l f_l\} \delta_{\tau' > \tau} - \sum_{l=1}^{\tau'-1} y_l f_l \delta_{\tau' > 1}]. \qquad (4.3.4.6)$$

Again, these formulae become simpler for the current-period consumption:

$$\frac{\partial c_1}{\partial y_{\tau'}} = \alpha_1 (1 + \tilde{r}_{\tau'}) \prod_{\tau=1}^{\tau'-1} (1 + \tilde{r}_{\tau+1})^{-1} \qquad (4.3.4.7)$$

$$\frac{\partial c_1}{\partial K_0} = \alpha_1 (1 + \tilde{r}_{L+1}) \prod_{\tau=1}^{L} (1 + \tilde{r}_{\tau+1})^{-1} A_L \qquad (4.3.4.8)$$

$$\frac{\partial c_1}{\partial r_{\tau'}} = -\alpha_1 (1 + \tilde{r}_{\tau'})^{-1} [(K_0 A_L - K_L)(1 + \tilde{r}_{L+1}) \prod_{\tau=1}^{L} (1 + \tilde{r}_{\tau+1})^{-1} + \sum_{l=2}^{\tau'} y_l (1 + \tilde{r}_l) \prod_{\tau=1}^{l-1} (1 + \tilde{r}_{\tau+1})^{-1} \delta_{\tau' > 1}]. \qquad (4.3.4.9)$$

Apart from the reformulation of the discount factors, (4.3.4.4) is identical to (4.2.3.1), while (4.3.4.5) differs from (4.2.4.1) by the factor A_L alone. An essential discrepancy, however, appears between (4.3.4.6) and (4.2.5.1). The reason is clearly that a change in the rate of interest relating to an *isolated* period τ' affects consumption and savings through the discount factors

$$(1 + \tilde{r}_{\tau_{\max}+1})^{-1} \prod_{\tau'=\tau_{\min}}^{\tau_{\max}} (1 + \tilde{r}_{\tau'+1}) \quad \text{or their reciprocals}$$

if and only if $\tau_{\min} < \tau' < \tau_{\max}$, i.e. within the product range; in formulae (4.3.4.6) and (4.3.4.9) these restrictions on the effectiveness of the one-period changes are expressed by means of the Kronecker deltas. Even then, a change in the rate of interest counts only once instead of in multiples $((L - \tau)$ or $(l - \tau)$, as in (4.2.5.1)).

Evidently, the change-in-personal wealth sub-effect of a prospective change in a single-period rate of interest is operative only as far as consumption *preceding* that change is concerned. In the latter case, this component of the interest effect is positive or negative according as K_L is larger or smaller than $K_0 A_L$, respectively; in a qualitative sense, this agrees with the conclusion reached in section 4.2.5.

This sub-effect should be distinguished from the wealth accumulation (or decumulation) compont of the interest effect

$$\left(\frac{\partial c_\tau}{\partial r_{\tau'}}\right)_{\text{II}} = \alpha_\tau f_\tau^{-1}(1 + r_{\tau'})^{-1} \left(\sum_{l=1}^{\tau'-1} y_l f_l - \hat{a}_{\tau'-1} R_L\right) \delta_{\tau'>1} \qquad (4.3.4.10)$$

resulting from (3.4.2) for $\alpha_l(C_l) = \alpha_l \ln C_l$.

The complementary substitution effect:

$$\left(\frac{\partial c_\tau}{\partial r_{\tau'}}\right)_{\text{I}} = \alpha_\tau f_\tau^{-1} (1 + r_{\tau'})^{-1} R_L (\delta_{\tau'>\tau} - \hat{a}_{\tau'-1} \delta_{\tau'>1}), \qquad (4.3.4.11)$$

similarly resulting from (3.4.1) appears to be positive or negative, according as $\tau' > \tau$ or $\tau' \leq \tau$, respectively; in other words, savings are stimulated (and consumption is deterred) in the time-interval preceding the period in which the rate of interest is supposed to increase, whereas for later periods the opposite is true. In this manner, the individual can reap the full benefit of higher interest receipts (or lower interest payments) on a higher amount of accumulated savings (or less dissavings) immediately after the transitory rise in the rate of interest.

On the first (current-)period consumption, an increase in the current rate of interest will have no effect, while a later change tends to have a mere positive effect on savings.

Mutatis mutandis, the same considerations apply to effects of (isolated) changes in asset price levels and – in the opposite direction – of (isolated) changes in consumer price levels.

4.3.5. CONTINUOUS VERSION

Replacing $\alpha_l(C_l)$ in section 3.1.1 by $\alpha_l \ln C_l$ in section 4.1.2 corresponds to the substitution of $\varphi\,\{C(\tau)\}$ in the utility function (3.7.1.1) by $\alpha(\tau) \ln \{C(\tau)\}$, resulting in:

$$\omega = \int_0^L \alpha(\tau) \ln C(\tau)\, d\tau \qquad (4.3.5.1)$$

with

$$\int_0^L \alpha(\tau)\, d\tau = 1.$$

Maximization of (4.3.5.1) subject to (3.7.1.3) results in:

$$C(\tau) = \alpha(\tau)\, R(\tau), \qquad (4.3.5.2)$$

with

$$R(\tau) = R(L)\, \delta^{-1}(\tau) = R(L) \cdot \exp\{(\tau - L)\varrho\}$$

and

$$R(L) = K_0 - K_L + \int_0^L Y(\tau)\, \delta(\tau)\, d\tau,$$

as lifetime financial resourses discounted till the expected end of life.

Evidently, the second-order condition (3.10.2.3) for a proper utility maximum is satisfied:

$$\varphi_{CC}(\tau) = -\alpha(\tau)\, C^{-2}(\tau) < 0. \qquad (4.3.5.3)$$

For the effects of changes in income parameters, in initial personal wealth, and in the rate of interest on the rate of consumption, we derive from (4.3.5.2):

$$C_{\text{par } Y}(\tau') = \alpha_{\tau'} \int_0^L Y_{\text{par } Y}(\tau)\, \delta^{-1}(\tau' - \tau + L)\, d\tau \qquad (4.3.5.4)$$

$$C_\varrho(\tau') = -\alpha_{\tau'} \Bigg[(K_0 - K_L)(L - \tau')\, \delta^{-1}(\tau') + \int_0^L Y(\tau)(\tau' - \tau)\delta^{-1}(\tau' - \tau + L)\, d\tau \Bigg] \qquad (4.3.5.5)$$

and

$$C_{K_0}(\tau') = -C_{K_L}(\tau') = \alpha_{\tau'} \delta^{-1}(\tau') \qquad (4.3.5.6)$$

respectively[7].

[7] These formulae too may be derived from more general ones, viz. those of section 3.7.3.

4.3.6. OPERATIONAL SIGNIFICANCE OF THE MODIFICATIONS

Whether the modifications proposed above – as well as other possible versions of the consumption and savings functions – are operationally significant, i.e. applicable to empirical data, depends on:

(1) whether these functions can be handled mathematically and computationally, and

(2) whether the (additional) variables required can be measured statistically.

The second condition appears to be more restrictive than the first one, especially since mathematical difficulties may be overcome by carrying out iterative procedures on a computer. On the other hand, needless complications should obviously be avoided.

In the present case, the problem of finding numerical values for the variables is aggravated by the particular nature of most of them, viz. as *expectations* about *future* values of economic concepts, like income, prices and 'urgency to consume'.

Fortunately, these variables need not always be quantified directly; the manner in which they may be approximated indirectly is shown in chapter 6, applying the micro-savings theory to Dutch survey data. Nevertheless, a number of variables have so far eluded statistical observation, either directly or indirectly; this holds good, inter alia, for expectations about consumer and asset price levels, and the lifetime pattern of the people's private rate of interest. For this reason, the versions of the consumption and savings functions dealt with in section 4.3.4 had to be shelved provisionally.

The minimum consumption levels, introduced in section 4.3.2, might perhaps be estimated a posteriori, as parameters. However, the improvement which might possibly result was not considered worth the additional trouble involved. One should bear in mind that these minimum consumption levels differ between periods and between individuals, and that they are linked up with the latters' α-values as indicators of their 'urgency to consume'; an additional problem would therefore be to disentangle these two types of 'personal parameters'.

On the other hand, survival rates (introduced in section 4.3.3) *have* been incorporated in the savings function that is put to an empirical test in chapter 6; actually, this apparent complication proved to be easier to handle computationally than the single life expectancies, entailing inter-individual differences in upper limits of summation.

Notwithstanding its indisputable superiority from a theoretical point of view, the continuous consumption and savings functions are unfit for empirical application. This would require continuous observation of the flow rates or instantaneous values of the flow or stock variables involved, respectively, just as in electricity generation amperage or voltage are registered continuously, viz. on graph paper. Since the latter is not applicable to the former, we have to consider the continuous version of the savings function as pure theory (for the time being).

Practically, however, the continuous version of the savings model will not deviate much from its discrete counterpart, unless the unit of time used in the latter exceeds (say) one year.

4.4. Lifetime pattern of personal wealth implied by the micro-savings model

Equation (4.1.3.7) enables us to calculate prospective personal wealth K_τ at (the end of) any future period τ, on the basis of given initial personal wealth K_0.

In order to gain further insight into the possible time patterns of K_τ we rewrite it, according to (4.1.3.7), as a sum of two components:

$$K_\tau = K_{1\tau} + K_{2\tau}, \tag{4.4.1}$$

such that

$$\begin{aligned} K_{1\tau} &= \{1 - \hat{\alpha}_\tau (1 + r)^{\tau - L}\} K_0 + \hat{\alpha}_\tau (1 + r)^{\tau - L} K_L \\ &= K_0 + \hat{\alpha}_\tau (1 + r)^{\tau - L} (K_L - K_0) \end{aligned} \tag{4.4.2}$$

and

$$K_{2\tau} = \sum_{l=1}^{\tau} Y_l (1 + r)^{\tau - l} - \hat{\alpha}_\tau \sum_{l=1}^{L} Y_l (1 + r)^{\tau - l}. \tag{4.4.3}$$

Since $K_{1\tau}$ moves from K_0 (for $\tau = 0$) to K_L (for $\tau = L$), while $K_{2\tau}$ is zero for these values of τ, $K_{1\tau}$ may be interpreted as the 'inter-terminal' component; $K_{2\tau}$, on the other hand, plays the rôle of income accumulator-decumulator.

According to the second member of (4.4.2), the weights of K_0 and K_L increase and decrease respectively (while remaining within the range (0, 1)) for τ going from 0 to L. If these weights are linear functions of τ, (4.4.2) would represent a series of points (τ, K_τ) on a straight line between (0, K_0) and (L, K_L). In general, however, (4.4.2) represents a sequence of points which can lie either all above or all below, or partly above and partly below, as well as right on that straight line – in addition to the first and last points, of course.

Anyhow, K_1 moves monotonically from K_0 to K_L, increasing, decreasing or remaining horizontal according as $K_L - K_0$ is positive, negative or zero.

For K_0 and K_L both positive or both negative, $K_{1\tau}$ will have the same sign within the entire range $0 \leq \tau \leq L$; for $K_0 > 0 > K_L$ or $K_0 < 0 < K_L$, K_τ will descend from positive to negative values or ascend from negative to positive values respectively, crossing the zero-line where $\tilde{\alpha}_\tau (1 + r)^{\tau - L} = K_0/(K_0 - K_L)$ for $K_0 \neq K_L$.

$K_{2\tau}$, on the other hand, need not, and generally will not be a monotonic function of τ, since it is the difference of two ever-positive terms, both being on the upgrade with increasing τ: the first one because summation of discounted income is extended over a longer time-interval, the second one because both $\hat{\alpha}_\tau$ (likewise covering a longer timespan) and the discount factors rise. This (means that) $K_{2\tau}$ may be positive, zero or negative for $\tau = 1, \ldots, L - 1$. Since:

$$K_{2\tau} = (1 - \hat{\alpha}_\tau) \sum_{l=1}^{L} Y_l (1 + r)^{\tau - l} - \sum_{l=\tau+1}^{L} Y_l (1 + r)^{\tau - l} \qquad (4.4.4)$$

eventually both terms at the right-hand side of (4.4.4) will vanish, hence $K_{2\tau}$ will return to zero, the value at which it started. Before that, however, $K_{2\tau}$ may change sign, even several times.

Hence, $K_{2\tau}$ may be positive, zero or negative – like $K_{1\tau}$, but independently, and with a less regular course. Consequently, its sum K_τ may also be positive, zero as well as negative.

Still, there might be a limit, say $\underline{K}_\tau$, below which K_τ is not allowed to drop:

$$K_\tau \geq \underline{K}_\tau \quad \text{for } \tau = 1, \ldots, L; \qquad (4.4.5)$$

$\underline{K}_\tau$ represents the minimum amount of personal wealth (or rather the maximum amount of debt) which the person in question can get away with, at the end of period τ. The latter value may depend, inter alia, upon the financial prospects of that person at the time (for instance, with regard to his income expectations and future needs).

Boundary conditions (4.4.5) – if effective for at least one period τ – will alter the savings- and consumption-functions; in such a case, the utility function (4.1.2.2) would have to be maximized subject to inequalities (4.4.5) as well as to a budget equation. This may be treated as a particular kind of dynamic programming problem, for which solutions were outlined by Beckmann [1959] and by van Praag [1968].

Without numerical specifications, however, nothing much can be said about the resulting lifetime patterns of prospective savings and personal wealth. Since the outcome depends on expectations (for the future) rather than on the observable present, this problem will have to be approached in an experimental way, by means of variously combined specifications of the time-paths of the exogenous variables, such as expected income and urgency to consume.[8]

Anyhow, the (optimal) lifetime pattern of personal wealth will not be fixed once and for all; on the contrary, it will change with the passing of (real) time, according as the planning of lifetime allocation of financial resources to consumption and saving shifts forward continuously, or at least regularly.

This may be shown most simply by considering personal wealth as accumulated savings. If we denote the value of x envisaged at actual time t for future time $t + \tau$ by $x_{t\tau}$, and the current value of x of time t by x_t $(= x_{t0})$, $x_{t\tau}$, $x_{t+1,\tau-1}$, $x_{t+2,\tau-2}$ etc. all refer to the same (future) time $t + \tau$ but originate from different moments of planning. In general, those values will mutually differ. This also applies to personal wealth; for instance:

$$K_{t2} = K_t + S_{t1} + S_{t2} \neq K_{t+1} + S_{t+1,1} = K_{t+1,1}; \qquad (4.4.6)$$

this means that personal wealth envisaged at the beginning of period t for the beginning of period $t + 2$ will generally deviate from next year's forecast for the same moment.

This is true even if $S_{t1} = K_{t+1} - K_t$, i.e. even if first-year savings come off exactly according to the plan drawn up at the beginning of this period. The reason is that in general $S_{t2} \neq S_{t+1,1}$, which may be shown when (4.1.3.8) is rewritten as:

$$S_{t\tau} = Y_{t\tau} + r_t \sum_{l=1}^{\tau-1} Y_{tl} (1 + r_t)^{\tau-l-1} \delta_{\tau>1}$$
$$- (r_t \hat{\alpha}_{t,\tau-1} \delta_{\tau>1} + \alpha_{t\tau}) [(K_t - K_{tL_t}) (1 + r_t)^{\tau-L_t} + \sum_{l=1}^{L_t} Y_{tl} (1 + r_t)^{\tau-l}]. \qquad (4.4.7)$$

Replacing $S_{t\tau}$ by $S_{t+1,\tau-1}$ in (4.4.7) means shifting the following variables one year ahead in real time:

(a) the rate of interest $(r_t \rightarrow r_{t+1})$;
(b) initial personal wealth $(K_t \rightarrow K_{t+1})$;

---

[8] For details, cf. Appendix A to this chapter.

(c) income expectations ($Y_{t\tau} \rightarrow Y_{t+1,\tau-1}$ and $Y_{tl} \rightarrow Y_{t+1,l-1}$);
(d) life expectancy ($L_t \rightarrow L_{t+1}$);
(e) 'urgencies to consume' ($\alpha_{t\tau} \rightarrow \alpha_{t+1,\tau-1}$ and $\hat{\alpha}_{t,\tau-1} \rightarrow \hat{\alpha}_{t+1,\tau-2}$),
while:
(f) the upper limits of prospective time in the summation terms are reduced from $\tau - 1$ to $\tau - 2$ and from L_t to L_{t+1}, and
(g) the power of the discount factor corresponding to intended change in personal wealth is cut down from $\tau - L_t$ to $\tau - 1 - L_{t+1}$.

Whereas the shifts mentioned under (a) through (c) above may (accidentally) leave the variables unchanged, a reduction of the life horizon is irrevocable: life expectancy diminishes with increasing age (because of increasing mortality risk) but less rapidly (because of intervening deaths), i.e.:

$$1 > L_t - L_{t+1} > 0.^{9} \tag{4.4.8}$$

As a result, urgencies to consume tend to rise with increasing age, by virtue of

$$\sum_{l=1}^{L_t} \alpha_{tl} = \sum_{l=1}^{L_{t+1}} \alpha_{t+1,l} = 1.$$

Consequently, the time-pattern of (optimal) personal wealth changes inevitably with the ageing of its possessor: at each plan-revision, new curves branch off from (and break off) the former, as exemplified in graph 4.1.

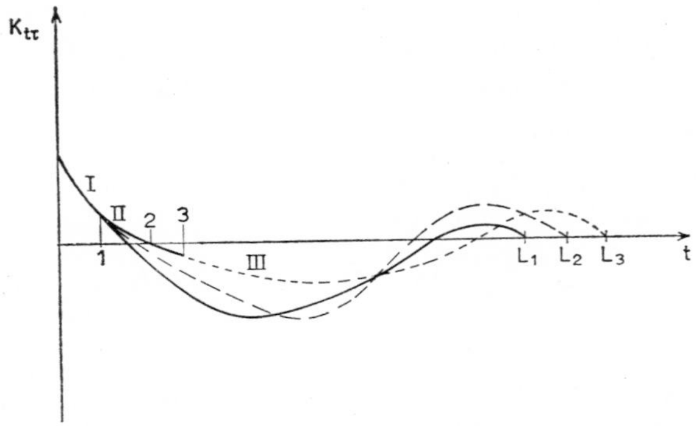

Graph 4.1. Possible changes in optimal lifetime patterns of personal wealth, with increasing age.

---

[9] At least, this applies to the majority of income recipients, having passed the age (of about 5 years in the Netherlands) at which the mortality rate is lowest.

APPENDIX A TO CHAPTER 4

EFFECTS OF DEBT RESTRICTION ON OPTIMAL LIFETIME CONSUMPTION AND PERSONAL WEALTH PATTERNS

So far, only a few experiments have been carried out on the basis of very simple assumptions about the exogenous variables; in particular we assumed $K_0 = K_L = 0$, α_t to decrease and Y_t to increase linearly over the life horizon. The resulting optimum lifetime pattern of consumption implies an age pattern of personal wealth like the one represented by the dotted line in graph 4A.1: first decreasing towards a minimum and afterwards increasing towards to the initial and eventual zero level, hence remaining negative all the time in between. The time at which minimum personal wealth (or maximum debt) will be reached depends on the rates of change of α_t and of Y_t assumed. If that minimum is below the acceptable level of debt ($\underline{K}_t$), imposition of the latter appears to raise the entire personal wealth curve to such an extent that the effectiveness of the restriction *seems* to be reduced to a minimum (period of time).

Perhaps one might have expected a restricted personal wealth curve to run closer to the unrestricted one, e.g. near the curve OA, along the straight line AB, and again along a curve near to BL. One should realize, however, that the lifetime pattern of *consumption* rather than of personal wealth is optimalized. This means that *overall* the *restricted* optimal consumption pattern (rather than the personal wealth pattern) should be as close as possible to the unrestricted one; for this purpose, one should keep in mind the particular (addi-log) form of the utility function – implying that efforts be made to reduce relative rather than absolute deviations.

Since consumption – as a flow variable – is related to the rate of change in personal wealth, the restricted optimal personal wealth curve should resemble the unrestricted one with respect to its slope (at the same time) more than with respect to its location.

A smooth curve like the 'restricted' uninterrupted line in graph 4A.1 seems to meet that criterion more closely than (say) curves OA and BL connected by the straight segment AB: coincidence on the stretch OA, implying coincidence of consumption too, apparently does not compensate sufficiently for deviations in the time-interval AB, especially in the neighbourhood of A (to the right) and of B (to the left); moreover, coincidence of the restricted

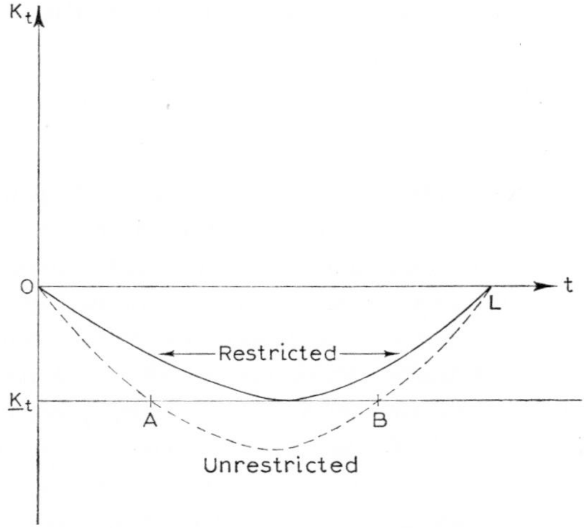

Graph 4 A.1. Possible effect of the imposition of a debt maximum ($-\underline{K}_t$) on the lifetime pattern of personal wealth corresponding to an optimal lifetime consumption pattern.

and the unrestricted personal wealth curves between B and L imply coincidence of the savings curves but *not* of the consumption curves, because preceding deviations between the personal wealth curves generally entail deviations in interest receipts (or payments, as in the case envisaged here).

Still, one should not forget that the single tentative conclusion reached here is based on very special, hence shaky assumptions, in need of reconsideration and amplification. Consequently, much more experimentation along the lines indicated above is in order.

CHAPTER 5

MACRO-SAVINGS THEORY

5.1. Derivation of a macro-savings function

5.1.1. PRELIMINARIES

In section 4.1.3 we derived a simple micro-savings function, by definition relating to separate persons, and for a single period of time only. Hence, there was no need to identify either the anonymous individual, or actual time – in contradistinction to prospective time.

In the present chapter, however, we derive a macro-savings function – i.e. relating to a group of individuals – and applicable to successive periods of time. This is done on the basis of the micro-savings function (4.1.3.4) by aggregating over individuals, and by including actual time. This requires identification of the variables and the parameters entering the micro-functions by subscripts i (= 1, ..., I) for the individuals constituting the group in question and by subscripts t (= 1, ..., T) for the time periods. For simplicity's sake, however, the double time-script '$t0$' for denoting the current period, i.e. if prospective time l coincides with actual time t, is reduced to a single t. Thus, the savings function (4.1.3.5) is specified more fully by:

$$S_{it} = (1 - \alpha_{it})\, Y_{it} - \alpha_{it}\, [(K_{it} - K_{it,L_{it}})\,(1 + r_{it})^{1-L_{it}} + \sum_{l=2}^{L_{it}} Y_{itl}\,(1 + r_{it})^{1-l}] \quad \text{for } t = 1, 2, \ldots, T; \qquad (5.1.1.1)$$

Y_{it} (= Y_{it0}) and Y_{itl} denote i's current income for period t and income expected at the beginning of period t for periods $t + l$ (l = 1, ..., $L_{it} - 1$) respectively; L_{it} represents the life expectancy of i, again at the beginning of period t, mainly determined by his or her age; α_{it}, depending, inter alia, on L_{it}, stands for the relative urgency to consume in the current period t; r_{it} denotes the uniform rate of interest assumed to apply to person i at the beginning of period t for discounting *all* future values, i.e. irrespective of the prospective time periods $t + l$ to which they relate; finally, K_{it} and $K_{it,L_{it}}$

symbolize 'initial' personal wealth (i.e. at the beginning of period t) and at that time desired final personal wealth (for the expected time of death, $t + L_{it}$), respectively.

We now endeavour to aggregate savings functions over all individuals $i (= 1, \ldots, I_t$ in periods t) in such a way that resulting total savings $S_t (= \sum_{i=1}^{I} S_{it})$ are expressed – at least approximately – in terms of (nothing but) *aggregates* of variables at the right-hand side of (5.1.1.1).

This problem is difficult, in particular because of the various ways in which life expectancies L_{it} appear in (4.1.3.5), viz. in a power, as a subscript attached to K, and as an upper limit of summation – all three of them awkward from the aggregation point of view. Since, however, L_{it} depends on a more limited set of characteristics of people (at the beginning of period t) – in particular age and sex (and possibly occupational status) – than the one with which α_{it} is connected, we intend to overcome those difficulties by carrying out the aggregation in two steps, viz.:

first, by grouping together individuals according to characteristics like age, sex and occupation such that they all have (about) the same life expectancy, and summing the micro-savings functions over all individuals constituting these groups to (age-, sex- etc. specific) *group* savings functions, and

second, by summing these group-savings functions over all groups constituting an entire region or nation to regional or national savings functions. This is done in subsections 5.1.2 and 5.1.3 respectively.

5.1.2. FIRST-STAGE AGGREGATION

Here, we sum (5.1.1.1) over all i belonging to the same age–sex group (a, s):[1]

$$S_{ast} = \sum_{i \in \{a,s\}} S_{it} = \sum_{i \in \{a,s\}} (1 - \alpha_{it}) Y_{it} - \sum_{i \in \{a,s\}} \alpha_{it} (K_{it} - K_{it,L_{it}}) (1 + r_{it})^{1 - L_{it}}$$

$$- \sum_{i \in \{a,s\}} \alpha_{it} \sum_{l=2}^{L_{it}} Y_{itl} (1 + r_{it})^{1-l} \qquad (5.1.2.1)$$

for $a = 1, \ldots, A$ and $s =$ m(ale), f(emale).

First, we replace L_{it} by $\bar{L}_{ast}$, i.e. the (average) life expectancy of individuals of age a and sex s at the beginning of period t. Secondly, we replace also the subscript i attached to the other variables by 'as', thus rendering (5.1.2.1)

[1] It should be noted that the age-sex groups (a, s) of individuals change in size (n_{ast}) as well as in composition over time.

into:

$$S_{ast} = (1 - \bar{\alpha}_{ast})\, Y_{ast} - \bar{\alpha}_{ast}\,(K_{ast} - K_{as,t+L_{as}})\,(1 + \bar{r}_{ast})^{1-\bar{L}_{ast}} - \bar{\alpha}_{ast} \sum_{l=1}^{\bar{L}_{ast}-1} Y_{astl}\,(1 + \bar{r}_{ast})^{-l}, \qquad (5.1.2.2)$$

with the barred variables representing means and the unbarred variables representing sums (over all n_{ast} individuals constituting the a,s-group in period t); e.g.

$$\bar{\alpha}_{ast} = n_{ast}^{-1} \sum_{i \in \{a,s\}} \alpha_{it}$$

and

$$Y_{astl} = \sum_{i \in \{a,s\}} Y_{itl}.$$

Thus, the sums of products of variables relating to individuals i in the third member of (5.1.2.1) are replaced by products of means and totals of variables for groups $\{a, s\}$ of individuals in the second member of (5.1.2.2). However, this is allowed only in the case where these variables are uncorrelated over the individuals $i \in \{a, s\}$ in question[2].

For $i \in \{a, s\}$, it seems likely that the latter condition is satisfied approximately; at least, there is no reason why *for* $i \in \{a, s\}$ α_{it} would be correlated with Y_{it}, either in a positive or in a negative sense. On the other hand, *over all* i, i.e. not confined to a particular age–sex group, α_{it} and Y_{it} would generally be correlated in a positive sense, since both α_{it} and Y_{it} tend to be higher according as people get older. This is an additional reason for confining aggregation provisionally to fairly homogeneous age–sex groups.

On the other hand, zero correlation between the variables does not suffice to replace a sum of products of *more than two* variables by the product of the number of its terms and the means of those variables[2a]. Therefore, replacing

---

[2] $$\sum_{i=1}^{n} x_i y_i = \sum_{i=1}^{n} (\bar{x} + \Delta x_i)(\bar{y} + \Delta y_i) = n\bar{x}\bar{y} + \sum_{i=1}^{n} \Delta x_i \Delta y_i$$

$$= \bar{x}\,(\sum_{i=1}^{n} y_i) \text{ if and only if } \sum_{i=1}^{n} \Delta x_i \Delta y_i = 0,$$

with $\bar{x} = n^{-1} \sum_{i=1}^{n} x_i$, and likewise $\bar{y}$, $\Delta x_i = x_i - \bar{x}$, and likewise Δy_i; $\sum_{i=1}^{n} \Delta x_i \Delta y_. = 0$ means zero correlation between x_i and y_i for $i = 1, \ldots, n$.

[2a] For instance, $\sum_i x_i y_i z_i = n\bar{x}\bar{y}\bar{z}$ requires not only:

$$\sum_i \Delta x_i \Delta y_i = \sum_i \Delta x_i \Delta z_i = \sum_i \Delta y_i z_i = 0,$$

i.e. zero correlation between the variables, but additionally:

$$\sum_i \Delta x_i \Delta y_i \Delta z_i = 0.$$

r_{it} by $\bar{r}_{ast}$ (as an arithmetic mean of the r_{it}) in the discount factors incorporated in (5.1.2.1) and (5.1.2.2) respectively is not entirely correct; still, it may be a good enough approximation, provided the coefficient of variation of r_{it} (for $i \in \{a, s\}$ and fixed t) is sufficiently small.

5.1.3. SECOND-STAGE AGGREGATION

The function for all personal savings may be written as the sum of the group savings functions:

$$S_t = \sum_{a=1}^{A} \sum_{s=m,v} S_{ast} = \sum_{a,s} (1 - \bar{\alpha}_{ast})\, Y_{ast} - \sum_{a,s} \bar{\alpha}_{ast}\, (K_{ast} - K_{as,t+Las})\, (1 + \bar{r}_{ast})^{1-\bar{L}_{ast}} - \sum_{a,s} \bar{\alpha}_{ast} \sum_{l=2}^{\bar{L}_{ast}} Y_{astl}\, (1 + \bar{r}_{ast})^{1-l} \qquad (5.1.3.1)$$

In order to get rid of the summation over a and s in (5.1.3.1), i.e. such that the variables explaining over-all savings are over-all totals (or means) themselves, a number of somewhat questionable assumptions about time-patterns of the group variables must be made.

First, we assume invariance of the life expectancies over the time period covered by the analysis:

$$\bar{L}_{ast} = \bar{L}_{as} \quad \text{for all } a, s.^3 \qquad (5.1.3.2)$$

Secondly, we assume that the time paths of $\bar{\alpha}_{ast}$ – the average urgencies to consume – may be linearly approximated over relatively small intervals of time[4]:

$$\bar{\alpha}_{ast} = \bar{\alpha}_{aso} + \gamma_{as} t, \qquad (5.1.3.3)$$

---

[3] In the past, life expectancies have shown a tendency to *increase* (inter alia, because of progress in medical science and practice); lately, however, the increasing incidence of traffic fatalities and heart failure counteract the former effect to the extent of possible overcompensating it in the near future, at least in particular age brackets (say, between 50 and 60 years, for men).

[4] The time-limitation is obligatory, since: $0 < \bar{\alpha}_{ast} < 1$ should be satisfied, whereas with t increasing unlimitedly, (5.1.3.2) would eventually yield $\bar{\alpha}_{as}$ exceeding 1 or becoming negative according as γ_{as} is positive or negative respectively. Such consequences could, of course, be avoided, even without any time-limitations, if (5.1.3.2) is replaced by a function of time which would keep $\bar{\alpha}_{ast}$ within the (0, 1)-range. For this purpose, e.g. logistic time-paths of $\bar{\alpha}_{ast}$ may be considered. However, the analytical and computational complications arising from such an alternative choice appear to be prohibitive.

with constants $\bar{\alpha}_{aso}$ positive and γ_{as} positive or negative. As a limiting case, γ_{as} may be zero, hence $\bar{\alpha}_{ast} = \alpha_{aso}$ (constant).

Thirdly, we assume constant shares of the age–sex groups in total current income Y_t:

$$Y_{ast}/Y_t = y_{as} \quad \text{for all } a, s \text{ and } t \tag{5.1.3.4}$$

with

$$\sum_{a,s} y_{as} = 1 .$$

Fourthly, we assume constant ratios of prospective to current income of age–sex groups:

$$Y_{astl}/Y_{ast} = \bar{\varepsilon}\, y_{l|as}, \tag{5.1.3.5}$$

with $y_{l|as} = \bar{Y}_{a+l,\, st}/\bar{Y}_{ast} = Y_{a+l.st}/Y_{ast}$

the ratio of mean income (with bar) or total income (without bar) expected for l years hence to current mean and total income, respectively, of people belonging to age–sex group (a, s), supposedly invariant over time,

and $\bar{\varepsilon}$ = the mean elasticity of income expectation – likewise supposed to be invariant over time in agreement with the implicit definition of ε in (4.2.3.5):

$$\frac{\mathrm{d}Y_{as,tl}}{\mathrm{d}Y_{as,t}} \overset{\text{def}}{=} \lim_{\Delta t \to 0} \frac{Y_{as,tl} - Y_{as,t-\Delta t,l}}{Y_{as,t} - Y_{as,t-\Delta t}} = \bar{\varepsilon}\, Y_{as,tl}/Y_{as,t}. \tag{5.1.3.6}$$

Together, (5.1.3.4) and (5.1.3.5) imply:

$$Y_{astl}/Y_t = y_{asl} \tag{5.1.3.7}$$

with $y_{asl} = \bar{\varepsilon} \cdot y_{l|as} \cdot y_{as}$ independent of t.

Fifthly, we may not be altogether wrong in assuming that:

$$K_{as,t+\bar{L}_{as}} \approx 0.^{5} \tag{5.1.3.8}$$

Moreover, this variable would not have much influence on current savings anyway, in particular because of the severely reducing effect exerted by the discount factor $(1 + r_{as})^{1-L_{as}}$.

---

[5] Unfortunately, we do not have any direct information on *intended* final personal wealth. The inheritance tax statistics, however, show that in the Netherlands only about one third of the deceased left property such that the tax inspector considered it worth his attention (exceeding or nearing the exemption limits); of this minority, a major part may have died prematurely or may have over-estimated its life expectancy. Anyhow, these observations and considerations support our hypothesis (5.1.3.8).

Sixthly, with respect to initial personal wealth – as with respect to total income – we assume that the shares of the age–sex groups remain constant over time:

$$K_{ast}/K_t = k_{as} \quad (K_t \neq 0). \tag{5.1.3.9}$$

Finally, we assume that the age–sex specific average discount factors $(1 + \bar{r}_{ast})^{-1}$ bear a constant relation to the general discount factors $(1 + \bar{r}_t)^{-1}$, corresponding to a particular market rate of interest r_t, i.e.

$$(1 + \bar{r}_{ast})^{-1} = d_{as}\,(1 + \bar{r}_t)^{-1} \tag{5.1.3.10}$$

with d_{as} positive constants for all a, s and t, generally near to 1.

Substitution of (5.1.3.2) through (5.1.3.10) into (5.1.3.1) yields:

$$\begin{aligned} S_t = {} & Y_t\,[1 - \sum_{a,s} \{\bar{\alpha}_{aso} + \gamma_{as}t\}\, y_{as}] \\ & - K_t \sum_{a,s} \{\bar{\alpha}_{aso} + \gamma_{as}t\}\, k_{as}\, \{d_{as}\,(1 + \bar{r}_t)\}^{1-L_{as}} \\ & - Y_t \sum_{a,s} \{\bar{\alpha}_{aso} + \gamma_{as}t\} \sum_{l=1}^{L_{as}-1} y_{asl}\, \{d_{as}\,(1 + \bar{r}_t)\}^{-l}. \end{aligned} \tag{5.1.3.11}$$

In order to extricate r_t from under the summation signs in (5.1.3.11), we make use of the following approximation:

$$\begin{aligned} (1 + \bar{r}_t)^{-l} & = (1 + \bar{r})^{-l}\,(1 + r_t')^{-l} \\ & \approx (1 + \bar{r})^{-l}\,(1 - l r_t') \end{aligned} \tag{5.1.3.12}$$

with $r_t' = (r_t - \bar{r})/(1 + \bar{r})$ and $\bar{r} = T^{-1} \sum_{t=1}^{T} r_t$, provided $l r_t' \ll 1$ for $l = 1, \ldots, L_{as} - 1$.[6] By substituting (5.1.3.12) into

[6] (5.1.3.12) may be looked upon as a Taylor series expansion of $(1 + r_t')^{-1}$ truncated after the second term with respect to either r_t', i.e.:

$$1 - l r_t' [+\tfrac{1}{2} l\,(l + 1)\,(r_t')^2 - \tfrac{1}{6} l\,(l + 1)\,(l + 2)\,(r_t')^3 + \text{etc.}]$$

or l, i.e.:

$$1 - l \cdot \ln{(1 + r_t')}\, [+\tfrac{1}{2} l^2 \ln{(1 + r_t')}^2 - \tfrac{1}{6} l^3 \ln{(1 + r_t')}^3 + \text{etc.}];$$

in the latter case $\ln{(1 + r_t')}$ may in turn be approximated by r_t' for $|r_t'| \ll 1$. More generally, for the purpose at hand (approximate) decomposition of the discount factors as sums of products of functions f_k of r_t' alone and g_k of l alone, i.e. $(1 + r_t')^{-l} \approx \sum_{k=1}^{K} f_k(r_t') \cdot g_k(l)$, would suffice. In principle, this may also be accomplished by means of truncated series other than Taylor's. Although such other series might fit $(1 + r_t')^{-l}$ better near particular values of l and r_t', the overall-performance of (5.1.3.12) is hard to surpass; this holds good, especially in view of the summations applied, averaging out differently directed approximation errors. Trailing along higher-order terms of the series seems inadvisable in view of the computational complications it would entail, as well as the difficulties it would cause in estimating the parameters by contributing to the already high degree of multi-collinearity between the variables; anyhow, it would not be worth the (questionable) benefit we might derive from it.

(5.1.3.11), we obtain:

$$S_t \cong (A_1 + A_2 r_t') Y_t + (B_1 + B_2 r_t') K_t + (C_1 Y_t + C_2 K_t) t + (D_1 Y_t + D_2 K_t) r_t' t, ^7 \quad (5.1.3.13)$$

with

$$\left.\begin{aligned}
A_1 &= 1 - \bar{\alpha}_0 - \sum_{a,s} \bar{\alpha}_{as0} \sum_{l=1}^{L_{as}-1} y_{asl} \{d_{as}(1+\bar{r})\}^{-1} \\
&\qquad (\bar{\alpha}_0 = \sum_{a,s} \bar{\alpha}_{as0} y_{as}) \\
A_2 &= \sum_{a,s} \bar{\alpha}_{as0} \sum_{l=1}^{L_{as}-1} y_{asl} l \{d_{as}(1+\bar{r})\}^{-l} \\
B_1 &= -\sum_{a,s} \bar{\alpha}_{as0} k_{as} \{d_{as}(1+\bar{r})\}^{1-L_{as}} \\
B_2 &= \sum_{a,s} \bar{\alpha}_{as0} k_{as} (L_{as}-1) \{d_{as}(1+\bar{r})\}^{1-L_{as}} \\
C_1 &= -\bar{\gamma} - \sum_{a,s} \gamma_{as} \sum_{l=1}^{L_{as}-1} y_{asl} \{d_{as}(1+\bar{r})\}^{-l} \\
&\qquad (\bar{\gamma} \overset{\text{def}}{=} \sum_{a,s} \gamma_{as} y_{as}) \\
C_2 &= -\sum_{a,s} \gamma_{as} k_{as} \{d_{as}(1+\bar{r})\}^{1-L_{as}} \\
D_1 &= \sum_{a,s} \gamma_{as} \sum_{l=1}^{L_{as}-1} y_{asl} l \{d_{as}(1+\bar{r})\}^{-l} \\
D_2 &= \sum_{a,s} \gamma_{as} k_{as} (L_{as}-1) \{d_{as}(1+\bar{r})\}^{1-L_{as}}
\end{aligned}\right\} \quad (5.1.3.14)$$

---

[7] It would be easy to rewrite (5.1.3.16) – couched in terms of deviations of interest rates r_t from their mean $\bar{r}$ – in terms of r_t themselves, viz. as:

$$S_t = (A_1' + A_2 r_t) Y_t + (B_1' + B_2 r_t) K_t + (C_1' Y_t + C_2' K_t) t + (D_1 Y_t + D_2 K_t) r_t t, \quad (5.1.3.13')$$

with

$$A_1' = A_1 - A_2 \bar{r} \qquad C_1' = C_1 - D_1 \bar{r},$$

$$B_1' = B_1 - B_2 \bar{r}, \qquad C_2' = C_2 - D_2 \bar{r},$$

whereas the other coefficients (A_2, B_2, D_1 and D_2) are left unchanged. However, such a reformulation does not have any advantage over (5.1.3.16). On the contrary, e.g. A_1 and B_1 may be interpreted as the effects of income and of personal wealth respectively on savings at an average rate of interest $\bar{r}$ – apart from explicit time effects – whereas A_1' and B_1' in (5.1.3.13) are more difficult to interpret. Therefore, we shall keep to (5.1.3.13) in the discussions below (cf. section 5.2.4).

5.2. Properties of the macro-savings function

5.2.1. GENERAL CONCLUSIONS

Equation (5.1.3.14) represents a linear and homogeneous function of current savings S_t in terms of current income Y_t and current personal wealth K_t – i.e. apart from effects of the rate of interest and of time.

Apparently, this property, also inherent to the micro-savings function (cf. section 4.2.1), is left intact by aggregation. With the micro-model, the macro-model likewise shares the property that the rate of interest does not have a separate effect on savings but one combined with the effects of income and of personal wealth. On the other hand, the latter joint effects in the macro-model are somewhat different from those found in the micro-model, due to the linearizations according to (5.1.3.12) applied to the discount factors, in order to attain a tractable macro-model. Therefore, one should keep in mind that the macro-savings function (5.1.3.13) is at best an approximation. This applies equally to the introduction of *actual* time in the model, again not independently but incorporated in products with the other variables, in order to take account of possible gradual changes in relative urgencies to consume. Contrariwise, *prospective* time, occupying a prominent place in the micro-model, has been eliminated from the macro-model, by means of the assumptions specified in section 5.1.3, in order to make the model operational.

5.2.2. DIMENSIONS, SIGNS AND ORDERS OF MAGNITUDE OF THE PARAMETERS

By comparing the dimensions of the variables

$$\left.\begin{array}{lll} S_t\colon [\mathrm{M}]\,[\mathrm{T}]^{-1}, & r_t'\colon [\mathrm{T}]^{-1}, & \\ Y_t\colon [\mathrm{M}]\,[\mathrm{T}]^{-1}, & t\colon [\mathrm{T}], & K_t\colon [\mathrm{M}] \end{array}\right\} \qquad (5.2.2.1)$$

we find for the dimensions of the parameters:

$$\left.\begin{array}{llll} A_1\colon [1], & B_1\colon [\mathrm{T}]^{-1}, & C_1\colon [\mathrm{T}]^{-1}, & D_1\colon [1], \\ A_2\colon [\mathrm{T}], & B_2\colon [1], & C_2\colon [\mathrm{T}]^{-2}, & D_2\colon [\mathrm{T}]^{-1} \end{array}\right\} \qquad (5.2.2.2)$$

(cf. de Jong [1967]).

The apparent simplicity of these dimensions adds to the plausibility of the macro-model, if only as an approximation.

With regard to the expected *signs* of the parameters, the following conclusions may be drawn from (5.1.3.14).

The parameter A_1 for the income effect *sec* will most likely be positive, but not exceed 1; A_1 would become negative only in the case where the values of y_{ast} generally exceed the reciprocals of the corresponding discount factors $d_{as}(1+\bar{r})^{-t}$, i.e. rise fairly steeply and continuously, and/or in the case where α_{aso} are relatively large (at least $> L_{as}^{-1}$). Moreover, A_1 cannot exceed 1. On the other hand, B_1 for the personal wealth effect sec will certainly be negative.

Contrariwise, the signs of A_2 and B_2, for the effects of the rate of interest combined with income and with personal wealth respectively, will both be positive. In short:

$$\left.\begin{array}{ll} 0 < A_1 < 1, & B_1 < 0 \\ A_2, B_2 > 0 & \text{in general.} \end{array}\right\} \qquad (5.2.2.3)$$

About the signs of the last four parameters (C_1, C_2, D_1 and D_2), however, not even tentative – let alone definitive – statements may be made. The reason is that the γ_{as} can be positive or negative, depending, inter alia, on *a* and *s*. Therefore, the resulting signs of C_1 through D_2 depend upon the 'weights' of the γ_{as}, represented by those parts of the right-hand expressions in (5.1.3.14) that follow the γ_{as}.

As regards the order of magnitude of A_1, we note that it cannot exceed 1 for (assumedly) positive values of y_{ast}; on the contrary, we may expect A_1 to be nearer to 0 than to 1, since A_1 in the macro-model (cf. (5.1.3.13)) is comparable with the total derivative:

$$\frac{\mathrm{d}S_1}{\mathrm{d}Y_1} = 1 - \alpha_1 - \alpha_1 \varepsilon \sum_{t=2}^{L} (Y_t/Y_1)(1+r)^{1-t}$$

in the micro-model (cf. (4.2.3.6)) rather than with $\partial S_1/\partial Y_1 = 1 - \alpha_1$ (cf. (4.2.3.7)).

In an absolute sense, A_2 is larger than the third term at the right-hand side of the expression for A_1:

$$A_1 + A_2 > 1 - \alpha_0 . \qquad (5.2.2.4)$$

Moreover, we expect $|B_1| < \sum_{a,s} \bar{\alpha}_{aso} k_{as} \stackrel{\text{def}}{=} \bar{a}_0'$, since the discount factors $d_{as}(1+\bar{r})^{1-L_{as}}$ are nearly always less than 1, and for large L_{as} even *much* less; $\bar{a}_0'$ is comparable with $\bar{\alpha}_0$, the second term in the right-hand expression of A_1. These two averages differ in the sets of weights applied to the α_{aso}, viz. the y_{as} and the k_{as} respectively. Still, we may conclude fairly safely that $|B_1| < \alpha_0$, i.e. unless the range of the $\bar{\alpha}_{aso}$ is abnormally large, unless weighting by the k_{as} yields a value of $\bar{\alpha}_0'$ near the highest of the $\bar{\alpha}_{aso}$ values, and unless weighting by the y_{as} yields a value of $\bar{\alpha}_0$ near the lowest of the $\bar{\alpha}_{aso}$ values – which would be extremely unlikely anyhow. Therefore, we also conclude:

$$1 - A_1 + B_1 > 0. \qquad (5.2.2.5)$$

Since B_2 differs from B_1 only in the additional time factor $(L_{as} - 1)$ – which is generally larger than 1 –:

$$B_2 > -B_1. \qquad (5.2.2.6)$$

Similarly, but less conclusively because of differences in weights, we may expect:

$$A_2 > -B_1, \qquad (5.2.2.7)$$

since the discount factor $(1 + \bar{r})^{1-L_{as}}$ in A_2 is never larger and generally smaller than the $(1 + \bar{r})^{-l}$ in B_1; anyhow, (5.2.2.3), (5.2.2.4) and (5.2.2.7) imply $2A_2 > -B_1 - \alpha_0$.

With respect to the parameters C_1, C_2, D_1 and D_2 we presume that the γ_{as} are generally smaller – in an absolute sense – than the corresponding $\bar{\alpha}_{aso}$, provided the unit of time is one year or less; moreover, if the γ_{as} are not all of the same sign, positive and negative values will offset each other at least partially in the weighted sums of these parameters over a and s. Hence, we expect:

$$\left.\begin{array}{ll} |C_1| < |1 - A_1|, & |C_2| < |B_1| \\ |D_1| < |A_2|, & |D_2| < |B_2|. \end{array}\right\} \qquad (5.2.2.8)$$

5.2.3. SIGNS AND ORDERS OF MAGNITUDE OF THE VARIABLES AND THEIR CONTRIBUTIONS TO SAVINGS

Not only the parameters, but also the variables to which they are attached, determine sign and size of savings S_t.

In micro-savings functions, like (4.1.3.5), personal wealth, and even income, may sometimes be negative. For particular groups of people, one or both of the corresponding aggregates too may be negative occasionally. In macro-savings functions, like (5.1.3.13), however, aggregate income Y_t and aggregate personal wealth K_t are nearly always positive. On the other hand, the r'_t – defined as deviations from a mean (cf. (5.1.3.12)) – will have varying signs. Accordingly, r'_tY_t, r'_tK_t, r'_tY_tt and r'_tK_tt too may be negative as well as positive. Consequently, the additive terms in which the latter four composite variables appear, may also be positive or negative, according as the signs of the variables coincide with or differ from those of their coefficients.

Contrariwise, the remaining four variables, viz. Y_t, K_t, Y_tt and K_tt are always non-negative, seeing that $t\,(= 1, \ldots, T)$ is defined in an ever-positive sense. With respect to the terms in which the latter four variables appear:

$A_1 Y_t$ will always be positive,

$B_1 K_t$ will always be negative,

while $C_1 Y_t t$ and $D_1 K_t t$ may be positive or negative according as C_1, D_1 are positive or negative.

Therefore, S_t may be negative as well as positive. Empirically, positive values for aggregate savings are more frequent than negative ones (at least for the set of natural persons constituting a nation). Still, negative aggregate personal savings have been observed – for instance, in years of recession (cf. also appendix A to chapter 7); for particular groups, say of pensioners, aggregate *dis*savings may even be the rule.

The relative importance of each of the 8 additive components contributing to savings according to (5.1.3.13) cannot be gauged a priori; moreover, it may change over time. Differences in size of the parameters as discussed in section 5.2.2 may be offset (rather than re-inforced) by differences in size of the variables. Even in the case where one or more of the 8 additive components of S_t are small in an absolute sense, those terms may be more important than larger ones for explaining changes in aggregate savings over time; this would happen if the variables included in the former terms show stronger movements than those included in the latter terms. However, even for the same absolute change in the explanatory variables, the effect may depend on values of other variables, viz. of those with which the changing variable is combined; this will be shown in the next sub-section.

5.2.4. EFFECTS OF THE EXPLANATORY VARIABLES ON AGGREGATE SAVINGS

From (5.1.3.13) we derive:

$$\frac{\partial S_t}{\partial Y_t} = A_{1t} + A_{2t} r'_t \qquad (5.2.4.1)$$

$$\frac{\partial S_t}{\partial K_t} = B_{1t} + B_{2t} r'_t \qquad (5.2.4.2)$$

$$\frac{\partial S_t}{\partial r'_t} = A_{2t} Y_t + B_{2t} K_t \qquad (5.2.4.3)$$

$$\frac{\partial S_t}{\partial t} = (C_1 + D_1 r'_t)\, Y_t + (C_2 + D_2 r'_t)\, K_t, \qquad (5.2.4.4)$$

with

$$\left.\begin{aligned} A_{1t} &= A_1 + C_1 t \\ A_{2t} &= A_2 + D_1 t \\ B_{1t} &= B_1 + C_2 t \\ B_{2t} &= B_2 + D_2 t \end{aligned}\right\} \text{ representing } \left.\begin{aligned} A_1 \\ A_2 \\ B_1 \\ B_2 \end{aligned}\right\} \text{ after } \alpha_{ast} \text{ has been substituted for } \alpha_{as0}.$$

Expressions (5.2.4.1) and (5.2.4.2), as well as (5.2.4.3) and (5.2.4.4), pairwise resemble each other. The first two partial derivatives depend on time and the rate of interest, and the last two on income and personal wealth, in combination with time and rate of interest respectively.

With regard to the signs of those income, personal wealth, interest rate and time effects, we may draw upon the results arrived at in section 5.2.2. Therefore, in general:

$$\partial S_t/\partial Y_t > 0, \tag{5.2.4.5}$$

$$\partial S_t/\partial K_t < 0, \tag{5.2.4.6}$$

and

$$\partial S_t/\partial r_t' > 0. \tag{5.2.4.7}$$

On the other hand, $\partial S_t/\partial t$ may be positive as well as negative, due to the a priori indeterminateness of C_1, C_2, D_1 and D_2.

The results obtained with respect to the macro-model generally agree – at least, never disagree – with those derived for the micro-model in sections 4.2.3 through 4.2.5. For the micro-model too, the income effect is generally positive, and the initial personal wealth effect is always negative. On the other hand, the interest effect on aggregate savings would always be positive, whereas its effect on savings by individuals may be positive, zero or negative. The latter difference is due to the circumstance that for the macro-model final desired personal wealth has been assumed to vanish (cf. (5.1.3.8)), whereas for the micro-model signs and values of both that dream-variable K_L and the observed K_0 have been left indeterminate; for $K_L \leq K_0$, the micro-model too would always yield a positive effect of an increase in the rate of interest on current savings.

On the other hand, for the micro-model a more definite conclusion could be drawn about the order of magnitude of income and wealth effects, viz. that the former would exceed the latter (cf. section 4.2.4) – numerically as well as algebraically – more than would be allowed for by the macro-model. The reason is that for the macro-model the effects of prospective and current income are lumped together by assumptions (5.1.3.4) and (5.1.3.5), whereas for the micro-model primarily the effect of an *isolated* change in current income on current savings is evaluated. Therefore, the income effect for the macro-model according to (5.2.4.1) should more appropriately be compared with the 'overall' income effect:

$$\frac{dS_1}{dY_1} = 1 - \frac{dC_1}{dY_1} = (1 - \alpha_1) - \alpha_1 \sum_{l=2}^{L} (1 + r)^{1-l} (Y_l/Y_1), \tag{5.2.4.8}$$

derived from (4.2.3.6) in the micro-model after replacement of ε by 1, i.e. on the assumption of strict proportionality between prospective and current income over actual time.

5.3. *A growth model of aggregate personal wealth*

In section 4.4 we analyzed the individual's prospective time-pattern of personal wealth; here, we deal with the (likewise theoretical) course of *aggregate* personal wealth over *actual* time.

Again disregarding possible changes in asset prices, we write:

$$S_t = K_{t+1} - K_t,^{8} \quad \text{for } t = 1, \ldots, T \tag{5.3.1}$$

by definition.

Substitution of (5.3.1) into (5.1.3.13) and rearrangement of the term results in the following linear first-difference equation in K_t:

$$K_{t+1} = \varphi_t \, [K_t + \Psi_t Y_t], \tag{5.3.2}$$

with

$$\begin{aligned} \varphi_t &= 1 + (B_1 + C_2 t) + (B_2 + D_2 t)\, r_t' \\ &= 1 - \sum_{a,s} \alpha_{ast} k_{as} \{d_{as}(1 + \bar{r})\}^{1 - L_{as}} \{1 - (L_{as} - 1)\, r_t'\}, \end{aligned} \tag{5.3.3}$$

after substitution of (5.1.3.14) for B_1, B_2, C_2 and D_2, while taking account of (5.1.3.3) for α_{ast}, and

$$\begin{aligned} \Psi_t &= [(A_1 + C_1 t) + (A_2 + D_1 t)\, r_t']\, \varphi_t^{-1} \\ &= \left[1 - \bar{\alpha}_t - \sum_{a,s} \alpha_{ast} \sum_{l=1}^{L_{as}-1} y_{asl} \{d_{as}(1 + \bar{r})\}^{-1} (1 - l r_t')\right] \varphi_t^{-1}, \end{aligned} \tag{5.3.4}$$

---

[8] In view of the definition of K_t in section 5.1.1, the timing of this variable in the savings identity differs from the one adopted for prospective time in (4.1.3.6).

after substitution of (5.1.3.14) for A_1, A_2, C_1 and D_1, while again taking account of (5.1.3.3) and writing $\bar{\alpha}_t = \bar{\alpha}_0 + \bar{\gamma}t$.

The solution of (5.3.2) is:

$$K_{t+1} = K_1 \prod_{\tau=1}^{t} \varphi_\tau + \sum_{\tau=1}^{t} \Psi_\tau Y_\tau \prod_{\tau'=\tau}^{t} \varphi_{\tau'}, \tag{5.3.5}$$

with the first and second term of the right-hand member representing the endogenous and exogenous components respectively.

Consequently, the time path of K_t depends on the signs and numerical values assumed by φ_τ and $\Psi_\tau Y_\tau$ for $\tau = 1, \ldots, t$, while t increases indefinitely. According to (5.3.3), $0 < \varphi_\tau < 1$ for all τ. Most likely, $\varphi_\tau \Psi_\tau$ too will lie between 0 and 1, for the same reasons as those advanced in section 5.2.2 for explaining why A_1 should be confined to the same range. Both the endogenous component and the summands of the exogenous component will be reduced by the φ_τ, the more so according as t is larger.

As a consequence, the endogenous component will monotonically decrease towards zero (over time). The reducing effect of the $\varphi_{\tau'}$ (with increasing t) on the exogenous component, however, is counteracted by the ensueing increase in the number of (positive) summands.

The overall effect of these two opposing forces on the exogenous component may be positive, negative or zero; its sign may even vary over time. Actually, the difference in value of that component between successive periods t and $t - 1$ is:

$$\sum_{\tau=1}^{t} \Psi_\tau Y_\tau \prod_{\tau'=\tau}^{t} \varphi_{\tau'} - \sum_{\tau=1}^{t-1} \Psi_\tau Y_\tau \prod_{\tau'=\tau}^{t-1} \varphi_{\tau'} = \Psi_t Y_t \varphi_t - (1 - \varphi_t) \sum_{\tau=1}^{t-1} \Psi_\tau Y_\tau \prod_{\tau'=\tau}^{t-1} \varphi_{\tau'} \tag{5.3.6}$$

$$\gtreqless 0 \quad \text{according as}$$

$$1 - \varphi_t \lesseqgtr \frac{\Psi_t Y_t}{\sum_{\tau=1}^{t-1} \Psi_\tau Y_\tau \prod_{\tau'=1}^{t-1} \varphi_{\tau'} + \Psi_t Y_t \varphi_t}.$$

Consequently, the exogenous component of K_{t+1} may rise or decline monotonically or alternatingly.

The same could apply to the sum of the endogenous and the exogenous components; the decreasing tendency of the endogenous component, however, may dominate possible incidental or continuing rises in the exogenous component.

It is interesting to compare these dynamics of aggregate personal wealth with the time-path of individual personal wealth. For this purpose we try to write K_τ in terms of a first-order linear difference equation, like K_{t+1} according to (5.3.2). For that purpose, we rewrite (4.1.3.6) as:

$$S_\tau = K_\tau - K_{\tau-1} = r_\tau K_{\tau-1} + (Y_\tau - C_\tau - r_\tau K_0) \qquad (5.3.7)$$

(replacing the constant r by a variable r_τ);

or,

$$K_\tau = (1 + r_\tau)\{K_{\tau-1} + (1 + r_\tau)^{-1}(Y_\tau - C_\tau - r_\tau K_0)\}. \qquad (5.3.8)$$

Equation (5.3.8) is formally equivalent to (5.3.2), with $(1 + r_\tau)$ corresponding to φ_τ and $(1 + r_\tau)^{-1}(Y_\tau - C_\tau - r_\tau K_0)$ corresponding to $\Psi_\tau Y_\tau$. Therefore, the 'solution' of (5.3.8) may be written in the form of (5.3.5), i.e. as:

$$K_\tau = K_0 \prod_{\tau'=1}^{\tau} (1 + r_{\tau'})$$
$$+ \sum_{\tau'=1}^{\tau} (Y_{\tau'} - C_{\tau'} - r_{\tau'} K_0)(1 + r'_{\tau+1})^{-1} \prod_{\tau''=1}^{\tau'} (1 + r_{\tau''+1}). \qquad (5.3.9)$$

The first term in the second member of (5.3.9) might suggest that with increasing τ and for positive $r_{\tau'}$ the effect of K_0 on K_τ would grow forever. Such an interpretation, however, disregards the presence of K_0 in the second term of that member, both explicitly and implicitly in the $C_{\tau'}$. Taking account of this structure results in (4.4.1) through (4.4.4), implying a decreasing but positive effect of K_0 – as represented by

$$1 - \hat{\alpha}_\tau (1 + r)^{\tau - L} \quad \text{– on } K_\tau.$$

For aggregate savings, equation (5.3.5) likewise ensures a reduction of the impact of initial personal wealth (K_1) on personal wealth in later periods, by virtue of $\varphi_\tau < 1$. Still, dissimilarities in time-paths between aggregate and individual personal wealth may arise, due to differences in the way they are brought about. The main reason is that the former relate to *actual* time and the latter to *prospective* time; an additional reason, related to the former one, is that in the aggregate intertemporal relationships the set of individuals changes over time, by young people and immigrants becoming income recipients on the one hand, and older people dying or emigrating on the other hand. A minor reason is the approximation bias – inherent in the aggregate relationships – because of the assumptions made and linearizations applied.

As shown in section 4.4 above, the individuals' actual lifetime pattern of personal wealth will deviate from its prospective patterns, the most essential reason being that with the passing of actual time, the individual's life is either cut off or extended in expectation. The prospective lifetime pattern of personal wealth has two assumedly fixed points, viz. $(0, K_0)$ and (L, K_L). The time-curve of aggregate personal wealth, however, does not have such a 'dead end', since it is based on the idea (if not ideal) of a perennial (and possibly growing) population and economy.

Another important, but outwardly invisible difference between the micro- and the macro-growth models of personal wealth stems from the nature of their variables. In the micro-model, the explanatory variables, like income and the rate of interest, may well be considered as exogenous with respect to savings; although feedback effects of prospective savings on income expectations through varying intended work and training efforts are not inconceivable, they do not seem strong enough to be taken into consideration. In the macro-model, however, income is in turn, at least partly, determined by savings, viz. by adding to physical capital as an important factor of production. Apart from population growth, that is the main explanation of the usual upward trend in the aggregate capital stock, whereas equation (5.3.5) might result in a decrease in personal wealth.

As a consequence, disregard of a production function may impair the significance of the dynamic analysis of the development of aggregate personal wealth presented above. Therefore, we now endeavour to remedy that omission.

Suppose that total personal income Y_t and total personal wealth K_t may be considered as appropriate measures of the total volume of production and total physical capital for periods t respectively, one may assume a simple production function of the Cobb–Douglas type, for instance:

$$Y_t = c_t K_{t+1/2}^{\varkappa} \cdot N_{t+1/2}^{\nu} \tag{5.3.10}$$

with $N_{t+1/2}$ and $K_{t+1/2}$ representing the mid-period labour force and capital stock both standardized for variations in composition with respect to quality, c_t a technological progress factor, and $\varkappa$ and ν denoting positive constants, presumably less than 1; both N_t and c_t are considered as exogenous with respect to the variables in the savings function.

Substitution of (5.3.10) into (5.3.2) yields:

$$K_{t+1} = \varphi_t \,(K_t + \chi_t K_{t+1/2}^{\varkappa}) \quad \text{for } t = 1, \ldots, T \tag{5.3.11}$$

with $\chi_t = \Psi_t c_t N_{t+1/2}^{\nu}$.

Equation (5.3.11) is a homogeneous, non-linear second-order difference equation in $K_{t/2}$, with χ_t – like φ_t – exogenous. Equation (5.3.11) does not have an exact analytical solution, except in the case where φ_τ and χ_τ are very special functions of time (or are constant), and $\varkappa$ assumes a special value (like 1).

None of these eventualities, however, is likely to prevail here. Still, for φ_t and χ_t as given functions of time, and with K_0 and $\varkappa$ as data, the time path of K_τ may be traced by repeated application of (5.3.11).

First, for $t = 1$, K_1 may be solved numerically if $K_{1/2}^{\varkappa}$ is approximated by $\frac{1}{2}\, K_0^{\varkappa}\{(2 - \varkappa)\, K_0 + \varkappa K_1\}$ for given K_0 and $\varkappa$;[9] then, for $t = 2$, it may be inserted into (5.3.11) for computing K_2; etc.

Unfortunately, however, the preceding reasoning disregards differences in meaning (hence in value) of variables K_t and Y_t between (5.1.3.13) and (5.3.1) on the one hand, and (5.3.10) on the other hand.

In the former two equations, K_t denotes *financial* capital (or personal wealth), whereas in the latter relationship K_t designates physical capital; in the first equation Y_t means income, whereas in the last one it stands for production (value added).

In at least two respects physical capital may differ from financial personal wealth. The main reason is that the former but not the latter is specifically relevant to physical production: personal wealth measures the present value of *future* contributions of physical capital to personal income, whereas for *current* production only the present-time technical efficiency is decisive. Empirically, this difference amounts to the following: with increasing age of the machinery and other fixed capital, the expected future stream of productive contributions diminishes along with decreasing life expectancy; on the other hand, productive efficiency of machines may remain at (approximately) the same level till after a certain time it drops rapidly, dooming the machines to reserve functions and the scrap-heap eventually. Hence, in general, physical capital and personal wealth will not develop in a parallel way, especially in the case of substantial changes in the age composition of productive equipment – as first observed by Griliches [1963].

For open groups there is an additional cause of difference, viz. that personal wealth owned by people belonging to a certain group, such as a nation, may have been invested at least partly outside the group, while production by

---

[9] A numerical solution of an analogous problem was also adopted by Qayum [1966, ch. III], when dealing with a growth model for a developing economy.

the group may be carried out by means of capital invested – at least partly – by people outside the group.

If the economy is open, this may give rise to a similar difference between the two Y_t concepts in the sense that part of a country's production may accrue to foreigners, whereas its residents may receive income from abroad.

True, one can try to interrelate the two kinds of K_t, as well as the two kinds of Y_t, albeit by means of still other variables.

Denoting aggregate physical ('*p*roductive') capital and personal wealth ('*f*inancial' capital) at the end of periods t by K_{pt} and K_{ft} respectively, the former may be represented by:

$$K_{pt} = \sum_{\tau=t-T}^{t} I_\tau (1 - \sum_{\tau'=\tau}^{t} \delta_{\tau\tau'}) \pi_{\tau/0}, \tag{5.3.12}$$

with I_τ = investments in period τ,
T = maximum lifetime of capital goods,
$\delta_{\tau\tau'}$ = physical, productivity reducing deterioration in period τ' of capital goods invested in period $\tau \leq \tau'$,
$\pi_{\tau/0}$ = index number of technological productivity of capital goods manufactured and invested in period τ compared with (an arbitrary) base period 0.

Thus, the indicator of physical capital K_{pt} takes account of the cumulative process of investments physically deteriorating by wear-and-tear (or simply ageing) but technically improving from earlier to later vintages.

In a closed economy:

$$I_\tau \equiv S_\tau (= K_{f\tau} - K_{f,\tau-1}), \tag{5.3.13}$$

so that substitution of (5.3.13) into (5.3.12) links physical to financial capital:

$$K_{pt} = \sum_{\tau=t-T}^{t} (K_{f\tau} - K_{f,\tau-1}) (1 - \sum_{\tau'=\tau}^{t} \delta_{\tau\tau'}) \pi_{\tau/0}. \tag{5.3.14}$$

In a open economy, however, (5.3.13) would have to be replaced by:

$$I_\tau + I_{e\tau} - I_{i\tau} \equiv S, \tag{5.3.15}$$

with $I_{e\tau}$ and $I_{i\tau}$ representing *e*xport and *i*mport of capital funds respectively.

Likewise, if we denote by Y_{pt} and Y_{ft} domestic production and domestic income, and by Y_{et} and Y_{it} income transfers to and from foreign countries, respectively, these variables are linked by the identity:

$$Y_{pt} \equiv Y_{ft} - Y_{et} + Y_{it}. \tag{5.3.16}$$

The (generally important) capital income components of Y_{et} and Y_{it} are the cumulated and financially depreciated values of I_{et} and I_{it} multiplied by their corresponding yields, respectively; other components of Y_{et} and Y_{it}, such as personal remittances to or from relatives abroad depend on the incidence of international migration, differences in levels of income, as well as on less tangible factors such as intensity of family ties. In turn, $I_{e\tau}$ and $I_{i\tau}$ depend, inter alia, on international differences in capital yield, speculative motives based on expectations in regard to currency devaluations or revaluations, etc. Tracing these effects would require the introduction of such a multitude of other variables that its core, viz. the original three-equation model, consisting of (5.1.3.13), (5.3.1) and (5.3.10) would soon become entangled in a proliferation of international financial relationships.

Still, this is the least of our troubles, since we might treat capital and income exports and imports as exogenous without undue violation of our scientific conscience: these international variables are generally of relatively small importance, cancelling each other at least partly, and depending to a great extent on exogenous variables in a stricter sense and/or having their origin in the remote (predetermined) past. In contradistinction, relationships (5.3.15) are much more troublesome. Disregarding (numerical) differences between Y_{pt} and Y_{ft}, but retaining the distinction between K_{pt} and K_{ft}, requires the modification of (5.3.11) into:

$$K_{ft} = \varphi_t\,[K_{f,t-1} + \chi_t K^{\varkappa}_{p,t-1/2}]. \tag{5.3.17}$$

Substitution of (5.3.14) into (5.3.17) results in:

$$K_{ft} = \varphi_\tau K_{f,t-1} + \varphi_t \chi_t \{\sum_{\tau=t-1/2-T}^{t-1/2} (K_{f,\tau} - K_{f,\tau-1})\,(1 - \sum_{\tau'=\tau}^{t-1/2} \delta_{\tau\tau'})\,\pi_{\tau/0}\}^{\varkappa}, \tag{5.3.18}$$

an implicit difference equation of unknown and unknowable order (unless $\varkappa^{-1}$ is a rational number) in $K_{f,t/2}$.

The upshot of it all is that if we let ourselves be lured by the sirens of scientific perfection, we could never extricate ourselves from the fascinating intricacies of (5.3.18): lest we forget about homecoming, we had better harden ourselves against the charm of over-theorizing, and confine ourselves to the savings equation (5.1.3.13) pure and simple. Taking the middle course of (5.3.11) instead of going the whole hog is just not good enough; even if it seems to be a model of simplicity compared with (5.3.18), it causes us sufficient trouble, especially from the point of view of parameter estimation, to keep clear of it.

5.4. Interim appraisal of the macro-savings function

In view of the many assumptions made and the approximations adopted for deriving the macro-savings functions on the basis of the micro-model, the latter apparently is more sophisticated than the former. Since, moreover, those assumptions and approximations are mainly concentrated in the second stage of the aggregation process, possible resulting distortions tend to be more serious with respect to the 'overall' savings function compared with the 'sex–age' group savings functions.

The magnitude and effects of the resulting discrepancies depend, of course, on the extent to which reality deviates from the assumptions. However, nothing much is known about it (otherwise it would not have been necessary to make these assumptions in the first place!).

On the other hand, the set of assumptions introduced in section 5.1 is somewhat too strict; in particular, expressions within sums relating to different individuals (i, i') within the same group (a, s), or to different groups (a, s), (a', s') within the whole 'nation', are allowed to swap values in (5.1.2.1) and in (5.1.3.13) respectively, without altering group or national savings. In as far as such reshuffling does not fully compensate for possible empirical violation of assumptions, the latter may be taken care of by the introduction of 'disturbances' into the models, provided they are stochastic rather than systematic. Indeed, such disturbances will be introduced in chapter 7 for the analysis of savings on the basis of macro-economic time series.

Approximate linearization of the discount factors, however, might give rise to *bias* (according to (5.1.3.12)) under the provisions made. In a relative sense, this bias is more serious according as $r'l$ is larger; on the other hand, the incomes to which these linearizations are applied are reduced more strongly by the 'average' discount factors $(1 + \bar{r})^{1-l}$ according as l assumes a higher value, i.e. according as they relate to a future that is farther removed from the present.

Finally, the macro-model may suffer from over-simplification of the basic micro-model. In general, choice of a more sophisticated micro-model, for which suggestions have been made in chapters 2 and 3, would be non-operational as a basis for macro-models. The reason is the lack of empirical information, especially with respect to prospective values of the relevant variables. It necessitates the adoption of strong assumptions with respect to the simplest micro-savings function (4.1.3.4), and a fortiori with respect to more intricate models.

EMPIRICAL PART

CHAPTER 6

APPLICATION OF THE MICRO-SAVINGS FUNCTION TO SURVEY DATA

6.1. Empirical basis: the 1960 Savings Survey of the Netherlands

6.1.1. SCOPE AND SIZE OF THE SAMPLE

During 1961 the Netherlands Central Bureau of Statistics carried out a savings survey in the Netherlands for 1960 as the reference period. This survey was confined to households of employees and pensioners. The reason for this limitation of the scope of the survey is that obtaining complete and reliable data from employers and self-employed persons was considered too difficult, especially since at that time this survey was the first of its kind in the Netherlands. This restriction should be kept in mind when considering the set-up and the results of the analysis.

About 2300 households headed by employees, 1100 pensioners' households and 150 households headed by independent workers but including members working as employees, were incorporated in the sample; of the households headed by employees about 2 percent included employers or self-employed. The households enumerated above also comprised some 600 single persons. The probabilities of households being drawn into the sample differed according to occupational status and income of the heads of the households (including single persons); sample fractions were higher in the upper income classes than in the lower ones.

In this survey, savings and related data were collected for all members of the households, either separately or collectively. Separate questionnaires were completed for all members of 15 years of age or over, receiving income (independently), on the basis of personal interviews. In case, however, the *labour* income of a member earned in 1960 was less than 250 guilders, it was added to that of the head of the household; in such a case, no separate worksheet was drawn up for that person. In this way, worksheets were completed for nearly 5000 heads and other members of households, summarizing, inter alia, data on income and savings. These worksheets provided the basic data for the savings analysis to be explained below. For a fuller description of the savings survey in question, and its tabulated results, cf. the series of pertinent publications prepared by the Netherlands Central Bureau of Statistics [1963, 1964].

6.1.2. REFERENCE UNITS

In processing the information collected from the persons interviewed in the Savings Survey, the Central Bureau of Statistics generally adopted *households* (including single persons) as reference units; therefore, the published tables present results mainly in terms of average savings *per household*, classified according to various characteristics, such as income and size of the household and the occupational status of the head of the household.

Since the household was already chosen as a sample unit – mainly for practical reasons –, the same kind of unit was retained for processing and tabulation purposes as well[1]. In this way, moreover, time and costs incurred by these operations were reduced, compared with the alternative of adopting separate persons as units.

A more essential reason for preferring the former to the latter kind of unit might have been the idea that decisions about savings are made by the household as a whole (either autocratically by the head of the household or the housewife, or democratically as a 'committee') rather than by individual members. The fact, however, that it was deemed necessary (and rightly so) to ask the individual income receiving members of the household about their own savings and its determining factors, such as income, is at variance with that view.

The theory set forth above provides even stronger arguments in favour of choosing individual income recipients instead of households as reference units. This theory shows clearly the paramount importance of personal characteristics, such as age and sex, in particular since the latter principally fix the life expectancy as one of the most important determinants of savings.

---

[1] On the basis of an analogous conception with respect to consumer expenditures, viz. that the latter would be decided upon by the household as a unit, Barten [1964] based his theory of family composition effects on expenditure allocation as quasi-price effects.

For analytical purposes, choice of individual persons instead of households has the additional advantage of enhancing the probability of arriving at significant results (at fixed confidence levels) by increasing the number of units of observation.

Indeed, the one and only criterion relevant for including members of the household as 'savers' (or dissavers) is that they possess the characteristics essential for allowing them to draw up their own 'savings plan'. For this purpose they should have attained a certain minimum age, earn at least a certain income, and show a sufficient degree of financial independence. Presumably, these criteria are approximately met by persons for whom worksheets have been completed, viz.:

(a) being 15 years of age or over, on January 1, 1960,
(b) having earned at least 250 Dutch guilders during 1960, and consequently:
(c) enjoying reasonable financial independence in general[2].

On the other hand: of the persons for whom no worksheet was completed, a negligible fraction only would satisfy those criteria (viz. women married under a marriage contract and adult members of the household, both with income from property, unoccupied but nevertheless financially independent).

Last but no least, basing the savings analysis on *individuals* enables us to study the relationships between savings behaviour of persons belonging to the same household (cf. sections 6.5.3 and 6.6.7).

6.1.3. FURTHER DELIMITATION OF THE REFERENCE GROUP

In principle, all persons for whom a worksheet was completed were included in the analysis. In addition to the reasons just mentioned, the practical advantage (or even necessity) of such a procedure was that in this way the data required for the analysis was available separately.

For various reasons, however, this set of observational units has to be restricted. First, all those people had to be left out for whom no (complete and sufficiently reliable) data was at our disposal for calculating the 'urgencies to consume' α_1, to be analyzed. It appeared, however, that this excluded

---

[2] By civil code also married women and minors may freely dispose of the wages and salaries they receive.

only those persons (165) who did not state (in a reasonably correct way) their personal wealth[3].

Secondly, all those people were excluded from the analysis for whom computation of the present value of the flow of expected future income would meet with insurmountable difficulties. In particular, this applied to men under 60 (police officers and military staff) and miners under 50 years of age who stated their intention to stop working within the next five years, as well as to students or trainees planning to start working within the next three years. Such a situation appeared to prevail for about 100 persons included in the Savings Survey sample. In this case, no attempt was made to approximate the present value of the flow of expected future income: in view of the inevitable crudeness of such an estimate, the additional effort required did not seem justified. As a result, however, the group of people in training or receiving advanced education – hence, belonging to the lowest age class – may well be under-represented.

On the other hand, the problem of computing the income term in the savings function could be solved reasonably well for the large majority of the more than 250 cases in which persons earned their living during a part of the year (1960) only; specifically, this applied on the one hand to people starting work for the first time or after a period of unemployment, and on the other hand to people becoming unemployed or being pensioned off in 1960. No satisfactory solution, however, could be found for the approximately 50 persons experiencing a change in income (within the same occupation) or changing jobs during 1960.

The few cases of persons stating a negative income (e.g. by losses incurred in plying a trade or practising a profession) were likewise excluded; the reason is that the only practicable method adopted here for estimating the present value of the flow of expected future income, would result in a – logically inacceptable – negative figure for such a value (cf. sections 6.2.2 and 6.2.8).

For obvious reasons, we also had to reject people whose (positive) savings purportedly exceeded their income, thus apparently implying negative consumption. Presumably, these anomalous situations were brought about by donations bestowed by one marriage partner on the other, not shown

[3] Information about income from property might have enabled a rough approximation of personal wealth at the beginning of the year, by applying a certain yield estimate. Such a procedure, however, was omitted in view of the resulting uncertainty of the personal wealth estimate, and considering that we were still left with a sufficiently large number of units.

on the questionnaire (inter alia, because of the existence of a joint bank account).

Finally, we eliminated the few holiday workers not yet 15 years old but still represented by work-sheets.

Eventually, we were left with 4412 cases apparently suitable for econometric analysis.

6.1.4. CONTENTS OF THE SURVEY QUESTIONNAIRE AND ITS USE IN THE SAVINGS ANALYSIS

In the Savings Survey, information was obtained about, inter alia:

1°. *personal characteristics* of the head and other members of the household, relating to December 31, 1960, viz.:

(a) sex
(b) age
(c) marital status
(d) year of marriage[4]
(e) status in household
(f) number of members of the household
(g) occupation
(h) industry
(i) whether or not student or trainee
(j) plans with respect to beginning of economic activity[4]
(k) plans with respect to ending of economic activity[4]
(l) motives for saving
(m) whether or not owner of the dwelling
(n) place of residence.

2°. *financial flow variables* relating to the year 1960, viz.:

(a) income distinguished by source (including income transfers and pensions),
(b) savings and investments, distinguished by nature, mode and destination,
(c) rent (or rental value) of dwellings,
(d) financial transactions possibly concluded for purchasing durable consumer goods,

---

[4] When applicable.

(e) extraordinary expenses[5],
(f) one-sided capital transfers,
(g) changes in the composition of personal wealth.

3°. *personal wealth*, distinguished by mode of investment, on December 31, 1960.

Moreover, data about members of the household, appearing, inter alia, on the cover sheet of the household questionnaire, in addition to 1° (f), provide information on the household's size and composition.

For the savings analysis applied here, only part of the information has been used, viz.:

A. for the computation of α_1:
2° (a). (income),
2° (b). (total savings),
3°. (personal wealth on December 31, 1959),

and

B. for the analysis of α_1:
1° (a). through (e) (supplemented by household data), (g) and (m),
2° (e),

for reasons to be explained in sections 6.2 and 6.3, respectively.

The data referred to under 1° (i) through (k) merely serve the purpose of eliminating persons interviewed who are exceptional with respect to their economic activity.

Savings motives – in the sense of intended destination of savings – are disregarded, since they do not fit into the savings model. The popular notion that people save for specific purposes may look plausible because of the existence of various savings arrangements for specific purposes, such as offered by building societies for eventually acquiring a house. On the other hand, such a notion fails to acknowledge the fluidity and universal applicability of savings. Intentions about spending accumulated savings may – and do – change overnight; this is precisely the outstanding characteristic of savings proper, in contradistinction to purchases of durable consumer goods, for instance, which may be considered as part-investment. Moreover, what may

[5] In 1960, comprising medical expenses exceeding a certain minimum level and (financial) support of close relatives (excluding children for whom children's allowance is received and tax deduction is granted).

seem to be savings for a special purpose, by means of a separate 'piggy bank', might be compensated by dissavings elsewhere, or less savings along different channels than might have been effected otherwise.

Finally, 'savings motives' do not have a logical counterpart in 'dissavings'-motives. Theoretically, savings differ from dissavings only in value, or at most with respect to the relevant rate of interest.

According to the savings theory set forth in chapters 2 through 4, the savings-dissavings pattern over time is aimed at maximizing the utility of *total* consumer expenditures over time, subject to the lifetime budget constraint. In this theory, there is no place for specific purposes of savings; allocation of the total amount of money earmarked for spending in a certain period to specific budget items is determined by second-stage optimization following the first-stage allocation of total resources over time to savings and consumption.

On the other hand, for computing the individual α_1, the data mentioned above under 1° through 3°, as collected in the Savings Survey, are still insufficient. Specifically, we need additional information about:

4°. income expectations,
5°. survival rates and life expectancies,
6°. rate(s) of discounting,
7°. desired final personal wealth,
and possibly:
8°. prospective levels of consumer and asset prices.

The reliability of the results of the savings analysis might have been enhanced if the completed questionnaires could also have supplied at least some information about 4° through 8°.

Still, such figures (if at all provided by individuals), would not have been very dependable either: many people do not cherish numerically specified expectations about their income, lifetime etc., and less so according as the reference period is farther removed from the present; on the other hand, the discount factors reduce the importance of data according as they relate to the more distant future – as pointed out in section 5.4.

Proposals for asking additional pertinent questions were rejected for fear that they would jeopardize the success of the entire survey. For this reason, the gap in our information about the aforementioned items has to be filled by means of non-individualized outside data, in the manner explained in section 6.3.

As stated above, questions about possible premature termination of economic activity were inserted in the questionnaire, mainly in order to preclude inappropriate standard treatment in such exceptional cases. According to the instructions accompanying the questionnaire, however, these questions were not put to unoccupied persons, to persons under 50 years of age, nor to married women. Consequently, no account could be taken of the usual case of young women's intentions to terminate paid activity soon after the conclusion of a contemplated marriage[6].

In such cases, adoption of standard procedures, viz. application of the age pattern of income relating to the minority of women still working at higher ages might give an upward bias to the present value of future income expected by the majority of women. For this reason, less importance should be attached to the savings analysis' results for women, compared with those for men. For the overall success of the analysis, however, the circumstance that only about one-fourth of the persons interviewed in the Savings Survey consisted of women, should be considered as a blessing in disguise.

6.2. Quantification of the variables in the micro-savings function

6.2.1. CURRENT INCOME, SAVINGS AND CONSUMPTION

Current (value of) consumption cannot directly be taken from the worksheets, but has to be calculated as the difference between income and savings thereupon recorded.

In the C.B.S.-publications on the methodology and the results of the 1960 Savings Survey of the Netherlands [1963, 1964], the mutually consistent National Accounts definitions of personal (disposable) income, consumption and savings were largely retained. Some minor modifications, however, were adopted, viz. by adding to personal disposable income:

(a) Pension Fund benefits,
(b) employers' and employees' contributions to Sick Fund,
as well as:
(c) imputed interest on contractual savings,
and *subtracting*:
(d) employers' and employees' contributions to Pension Fund.

[6] At least in the Netherlands!

For the present purpose, the National Accounts definition of personal savings has been adjusted accordingly by (again):

(a) adding Pension Fund benefits, and

(b) subtracting Pension Fund premiums.

True, the value of consumption is unaffected by these self-same changes in both income and savings. However, they still have an impact on current income, as well as on future income computationally based on it (cf. section 6.2.2).

The adjustments underlying the redefinition of disposable income were aimed at approximating as closely as possible the amounts income recipients could freely dispose of, either for immediate consumption, or for saving – per unit of time. Savings have been redefined in such a way as to represent amounts forthcoming (per unit of time) for, or withheld from spending on future consumption, according as they are positive or negative (: dissavings), respectively.

Moreover, the definitions of disposable income and of savings agree mutually and with the definition of initial personal wealth (cf. section 6.2.3). Specifically, Pension Fund benefits have been added to income, and Pension Fund premiums have been subtracted from it, since the former can, but the latter cannot be freely disposed of. According to the system of National Accounts, however, those items are considered as savings and dissavings, respectively. Accordingly, such past cumulated or decumulated savings would have to be incorporated in initial personal wealth. On the other hand, it is well-nigh impossible to evaluate the claims of the respondents in the Savings Survey on total wealth administered by the Pension Funds. For this practical reason, in addition to the more fundamental reasons mentioned above, pensions are considered as income (of pensioners) and pension premiums as costs of acquiring this kind of income (perhaps, later on).

Employers' and employees' contributions to Sick Funds (b) were considered as payments for 'medicare', hence as components of both disposable income and consumption. The lag between receipts of Sick Fund premiums and payments for medicare is short enough to be neglected if years are chosen as units of time. Since the value of medical care received by individuals eludes direct observation, the amount of premium paid by or for these persons is adopted as a proxy.

Imputed interest (d) on contractual savings (e.g. for old-age pensions) should be conceived of as disposable income, since it raises the surrender and loanable value of the policy, security or other evidence of cumulated savings in question. Again, the latter correction too is needed for ensuring logical consistency between the concepts of income, savings and personal wealth. Accumulated contractual savings, e.g. as life insurance premiums, are included in initial personal wealth. Moreover, in those premiums interest is taken account of. Consequently, future expenditures would exceed future income and change in personal wealth – all duly discounted – if imputed interest on contractual savings is not included in income. For this reason, current income is augmented by interest on wealth invested in (life) insurance.

6.2.2. EXPECTED TIME PATTERN OF FUTURE INCOME

For approximating the expected course of future income[7], different assumptions are made about the time patterns of:

Y_{at} = labour income (wages, salaries, remuneration of entrepreneurial activity as well as pensions), and

Y_{ot} = capital income (interest, dividends, rents, rental value of owner-occupied dwelling, and imputed rent on contractual savings).

Therefore, these two types of income are dealt with separately in sections 6.2.2.1 and 6.2.2.2, respectively.

6.2.2.1. Labour income. With respect to prospective labour income, the assumption is made that the ratio $\hat{Y}_{i\in b,a,s;\tau}$ between the labour income expected for the period τ years hence to current income of an individual i with occupation b, age a (in the current period) and sex s, equals the ratio between the *mean* 'typical' (labour) income $\bar{Y}_{b,a+\tau,s}$ in the current period at age $a+\tau$ to ditto ($\bar{Y}_{bas}$) at age a, for people with occupation b and sex s; in formula:

$$\hat{Y}_{i\in b,a,s;\tau} = \bar{Y}_{b,a+\tau,s}/\bar{Y}_{b,a,s}. \qquad (6.2.2.1.1)$$

The latter two averages were derived from basic data[8] underlying the statistics on income distribution relating to the year nearest to the reference

---

[7] We remind the reader that possible interest receipts or payments of interest on net savings or dissavings accumulated since the beginning of the reference period are excluded from 'expected income' by definition (cf. section 2.4, table 2.1 and diagram 4.2 above).

[8] Indeed, the Netherlands Central Bureau of Statistics did publish income data, but not of the kind directly needed for the kind of analysis envisaged by us, i.e.:

1°. for income recipients classified by occupation, age and sex simultaneously (instead of by mere pairs of such characteristics), and

2°. relating to typical income instead of to total income.

period for which this kind of information was available at the time this econometric analysis started; the former proved to be 1958.

The basic assumption underlying (6.2.2.1.1) is that men and women base their lifetime income expectations on cross-section data, i.e. on current differences in mean income between age-classes, within the category comprising their occupation.

This hypothesis is questionable for at least two reasons. First, people belonging to the same occupational category may differ between age classes, e.g. because the younger generation is better educated than the older one, even if they perform the same kind of work. This tends to result in a downward bias in income expectations. Second, *future* age-patterns of income may vary from the present ones, due to both specific and general factors. The specific factors affecting future mean income *per* group of *occupation* for each sex and age-class are those determining demand for and supply of men and women of different ages to be active in various jobs; in turn, pertinent wage rates or mean incomes are part of these determinants. General factors – relating to all occupations alike – are trends and fluctuations in levels of prices and real income in general.

Such considerations, however, are hard or impossible to express in quantitative terms. True, a number of studies appeared about the future of markets for particular occupations, especially the academic professions (cf. e.g. Dalmulder [1959]); in addition, projections published by the Netherlands Central Planning Bureau present expected developments of the most important economic variables (such as real per capita income) for the next ten to fifteen years. Nevertheless, these prognostic studies are too limited in scope to be of much value for our purpose.

Of decisive importance, however, is that the expectations relevant here should reflect the ideas that individuals may have about their future income on which they base their savings behaviour; contrariwise, future developments considered most likely by economic experts are irrelevant in that respect unless accepted by the income recipients – which is hardly plausible: the majority of them does not read publications written for specialists, but is swayed by general, readily available information, however misleading it might be. In this respect, crude but comprehensive and general cross-section means, as processed in the way outlined above, has a definite advantage over more special figures from various other and usually more obscure sources.

Finally, one should keep in mind that whereas the *relative* prospective future incomes are computed in a collectivistic way, the income recipient's current income on which those expected income ratios are grafted, is individualized.

These considerations are the reason why we adopted the cross-section data[9] as the basis for computing the present value of expected future income, notwithstanding the theoretical objections that can be raised to it.

The reason for preferring typical to total income in order to estimate prospective future income is that total income includes 'other' income, which is dealt with separately. True, this 'other' income is part of entrepreneurial income of independent workers, consisting of both labour and capital income. In this Savings Survey, however, entrepreneurs were infrequent, i.e. appearing but occasionally as members of households headed by employees, pensioners or unemployed. In addition, even to entrepreneurial income (in the Netherlands), capital income does not contribute more than about 10 per cent.[10] The only category of persons whose typical income – by definition – consists entirely of capital income are the (rare) income recipients without occupation.

Altogether, but 14 socio-economic (occupational) classes could be distinguished (cf. table 6C.1). On the one hand, such a broad classification gives rise to heterogeneity of the categories, and might entail 'aggregation bias' (e.g. because the composition of these categories by detailed occupation may differ according to age and sex, and thus affect the course of mean income from one age class to the next one). On the other hand, it allows for the rather frequent change of occupation within the same broad class, the latter being a prerequisite for the application of this method.

The income data for the Netherlands, 1958, had to be adapted to our analysis, in two ways:

(α) all quinquennial or decennial age-class data had to be detailed to age–year data, and

(β) corrections had to be made in cases where people had stated their intention to stop working before the normal age of retirement.

The methods adopted for these adaptations are described in appendices A and B to this chapter, respectively. On the other hand, pensions are considered as deferred labour income and assumed to be constant from the time of

---

[9] Cross-section income data are used for the same or similar purposes by other economists as well; cf. e.g. Houthakker [1959], Wilkinson [1966], Fase [1969] and the other publications the latter refers to.

[10] Cf. Somermeyer [1965, table 3].

retirement onwards. The resulting age pattern of mean labour income by occupation and sex is depicted in graphs 6C.1 through 13, and commented upon in appendix 6C.2, as a byproduct of this analysis.

6.2.2.2. Capital income. By definition, those parts of income resulting from (dis)savings effectuated after the initial date of the savings plan, are excluded from the concept of income used here (cf. footnote 7 to this chapter). Besides being operationally necessary for the reasons mentioned in section 2.4, this restriction has the additional advantage that prospective capital income may be considered as invariant over time, provided the same applies to the prospective yield.

Consequently, individuals' capital income over 1960, as reported in the Savings Survey, may also be considered as expected capital income for all future years within his or her life horizon. This capital income comprises interest (received (+) and/or paid (−)), dividends, rents or rented value of owner–occupied dwelling; it includes imputed interest on contractual savings (cf. section 6.2.1), but excludes interest received or paid on savings or dissavings cumulated since the beginning of the current period.

6.2.3. INITIAL PERSONAL WEALTH

For this savings analysis, (initial) personal wealth – like disposable income – is defined in generally the same way as adopted in the Savings Survey itself (cf. section 6.2 of the pertinent publication issued by the C.B.S. [1963]) – viz. as the total value of all assets, net of liabilities, at a person's disposal in the private sphere. Hence, for both purposes, real estate as well as all kinds of liquid assets (such as cash, bank balances, bonds and shares) are included, whereas durable consumer goods are excluded (indeed, no pertinent data was collected).

On the other hand, savings invested in annuities and in voluntarily contracted pension schemes – included in the Savings Survey concept of personal wealth – were left out of the valuation adopted for the present savings analysis. Instead, for the latter purpose, the savings components were subsumed among the second type of resources at the disposal of consumers, viz. future income. In this way, consistency with the likewise modified definition of income (cf. section 6.2.2) has been maintained.

Other cumulated contractual savings, however, are incorporated in the 'analysis' as well as in the 'Survey' concept of personal wealth.

Personal wealth on January 1, 1960, was not known directly, but was derived from personal wealth on December 31, 1960, by deducting changes in personal wealth during 1960, the latter two being stated on the worksheets. Since accurate data on savings invested in life insurance was unavailable, pertinent estimates based on general assumptions had to take its place (cf. section 6.3.3 of the C.B.S.-publication [1963]).

2.2.4. INTENDED FINAL PERSONAL WEALTH

The following considerations are at the basis of estimates of people's intended final personal wealth. Due to lack of pertinent direct information, we had to figure out people's presumable intentions. The fact that occasionally the assets of the deceased are found to exceed their liabilities was taken as an indication that most of them died unexpectedly if not prematurely; otherwise they might have used up their personal wealth. The only types of assets that may be regarded – with reasonable certainty – as intended to be left behind are the ones becoming available only *after* the death of the person concerned, viz. life insurance and burial-society benefits. Its present value was calculated on the basis of the premiums paid for or sums of those types of insurance purchased in 1960, in combination with the individual's age, according to insurance tables used at the time. The practical advantage of such an approach is its simplicity and unambiguity. Even if one assumes that people might intend to leave part of their present personal wealth to relatives, no one could tell what part (say 10, 50 or perhaps 200 per cent).

Fortunately, however, the results of this analysis are not very sensitive to errors in estimates of changes in personal wealth, possibly due to misinterpretation of people's intentions. The reason is that the contribution of intended change in personal wealth to total consumer resources is generally a minor one, compared with the contribution of the flow of current and future income. Most income recipients do not have any personal wealth worth mentioning, as evidenced by the fact that in the Netherlands less than one tenth of the income recipients was assessed in property tax. Total personal wealth equals but 4 to 5 years' total personal income, i.e. much less than the average income recipient's life expectancy (which is nearer to 35 years). Moreover, even owner-occupied dwellings cannot be presumed – beyond reasonable doubt – to be left to survivors, since it may be mortgaged or sold long before death (e.g. for securing a place in a nursing home for the old-aged). Last but not least, discount factors have a stronger reducing effect on change in personal wealth than on future incomes, because the latter are generally nearer to the present than final personal wealth (cf. inequality (4.2.4.2)).

Consequently, intended final personal wealth K_{iL}^* is set equal to zero, unless the Savings Survey gave evidence of life-insurance or burial-society contracts; in the latter case, K_{iL}^* was equated to the actuarial value of the ensuing claims at death.

6.2.5. SURVIVAL RATES AND LIFE EXPECTANCIES

Since no direct questions were asked about the interviewees' survival rates and life expectancy, this key variable had to be imputed to them on the basis of the prime *general* factors determining life expectancy and known for all respondents individually, viz. age and sex. A third factor reported upon in the Survey, viz. occupation, might also affect life expectancy, albeit to a lesser degree – at least in an economically developed and socially advanced country like the Netherlands; on the other hand, no survival rates are calculated per occupation – combined with age and sex –, inter alia, because occupation may and does change over time.

Consequently, respondents' survival rates and life expectancies have been derived from pertinent tables, drawn up by the Netherlands Central Bureau of Statistics, on the basis of their age and sex alone [1967].

Computationally, it appears to be simpler to operate with survival rates than with life expectancies, since the former but not the latter allow us to retain a uniform upper limit of summation over future time, viz. the maximum age of 106 years. This means that for carrying out the computations we adopted the 'alternative' model of section 4.3.4 rather than the basic model of section 4.1.3. The difference between these two approaches for the present value of expected future income is analyzed theoretically in appendix D to this chapter.

6.2.6. PROSPECTIVE RATES OF INTEREST

Since (again) no direct information about the prospective rates of interest for discounting future values was available, an indirect approach was in order. As a result, no reasonable method could be devised for numerical distinction of prospective rates of interest between (future) periods; it proved already difficult enough to decide upon uniform rates of interest (valid for all future periods).

In principle, it would have been possible to choose individualized rates of interest. As such, the yields of personal wealth of the individuals, i.e. the ratios of capital income to personal wealth could have been adopted. These yields tend to increase with the individuals' size of personal wealth.[11] Thus, higher interest rates, entailing more rapid decrease of discount factors, would have to be applied according as the individuals are richer. Nevertheless, the validity of the latter conclusion may be questioned.

First, prospective personal wealth will not be constant over time, but will vary in such a way – between assumedly given initial and final values – as to maximize utility. The complications arising from the introduction of the dependence of the rate of interest on personal wealth have already been noted in sections 2.8.2.2 and 2.8.3.2. Nevertheless, we maintain that – generally speaking – the poor will remain poor because they are poor, whereas the rich tend to become still richer because they are rich. On the other hand, the poor are more apt to encounter high rates of interest – i.e. not to receive, but to pay, e.g. for hire purchase –, whereas such indebtedness may be avoided by the rich, cushioned by sizeable positive personal wealth.

Second, inter-individual differences in capital yields may be compensated for by capital gains or losses, and affected, inter alia, by differences in taxation (because in the Netherlands no capital gains tax exists for private persons).

Third, individual capital yields in any particular year, such as 1960, may be strongly disturbed by incidental or accidental factors then prevailing; moreover, they depend on liquidity preference, which tends to be stronger according as personal wealth is less, thus contributing to the explanation of differences in capital yields in relation to size of personal wealth, as noted above.

Fourth, for older people the capital yields are much lower than the reciprocals of their life expectancies to be considered as the minimum rates of interest at which they would be inclined to lend money (cf. (2.3.1)).

For all these reasons, the individual current yields can hardly be considered as representing people's prospective rates of interest for discounting future values. Therefore, arguments in favour of choosing individualized values on general principles were overruled, and a *general* market rate of interest was deemed more relevant for most people's discounting of future values. As such, the average yield of the most important nine Government bonds in 1960, viz.

---

[11] Cf. Somermeyer [1965, table 19].

4.08 per cent per annum, as calculated by the C.B.S.[12] was selected. However, it should be conceded that also the latter measure is far from ideal. For one thing, it could hardly be considered applicable to older people, for the reason mentioned in section 2.3. No attempt was made to replace it by the reciprocals of life expectancy, although this might have been better from a theoretical point of view.

Unfortunately, the present value of future resources for financing lifetime consumption, hence the values of the α_1 ('urgencies to consume') to be analysed, are rather sensitive to errors in the rates of interest imputed. This sensitivity increases according as life expectancies are higher and according as a steeper rise of income is envisaged (especially in the middle-long run). This may be ascertained as follows: let

$$z = \sum_{l=1}^{M-a} Y_l s_l (1 + r)^{1-l} \tag{6.2.6.1}$$

denote the present value of the flow of current and expected future income of an individual with age a, while M denotes the maximum attainable age; then, its 'interest sensitivity' is expressed by:

$$-z^{-1} \frac{\partial z}{\partial r} = z^{-1} \sum_{l=1}^{M-a} (l - 1)\, Y_l s_l (1 + r)^{-l} \tag{6.2.6.2}$$

$$= (1 + r)^{-1} \sum_{l=1}^{M-a} (l - 1) \frac{Y_l s_l (1 + r)^{-l}}{\sum_{l'=1}^{M-a} Y_{l'} s_{l'} (1 + r)^{-l'}}.$$

The latter expression means that this sensitivity measure is an average of the time-spans $l - 1$ over maximum remaining lifetime, weighted by shares of discounted future income per period l in the present value of all future expected incomes – apart from a reduction factor $(1 + r)^{-1}$, near 1. Since $M - a$ decreases pari passu with advancing age a, that average length of time too will decrease. Moreover, it will be higher according as the Y_l assume higher values for later periods l, i.e. show steeper rises, compensating for the reducing effects of decreasing survival rates s_l and discount factors $(1 + r)^{-l}$. Consequently, the sensitivity of the results of the analysis is generally higher for adolescents and twens (with high life expectancies and substantial prospective rise in income) than for the old-aged people.

---

[12] Central Bureau of Statistics [1961, table 2 on page 47].

6.2.7. PROSPECTIVE CONSUMER AND ASSET PRICE LEVELS

About people's ideas with respect to future development of consumer and asset prices still less is known than about all other variables dealt with before; most likely, the majority of people does not have any idea about it at all. This may be interpreted:

(a) either that people (implicitly) assume that in future the price levels will remain the same as in the current period,

(b) or that people already incorporated their price level forecasts (also implicitly) in their income expectations and in their change-in-personal-wealth intentions.

Practically, both assumptions lead to the same conclusion, viz. that we should *not* include consumer and asset price levels in the consumption or savings functions explicitly.

6.2.8. SUMMING-UP: TOTAL RESOURCES

The variables dealt with in sections 6.2.1 through 6.2.7 above affect current consumption and savings as combined in 'total resources' (at the beginning of the current period). Formerly defined by (4.1.3.4), it is now rewritten as:

$$R_{i1} = (K_{io} - K_{iL})(1 + r)^{1-L_i} + \sum_{l=1}^{M} Y_{il}s_{il}(1 + r)^{1-l}$$

$$= (K_{io} - K_{iL})(1 + r)^{1-L_{a,s(i)}} + Y_{A,i1}F_{a;b,a,s(i)} + Y_{O,i1}F_{O;a,s(i)}, \quad (6.2.8.1)$$

for individuals $i = 1, \ldots, I$, with:

K_{io} and K_{iL} = initial and final intended personal wealth of i calculated according to the rules explained in sections 6.2.3 and 6.2.4, respectively,

$Y_{A,i1}$ and $Y_{O,i1}$ = current labour and other income of i respectively, as distinguished in the prefatory part of section 6.2.2,

$F_{A;b,a,s(i)} = \sum_{\tau=a}^{M} \bar{Y}_{A\in b,a,s;\tau}s_{a,s(i);\tau}(1 + r)^{1-\tau}$

= the labour income capitalization factor, depending on the individual's occupation (b), age (a) and sex (s),

$$F_{0;a,s(i)} = \sum_{\tau=a}^{M} s_{a,s(i);\tau} (1 + r)^{a-\tau}$$

= the capital income capitalization factor, depending on the individual's age and sex only, corresponding to $Y_{A,i1}$ and $Y_{0,i1}$, and calculated in the manner explained in sections 6.2.2.1 and 6.2.2.2 respectively,

and comprising:

$\bar{Y}_{A\in b,a,s;\tau}$ = the ratio of mean labour income at age τ to mean labour income at age a, for people of occupational status b and sex a (cf. (6.2.2.1.1)),

r = the rate of interest, indiscriminately fixed at 4.08 per cent per annum,

$s_{a,s(i);l}$ = the probability that i, with age a and sex s, will survive l years, and

$L_{as(i)} = \sum_{l=1}^{M-a} s_{a,s(i);l}$ = the life expectancy of i, with age a and sex s, and

$M = 106$ = the maximum age reached in the Netherlands, i.e. 106 years.

6.3. *The 'urgency to consume' and its main determinants*

6.3.1. QUANTIFICATION OF THE 'URGENCY TO CONSUME'

As observed in section 4.2.1, the micro-consumption function for the current period (as well as for any prospective period) has but one 'parameter', viz. the α_1 (or generally, α_τ). Furthermore, this 'parameter' depends on a number of personal characteristics of the income recipient not (yet) made explicit. Hence, the 'urgency to consume' need not – and should not – be 'estimated' in the sense usual in econometrics, but can be computed directly, viz. as:

$$\alpha_{i1} = C_{i1}/R_{i1} \quad \text{for } i = 1, \ldots, I, \tag{6.3.1.1}$$

with C_{i1} and R_{i1} calculated in accordance with sections 6.2.1 and 6.2.8 respectively, for each individual separately.

6.3.2. MAIN DETERMINANTS OF THE 'URGENCY TO CONSUME'

6.3.2.1. Life expectancy. Effects of (expected) income and of (intended) change in personal wealth on current consumption and savings are already taken care of sufficiently by means of the comprehensive variable R_{i1}. Since, however, the α_{il} should sum up to 1 (either unweighted over l from 1 through L_i according to (4.1.2.3), or weighted by the s_i over l from 1 through M according to (4.3.3.1)), the α_{i1} – like the R_{i1} – still depend on L_i or s_i; hence, indirectly they depend on the latter's main determining factors, viz. primarily age and secondarily sex.

Hence, we shall deal with effects of age before discussing the expected impact of other factors on α_1.

6.3.2.2. Age. In order to clarify age effects, we rewrite (6.3.1.1) by means of (6.2.8.1) as follows:

$$\alpha_{i1} = \frac{1 - s_{i1}}{(k_{i0} - k_{iL})(1 + r)^{1 - L_{a,s(i)}} + y_{A,i1}F_{A;b,a,s(i)} + y_{0,i1}F_{0;a,s(i)}} \tag{6.3.2.2.1}$$

with s_{i1} k_{i0}, k_{iL}, $y_{A,i1}$ and $y_{0,i1}$ equaling the corresponding upper case variables divided by Y_{i1}; here, s_{i1} denotes the savings rate, and $y_{A,i1}$ and $y_{0,i1}$ are the labour and capital income shares in total current income, respectively.

With regard to the latter 5 variables, numerical measures are obtained for each individual separately, whereas the others differ only between groups, distinguished by 2 or 3 characteristics; thus $L_{a,s(i)}$ and $F_{0;a,s(i)}$ depend upon age and sex, and $F_{A;b,a,s(i)}$ on occupational status as well. For given b and s, F_A and F_0 (short for $F_{a;b,a,s(i)}$ and $F_{0;a,s(i)}$ respectively) decline with increasing age. The sensitivity of F_A and F_0 with respect to variations in age appears to be so large as to generally dominate concomitant variations in those 5 lower-case variables (cf. appendix C). Consequently, α_1 may be expected to bear a strong positive relation to age, in particular through the life expectancy, closely linked to it.

6.3.2.3. Other characteristics. Sex and occupational status too may affect F_A and F_0, as well as, inter alia, the savings rate and the relative intended change in personal wealth. The latter variables, hence the α_1 too, depend also on other characteristics of the income reeipients, though they do not affect the capitalization factors. Those characteristics include the individual's marital status, his (or her) status within the household (as head, wife, child or other type of dependent), and – merely with respect to the head of the household – its size and composition. By and large, these personal characteristics – in addition to age and sex – jointly determine the prospective lifetime course of wants and burdens. Accordingly, these characteristics were treated as one (joint) factor in the savings analysis.[13]

Occupational status – besides determining (together with age and sex) the prospective course of income – might also affect wants and burdens differently according to phase of the life-cycle, albeit to a lesser degree presumably.

Such a differential effect can hardly be attributed to *education received.* Although the nature and level of training tend to affect wants (e.g. for further education as well as for reading and recreation), no sufficient reason could be advanced for assuming that these effects would be different for the future compared with the current period.

For a similar reason, the individual's *residence* was left out of account, with respect to both location and degree of urbanization. In the case where there is no plan for or expectation of change of residence, the latter would be a constant factor. Even if intentions for such a change exist, its effect cannot be ascertained, because of lack of information about nature and location of the prospective future residence.

On the other hand, distribution of excess burdens over time may be different according as the individual is *owner or tenant* of the dwelling occupied by him. This may be due to redemption of (mortgage or other) debts incurred for building or buying the house, or for keeping it in good repair; for these purposes, funds may be set aside, i.e. money may be saved deliberately. *Extraordinary expenses* stated in the Savings Survey, in accordance with the definitions adopted for assessment in income tax and wage tax, comprise excess costs of medical care and support of near relatives. Such exceptional costs are generally of a temporary nature (almost by definition). Therefore, they may be expected to influence α_1.

About the direction – and a fortiori about the magnitude – of the effects of these personal characteristics on savings, economic literature provides but

---

[13] Strictly speaking, such a combination of factors could be avoided by introducing interactions as well as main effects into the model, but the method proposed above (and applied below) is simpler (cf. section 6.4.3). Since the estimates of main effects of factors belonging to one group are independent of those relating to another group, according to the 'unweighted' method of section 6.5.1, they belong to the factors outside the former group.

scanty information (cf. chapter 1). As far as empirical results are presented, they are of questionable quality and significance, in view of the theoretically objectionable form and contents of the savings models by means of which they are obtained.

The reason is that these models take no or insufficient account of the expected course of future income; moreover, they assume (implicitly, if not explicitly) that such characteristics as age, occupational status, etc. affect savings directly, and in particular additively, instead of multiplicatively, through the 'urgency to consume' – like in our own savings model.

Consequently, savings literature does not advance hypotheses about effects of such personal characteristics on the 'urgency to consume' as distinct from consumption. As observed above in connection with (6.3.2.2.1), these factors influence α_1 through the *F*-factors (as far as age, sex and occupational status are concerned) as well as through the savings, capital-change and income-ratios s_{i1}, $k_{i0} - k_{iL}$, and $y_{A,i1}$ and $y_{0,i1}$, respectively.

According to the considerations underlying the present study, a factor will have a positive or a negative effect on α_1, respectively, according as it will aggravate or alleviate these wants and burdens more or less in the present compared to the future.

This will be difficult to ascertain in practice. Still, we may tentatively assume:

(a) Extraordinary expenses (in the current period) will raise the α_1.

(b) Ownership in lieu of tenancy of the dwelling occupied by the individual in question will also tend to elevate the α_1, since the gradual redemption of mortgage debts incurred for financing the building or buying a house implies an alleviation of financial burdens in future compared to the present – as long as this development is not caught up by the trendlike increase of maintenance costs.

(c) Households with pre-school children (not yet 6 years of age) may expect an increase of their financial burdens in the (near) future; the reverse holds good for households with older children near the time at which the latter will become financially independent (or at least: less dependent) on their parents.

(d) Costs of food will decrease more for manual than for non-manual (e.g. clerical) workers between their present employment and their later retirement, in view of differences in physical requirements for work performance; thus, higher α-values may be expected for the former compared with the latter category.

Regarding the other factors included in the analysis, the authors do not venture any hypotheses about the sign of their effects; they merely assume that those factors may influence α_1 (to be tested against the null-hypothesis that α_1 is independent of those factors). These effects need not be monotonic, let alone linear; as far as those factors are attributive rather than distributive in nature, 'linearity' is not even logically permissible. For certain value regions of those factors, their effects on α_1 may be positive, and for others negative.

Moreover, people's characteristics need not affect the α_1 in a way independent of each other, or of additional factors, but may do so in a (perhaps intricate) relationship. This means that the effect of a factor on α_1 does not merely depend upon the value of this one factor but that it may depend upon the values of one or more other factors related to the former.

6.4. Model for inter-individual differences in 'urgency to consume'

6.4.1. VARIABLE TO BE EXPLAINED ($\alpha_1 L$)

The discussions in section 6.3.2.1 amount to the conclusion that the value of α_1 decreases according as L increases, approximately in inverse proportion. Since effects of factors (such as L) on variables (such as α_1) should be taken account of a priori as much as possible, $\alpha_1 L$ appears to be a more appropriate variable 'to be explained' than α_1 itself.

At least, one may surmise that the variance of $\alpha_1 L$ between individuals is smaller – in a relative sense – than the variance of α_1 alone. Whereas α_1 may range from (say) 0.02 for adolescents to values near 1 for centagenarians, $\alpha_1 L$ will keep closer to 1.

6.4.2. EXPLANATORY VARIABLES

The determinants of the 'urgency to consume', discussed in section 6.3.2 in a mere qualitative way, have to be 'quantified'. Of these factors only life expectancy and/or age are quantitative in nature, whereas all others are attributive. This means that at least the latter factors have to be represented by dummy variables; i.e. assuming values 1 and 0 according as a particular characteristic (say female, or bachelor) does or does not apply, respectively, within a certain set of characteristics (in the example: sex, or marital status).

Even measurable factors, such as life expectancy (or rather: age) will be reduced to (age-) classes for joint theoretical and practical reasons. First, age (or life expectancy) will affect the $\alpha_1 L$ in an unknown, but presumably non-monotonic way. Therefore, it is easier to operate with dummy variables for age classes than with complicated (say polynomial) age functions, which are approximations at best. Last but not least, the data required are not known for separate age-years, but for age-classes only. Even then, the number of classes has to be kept down to a strict minimum.

If the relationship between $\alpha_1 L$ and the factors affecting it is (made) separable (say in an additive or in a multiplicative way), the number of mutually independent explanatory dummy variables will equal the total number of characteristics distinguished minus the number of sets to which these characteristics belong, plus one. Already this number runs into two figures, although it would still be manageable.

Separability of such a relationship, however, is too much to be hoped for. On the contrary, one should expect 'interaction'. This means that we have to adopt a classification of individuals by more than one type of characteristics simultaneously. Consequently, the number of (dummy) variables would increase considerably.

If the individuals are to be distinguished by all 8 types of characteristics at the same time, the number of classes will become a multiple of the sample size. Of course, this would mean that most cells in such a multi-dimensional classification would remain empty (especially if representing improbable or even impossible combinations), while the others would show small numbers only. On the other hand, if we confine ourselves to first-order interactions between two types of characteristics only, 28 pairs of such interactions would be the result.

In order to simplify matters, the following compromise has been adopted:

(a) a number of alternative pairs of sub-sets, consisting of types of characteristics, is chosen for selected groups of individuals, such that:
(b) all types of characteristics are covered at least once, with frequencies roughly corresponding to their presumed importance for the groups in question, and
(c) interaction with respect to the urgency to consume may be expected *within* the sub-sets, but hardly any *between* the sub-sets.

Thus, interaction is already incorporated in the main (joint) effects, obviating the need of introducing *separate* interaction terms into the model.

For such a simplification, a price has to be paid, viz. in the form of restrictions on the validity of and the comparability between the results to be obtained for the groups selected, according to the dichotomies adopted.

Notwithstanding inclusion of the age effect in the variable to be explained ($\alpha_1 L$), by means of the life expectancy L, age itself is still considered a sufficiently important factor. In accordance with point (b) above, age is assigned the rôle of a primary criterion for either classifying people within a certain group, or separating people into (age) groups – especially people below the age of 25 and above the age of 64.

In accordance with point (c) above, types of characteristics would be combined into the sub-sets referred to before, as far as they would have anything to do with each other, i.e. interact. On the other hand, the sub-classifications are chosen in such a way that zero (or low) frequencies per cell are avoided as much as possible. This imposes limits on the degree of detail the classification could stand.

The resulting sub-divisions are presented in tables 6.1 through 6.5.

6.4.3. THE MODEL

Section 6.4.2 suggests that an analysis-of-variance model may be adopted for explaining inter-individual differences in the 'urgency to consume', viz.:

$$x_{gh,i} = \varkappa_g + \lambda_h + \mu + \varepsilon_{gh,i}, \qquad (6.4.3.1)$$

with $x_{gh,i} = \alpha_{1i} L_i$ for individuals $i = 1, \ldots, n$, classified according to non-overlapping sub-sets of characteristics $g = 1, \ldots, G$ and $h = 1, \ldots, H$, with frequencies n_{gh}, such that $\sum_g \sum_h n_{gh} = n$,

$\varkappa_g, \lambda_h$ = the effects of characteristic-mixes g and h respectively on $x_{gh,i}$,

μ = a constant, and

$\varepsilon_{gh,i}$ = an error term.

The specification of the g and h, as well as – and in accordance with – the delimitation of the set of individuals i varies between the alternative computations carried out.

The linearity of the model and the absence of a separate interaction term imply the assumption that the sub-sets of characteristics g and h affect $\alpha_{1i} L_i$ independently.

The following regression model is equivalent to (6.4.3.1):

$$x_{gh,i} = \sum_{g'=1}^{G} \varkappa_{g'}\delta_{g'g_i} + \sum_{h'=1}^{H} \lambda_{h'}\delta_{h'h_i} + \mu + \varepsilon_{gh,i}, \tag{6.4.3.2}$$

with

$$\delta_{k'k_i} = \begin{cases} 1 & \text{for } k' = k_i \\ 0 & \text{for } k' \neq k_i \end{cases}$$

and $k = g, h$.

Since $\sum_{g'=1}^{G} \delta_{g'g_i} = \sum_{h'=1}^{H} \delta_{h'h_i} = 1$, one of the dummy-variables of each subset, say $\delta_{1g_i} = 1 - \sum_{g'=2}^{G} \delta_{g'g_i}$ and $\delta_{1h_i} = 1 - \sum_{h'=2}^{H} \delta_{h'h_i}$ can be expressed in terms of the others; hence:

$$x_{gh,i} = \sum_{g'=2}^{G} (\varkappa_{g'} - \varkappa_1)\,\delta_{g'g_i} + \sum_{h'=2}^{H} (\lambda_{h'} - \lambda_1)\,\delta_{h'h_i} + \varkappa_1 + \lambda_1 + \mu + \varepsilon_{gh,i}. \tag{6.4.3.3}$$

In matrix notation, (6.4.3.2) and (6.4.3.3) become:

$$x = [Y \quad Z \quad \iota_n]\begin{bmatrix} \varkappa \\ \lambda \\ \mu \end{bmatrix} + \varepsilon = [Y_- \quad Z_- \quad \iota_n]\begin{bmatrix} \varkappa_{-1} - \varkappa_1 \cdot \iota_{G-1} \\ \lambda_{-1} - \lambda_1 \cdot \iota_{H-1} \\ \varkappa_1 + \lambda_1 + \mu \end{bmatrix} + \varepsilon, \tag{6.4.3.4}$$

with:

$$x = \begin{bmatrix} x_{11} \\ \vdots \\ x_{1H} \\ x_{21} \\ \vdots \\ x_{2H} \\ \vdots \\ x_{G1} \\ \vdots \\ x_{GH} \end{bmatrix}, \quad Y = \begin{bmatrix} \iota_{n_{11}} & & & & \\ \vdots & & & 0 & \\ \iota_{n_{1H}} & & & & \\ & \iota_{n_{21}} & & & \\ & \vdots & & & \\ & \iota_{n_{2H}} & \ddots & & \\ & & & & \iota_{n_{G1}} \\ & 0 & & & \vdots \\ & & & & \iota_{n_{GH}} \end{bmatrix}, \quad Z = \begin{bmatrix} \iota_{n_{11}} & & & 0 \\ & \iota_{n_{12}} & & \\ & 0 & \ddots & \\ \cdots & \cdots & \cdots & \iota_{n_{1H}} \\ \iota_{n_{21}} & & & \\ & \ddots & & \\ \cdots & \cdots & \cdots & \iota_{n_{2H}} \\ \iota_{n_{G1}} & \cdots & \cdots & \cdots \\ & \ddots & & 0 \\ & 0 & & \iota_{n_{GH}} \end{bmatrix}$$

of orders $n \times G$ and $n \times H$

$x' =$

$$\{x_{11,1} \cdots x_{11,n_{11}}, x_{12,1} \cdots x_{12,n_{12}} \cdots x_{1H,1} \cdots x_{1H,n_{1H}} \cdots x_{GH,1} \cdots x_{GH,n_{GH}}\}$$

a vector of length n,

$\iota'_{n_{gh}} = \{1 \cdots 1\}$ summation vectors of lengths n_{gh},

$$(g = 1, \ldots, G; \quad h = 1, \ldots, H),$$

$Y_- = Y$ minus the first column (hence of order $n \times (G-1)$),

$Z_- = Z$ minus the first column (hence of order $n \times (H-1)$),

$\varkappa'_{-1} = \{\varkappa_2 \cdots \varkappa_G\}$ a vector of length $G-1$,

$\lambda'_{-1} = \{\lambda_2 \cdots \lambda_H\}$ a vector of length $H-1$, and

$\varepsilon' =$ a vector of length n, corresponding to x.

6.5. *Estimation and testing*

6.5.1. ESTIMATING EFFECTS

Since the column ranks of both $[Y \quad Z \quad \iota_n]$ and $[Y_- \quad Z_- \quad \iota_n]$ are $G+H-1$ (in view of $\iota'_n Y \iota_G = \iota'_n Z \iota_H = \iota'_n \iota_n = n$), only the third member of (6.4.3.4) is suitable for estimation, viz. of the $1 \times (G+H-1)$ vector

$$\{(\varkappa_{-1} - \varkappa_1 \iota_{G-1})', (\lambda_{-1} - \lambda_1 \iota_{H-1})', \varkappa_1 + \lambda_1 + \mu\}.$$

With respect to the error vector ε, we may assume:

$$\mathrm{E}\varepsilon = 0, \tag{6.5.1.1}$$

$$\mathrm{E}\varepsilon_{gh,i} \cdot \varepsilon_{g'h',i'} = 0 \quad \text{for } i \neq i', \tag{6.5.1.2}$$

$$\text{and/or } g \neq g' \text{ and/or } h \neq h'$$

and either

$$\mathrm{E}\varepsilon^2_{gh,i} = \sigma^2 \quad \text{(case I)} \tag{6.5.1.3I}$$

or

$$\mathrm{E}n^{-1}_{gh}\,\varepsilon^2_{gh,i} = \sigma^2_*. \quad \text{(case II)} \tag{6.5.1.3II}$$

Zero-covariances between disturbances in savings behaviour relating to different individuals, as meant by (6.5.1.2), seem plausible, in view of their (rather wide) spatial dispersion.

Possibly, however, an exception has to be made in case i and i' belong to the same household – a contingency examined in sections 6.5.3 and 6.6.6.

Still, we expect that possible positive or negative values for intra-family error covariances are rare and/or small enough to be neglected without noticeable increase of the variances of the parameter estimates. According to (6.5.1.3 I) case I implies that the error variances would be independent of the numbers of the individuals in the sample falling into 'cells' (g, h) of characteristic-mixes. Case II, on the other hand, implies that these variances would be proportional to the sample frequencies[14].

In so far as larger cell frequencies are due to less detailed classification, resulting in a higher degree of heterogeneity, assumption II may not be worse, and may be even better than assumption I. Hence, the consequences of both assumptions will be examined below.

On the assumption that case I applies, the B.L.U. estimator of the parameters is

$$\text{est}\begin{bmatrix} \varkappa_{-1} - \varkappa_1 \cdot \iota_{G-1} \\ \lambda_{-1} - \lambda_1 \cdot \iota_{H-1} \\ \varkappa_1 + \lambda_1 + \mu \end{bmatrix} = \begin{bmatrix} Y'_- Y_- & Y'_- Z_- & Y'_- \iota_n \\ Z'_- Y_- & Z'_- Z_- & Z'_- \iota_n \\ \iota'_n Y_- & \iota'_n Z_- & \iota'_n \iota_n \end{bmatrix}^{-1} \begin{bmatrix} Y'_- \\ Z'_- \\ \iota'_n \end{bmatrix} x, \qquad (6.5.1.4)$$

with in the right-hand member

$$[\ ]^{-1} = \left[\begin{array}{ccc|ccc|c} n_{2.} & & 0 & n_{22} & \cdots & n_{2H} & n_{2.} \\ & \ddots & & & & & \vdots \\ 0 & & n_{G.} & n_{G2} & \cdots & n_{GH} & n_{G.} \\ n_{22} & \cdots & n_{G2} & n_{.2} & & 0 & n_{.2} \\ \vdots & & & & \ddots & & \vdots \\ n_{2H} & \cdots & n_{GH} & 0 & & n_{.H} & n_{.H} \\ n_{2.} & \cdots & n_{G.} & n_{.2} & \cdots & n_{.H} & n \end{array}\right]^{-1} .$$

---

[14] Strictly speaking, this would be true only in the case where the n_{gh}^{-1} are considered as fixed, so that they could be put in front of the expectation operator. In case, however, one would adopt the more realistic view of n_{gh}^{-1} being subject to sampling errors, the interpretation of (6.5.1.3 II) presented above, would hold good only approximately. If n_{gh}^{-1} and $\varepsilon^2_{gh,i}$ are stochastically independent,

$$\mathrm{E}n_{gh}^{-1} \cdot \varepsilon^2_{ghi} = (\mathrm{E}n_{gh}^{-1})\,(\mathrm{E}\varepsilon^{-2}_{g,hi}) = \sigma^2_*,$$

i.e. the variances would be proportional to the *expected* values of the reciprocals of the cell frequencies.

In general, the elements of this inverse will be complicated functions of all n_{gh} ($g = 1, \ldots, G; h = 1, \ldots, H$), i.e. unless all n_{gh} are equal.

This may be shown by separating the estimator of $\varkappa_1 + \lambda_1 + \mu$ from the estimator of the rest of the parameter vector, by re-measuring variables in terms of deviations from their original means, i.e. by pre-multiplying x, Y_- and Z_- by $(I_n - n^{-1} \cdot \iota_n \iota_n')$ in order to obtain $\underline{x}_-$, $\underline{Y}_-$ and $\underline{Z}_-$, respectively. Therefore,

$$\text{est}\begin{bmatrix} \varkappa_{-1} - \varkappa_1 \cdot \iota_{G-1} \\ \lambda_{-1} - \lambda_1 \cdot \iota_{H-1} \end{bmatrix} = \begin{bmatrix} Y_-' (I_n - n^{-1}\iota_n\iota_n') Y_- & Y_-' (I_n - n^{-1}\iota_n\iota_n') Z_- \\ Z_-' (I_n - n^{-1}\iota_n\iota_n') Y_- & Z_-' (I_n - n^{-1}\iota_n\iota_n') Z_- \end{bmatrix}^{-1} \times$$

$$\times \begin{bmatrix} Y_-' \\ Z_-' \end{bmatrix} [I_n - n^{-1}\iota_n\iota_n'] \bar{x}_{..} \qquad (6.5.1.5)$$

is equivalent to (6.5.1.4)[15].

In general, the four sub-matrices of the moment matrix to be inverted are still complicated expressions, unless it becomes block-diagonal, i.e. unless $Y' [I_n - n^{-1}\iota_n\iota_n'] Z = 0$. The necessary and sufficient condition for all elements of this matrix to become zero is that all elements of the $Y'Z$ matrix are equal, i.e. that $n_{gh} = (GH)^{-1} n$ for $g = 2, \ldots, G$ and $h = 2, \ldots, H$. In that case, moreover:

$$Y_-' (I_n - n^{-1}\iota_n\iota_n') Y_- = G^{-1} n (I_{G-1} - G^{-1}\iota_{G-1}\iota_{G-1}')$$

and

$$Z_-' (I_n - n^{-1}\iota_n\iota_n') Z_- = H^{-1} n (I_{H-1} - H^{-1}\iota_{H-1}\iota_{H-1}'),$$

so that:

$$\text{est}_1 (\varkappa_{-1} - \varkappa_1 \cdot \iota_{G-1}) = G^{-1}n (I_{G-1} - G^{-1}\iota_{G-1}\iota_{G-1}')^{-1} Y_-' (I_n - n^{-1}\iota_n\iota_n') x$$

$$= G^{-1}n (I_{G-1} + \iota_{G-1}\iota_{G-1}') Y_-' (I_n - n^{-1}\iota_n\iota_n') x, \qquad (6.5.1.5\text{a})$$

and likewise,

$$\text{est}_1 (\lambda_{-1} - \lambda_1\iota_{H-1}) = H^{-1}n (I_{H-1} + \iota_{H-1}\iota_{H-1}') Z_-' (I_n - n^{-1}\iota_n\iota_n') x. \qquad (6.5.1.5\text{b})$$

---

[15] For a proof, cf. appendix 6E.

In case II the system of equations (6.4.3.3) may be condensed into:

$$\bar{x}_{gh} = \sum_{g'=2}^{G} (\varkappa_{g'} - \varkappa_1)\, \delta_{g'g} + \sum_{h'=2}^{M} (\lambda_{h'} - \lambda_1)\, \delta_{h'h} + \varkappa_1 + \lambda_1 + \mu + \bar{\varepsilon}_{gh}, \quad (6.5.1.6)$$

with

$$\bar{x}_{gh} = n_{gh}^{-1} \sum_{i \in \{g,h\}} x_{gh,i} \quad \text{and} \quad \bar{\varepsilon}_{gh} = n_{gh}^{-1} \sum_{i \in \{g,h\}} \varepsilon_{gh,i},$$

while

$$\mathrm{E}\bar{\varepsilon}_{gh} = 0 \quad \text{by virtue of (6.4.3.1),}$$

and

$$\mathrm{E}\bar{\varepsilon}_{gh}\bar{\varepsilon}_{g'h'} = \begin{cases} \mathrm{E}n_{gh}^{-1}\sigma_{gh}^2 = \sigma_*^2 & \text{for } g = g',\ h = h' \quad \text{by virtue of (6.5.1.3 II)} \\ 0 \quad \text{for} \quad g \neq g' & \text{and/or} \quad h \neq h'. \end{cases}$$

In matrix notation:

$$\bar{x}_{..} = [\bar{Y}_- \quad \bar{Z}_- \quad \iota_{GH}] \begin{bmatrix} \varkappa_{-1} - \varkappa_1 \iota_{G-1} \\ \lambda_{-1} - \lambda_1 \iota_{H-1} \\ \varkappa_1 + \lambda_1 + \mu \end{bmatrix} + \bar{\varepsilon}_{..}, \quad (6.5.1.7)$$

with

$$\bar{Y}_- = \begin{bmatrix} 0 & \cdots & 0 \\ \iota_H & & 0 \\ & \ddots & \\ 0 & & \iota_H \end{bmatrix}, \quad \bar{Z}_- = \begin{bmatrix} 0 & \cdots & 0 \\ 1 & & \vdots \\ 0 & \ddots & \\ \vdots & & 0 \\ 0 & 0 & 1 \\ 0 & \cdots & 0 \\ 1 & & \\ 0 & \ddots & \\ \vdots & & 0 \\ 0 \cdots 0 & & 1 \\ & \vdots & \\ 0 & \cdots & 0 \\ 1 & & \vdots \\ 0 & \ddots & \\ \vdots & & 0 \\ 0 \cdots 0 & & 1 \end{bmatrix}$$

matrices of order $GH \times (G - 1)$ and $GH \times (H - 1)$, respectively, and

$$\bar{x}'_{..} = \{\bar{x}_{11} \cdots \bar{x}_{1H}, \bar{x}_{21} \cdots \bar{x}_{2H} \cdots\cdots \bar{x}_{G1} \cdots \bar{x}_{GH}\},$$

$$\bar{\varepsilon}'_{..} = \{\bar{\varepsilon}_{11} \cdots \bar{\varepsilon}_{1H}, \bar{\varepsilon}_{21} \cdots \bar{\varepsilon}_{2H} \cdots\cdots \bar{\varepsilon}_{G1} \cdots \bar{\varepsilon}_{GH}\}$$

vectors of length GH.

System (6.5.1.7) can also be obtained by premultiplying the members of (6.4.3.4) by D, with

$$D = \begin{bmatrix} \iota'_{n_{11}} \cdot n_{11}^{-1} & & & & & & & 0 \\ & \iota'_{n_{12}} \cdot n_{12}^{-1} & & & & & & \\ & & \ddots & & & & & \\ & & & \iota'_{n_{1H}} \cdot n_{1H}^{-1} & & & & \\ & & & & \ddots & & & \\ & & & & & \iota'_{n_{G1}} \cdot n_{G1}^{-1} & & \\ & & & & & & \ddots & \\ 0 & & & & & & & \iota'_{n_{GH}} \cdot n_{GH}^{-1} \end{bmatrix} \text{ a } GH \times n \text{ matrix.}$$

Then, the new parameter estimate is:

$$\text{est}_2 \begin{bmatrix} \varkappa_{-1} - \varkappa_1 \iota_{G-1} \\ \lambda_{-1} - \lambda_1 \iota_{H-1} \\ \varkappa_1 + \lambda_1 + \mu \end{bmatrix} = \begin{bmatrix} \bar{Y}'_- \bar{Y}_- & \bar{Y}'_- \bar{Z}_- & Y'_- \iota_G \\ \bar{Z}'_- \bar{Y}_- & \bar{Z}'_- \bar{Z}_- & \bar{Z}'_- \iota_H \\ \iota'_G \bar{Y}_- & \iota'_H \bar{Z}_- & \iota'_{GH} \iota_{GH} \end{bmatrix}^{-1} \begin{bmatrix} Y'_- \\ \bar{Z}'_- \\ \iota'_{GH} \end{bmatrix} \bar{x}_{..} \tag{6.5.1.8}$$

with the inverse of the moment matrix:

$$\left[\begin{array}{ccc|ccc|c} 1 & & 0 & 1 & \cdots\cdots & 1 & 1 \\ & \ddots & & \vdots & & \vdots & \vdots \\ 0 & & 1 & 1 & \cdots\cdots & 1 & 1 \\ \hline 1 & \cdots\cdots & 1 & 1 & & 0 & 1 \\ \vdots & & \vdots & & \ddots & & \vdots \\ 1 & & 1 & 0 & & 1 & 1 \\ \hline 1 & \cdots\cdots & 1 & 1 & \cdots\cdots & 1 & GH \end{array}\right]. \quad \text{Hence:}$$

$$\text{est}\,(\varkappa_{-1} - \varkappa_1 \iota_{G-1})$$

$$= (G-1)^{-1}\,[I_{G-1} + \iota_{G-1}\iota'_{G-1}]\,Y'_{-}\,[I_{GH} - (GH)^{-1}\iota_{GH}\iota'_{GH}]\,\bar{x}_{..} \quad (6.5.1.9\text{a})$$

$$\text{est}\,(\lambda_{-1} - \lambda_1 \iota_{H-1})$$

$$= (H-1)^{-1}\,[I_{H-1} + \iota_{H-1}\cdot\iota'_{H-1}]\,Z'_{-}\,[I_{GH} - (GH)^{-1}\,\iota_{GH}\iota'_{GH}]\,\bar{x}_{..}. \quad (6.5.1.9\text{b})$$

Under the assumptions made above, equations (6.5.1.5) and (6.5.1.9) yield the following scalar expressions for the estimates of the effects:

$$\text{est}\,(\varkappa_g - \varkappa_1) = \bar{x}_{g.} - \bar{x}_{1.}$$

$$= H^{-1}\sum_{h=1}^{H}(\bar{x}_{gh} - \bar{x}_{1h}) \quad \text{for } g = 2, \ldots, G, \quad (6.5.1.10\text{a})$$

$$\text{est}\,(\lambda_h - \lambda_1) = \bar{x}_{.h} - \bar{x}_{.1}$$

$$= G^{-1}\sum_{g=1}^{G}(\bar{x}_{gh} - \bar{x}_{g1}) \quad \text{for } h = 2, \ldots, H. \quad (6.5.1.10\text{b})$$

Obviously, these estimates satisfy the logical tests of identity, reversibility and triangularity, i.e:

$$\text{est.}\,(\varkappa_g - \varkappa_{g'}) = \text{est.}\,(\varkappa_g - \varkappa_1) - \text{est.}\,(\varkappa_{g'} - \varkappa_1); \quad (6.5.1.10\text{c})$$

m.m. the same applies to the estimates of the differences between the λ's. Therefore, it is inessential which of the $\varkappa$'s or λ's are taken as $\varkappa_1$ or λ_1, respectively. Still, in order to get rid of the asymmetry present in (6.5.1.10a/b), the latter may be replaced by:

$$\text{est}\,(\varkappa_g - \bar{\varkappa}) = \bar{x}_{g.} - \bar{x} \quad \text{for } g = 1, \ldots, G, \quad (6.5.1.11\text{a})$$

and

$$\text{est}\,(\lambda_h - \bar{\lambda}) = \bar{x}_{.h} - \bar{x} \quad \text{for } h = 1, \ldots, H, \quad (6.5.1.11\text{b})$$

with

$$\bar{\varkappa} = G^{-1}\sum_{g=1}^{G}\varkappa_g, \quad \bar{\lambda} = H^{-1}\sum_{h=1}^{H}\lambda_h \quad \text{and} \quad \bar{x} = G^{-1}\sum_{g=1}^{G}x_{g.} = H^{-1}\sum_{h=1}^{H}x_{.h}.$$

These estimates are unbiased (at least under assumption I) but need not have smallest variance (under assumption II); simplicity is their additional advantage.

They remain this way, even if an interaction term ν_{gh} is introduced into (6.4.3.1), (6.4.3.2) or (6.4.3.3):

$$\begin{aligned} x_{gh,i} &= \varkappa_g + \lambda_h + \nu_{gh} + \mu + \varepsilon_{gh,i} \\ &= \sum_{g'=1}^{G} \varkappa_{g'} \cdot \delta_{g'g_i} + \sum_{h'=1}^{H} \lambda_{h'} \cdot \delta_{h'h_i} + \sum_{g'=1}^{G} \sum_{h'=1}^{H} \nu_{g'h'} \delta_{g'g_i} \delta_{h'h_i} + \mu + \varepsilon_{gh,i} \\ &= \sum_{g'=2}^{G} (\varkappa_{g'} - \varkappa_1)\, \delta_{g'g_i} + \sum_{h'=2}^{H} (\lambda_{h'} - \lambda_1)\, \delta_{h'h_i} \\ &\quad + \sum_{g'=1}^{G} \sum_{h'=1}^{H} (\nu_{g'h'} - \nu_{11})\, \delta_{g'g_i} \delta_{h'h_i} + \varkappa_1 + \lambda_1 + \nu_{11} + \mu + \varepsilon_{gh,i}; \end{aligned} \tag{6.5.1.12}$$

or, equivalently, into (6.5.1.6):

$$\begin{aligned} \bar{x}_{gh} &= \sum_{g'=2}^{G} (\varkappa_{g'} - \varkappa_1)\, \delta_{g'g} + \sum_{h'=2}^{H} (\lambda_{h'} - \lambda_1)\, \delta_{h'h} \\ &\quad + \sum_{g'=1}^{G} \sum_{g'=1}^{H} (\nu_{g'h'} - \nu_{11})\, \delta_{g'g} \delta_{h'h} + \varkappa_1 + \lambda_1 + \nu_{11} + \mu + \bar{\varepsilon}_{gh}. \end{aligned} \tag{6.5.1.13}$$

Interactions introduced in such a way do not affect the estimates of the effects; the corresponding estimates of the interactions can be expressed most simply by:

$$\text{est}\,(\nu_{gh} - \bar{\nu}_{..}) = \bar{x}_{gh} - \bar{x}_{g.} - \bar{x}_{.h} + \bar{x}_{..} \tag{6.5.1.14}$$

In the case where one or more of the cells (g, h) is empty, the pertinent (i.e. non-existent) $\bar{x}_{gh}$ drop out of the summation over g or h in the preceding formulae; the point estimates of the parameters and the factors G^{-1} and H^{-1} are adjusted accordingly.

On the other hand, interactions to be estimated under the alternative hypothesis (6.5.1.3 I) would affect the estimates of the (main) effects as well as the interactions themselves.

The formulae derived above can easily be generalized to more than two dimensions. For instance, if we specify:

$$x_{ghk,i} = \varkappa_g + \lambda_h + \nu_k + \mu + \varepsilon_{ghk,i}, \tag{6.5.1.15}$$

with $k\ (= 1, \ldots, K)$ a third type of characteristic and ν_k its corresponding effect, the effects formulae corresponding to (6.5.1.10a and b) become:

$$\begin{aligned}\text{est}\,(\varkappa_g - \varkappa_1) &= \bar{x}_{g..} - \bar{x}_{1..}\\ &= (HK)^{-1} \sum_{h=1}^{H} \sum_{k=1}^{K} (\bar{x}_{ghk} - \bar{x}_{1hk}) \quad \text{for } g = 2, \ldots, G\end{aligned} \tag{6.5.1.16a}$$

$$\begin{aligned}\text{est}\,(\lambda_h - \lambda_1) &= \bar{x}_{.h.} - \bar{x}_{.1.}\\ &= (GK)^{-1} \sum_{g=1}^{G} \sum_{k=1}^{K} (\bar{x}_{ghk} - \bar{x}_{g1k}) \quad \text{for } h = 2, \ldots, H\end{aligned} \tag{6.5.1.16b}$$

$$\begin{aligned}\text{est}\,(\nu_k - \nu_1) &= \bar{x}_{..k} - \bar{x}_{..1}\\ &= (GH)^{-1} \sum_{g=1}^{G} \sum_{h=1}^{H} (\bar{x}_{ghk} - \bar{x}_{gh1}) \quad \text{for } k = 2, \ldots, K.\end{aligned} \tag{6.5.1.16c}$$

6.5.2. TESTING EFFECTS

The variances of the point estimates (6.5.1.11a/b) are:

$$\begin{aligned}\text{var}\,\{\text{est}\,(\varkappa_g - \bar{\varkappa})\} &= \text{E}\,\{\text{est}\,(\varkappa_g - \bar{\varkappa}) - (\varkappa_g - \bar{\varkappa})\}^2\\ &= H^{-2}\text{E}\left\{\sum_{h=1}^{H} (\bar{\varepsilon}_{gh} - \bar{\varepsilon}_{.h})\right\}^2 \quad \text{with } \bar{\varepsilon}_{.h} = G^{-1} \sum_{g=1}^{G} \bar{\varepsilon}_{gh}\\ &= H^{-2}\text{E} \sum_{h=1}^{H} (\bar{\varepsilon}^2_{gh} + \bar{\varepsilon}^2_{.h})\end{aligned} \tag{6.5.2.1}$$

(since all covariances vanish by virtue of 6.5.1.2).

The variances in the fourth member of (6.5.2.1) may be estimated by:

$$\text{est}\,\bar{\varepsilon}^2_{gh} = (n_{gh} - 1)^{-1} \sum_{i=1}^{n_{gh}} (x_{gh,i} - \bar{x}_{gh})^2 \quad \text{for } g = 1, 2, \ldots, G, \tag{6.5.2.2}$$

while:

$$\text{E}\bar{\varepsilon}^2_{.h} = \text{E}\left(G^{-1} \sum_{g=1}^{G} \bar{\varepsilon}_{gh}\right)^2 = G^{-2} \sum_{g=1}^{G} \text{E}\bar{\varepsilon}^2_{gh} \quad \text{(covariances being zero).}$$

Likewise,

$$\text{var}\,\{\text{est}\,(\lambda_h - \bar{\lambda})\} = G^{-2}\text{E} \sum_{g=1}^{G} (\bar{\varepsilon}^2_{gh} + \bar{\varepsilon}^2_{g.}). \tag{6.5.2.3}$$

Therefore, the *expected* variances of the point estimates of $\varkappa_g - \bar{\varkappa}$ and $\lambda_h - \bar{\lambda}$ appear to be the same for all g and h, respectively. On the other hand, the *estimates* of these variances as expressed by (6.5.2.1) and (6.5.2.2) still depend on g and h, respectively. These differences, however, may be *smoothed over* by averaging over g and h respectively (allowed for under the assumption of homoskedasticity), with the result:

$$\text{est}_* \operatorname{var} \{\text{est} (\varkappa_g - \bar{\varkappa})\} = 2G^{-1}H^{-2} \sum_{g=1}^{G} \sum_{h=1}^{H} \text{est}\, \bar{\varepsilon}_{gh}^2 \qquad (6.5.2.4)$$

and

$$\text{est}_* \operatorname{var} \{\text{est} (\lambda_h - \bar{\lambda})\} = 2G^{-2}H^{-1} \sum_{g=1}^{G} \sum_{h=1}^{H} \text{est}\, \bar{\varepsilon}_{gh}^2 . \qquad (6.5.2.5)$$

Likewise, we find for the estimates of the variances of the estimated effects of differences between pairs of characteristics (g, g'):

$$\text{est}_* \operatorname{var} \{\text{est} (\varkappa_g - \varkappa_{g'})\} = H^{-2} \sum_{h=1}^{H} (\bar{\varepsilon}_{gh}^2 + \bar{\varepsilon}_{g'h}^2)$$

$$\text{for} \quad g, g' = 1, \ldots, G \text{ and } g \neq g', \qquad (6.5.2.6)$$

$$\text{est}_* \operatorname{var} \{\text{est} (\lambda_h - \lambda_{h'})\} = G^{-2} \sum_{g=1}^{G} (\bar{\varepsilon}_{gh}^2 + \bar{\varepsilon}_{gh'}^2)$$

$$\text{for} \quad h, h' = 1, \ldots, H \text{ and } h \neq h'! \qquad (6.5.2.7)$$

In the case where one or more of the cells (g, h) is empty or has one element only, est $\bar{\varepsilon}_{gh}^2$ does not exist; hence it drops out of the summation in the variance formulae above, with corresponding adjustment of the G and H in the factors G^{-1}, G^{-2}, H^{-1} and H^{-2}.

Formulae (6.5.2.4) and (6.5.2.5) have the practical and aesthetical advantage of yielding the same variance estimates for all g and all h, respectively. On the other hand, using asymmetric formulae such as (6.5.2.3) does not require that E var $\bar{\varepsilon}_{gh}$ is independent of g and h.

The latter assumption might even be tested against the alternative hypothesis of E var $\bar{\varepsilon}_{gh}$ varying with g and/or h (cf. Rao [1965] pp. 226–227).

Whatever variance estimates are adopted, they may be used for testing the statistical significance of the parameters' point estimates. For testing the significance of $(\bar{\varkappa}_g - \bar{\varkappa})$ and $(\lambda_h - \bar{\lambda})$ for each g and h separately, Student's t-statistic may be adopted.

Formulae (6.5.2.2) through (6.5.2.7) for estimates of the variances of estimated effects can be generalized to more than two dimensions as easily as those for the estimates of the effects themselves. Specifically, for model (6.5.1.15) we find:

$$\text{est}_* \text{ var } \{\text{est } (\varkappa_g - \varkappa_{g'})\} = (HK)^{-2} \sum_{h=1}^{H} \sum_{k=1}^{K} (\bar{\varepsilon}_{ghk}^2 + \bar{\varepsilon}_{g'hk}^2), \quad (6.5.2.8)$$

and similar expressions for the estimates of var $\{\text{est } (\lambda_h - \lambda_{h'})\}$ and var $\{\text{est } (\nu_k - \nu_{k'})\}$.

6.5.3. TESTING INTRA-FAMILY (DIS-) SIMILARITIES IN SAVINGS BEHAVIOUR

Section 6.1.4 already listed income recipients' general characteristics asked for in the savings survey and taken account of in the savings analysis.

Savings behaviour, however, is also shaped by other, more idiosyncratic and less easily observable factors – or at least factors not included in the survey questionnaire; examples are people's state of health (unless reflected in 'extraordinary expenses') and their religion.

At this stage of the analysis we are interested in the way savings behaviour of members of the same household is affected by their living together and/or by kinship, i.e. whether they influence each other's savings behaviour in a positive sense, in a negative sense, or not at all.

Positive (negative) mutual influencing of household members means that if one member of a household shows more or less than average thriftiness or prodigality, the probability that the same would apply to one or more other members of the same household would be larger (smaller) than in case of mutual independence.

The 'more (less) than average' is indicated by the sign of the household member's α_1-value minus the average α_1-value for the group of people to which this income recipient belongs according to the characteristics listed in section 6.1.4, i.e. whether this difference is positive or negative. Thus, the effect of general factors, not specifically pertaining to the household as a unit, is eliminated as far as possible. In order to keep the analysis simple, *magnitudes* of such deviations – apart from sign – are disregarded.

The hypothesis of positive push or pull effects between members of the same household, either of different generations (such as parents and their children) or of the same generation (such as brothers and sisters) corresponds to the assumption of empirically corroborated positive hereditary educational and imitation effects; it also fits in with the theory that members of the same household are swayed in the same direction by the household's environment.

Such effects, moreover, tend to be reinforced by the fact that people generally choose marriage partners with social, educational and financial backgrounds similar to their own. All these factors, common to members of the same household, may predispose them towards short-sightedness or far-sightedness, towards optimism or pessimism.

On the other hand, the opposite hypothesis, viz. that of negative mutual influencing of household members may also be backed by introspection as well as by observation. Often, members of a household disagree with other members (especially with those of another generation) to the point of opposing each other. Heredity too may have ambivalent effects, particularly if father and mother have different inclinations (in accordance with Reik's psychological 'complementarity' theory of the choice of marriage partners, in contradistinction to the above-mentioned sociological 'similarity' theory); cf. Reik [1944, 1945].

Furthermore, household members' diversity in savings behaviour may be induced or reinforced for purely financial reasons: if one or more members of the family is either excessively thrifty or abnormally extravagant, other members could permit themselves more than average generosity or would be compelled to impose more than ordinary *economies* on themselves.

Therefore, plausible arguments may be advanced in favour of both positive and negative influences of household members on each other, at least with respect to their savings behaviour.

Nevertheless, the *authors* tend to support the assumption that positive effects outweigh the negative ones. Thus, the hypothesis of *positive* mutual influencing of the household members is tested against the null-hypothesis of mutual independence.

This alternative can be tested on the basis of the 1960 Savings Survey of the Netherlands. For 300 odd households with two or more income recipients, separate information was available about all variables entering the analysis.

The analysis was confined to households with two known income recipients; the number of households with three or more members for whom the α_1 can be calculated is so small that presumably no statistically significant results could be obtained from it anyhow.

For the sub-set of households with two known income recipients, the following table may be constructed:

Frequencies of households with two income receiving members classified according to above-normal (+) or below-normal (−) values of individual 'urgencies to consume'

		second member		
		+	−	total
first member	+	n_{++}	n_{+-}	$n_{+.}$
	−	n_{-+}	n_{--}	$n_{-.}$
	total	$n_{.+}$	$n_{.-}$	$n_{..}$

The members of the household may be ranked as 'first' or 'second' either at random or systematically (e.g. the elder member first and the younger one second, or vice versa).

Thus, n_{+-} and n_{-+} can differ in a random way and in a systematic fashion, respectively. A third ('confounding') method would consist of treating each household member twice, i.e. once as 'first', and once as 'second'; then the double dichotomy would become:

$2n_{++}$	$n_{+-} + n_{-+}$
$n_{-+} + n_{+-}$	$2n_{--}$

ensuring symmetry around the main diagonal.

Here, the systematic ranking is preferred, because it does not waste any information that may be incorporated in a possible relationship between savings behaviour and 'rank number' in the household.

For testing the hypothesis mentioned above, however, the *direction* of the ranking is immaterial; i.e. interchange of n_{+-} and n_{-+} does not affect the outcome of the test, being symmetrical with respect to the latter two frequencies.

In the case of mutual independence between the members of the household with respect to savings behaviour:

$$\mathrm{E}(t) = 0, \quad \text{with} \quad t = n_{++} - \frac{n_{+.} \cdot n_{.+}}{n_{..}} = n_{--} - \frac{n_{-.} \cdot n_{.-}}{n_{..}}$$

$$= \frac{n_{++} \cdot n_{--} - n_{+-} \cdot n_{-+}}{n_{..}} \quad \text{(the null-hypothesis).}$$

Hence, t may be used as a test statistic. For sufficiently large $n_{..}$ (considered as fixed), the distribution of t is approximately normal under the null-hypothesis, with zero mean, and variance

$$\sigma^2 = \frac{n_{++} \cdot n_{+-} \cdot n_{-+} \cdot n_{--}}{n_{..}^2 \, (n_{..} - 1)}.$$

This means that in the case of one-sided testing of the null-hypothesis H_0 against the alternative hypothesis H_+ of positive mutual influence, H_0 should be rejected in case $t/\sigma > \phi(\alpha)$, with ϕ a function of the significance level α. For the value 0.05 traditionally selected for α, $\phi(\alpha) = 1.65$.

The formula for t implies that if the income receiving members of the household are ranked in either a systematic or a random way, the null-hypothesis will be rejected as soon as, and in general sooner than if the 'confounding' method is adopted. The reason is that t would become smaller in case $n_{+-} \cdot n_{-+}$ would be replaced by $\frac{1}{4}\,(n_{+-} - n_{-+})^2$, since

$$\tfrac{1}{4}\,(n_{+-} + n_{-+})^2 - n_{+-} \cdot n_{-+} = \tfrac{1}{4}\,(n_{+-} - n_{-+})^2 \geq 0.$$

6.6. Results

6.6.0. TABULATION

6.6.0.1. Basic tables

6.6.0.1.1. Classification. Tables 6.1 through 6.5 are drawn up in accordance with the principles for classifying individuals by explanatory variables set out in section 6.4.2.

Specifically, this means that age is always singled out, either as a primary criterion for distinguishing people (tables 6.1 through 6.3) and/or for restricting the tables to selected age-classes; in particular, tables 6.4 and 6.5 relate to persons less than 25 years old and 65 years and over, respectively. The latter way of tabulation is adopted in cases where (secondarily) other types of characteristics are considered to be of special interest for the age groups concerned, i.e. participation or non-participation in bonus savings plans and living in owned or rented dwellings, respectively. The reason is that such participation and ownership appear most frequently among the lowest and highest age groups, respectively.

Table 6.3 is restricted to three age-classes only, since extraordinary expenses, according to which households are classified secondarily, are fairly rare among people below the age of 35 or above the age of 64.

On the other hand, in table 6.1 all age-classes are sub-divided by socio-economic group, viz. manual workers, non-manual workers and others (in particular, pensioners); the latter category (and merely this one), however, is separated in the highest age-class only.

More generally, individuals are cross-classified by characteristics that are considered to be relevant to each other, i.e. unless the cell frequencies would become too small (say 2 or 1, and a fortiori 0) too frequently.

Because of the latter constraint, tables 6.1 and 6.3 are confined to the most common group of income recipients, viz. male married heads of households, while tables 6.2 and 6.4 are restricted to people without children; contrariwise, table 6.5 is limited to children (of heads of households).

All these and some other restrictions imposed, as well as classifications adopted in tables 6.1 through 6.5 are summarized in table 6.6.

Columns R(estrictions) in this synopsis show that the income recipients, to whom these tables relate, overlap partly, and often considerably; this applies, in particular, to tables 6.1 and 6.3, both dealing with male heads of households. Tables 6.3, 6.5 and 6.4, however, are entirely disjoint; neither does table 6.5 have anything in common with tables 6.1 or 6.2.

On the other hand, a survey of the R-columns in table 6.6 reveals that groups of people with special, generally rare 'characteristic-mixes' are not represented at all in tables 6.1 through 6.5.

6.6.0.1.2. Contents. Tables 6.1 through 6.5 offer basic information per cell, determined by the pairs of characteristics (g, h) mentioned in the headings and the stubs, respectively, and derived from the sample of the 1960 Savings Survey of the Netherlands, as follows:

(1) sample frequencies, i.e. numbers of income recipients i observed in the sample;
(2) pertinent mean values $\overline{\alpha_1 L}$ of the $\alpha_{1i}L_i$;
(3) pertinent estimates of the standard errors (squared):

$$\hat{\sigma}^2_{(gh)} = (n_{gh} - 1)^{-1} \sum_{i \in \{g,h\}} (\alpha_{1i}L_i - \overline{\alpha_1 L})^2.$$

Naturally, $\overline{\alpha_1 L}$ and $\hat{\sigma}$ are presented only if n_{gh} is at least 1 and 2, respectively, i.e. not empty or near-empty.

The latter restriction also applies to the derived measures, likewise printed per cell, viz.:

(4) coefficients of variation $V = \hat{\sigma}/\overline{\alpha_1 L}$.

Furthermore, the horizontal blocks for 'totals' contain additionally:

(5) mean values $\bar{\alpha}_1$ of α_{1i}.

The reasons for this selection are:

Ad 1. The cell frequencies are important for the size of the standard errors; they co-determine the degree of significance of the estimates of the effects. On the other hand, this sample distribution does not represent the distribution of income recipients according to the characteristics (g, h) in the population; this is due to the differences in probabilities with which they are drawn from various strata distinguished according to occupational status and level of income of the interviewees.

Ad 2. $\overline{\alpha_1 L}$ is the variable on which this analysis is focussed, i.e. for which we wish to assess the extent to which it is affected by the characteristics (g, h). This means that the differences of $\overline{\alpha_1 L}$ between cells are of paramount importance, while the squares of these differences represent the between-cell component of the total variance of the $\alpha_{1i}L_i$.

Ad 3. The standard errors $\hat{\sigma}$ are a measure of the dispersion of the $\alpha_{1i}L_i$; the standard errors, together with the frequencies, determine the degree of significance of the effects; their squares represent the within-cell contributions of the $\alpha_{1i}L_i$ to their total variance.

Ad 4. The coefficients of variation indicate the degree of heterogeneity of the cells with respect to the $\alpha_{1i}L_i$.

Ad 5. The $\bar{\alpha}_1$ in themselves, as well as when compared with the $\overline{\alpha_1 L}$, are worth separate consideration; this applies, in particular, to age effects. Since, however, the $\bar{\alpha}_1$ are not the subject proper of our analysis, they are dealt with more summarily, viz. confined to the 'totals' per column. This is all the more justified because of the near-constancy of the ratios between $\overline{\alpha_1 L}$ and $\bar{\alpha}_1$ (cf. section 6.6.2.2), as well as the near-equality of their coefficients of variation, both per age-sex class[16].

6.6.0.2. Effects' tables

6.6.0.2.1. Classification. Tables 6.9 through 6.14 present the effects of the types of characteristics mentioned under *a* through *i* in table 6.6. on $\overline{\alpha_1 L}$.

---

[16] The reader interested in more detailed information about the α_1, including their standard errors, is referred to Bannink a.o. [1966, tables Ia through Va], corresponding to tables 6.1 through 6.5 above, respectively.

TABLE 6.1.

Mean values of $\alpha_{1i}L_i$ and their estimated standard errors ($\hat{\sigma}$), in addition to the sample frequencies (n_{gh}) of male married heads of households of 25 years aged and over, by composition of the household, age-class and occupational status, compared with $\bar{\alpha}_1$

Composition of the household	Variables	25–34				35–44				45–54	
		Total	other	man.	non-man.	Total	other	man.	non-man.	Total	other
Without children	n_{gh}	76		34	42	49		23	26	73	1
	$\overline{\alpha_1 L}$	1.93		2.11	1.78	2.11		2.16	2.06	1.92	0.51
	$\hat{\sigma}$	0.55		0.52	0.53	0.78		0.32	1.03	0.57	
	V	0.28		0.25	0.30	0.37		0.15	0.50	0.30	
With 1 child <15 years	n_{gh}	145		83	62	81		40	41	45	1
	$\overline{\alpha_1 L}$	1.95		2.14	1.69	1.98		2.19	1.78	1.91	2.00
	$\hat{\sigma}$	0.47		0.37	0.48	0.38		0.20	0.40	0.42	
	V	0.24		0.17	0.28	0.19		0.09	0.22	0.22	
With 1 child ≧15 years	n_{gh}	1			1	7		2	5	52	
	$\overline{\alpha_1 L}$	2.31			2.31	2.02		2.00	2.03	1.88	
	$\hat{\sigma}$					0.29		0.27	0.32	0.32	
	V					0.14		0.14	0.16	0.17	
With 2 children both ≦5 years	n_{gh}	78	1	34	43	22	1	9	12	2	
	$\overline{\alpha_1 L}$	1.93	1.69	2.08	1.82	1.87	1.63	2.12	1.70	1.45	
	$\hat{\sigma}$	0.31		0.23	0.33	0.31		0.21	0.25	0.28	
	V	0.16		0.11	0.18	0.17		0.10	0.15	0.19	
With 2 children >5 years	n_{gh}	38		26	12	132	1	68	63	100	2
	$\overline{\alpha_1 L}$	2.03		2.17	1.72	1.97	1.54	2.17	1.77	1.89	1.56
	$\hat{\sigma}$	0.32		0.10	0.42	0.40		0.22	0.44	0.35	0.25
	V	0.16		0.05	0.24	0.20		0.10	0.25	0.19	0.16
With 3–4 children <15 years	n_{gh}	71		47	24	177	1	87	89	45	1
	$\overline{\alpha_1 L}$	2.05		2.15	1.85	1.98	0.72	2.14	1.84	1.82	2.21
	$\hat{\sigma}$	0.27		0.17	0.32	0.34		0.23	0.33	0.31	
	V	0.13		0.08	0.17	0.17		0.11	0.18	0.17	
With 3–4 children ≧15 years	n_{gh}	2		1	1	63	2	32	29	101	2
	$\overline{\alpha_1 L}$	2.06		2.20	1.93	1.97	1.63	2.11	1.84	1.96	1.92
	$\hat{\sigma}$	0.19				0.29	0.65	0.16	0.30	0.27	0.05
	V	0.09				0.15	0.40	0.08	0.17	0.14	0.03
With 5 or more children	n_{gh}	15		12	3	72	1	41	30	67	
	$\overline{\alpha_1 L}$	2.09		2.14	1.90	2.02	1.97	2.19	1.79	1.85	
	$\hat{\sigma}$	0.21		0.20	0.10	0.30		0.20	0.27	0.33	
	V	0.10		0.09	0.05	0.15		0.09	0.15	0.18	
Total	n_{gh}	426	1	237	188	603	6	302	295	485	7
	$10^4\bar{\alpha}_1$	453		487	410	571		617	525	732	
	$\overline{\alpha_1 L}$	1.97	1.69	2.13	1.77	1.99	1.52	2.16	1.83	1.90	1.67
	$\hat{\sigma}$	0.41		0.32	0.43	0.40	0.51	0.22	0.46	0.38	0.57
	V	0.21		0.15	0.24	0.20	0.34	0.10	0.25	0.20	0.34

man. = manual worker; non-man. = non-manual worker.

45–54		55–64				65+				Total			
man.	non-man.	Total	other	man.	non-man.	Total	other	man.	non-man.	Total	other	man.	non-man.
39	33	182	31	78	73	364	343	8	13	744	375	182	187
2.12	1.72	1.67	1.69	1.76	1.56	1.15	1.17	1.16	0.83	1.50	1.21	1.93	1.66
0.51	0.52	0.41	0.41	0.29	0.49	0.35	0.35	0.36	0.42	0.57	0.38	0.47	0.66
0.24	0.30	0.25	0.24	0.17	0.31	0.31	0.30	0.31	0.50	0.38	0.32	0.24	0.40
25	19	17		8	9	1			1	289	1	156	132
2.08	1.68	1.85		1.96	1.75	1.71			1.71	1.94	2.00	2.13	1.72
0.16	0.55	0.30		0.26	0.31					0.43		0.31	0.45
0.08	0.33	0.16		0.14	0.17					0.22		0.14	0.26
31	21	58	6	28	24	68	60	7	1	186	66	68	52
1.97	1.76	1.76	1.56	1.76	1.81	1.29	1.28	1.33	1.41	1.63	1.30	1.82	1.81
0.22	0.41	0.48	0.73	0.32	0.57	0.27	0.27	0.23		0.45	0.34	0.33	0.48
0.11	0.23	0.27	0.47	0.18	0.31	0.21	0.21	0.18		0.28	0.26	0.18	0.27
1	1									102	2	44	56
1.65	1.25									1.91	1.66	2.08	1.78
										0.32	0.04	0.23	0.32
										0.17	0.03	0.11	0.18
48	50	48	2	30	16	19	18	1		337	23	173	141
2.06	1.74	1.76	1.85	1.87	1.54	1.29	1.28	1.58		1.89	1.36	2.08	1.73
0.18	0.40	0.38	0.14	0.27	0.47	0.26	0.26			0.40	0.30	0.24	0.43
0.09	0.23	0.21	0.07	0.15	0.30	0.20	0.20			0.21	0.22	0.11	0.25
20	24	4		2	2					297	2	156	139
1.98	1.66	1.76		1.88	1.64					1.97	1.47	2.12	1.81
0.29	0.25	0.21		0.15	0.23					0.32	1.05	0.23	0.32
0.14	0.15	0.12		0.08	0.14					0.16	0.72	0.11	0.18
52	47	30	2	18	10	6	6			202	12	103	87
2.05	1.86	1.74	1.45	1.75	1.79	1.37	1.37			1.91	1.52	2.02	1.84
0.20	0.30	0.40	0.06	0.43	0.37	0.25	0.25			0.32	0.33	0.27	0.31
0.10	0.16	0.23	0.04	0.25	0.21	0.18	0.18			0.17	0.22	0.14	0.17
40	27	12	2	6	4	4	3		1	170	6	99	65
1.91	1.76	1.86	1.82	1.92	1.78	1.20	1.06		1.63	1.93	1.47	2.06	1.78
0.30	0.37	0.16	0.05	0.19	0.15	0.55	0.58			0.34	0.58	0.28	0.30
0.16	0.21	0.09	0.03	0.10	0.08	0.46	0.54			0.18	0.39	0.13	0.17
256	222	351	43	170	138	462	430	16	16	2327	487	981	859
780	677	955		990	897	1208	1231	1016	758	767		691	642
2.03	1.75	1.72	1.67	1.80	1.64	1.18	1.19	1.26	0.98	1.77	1.24	2.04	1.75
0.29	0.40	0.41	0.44	0.31	0.48	0.34	0.34	0.31	0.49	0.49	0.38	0.33	0.46
0.14	0.23	0.24	0.26	0.17	0.29	0.29	0.28	0.25	0.50	0.28	0.31	0.16	0.26

TABLE 6.2.

Mean values of $\alpha_{1i}L_i$ and their estimated standard errors ($\hat{\sigma}$), in addition to the sample frequencies (n_{gh}) of single persons, heads of households and spouses aged 25 years and over without children, by sex, marital status and age-class, compared with $\bar{\alpha}_1$

Sex	Marital Status	Vari-ables	age in years 25–34	35–44	45–54	55–64	65+	Total
MEN	Total	n_{gh}	95	56	88	210	454	903
		$\bar{\alpha}_1$	0.0436	0.0595	0.0769	0.1019	0.1259	0.1023
		$\overline{\alpha_1 L}$	1.91	2.11	1.92	1.75	1.15	1.51
		$\hat{\sigma}$	0.59	0.73	0.53	0.99	0.37	0.72
		V	0.31	0.35	0.27	0.56	0.32	0.48
	single	n_{gh}	19	4	11	14	26	74
		$\overline{\alpha_1 L}$	1.84	1.98	1.91	2.72	1.02	1.74
		$\hat{\sigma}$	0.77	0.14	0.21	3.48	0.44	1.66
		V	0.41	0.07	0.11	1.28	0.43	0.96
	having been married	n_{gh}		2	2	5	2	11
		$\overline{\alpha_1 L}$		2.37	1.94	1.74	1.25	1.80
		$\hat{\sigma}$		0.42	0.15	0.17	0.21	0.41
		V		0.18	0.08	0.10	0.17	0.23
	widower	n_{gh}			1	7	58	66
		$\overline{\alpha_1 L}$			2.00	1.94	1.19	1.28
		$\hat{\sigma}$				0.09	0.37	0.43
		V				0.05	0.32	0.34
	non-married	n_{gh}	19	6	14	26	86	151
		$\overline{\alpha_1 L}$	1.84	2.11	1.92	2.32	1.14	1.54
		$\hat{\sigma}$	0.77	0.29	0.19	2.55	0.40	1.22
		V	0.42	0.14	0.10	1.10	0.35	0.79
	married	n_{gh}	76	50	74	184	368	752
		$\overline{\alpha_1 L}$	1.93	2.10	1.92	1.67	1.16	1.50
		$\hat{\sigma}$	0.55	0.77	0.57	0.41	0.36	0.57
		V	0.28	0.36	0.30	0.25	0.31	0.38
WOMEN	Total	n_{gh}	68	77	57	131	241	574
		$\bar{\alpha}_1$	0.0461	0.0549	0.0765	0.0957	1.198	0.0979
		$\overline{\alpha_1 L}$	2.25	2.12	1.96	1.92	1.25	1.71
		$\hat{\sigma}$	1.11	0.59	0.49	0.85	0.37	0.77
		V	0.50	0.28	0.25	0.44	0.30	0.45
	single	n_{gh}	22	29	21	29	46	137
		$\overline{\alpha_1 L}$	1.73	2.01	1.88	1.64	1.17	1.59
		$\hat{\sigma}$	0.49	0.42	0.57	0.48	0.42	0.56
		V	0.28	0.21	0.30	0.29	0.36	0.35
	having been married	n_{gh}	1	1	1	9	2	14
		$\overline{\alpha_1 L}$	2.39	2.17	1.86	2.18	1.48	2.07
		$\hat{\sigma}$				0.36	0.12	0.39
		V				0.17	0.08	0.19

TABLE 6.2.
(cont.)

Sex	Marital Status	Variables	age in years					
			25–34	35–44	45–54	55–64	65+	Total
WOMEN	widow	n_{gh}		2	8	74	184	268
		$\overline{\alpha_1 L}$		2.50	2.08	2.01	1.28	1.51
		$\hat{\sigma}$		0.18	0.30	1.02	0.36	0.71
		V		0.07	0.14	0.51	0.28	0.47
	non-married	n_{gh}	23	22	30	112	232	419
		$\overline{\alpha_1 L}$	1.76	2.06	1.93	1.93	1.26	1.55
		$\hat{\sigma}$	0.50	0.41	0.50	0.89	0.38	0.66
		V	0.28	0.20	0.26	0.46	0.30	0.43
	married	n_{gh}	45	55	27	19	9	155
		$\overline{\alpha_1 L}$	2.50	2.14	1.99	1.83	1.16	2.12
		$\hat{\sigma}$	1.26	0.65	0.49	0.60	0.34	0.89
		V	0.50	0.30	0.24	0.33	0.30	0.42
BOTH SEXES	Total	n_{gh}	163	133	145	341	695	1477
		$\bar{\alpha}_1$	0.0450	0.0565	0.0732	0.0987	0.1253	0.0990
		$\overline{\alpha_1 L}$	2.05	2.11	1.94	1.82	1.19	1.58
		$\hat{\sigma}$	0.86	0.65	0.51	0.94	0.37	0.75
		V	0.42	0.31	0.26	0.52	0.31	0.47
	single	n_{gh}	41	23	32	43	72	211
		$\overline{\alpha_1 L}$	1.78	2.01	1.89	1.99	1.12	1.64
		$\hat{\sigma}$	0.63	0.38	0.47	2.04	0.43	1.08
		V	0.35	0.19	0.25	1.03	0.39	0.66
	having been married	n_{gh}	1	3	3	14	4	25
		$\overline{\alpha_1 L}$	2.39	2.30	1.91	2.02	1.37	1.95
		$\hat{\sigma}$		0.32	0.12	0.37	0.19	0.41
		V		0.14	0.06	0.18	0.14	0.21
	widow(er)	n_{gh}		2	9	81	242	334
		$\overline{\alpha_1 L}$		2.50	2.07	2.01	1.25	1.47
		$\hat{\sigma}$		0.18	0.28	0.98	0.37	0.67
		V		0.07	0.13	0.49	0.29	0.46
	non-married	n_{gh}	42	28	44	138	318	570
		$\overline{\alpha_1 L}$	1.79	2.08	1.93	2.00	1.22	1.55
		$\hat{\sigma}$	0.63	0.39	0.42	1.36	0.38	0.85
		V	0.35	0.19	0.22	0.68	0.31	0.55
	married	n_{gh}	121	105	101	203	377	907
		$\overline{\alpha_1 L}$	2.14	2.12	1.94	1.69	1.16	1.61
		$\hat{\sigma}$	0.92	0.70	0.55	0.43	0.36	0.68
		V	0.43	0.33	0.28	0.26	0.31	0.42

TABLE 6.3.

Mean values of $\alpha_{1i} L_i$ and their estimated standard errors ($\hat{\sigma}$), in addition to the sample frequencies (n_{gh}) of male married heads of households aged 35–64 years, by composition of the household, age-class and presence or absence of extraordinary expenses (E.E.), compared with $\bar{\alpha}_1$

Composition of household	Variables	age in years 35–44 E.E. no	35–44 E.E. yes	35–44 Total	45–54 E.E. no	45–54 E.E. yes	45–54 Total	55–64 E.E. no	55–64 E.E. yes	55–64 Total	Total E.E. no	Total E.E. yes	Total Total
no child	n_{gh}	71	17	88	82	15	97	67	8	75	220	40	260
	$\overline{\alpha_1 L}$	1.98	1.99	1.98	1.89	1.91	1.90	1.78	1.75	1.78	1.89	1.91	1.89
	$\hat{\sigma}$	0.39	0.28	0.37	0.37	0.37	0.37	0.46	0.35	0.44	0.41	0.33	0.40
	V	0.20	0.14	0.19	0.20	0.20	0.20	0.26	0.20	0.25	0.22	0.17	0.21
1–2 children	n_{gh}	140	14	154	85	17	102	41	7	48	266	38	304
	$\overline{\alpha_1 L}$	1.95	2.05	1.96	1.89	1.83	1.88	1.73	1.91	1.76	1.90	1.92	1.90
	$\hat{\sigma}$	0.39	0.33	0.39	0.36	0.34	0.35	0.38	0.33	0.38	0.39	0.34	0.38
	V	0.20	0.16	0.20	0.19	0.19	0.19	0.22	0.18	0.21	0.20	0.18	0.20
3–4 children	n_{gh}	214	26	240	121	25	146	25	9	34	360	60	420
	$\overline{\alpha_1 L}$	1.98	1.99	1.98	1.92	1.91	1.91	1.69	1.89	1.74	1.94	1.94	1.94
	$\hat{\sigma}$	0.32	0.36	0.32	0.29	0.29	0.29	0.40	0.30	0.38	0.32	0.32	0.32
	V	0.16	0.18	0.16	0.15	0.15	0.15	0.23	0.16	0.22	0.17	0.17	0.17
≥5 children	n_{gh}	65	7	72	57	10	67	10	2	12	132	19	151
	$\overline{\alpha_1 L}$	2.01	2.11	2.02	1.85	1.87	1.85	1.88	1.78	1.86	1.93	1.95	1.93
	$\hat{\sigma}$	0.31	0.14	0.30	0.36	0.17	0.33	0.15	0.26	0.16	0.33	0.20	0.32
	V	0.16	0.07	0.15	0.19	0.09	0.18	0.08	0.14	0.09	0.17	0.10	0.17
Total	n_{gh}	490	64	554	345	67	412	143	26	169	978	157	1135
	$10^4\bar{\alpha}_1$	570	575	571	735	717	732	952	985	955	719	718	719
	$\overline{\alpha_1 L}$	1.97	2.01	1.98	1.89	1.88	1.89	1.76	1.84	1.77	1.91	1.93	1.92
	$\hat{\sigma}$	0.35	0.31	0.35	0.34	0.31	0.33	0.41	0.31	0.40	0.36	0.32	0.36
	V	0.18	0.15	0.18	0.18	0.16	0.18	0.23	0.17	0.22	0.19	0.16	0.19

TABLE 6.4.

Mean values of $\alpha_{1i}L_i$ and their estimated standard errors ($\hat{\sigma}$), in addition to the sample frequencies of persons aged 65 years and over, by sex, marital status and owning or not owning their dwelling (O.D.)

Sex	Variables	Marital status															Total		
		single			having been married			widow(er)			not married			married					
		O.D.		total	O.D.		total	O.D.		total	O.D.		total	O.D.		total	O.D.		total
		no	yes		no	yes		no	yes		no	yes		no	yes		no	yes	
Men	$^*n_{gh}$	22	13	35	1	1	2	74	24	98	97	38	135	301	166	467	398	204	602
	$\overline{\alpha_1 L}$	1.14	0.92	1.06	1.40	1.11	1.25	1.32	0.63	1.15	1.28	0.74	1.13	1.33	0.93	1.18	1.32	0.89	1.17
	$\hat{\sigma}$	0.47	0.41	0.45			0.21	0.25	0.33	0.40	0.32	0.38	0.42	0.25	0.35	0.35	0.27	0.36	0.36
	V	0.41	0.44	0.43			0.17	0.19	0.53	0.35	0.25	0.52	0.37	0.19	0.37	0.29	0.21	0.40	0.31
Women	$^*n_{gh}$	44	16	60	3		3	220	65	285	267	81	348	5	5	10	272	86	358
	$\overline{\alpha_1 L}$	1.26	0.97	1.18	1.37		1.37	1.38	0.95	1.28	1.36	0.95	1.26	1.35	0.84	1.10	1.36	0.94	1.26
	$\hat{\sigma}$	0.44	0.44	0.45	0.22		0.22	0.36	0.57	0.45	0.37	0.55	0.45	0.28	0.31	0.39	0.37	0.53	0.45
	V	0.35	0.45	0.38	0.16		0.16	0.26	0.61	0.35	0.27	0.58	0.36	0.21	0.37	0.36	0.27	0.57	0.36
Men and women	$^*n_{gh}$	66	29	95	4	1	5	294	89	383	364	119	483	306	171	477	670	290	960
	$\overline{\alpha_1 L}$	1.22	0.95	1.14	1.37	1.11	1.32	1.36	0.86	1.25	1.34	0.88	1.23	1.33	0.93	1.18	1.33	0.91	1.21
	$\hat{\sigma}$	0.45	0.42	0.45	0.18		0.20	0.33	0.54	0.44	0.36	0.51	0.45	0.25	0.35	0.35	0.31	0.42	0.40
	V	0.37	0.44	0.40	0.13		0.15	0.25	0.62	0.36	0.27	0.58	0.36	0.19	0.37	0.29	0.24	0.46	0.33

TABLE 6.5.

Mean values of $\alpha_{1l}L_l$ and their estimated standard errors ($\hat{\sigma}$), in addition to the sample frequencies of persons under the age of 25 years, sex, participation or non-participation in a bonus savings plan, and occupational status

Sex	Variables	Participation in savings plan											
		No				Yes				Total			
		Total	other	manual	non-manual	Total	other	manual	non-manual	Total	other	manual	non-manual
Men	n_{gh}	252	12	194	46	76	3	55	18	328	15	249	64
	$10^4\bar{\alpha}_1$	254		262	182	222		233	197	247		256	186
	$\overline{\alpha_1 L}$	1.35	2.22	1.39	0.95	1.17	0.83	1.24	1.02	1.31	1.94	1.36	0.97
	$\hat{\sigma}$	0.52	0.60	0.46	0.39	0.35	0.35	0.33	0.32	0.49	0.80	0.44	0.37
	V	0.39	0.27	0.33	0.41	0.29	0.42	0.27	0.32	0.38	0.41	0.32	0.38
Women	n_{gh}	255	1	131	123	117	1	51	65	372	2	182	188
	$10^4\bar{\alpha}_1$	263		315	206	222		293	168	250		309	193
	$\overline{\alpha_1 L}$	1.53	2.23	1.84	1.19	1.30	0.80	1.73	0.98	1.46	1.52	1.81	1.12
	$\hat{\sigma}$	0.46		0.29	0.36	0.48		0.30	0.30	0.48	1.01	0.30	0.35
	V	0.30		0.16	0.30	0.37		0.18	0.31	0.33	0.67	0.16	0.32
Men and women	n_{gh}	507	13	325	169	193	4	106	83	700	17	431	252
	$10^4\bar{\alpha}_1$	259		283	200	222		260	174	248		278	191
	$\overline{\alpha_1 L}$	1.44	2.22	1.57	1.13	1.25	0.82	1.48	0.99	1.39	1.89	1.55	1.08
	$\hat{\sigma}$	0.50	0.58	0.46	0.38	0.44	0.29	0.40	0.31	0.49	0.80	0.44	0.36
	V	0.35	0.26	0.29	0.34	0.35	0.35	0.27	0.31	0.35	0.42	0.29	0.34

man. = manual worker
non-man. = non-manual worker

TABLE 6.6.

Synopsis of restrictions (R) and classifications (C) applying to tables 6.1 through 6.5

	Type of characteristic	6.1		6.2		6.3		6.4		6.5	
		R	C	R	C	R	C	R	C	R	C
a	Sex	male			x	male			x		x
b	Age	≥25	x	≥25	x	35–64	x	≥65		<25	
c	Marital status	married			x	married			x	single	
d	Status in household	head				head				child	
e	Size and composition of household		x	without children			x	without children			
f	Socio-economic status		x								x
g	Extra-ordinary expenses						x				
h	Ownership of dwelling								x		
i	Participation in bonus savings plan										x

The effects are analyzed separately for various characteristics, associated with the one under consideration, according to tables 6.1 through 6.6. The most elaborate cross-classification is applied to age, because of the key position taken up by this variable in tables 6.1 through 6.3, and the high degree of cross-classification adopted therein.

6.6.0.2.2. Pairing of characteristics for estimating effects. In principle, effects can be estimated for the $\frac{1}{2}G\,(G-1)$ different pairs of the G characteristics of the same type. Once the effects of an arbitrary 'base' of $G-1$ pairs of characteristics are estimated, the triangularity conditons (6.5.1.10c) determine the effects of the $\frac{1}{2}\,(G-1)\,(G-2)$ other pairs of characteristics. The inevitable appearance of (near-) empty cells may, however, impair these relationships.

In order to reduce the number of effects to be calculated and reproduced, we have to make a choice of $G-1$ pairs of characteristics. For $G = 2$ (the two sexes, and the dichotomies with respect to ownership of dwelling, participation in bonus savings plan and burdening by extraordinary expenses), there is no choice, hence no problem. For specific types of characteristics of a quantitative nature (age, size of household) a one-dimensional ordering is possible; nevertheless, the ages of the children have a bearing on the composition of the household. This suggests that in the latter case effects are calculated with respect to pairs of successive characteristics; indeed, this is done in tables 6.10 and 6.12.

Still, if there is a definite pattern in the point estimates of the effects between successive pairs of characteristics, in particular if they are (nearly) all of the same sign, the difference between the extremes may be statistically significant, whereas the successive difference may be insignificant.

For this reason, tables 6.9 and 6.10 present effects for the extremes (between ages and household sizes, respectively), in addition to effects for the successive pairs.

Such unambiguous ranking is, however, impossible for marital status: as regards their conditions of life persons having been married (either widowed or divorced) resemble both married and single people, but in different respects; therefore, effects are presented between all three pairs of marital statuses distinguished (single, married, having been married), as well as between married and unmarried (single and having been married taken together).

6.6.0.2.3. Contents. Two kinds of numerical information is provided in these tables, viz.:

(a) the effects themselves, as unweighted mean differences between means of $\alpha_{1i} \cdot L_i$, and
(b) the corresponding estimates of standard errors.

In the case where tables 6.9 through 6.14 present estimates separately for factors distinguished in the corresponding basic table, the three-way classification adopted in the latter is reduced to a two-way classification. This means that the effects are estimated according to (6.5.1.10a and b), and their corresponding standard errors according to (6.5.2.6) and (6.5.2.7).

Where, however, no such sub-division is made, i.e. for 'totals', the three-dimensional analysis of variance model (6.5.1.15) should be used; hence, these effects are estimated according to (6.5.1.16a) through (6.5.1.16c) and their corresponding standard errors according to (6.5.2.8) etc.

Also the latter estimates are, of course, related to the former ones, viz. the 'total' means as unweighted averages of the means for the sub-divisions, and the standard errors of the 'total' means as square roots of the sums of standard errors of the subordinated means divided by their number. This makes for less unreliability of the 'total' means compared with the former means.

Occasionally, a distinction is made according to two types of characteristics (such as sex and marital status) simultaneously; then, a one-dimensional analysis of variance model applies, and the effects and their standard errors are estimated accordingly, viz. as

$$\varkappa_{g(hk)} - \varkappa_{1(hk)} = \bar{x}_{ghk} - \bar{x}_{1hk}. \qquad (6.6.0.2.3.1)$$

Throughout, we adopted the usual 95 per cent confidence level as the criterion for significance. This means that we accept a probability of 5 per cent for considering insignificant effects as significant, i.e. of erroneously rejecting the null-hypothesis in 1 out of every 20 effects' estimates considered.

6.6.1. CELL FREQUENCIES

According to tables 6.1 through 6.5, the frequencies n_{gh} vary widely between the cells: from zero (empty cells) to over 200. Larger maximum frequencies appear in tables 6.4 and 6.5 than in table 6.1 through 6.3, though the former two relate to smaller sub-samples than the latter three. In addition to less detail in the (sub-) classification applied to tables 6.4 and 6.5, compared with the others, people are less evenly distributed over the alternatives offered: owning a dwelling or participating in a bonus savings plan are more rare than their opposites.

Notwithstanding adaptation of the criteria for classification (cf. section 6.6.0.1.1), aimed, inter alia, at reducing the occurrence of (near-) empty cells, the latter still appear in most of the tables.

6.6.2. MEANS

6.6.2.1. Means of $\alpha_{1i}L_i$. An examination of tables 6.1 through 6.5 prompts the following impressions:

1. With respect to the *level* of the $\overline{\alpha_1 L}$, we notice that:

(a) $\overline{\alpha_1 L}$ rarely assumes values below par, and generally exceeds 1 considerably, with values ranging to maxima of about 2;

(b) compared with people between the ages of 25 and 65, the old-aged (65^+) generally show lower values of $\overline{\alpha_1 L}$ – as appears from table 6.4 in contrast to tables 6.1 through 6.3;

(c) curiously enough, the younger generation (children under the age of 25) also present relatively low values of $\overline{\alpha_1 L}$ – as appears from table 6.5 compared with tables 6.1 through 6.3.

This brings us to:

2. *differences* in $\overline{\alpha_1 L}$-values between cells; in accordance with point 1(b) above – but disregarding point 1(a) for the time being – we notice:

(d) a general decline in values of $\overline{\alpha_1 L}$ with increasing age.

Indeed, it appears that:

(e) the $\overline{\alpha_1 L}$ are affected more strongly by age than by any other type of characteristic.

In a sense, this seems peculiar, because with respect to age, α_1 and L compensate each other to a certain extent: L decreases, while (therefore) α_1 increases with advancing age.

Besides, the tables suggest minor differences in $\overline{\alpha_1 L}$ with respect to other factors, in the sense that generally higher values are found for:

(f) owners of dwellings compared to renters,

(g) heads of households without children compared to those with children,

(h) manual workers compared to non-manual workers,

(i) participants compared to non-participants in bonus savings plans.

The latter conclusions should be considered as tentative only; they are examined more thoroughly in sections 6.6.4 and 6.6.5. The above-par level of the $\overline{\alpha_1 L}$, however, seems beyond reasonable doubt.

Apparently, the assumption adopted in section 4.2.3, viz, that α_1 would be of the order L^{-1} in magnitude, represents an under-estimation of these quasi-parameters; at least, this applies to employees and pensioners, to whom the savings survey and savings analyses are confined almost entirely.

On the one hand, a constant value L^{-1} for α_τ $(\tau = 1, \ldots, L)$ implies $C_\tau = L^{-1} R_1 (1 + r)^{\tau - 1}$, according to (4.1.3.3); this means that consumption would increase exponentially over prospective time τ, at a rate of growth r. On the other hand, invariance of prospective future consumption implies $\alpha_\tau = r(1 + r)^{L-\tau}/\{(1 + r)^L - 1\}$, again according to (4.1.3.3); this means an exponential decrease of α_τ, at a rate $1/(1 + r)$, ensuring $\sum_{\tau=1}^{L} \alpha_\tau = 1$.

For $\tau = 1$ in particular, we obtain:

$$\alpha_1 = r/\{1 + r - (1 + r)^{1-L}\}, \qquad (6.6.2.1.1)$$

implying $\alpha_1 > r/(1 + r)$.

According to this formula, values of α_1 and $\alpha_1 L$ are calculated for the approximate centres of the age-classes distinguished here, and presented in table 6.7.

Comparing the empirical values in the last column with the "hypothetical" ones in the last-but-one columns, we find a rough correspondence in level

TABLE 6.7.

Hypothetical values of α_1* and $\alpha_1 L$ at the centres of the age-classes, with corresponding life expectancies for the male population of the Netherlands around 1960 and $r = 4.08$ per cent per annum, compared with empirical $\alpha_1 L$ values†

Age-class	average age	Life expectancy (L)	$10^3\alpha_1$	$\alpha_1 L$	$\alpha_1 L$
	years		hypothetical*		empirical†
<25	22	52	44.9	2.33	1.31
25–34	30	44	47.4	2.09	1.97
35–44	40	35	52.0	1.82	1.99
45–54	50	26	60.6	1.58	1.90
55–64	60	18	76.4	1.38	1.72
65+	72	10	118.9	1.19	1.18

* according to formula $\alpha_1 = r/\{1 + r - (1 + r)^{1-L}\}$.

† from 'totals' of tables 6.1 and 6.5.

for ages between 25 and 45 years, and from 65 years upwards. In between, however, the empirical values of $\overline{\alpha_1 L}$ stay at nearly the same level till the age of 55, whereas they drop steeply around the age of 65. The largest discrepancy is found for people below the age of 25, with hypothetical values of $\alpha_1 L$ far exceeding the empirical ones. A part of this difference might perhaps be ascribed to the particular position of these people, viz. children still living at home.

Nevertheless, we conclude that neither the Modiglianian invariance hypothesis ($\alpha_\tau = L^{-1}$) nor the discounting hypothesis (α_τ declining exponentially) appears to fit the facts. Consequently, we are left with the concept of $\alpha_{\tau i}$ as a priori unspecifiable functions of τ, but depending on characteristics of persons i. This applies, in particular, to the α_{1i}.

6.6.2.2. Means of α_{1i}. As mentioned in section 6.6.0.1.2, the α_1-values are published for the horizontal totals only. Apparently, this suffices, especially since the values of L vary only slightly between groups of income recipients with different characteristics but belonging to the same age–sex class; the largest variations (in a relative sense) are found, of course, for the upper age-class 65$^+$. For the same reason, we find the ratios between $\overline{\alpha_1 L}$ and $\bar{\alpha}_1$ to be nearly constant within the same age–sex class; at least in:

$$\overline{\alpha_1 L}/\bar{\alpha}_1 = \bar{L}(1 + V_{\alpha_1} V_L r_{\alpha_1,L}) < \bar{L}, \qquad (6.6.2.2.1)$$

the coefficients of variation V_{α_1} and V_L of α_{1i} and L_i, respectively, and their coefficient of correlation $r_{\alpha_1,L}$ for all i belonging to the same cell will not vary much between cells within the same age column. Furthermore, V_L is generally small, except perhaps for the highest age brackets; assuming rectangular distributions of L_i within the 10-years wide age brackets, $\sigma_{L_i} = 10/\sqrt{12} = 2.9$ years, an overestimate of its actual standard deviation. For L = (say) 35, the age bracket of 35–44 years, $V_{\alpha_i} = 0.25$ and $V_{\alpha_i,L}$ = (say) 0.8: $\overline{\alpha_1 L}/\bar{\alpha}_1 = 0.984\bar{L}$; it even justifies approximation of $\overline{\alpha_1 L}/\bar{\alpha}_1$ by $\bar{L}$ for most practical purposes. Anyhow, dealing with $\bar{\alpha}_1$ per age–sex class amounts to dealing with $\overline{\alpha_1 L}$ reduced by a scale factor that is nearly constant and approximately equal to L^{-1}. The latter value differs, however, according to sex: at each age attained by income recipients, women may expect to live longer than men. Moreover, the mean age of women in most income brackets (except the highest one) is usually lower than that of men; the reason is women's flight from paid work into unpaid household chores, following marriage, and particularly child-bearing. At least this was the normal situation in the Netherlands around 1960, with a mere fourth of the married women being gainfully occupied.

Between age brackets, $\bar{\alpha}_1$ varies strongly, even if somewhat less than in proportion to $\bar{L}^{-1}$.

6.6.3. DISPERSIONS

6.6.3.1. Dispersion of $\alpha_{1i}L_i$. In general, the estimated standard errors of $\alpha_{1i}L_i$ remain below 1, and the majority even below $\frac{1}{2}$. Since their means are usually well above 1, most of the coefficients of variation are between 0.20 and 0.40. This means that the cells are fairly homogeneous in general. In view of the manner in which the α's are calculated according to (6.3.2.2.1), i.e. as the ratios of current income to the present values of future expected income and of the intended change in personal wealth, the comparative stability of the α's may be ascribed to the stickiness of savings rates and wealth-income ratios.

Naturally, the $\hat{\sigma}$, hence the V, are higher for totals than for sub-divisions, because of the variance-raising effect of between-cell contributions.

The pattern of the $\hat{\sigma}$'s – if there is any – is more irregular than that of the $\overline{\alpha_1 L}$; occasionally, it gives the impression of being spurious. This is quite usual, however: compared with means, standard errors are much more sensitive to incidental extremes, because of the squaring involved in the calculation of variances. Thus, we find some extremely high $\hat{\sigma}$-values, in particular in table 6.2, among older single men and married women; indeed, it seems that table 6.2 shows a larger number of high $\hat{\sigma}$-values than any of the other tables. Evidently, such extremes lower the chance of finding significant effects of factors at a pre-determined confidence level. Notwithstanding these irregularities with respect to standard errors, tables 6.1 through 6.5 suggest some tendencies with respect to the *relative* errors; in particular, they give the impression that coefficients of variation are higher

for	than for
a. non-manual workers	manual workers
b. heads of households without children	heads of households with children
c. men under 25 or over 64	ditto women
d. people aged 65+ owning dwellings	ditto not owning dwellings
e. male adolescents not participating in bonus savings plans	ditto participating in same
f. heads of household without extraordinary expenses	ditto with such expenses

This means that the groups at the left-hand side would be more heterogeneous than those at the right-hand side. In general, these differences in sign seem plausible:

ad a. the group of non-manual workers is much more diverse – comprising high-ranking technical experts as well as low-level clerks, highly successful businessmen and top managers as well as small-time farmers;

ad c. lesser variations among women compared with men is also observed in other respects, such as length and intelligence; moreover, as income recipients, they form a special, auto-selected group;

ad d. through f. some of the positive alternatives (participating in a savings plan having extraordinary expenses) appear to have a homogenizing effect on the α_1-values.

Furthermore, one might presume a positive correlation between corresponding standard errors and means, as is often observed in other surveys; in particular, this would entail generally lower $\hat{\sigma}$-values for the 65^+-age class. Although there appears to be some tendency in that direction, it is not strong enough to yield statistically significant results at (say) a 95 per cent confidence level.

More promising is the consideration that standard errors are measures of heterogeneity, and that heterogeneity tends to become more pronounced according as less detailed classification is applied to a given sample (generally resulting in larger cell frequencies). This reasoning underlies assumption (6.5.1.3 II), stating that the expected value of the ratio of variance to frequency is equal for all cells[17] in the same table; the (more usual) alternative assumption (6.5.1.3 I) is that all cell variances as such are equal. In a less precise, but operational manner, we tested the hypothesis that the standard errors per cell are proportional to the square roots of the sample frequencies against the alternative hypothesis that the two would be stochastically independent.

One manner in which to test both hypotheses is to estimate the parameters γ_0 and γ_1 as well as their sampling variances s_a^2 and s_b^2 of the regression equation:

$$\hat{\sigma}_{gh} = \gamma_0 + \gamma_1 \sqrt{n_{gh}}. \tag{6.6.3.1.1}$$

If – at a predetermined probability level of (say) 95 per cent – $\hat{\gamma}_0$ is found not to differ significantly from zero and a significantly positive $\hat{\gamma}_1$ is obtained,

[17] By 'cells' we mean the smallest sub-divisions only, excluding (sub-) totals of any kind as well as empty cells.

we accept the proportionality hypothesis (6.5.1.3II) and reject the constancy hypothesis (6.5.1.3I).

If, on the other hand, $\hat{\gamma}_1$ is found not to be significantly positive (it might even be negative!), but a $\hat{\gamma}_0$ value is obtained that differs significantly from zero, we accept (6.5.1.3I) and reject (6.5.1.3II).

The results of applying (6.6.3.1.1) to tables 6.1 through 6.5, however, left us undecided, because in all cases both $\hat{\gamma}_0$ and $\hat{\gamma}_1$ appeared to be significant at the 95 per cent confidence level. This means that we can accept neither the proportionality hypothesis nor the homoskedasticity hypothesis; that we cannot reject the hypothesis of a linear relationship is not relevant to our problem.

Nevertheless, we should like to know which of the two hypotheses is the least objectionable one; or, more specifically, which of the two measures, i.e. either $\hat{\sigma}_{gh}$ or $\hat{\sigma}_{gh}/\sqrt{n_{gh}}$, shows the smallest coefficient of variation.

Table 6.8 answers this question in favour of the first alternative. For all tables 6.1 through 6.5 the $\hat{\sigma}_{gh}/\sqrt{n_{gh}}$ are more heteroskedastic than the $\hat{\sigma}_{gh}$ themselves. On the other hand, this means that the estimation of the effects according to (6.5.1.10a + b) and based on (6.5.1.3II) was less efficient – though more practical – than estimation according to (6.5.1.5) and based on (6.5.1.3I) would have been. Fortunately, however, the differences in efficiency are smallest where it matters most, i.e. where heteroskedasticity is strongest.

This table confirms the presumption that the standard errors of table 6.2 behave much more erratically than those of the other tables. The rank-order of the tables with respect to heteroskedasticity is the same, according to both criteria.

TABLE 6.8.

Coefficients of variation of $\hat{\sigma}_{gh}$ and of $\hat{\sigma}_{gh}/\sqrt{n_{gh}}$, relating to the α_{1i}/L_i, between the cells of tables 6.1 through 6.5

Table	Coefficient of variation	
	$\hat{\sigma}_{gh}$	$\hat{\sigma}_{gh}/\sqrt{n_{gh}}$
6.1	0.66	0.87
6.2	1.32	1.47
6.3	0.24	0.53
6.4	0.57	0.75
6.5	0.16	0.35

6.6.3.2. Dispersions of α_{1i}. The coefficients of variation $V_{\alpha_1 L}$ of $\alpha_{1i}L_i$ are related to those of α_{1i} (V_{α_1}) and L_i (V_L) by:

$$\begin{aligned} V^2_{\alpha_1 L} &= (1 + V_{\alpha_1} V_L r_{\alpha_1,L})^{-2} (V^2_{\alpha_1} + V^2_L + 2V_{\alpha_{1i}} V_L r_{\alpha_1,L}) \\ &\approx \{1 + 2V_L (V^{-1}_{\alpha_1} - V_{\alpha_1}) r_{\alpha_1,L}\} V^2_{\alpha_1} \\ &\quad + (1 - 2V_{\alpha_1} V_L r_{\alpha_1,L}) V^2_L, \end{aligned} \qquad (6.6.3.2.1)$$

on account of $|V_{\alpha_1} V_L r_{\alpha_1,L}| \ll 1$ for reasons explained in section 6.6.2.2. Since one of the reasons is $V_L \ll V_\alpha < 1$ (in general), the term with $V^2_{L_1}$ in (6.6.3.2.1) is usually negligible compared to the term with $V^2_{\alpha_1}$; and since $\{1 + 2V_L (V^{-1}_\alpha - V_{\alpha_1}) r_{\alpha_1,L}\}$ tends to be nearly 1:

$$V_{\alpha_1} \approx \{1 - V_L (V^{-1}_{\alpha_1} - V_{\alpha_1}) r_{\alpha_1,L}\} V_{\alpha_1 L}, \qquad (6.6.3.2.2)$$

it means that the coefficient of variation of the α_{1i} is but slightly higher than that of the $\alpha_{1i}L_i$, with $V^{-1}_\alpha > 1 > V_\alpha$ and $r_{\alpha_1,L} < 0$.

This theoretically obtained result is corroborated empirically: the coefficients of variation of the α_{1i} appearing in Bannink a.o. [1966, tables I through V] are usually somewhat (but not by more than 5 per cent) higher than those of the $\alpha_{1i}L_i$ appearing in the corresponding tables 6.1 through 6.5.

This means that not only the averages but also the standard errors of α_{1i} and $\alpha_{1i}L_i$ are nearly proportional to each other, within the same age–sex class; and since with rising age, $\bar{\alpha}_1$ increases much more rapidly than $\overline{\alpha_1 L}$, the standard errors of α_{1i} also go up steeply, whereas those of $\alpha_{1i}L_i$ hardly show any systematic relationship with age (cf. section 6.6.2.2).

6.6.4. MAIN EFFECTS

6.6.4.1. General observations. First, it appears that the absolute values of the estimated effects are rarely much larger, and sometimes even smaller than the corresponding standard errors. On the one hand, the point estimates of the effects are comparatively small, because they result from subtractions of mean, ever-positive $\bar{\alpha}_1$-values; on the other hand, the corresponding estimates of the standard errors of the effects are comparatively large, because they result from *additions* of variances, insufficiently reduced by the generally small numbers of cells involved. The frequent occurrence of (near-) empty cells, resulting in loss of information, is an aggravating factor in that respect. Consequently, a large number of effects of *separate* characteristics – of the same type – appears to be non-significant at a 95 per cent confidence level.

The standard errors of the effects estimated without cross-classification according to other types of characteristics are generally lower than the corresponding effects for the sub-divisions; this, of course, is due to the larger number of cells involved in the former effects compared with the latter. Since the point estimates of the effects for the sub-divisions may not agree in sign, the effects of types of characteristics not cross-classified need not always be more significant than those for the sub-divisions. Nevertheless, it appears to be the rule. The reason is that effects of characteristics show a slight tendency to be of the same sign for the various sub-divisions. It stands to reason that this tendency is more pronounced according as the ratios of the estimated standard errors to the corresponding point estimates are smaller, i.e. according as the latter are more reliable. This presumption is corroborated by the outcome of our calculations: the concordance of signs of effects is perfect for a relatively strong factor such as socio-economic status, (table 6.13). On the other hand, it is virtually non-existent with respect to a weak factor such as sex (table 6.9).

6.6.4.2. Sex. Indeed, in no case do we find a significant effect of sex on the $\alpha_{1i}L_i$; moreover, the point estimates vary in sign (according to table 6.9). On the other hand, Bannink [1967, text table 1] found consistently lower values of the α_{1i} for men compared with women, implying a just-significant total sex effect. A plausible explanation of this paradox is that what has been considered as a sex effect is really a life-expectancy effect: the apparently lower urgencies to consume of women compared with men may be largely due to women's longevity, in this respect beating men by a couple of years (cf. section 6.6.2.2).

6.6.4.3. Age. Between successive age classes, the effects of age on the $\alpha_{1i}L_i$ look unimpressive, according to table 6.10; between the extreme age classes distinguished, i.e. between 65^+ and 25–34 years, however, a significant negative overall age effect on the $\alpha_{1i}L_i$ is obtained[18]. This corroborates the impression mentioned in section 6.6.1.1 and based on table 6.1, viz. that in the long run the $\alpha_{1i}L_i$ tend to decline with increasing age. This tendency seems to set in already near the age of 55. It is perhaps a sign of fear or a foreboding that ageing people may have of still more urgent needs ahead of them – in

---

[18] Because of the scattering of empty cells, the age effects for 65^+ compared with 25–34 do not equal the sums of the preceding age effects between the successive age classes.

TABLE 6.9.

Effects of sex on the values of $\overline{\alpha_1 L}$ (males compared with females)

No.	Source: basic table	Delimitation of groups					$10^3 \times \Delta \overline{x_1 L}$
		Marital status	Compos. of househ.	Status in househ.	Age (yrs)	Socio-econ. status	
1a	6.2		without child		25+		−19 (293)
b		married					−168 (412)
c		unmarried					110 (367)
d		single					208 (751)
e		having been married					−98 (230)
2a	6.4		without child		65+		−55 (260)
b		married					35 (300)
c		unmarried					−145 (414)
		single					−85 (441)
3a	6.5	single		child	<25		−187 (232)
b						manual	−470 (352)
c						non-manual	−100 (344)

Between brackets: estimated standard errors.

particular, on account of illness or disability. Alternatively or additionally, it may also be due to a common over-estimation of their life expectancies.

The estimated age effects appear to be unanimous as regards their negative signs between age classes 45–54 and 35–44, as well as between 65^+ and 55–64. Occasional positive (albeit statistically insignificant) effects are found between age classes 35–44 and 25–34, and between 55–64 and 45–54 for

TABLE 6.10. Age effects on the values of $\overline{\alpha_1 L}$ (higher age classes compared with lower ones)

No.	Source: basic table	Delimitation of groups						$10^3\Delta\,\overline{\alpha_1 L}$				
								Age classes (years)				
		Sex	Marital status	Compos. of househ.	Status in househ.	Age (yrs)	Socio-econ. status	35–44 25–34	45–54 35–44	55–64 45–54	65+ 55–64	65+ 25–34
1a	6.1	M	married		head	25+		−10 (154)	−42 (129)	−34 (117)	−404 (150)	−607 (101)
b							manual	−13 (147)	−158 (136)	−181 (153)	−440 (239)	−770 (122)
c							non-manual	−24 (233)	−173 (231)	−44 (216)	−330 (446)	−535 (449)
2a	6.2	M	single	without child	head	25+		155 (558)	−227 (362)	75 (902)	−863 (895)	−795 (505)
b		F						−100 (726)	−253 (378)	−38 (428)	−643 (371)	−937 (696)
c		M+F						28 (458)	−241 (262)	19 (499)	−753 (484)	−866 (430)
a		M	having been married					270 (823)	−190 (347)	400 (2557)	−1180 (2581)	−700 (868)
b		F						300 (647)	−130 (647)	0	−670 (968)	−500 (628)
c		M+F						285 (523)	−160 (367)	200 (1277)	−925 (1378)	−600 (535)
a		M	married					170 (946)	−180 (792)	−250 (702)	−510 (546)	−770 (657)
b		F						−360 (1418)	−150 (814)	−160 (775)	−670 (690)	−340 (1305)
c		M+F						−95 (853)	−165 (568)	−205 (523)	−590 (411)	−1055 (731)
3a	6.3	M	married			35–64			−248 (325)	−165 (333)		
b		M		with E.E.		35–64			−155 (209)	−48 (217)		
c		M		without E.E.		35–64			−93 (248)	−118 (252)		

E.E. = extraordinary expenses

particular combinations of sex and marital status, but the negative effects of age on $\alpha_{1i}L_i$ keep a solid majority.

Contrariwise, Bannink [1967, text table 2] showed predominantly positive effects of age on α_{1i}. The obvious reason is that the $\alpha_{\tau i}$ for $\tau = 1, \ldots, L$ must add up to 1 over life horizons that recede with rising age.

Together, these observations imply that multiplying the α_{1i} by L_i somewhat over-compensated the positive effect of age on α_{1i}, i.e. with the result of a negative effect of age on $\alpha_{1i}L_i$.

6.6.4.4. Marital status. No systematic, and a fortiori no significant separate effects of marital status on $\alpha_{1i}L_i$ can be detected in table 6.11. Perhaps, the picture of such possible effects is blurred by the heterogeneity of the groups of both the married people and the people having been married.

6.6.4.5. Household size and composition. Table 6.12 hardly confirms the impression imparted by table 6.1, viz. that the $\alpha_{1i}L_i$ tend to increase with increasing size of the household and ages of the children: positive estimates for effects of an increase in size of the households or in age of the child(ren) are alternated by negative estimates for such effects. Sometimes, but not always, such a dip in the value of $\alpha_1 L$ (or of α_1) is understandable (even though not necessarily true!). For instance, two children both under 5 may entail less *present* urgency to consume than one child over 15. For one thing, the younger of the two tots (not twins) may step into the older one's shoes or trousers, especially if they are of the same sex – meaning economies of scale (cheaper by the pair, if not by the dozen). For another thing, one should bear in mind throughout that urgency to consume is a relative concept, meaning that present needs are weighted against future needs; specifically, the relatively high value of α_1 (or $\alpha_1 L$) for the household with one child over 15 may also be explained in view of prospective relief in the near future, viz. when this child will leave home or will start to earn its own upkeep; on the other hand, the household with the two small children is in for more difficult times ahead, due to the growing-up of their offspring, entailing increasing costs of living.

Comparing households of manual workers with those of non-manual workers, the latter indeed suggest an overall, albeit slight, increase in the 'urgency to consume' with increasing size and rising ages of the children, whereas the former do not. A partial explanation may be that manual workers' children tend to receive a shorter and cheaper schooling than the children

TABLE 6.11.

Effects of marital status on the values of $\overline{\alpha_1 L}$

No.	Source: basic table	Delimitation of groups: Sex	Delimitation of groups: Compos. of household	Delimitation of groups: Age (yrs)	$10^3\Delta\overline{\alpha_1 L}$ — Difference in marital status — married compared with: unmarried	married compared with: single	married compared with: having been married	having been married comp. with single
1a	6.5	M + F	without child	25+	6 (302)	52 (376)	−188 (219)	240 (354)
b		M		25+	−110 (596)	−138 (761)	−113 (279)	−83 (732)
c		F		25+	136 (416)	238 (394)	−92 (381)	330 (286)
2a	6.4	M + F		65+	20 (268)	45 (265)	−110 (198)	155 (252)
b		M		65+	120 (329)	100 (379)	−125	225
c		F		65+	−60 (392)	−20 (375)	−20 (303)	110 (381)

TABLE 6.12.

Effects of household size and composition on the values of $\overline{\alpha_1 L}$

No.	Source: basic table	Sex	Marital status	Status in household	Age (yrs)	Socio-economic status	without children vs 1 child <15	1 child <15 vs 1 child ≥15	1 child ≥15 vs 2 children both ≤5	2 children both ≤5 vs 2 children not both ≤5	2 children not both ≤5 vs 3–4 children not all <15	3–4 children not all <15 vs 3–4 children all <15	3–4 children all <15 vs 5+ children	5+ children vs without children
							$10^3\Delta\overline{\alpha_1 L}$: Differences in household composition; comparisons ↑↓							
1a	6.1	M	married	head	25+		237 (196)	26 (238)	−306 (187)	131 (160)	−7 (130)	101 (137)	24 (136)	85 (173)
b						manual	55 (225)	−167 (185)	−100 (204)	183 (186)	−30 (148)	−10 (199)	13 (638)	3 (216)
c						non-manual	132 (361)	142 (340)	−443 (330)	153 (300)	55 (260)	108 (236)	−48 (224)	182 (310)

No.	Source: basic table	Age (yrs)		1 child vs 2 children	2 children vs 3–4 children	3–4 children vs 5+ children
2a	6.3	35–64	with E.E.	47 (273)	0	−10 (216)
b			without E.E.	−27 (321)	7 (293)	50 (257)

E.E. = extraordinary expenses

from non-manual workers' homes. The reader should, however, be cautioned that the preceding reasoning is highly speculative, and prompted by point estimates that are not even significantly different from zero.

6.6.4.6. Occupational status. Compared with non-manual workers, labourers appear to have significantly higher values of $\alpha_{1i}L_i$, as evidenced by table 6.13; this also holds good for the separate age classes, although not significantly. This means that apparently occupation, like sex and age, were not sufficiently accounted for in the estimates of the present value of financial resources. It is, however, doubtful whether this may be attributed to less foresight on the side of manual workers, compared with non-manual workers – as claimed by Watts [1958] on account of differences in years of schooling received.

TABLE 6.13.

Effects of occupational status on the values of $\overline{\alpha_1 L}$ (manual workers compared with non-manual workers)

No.	Source basic table	Delimitation of groups					$10^3 \times \Delta\overline{\alpha_1 L}$
		Sex	Marital status	Status in house-hold	Age (yrs)	Particip. in bonus savings plan	
1a	6.1	M	married	head	> 25+		235
							(149)
b					25–34		329
							(201)
c					35–44		284
							(189)
d					45–54		299
							(190)
e					55–64		147
							(184)
f					65+		125
							(636)
	6.5		single	child	< 25		515
							(246)
2a						yes	485
							(313)
b						no	545
							(380)

6.6.4.7. Extraordinary expenses. It is plausible that present-day extraordinary expenses – on account of illness as well as financial support of children receiving higher education – raise the $\alpha_{1i}L_i$ as well as the α_{1i}. Though positive point estimates, at least for all heads of household of 35–64 years, dominate, they do not differ significantly from zero, according to table 6.14. One should bear in mind, however, that the extraordinary expenses raise α_{1i} or $\alpha_{1i}L_i$ only if they are considered as merely temporary instead of continuing or even escalating.

6.6.4.8. Participation in a bonus savings plan and ownership of a dwelling. According to table 6.14, the $\alpha_{1i}L_i$ appear to be negatively associated with both participation in a bonus savings plan and ownership of the dwelling. Both have in common that they imply investment of a kind, and may be interpreted in causally opposite ways. On the one hand, participation in a bonus savings plan or ownership of a dwelling may stimulate the urgency to save rather than the urgency to consume (qualitatively, the effects on $\alpha_{1i}L_i$ and α_{1i} are the same). The negative effect of participation in a bonus savings plan on the urgency to consume may be considered, at least partly, as a positive interest effect on savings, since the interest equivalent of the bonus has not been incorporated in the discount factors. A similar interpretation of the effect of ownership of the dwelling is not possible, however, except in the case where it entails fiscal savings.

On the other hand, one may reverse the causal relationship by reasoning that those younger people who do participate in a bonus savings plan or those older people who do own their dwellings may be the very men and women who by nature are more than normally inclined to save. Unfortunately, one cannot separate these forces on the basis of the present data collected.

6.6.5. OVERALL PERFORMANCE OF THE THREE-WAY CLASSIFICATION

How much do the 8 types of characteristics distinguished here contribute to the variance of our key variable, $\alpha_{1i}L_i$, as compared with the variance of α_{1i}? This question is answered in table 6.15.

First, it appears that these characteristics contribute less than one-half to the total variance of the variable to be explained; the only exception is presented by young women. This is not a novel phenomenon; for instance, it was also observed by Somermeyer [1965], in a case where partly the same plan – compared with their opposites – on the values of $\overline{\alpha_1 L}$

No.	Source: basic table	Effect of:	Delimitation of groups: Sex	Marital status	Compos. of household	Status in household	Age (yrs)	$10^3\Delta\overline{\alpha_1 L}$
1a	6.3	E.E.	M	marr.		head	35–44	27 (229)
b							45–54	−8 (230)
c							55–64	63 (241)
2a	6.4	Owning dwelling	M		without child		65+	−400 (288)
b			F					−410 (311)
c			M + F					−405 (212)
d			M			not married		−540 (497)
e			F					−410 (663)
f			M + F					−475 (412)
g			M			married		−400 (430)
h			F					−510 (418)
i			M + F					−455 (295)
3	6.5	Participation in savings plan		unmarr.		child	< 25	−537 (241)

TABLE 6.15.

Percentage contributions of between-cell variances to total variances of $\alpha_{1i}L_i$ and α_{1i}, and the coefficients of variation of these variables

Basic table: This book	Basic table: Bannink [1967]	Delimitation of income recipients	Type of characteristic distinguished	Percentage contribution of the characteristics to total variance: $\alpha_{1i}L_i$	Percentage contribution of the characteristics to total variance: α_{1i}	Coefficients of variation (per cent): $\alpha_{1i}L_i$	Coefficients of variation (per cent): α_{1i}
6.1	I A	Male heads of households, 25 years of age and over (married)	Age Household composition Occupational status	48	25	28	47
6.2	II A	Men and women 25 years of age and over, without children	Sex Age Marital status	31	34	47	57
6.3	III A	Male heads of households, 35–64 years (married)	Age Household composition Extraordinary expenses	5	46	19	31
6.4	IV A	Men and women 65 years of age and over, without children	Sex Age Ownership of dwelling	26	26	33	47
6.5	V A	Children under 25 years of age	Sex Occupational status Partic. in Savings Plan	42	29	35	37

explanatory variables (age, sex, occupation) were brought into play for the explanation of inter-individual differences in income.

As suggested in section 6.6.3.2, the coefficients of variation of the $\alpha_{1i}L_i$ are uniformly smaller than those of the α_{1i}. The main reason is that the latter variable declines with increasing age, somewhat less than proportionately; therefore, variability is reduced by multiplying it by L_i. Consequently, we find that, as a rule, the differences in coefficients of variation are largest according as age plays a more important rôle. Consequently, the deviations are more pronounced in table 6.1 with a wide range of ages than in table 6.3 with the age range restricted to 35–64 years, and even more so in table 6.5 confined to younger people. The only expectation is shown by table 6.2, which covers as wide an age range as table 6.1, yet shows a smaller difference in coefficients of variation; irregularities in the age pattern of the α_i may be at the base of this phenomenon.

It seems anomalous that the three characteristics (among which age) distinguished in table IA of Bannink a.o. [1966] account for a much smaller share of the variance of α_{1i} than the same characteristics distinguished in the corresponding table 6.1 with respect to $\alpha_{1i}L_i$; one might expect the contrary, in view of the greater sensitivity of α_{1i}, compared with $\alpha_{1i}L_i$, to variations in age. Precisely because of its relatively smaller variations, however, less variance of $\alpha_{1i}L_i$, compared with α_{1i}, has to be accounted for.

Anyhow, it is noteworthy that nearly one-half of the variation of the $\alpha_{1i}L_i$ is explained by age, followed at a distance by the other two factors.

It stands to reason that the restriction of the age range in table 6.3 compared with table 6.1 reduces the part of total variance explained by age and two other factors; still, one might have expected a somewhat better performance than a mere 5 per cent.

On the other hand, much improvement is neither necessary nor possible, in view of the already low coefficient of variation of the $\alpha_{1i}L_i$. Contrariwise, it is less obvious that the same three characteristics account for nearly one half of the variance of α_{1i} – even though relatively larger than that of $\alpha_{1i}L_i$.

Differences in importance of the factors with respect to their impact on $\alpha_{1i}L_i$ are, of course, reflected in other tables besides table 6.3. Occupational status helps to boost the between-cell contributions to variance in table 6.5 as well as in table 6.1; in table 6.4 the one-quarter explanation of the variance is largely due to the factor 'ownership of dwelling'.

With the exception of table 6.3, the basic tables feature triplets of factors –

drawn from a total of eight, and repeatedly reshuffled – with amply significant joint effects on the variable $(\alpha_{1i}L_i)$ under consideration.

Finally, it is gratifying to note:

(1) that at least part of the variance of α_{1i} is taken care of by L_i, and
(2) that a considerable, even if not a major, part of the remaining variance can be attributed to the effects of a number of personal characteristics.

6.6.6. INTRA-FAMILY (DIS-) SIMILARITIES IN SAVINGS BEHAVIOUR

For the 297 households with two income receiving members included in the Savings Survey and retained for the present analysis, the dummy table presented in section 6.5.3 was completed. The result is as follows:

TABLE 6.16.

Frequencies of households with two income receiving members classified according to above-normal (+) or below-normal (−) values of individual 'urgencies to consume'

		older member		
		+	−	total
younger member	+	55 (50.9)	68 (72.1)	123
	−	68 (72.1)	106 (101.9)	174
	total	123	174	297

The figures between brackets denote the expected frequencies in case the null-hypothesis would hold; these theoretical frequencies per cell are calculated as the products of the corresponding row and column marginal totals divided by the grand total (297).

Comparison between the empirical and the theoretical frequencies shows a small excess of empirical over theoretical frequencies on the main diagonal, and the opposite on the subsidiary diagonal; by definition, the differences between the empirical and the theoretical frequencies in both the northwestern and the southeastern cells equal t. This suggests a slight net positive association between household members as regards savings behaviour, in accordance with the alternative hypothesis stated in section 6.5.3.

For testing the latter hypothesis against the null-hypothesis, we first ascertain that the total sample size (297) is sufficient for justifying the approximation of the t-statistic by a normal distribution. Its mean is zero, and $\sigma = 4.2$, while $t = 55 - 50.9 = 106 - 101.9 = 4.1$.

In a one-sided test (of the null-hypothesis against the alternative hypothesis), these results imply a probability of 18 per cent for such a high or a higher value of t to be brought about by pure chance.

On the one hand, this implies that with regard to savings behaviour, positive agreement between household members is more likely than independence or disagreement. On the other hand, such a low level of significance is generally considered as insufficient for rejecting the null-hypothesis.

This inconclusiveness might be due to insufficient homogeneity of the pairs of household members included in table 6.16. Therefore, the same kind of analysis has been carried out once more, this time restricted to parent–child pairs of household members, with the following result:

TABLE 6.17.

Frequencies of households with one parent and one child as the two income receiving members classified according to above-normal (+) or below-normal (−) values of the 'urgencies to consume'

		Parent		
		+	−	total
child	+	52 (48.8)	67 (70.2)	119
	−	64 (67.2)	100 (96.8)	164
	total	116	167	283

Contrary to expectations, the latter restricted (but only slightly smaller) group yielded less instead of more significant results (although still in favour of the hypothesis of 'positive mutual agreement').

Similar analyses carried out for pairs of children in households with 2, 3 or 4 income receiving members led to qualitatively similar conclusions.

The net outcome of the analyses presented above need not surprise us, in view of the co-existence of arguments in favour of both similarity and dissimilarity in savings behaviour, such that the former seems to outweigh the latter only slightly.

APPENDIX A TO CHAPTER 6

GRAPHICAL SMOOTHING OF DATA ON TYPICAL INCOME FROM AGE-CLASS TO AGE-YEAR DISTRIBUTIONS

6A.1. Methodological considerations

For computing present values of expected future typical income[1], means per age-class (covering 5 or 10 age-years) are much too crude. The reason is that mean (typical) income does not remain constant within any age-class in order to change abruptly between classes, but varies gradually between as well as within them.

This drawback of the age-class approach is particularly awkward for calculating present values of income flows. Indeed, by applying indexnumbers of mean typical income per age-class, the present value of the entire flow of expected future income would gradually and slowly fall with age increasing *within the same age-class*, whereas it would change abruptly by passing to the next age-class.

Therefore, it was deemed necessary to approximate mean typical income per age-*year*. In principle, it would have been possible to derive a distribution of income recipients per age-year; however, the additional processing of the collected data would have been too expensive in view of its limited usefulness: the number of persons per cell (identified by age-year, occupational group and sex) would occasionally become so small (especially among women, and in the lowest age bracket) that the mean typical incomes per occupational group and per sex would largely show mere erratic fluctuations over the age-years. Since such fluctuations would have to be ironed-out anyhow, it seemed more natural as well as efficient to apply such a smoothing procedure to the income means per age-class *directly*.

---

[1] 'Typical' income is the income derived from the *main* source of income, depending on the person's occupational status; e.g. the typical incomes of employees, entrepreneurs and the rare 'men of property' are wages and salaries, profits, and capital income respectively.

For this purpose, a graphical method was adopted. First, the relationships – per occupational group per sex – between mean typical income and age-class – were depicted by means of step-lines. Next, free-hand curves were drawn through and around these step-lines in such a way that within each age-class the area below the curve (and bounded by the vertical lines of division between the classes, in addition to the base) would represent about the same total income as the area of the original rectangle below the horizontal section of the step-line. Obviously this cannot be done in an exact manner, since the distribution of income recipients – for each occupational group and sex per age-*year* – is unknown. If such a distribution is not too skew (as we may safely assume), i.e. if the age-class is not too wide (at most 10 years, since there is no need of adjustment above the age of retirement) and if the adjusted line is monotonically falling or rising and not too crooked, the smooth curve will intersect the horizontal parts of the stepline near the middle of the classes. Obviously, an exception should be made for the modal age-class, where the adjustment curve will intersect the horizontal part of the step-line at least twice (i.e. from below and from above).

Difficulties arise merely at the lowest age-class (under 21 years), at the age-class within which or at whose end the age of retirement (65, 55 or 70 years) is situated, and in the case where the relationship between mean income and age is fickle; the latter applies especially to women belonging to occupational groups in which they are but scantily represented.

Particular attention should be paid to the lowest age-class, since:

(a) mean typical income in that class is often but a fraction (say less than one half) of what it amounts to in the next-higher age-class, because of which:
(b) the present value of the flow of expected future income at any point in the lowest age-class is rather sensitive to even relatively small errors in estimating the income pattern within this class, while:
(c) the distribution of income recipients by age-year within this class is very skew (i.e. relative frequencies rising steeply with age increasing from 15 to 21 years), and finally:
(d) the curve at its lower side is open-ended, since the lower age-limit can only be guessed at or fixed arbitrarily (at ages varying between 14 and 17 years, depending upon the occupational group in question).

Considering point (c), we took account of the distribution of economically active minors by age-year per occupational group per sex, as derived from the 1960 Population Census of the Netherlands, in order to draw reasonably dependable income curves for the lowest age-bracket.

The difficulty in determining income development in the age-class comprising or adjoining the age of retirement is the usually steep decline of typical income to the (at least 30 per cent) lower level of pension, causing a sharp bend in the income line around that age. This means that till a point near the age of retirement, the curve lies slightly above the horizontal section of the stepline, while immediately after, it plunges headlong to the pension level. As observed in section 6.2.2.1, from the age of retirement onwards deferred labour income alias pension income is assumed to be constant. Thus, no adjustment is needed for this age-class, with a continuous horizontal income line.

On the other hand, this implies that at the age of retirement the income line is kinked.

Because of this peculiarity, the relationship between present value of expected future incomes and age shows an unmistakable – albeit minor – leap upward at the transition from economic activity to economic inactivity.

An irregular course of mean typical income over the age-classes usually conveys uncertainty about its real course. Since the adjusted income line should follow the ups and downs of the step-line for the age-classes rather closely, that curve will show many bends in such a case. This reduces further its degree of realism. Fortunately, the basic cause of all these uncertainties – viz. the small numbers in the sample – confines these contingencies to a mere pittance of cases (concentrated among minors and gainfully occupied women).

6A.2. Graphical results

Graphs 6A.1 through 6A.8 and 6A.10 through 6A.12 show the results of the smoothing process described in section 6A.1 for men and women, respectively[2].

In all, 14 occupational groups are distinguished; their allocation to graphs was not based on any theoretical consideration, but was merely meant to keep the occupation-specific lines apart.

The thin step-lines depict the income means presented in the C.B.S. statistics on the 1960 distribution of income in the Netherlands; the dashed lines connect the middles of the horizontal thin lines, but stop at retirement; finally, the uninterrupted lines represent the result of the smoothing process.

---

[2] These graphs were borrowed from Bannink and Somermeyer [1966, pp. 101–104].

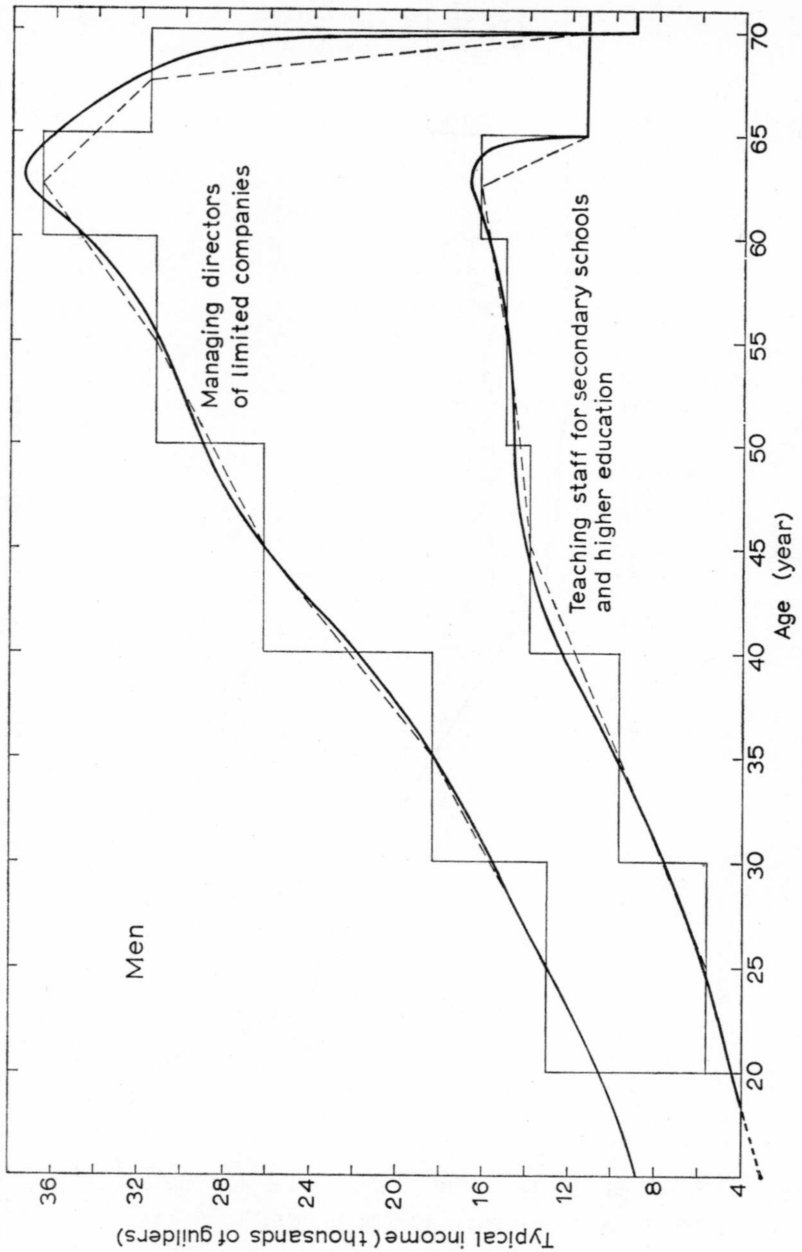

Graph 6A.1. Graphical interpolation of typical income by age.

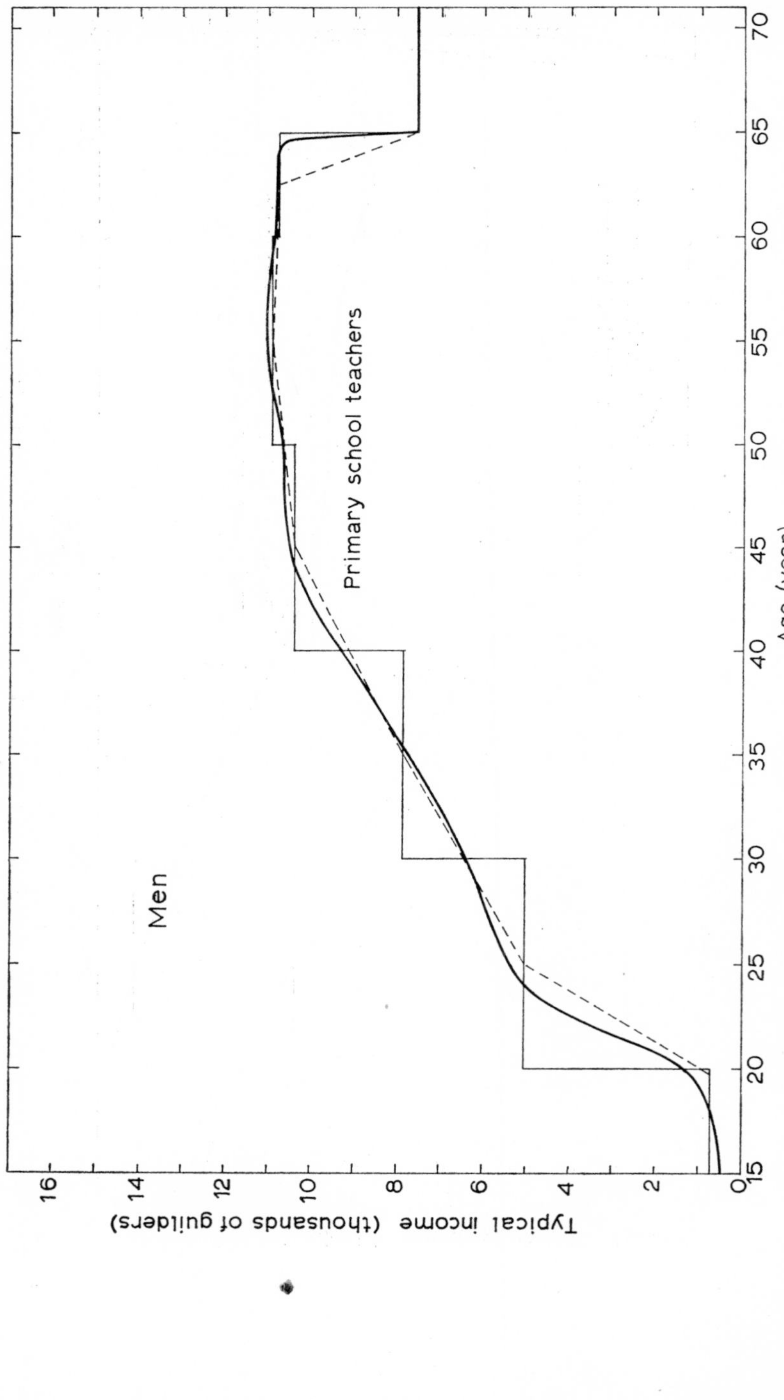

Graph 6A.2. Graphical interpolation of typical income by age.

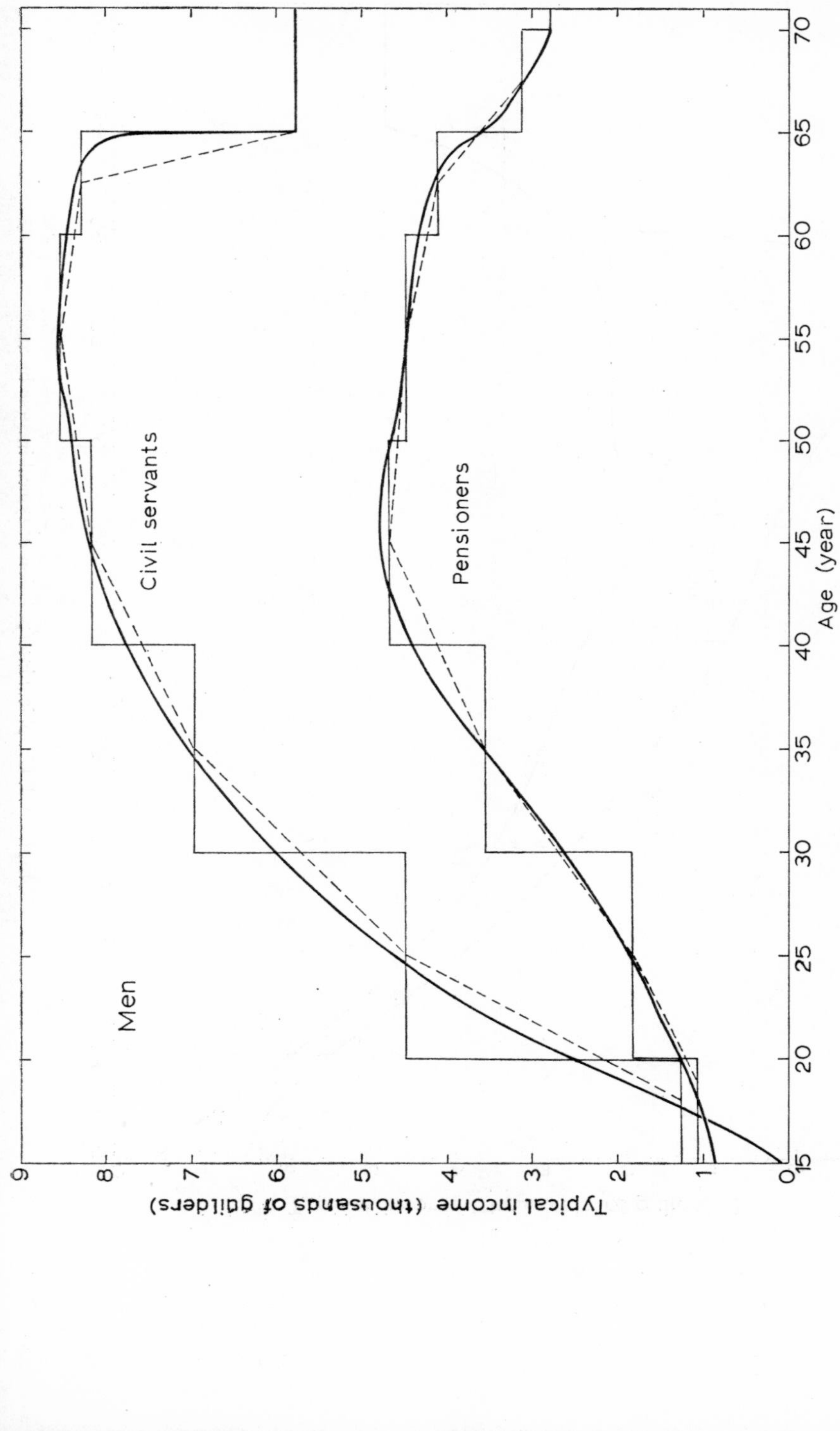

Graph 6A.3. Graphical interpolation of typical income by age.

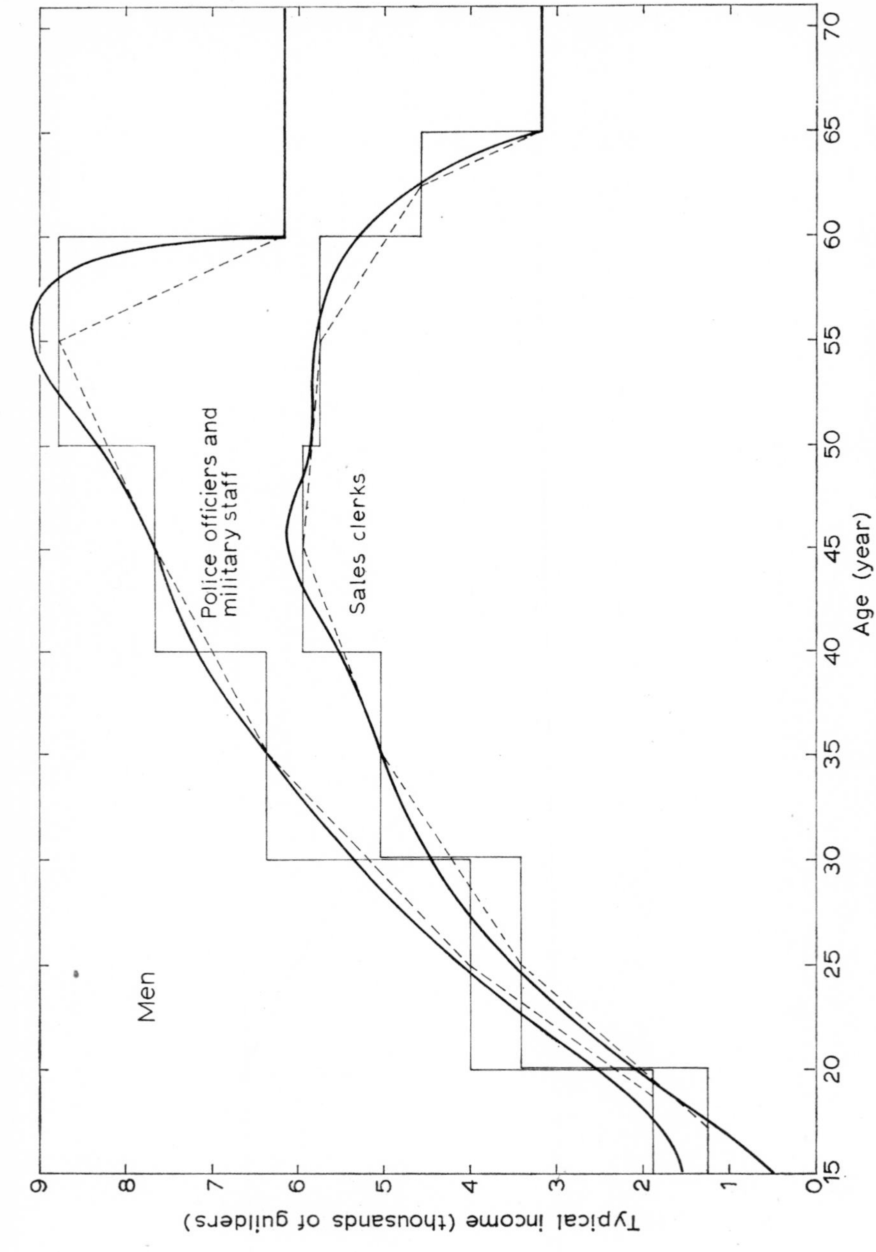

Graph 6A.4. Graphical interpolation of typical income by age.

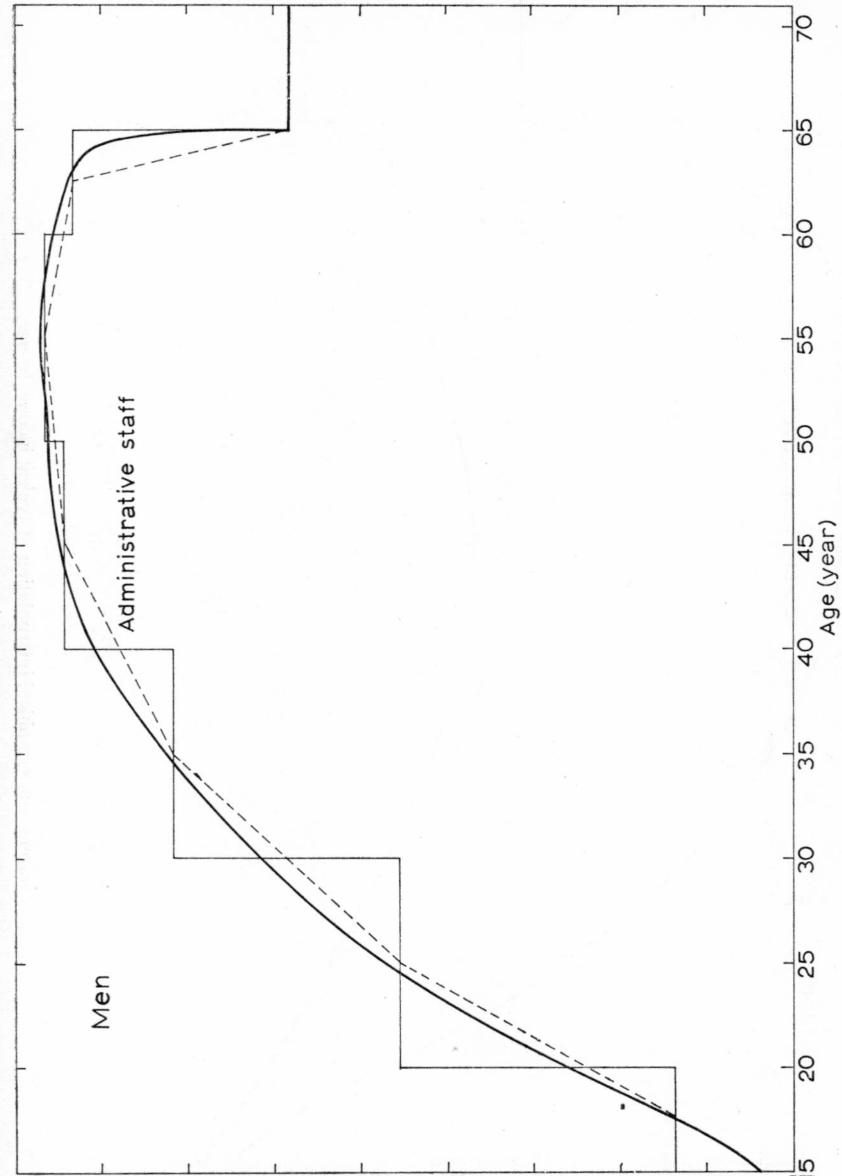

Graph 6A.5. Graphical interpolation of typical income by age.

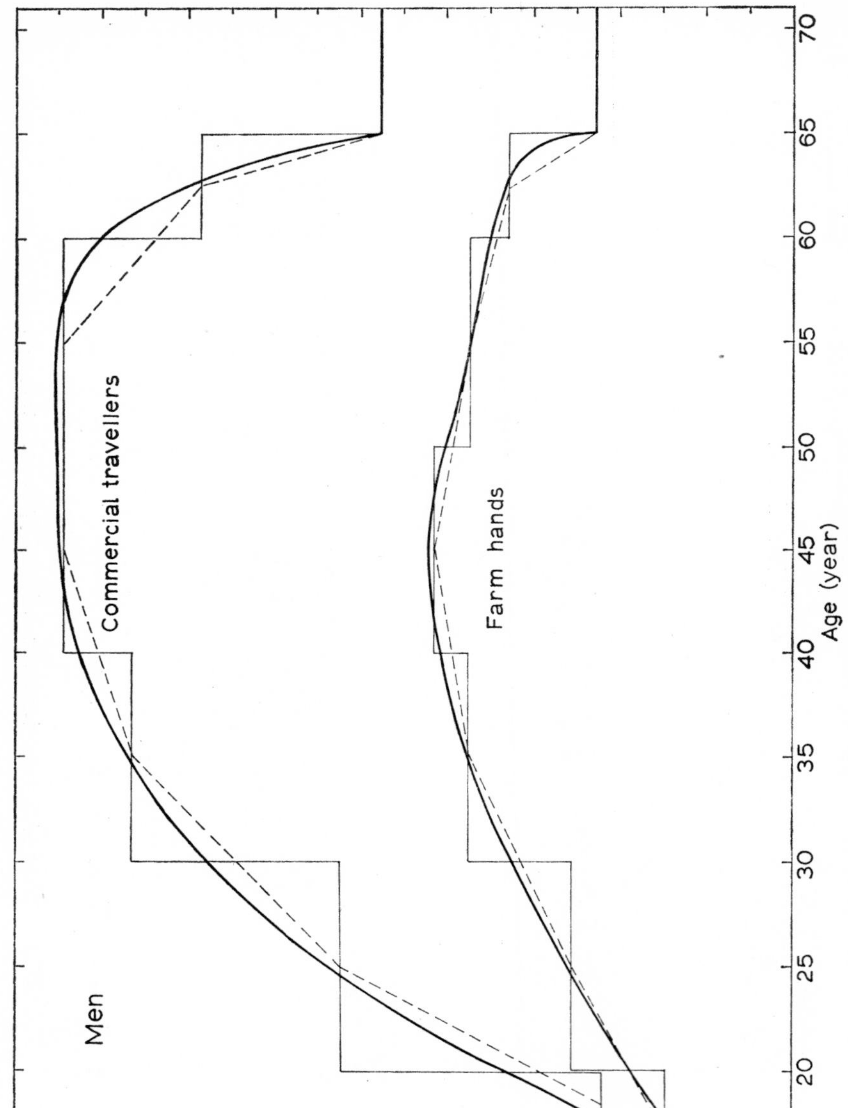

Graph 6A.6. Graphical interpolation of typical income by age.

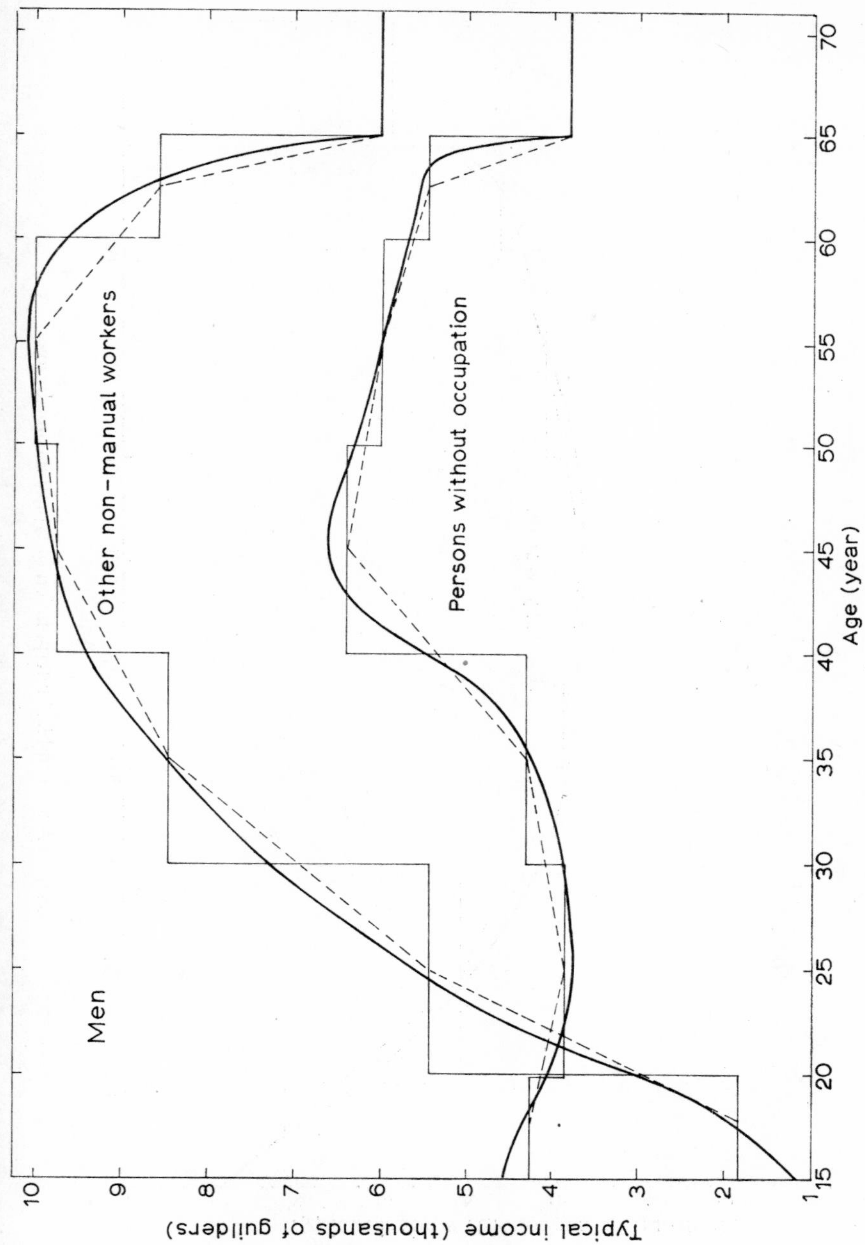

Graph 6A.7. Graphical interpolation of typical income by age.

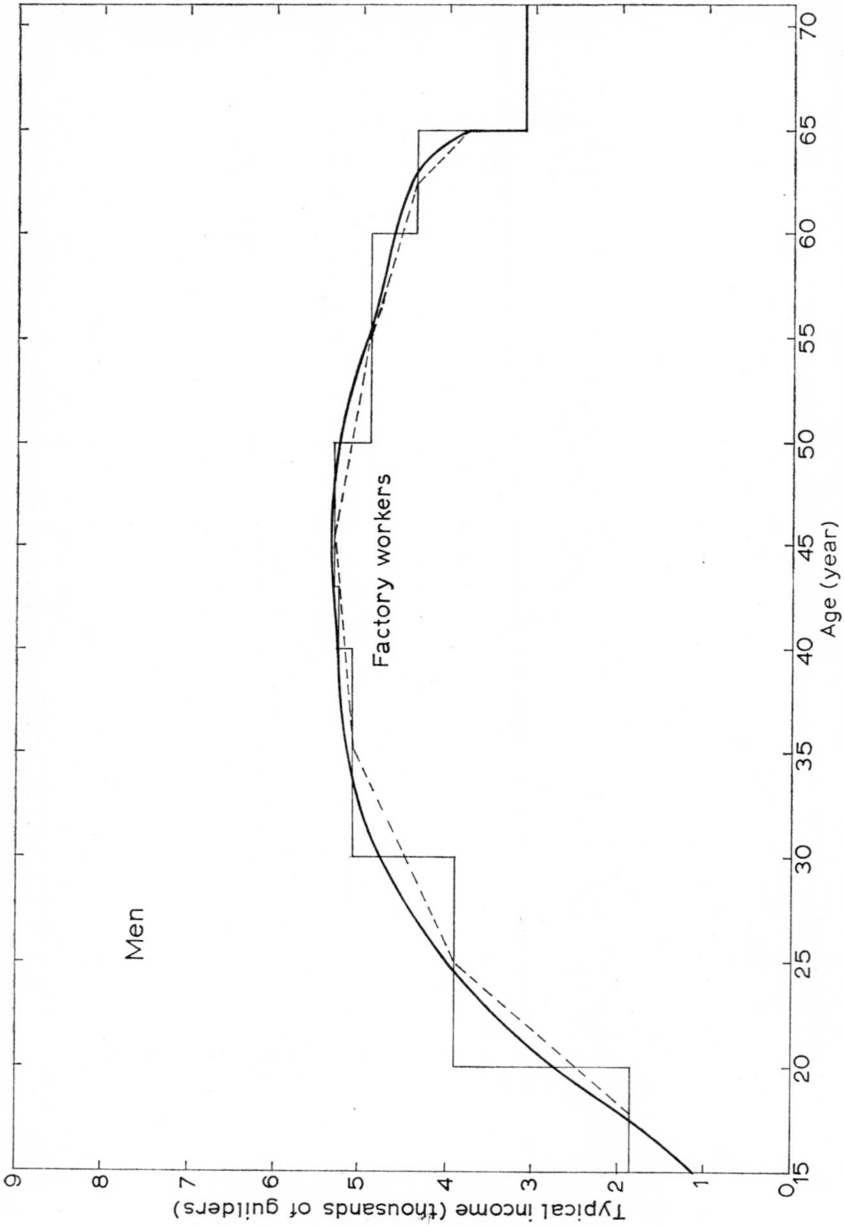

Graph 6A.8. Graphical interpolation of typical income by age.

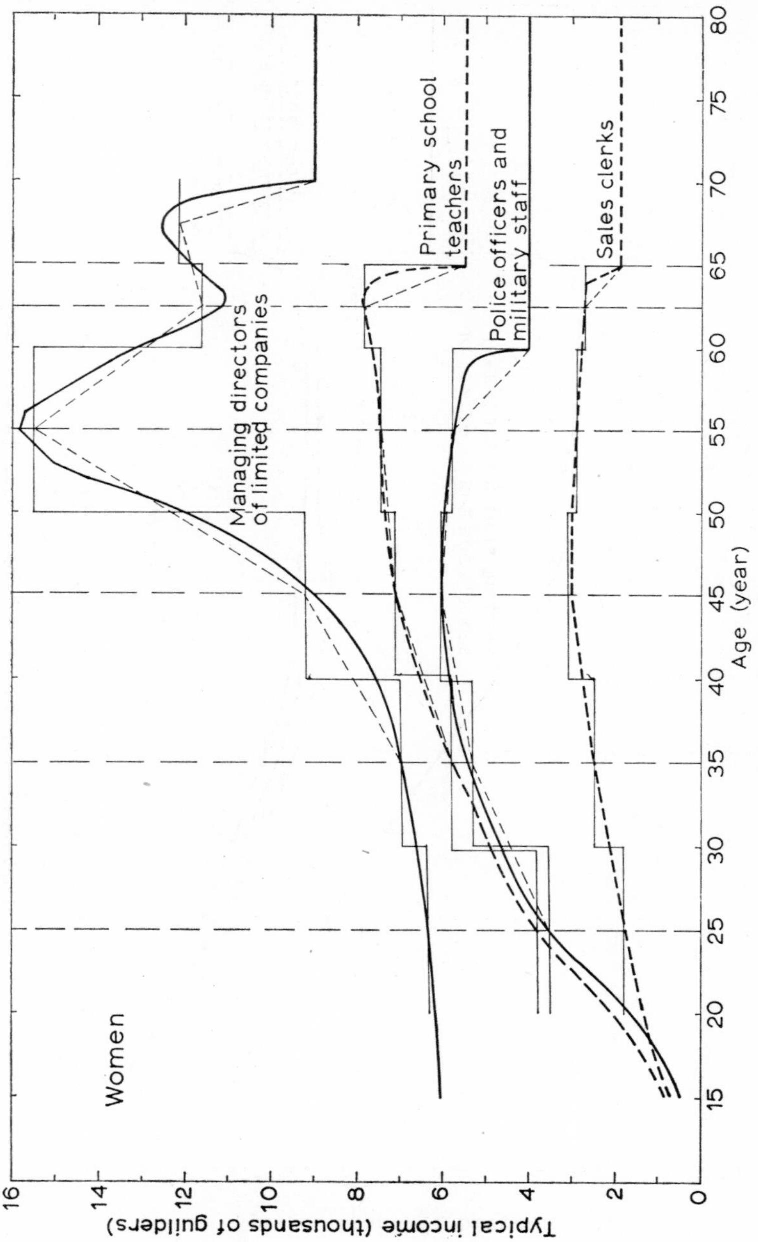

Graph 6A.9. Graphical interpolation of typical income by age.

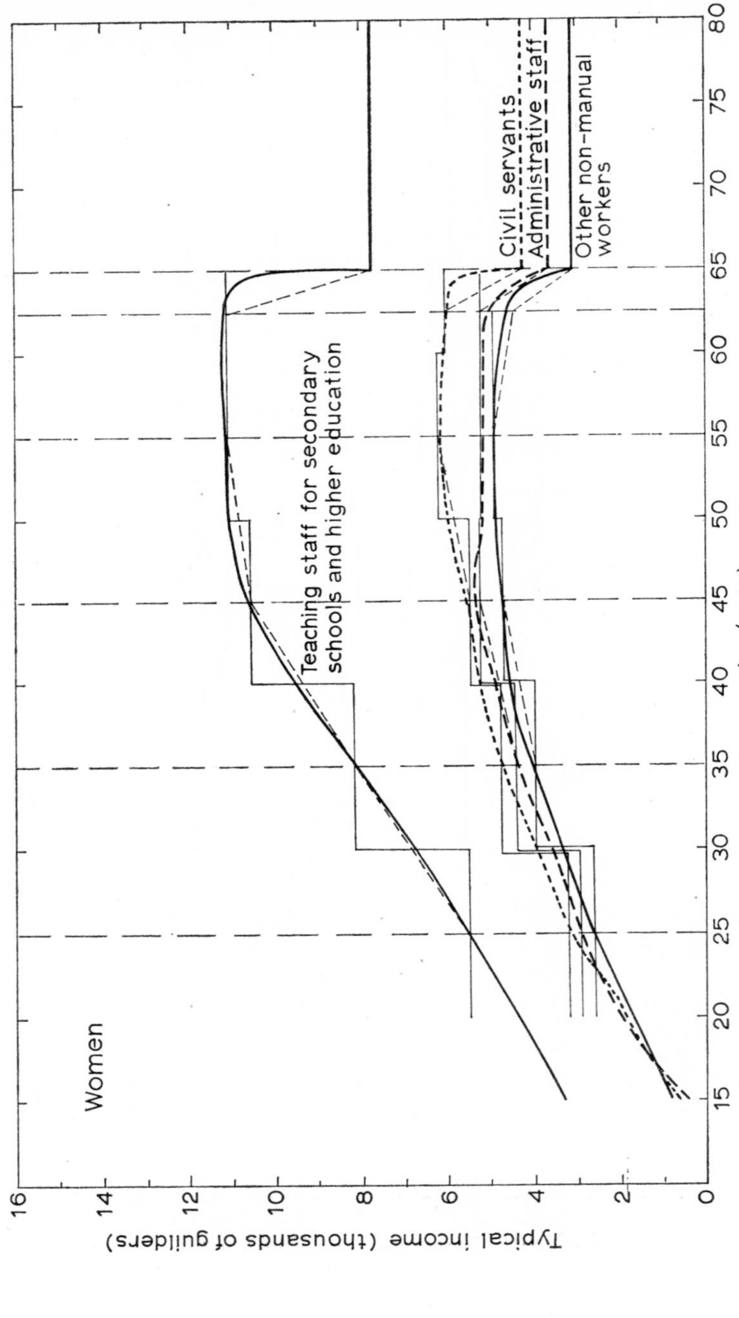

Graph 6A.10. Graphical interpolation of typical income by age.

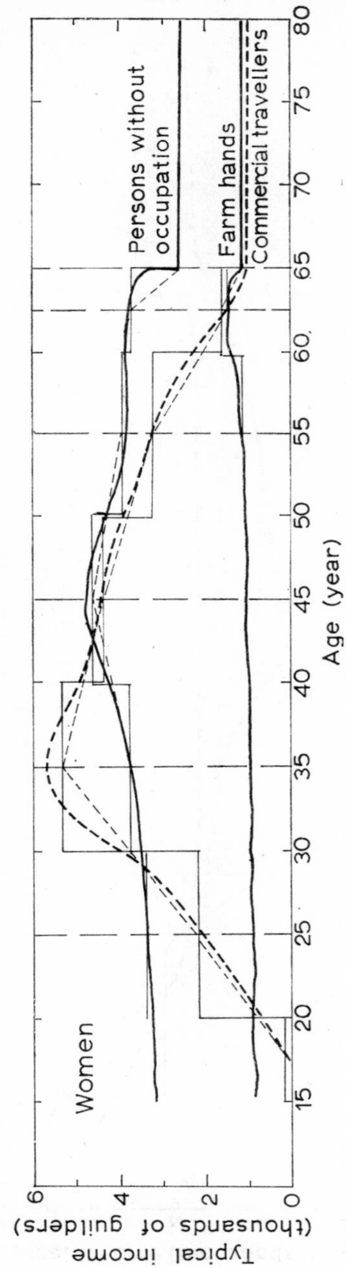

Graph 6A.11. Graphical interpolation of typical income by age.

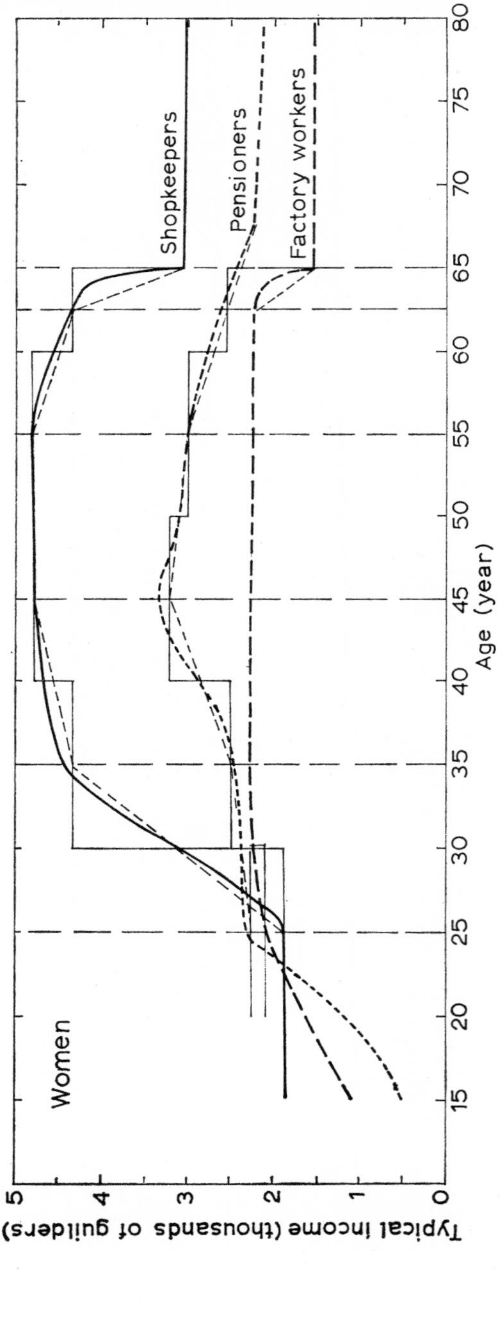

Graph 6A.12. Graphical interpolation of typical income by age.

The general impression created by the picture of the age-pattern of typical income is one of 'rise and decline'; the differences between the occupational groups relate to the levels at which these developments take place (and end at retirement), the steepness of ascent and eventual descent, and the age at which a maximum level of income is reached[3].

Levels of income appear to be highest for managing directors of companies limited, followed at a considerable distance by the teaching staff of secondary schools and universities, primary school teachers, other non-manual workers, civil servants, administrative staff and travelling salesmen, approximately in this order. In general, non-manual workers receive higher remuneration than manual workers, comprising a.o. factory workers and farm hands; in general, the level of remuneration corresponds roughly to the level of education (say, years of schooling completed) required for practising the occupation in question, rather than the education actually received (meaning that for jobs such as clerical work, people may be overqualified as well as underqualified).

This ranking of occupations by level of typical income is about the same for men and women; in comparable occupations, however, women are paid less than men, such that mean income of women in 'higher' occupations corresponds to men's mean income in 'lower' occupations.

Within each sex, there are but few marked differences in steepness of income movements in its ascending phase between occupations proper; a notable exception are the farm labourers, whose income from adolescence onwards is rising more slowly than that of other manual workers (and non-manual workers a fortiori). On the other hand, the rather flat course of the income curves for pensioners and (other) unoccupied persons should not surprise us.

Within the same occupational class, women's curves are flatter than men's ditto, meaning that career opportunities open to women are more restricted than those available to men. In this respect, women are least discriminated against in the teaching profession.

In non-manual occupations, the maximum income appears to be reached at later ages (often near the age of retirement) than in the manual occupations, where waning productivity at middle age tends to depress remuneration on a piece-rate basis. As a result of the same phenomenon, however,

[3] A warning is in order that the vertical scales differ between graphs, hampering intergraph comparisons.

non-manual workers seem to experience a relatively more pronounced drop in income at the time of retirement than manual workers.

Income data, and consequently income curves, suggest a more regular income pattern for men than for women. This may be ascribed, at least partly, to smaller numbers of women (compared with men) working in most occupations (except primary school teaching), and especially as managing directors; the smaller the numbers, the larger the relative effect of accidental factors on the determination of income. In such cases of a capricious course of mean income, the conclusions based on it should be used with caution.

Fortunately, averaging the derived or imputed income estimates over lifetime in order to calculate the labour income capitalization factors, smoothes away at least some of the irregularities inherent in age-specific data.

APPENDIX B TO CHAPTER 6

CONSEQUENCES OF TERMINATING OR CHANGING ECONOMIC ACTIVITY FOR THE PROSPECTIVE TIME PATTERN OF INCOME

In forecasting their (future) income path, people (particularly the young ones) presumably have in mind the time at which they will join the labour force – if they did not yet do so, e.g. because of study; moreover, they are assumed to be aware that after having been active in an occupation, they will have to give it up at some time[1]. The latter consideration, of course, applies to retirement in particular; in addition, single women's marriage prospects frequently induce them to quit their job soon after the marriage vows have been exchanged – at least in the Netherlands. Anyhow, this means that at a certain age people will pass from a 'proper' occupational group to the class of pensioners or of "unoccupied persons".

The latter two categories, however, are extremely heterogeneous, without any visible relations to the occupations practised before. In order to meet this difficulty, the income related to each 'proper' occupational group for ages exceeding the corresponding normal age of retirement is fixed at an estimated constant pension level. In the income statistics (by occupation, sex and age), a sudden steep fall in the number of men or women (plying a trade or practising a profession) from one age-class to the next higher one is a sure sign of the usual age of retirement being near the dividing line between the two classes – i.e. if such a reduction in numbers is significantly more pronounced than might be expected on the basis of deceases and the trend-like increase of the gainfully occupied population alone. Thus, by calculating the ratios between numbers of individuals of the same sex and belonging to the same occupational group but in successive age brackets, and interpolating, one may approximate the age around which the exodus from economic

[1] If remunerated work is begun or ended between the beginning and the end of a calendar year, i.e. of this remuneration is earned during m months of that year only, it is multiplied by $12/m$ in order to arrive at an equivalent annual income.

activity – i.e. either from a particular occupation or altogether – is concentrated. Notwithstanding the rather crude age classification adopted in Dutch statistics on income distribution, such a method works out rather well. The reason is that for certain occupational groups (such as civil servants and teachers) the age of retirement is fixed statutorily, while a number of employees in other branches of economic activity follow suit either by rule or according to custom. Application of this procedure is facilitated further by the circumstance that the most common age of retirement, viz. 65 years, coincides with the delimitation between the highest and the highest but one age-class – intentionally rather than accidentally.

It means that 65 years is considered as the general age of retirement unless the contrary is in evidence. Specifically, exceptions are made for:
Group 2: managing directors of companies limited, for whom the age of 70 was considered a likely average age of retirement, and
Group 6: police staff and military personnel, for whom the age of retirement is fixed statutorily at 55.

The expected pension was assumed to bear a uniform constant ratio to the mean typical income for the age-class immediately preceding the age of retirement; on the analogy of regulations applying to civil servants, it was fixed at 70 per cent. Even where such a – relatively favourable – superannuation scheme did not (yet) exist in 1960, people presumably count on its prevailance at the time when most of them will retire.

For managing directors of limited companies, however, a different approach had to be adopted. The reason is that the pension schemes of those executives are generally administered by life insurance companies, resulting in annuity expectations; as usual, the benefits to be derived therefrom can be calculated on the basis of premium and age data stated on the worksheets. Moreover, after retiring as managing directors, the latter may generally expect to be appointed on the Board of Directors, and to draw income as such.

According to the Netherlands 'Statistics of Limited Companies' in 1956 – comparable to 1960 as regards the business situation – the average remuneration of Governing Directors appeared to be about 8000 guilders per year (Central Bureau of Statistics [1963]); the underlying assumption is that on the average the Companies Ltd (with paid-up capital of at least 1 million guilders) would have 4 to 5 members on their Boards of Governors[2]. General

---

[2] About limited companies with paid-up capital of less than one million guilders, no information is available.

old-age pension is added to the remuneration for the directorship, resulting – for 1960 – in a mean income of about 9000 guilders per annum (exclusive of annuities) for former managing directors being 70 years of age or older.

The retirement income of the (few) independent workers of 70^+ years of age is again fixed at 70 per cent of their mean income estimated for the highest-but-one age-class, i.e. up to 65 years.

The mean values of pensions thus computed exceed considerably the means of typical incomes (= pension) found for pensioners of 65 years and over, as derived from income distribution statistics.

This discrepancy is due to the following circumstances:

(a) a major part of the pensioners in 1960 (or rather 1958) has been pensioned off at a time when pension schemes were not yet as favourable as those applying to people having become inactive in a later period nor (a fortiori) as favourable as those becoming effective for people still working in the reference period;

(b) a (minor) part of the pensioners has been pensioned off at a lower than normal age (for instance because of disablement), so that they were not yet entitled to the normally attainable maximum pension.

Apart from the particular way of imputing expected pensions to people economically active in 1960, as outlined above, formula (6.2.2.1.1) is applied to the mean values of typical incomes (for each sex and occupational group) derived from income distribution statistics (Central Bureau of Statistics [1962ff]). Such an approach presupposes that, in general, income recipients expect to remain within the same occupational group to which they belonged in 1960 till the end of their economically active life.

Obviously, the latter assumption will be satisfied more frequently according as the classification of workers by occupation is less detailed, i.e. according as the occupations between which income recipients may move, are more highly aggregated. Thus, only a single group 'civil servants' is distinguished, irrespective of rank, hence leaving free scope for promotion. Combining other labourers with 'labourers in manufacturing industry' allows for the contingency that employees in either branch of economic activity move to the other one.

A further argument in favour of avoiding detail in occupational classification is the inaccuracy inherent in the description of the occupation reported on the income tax forms, completed by the public and underlying the income distribution statistics: since the tax authorities do not cherish occupation as a crucial piece of information, it is generally left unchecked.

In as far as transition from one occupational group to another may be expected, it will usually take place between mutually related occupational groups (such as between the Civil Service and clerical work outside the State or Municipical Government Service, or between manual work in agriculture and in manufacturing industry); much more rarely will it happen between such diverse occupational groups as independent workers and various types of employees. Anyhow, possible transition from one occupational group to another one will be accompanied by a more propitious rather than by a less promising course of income than would have been expected in case the original occupational status would *not* have been abandoned. This means that the assumed constancy of occupational group would result in a downward rather than in an upward bias of the present value of expected future incomes, calculated according to the rules outlined above.

Such a consequence, however, need not be held against the method explained above. Indeed, the only question relevant to savings is whether our estimates of expectations about the future course of the variables such as income agrees with *expectations actually nourished;* whether or not they agree with *reality* – which, incidentally, is co-determined by expectations – is irrelevant.

INCOME CAPITALIZATION FACTORS, AGE PATTERNS OF TYPICAL INCOME, AND THEIR DEPENDENCE ON OCCUPATION, AGE AND SEX

6C.1. Theoretical analysis

6C.1.1. LABOUR INCOME CAPITALIZATION FACTOR (LICF)

In section 6.2.8, the labour income capitalization factor (LICF) is defined as:

$$F_{A(i)} = \sum_{l=0}^{M} (\bar{Y}_{b,a+l,s}/\bar{Y}_{b,a,s})\, s_{a,s;l}\,(1+r)^{1-l}$$

$$= \sum_{\tau=a}^{M} \left(\frac{\bar{Y}_{b,\tau,s}}{\bar{Y}_{b,15,s}} \Bigg/ \frac{\bar{Y}_{b,a,s}}{\bar{Y}_{b,15,s}}\right) s_{a,s;\tau-a}\,(1+r)^{1+a-\tau}, \tag{6C.1.1.1}$$

with $F_{A(i)}$ short for $F_{A,b,a,s(i)}$.

The difference between the second and third members of (6C.1.1.1) is that the summation is extended over (current and future) ages τ and age-increments l respectively; the upper limit of the summation can remain the same, because $s_{a,s;M} = s_{a,s;M-a} = 0$ by definition of M as the maximum age to be reached. Moreover, the income ratio in the second member is rewritten as a ratio of income ratios, with occupation–sex specific income at the age of 15 as the common base – 15 years being the minimum age at which people might be employed in the Netherlands in 1960.

This means that occupation, age and sex affect the LICF through the age pattern of income (per occupation, per sex), as well as the survival rate and the discount factor, depicted in diagram 6C.1; in addition, the latter three kinds of variables are summed over future age years, as designated by the plusses.

DIAGRAM 6 C.1.

Effects of occupation, age and sex through the age pattern of income, discount rates and survival rates on labour income capitalization factors

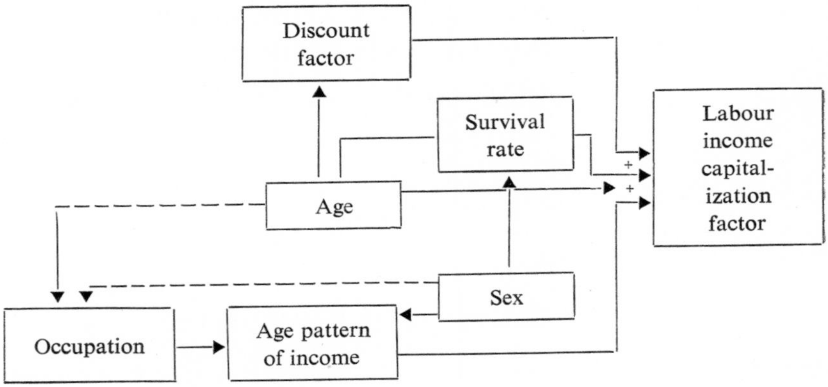

6 C.1.2. OCCUPATION

Equation (6C.1.1.1) implies that – for given initial age (a) and sex (s) –, $F_{A(i)}$ will be larger according as $\bar{Y}_{b,a+\tau,s}/\bar{Y}_{b,a,s}$, i.e. the ratio of later-age income to current income, will be higher when averaged over prospective lifetime. Since these ratios are multiplied by discount factors as well as by survival rates, both of which are less than one and decreasing with advancing age, the income ratios at lower ages are more important than those at higher ages. This means that an increase of income at a later age contributes less to the LICF, hence to 'financial resources' (R_τ) than the same increase at an earlier age.

6 C.1.3. AGE

As mentioned under 6C.1.1, the effect of age on the LICF is rather complicated, viz. through the income ratios, the survival rate, the discount factor and the range of summation. In order to simplify the (theoretical) analysis of the age effect, we replace the sum by an integral, drop the subscripts for occupation and sex, and redefine the LICF as a function of initial age by:

$$F_A(a) = \int_a^M \{\bar{Y}(\tau)/\bar{Y}(a)\}\, s\,(a, \tau - a) \exp\{(a - \tau)\varrho\}\, d\tau, \qquad (6C.1.3.1)$$

with ϱ the continuous rate of interest corresponding to r. Then, the sensitivity of $F_A(a)$ with respect to a change in age is expressed by:

$$\frac{\mathrm{d}F_A(a)}{\mathrm{d}a} = -1 - F_A(a)\left\{\frac{\mathrm{d}\ln \bar{Y}(a)}{\mathrm{d}a} - \varrho\right\} - \int_a^M \{\bar{Y}(\tau)/\bar{Y}(a)\}\frac{\mathrm{d}s}{\mathrm{d}a}\exp\{(a-\tau)\varrho\}\,\mathrm{d}\tau, \qquad (6C.1.3.2)$$

with $\lim_{\tau \to a} s(a, \tau - a) = 1$.

The growth rate of income $\mathrm{d}\ln Y(a)/\mathrm{d}a$ may exceed ϱ in some (especially lower) income range, but is bound to decline and become negative from a certain age upwards; the third term is negative, since $\mathrm{d}s/\mathrm{d}a \leq 0$ for the relevant age range (say, from 15 through 105 years). This means that in principle $\mathrm{d}F_A(a)/\mathrm{d}a$ may be positive as well as negative or zero. Still, in general, a negative value of this derivative seems more plausible than a positive one, for the following reasons. Since in an absolute sense $\mathrm{d}s/\mathrm{d}a$ will be small in nearly the entire range of ages, the integral term in (6C.1.3.2) will usually be negligible compared to the other terms; and though $\mathrm{d}\ln \bar{Y}(a)/\mathrm{d}a$ may be less than ϱ, their difference will seldom be smaller than $-\{F_A(a)\}^{-1}$.

The latter contingency, however, may – and does occasionally – appear, viz. in case of a sudden, sharp decline of income, such as used to occur at the time of retirement. Consequently, the $F_A(a)$ curve is generally downward sloping, with an induction current hitch at the time when economic activity is switched off. On the other hand, for a growth rate of $Y(a)$ exceeding ϱ – especially at lower ages –, we get $\mathrm{d}F_A(a)/\mathrm{d}a < -1$, i.e. a steeply declining $F_A(a)$ curve.

In order to gain further insight into the behaviour of $F_A(a)$ as a function of a, and especially into its curvature, we examine its second-order derivative:

$$\frac{\mathrm{d}^2F_A(a)}{\mathrm{d}a^2} = \left(\frac{\mathrm{d}\ln \bar{Y}(a)}{\mathrm{d}a} - \varrho\right) + F_A(a)\left(\frac{\mathrm{d}\ln \bar{Y}(a)}{\mathrm{d}a} - \varrho\right)^2 - F_A(a)\frac{\mathrm{d}^2\ln \bar{Y}(a)}{\mathrm{d}a^2} - \int_a^M \{\bar{Y}(\tau)/\bar{Y}(a)\}\frac{\mathrm{d}^2 s}{\mathrm{d}a^2}\exp\{(a-\tau)\varrho\}\,\mathrm{d}\tau \qquad (6C.1.3.3)$$

assuming that

$$\lim_{\tau \to a} \frac{\mathrm{d}s(a, \tau - a)}{\mathrm{d}a} = 0.$$

TABLE 6 C.1.

Capitalization factors μ for calculating the present value of expected future labour income from current labour income, for selected ages, according to occupational group and sex

No.	Occupational group	Sex	Age in years								
			15	25	35	45	55	65	75	85	95
1	Entrepreneurs	M	81.8	26.7	19.1	14.1	10.4	9.6	6.0	3.1	1.4
		F	50.8	41.3	18.6	15.1	11.1	10.0	6.3	3.4	1.6
2	Managing directors	M	36.3	32.7	25.3	17.0	11.5	5.0	6.0	3.1	1.4
	of limited companies	F	22.8	28.6	28.1	22.4	10.6	8.8	6.3	3.4	1.6
3	Primary school teachers	M	255.1	30.8	22.8	15.3	11.2	9.6	6.0	3.1	1.4
		F	123.4	31.6	21.9	16.2	12.3	10.1	6.3	3.4	1.6
4	Teaching staff for secondary schools	M	49.6	37.4	24.1	16.0	12.0	9.6	6.0	3.1	1.4
	and higher education	F	39.7	31.8	22.6	16.0	11.9	10.1	6.0	3.4	1.6
5	Civil servants	M	914.1	29.9	20.1	15.2	11.1	9.6	6.0	3.1	1.4
		F	116.5	30.4	21.2	16.6	11.8	10.1	6.3	3.4	1.6
6	Police officers	M	70.6	31.4	21.0	15.8	9.9	9.5	5.9	3.1	1.4
	and military staff	F	172.7	28.8	18.9	14.5	10.9	10.2	6.3	3.4	1.6
7	Administrative staff	M	281.0	29.6	20.1	15.0	11.0	9.6	6.0	3.1	1.4
		F	166.1	30.6	20.7	15.1	12.1	10.1	6.3	3.4	1.6
8	Sales clerks	M	159.4	27.6	19.2	13.4	9.8	9.6	6.0	3.1	1.4
		F	63.4	28.2	20.4	14.9	11.4	10.1	6.3	3.4	1.6
9	Commercial travellers	M	89.3	26.5	18.3	14.1	9.9	9.6	6.0	3.1	1.4
	and insurance agents	F	566.1	34.7	12.2	10.6	7.9	10.4	6.5	3.5	1.6
10	Other non-manual workers	M	101.4	29.0	19.5	14.6	10.3	9.6	6.0	3.1	1.4
		F	76.3	31.1	20.1	15.6	11.3	10.1	6.3	3.4	1.6
11	Factory workers	M	69.6	23.5	17.3	13.7	10.6	9.6	6.0	3.1	1.4
		F	38.5	21.2	17.9	15.3	11.9	10.2	6.3	3.4	1.6
12	Farm hands	M	60.4	26.6	18.0	13.3	10.5	9.6	6.0	3.1	1.4
		F	23.6	23.1	21.2	18.7	14.8	9.9	6.1	3.3	1.5
13	Pensioners	M	67.6	47.2	21.4	13.9	10.8	7.8	5.9	3.1	1.4
		F	95.7	24.0	21.9	14.4	11.6	9.0	5.9	3.2	1.5
14	Persons without occupation	M	21.7	26.1	23.5	13.5	10.7	9.6	6.1	3.1	1.4
		F	25.0	22.7	19.7	13.1	11.6	10.1	6.3	3.4	1.6

Of the four terms at the right-hand side of (6C.1.3.3), only the second one has a fixed sign, viz. positive The first term will be positive. at lower ages, but negative at higher ages, as observed above. This entails that the term: $-F_A$ (d^2 ln $\bar{Y}(a)$/da^2) will be positive over a wide range of ages. The fourth term may be positive, negative or zero; although a negative value – corresponding to $d^2s/da^2 > 0$ – seems most likely for the greater part of the relevant interval of ages, it is probaly negligible compared with the other terms.

We conclude that $d^2F_A(a)da^2$ may be positive, negative or zero; a positive value is, however, most likely, since we expect the general decline in the growth rate of expected income (third term) to dominate the scene, in addition to the ever-positive second term.

6 C.1.4 SEX

For women, career opportunities are generally less favourable than for men. Therefore, one might expect that the income ratios $\bar{Y}_{b,a+l,f}/\bar{Y}_{b,a,f}$ for females are generally less than the corresponding ratios $\bar{Y}_{b,a+l,m}/\bar{Y}_{b,a,m}$ for males. The differences, however, are compensated to some extent by higher survival rates of women compared with men, the more so according as the initial age is higher. Eventually – at the latest at the age of retirement – women's LICF rise above those of men (in the same occupational group).

6 C.2. Numerical and graphical results

According to the method outlined above, 2464 values of $F_{A(i)}$ have been calculated, i.e. for 2 sexes × 14 occupational groups × 88 age-years. These values are shown in continuous version in graphs 6C.1–6C.14, while table 6C.1 presents values of $F_{A(i)}$ for ages at ten-year intervals.

The graphs and the table corroborate the anticipations expressed in section 6C.1.3, viz. that as a rule the $F_A(a)$ is a decreasing function of age a, convex to the origin. This decrease is near-exponential, and mainly due to the shortening of the life horizon (with advancing age) over expected discounted future income, totalized according to (6C.1.1.1). As predicted,exceptions appear at retirement ages (from 55 to 70 according to occupation, but mostly at 65 years); here the LICF leaps up, following a sharp decline in income. Since afterwards the expected 'labour' incomes, turned into pensions, are

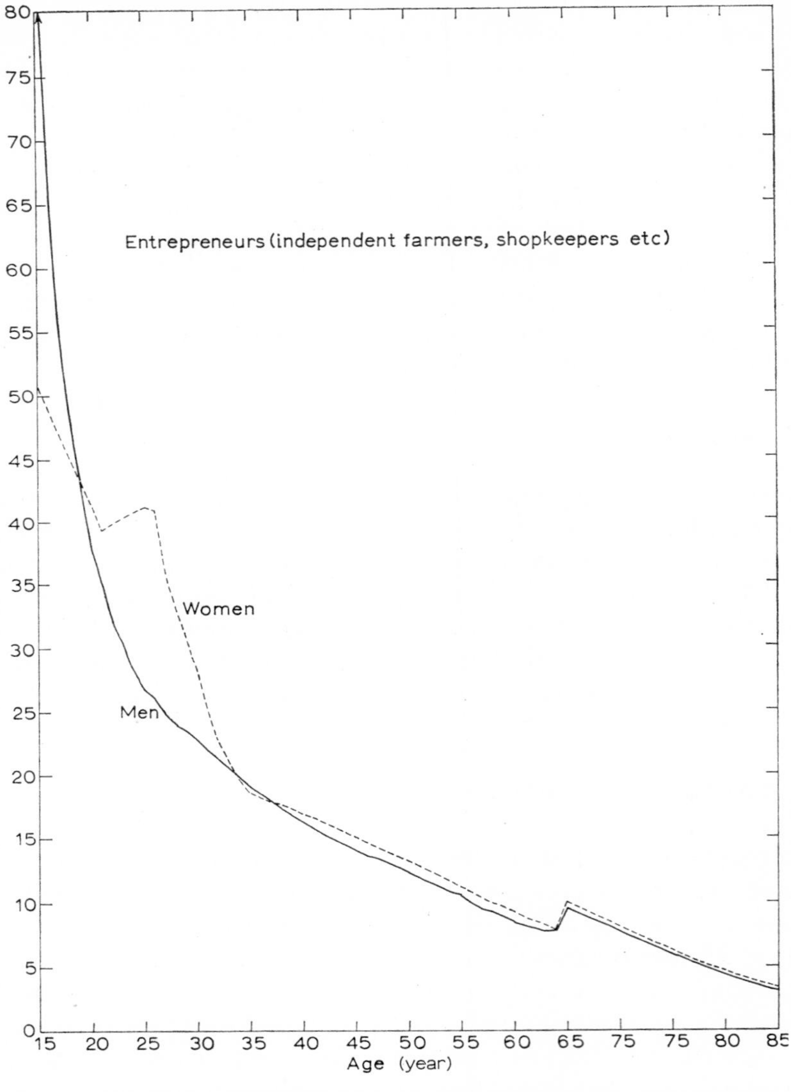

Graph 6C.1. Labour income capitalization factors, according to occupation and sex, at selected ages.

[At particular (lower) ages no figures are cited in cases where numbers of people are too small.]

assumed to remain constant, the LICF resume their near-exponential decline. Therefore, the LICF values at the normal age of retirement are nearer those for 55 than for 75 years, as shown by the table and the graphs.

Otherwise, the levels of the income capitalization factors are higher, and their decline per age year is more pronounced, according as income rises more rapidly (or falls more slowly) with increasing age. Accordingly, among

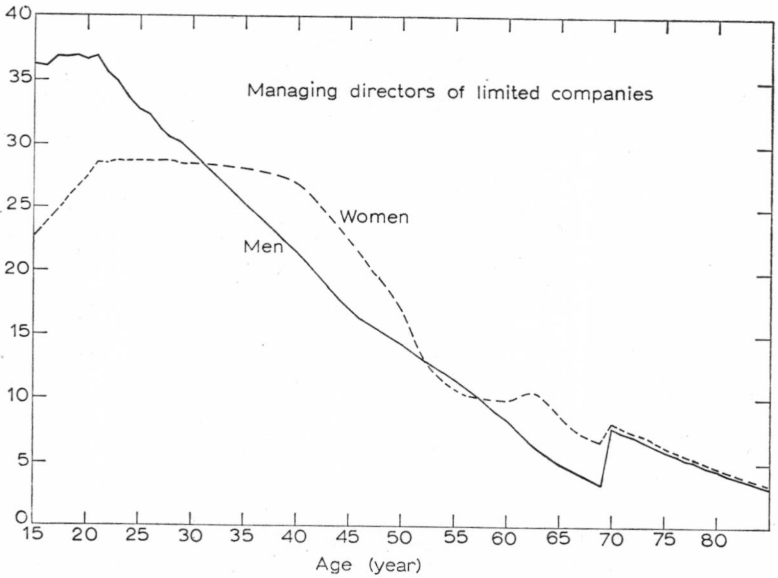

Graph 6C.2. Labour income capitalization factors, according to occupation and sex, at selected ages.

[At particular (lower) ages no figures are cited in cases where numbers of people are too small.]

non-manual workers, and especially among entrepreneurs and managing directors, we find both higher and more strongly decreasing LICF than among manual workers. This applies to both men and women; within the same occupational group, however, men's LICF are higher at lower ages and come down faster than women's, till at the latest from the age of retirement onwards, women's LICF are more elevated than men's (at the same age). The reason for the latter phenomenon is that survival rates of women exceed those of men, the more so according as the age is higher; moreover, the expected pensions are assumed to be constant.

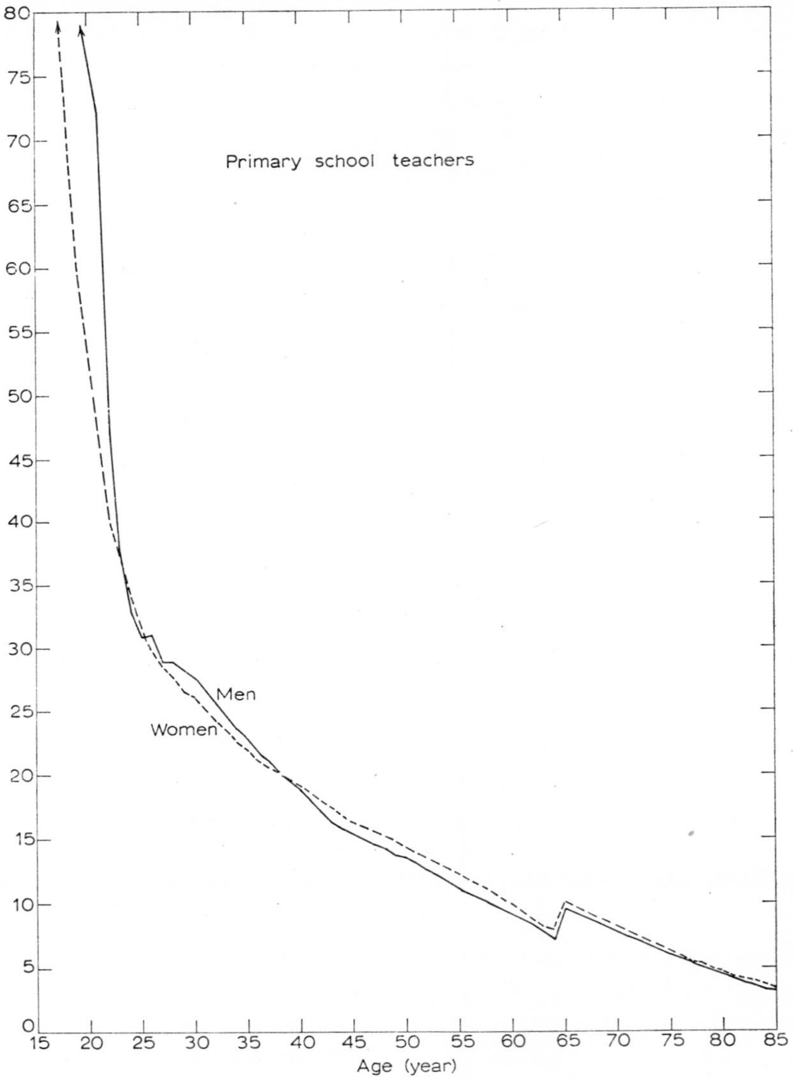

Graph 6C.3. Labour income capitalization factors, according to occupation and sex, at selected ages.

[At particular (lower) ages no figures are cited in cases where numbers of people are too small.]

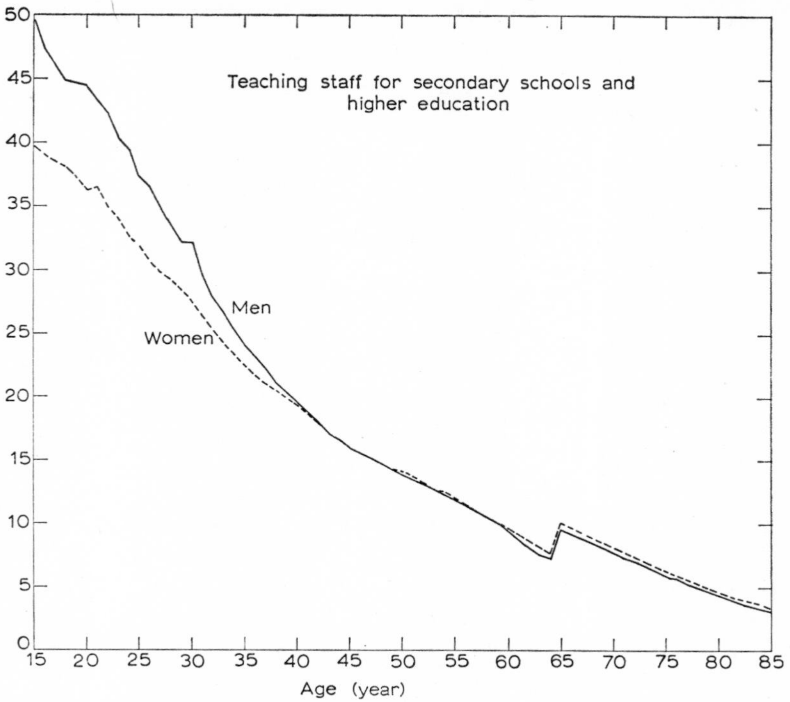

Graph 6C.4. Labour income capitalization factors, according to occupation and sex, at selected ages.

[At particular (lower) ages no figures are cited in cases where numbers of people are too small.]

The latter circumstance is also responsible for the convergence of the LICF, relating to different occupational groups, with increasing age, such that from age 70 onwards pertinent inter-occupational differences have virtually disappeared: apparently, approaching death is the great equalizer.

6C.3. Other income

Since by definition of Y_0 other (capital) income consists of the yield of *initial* personal wealth only, this kind of income too can be treated as constant, provided the rate of interest too is expected to remain the same in future. Thus, the matching capitalization factor $F_{0(i)}$ is essentially the same as $F_{A(i)}$ – i.e. for constant income, hence analogous to the $F_{A(i)}$ applied to pensions, but not restricted to post-retirement ages.

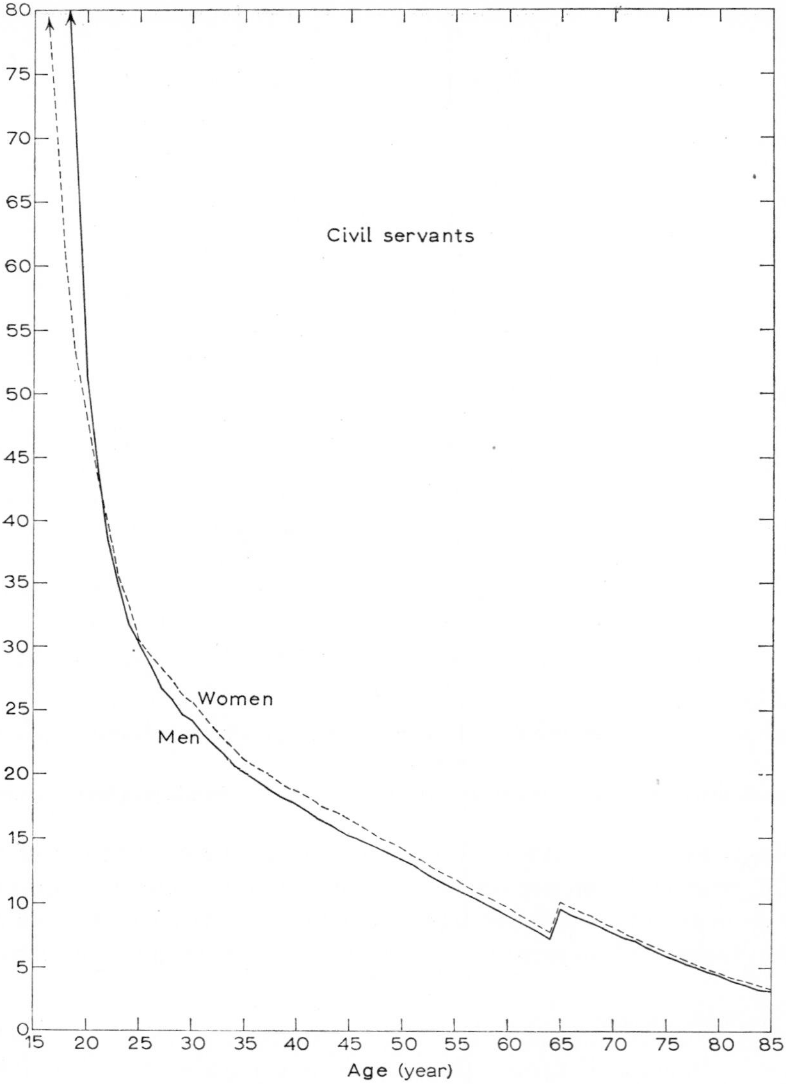

Graph 6C.5. Labour income capitalization factors, according to occupation and sex, at selected ages.

[At particular (lower) ages no figures are cited in cases where numbers of people are too small.]

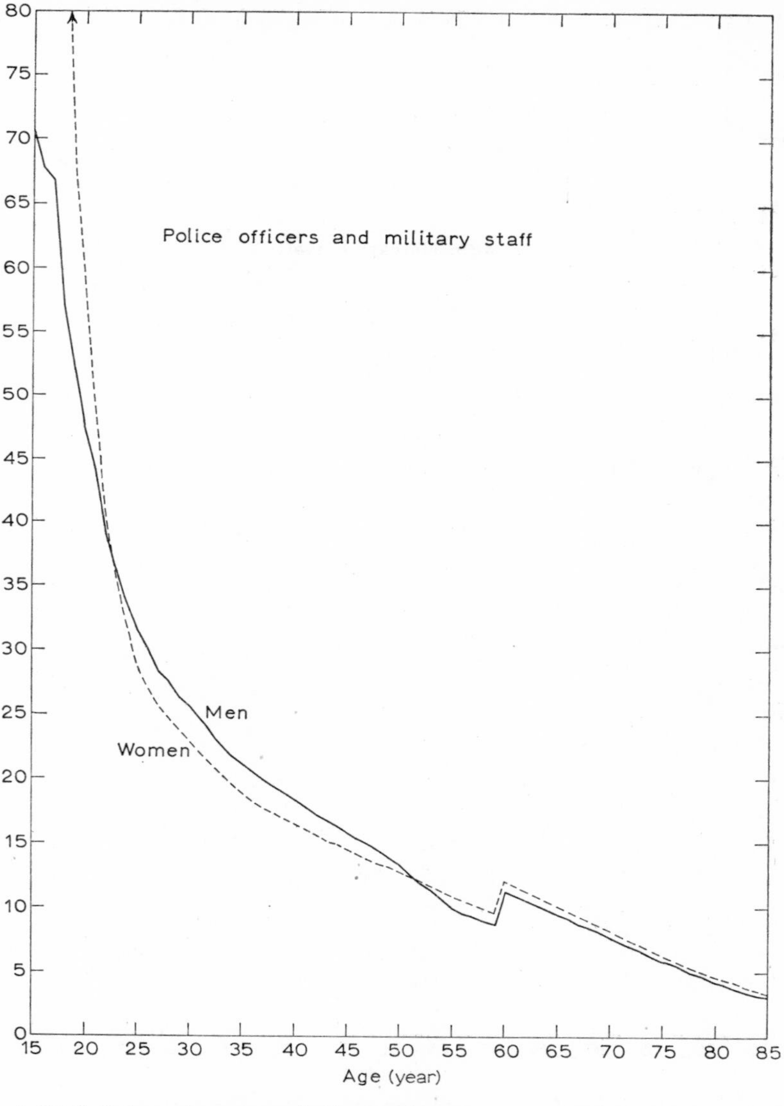

Graph 6C.6. Labour income capitalization factors, according to occupation and sex, at selected ages.

[At particular (lower) ages no figures are cited in cases where numbers of people are too small.]

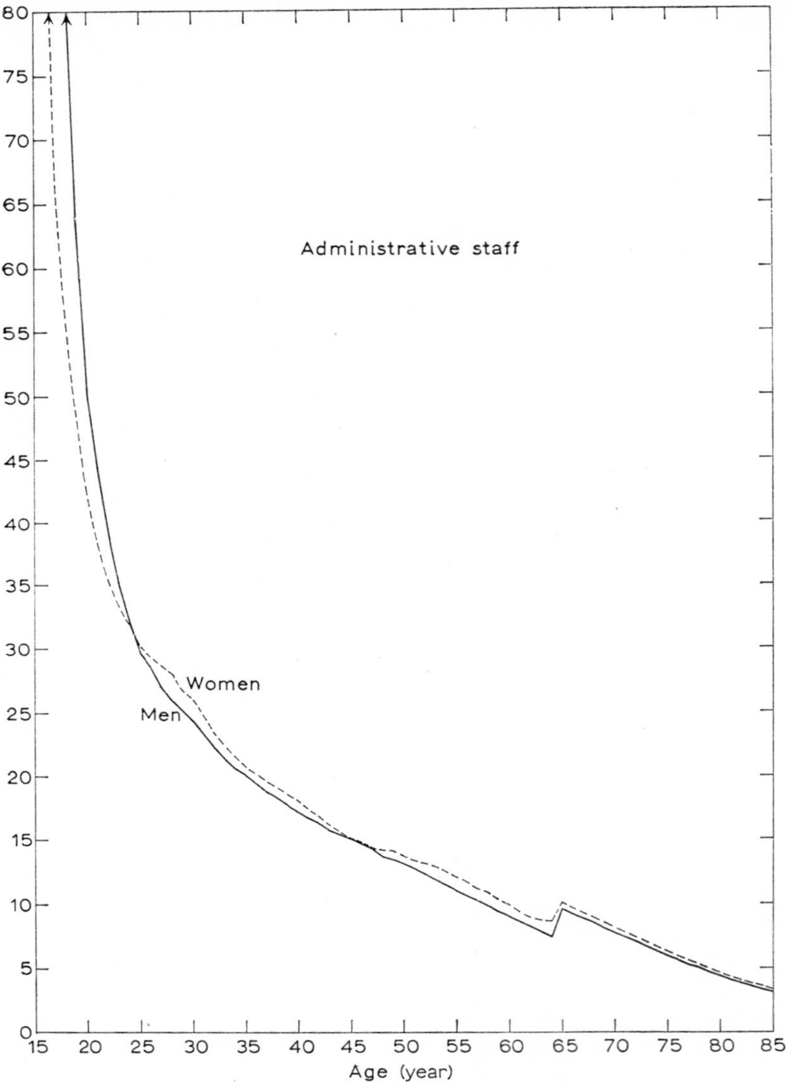

Graph 6C.7. Labour income capitalization factors, according to occupation and sex, at selected ages.

[At particular (lower) ages no figures are cited in cases where numbers of people are too small.]

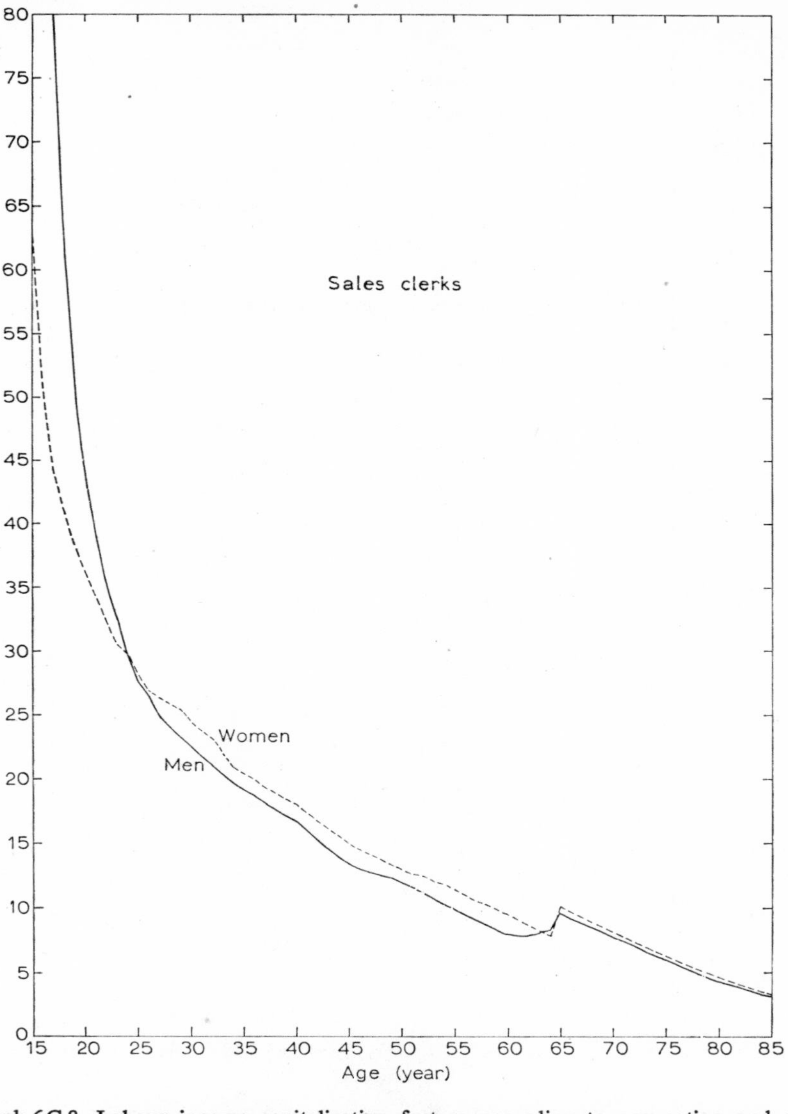

Graph 6C.8. Labour income capitalization factors, according to occupation and sex, at selected ages.

[At particular (lower) ages no figures are cited in cases where numbers of people are too small.]

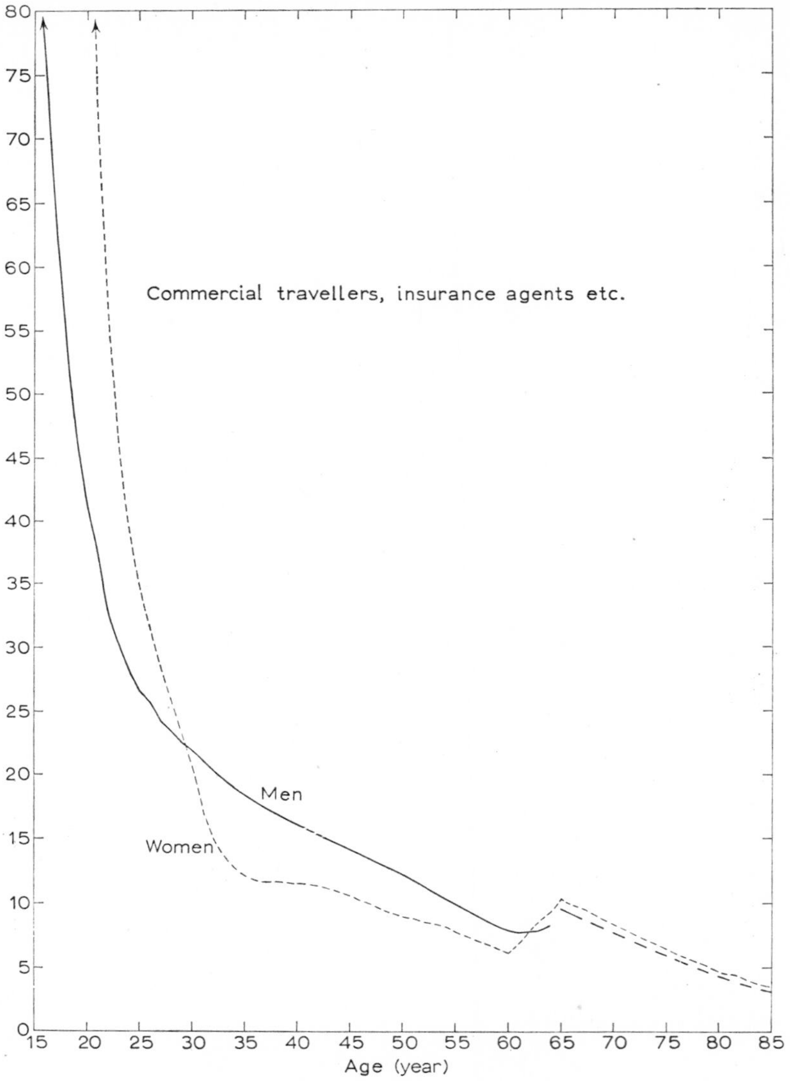

Graph 6C.9. Labour income capitalization factors, according to occupation and sex, at selected ages.

[At particular (lower) ages no figures are cited in cases where numbers of people are too small.]

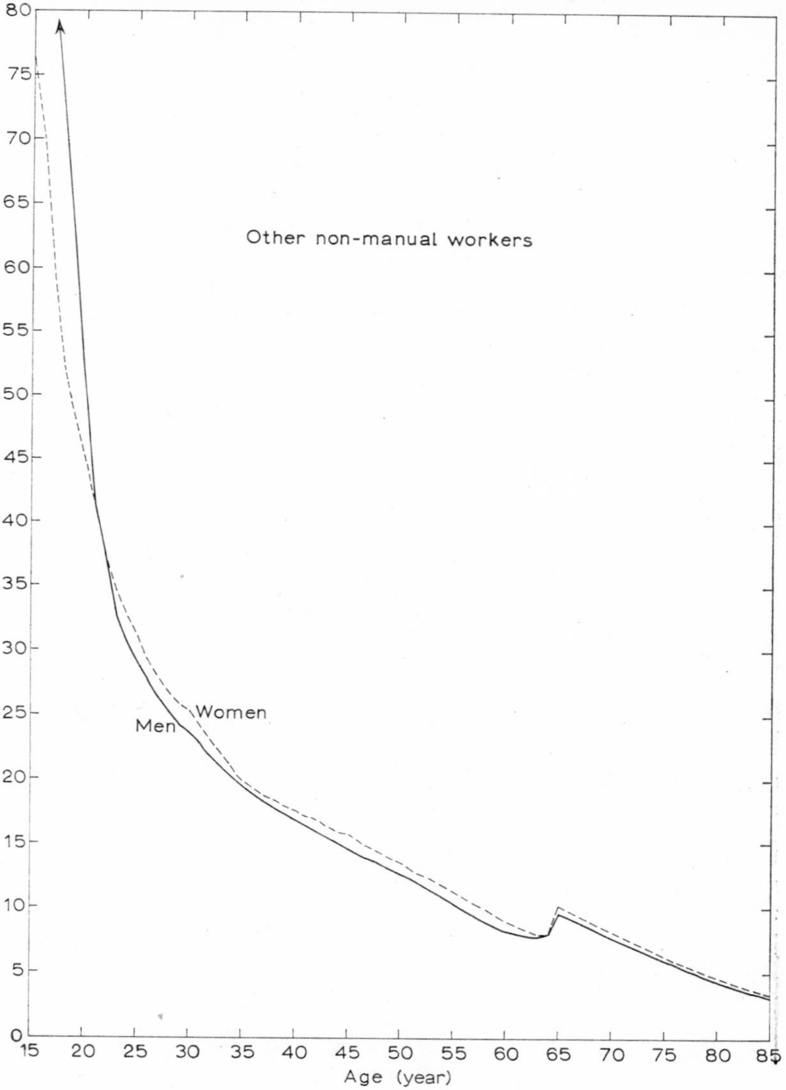

Graph 6C.10. Labour income capitalization factors, according to occupation and sex, at selected ages.

[At particular (lower) ages no figures are cited in cases where numbers of people are too small.]

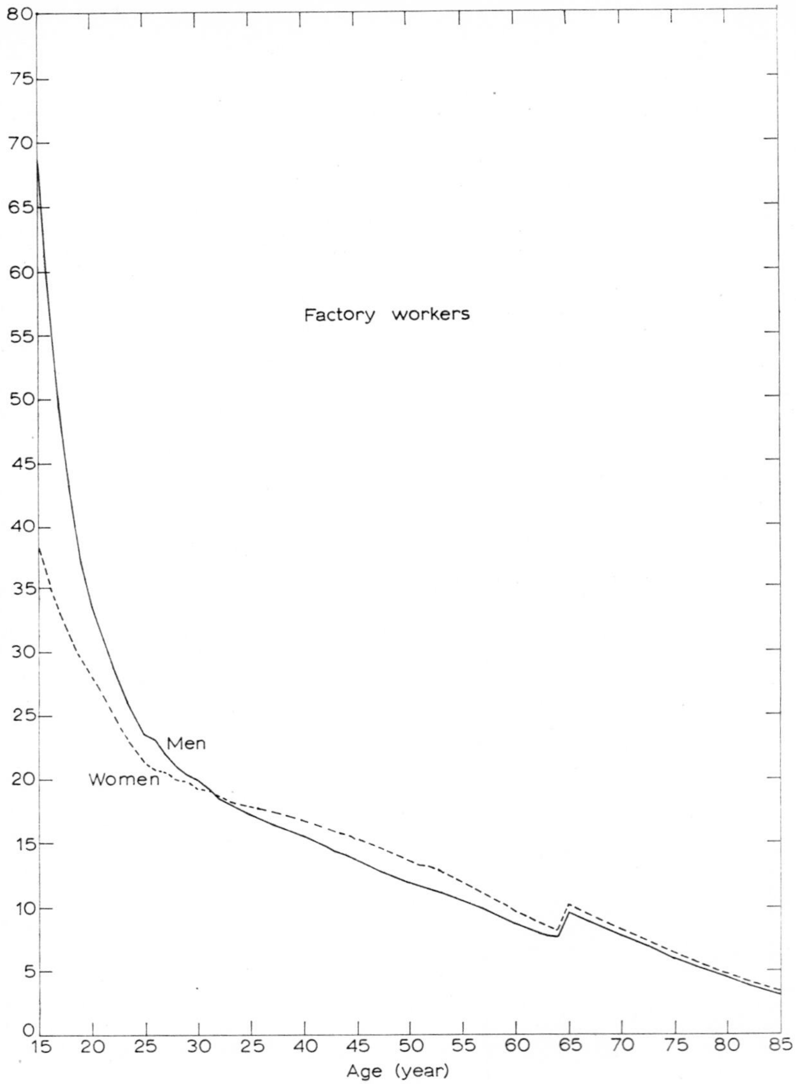

Graph 6C.11. Labour income capitalization factors, according to occupation and sex, at selected ages.

[At particular (lower) ages no figures are cited in cases where numbers of people are too small.]

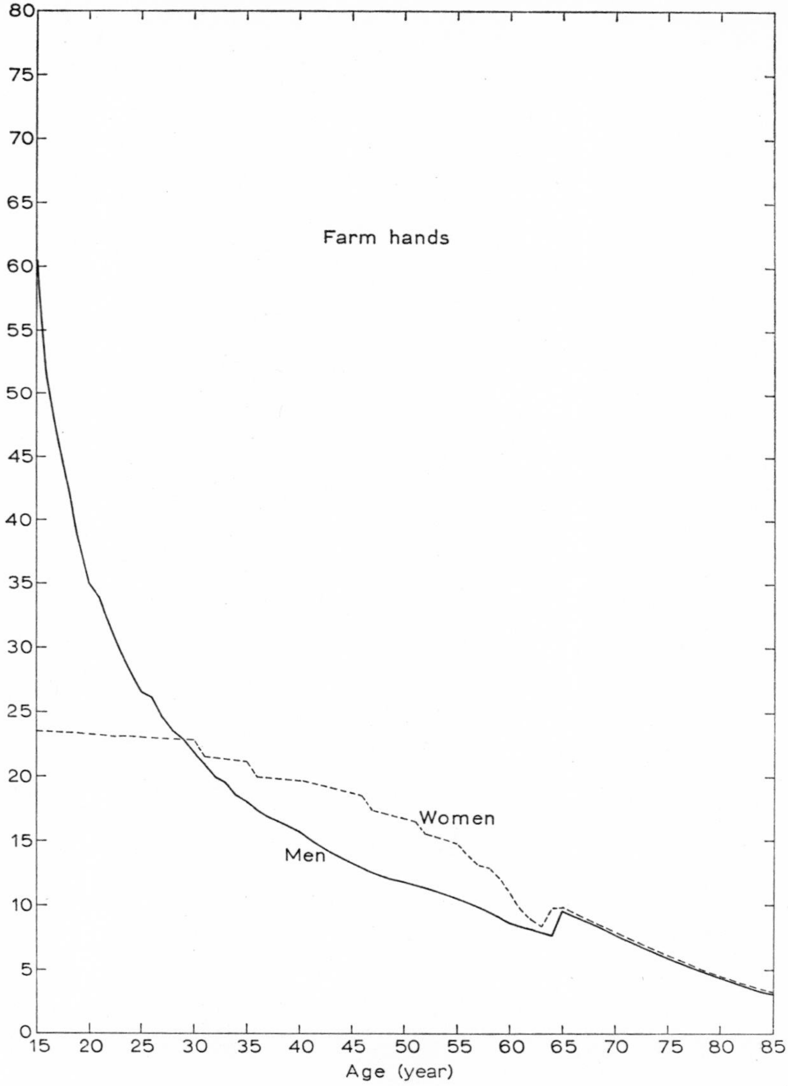

Graph 6C.12. Labour income capitalization factors, according to occupation and sex, at selected ages.

[At particular (lower) ages no figures are cited in cases where numbers of people are too small.]

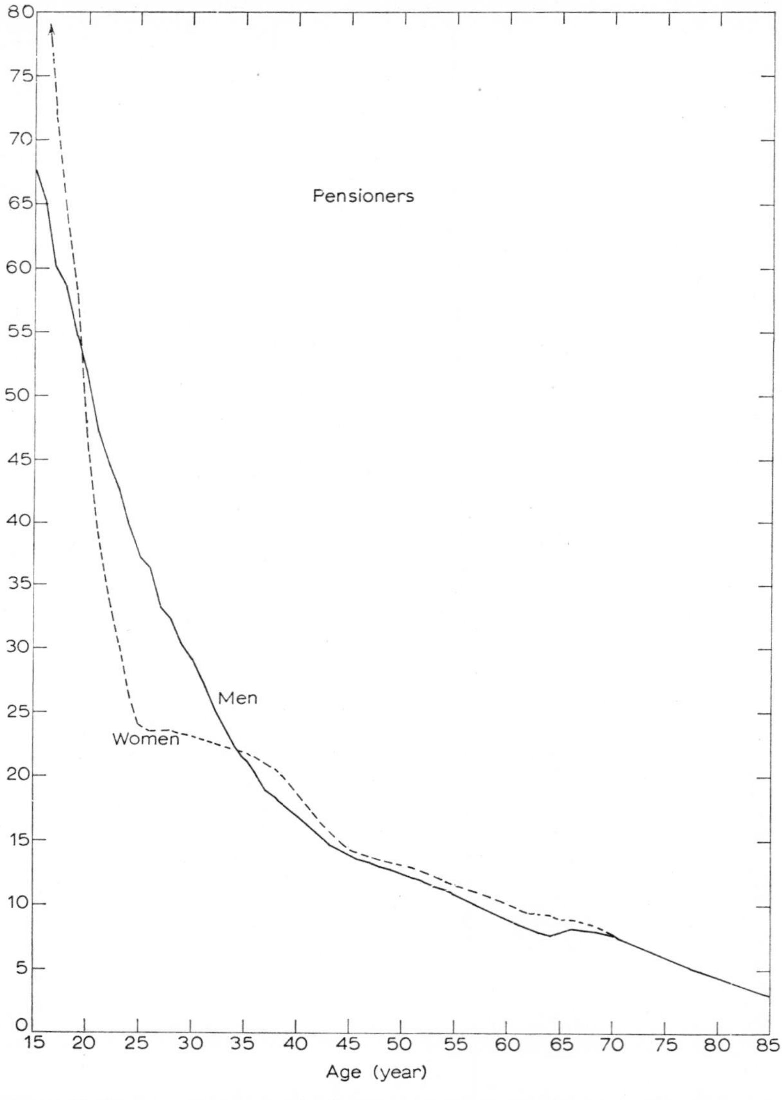

Graph 6C.13. Labour income capitalization factors, according to occupation and sex, at selected ages.

[At particular (lower) ages no figures are cited in cases where numbers of people are too small.]

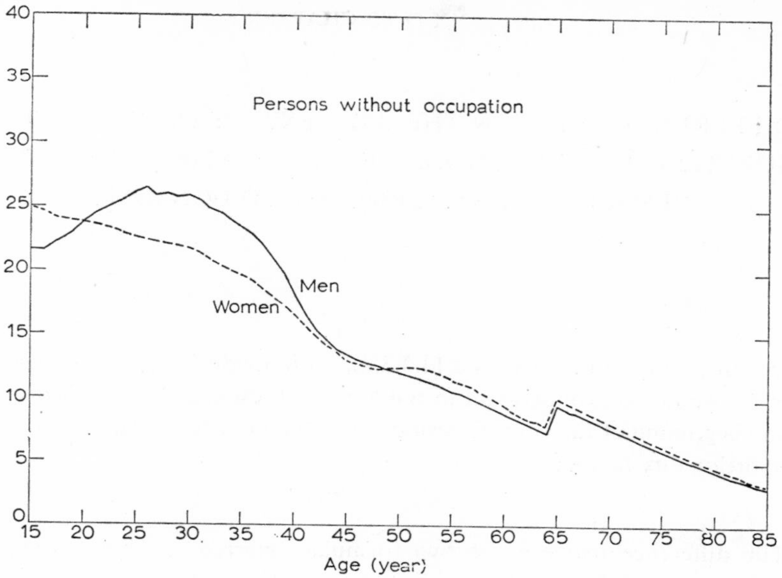

Graph 6C.14. Labour income capitalization factors, according to occupation and sex, at selected ages.

[At particular (lower) ages no figures are cited in cases where numbers of people are too small.]

DIFFERENCE BETWEEN THE 'LIFE-EXPECTANCY' AND THE 'SURVIVAL RATE' METHODS OF CALCULATING 'FINANCIAL RESOURCES' AND 'URGENCY TO CONSUME'

According to both (4.1.3.4) and (4.3.3.2), an individual's current consumption C_1 would be proportional to the 'financial resources' R_1 at his disposal at the beginning of the current period, with "urgency to consume" α_1 as the proportionality factor:

$$C_1 = \alpha_1 R_1 . \tag{6D.1}$$

The difference between the two formulae referred to above is that in (4.1.3.4) and (4.3.3.2) R_1 is calculated on the basis of the individual's life expectancy (L) and his entire survival rate pattern (s_l, for $l = 1, \ldots, M$) respectively. Since C_1 remains the same in both cases, α_1 changes in inverse proportion to R_1 if one method of calculation is substituted for the other.

According to (4.1.3.4) and (4.3.3.2), the two variables R_1, distinguished by additional sub-scripts (L) and (s), in order to denote calculation by the 'life-expectancy' and by the 'survival rate' method, respectively, are expressed by:

$$R_{1(L)} = (K_0 - K_L)(1 + r)^{1-L} + \sum_{l=1}^{L} Y_l (1 + r)^{1-l} \tag{6D.2}$$

and

$$R_{1(s)} = (K_0 - K_F)(1 + r)^{1-M} + \sum_{l=1}^{M} Y_l (1 + r)^{1-l} s_l \tag{6D.3}$$

Hence, the differences between the two "financial resources" concepts may consist of differences in the 'wealth accumulation' (or decumulation) component and/or in the income component.

The first component would be equal in (6D.2) and (6D.3) if $K_0 - K_F$ equals $(K_0 - K_L)(1 + r)^{M-L}$. This means that in an absolute sense, $K_0 - K_F$ would increase according as a higher value would be assigned to M. With M tending to infinity, the wealth accumulation component of $R_{1(s)}$ would tend to zero.

For $K_L = K_F > K_0$, $R_{1(L)}$ will have a larger wealth accumulation component than $R_{1(s)}$, i.e. $R_{1(L),1} > R_{1(s),1}$.

For the difference between the income components of (6D.3) and (6D.2), we may write:

$$R_{1(s),2} - R_{1(L)2,} = \sum_{l=1}^{M} Y_l (1+r)^{1-l} s_l - \sum_{l=1}^{L} Y_l (1+r)^{1-l}$$

$$= \sum_{l=L+1}^{M} Y_l (1+r)^{1-l} s_l - \sum_{l=1}^{L} Y_l (1+r)^{1-l} (1-s_l)$$

$$= \sum_{l=1}^{L} \{Y_{l+L} (1+r)^{-L} s_{l+L} - Y_l (1-s_l)\} (1+r)^{1-l}$$

$$+ \sum_{l=L+1}^{M-L} Y_{l+L} (1+r)^{1-l-L} s_{l+L} \delta_{M>2L} \qquad (6D.4)$$

with

$$\delta_{M>2L} = \begin{cases} 1 & \text{for } M > 2L \\ 0 & \text{for } M \leq 2L. \end{cases}$$

As a rule, the last term in the last member of (6D.4) will vanish, i.e. unless the individual's age is nearing or exceeding the life-expectancy at birth (say around 70 years) – cf. table 6D.1.

TABLE 6D.1.

Maximum ages to be reached after doubling life expectancies at selected ages of male and female residents of the Netherlands, 1961/65, in years

starting age (a)	life expectancy (L)		$a_{max} = a + 2L$	
	males	females	males	females
20	53	57	127	135
40	34	38	109	116
60	17	20	95	100
80	6	7	92	93

Source: Central Bureau of Statistics (Netherlands) [1967].

As regards the first term in the fourth member of (6D.4), $Y_{l+L}(1+r)^{-L}s_{l+L}$ is likely to decrease monotonically with increasing l. On the other hand, $Y_l\,(1-s_l)$ tends to increase with advancing age, although at a higher level of l it may decrease eventually: whereas Y_l will grow, at least initially, at lower age levels, and $1 - s_l$ will continue to increase towards its maximum level 1, it may be caught up by a final decline of Y_l. Nevertheless, it seems likely that in the first summation term in the fourth member of (6D.4), $Y_l(1 - s_l)$ will generally exceed $Y_{l+L}(1+r)^{-L}s_{l+L}$, for the following reasons:

(a) the added incomes, i.e. the $Y_{\tau>L}$ to be expected beyond L, are probably small compared with income $Y_{\tau<L}$ to be received before L;
(b) the $Y_{\tau>L}$ are more heavily discounted than the $Y_{\tau<L}$, and
(c) the $Y_{\tau>L}$ are even more reduced by the $s_{\tau>L}$ than the $Y_{\tau<L}$ are toned down by the larger $s_{\tau<L}$.

Argument (c) might be countered by noting that if the $s_{\tau<L}$ are near to 1 but a small contribution from ages $\tau > L$ to $R_{1(s),2}$ would be needed in order to compensate for the loss arising from the difference between 1 and $s_{\tau<L}$. On the other hand, in such a case the latter contribution *could* not be substantial anyhow, since values of $s_{\tau<L}$ close to 1 would have to be offset by low values of $s_{\tau-L}$ in order to yield a life expectancy of L.

For a special case, the sign conditions of the difference $R_{1(s),2} - R_{1(L),2}$ can be stated exactly, viz. if incomes Y_l follow an exponential growth path:

$$Y_l = Y_1 (1 + g)^{l-1} \quad \text{for} \quad l = 1, \ldots, M, \tag{6D.5}$$

with g the growth rate per unit of time. Substitution of (6D.5) into (6D.4) yields:

$$R_{1(s),2} - R_{1(L),2} = Y_1 \{\sum_{l=1}^{M} \gamma^{l-1} s_l - \sum_{l=1}^{L} \gamma^{l-1}\}$$

$$= Y_1 \{ \sum_{l''=L+1}^{M} \gamma^{l''-1} s_{l''} - \sum_{l'=1}^{L} \gamma^{l'-1} (1 - s_{l'})\}, \tag{6D.6}$$

with $\gamma = (1 + g)/(1 + r)$.

In order to examine the sign of $R_{1(s),2} - R_{1(L),2}$, we distinguish three cases according to the sign of $g - r$.

I. $g > r$, hence $\gamma > 1$

According to (6D.6), the minimum of $R_{1(s),2} - R_{1(L),2}$ is reached for $s_{l''}$ minimal, i.e. all zero, implying $s_{l'}$ all unity; only thus, the contribution of the $\gamma^{l''-1} s_{l''}$ is reduced as much as possible compared with the contribution of $\gamma^{l'-1} s_{l'}$ – in view of $\gamma^{l''-1} > \gamma^{l'-1}$ and considering that the s_l ($s_{l'}$, $s_{l''}$) should satisfy the monotonicity condition (2.7.4).

Consequently:

$$\underset{s_l}{\operatorname{Min}} \{R_{1(s),2} - R_{1(L),2}\} = 0 \quad \text{for } \gamma > 1. \tag{6D.7}$$

II. $g = r$, hence $\gamma = 1$

In this case, (6D.6) becomes:

$$R_{1(s),2} - R_{1(L),2} = Y_1 \left(\sum_{l=1}^{M} s_l - \sum_{l=1}^{L} 1\right) = Y_1 (L - L) = 0. \tag{6D.8}$$

III. $g < r$, hence $\gamma < 1$

According to (6D.6), the *maximum* of $R_{1(s),2} - R_{1(L),2}$ is reached for (again) $s_{l'}$ maximal, i.e. all 1, implying $s_{l''} = 0$: only thus the reducing effect of $\gamma^{l''-1} < \gamma^{l'-1}$ is counteracted as much as possible, under condition (2.7.4), as in case I.

Consequently:

$$\underset{s_l}{\operatorname{Max}} \{R_{1(s),2} - R_{1(L),2}\} = 0 \quad \text{for } \gamma < 1. \tag{6D.9}$$

These extremes, found in cases I and III, are, of course, highly unlikely, since $s_{l'} = 1$ and $s_{l''} = 0$ means that at a certain age everyone would be expected to live precisely L units of time and die immediately afterwards.

Together, (6D.7) through (6D.9) imply:

$$R_{1(s),2} - R_{1(L),2} \gtreqless 0 \quad \text{according as } g \gtreqless r. \tag{6D.10}$$

Since, however, the expected future course of income will rarely be exponential, condition (6D.10) can hardly ever be applied exactly. On the other hand, it might be applied approximately if g is replaced by $\bar{g}$, an average of the age-specific rates of growth of income.

Since $r > \bar{g}$ seems more likely than $r \leq \bar{g}$ – over the entire, maximal lifetime –, a negative value of $R_{1(s),2} - R_{1(L),2}$ is again more plausible than a positive one.

Thus, with $R_{1(s),1} \leq R_{1(L),1}$ and $R_{1(s),2} < R_{2(L),2}$, in general $R_{1(s)}$ is less than $R_{1(L)}$, implying $\alpha_{1(s)} > \alpha_{1(L)}$. This may seem strange, in view of the larger number of $\alpha_{l(s)}$ compared with the number of $\alpha_{l(L)}$; the solution of this paradox, however, is that not the $\alpha_{l(s)}$ themselves, but their products with the corresponding factors s_l (< 1) must add up to 1.

The continuous version of the consumption-savings model enables a more elegant, but essentially similar way of treating this problem: for such a model, the difference between the two concepts of 'financial resources' becomes:

$$R_{(s)} - R_{(L)} = (K_0 - K_F)(1 + r)^{1-M} - (K_0 - K_L)(1 + r)^{1-L}$$

$$+ \int_0^L [Y(l + L)\, s\,(l + L) \exp(-\varrho L) - Y(l)\,\{1 - s(l)\} \times$$

$$\times \exp\{(1 - l)\varrho\}]\, dl$$

$$+ \int_L^{M-L} Y(l+L) \cdot s\,(l+L) \cdot \exp\{(1 - l - L)\varrho\} \cdot dl. \quad (6D.11)$$

From (6D.11) the same (tentative) conclusions may be drawn as from (6D.3) through (6D.4).

APPENDIX E TO CHAPTER 6

ELIMINATION OF THE INTERCEPT FROM LEAST SQUARES PARAMETER ESTIMATION

Assume that the following linear model is given:

$$x = [W \quad \iota_N] \begin{bmatrix} \beta \\ \mu \end{bmatrix} + \varepsilon, \tag{6E.1}$$

with x = an $N \times 1$ vector of observations on the variable x_n to be explained.
W = an $N \times \Lambda$ matrix of N observations on the Λ explanatory variables $x_{n\lambda}$,
ι_N = a summation vector of length N,
β = a $\Lambda \times 1$ vector of parameters,
μ = an intercept, and
ε = an $N \times 1$ vector of disturbances.

Pre-multiplication of (6E.1) by

$$\begin{bmatrix} W' \\ \iota_N' \end{bmatrix} [I_N - N^{-1}\iota_N\iota_N'] \quad \text{yields}$$

$$\begin{aligned} \begin{bmatrix} W' \\ \iota_N' \end{bmatrix} [I_N - N^{-1}\iota_N\iota_N']\, x &= \begin{bmatrix} W' \\ \iota_N' \end{bmatrix} [I_N - N^{-1}\iota_N\iota_N']\, [W \quad \iota_N] \begin{bmatrix} \beta \\ \mu \end{bmatrix} \\ &\quad + \begin{bmatrix} W' \\ \iota_N' \end{bmatrix} [I_N - N^{-1}\iota_N\iota_N']\, \varepsilon \\ &= \begin{bmatrix} W' \\ \iota_N' \end{bmatrix} [I_N - N^{-1}\iota_N\iota_N']\, [W \quad \iota_N] \begin{bmatrix} b \\ m \end{bmatrix}, \end{aligned} \tag{6E.2}$$

if b and m are estimates of β and μ respectively, W is non-stochastic and $\mathrm{E}\varepsilon = 0$; or:

$$W' [I_N - N^{-1}\iota_N\iota_N']\, x = W' [I_N - N^{-1}\iota_N\iota_N']\, Wb \tag{6E.3}$$

and

$$0 \equiv 0,$$

since

$$[I_N - N^{-1}\iota_N\iota_N']\,\iota_N = \iota_N - \iota_N = 0.$$

Hence,

$$b = [W'\{I_N - N^{-1}\iota_N\iota_N'\}\,W]^{-1}\,W'\,[I_N - N^{-1}\iota_N\iota_N']\,x \qquad (6\text{E}.4)$$

and

$$m = \iota_N'\,[x - Wb] \qquad (6\text{E}.5)$$

may be computed successively, with $\{I_N - N^{-1}\iota_N\ \ \iota_N'\}$ an averaging, idempotent matrix, i.e. converting the matrix W and the vector x in terms of deviations of the variables from their original (sample) means.

CHAPTER 7

A MACRO-SAVINGS FUNCTION FOR THE NETHERLANDS, 1949–1966

In chapter 5 a macro-savings model was developed, especially for time series analysis. This model was applied to the Netherlands post-war economy.

7.1. Coverage

7.1.1. REFERENCE PERIOD

The years 1949 through 1966 were chosen as the time-interval for which the macro-savings functions of the Netherlands should be estimated; 1949 was selected as the initial year, since it was the first post-war year in the Netherlands without rationing (affecting savings); 1966 had to be the terminal year, being the most recent one for which information was available on all variables included in the model at the time (spring 1968) the analysis was started.

7.1.2. UNITS OF TIME

The choice of calendar years rather than shorter periods of time (such as quarters or months) was prompted by theoretical as well as practical considerations. From a theoretical point of view, the use of data relating to periods shorter than one year was precluded, because the savings model applied does not account for seasonal fluctuations in, inter alia, the 'urgency to consume' (α). From a practical point of view – which is ultimately decisive –, short-period information on a number of variables is either absent (for K_t) or less reliable (for S_t and Y_t) than annual data; this means that enlargement of the equivalent amount of information and corresponding improvement of parameter estimates would be foiled.

7.1.3. SECTOR(S)

Both the micro-model and the corresponding macro-model have primarily been developed with respect to the savings of *private income recipients*, individually and in the aggregate, respectively. One may argue, however, that all savings, irrespective of the sector of the economy in which they originate, might be imputed to private income recipients, because ultimately all national wealth belongs to them. In a statistical sense, moreover, no clear-cut distinction can be made between the finances of non-incorporated business and those of private households of own-account workers like farmers and independent tradesmen.

Consequently, separate regression analyses have been carried out alternatively for personal and for national savings; i.e. for the household sector, and for all sectors of the Dutch economy combined.

7.2. *Variables*

7.2.1. MUTUAL CONSISTENCY

Ideally, the data used in any analysis should be mutually consistent, i.e. it should fit into the same conceptual and statistical framework. Fortunately, this is true both of the personal and the national data on savings and on income, since all are derived from the same system of National Accounts.

Figures on national wealth can also be dovetailed into National Account figures, viz. by requiring that changes in real values of capital goods equal net investments (= savings), i.e. apart from changes in prices of the capital goods.

The only variable in the savings model that cannot and need not fit directly into the system of national accounts is the rate of interest for converting future to present values.

All basic data and the resulting variables used in the regression analyses are presented in appendix A to this chapter.

7.2.2. SAVINGS

In accordance with section 7.1.2 two alternative savings concepts were used in the analyses, viz. personal savings and national savings. For both, the series have been copied from the annual publications on 'National Accounts' prepared by the Central Bureau of Statistics of the Netherlands. The main difference between the personal and the national savings series is due to the business sector (savings by way of undistributed profits made by incorporated enterprise or dissavings in the case where dividends exceed profits) and to Government savings or dissavings. In principle, savings may be negative in any sector.

7.2.3. INCOME

Personal and national savings are primarily related to the corresponding income concepts, viz. (personal) disposable income and national income (at market prices), respectively. The main difference between national and personal income is income accrueing to other sectors; in addition, net transfers from other sectors (like relief provided by Government and remittances sent by or to relatives abroad) are included in personal income. Deduction of direct taxes from personal income leaves disposable income. The latter concept is adopted as the counterpart of personal savings, since the savings theory underlying the macro-model presupposes that income can be disposed of freely; this means that it is either saved or consumed but not spent on ineluctable direct taxes, such as income tax.

7.2.4. WEALTH

Ideally, two alternative wealth concepts, viz. personal wealth and national wealth, corresponding to the two alternative savings and income concepts, should be adopted for explaining fluctuations in personal savings and in national savings, respectively.

Unfortunately, however, series on personal or national wealth available for the Netherlands do not cover the entire time-span of the analysis; even more seriously, those figures are inconsistent with the savings data. For the sake of consistency an indirect approach was made along the following lines.

If for any moment 0 (= the end of period 0) personal or national wealth K_0 is known, the value K_t of K at any later date (i.e. the end of periods t) could be derived from:

$$K_t = K_0 + \sum_{\tau=1}^{t} S_\tau \quad \text{for } t = 1, \ldots, T, \tag{7.2.4.1}$$

if S_τ are the known values of savings in periods $\tau = 1, \ldots, t$, and prices of capital goods do not change in the meantime. The latter assumption is obviously unrealistic. Taking into account changes in the prices of capital goods, as represented by index numbers P_t, relating to the end of periods t (= 0, 1, ...), equation (7.2.4.1) would have to be replaced by

$$\frac{K_t}{P_t} = \frac{K_0}{P_0} + \sum_{\tau=1}^{t} \frac{S_\tau}{P_{\tau-1/2}}, \tag{7.2.4.2}$$

with $P_{\tau-1/2}$ approximating the mean price level relating to the savings flows within periods τ. The S_t may be represented by the same series on personal and national savings, respectively, as discussed in section 7.2.2. For the P_t and $P_{t-1/2}$, the 'implicit' index-number of the price of investment goods, as the ratio between investment at current and at constant prices, has been chosen.

For lack of information on fluctuations of investments within calendar years, the $P_{t-1/2}$ are calculated simply as unweighted arithmetical averages of P_{t-1} and P_t.

K_0, however, is still indeterminate. One of two possible lines of approach could be adopted (alternatively):

(a) for a particular point of time – subsequently labeled 0 – an available estimate of national or personal wealth could be accepted as K_0, or

(b) K_0 could be left indeterminate, to be estimated as a parameter in conjunction with the ordinary coefficients of regression.

With respect to the first method, we select an estimate of wealth for a point of time at which it seems most reliable, i.e. for the end of 1958; then, the figures for the ends of the other periods covered by the analysis are found by adding or subtracting savings to or from that benchmark.

On the other hand, the particular specification of the original savings equation, viz. the exclusion of a constant term enables application of method (b). Since by (7.2.4.1) and (7.2.4.2) the term $B_1 K_t/Y_t$ in (7.3.1.2) is replaced by $B_1 (K_0/P_0)/Y_t + B_1 \sum_{\tau=1}^{t} (S_\tau/P_{\tau-1/2})/Y_t$, estimates of B_1 and $B_1 K_0/P_0$ as parameters may be obtained. Together they yield an estimate of K_0:

$$\hat{K}_0 = \frac{\widehat{(B_1 K_0/P_0)}}{\hat{B}_1} \cdot P_0; \tag{7.2.4.3}$$

m.m. the same applies to other terms involving K_t.

In the latter case, the accumulation (or decumulation) process could start at an arbitrary moment, since the estimates of parameters in the savings model are unaffected by the choice of the point of departure.

7.2.5. RATE OF INTEREST

In the present context, a statistical indicator for the rate of interest should reflect what people, on the average, have in mind for discounting expected future values to present ones. The actual choice has been made on the basis of the opportunity cost principle, i.e. by adopting the rate of interest people might reasonably expect to receive as a remuneration for postponing part of their consumption. The yield of a sufficiently safe, readily accessible and easily negotiable investment of money – to wit in Government bonds – seems to be a fair measure of such a concept. For this purpose, a number of pertinent time-series, as broad and as similar in coverage as possible – given the limited availability of data – were linked.

7.3. Estimation methods

7.3.1. ORDINARY LEAST SQUARES (OLS) AND SPECIFICATION OF THE REGRESSION EQUATION

The savings equation whose coefficients should be estimated is:

$$\begin{aligned} S_t = A_1 Y_t + A_2 r_t' Y_t + B_1 K_t + B_2 r_t' K_t + C_1 Y_t t \\ + C_2 K_t t + D_1 Y_t r_t' t + D_2 K_t r_t' t + v_t \qquad (7.3.1.1) \end{aligned}$$

with v_t representing possible errors.

In order to reduce presumed heteroskedasticity of the v_t in (7.3.1.1), we divide both sides of (7.3.1.1) by Y_t; thus the following relationship results:

$$\begin{aligned} S_t/Y_t = A_1 + A_2 r_t' + B_1 K_t/Y_t + B_2 r_t' K_t/Y_t + C_1 t \\ + C_2 (K_t/Y_t) \cdot t + D r_t' t + D_2 K_t/Y_t \cdot r_t' t + u_t, \qquad (7.3.1.2) \end{aligned}$$

with $u_t = v_t/Y_t$, and

$$\mathrm{E}(u_t) = 0$$

$$\mathrm{E}(u_t u_{t+s}) = \begin{cases} \sigma^2 & \text{if} \quad s = 0 \\ 0 & \text{if} \quad s \neq 0 \end{cases}$$

$$\text{for } 1 \leq t \leq T - s \leq T;$$

the latter two conditions express the assumptions of homoskedasticity and absence of auto-correlation among the errors.

Equation (7.3.1.2) may be rewritten in a more concise notation as follows:

$$s_t = A_1 + A_2 r_t' + B_1 k_t + B_2 r_t' k_t + C_1 t + C_2 k_t t + D_1 r_t' t + D_2 r_t' k_t t + u_t, \qquad (7.3.1.3)$$

with $s_t = S_t/Y_t$ and $k_t = K_t/Y_t$.

Since four of the explanatory variables appearing in (7.3.1.3) are products of two or three of the 'basic' variables (k_t, r_t' and t) one may expect a high degree of multicollinearity between the composite variables and the basic variables, and among the composite variables themselves. This will appear from a relatively low value of the determinant Δ of the moment matrix $X'X$ – i.e. compared with the determinants $\Delta_g, \Delta_{gh}, \Delta_{ghi}$ of the moment matrix if one or more of those composite variables ($g, h, i = k_t r_t', k_t t, r_t' t$ or $k_t r_t' t$) are left out.

In order to make Δ comparable with the latter determinants, however, they should be multiplied by the sum(s) of squares Q of the variable(s) excluded. Thus, the ratios of Δ to $\Delta_g Q_g$ etc., as shown in table 7.1, may serve as criteria

TABLE 7.1.

Ratios of Δ to $\Delta_g Q_g$, $\Delta_{gh} Q_g Q_h$, and $\Delta_{ghi} Q_g Q_h Q_i$*

	Composite variables+ g, h, i	Personal savings	National savings
1	$k \cdot r$	0.45×10^{-4}	0.63×10^{-4}
2	$k \cdot t$	0.23×10^{-3}	0.69×10^{-4}
3	$r \cdot t$	0.41×10^{-3}	0.55×10^{-4}
4	$k \cdot r \cdot t$	0.58×10^{-3}	0.61×10^{-4}
5	$k \cdot r, k \cdot t$	0.13×10^{-6}	0.10×10^{-7}
6	$k \cdot r, r \cdot t$	0.23×10^{-6}	0.17×10^{-7}
7	$k \cdot r, k \cdot r \cdot t$	0.14×10^{-6}	0.16×10^{-7}
8	$k \cdot t, r \cdot t$	0.27×10^{-6}	0.51×10^{-8}
9	$k \cdot t, k \cdot r \cdot t$	0.28×10^{-6}	0.50×10^{-8}
10	$r \cdot t, k \cdot r \cdot t$	0.18×10^{-5}	0.96×10^{-6}
11	$k \cdot r, k \cdot t, r \cdot t$	0.23×10^{-9}	0.45×10^{-11}
12	$k \cdot r, k \cdot t, k \cdot r \cdot t$	0.16×10^{-9}	0.39×10^{-11}
13	$k \cdot t, r \cdot t, k \cdot r \cdot t$	0.12×10^{-8}	0.90×10^{-10}

* In appendix B to this chapter, it is shown that the determinants of the moment matrices are independent of the way in which the variables are measured.

\+ Points (·) denote multiplication between corresponding elements of the $T \times 1$ vectors of the variables.

when deciding which composite variable(s) to drop, lest the results be foiled by an excessive degree of multicollinearity. In this process of elimination, one may start by combining variables for which the ratio as defined above is lowest, and continue eliminating variables till the standard errors of the parameters – being proportional to the square roots of the elements on the main diagonal of $(X'X)^{-1}$ – will have come down to acceptable levels.

Thus, all (combinations of) composite variables listed in table 7.1, with the exception of $r_t't$ on line 3, were eliminated forthwith. In view of the fairly high correlation between k_t and t, alternatively t was left out too; since in this case it does not make sense to retain a composite variable of which one or more components are eliminated as basic variables, $r_t't$ was dropped together with t.

Using this information we estimated the parameters of the following four 'condensed' equations, using personal and national data:

$$s_t = A_1 + A_2 r_t' + B_{10} k_{0t}^* + B_{11} k_{1t}^* + C_1 t + D_1 r_t' t + u_t, \quad (7.3.1.4)$$

$$s_t = A_1 + A_2 r_t' + B_1 k_t + C_1 t + D_1 r_t' t + u_t, \quad (7.3.1.5)$$

$$s_t = A_1 + A_2 r_t' + B_{10} k_{0t}^* + B_{11} k_{1t}^* + u_t, \quad (7.3.1.6)$$

$$s_t = A_1 + A_2 r_t' + B_1 k_t + u_t. \quad (7.3.1.7)$$

The parameters in (7.3.1.5) and (7.3.1.7) correspond approximately to the homonymous parameters in the basic macro-savings function (7.3.1.3) in the way shown in table 7.2.

TABLE 7.2.

Approximate correspondence between parameters in equations (7.3.1.7), (7.3.1.5) and (7.3.1.3)

Condensed equations (7.3.1.7)	Condensed equations (7.3.1.5)	Basic equation (7.3.1.3)
A_1		A_1
A_2		$A_2 + B_2\bar{k}$
B_1		B_1
	C_1	$C_1 + C_2\bar{k}$
	D_1	$D_1 + D_2\bar{k}$

Note: $\bar{k}$ represents an average of the k_t.

The variable k corresponds to the wealth concept meant under point (a), and k^* corresponds to the wealth concept meant under (b), both in section 7.2.4:

$$B_{10}k^*_{0t} + B_{11}k^*_{1t} = \left(B_1 \frac{K_0}{P_0}\right)\frac{P_t}{Y_t} + (B_1)\frac{P_t}{Y_t}\sum_{\tau=1}^{t}\frac{S_\tau}{P_{\tau-1/2}}. \qquad (7.3.1.8)$$

If the assumption of a scalar covariance matrix of the disturbances must be rejected on a theoretical or on a statistical basis, then the OLS method for estimating parameters is no longer the most efficient one.

Since savings rates instead of absolute savings are the dependent variables, heteroskedasticity is probably the least of our worries. On the other hand, an appreciable amount of (positive) autocorrelation of the disturbances is quite likely. In order to cope with this problem efficiently, we may apply:

7.3.2. GENERALIZED LEAST SQUARES (GLS)

7.3.2.1. Transformation. First, the variables are transformed according to a particular autoregressive structure assumed. As usual, we suppose that the latter is simply of the first order, i.e.:

$$u_t = \varrho u_{t-1} + \varepsilon_t, \qquad (7.3.2.1.1)$$

with

$$|\varrho| < 1$$

$$\left.\begin{aligned} E(\varepsilon_t) &= 0 \\ E\varepsilon_t^2 &= \sigma_\varepsilon^2 \end{aligned}\right\} \text{ for all } t$$

$$E(\varepsilon_t \varepsilon_{t+s}) = 0 \quad \text{for all } t \text{ and } s \neq 0.$$

Secondly, ordinary least squares are applied to the regression equation in the transformed variables.

Consider the model:

$$y = X\beta + u, \qquad (7.3.2.1.2)$$

where y is a $T \times 1$ vector of successive observations on the dependent variable, X is a $T \times \Lambda$ matrix (with rank Λ) of T successive observations on the Λ independent variables (regarded as fixed), and u is a $T \times 1$ random vector of disturbances with zero expectations. The disturbances are assumed to follow the autoregressive process mentioned in (7.3.2.1.1).

According to those assumptions:

$$\mathrm{E}uu' = \frac{\sigma_\varepsilon^2}{1-\varrho^2} R, \quad \text{with } R = \begin{bmatrix} 1 & \varrho & \varrho^2 & \cdots & \varrho^{T-1} \\ \varrho & 1 & \varrho & \cdots & \varrho^{T-2} \\ \vdots & \vdots & \vdots & & \vdots \\ \varrho^{T-1} & \varrho^{T-2} & \varrho^{T-3} & \cdots & 1 \end{bmatrix}$$

(7.3.2.1.3)

and

$$R^{-1} = \frac{1}{1-\varrho^2} \begin{bmatrix} 1 & -\varrho & 0 & \cdots & 0 & 0 \\ -\varrho & 1+\varrho^2 & -\varrho & \cdots & 0 & 0 \\ 0 & -\varrho & 1+\varrho^2 & \cdots & 0 & 0 \\ \vdots & \vdots & \vdots & & \vdots & \vdots \\ 0 & 0 & 0 & \cdots & 1+\varrho^2 & -\varrho \\ 0 & 0 & 0 & \cdots & -\varrho & 1 \end{bmatrix}. \qquad (7.3.2.1.4)$$

Furthermore, (7.3.2.1.2) may be converted to a standard linear regression model with scalar covariance matrix by means of the following transformations:

$$y^* = Fy, \quad X^* = FX, \quad u^* = Fu, \qquad (7.3.2.1.5)$$

with:

$$F = \begin{bmatrix} (1-\varrho^2)^{1/2} & 0 & 0 & \cdots & 0 & 0 & 0 \\ -\varrho & 1 & 0 & \cdots & 0 & 0 & 0 \\ \vdots & \vdots & \vdots & & & & \\ 0 & 0 & 0 & \cdots & -\varrho & 1 & 0 \\ 0 & 0 & 0 & \cdots & 0 & -\varrho & 1 \end{bmatrix} \qquad (7.3.2.1.6)$$

of order $T \times T$,[1]

and $F'F = (1-\varrho^2) R^{-1}$ if ϱ is known. The new model has a scalar covariance matrix:

$$\begin{aligned} \mathrm{E}\,[u^*(u^*)'] &= \mathrm{E}\,(Fuu'F') = F\,[\mathrm{E}uu']\,F' \\ &= \frac{\sigma_\varepsilon^2}{1-\varrho^2} FRF' = \frac{\sigma_\varepsilon^2}{1-\varrho^2}(1-\varrho^2)\,I = \sigma_\varepsilon^2 \cdot I. \end{aligned} \qquad (7.3.2.1.7)$$

[1] With the help of this matrix the estimation method produces the so-called Prais-Winston estimator, which is relatively more efficient than the Cochrane-Orcutt estimator, by using one observation more.

Consequently, we may apply ordinary least squares provided the symbols of (7.3.2.1.2) are replaced by ditto with an asterisk. If the assumptions on the disturbances ε_t stated in connection with (7.3.2.1.1) have to be rejected (i.e. $\mathrm{E}\varepsilon\varepsilon' \neq \sigma_\varepsilon^2 I$), then the transformed variables are transformed a second time according to a new autoregressive structure, such as

$$\varepsilon_t = \varrho_\varepsilon \varepsilon_{t-1} + \eta_t, \tag{7.3.2.1.8}$$

with η_t assumedly having a scalar covariance matrix. Provided ϱ, ϱ_ε, ϱ_η, ... tend to zero, this method may be applied repeatedly, till the autocorrelation of the disturbances becomes insignificant. In practice, however, this procedure is already stopped after the second iteration.

7.3.2.2. Estimation of the coefficient(s) of autocorrelation. For carrying out the procedure outlined above, we need an estimate of ϱ. The simplest estimator of ϱ is:

$$\hat{\varrho} = \frac{\sum_{t=2}^{T} \hat{u}_t \hat{u}_{t-1}}{\sum_{t=2}^{T} \hat{u}_{t-1}^2} \tag{7.3.2.2.1}$$

with $\hat{u}' = \{\hat{u}_1, \ldots, \hat{u}_T\}$ resulting from application of OLS to (7.3.2.1.2), i.e. as:

$$\hat{u} = [I - X'(X'X)^{-1}X]\, y. \tag{7.3.2.2.2}$$

In the case where significant autocorrelation (of a second order) would still be left, viz. in the ε's satisfying (7.3.2.1.8), ϱ_ε might be estimated in a way analogous to (7.3.2.2.1), i.e. by:

$$\hat{\varrho}_\varepsilon = \frac{\sum_{t=2}^{T} \hat{\varepsilon}_t \hat{\varepsilon}_{t-1}}{\sum_{t=2}^{T} \hat{\varepsilon}_{t-1}^2}, \tag{7.3.2.2.3}$$

with $\hat{\varepsilon}' = \{\hat{\varepsilon}_1, \ldots, \hat{\varepsilon}_T\}$ resulting from application of OLS to:

$$y^* = X^* \beta^* + \varepsilon, \tag{7.3.2.2.4}$$

with $\varepsilon \equiv u^*$ according to the transformations (7.3.2.1.5) if F is defined by (7.3.2.1.6); then:

$$\hat{\varepsilon} = [I - (X^*)' \{(X^*)' X^*\}^{-1} X^*]\, y^*. \tag{7.3.2.2.5}$$

Alternatively, ϱ and ϱ_ε may be estimated simultaneously. Substitution of (7.3.2.1.8) into (7.3.2.1.1) yields the following second-order autoregressive scheme:

$$u_t = (\varrho + \varrho_\varepsilon)\, u_{t-1} - \varrho\varrho_\varepsilon u_{t-2} + \eta_t, \tag{7.3.2.2.6}$$

with the η's assumedly having a scalar covariance matrix.

Application of OLS to (7.3.2.2.6) yields estimates of $\varrho + \varrho_\varepsilon$ and $\varrho\varrho_\varepsilon$, say:

$$\begin{cases} \text{est.}\,(\varrho + \varrho_\varepsilon) = a_1 \\ \text{est.}\,\varrho\varrho_\varepsilon = a_2 . \end{cases} \tag{7.3.2.2.7}$$

Estimates of ϱ and ϱ_ε *separately* may be solved from (7.3.2.2.7), viz. as:

$$\begin{cases} \text{est.}\,\varrho = \tfrac{1}{2}\,\{a_1 \pm \sqrt{a_1^2 - 4a_2}\} \\ \text{est.}\,\varrho_\varepsilon = \tfrac{1}{2}\,\{a_1 \mp \sqrt{a_1^2 - 4a_2}\} \end{cases} \tag{7.3.2.2.8}$$

with ϱ and ϱ_ε having opposite signs for $\sqrt{a_1^2 - 4a_2}$, provided $a_1^2 \geq 4a_2$, lest the roots be complex.

One may expect that two steps in the iterative procedure will suffice, i.e. that after the second stage no significant autocorrelation between the disturbances in the transformed regression equations is left at a predetermined confidence level of (say) 95 per cent. In order to check this assumption, we used the 'improved' Durbin-Watson test-statistic, developed by Abrahamse [1969].

Instead of being estimated *separately*, the coefficients of autocorrelation ϱ may be estimated together with the regression coefficients, according to the method outlined in section 7.3.3. While all estimates of ϱ are biased but consistent, the latter method might be more efficient under certain conditions.

The outcome of applying the latter method may be used in its entirety; in tables 7.4 through 7.7 these results are labeled 'DLS'. Alternatively, however, the ϱ-estimate obtained by the DLS-method is adopted only for computing the F-matrix to be used in GLS.

Thus, four kinds of GLS-estimates will be presented in tables 7.3 through 7.7, viz.:

$\hat{\varrho}$ for *F*-matrix		first stage	second stage
estimated	separately	GLS 1	GLS 2
	jointly with β's	GLS 1*	GLS 2*

7.3.3. JOINT ESTIMATION OF THE COEFFICIENTS OF REGRESSION AND OF AUTOCORRELATION

The joint estimation procedure was first proposed by Durbin [1960] and further developed by Gupta [1969] as follows:

Assume

$$y^- = X^-\beta + u; \tag{7.3.3.1}$$

y^- = a $(T-1) \times 1$ vector of the dependent variables,

X^- = a $(T-1) \times \Lambda$ matrix of the (non-stochastic) independent variables,

β = a $\Lambda \times 1$ vector of coefficients,

u^- = a $(T-1) \times 1$ vector of errors,

with the superscript $^-$ denoting that the observations for period 1 are omitted.

The u^- should satisfy:

$$\mathrm{E}u^- = 0 \tag{7.3.3.2}$$

and

$$u^- = \varrho u^-_{-1} + \varepsilon^- \quad \text{with} \quad \mathrm{E}\varepsilon^- = 0 \quad \text{and} \quad \mathrm{E}\varepsilon^- (\varepsilon^-)' = \sigma^2 I_{T-1} \tag{7.3.3.3}$$

and

$$\begin{cases} u^{-\prime} = \{u_2, \ldots, u_T\}' \\ u^{-\prime}_{-1} = \{u_1, \ldots, u_{T-1}\}'. \end{cases}$$

Substitution of (7.3.3.3) into (7.3.3.1) yields:

$$y^- = X^-\beta + \varrho u^-_{-1} + \varepsilon. \tag{7.3.3.4}$$

Since u^-_{-1} is unknown, however, it is provisionally replaced by $\hat{u}^-_{-1}$, $\hat{u}^-$ being defined by:

$$\hat{u}^- = [I - X^- \{(X^-)' X^-\}^{-1} (X^-)'] \, y^-, \tag{7.3.3.5}$$

resulting from the application of OLS.

Hence, the parameters β and ϱ may be estimated simultaneously by application OLS to:

$$y^- = [X^- \quad \hat{u}^-_{-1}] \begin{bmatrix} \beta^- \\ \varrho \end{bmatrix} + \varepsilon^-. \tag{7.3.3.6}$$

Consequently, we obtain:

$$\begin{bmatrix} \hat{\beta}^- \\ \hat{\varrho} \end{bmatrix} = \begin{bmatrix} X^{-\prime}X^- & X^{-\prime}\hat{u}^-_{-1} \\ \hat{u}^{-\prime}_{-1}X^- & \hat{u}^{-\prime}_{-1}\hat{u}^-_{-1} \end{bmatrix}^{-1} \begin{bmatrix} X^{-\prime} \\ \hat{u}^{-\prime}_{-1} \end{bmatrix} y^-, \tag{7.3.3.7}$$

with asymptotic covariance matrix

$$\operatorname{plim} \begin{bmatrix} \hat{\beta}^- - \mathrm{E}\hat{\beta}^- \\ \hat{\varrho} - \mathrm{E}\hat{\varrho} \end{bmatrix}' \begin{bmatrix} \hat{\beta}^- - \mathrm{E}\hat{\beta}^- \\ \hat{\varrho} - \mathrm{E}\hat{\varrho} \end{bmatrix} = \hat{\sigma}^2 \begin{bmatrix} (X^{-\prime}X^-)^{-1} & 0 \\ 0 & (\hat{u}^{-\prime}_{-1}\hat{u}_{-1})^{-1} \end{bmatrix} \tag{7.3.3.8}$$

and

$$\hat{\sigma}^2 = \frac{\hat{\varepsilon}'\hat{\varepsilon}}{T - \Lambda - 2},$$

with $\hat{\varepsilon}$ the vector of residuals resulting from application of OLS to (7.3.3.4), and Λ the number of coefficients of regression to be estimated.

7.3.4. A SIMULTANEOUS EQUATIONS APPROACH?

Application of one of the 'single-equation' estimation methods outlined in sections 7.3.1 through 7.3.3 means that all 'explanatory variables' in the savings equations are considered as exogenous or that the endogenous nature of one or more of these variables is disregarded. This applies to (at least) Y_t and K_t, as explained in section 5.3; even r_t may be considered as an endogenous variable, since it is affected not only by the demand for investment funds but also by the amount of savings (S_t) offered in the capital market.

Section 5.3 outlined ways in which the savings model can be amplified in order to take account of the endogenous nature of explanatory variables in the savings equations. It also makes clear, however, that the complications resulting from such an extension of the model well-nigh preclude its application, especially if a distinction is made between physical capital and financial capital otherwise known as personal wealth. Even if such a distinction is dropped, the resulting difficulties of obtaining parameter estimates, e.g. by maximum likelihood methods, are considerable if not insurmountable.

Experiments were carried out on a model consisting of the following three equations:

$$S_t = A_1 Y_t + A_2 r_t' Y_t + B_1 K_t + Y_t u_t \tag{7.3.4.1}$$

$$S_t = K_t - K_{t-1} \tag{7.3.4.2}$$

$$Y_t = c \cdot L^{\lambda}_{t-1/2} \cdot K^{\varkappa}_{t-1/2} \cdot \exp(dt + w_t), \tag{7.3.4.3}$$

with u_t and w_t assumed to have zero expectations and scalar covariance matrices, with $Eu_t w_{t'} = 0$ for $t, t' = 1, \ldots, T$ $(t \neq t)$, and d a (positive) constant representing disembodied technological change. The results obtained suggest that simultaneous estimation of all parameters yields inacceptable figures for at least a couple of them – in particular λ and $\varkappa$, coming up with either excessively high or excessively low (or even negative) values. This may be due to imperfections of the model – in particular because of confusing physical capital with personal wealth – as well as to imperfections of the iterative procedure adopted for successive approximation of the parameter values. Such a disappointing outcome need not surprise us, since it is common experience that more sophisticated methods, being more sensitive to both specification and measurement errors, often produce results that are less reliable and plausible than those obtained by simpler, theoretically inferior but robuster procedures.

For these reasons we confined ourselves – at least for the time being – to single-equation estimation of the parameters in alternatively specified savings equations (7.3.1.3) through (7.3.1.7).

7.4. Empirical results

7.4.1. SYNOPSIS

The results of applying the estimation methods outlined in section 7.3 to equations (7.3.1.3) through (7.3.1.7) are presented in tables 7.3 through 7.7, respectively; the 'a'-tables relate to personal savings, and the 'b'-tables relate to national savings.

These tables enable us to make comparisons:

(1) between various specifications of the savings functions, for the same scope of savings, estimated according to the same method;
(2) between personal and national savings, according to functions specified and estimated in the same manner;
(3) between various methods applied to identically specified functions for the same scope of savings.

These comparisons are made with respect to:

(α) signs and orders of magnitude of the estimated regression coefficients,
(β) reliability (standard errors) of these point estimates, and
(γ) goodness of fit.

7.4.2. COMPARISON BETWEEN VARIOUS SPECIFICATIONS OF THE SAVINGS FUNCTIONS

A comparison between corresponding results presented in tables 7.3 through 7.7 shows that in general:

(a) the appearance of incorrect signs of the coefficients (as discussed in section 5.2.2) is less frequent according as the savings functions are specified in a more condensed way;
(b) the reliability (as measured by the ratios of the point estimates to their standard errors) is higher for the more concisely specified savings functions than for the more detailed ones;
(c) the goodness of fit of the equations (as measured by the coefficient of multiple correlation) declines but slightly according as the savings functions are specified in a less detailed way;
(d) the results obtained by means of wealth series with pre-determined level are generally more satisfactory in all respects mentioned above than those obtained by means of wealth series with indeterminate level (cf. table 7.5 with table 7.4, and table 7.7 with table 7.6).

Conclusions (a), (b) and (c) should not surprise us, in view of the observations made with regard to multicollinearity between (composite and/or single) variables in the most detailed model (7.3.1.3) – cf. table 7.1. These considerations led to alternative, more concise specifications of the savings functions. Apparently, the advantage of reducing multicollinearity by eliminating a number of (composite) variables outweighed the disadvantage of thereby introducing specification errors.

In particular, it appears that dropping terms with $k_t r_t'$ represents a profit rather than a loss. The relationships between corresponding coefficients in variously specified savings functions, as presented in table 7.2, tally fairly well, at least between tables 7.5 and 7.7; because of the unreliability of parameter estimates according to specifications other than those underlying tables 7.5 and 7.7, the relations shown by table 7.2 do not fit the point estimates of the coefficients between other pairs of tables.

As might be expected, the estimates of A_1 are more reliable than those of all other coefficients; the former are always positive, and never exceed 1. The second and third best estimates are those of B_1 (or B_{10} and B_{11}) and of A_2, respectively: their point estimates are nearly always negative and positive, respectively, in accordance with (5.2.2.3). Presumption (5.2.2.7), viz. that in

TABLE 7.3.

Explanation of personal savings' and of national savings' rates according to formula (7.3.1.3) by ordinary least squares (OLS)

Variables to be explained	Coefficients of regression (and their standard errors)								Coefficient of correlation
	A_1	A_2	B_1	B_2	C_1	C_2	D_1	D_2	R
Personal savings rate	0.711	18.2	−0.109	−1.8	−0.040	0.008	1.3	−0.43	0.965
	(0.358)	(48.0)	(0.065)	(8.5)	(0.027)	(0.005)	(1.8)	(0.35)	
National savings rate	0.406	−19.1	−0.052	6.1	−0.028	0.007	5.5	−1.5	0.758
	(0.617)	(76.5)	(0.141)	(17.7)	(0.054)	(0.012)	(5.5)	(1.3)	

TABLE 7.4.
Explanation of savings' rates according to formula (7.3.1.4) by various methods

Method used	Coefficients of regression (and their standard errors)						Coefficient of autocorrelation	Coefficient of correlation*
	A_1	A_2	B_{10}	B_{11}	C_1	D_1	ϱ	R
a. *Personal savings*								
OLS	0.277	6.74	−64.5	−0.24	0.021	−0.475		0.964
	(0.140)	(1.97)	(29.1)	(0.05)	(0.007)	(0.114)		
GLS 1	0.246	5.88	−58.2	−0.24	0.022	−0.414	0.245	
	(0.145)	(2.21)	(30.0)	(0.06)	(0.008)	(0.129)	(0.238)	
GLS 1*	0.169	3.49	−43.9	−0.24	0.024	−0.248	0.624	
	(0.146)	(2.60)	(29.4)	(0.07)	(0.009)	(0.161)	(0.360)	
GLS 2	0.227	5.31	−52.3	−0.23	0.022	−0.372	0.160	
	(0.149)	(2.38)	(30.6)	(0.06)	(0.008)	(0.140)	(0.245)	
GLS 2*	0.153	2.82	−40.6	−0.24	0.025	−0.189	0.179	
	(0.151)	(2.79)	(29.9)	(0.08)	(0.009)	(0.176)	(0.450)	
DLS	0.099	7.46	−34.3	−0.36	0.036	−0.486	0.624	0.973
	(0.146)	(1.76)	(29.6)	(0.07)	(0.009)	(0.105)	(0.360)	
b. *National savings*								
OLS	0.136	3.89	5	−0.05	0.011	−0.366		0.738
	(0.219)	(3.05)	(63)	(0.11)	(0.017)	(0.219)		
GLS 1	0.181	3.0	−11	−0.07	0.012	−0.291	0.478	
	(0.206)	(2.7)	(59)	(0.11)	(0.017)	(0.187)	(0.217)	
GLS 1*	0.177	2.4	−11	−0.09	0.014	−0.250	0.614	
	(0.203)	(2.6)	(58)	(0.11)	(0.017)	(0.182)	(0.293)	
GLS 2	0.207	2.7	−20	−0.10	0.013	−0.259	0.277	
	(0.203)	(2.6)	(58)	(0.11)	(0.018)	(0.179)	(0.234)	
GLS 2*	0.196	2.2	−19	−0.10	0.015	−0.219	0.248	
	(0.202)	(2.6)	(58)	(0.11)	(0.018)	(0.179)	(0.314)	
DLS	0.163	3.5	−0.2	−0.05	0.008	−0.267	0.614	0.811
	(0.213)	(2.9)	(61)	(0.11)	(0.017)	(0.218)	(0.293)	

* *General:* In tables 7.4–7.7 the coefficients of correlation are corrected for degrees of freedom.

TABLE 7.5.

Explanation of savings' rates according to formula (7.3.1.5) by various methods

Method used	Coefficients of regression (and their standard errors)					Coefficient of auto-correlation	Coefficient of correlation*
	A_1	A_2	B_1	C_1	D_1	ϱ	R
a. *Personal savings*							
OLS	0.539	7.47	−0.072	−0.002	−0.520		0.929
	(0.167)	(2.72)	(0.024)	(0.004)	(0.158)		
GLS 1	0.406	5.77	−0.054	0.002	−0.405	0.493	
	(0.162)	(2.98)	(0.023)	(0.005)	(0.179)	(0.213)	
GLS 1*	0.320	3.91	−0.044	0.004	−0.274	0.762	
	(0.155)	(3.09)	(0.021)	(0.005)	(0.198)	(0.266)	
GLS 2	0.380	5.20	−0.051	0.002	−0.352	0.265	
	(0.158)	(3.14)	(0.022)	(0.005)	(0.193)	(0.232)	
GLS 2*	0.320	3.92	−0.044	0.004	−0.275	−0.003	
	(0.155)	(3.09)	(0.021)	(0.005)	(0.198)	(0.293)	
DLS	0.351	7.26	−0.042	0.000	−0.431	0.762	0.957
	(0.144)	(2.18)	(0.021)	(0.004)	(0.129)	(0.266)	
b. *National savings*							
OLS	0.231	3.54	−0.017	0.003	−0.322		0.760
	(0.172)	(2.56)	(0.035)	(0.003)	(0.152)		
GLS 1	0.268	2.96	−0.026	0.003	−0.261	0.478	
	(0.145)	(2.65)	(0.029)	(0.003)	(0.160)	(0.213)	
GLS 1*	0.273	2.56	−0.028	0.003	−0.225	0.611	
	(0.138)	(2.68)	(0.028)	(0.003)	(0.166)	(0.262)	
GLS 2	0.307	3.17	−0.035	0.003	−0.253	0.254	
	(0.133)	(2.68)	(0.027)	(0.003)	(0.166)	(0.233)	
GLS 2*	0.307	2.82	−0.035	0.003	−0.222	0.209	
	(0.129)	(2.71)	(0.026)	(0.003)	(0.172)	(0.304)	
DLS	0.221	3.25	−0.012	0.002	−0.234	0.611	0.838
	(0.145)	(2.18)	(0.030)	(0.002)	(0.133)	(0.262)	

TABLE 7.6.

Explanation of savings' rates according to formula (7.3.1.6) by various methods

Method used	Coefficients of regression (and their standard errors)				Coefficient of auto-correlation	Coefficient of correlation*
	A_1	A_2	B_{10}	B_{11}	ϱ	R
. *Personal savings*						
OLS	0.633	0.63	−140	−0.128		0.872
	(0.147)	(1.65)	(36)	(0.065)		
GLS 1	0.451	0.92	−96	−0.065	0.632	
	(0.129)	(1.46)	(31)	(0.063)	(0.191)	
GLS 1*	0.399	1.10	−83	−0.055	0.802	
	(0.122)	(1.37)	(29)	(0.063)	(0.206)	
GLS 2	0.422	1.30	−89	−0.061	0.331	
	(0.121)	(1.43)	(28)	(0.063)	(0.217)	
GLS 2*	0.392	1.30	−82	−0.057	0.171	
	(0.120)	(1.37)	(28)	(0.064)	(0.248)	
OLS	0.504	2.16	−103	−0.105	0.802	0.946
	(0.110)	(1.19)	(28)	(0.047)	(0.206)	
. *National savings*						
OLS	0.083	−1.18	−13	0.061		0.712
	(0.131)	(1.04)	(30)	(0.037)		
GLS 1	0.221	−0.87	−28	0.021	0.451	
	(0.115)	(1.02)	(35)	(0.033)	(0.206)	
GLS 1*	0.254	−0.77	−38	0.011	0.569	
	(0.109)	(1.01)	(33)	(0.032)	(0.233)	
GLS 2	0.290	−0.54	−49	0.001	0.282	
	(0.105)	(1.03)	(32)	(0.031)	(0.221)	
GLS 2*	0.318	−0.30	−58	−0.008	0.320	
	(0.098)	(1.01)	(30)	(0.029)	(0.255)	
OLS	0.202	−0.54	−17	0.018	0.569	0.823
	(0.112)	(0.87)	(33)	(0.033)	(0.233)	

an absolute sense A_2 exceeds B_1, holds good throughout tables 7.3–7.7. In addition $|A_2|$ also exceeds A_1.

On the other hand, the standard errors of the point estimates of B_1 – and even more so those of A_2 – are still rather high; only table 7.7 – with r_t' and k_t as the sole explanatory variables for the savings rates s_t – shows fairly reliable B_1 – estimates.

The coefficients in terms incorporating t as an explicit variable are rather weak, and (consequently) vary in sign. This suggests that the values of γ_{as} in (5.1.3.3), even if significantly differing from zero for separate (a, s)-groups,

TABLE 7.7.

Explanation of savings' rates according to formula (7.3.1.7) by various methods

Method used	Coefficients of regression (and their standard errors) A_1	A_2	B_1	Coefficient of auto-correlation ϱ	Coefficient of correlation* R
a. *Personal savings*					
OLS	0.530	−0.19	−0.077		0.885
	(0.075)	(1.34)	(0.014)		
GLS 1	0.444	0.89	−0.063	0.661	
	(0.076)	(1.09)	(0.014)	(0.171)	
GLS 1*	0.408	1.07	−0.057	0.797	
	(0.081)	(1.06)	(0.015)	(0.164)	
GLS 2	0.422	1.27	−0.060	0.311	
	(0.079)	(1.11)	(0.014)	(0.216)	
GLS 2*	0.402	1.18	−0.056	0.112	
	(0.082)	(1.08)	(0.015)	(0.243)	
DLS	0.406	1.25	−0.053	0.797	0.962
	(0.050)	(0.83)	(0.009)	(0.164)	
b. *National savings*					
OLS	0.310	1.19	−0.031		0.402
	(0.146)	(0.97)	(0.034)		
GLS 1	0.325	0.67	−0.036	0.694	
	(0.105)	(0.84)	(0.024)	(0.145)	
GLS 1*	0.322	0.61	−0.035	0.750	
	(0.102)	(0.85)	(0.024)	(0.145)	
GLS 2	0.346	0.87	−0.042	0.312	
	(0.098)	(0.87)	(0.022)	(0.204)	
GLS 2*	0.333	0.72	−0.039	0.151	
	(0.099)	(0.86)	(0.023)	(0.239)	
DLS	0.200	1.02	−0.004	0.750	0.876
	(0.080)	(0.52)	(0.018)	(0.145)	

compensate each other to such a degree that their overall effect (through changes in the 'urgency to consume' over time) is negligible.

Conclusion (d) is not as obvious as the preceding conclusions, in view of justifiable doubts regarding the accuracy of the absolute wealth figures used; our confidence in this series, however, is reinforced by the observation that results thus obtained are nevertheless superior to those reached by leaving the 'level' of the series indeterminate.

The final conclusion of this sub-section is that the outcome according to the specification of the savings functions underlying table 7.7 is more trustworthy than that attained for alternative, more detailed specifications, presented in tables 7.3–7.6.

7.4.3. COMPARISON BETWEEN PERSONAL SAVINGS AND NATIONAL SAVINGS

Results obtained for national savings are inferior to those obtained for personal savings. This holds good for all specifications adopted, all methods applied, and in all respects, in particular with regard to the reliability of the point estimates and the goodness of fit.

This outcome might be expected, since the macro-savings model is derived from a micro-savings model developed for *private* persons and their *individual* savings.

In an absolute sense, the point estimates of both B_1 and A_1 are invariably higher for personal savings than for national savings; in this regard, no definitive conclusion may be drawn with respect to A_2.

7.4.4. COMPARISON BETWEEN ESTIMATION METHODS

Table 7.3 is confined to results obtained by OLS only, because application of more sophisticated methods would not be worthwhile here.

Tables 7.4 through 7.7, however, present the outcome of applying generalized least squares, with coefficients of autocorrelation estimated separately or jointly with the other parameters (cf. section 7.3.2), determining the transformation matrix F according to (7.3.2.1.6); these two versions are denoted without and with an asterisk, respectively. This process is carried out twice (indicated by 1 and 2, respectively), at the second stage with coefficients of autocorrelation estimated for the ε-disturbances left at first-stage GLS.

Finally, the results on the 'DLS'-lines represent the estimates of both the ordinary parameters and the coefficient of autocorrelation obtained jointly according to section 7.3.3.

One may expect that the more sophisticated methods yield better results than the less refined ones; in particular, that the standard errors of the point estimates, in an absolute (if not in a relative) sense, generally decrease along the following lines:

$$\text{OLS} \begin{cases} \nearrow & \text{GLS 1} \rightarrow \text{GLS 2} \\ \longrightarrow & \text{GLS 1*} \rightarrow \text{GLS 2*} \\ \searrow & \text{DLS} \end{cases}$$

These expectations, however, are not entirely corroborated by the results. This may be partly due to the bias in the estimates of the variances, computed as if no autocorrelation of the disturbances exists. Anyhow, the tendency of the standard errors to decrease from OLS to GLS and to DLS, as well as from GLS 1* to GLS 2* is shown more clearly in tables 7.6 and 7.7, dealing with the simpler versions of the savings function, than in the preceding tables, dealing with the more complicated ones.

In tables 7.6 and 7.7, the DLS method appears to be the best performer[2]; in the other tables, however, it does not compare as favourably with the versions of the GLS method. This should not surprise us, since the positive effect of the *additional* reduction in the number of degrees of freedom, by the simultaneous estimation of the coefficients of autocorrelation, on the parameter variances is more pronounced according as the number of ordinary parameters to be estimated is larger; this holds good in particular because of the rather small number of periods of observation (18 years), compared with the relatively large number of parameters to be estimated (ranging from 8 to 3).

The estimates of the coefficients of autocorrelation naturally decrease between the two stages of GLS. They do so more rapidly between GLS 1* and 2* than between GLS 1 and 2, especially since both the GLS 1* estimates (equalling the DLS estimates) of the ϱ are higher than the GLS 1 estimates, and the GLS 2* estimates are lower than the GLS 2 estimates.

---

[2] We like to stress that this judgement in favour of the DLS-method is *not* based – and should not be based – on the values of the coefficient of multiple correlation R – as measures of goodness of fit. True, in each table the DLS-R is higher than the OLS-R, but this difference is due to the inclusion of lagged residuals, initially estimated by OLS, as improper 'explanatory' variables into the regression equations. As explained by Koerts and Abrahamse [1970], it is dangerous to compare correlation coefficients belonging to different models, because their distributions depend on the X-matrices. At most, the coefficients of correlation reproduced give a *rough* indication of the difference in *levels* of goodness of fit between explanations of personal savings and national savings, and to what extent the 'fit' deteriorates according as variables are dropped because of multicollinearity (cf. the first paragraph of section 7.4.3 and point (c) in section 7.4.2, respectively).

This suggests that the estimates of ϱ, obtained together with the estimates of the regression coefficients are nearer the true values of ϱ than the $\hat{\varrho}$ estimated separately. On the other hand, their standard errors are higher in the latter case compared with the former one; they even increase from the first to the second stage of GLS.

After application of the Abrahamse and Koerts' [1969] improved Durbin and Watson test on coefficients of autocorrelation of the disturbances, the latter appear to differ significantly from zero (i.e. at a 95 per cent confidence level for the first stage in all tables 7.4b through 7.7a and b).

According as the probability of the null-hypothesis becomes smaller, point estimates of the regression coefficients become more reliable by passing from stage 1 to stage 2. Otherwise – as evidenced by table 7.4 – second-stage GLS-point estimates might even appear to be *less* reliable than the first-stage ditto. At the second stage, no significant autocorrelation between the disturbances appear to be left; therefore, stopping at this stage is justified in all cases.

With respect to the most important parameter A_1, the DLS-estimates are generally lower than the GLS-estimates for both personal and national savings. On the other hand, for personal savings OLS-estimates exceed GLS- (and DLS-) estimates, whereas for national savings OLS-estimates fall below GLS-estimates. In general, the lower values of A_1 seem to be more plausible than the higher ones[3].

In tables 7.5a and 7.7a for personal savings, B_1 estimates decrease in an absolute sense between OLS and GLS, and between OLS or GLS and DLS; the same applies to the B_{10}- and B_{11}-estimates in table 7.6a. For national savings, the B-estimates show a less regular pattern. For the estimates of the other parameters too, no general conclusions can be drawn as far as their variations between methods are concerned.

In section 7.4.3, the specification of the savings function underlying table 7.7 was already singled out as the one for which the most reliable results were obtained. Taking account of the preceding considerations, we now conclude that within table 7.7 the DLS-estimates appear to be the most reliable ones.

---

[3] When comparing tables, the equivalences of table 7.2 should, of course, be taken into account.

7.4.5. A GRAPHICAL REPRESENTATION OF THE 'BEST' EQUATION

Graph 7.1 depicts this 'best' explanation of s_t – represented as an uninterrupted line, by:

$$s_t^* = 0.406 + 1.25r_t' - 0.053k_t, \qquad (7.4.5.1)$$

represented as a dashed line, and taken from the DLS-row of table 7.7a.

Obviously, the savings rate s_t is affected more strongly by the wealth-income ratio k_t – in an inverse sense – than by the rate of interest – in a positive sense. Moreover, comparison of the point estimates of the parameters with their estimated standard errors shows that the impact of r_t on s_t is not only weaker, but – for related reasons – also known less accurately than the effect of k_t on s_t.

The uncertainty of the parameter estimates – for r_t, but to a lesser degree for k_t too – is partly due to a high degree of correlation between these two explanatory variables. In turn, this interrelationship is largely the result of the trend-like movements (upward for r_t, downward for k_t) displayed by these variables in the period observed; together, they give rise to the upward trend of s_t, as appears from graph 7.1.

The fact that not yet 80 per cent of the variance of s_t is explained by the joint effects of k_t and r_t is expressed by the fairly large deviations between the actual savings rates s_t and the calculated ones s_t^*. Although the trend of s_t is followed rather closely by that of s_t^* at least from 1952 onwards[4], the short-run changes of s_t^* around its trend do not correspond as well to those of s_t.

As mentioned in footnote 2 to this chapter, the fact that table 7.7a nevertheless shows a coefficient of multiple correlation of 0.962 on the DLS-line is due to the inclusion of another "explanatory" variable in the regression equation, viz. the lagged OLS-estimate of the residuals ($\hat{u}_{t-1}$), extending (7.4.5.1) to:

$$s_t^{**} = 0.406 + 1.25r_t' - 0.053k_t + 0.797\hat{u}_{t-1}. \qquad (7.4.5.2)$$

The coefficient 0.797 preceding $\hat{u}_{t-1}$ indicates a high degree of auto-correlation between successive disturbances. This appears from graph 7.1 by the

[4] The large savings 'deficit' for 1949 and 1950, already reduced in 1951 and disappeared in 1952, might be ascribed – at least partly – to post-war back-log demand; the same phenomenon was also observed in other countries, like the U.S.A. On the other hand, a Korea boom effect was hardly noticeable in the Netherlands.

relatively small numbers of intersections between the lines for s_t and for s_t^* such that $s_t - s_t^*$ changes sign only four times instead of the expected 8 or 9 times; on the other hand, $s_t^{**} - s_t$ changes sign 7 times out of 16. Furthermore, $|s_t^{**} - s_t|$ is, of course, generally smaller than $|s_t{}^* - s_t|$, meaning that s_t^{**} nestles more closely to s_t.

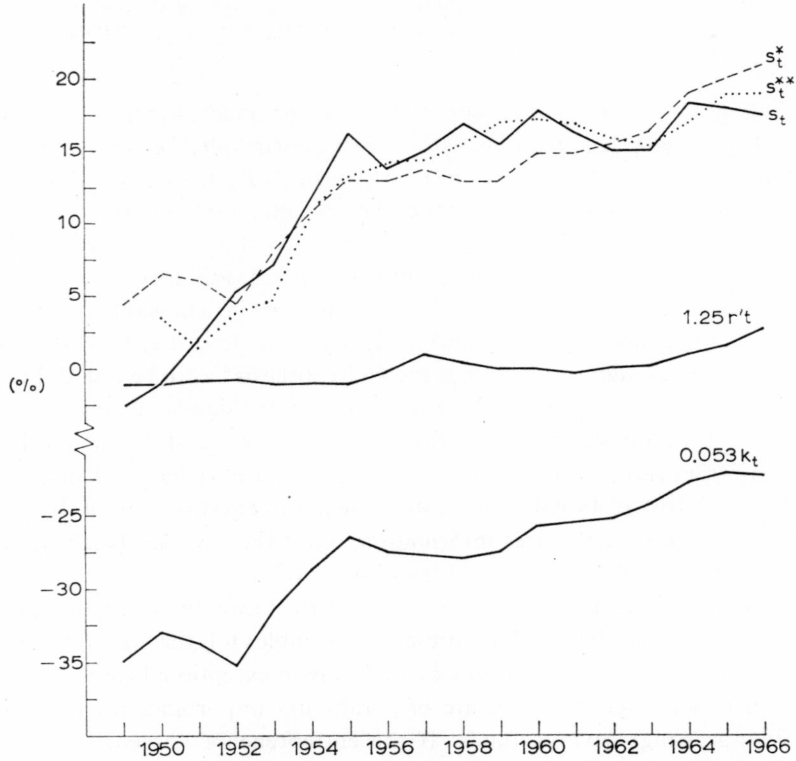

Graph 7.1. Explanation of the personal savings rate in the Netherlands, 1949–1966, according to formula $s_t = 0.406 + 1.25r_t' - 0.053k_t$ (cf. table 7.7a, DLS); s_t: observed savings rates, s_t^*: savings rate calculated according to (7.4.4.1), s_t^{**}: savings rate calculated according to (7.4.4.2).

Those who might feel distressed by the rather poor performance of the savings model *as far as savings rates are concerned* should consider that the denominators of the latter fractions already take care of the most important variable affecting savings, viz. income. The stability of the savings-income ratio – 'corrected' for the wealth- and rate of interest effects – is borne out by the relatively low value (0.050) of the standard error of the intercept, compared with its point estimate (0.406).

7.4.6. APPROXIMATION OF THE PARAMETERS OF THE MACRO-SAVINGS FUNCTION BY MEANS OF RESULTS OF THE CROSS-SECTION ANALYSIS

According to (5.1.3.14), the parameters of the macro-savings functions (5.1.3.13) can be calculated directly – at least in principle. The prerequisite is that the elements of the expressions for A_1 through D_2 are known; if we confine ourselves, however, to the condensed and favoured equation (7.3.1.7), knowledge of the elements of A_1, $\bar{A}_2$ ($= A_2 + B_2\bar{k}$) and B_1 suffices.

The reason why we did not do so in the first place is that we were not sure beforehand that the "time"-parameters would be insignificant to such an extent that they could (and should) be disregarded. It is true that we could have assumed as much a priori, but such a hypothesis has to be tested. In the case that the outcome of the test would have revealed significant autonomous effects of time on savings, i.e. values of C_1, C_2, D_1 and D_2 significantly differing from zero, the latter parameters could not have been calculated on the basis of cross-section data for a single year alone: estimation of the time-shift parameters γ_{as} requires information about the α-values (such as provided by Savings Surveys) for at least two periods.

Even for the calculation of A_1, A_2, B_1 and B_2, however, the requisite data is deficient. First, the α-values presented in tables 6.1 through 6.5 relates mainly to employees and pensioners, and only in exceptional cases to entrepreneurs – although the latter are of paramount importance for providing (or withdrawing) savings funds. If the entrepreneurs' 'urgencies to consume' deviate from those of the employees, it would presumably be downwards rather than upwards. Second, we are incompletely informed about the shares of the age–sex groups in total personal wealth of the Netherlands, because of the relatieely high exemption limits granted by the property tax law: since the distribution of wealth statistics are based on tax reports, they are confined to the less than 10 per cent income recipients completing such reports. As the percentage coverage increases with age, at least up to 65 years, the wealth shares of the lower age-classes tend to be underestimated on the basis of registered personal wealth data. On the other hand, the bias is limited, because the greater part of personal wealth is owned by the minority represented in the pertinent statistics. Therefore, we took the latter's share in personal wealth, for lack of something better.

Third, the calculation of A_1 and A_2 requires that assumptions are made about the factors $y_{asl} = \bar{\varepsilon} y_{l|as} y_{as}$ such that they can be computed by means of published data. Since the statistics on the distribution of income distinguish income recipients according to age (a), sex (s) and occupation (b), we write:

$$\begin{aligned} Y_{astl}/Y_{ast} &= \bar{\varepsilon} \sum_b Y_{bastl}/Y_{ast} \\ &= \bar{\varepsilon} y_{as}^{-1} \sum_b y_{bas,t} \cdot \hat{Y}_{l,bas,t}, \end{aligned} \tag{7.4.6.1}$$

with

$$y_{bas,t} = (Y_{bast}/Y_{ast})(Y_{ast}/Y_t) = (Y_{bast}/Y_{ast})\, y_{as}, \quad \text{by virtue of (5.1.3.4),}$$

and

$$\hat{Y}_{l,bas,t} = Y_{b,a+l,s,t}/Y_{bast}, \quad \text{while } Y_{b,a+l,st} = Y_{bastl}.$$

Because of shifts in the labour force from independent towards dependent employment, and from manual towards non-manual work, the $y_{bas,t}$ too will show changes over time; probably, these will be larger than variations in the income ratios $\hat{Y}_{l|bas,t}$. Still, the sum of products of these ratios with the corresponding weights may be nearly constant, provided that systematic relationships between the size of the ratios and the movements of the weights (upwards or downwards) are absent. Since the latter presumption seems reasonable, we feel justified in calculating the third member of (7.4.6.1) for any period t_0 for which the data is available; the particular choice of the period will not make much difference, according to assumption (5.1.3.5).

Hence, we state:

$$Y_{astl}/Y_{ast} \approx \bar{\varepsilon} y_{as}^{-1} \sum_b y_{bas,t_0} \hat{Y}_{l|bas,t_0}. \tag{7.4.6.2}$$

In order to minimize the deviations in general, we take $t_0 = 1959$, i.e. near the middle of the reference period 1949–1966; moreover, it is close to 1960, for which the corresponding α's were calculated.

The most difficult problem remaining is the valuation of $\bar{\varepsilon}$. According to section 4.2.3, the elasticities of income expectation would have to assume highly unlikely values of $\bar{\varepsilon}$, i.e. exceeding 1, in order to yield acceptable values of the marginal propensity to consume. On the other hand, section 6.6.2.1

showed that the α-values presented there are almost double the reciprocals of life expectancy, adopted in chapter 4 as provisional approximations of α_1.

Therefore, we conclude that presumably $\bar{\varepsilon}$ lies somewhere between $\frac{1}{2}$ and 1. Since any attempt at a narrower limitation of $\bar{\varepsilon}$ is bound to be spurious, we experiment with both supposedly extreme values, viz.:

$$\bar{\varepsilon} = 1 \tag{7.4.6.3a}$$

and

$$\bar{\varepsilon} = 0.5. \tag{7.4.6.3b}$$

In view of such uncertainty, there does not seem much risk involved in fixing:

$$d_{as} = 1 \quad \text{for all } a, s, \tag{7.4.6.4}$$

i.e. at the value around which it ripples, as a corrective multiplier of the normal discount factors $(1 + \bar{r})^{-l}$.

Then, by virtue of (7.4.6.1), (7.4.6.2) and (7.4.6.4), we can calculate:

$$A_1 = 1 - \bar{\varepsilon} \sum_{a,s} \bar{\alpha}_{as} \sum_{b} \mu_{bas} \cdot y_{bas,t_0}, \tag{7.4.6.5}$$

with $\bar{\varepsilon}$ assuming values according to either (7.4.6.3a) or (7.4.6.3b), and

$$\mu_{bas,t_0} = \sum_{l=1}^{L_{as}} \hat{Y}_{l-1|bas,t_0} (1 + \bar{r})^{1-l} \quad (t_0 = 1959)$$

where $\hat{Y}_0|_{bas,t_0} \stackrel{\text{def}}{=} 1$, and $\gamma_{as} = 0$ for all a, s.

The other coefficients can be calculated as follows:

$$A_2 = 1 - \bar{\alpha}_0 - A_1 \tag{7.4.6.6}$$

$$B_1 = - \sum_{a,s} \bar{\alpha}_{as} k_{as} (1 + \bar{r})^{1-L_{as}} \tag{7.4.6.7}$$

$$B_2 = \sum_{a,s} \bar{\alpha}_{as} k_{as} (L_{as} - 1)(1 + \bar{r})^{1-L_{as}} \tag{7.4.6.8}$$

$$\bar{A}_2 = A_2 + B_2 \bar{k} \quad \text{(cf. table 7.2).} \tag{7.4.6.9}$$

The values of the parameters thus calculated are reproduced in table 7.8, under the heading 'C.S.' (meaning: based on results of the cross-section analysis), with I and II relating to the alternatives $\bar{\varepsilon} = 1$ and 0.5, respectively. For the sake of comparison, we reproduced the estimates of the time-series analysis in the same table, under the heading "T.S.".

The signs of the coefficients appear to be the same according to both methods of valuation, and for both values of $\bar{\varepsilon}$. For the rest, the three columns of parameter values show wide discrepancies. The A_1-values differ most between C.S.-II and C.S.-I, with the T.S.-estimate being closer to the former than to the latter alternative value. Thus, the A_1-estimate appears to be extremely sensitive with respect to the value of $\bar{\varepsilon}$ adopted. In an absolute sense, $\bar{A}_2$ is as subject to variations in $\bar{\varepsilon}$ as A_1, but in the opposite direction, and less so in a relative sense. A fortiori, this applies to $\bar{A}_2$, the coefficient of the interest rate, because B_2 – like B_1 – is independent of $\bar{\varepsilon}$. This means that the $\bar{A}_2$ value according to C.S.-II is still much larger than its T.S.-counterpart, though less than the C.S.-I value.

B_2, the wealth coefficient is the only one whose order of magnitude is the same for the C.S.-valuation and the T.S.-estimation, taking account of its variance.

The set of C.S.-I parameters is inacceptable because they imply savings rates that on the average lie 0.28 below the corresponding observed rates. This means that over the reference period 1949–1966 all savings rates cal-

TABLE 7.8.

Parameter values for the macro-savings function (7.3.1.7) calculated according to (7.4.6.5) through (7.4.6.9) on the basis of results of the cross-section analysis (C.S.) and estimated in time-series analysis (T.S.), respectively

parameter	C.S.		T.S.
	I $\bar{\varepsilon} = 1$	II $\bar{\varepsilon} = 0.5$	point estimates
A_1	0.080	0.540	0.406
A_2	0.852	0.392	
B_1	−0.044		−0.053
B_2	0.502		
$\bar{A}_2$	3.50	3.04	1.25

Sources:

C.S.:
- α_{as} averaged from tables 6.1 through 6.5,
- μ_{bas} from table 6C.1,
- y_{bas} from table 14 } Central Bureau of
- k_{as} from table 11 } Statistics [1963],

T.S.: table 7.7a (line DLS).

culated on that basis are negative, whereas all but the first two of the observed rates are positive. Contrariwise, the savings rates based on the C.S.-II parameter values lie around 0.09 *above* both the observed rates and the rates based on T.S. parameter estimates: whatever the defects of the latter might be, at least they ensure a correct level of theoretical savings rates based thereon.

This raises the question as to what level of $\bar{\varepsilon}$ would likewise ensure that theoretical savings rates are 'on the level' with the observed ones; the answer is the solution of the equation:

$$(1 - \bar{\varepsilon}^*)(1 - 0.080) = 0.280,$$

with 0.080 the value of A_1 for $\bar{\varepsilon} = 1$ and 0.280 the downward bias of theoretical savings rates according to C.S.-I, yielding

$$\bar{\varepsilon}^* = 0.70.$$

The latter value is near the centre of the range ($\frac{1}{2}$, 1), considered as a priori acceptable. Consequently, the corresponding values $A_1^* = 0.35$ and $\bar{A}_2^* = 3.23$ are almost halfway between the C.S.-I and C.S.-II extremes. Anyhow, it is gratifying that the T.S. point estimate of A_1 is approximated more closely by the new A_1^*-value than by either its C.S.-II or (a fortiori) its C.S.-I value; accordingly, the in-between set of values assigned to the parameters results in a better performance of the macro-savings model than the alternative C.S.-I and C.S.-II sets, and not much worse than the still superior T.S.-estimates.

It should be noted that, as regards the intensity of the fluctuations of the theoretical savings rates, the lower absolute value of B_1 and the higher value of $\bar{A}_2$ obtained as C.S.-values – compared with T.S.-estimates – compensate each other to a certain degree. Consequently, the success of the C.S.-valuation of the parameters of the macro-savings model appears to depend mainly on the appropriate assessment of $\bar{\varepsilon}$; unfortunately, however, such a choice cannot be made a priori unless we have quantitative empirical information about people's expectational attitudes.

Apart from this, the results of the C.S.-valuations may be impaired by mis-estimations of $\bar{\alpha}_{as}$ and/or μ_{as}; in contradistinction to $\bar{\varepsilon}$ and the μ_{as}, possible errors in the α_{as} affect not only A_1 and A_2, but also B_1 and B_2.

The $\bar{\alpha}_{as}$ obtained in the cross-section analysis may have been over-estimated because of the virtual exclusion of entrepreneurs, with presumably lower values of α_1. However, the effect of this possible bias on A_1 and $\bar{A}_2$ is certainly less than an error in the numerical specification of $\bar{\varepsilon}$. This also applies to possible over-estimation of μ, due to neglecting differential effects of income tax, reducing gross income to disposable income; or, the subjective rate of interest may have exceeded the official one adopted for our calculations.

7.4.7. IMPLICATIONS FOR INCOME AND WEALTH EFFECTS

According to (7.3.1.7), the marginal propensity to consume equals:

$$\frac{\partial S_t^*}{\partial Y_t} = 1 - \frac{\partial C_t^*}{\partial Y_t} = A_1 + A_2 r_t'. \qquad (7.4.7.1)$$

Table 7.9 presents its values for the best numerical specifications based on cross-section analysis and obtained in time-series analysis, respectively. Because of its higher coefficient for the rate of interest, the range of marginal

TABLE 7.9.

Marginal propensities to save, based on the 'best' results of cross-section and time-series analyses

Kind of value	Value		Reached in
	Cross-section ($\varepsilon = 0.70$)	Time-series	
Minimum	0.32	0.40	1949
Maximum	0.42	0.44	1966
Average	0.35	0.41	1960

propensities to save (or to consume) appears to be higher for the C.S.-specification than for the T.S.-estimation.

Nevertheless, the C.S.-values always stay below the corresponding T.S.-values, with extremes reached simultaneously.

The lower C.S.-value – compared with the T.S.-value – for the marginal rate of savings still exceeds most of the pertinent values found in other empirical analyses. However, this is usually due to the neglect of the (reducing) effect of wealth on savings. For the same reason, the average savings rate:

$$\tfrac{1}{18} \sum_{t=1949}^{1966} (S_{pt}/Y_{pt}) = 0.12$$

underbids the marginal rate by values varying from $0.044k_t$ to $0.053k_t$, or between 0.24 and 0.28 on the average.

Indeed, the effect of personal wealth on savings and consumption according to (7.3.1.7) equals:

$$\frac{\partial S_t}{\partial K_t} = -\frac{\partial C_t}{\partial K_t} = B_1, \tag{7.4.7.2}$$

with values vacillating between -0.044 and -0.053 according to the C.S. and T.S. specifications respectively.

Comparing mean effects of income with those of personal wealth on consumption, we find:

$$\left|\frac{\partial C_t}{\partial Y_t}\bigg/\frac{\partial C_t}{\partial K_t}\right| = -(1 - A_1)/B_1$$

$$= \bar{\varepsilon}\, \frac{\sum_{a,s} \bar{\alpha}_{as} \sum_b \mu_{bas} y_{bas}}{\sum_{a,s} \bar{\alpha}_{as} k_{as} (1 + \bar{r})^{1-L_{as}}} \tag{7.4.7.3}$$

(by virtue of (7.4.6.5) and (7.4.6.7))

$$= \bar{\varepsilon}\bar{\bar{\mu}} w_{y/k} (1 + \bar{r})^{\bar{\bar{L}}-1},$$

with

$$\bar{\bar{\mu}} = \frac{\sum_{a,s} \bar{\alpha}_{as} y_{as} \bar{\mu}_{as}}{\sum_{a,s} \bar{\alpha}_{as} y_{as}}, \quad \text{where } \bar{\mu}_{as} = \sum_b \mu_{bas} y_{bas}/y_{as},$$

$$w_{y/k} = \frac{\sum_{a,s} \bar{\alpha}_{as} y_{as}}{\sum_{a,s} \bar{\alpha}_{as} k_{as}},$$

and

$$(1 + \bar{r})^{\bar{\bar{L}}-1} = \frac{\sum_{a,s} \bar{\alpha}_{as} k_{as}}{\sum_{a,s} \bar{\alpha}_{as} k_{as} (1 + \bar{r})^{1-L_{as}}}.$$

While $\bar{\mu}_{as}$ denote mean age–sex specific income capitalization factors (averaged over occupations b), $\bar{\bar{\mu}}$ may be interpreted as an overall mean income capitalization factor; $w_{y/k}$ represents a change-in-weights correction factor, affected by variations in the ratios y_{as}/k_{as} of income-to-wealth shares between age–sex groups; finally, $(1 + \bar{r})^{\bar{\bar{L}}-1}$ is a weighted harmonic mean of the $(1 + \bar{r})^{L_{as}}$, implying $\bar{\bar{L}}$ as a 'powered' harmonic mean of the L_{as}.

This macro-effects ratio is more complicated than its micro-economic counterpart:

$$\frac{\partial C_1}{\partial Y_1} \bigg/ \frac{\partial C_1}{\partial K_0} = (1 + r)^{L-1} \tag{7.4.7.4}$$

implied by (4.2.3.3) and (4.2.4.1): in contradistinction to the latter, (7.4.4.3) takes account of 'halo' effects of changes in current income on expected future income, acting upon capitalization factors (μ_{as}) through the diffusing elasticities of income expectation ($\bar{\varepsilon}$). Differences in income and wealth patterns according to occupation and sex contribute to the complexity of the expressions, especially through the change-in-weight correction factors $w_{y/k}$.

With the C.S.-values of A_1 and B_1 corresponding to $\bar{\varepsilon} = 0.70$, we find 14.7 for the income-to-wealth effects ratio; it is the product of $\bar{\varepsilon} = 0.70$, $\bar{\bar{\mu}} = 13.5$, $w_{y/k} = 0.72$ and $(1 + \bar{r})^{\bar{\bar{L}}-1} = 2.14$, yielding $\bar{\bar{L}} = 20$ for $\bar{r} = 0.0408$.

In order of magnitude, that value of $\bar{\bar{\mu}}$ corresponds to the values of the μ_{bas} attained at ages between 45 and 50 years, as shown in table 6C.1. The value of $\bar{\bar{L}}$ agrees with the life expectancy of men around the age 55. The former, and a fortiori the latter ages seem rather high with regard to the 'average' income recipient; one should take into account, however, that they result from the application of weights $\bar{\alpha}_{as}y_{as}$ and $\bar{\alpha}_{as}k_{as}$, increasing with rising age, because all their components do so. Since this applies to the wealth shares k_{as} more strongly than to the income shares y_{as}, the age corresponding to $\bar{\bar{L}}$ is even higher than that to which $\bar{\bar{\mu}}$ relates; it also finds expression in the value of the change-in-weights correction factor $w_{y/k}$, being considerably below par.

On the other hand, the T.S. parameter estimates imply a somewhat lower value of the income-to-wealth effects ratio. Retaining the values of $\bar{\bar{\mu}}$ and $\bar{\bar{L}}$ just mentioned, the latter ratio requires an $\bar{\varepsilon}$ of 0.54 – still within the feasible region, albeit near its lower bound. One may only conjecture that the 'real' effects ratio is somewhere between 14.7 and 11.3; it may result from revisions of $\bar{\bar{\mu}}$ and/or $\bar{\bar{L}}$, but probably entails variations in $\bar{\varepsilon}$ as well.

Anyhow, such a difference implies that the "true" values of A_1 and B_1 differ from the T.S. point estimates and/or the C.S.-valuations. In particular, one should never lose sight of the stochastic nature of both the latter and the former, in addition to possible bias. In view of the variances of the α's underlying the C.S.-valuations and those of the T.S. point estimates, the two sets of parameter values do not differ significantly at a probability level of (say) 95 per cent. This accords a clean bill of health to the foundation of the empirical macro-savings function (7.3.1.7) on the micro-theory developed in chapter 4.

7.4.8. MAIN CONCLUSIONS

(1) Results obtained for the more condensed versions of the savings model, particularly those presented in table 7.7, are more reliable than those presented in the more extensively specified models;
(2) the point estimates for the intercept and the coefficients for the rate of interest have the expected positive sign, and the coefficients for the capital-income ratio have the expected negative sign, while all assume acceptable orders of magnitude, at least for the condensed version of the savings function underlying table 7.7;
(3) more reliable results are obtained for personal savings than for national savings;
(4) results obtained by means of the DLS-method appear to be superior to those obtained by means of other methods;
(5) parameters of the macro-savings function can also be calculated by means of results of the micro cross-section analysis such that the observed savings rates are approximated reasonably well; its prerequisite is fixation of the elasticity of income expectation at about 0.70.

APPENDIX A TO CHAPTER 7

TABLE 7 A.1.

Basic data underlying the savings model for the Netherlands, 1949–1966

Year	Savings		Disposable Income		Wealth[1]		Price Index[2] Number	Average yield of Gov't Bonds
	Private	National	Private	National	Private	National		
	S_{pt}	S_{nt}	Y_{pt}	Y_{nt}	K_{pt}	K_{nt}	P_t	r_t
	× 10^6 guilders				× 10^9 guilders		(1966 = 100)	percent per annum
1949	−283	1.714	11.301	15.432	74.8	69.1	49.7	3.19
1950	−125	1.996	12.667	17.168	78.7	74.8	52.5	3.19
1951	300	2.813	14.179	19.461	90.1	87.7	60.2	3.49
1952	786	3.263	14.765	20.285	98.4	98.4	65.5	3.47
1953	1.148	3.809	16.140	21.800	95.5	97.9	63.1	3.23
1954	2.149	4.428	18.418	24.516	99.8	104.6	65.0	3.25
1955	3.429	5.479	21.147	27.528	106.2	113.3	67.7	3.26
1956	3.109	5.111	22.655	29.587	117.5	127.6	72.7	3.93
1957	3.653	6.036	24.303	32.040	127.7	140.1	77.1	4.82
1958	4.268	6.150	25.310	32.407	133.1	148.0	78.2	4.38
1959	4.055	7.256	26.302	34.735	137.1	154.0	78.2	4.18
1960	5.248	8.823	29.417	38.823	143.0	163.1	79.2	4.18
1961	5.055	8.606	31.100	41.082	149.9	173.8	80.2	3.91
1962	5.032	8.327	33.401	43.972	158.5	186.4	82.1	4.18
1963	5.598	8.284	37.121	47.918	170.2	202.6	85.6	4.21
1964	7.979	11.228	43.633	56.695	186.8	223.9	91.1	4.99
1965	8.721	12.250	48.591	63.130	202.5	244.5	94.9	5.36
1966	9.275	12.990	52.725	68.620	222.1	260.8	100.0	6.35

[1] $K_{p,1958}$ and $K_{n,1958}$ have been estimated, the other figures were derived by adding or subtracting savings to these bench-marks.
[2] of investment goods.

APPENDIX B TO CHAPTER 7

INVARIANCE OF THE DETERMINANT OF A MOMENT MATRIX OF BASIC VARIABLES AND THEIR PRODUCTS AGAINST SHIFTING OF THE FORMER ONES, WITH THE LATTER ONES BECOMING PRODUCTS OF THE TRANSFORMED BASIC VARIABLES

Suppose the X-matrix of explanatory variables is specified by

$$X = [\iota \quad x_1 \quad x_2 \quad x_3],^1 \tag{7B.1}$$

ι, x_1, x_2 and x_3 being column vectors of length T, with

$$x_3 = \dot{x}_1 x_2 = \dot{x}_2 x_1$$

(in scalar notation: $x_{3t} = x_{1t}x_{2t}$; $t = 1, \ldots, T$) and $\dot{x}_1$, $\dot{x}_2$ denoting the diagonal matrices with the elements of x_1 and x_2 on the main diagonal.

Then, the determinant of the moment matrix becomes:

$$|X'X| = \begin{vmatrix} \iota'\iota & \iota'x_1 & \iota'x_2 & \iota'x_3 \\ x_1'\iota & x_1'x_1 & x_1'x_2 & x_1'x_3 \\ x_2'\iota & x_2'x_1 & x_2'x_2 & x_2'x_3 \\ x_3'\iota & x_3'x_1 & x_3'x_2 & x_3'x_3 \end{vmatrix}. \tag{7B.2}$$

Suppose now that the basic variables x_1 and x_2 are replaced by shifted variables z_1 and z_2 such that:

$$z_i = x_i - d_i\iota \quad \text{for } i = 1, 2, \tag{7B.3}$$

with d_i arbitrary constants.

---

1 The number of basic variables may be enlarged to 3 or more, and the number of composite variables may be likewise increased, without entailing any essential change in the proof.

Suppose further that the composite variable x_3 is replaced by $\mathring{z}_3$, such that:

$$\mathring{z}_3 = \dot{z}_1 z_2 = \dot{z}_2 z_1 . \tag{7B.4}$$

Then, we can prove that:

$$|Z'Z| = \begin{vmatrix} \iota'\iota & \iota' z_1 & \iota' z_2 & \iota'\mathring{z}_3 \\ z_1'\iota & z_1' z_1 & z_1' z_2 & z_1'\mathring{z}_3 \\ z_2'\iota & z_2' z_1 & z_2' z_2 & z_2'\mathring{z}_3 \\ \mathring{z}_3'\iota & \mathring{z}_3' z_1 & \mathring{z}_3' z_2 & \mathring{z}_3'\mathring{z}_3 \end{vmatrix} = |X'X| . \tag{7B.5}$$

Proof. The following sequence of operations transforms $|X'X|$ into $|Z'Z|$:

(a) Subtracting of d_1 and d_2 times the first row from the second and third row of the determinant at the right-hand side of (7B.2) results in $\{z_i'\iota \quad z_i'x_1 \quad z_i'x_2 \quad z_i'x_3\}$ for $i = 2, 3$, respectively, leaving the first and fourth rows unchanged.

(b) Adding $d_1 d_2$ times the first row, and subtracting d_2 times the second row plus d_1 times the third row of that determinant from its fourth row, becoming $\{\mathring{z}_3'\iota \quad \mathring{z}_3'x_1 \quad \mathring{z}_3'x_2 \quad \mathring{z}_3'x_3\}$, with the other rows remaining the same as left after the application of (a).

(c) Subsequent analogous application of (a) and (b) to columns instead of to rows results in the determinant expression of the middle member of (7B.5).

In particular, if $\bar{x}_1$ and $\bar{x}_2$ are considered as the new zero points of z_1 and z_2, i.e. if $\bar{x}_i = d_i$ and $\iota' z_i = 0$ for $i = 1, 2$, we obtain:

$$|Z'Z| = \begin{vmatrix} \iota'\iota & 0 & 0 & \iota'\mathring{z}_3 \\ 0 & z_1' z_1 & z_1' z_2 & z_1'\mathring{z}_3 \\ 0 & z_2' z_1 & z_2' z_2 & z_2'\mathring{z}_3 \\ \mathring{z}_3'\iota & \mathring{z}_3' z_1 & \mathring{z}_3' z_2 & \mathring{z}_3'\mathring{z}_3 \end{vmatrix}$$

$$= T \begin{vmatrix} z_1' z_1 & z_1' z_2 & z_1'\mathring{z}_3 \\ z_2' z_1 & z_2' z_2 & z_2'\mathring{z}_3 \\ \mathring{z}_3' z_1 & \mathring{z}_3' z_2 & \mathring{z}_3'\mathring{z}_3 \end{vmatrix} \tag{7B.6}$$

after subtraction of $\mathring{z}_3$ times the first row and the first column from the fourth row and from the fourth column, respectively.

CHAPTER 8

EFFECTS OF BIOLOGICAL AND DEMOGRAPHIC FACTORS ON SAVINGS IN THE NETHERLANDS AND IN MEXICO

8.1. Effects of extending life expectancy on individual savings in the Netherlands

In section 3.7.3.2 we examined effects of changes in life expectancy and in the time-pattern of survival rates on savings by means of a continuous model, i.e. purely theoretically. For practical purposes, however, and in particular for evaluating the effect of extending life expectancy by one period, i.e. from L to $L+1$, we revert to the discrete savings model (4.1.3.5), applied in chapter 6; in the present context, it yields a difference in savings equalling:

$$S_1^+ - S_1 = (\alpha_1 - \alpha_1^+) \sum_{l=1}^{L} Y_l (1 + r)^{1-l} - \alpha_1^+ Y_{L+1}^+ (1 + r)^{-L}$$
$$+ \{\alpha_1 (1 + r) - \alpha_1^+\} (K_0 - K_{L(+1)}) (1 + r)^{-L}; \quad (8.1.1)$$

for simplicity's sake, i-subscripts are deleted, while $^+$ superscripts denote variables and parameters in the case where L is replaced by $L+1$, and we assume that $K_{L+1} = K_L$ and $Y_l^+ = Y_l$ for $l = 1, \ldots, L$.

Presumably, the net effect of the three terms at the right-hand side of (8.1.1) is positive. In particular, if

$$L\alpha_1 \approx (L + 1)\, \alpha_1^+ \quad \text{(in view of } \sum_{l=1}^{L} \alpha_1 = \sum_{l=1}^{L+1} \alpha_1^+ = 1) \qquad (8.1.2)$$

and

$$Y_{L+1}^+ = K_{L(+1)} = 0, \qquad (8.1.3)$$

(8.1.1) is reduced to:

$$\Delta s_1 \approx \alpha_1 [\underbrace{(L + 1)^{-1} \mu}_{\text{I}} + \underbrace{\{(L + 1)^{-1} + r\} kv}_{\text{II}}], \qquad (8.1.4)$$

with

$\Delta s_1 = (S_1^+ - S_1)/Y_1$ as the change in the savings rate,

$k = K_0/Y_1$ as the wealth-income ratio,

$\mu = \sum_{l=1}^{L} (Y_l/Y_1)(1 + r)^{1-l}$ as the income capitalization factor,

and

$\nu = (1 + r)^{-L}$ as the 'final' discount factor.

According to (8.1.4), Δs_1, hence $S_1^+ - S_1$ is always positive.

By means of (8.1.4) we tried to approximate the effects of increasing life expectancies (by one year) on savings rates per age-class in the Netherlands; unfortunately, a further distinction of the α_1 by sex and marital status was impracticable, because of lack of pertinent data for computing other elements of Δs_1 (and s_1 itself) in such detail. Contrariwise, it required averaging of factors, such as those constituting $\bar{\alpha}_1$, $\bar{L}$ and $\bar{\mu}$ over their classifications by marital status, sex and/or occupational status (cf. table 8.1).

Table 8.1 shows that Δs_1 is not only positive (as implied by (8.1.4)), but that it also increases with advancing age, hence declining life expectancy, excepting the lowest age class. This phenomenon results mainly from the fact that wealth-income ratios k happen to increase with age; the reducing effect of ageing on L, hence on ν, as well as its tendency to raise α_1, is checked – at least partly – by declining values of μ. Thus, at lower ages, Δs_1 is determined largely by μ, with k playing a subordinate rôle, while at higher ages k gains importance – in addition to α_1, of course –; this effect is reinforced since ν increases (just as μ decreases) with age.

This development of changes in savings rates with advancing age is depicted in graph 8.1; here, the Δs_1 are proportional to the areas of the bars for each age-class. The bases of these rectangles are proportional to the α's, and the heights are proportional to the sum of $(L+1)^{-1}\mu$ (for part I) and $\{(L + 1)^{-1} + r\}\, k\nu$ (for part II).

With increasing age, the α's, of course, increase; $(L+1)^{-1}\mu$ decreases first rapidly, and later on more slowly from the lowest age-class (< 25 years) till the age-class of 45–54 years; from here on, the increase accelerates rapidly. $\{(L + 1)^{-1} + r\}\, k\nu$, on the other hand, appears to increase monotonically and forcefully with advancing age, since its three multiplicative components

TABLE 8.1.

Approximate effects of increasing life expectancies by one year on savings rates, in addition to its components according to equation (8.1.4), for income recipients (excluding independent workers) in the Netherlands, around 1960

Variables and parameters			Age-classes with approximate mean age in years					
Symbol	Meaning	Unit of measurement	<25	25–34	35–44	45–54	55–64	≥65
			20	30	40	50	60	75
$\overline{L}$	mean life expectancy	year	55	46	36	27	19	9
$\overline{\alpha}_1$	mean current urgency to consume	10^3 year^{-1}	25.5	40.2	56.3	70.4	95.2	125.4
$\overline{\mu}$	mean income capitalization factor	year	63.4	24.6	17.4	12.6	10.0	7.6
$\overline{\nu}$	discount factor	1	0.111	0.159	0.237	0.340	0.468	0.698
$\overline{r}$	rate of interest	% p.a.	←		4.08			→
$\overline{k}$	wealth-income ratio	year	0.325	0.802	1.121	1.516	1.509	7.53
Δs_1	change in savings rate due to increasing L by 1 year	%	2.89	2.14	2.75	3.45	5.37	18.8
s_1	savings rate	%	3.3	11.2	12.6	11.4	14.6	14.2
$\dfrac{\Delta s_1}{s_1}$	relative change in savings rate	1	0.88	0.19	0.22	0.30	0.37	1.32

Sources and ways of computation:

$\bar{L}$ mean life expectancies of men and women in the Netherlands, around 1960, according to C.B.S. [1967] text table 9, as unweighted averages of the figures for men and women, relating to 1956–1960 and 1961–1965, at mean ages;

$\bar{\alpha}_1$ means of average α's for people classified by sex and marital status, weighted by their frequencies for the Netherlands in 1960 as presented in C.B.S. [1964] text table 1, per age class;

$\bar{\mu} =$ means of income capitalization factors presented by Bannink a.o. [1966] text table 9, weighted by numbers of income recipients in 1958 classified by sex and socio-economic groups, presented by Somermeyer [1965] text table 9a, and subsequently interpolated geometrically, in order to derive approximate mean income capitalization factors relating to ages 20, 30, 40 etc. from those relating to ages 15, 25, 35, 45 etc. as centres of age classes <21, 21–29, 30–39, 40–49 etc.;

$\bar{\nu} = (1 + r)^{-L}$ discount factor;

$\bar{r}$ mean yield of 8 principal Government bonds in the Netherlands over 1960, as used by Bannink a.o. [1966];

$\bar{k}$ ratio of total personal wealth to total disposable income, derived from C.B.S. [1964] text tables 13A and 5A respectively, per age class;

Δs_1 calculated by means of $\bar{\alpha}_1$, $\bar{L}$, $\bar{\mu}$, ν, $\bar{r}$ and $\bar{k}$, according to formula (8.1.4.), per age class;

s_1 ratio of total savings to total disposable income derived from C.B.S. [1964] text table 5A, lines 3 and 1 respectively.

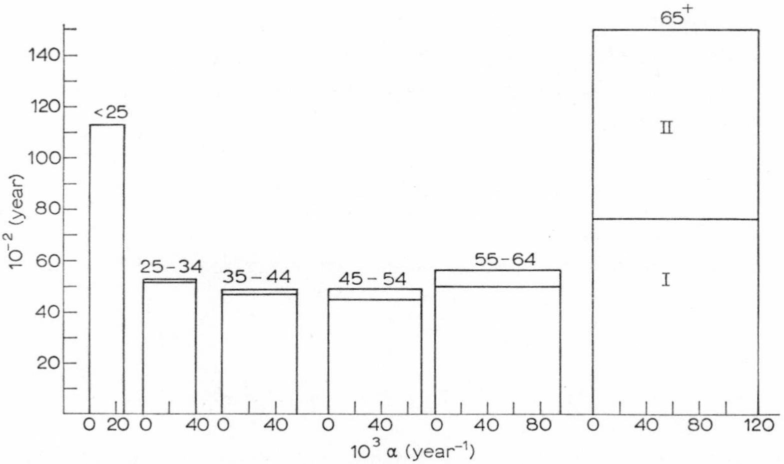

Graph 8.1. Effect of extending life expectancy by one year on the savings rates in the Netherlands, per age-class.

increase in that direction. Therefore, II evolves from a negligible component (for <25 years) to one that is of about equal importance as I (for 65$^+$ years).

With increasing age, I and II together first decline in height till a minimum is reached, again for the 'middle-age'-class 45–54, after which an increase sets in, even more pronounced than shown by I alone.

Savings rates themselves also appear to increase monotonically with age (although older people could afford to dissave). Since changes in savings rates due to a rise in life expectancies generally appear to increase more rapidly than savings rates themselves, the more so according as the age is higher, relative changes in savings rates too are increasing functions of age – again with the exception of the lowest age class.

8.2. Effects of variations in the composition of the population on aggregate savings rates

In order to illustrate the possible impact of population changes on savings, we tried to approximate differences in savings rates between Mexico and the Netherlands as far as they may be attributed to mutual differences in age distribution and in life expectancies only. This means that for such a comparison all other factors (in particular, those of an economic nature) are assigned the same values to both countries, viz. those relating to the Netherlands.

In order to render possible or facilitate the use of (5.1.2.2) for evaluating the impact of population changes on savings, we make the following simplifying assumptions:

$$K_{as,L_{as}} = 0 \tag{8.2.1}$$

$$\bar{r}_{as} = \bar{r}. \tag{8.2.2}$$

Then, for period $t = 1$ overall savings are expressed by:

$$\begin{aligned} S_1 &= \sum_a \sum_{s=m,v} S_{as,1} \\ &\approx \sum_a \sum_s \{(1 - \bar{\alpha}_{as}\mu_{as})\, Y_{as1} - \bar{\alpha}_{as} K_{as,0} \nu_{as}\}, \end{aligned} \tag{8.2.3}$$

with $\mu_{as} = \sum_{l=1}^{L_{as}} y_{asl}\,(1 + \bar{r})^{1-l}$ as the age-sex specific income capitalization factors, and $\nu_{as} = (1 + r)^{1-L_{as}}$ the 'final' discount factors.

As for the application of the micro-model, the macro-savings function

(8.2.3) is rewritten in terms of ratios[1] and the distinction according to sex is dropped, entailing the use of averages for males and females together[2]. Thus, the difference in all-over savings rates between Mexico and the Netherlands attributable to demographic differences only can be approximated by:

$$\bar{s}^*_{\mathrm{M}} - \bar{s}_{\mathrm{N}} \approx \sum_a [f_{a,\mathrm{M}} \{1 - \bar{\alpha}_{a,\mathrm{M}}\bar{\mu}^*_{a,\mathrm{M}} - \bar{\alpha}_{a,\mathrm{M}}\bar{k}_{a,\mathrm{N}} (1 + \bar{r}_{\mathrm{N}})\, \bar{v}_{a,\mathrm{M}}\}$$
$$- f_{a,\mathrm{N}} \{1 - \bar{\alpha}_{a,\mathrm{N}}\bar{\mu}_{a,\mathrm{N}} - \bar{\alpha}_{a,\mathrm{N}}\bar{k}_{a,\mathrm{N}} (1 + \bar{r}_{\mathrm{N}})\, \bar{v}_{a,\mathrm{N}}\}]\, (\bar{Y}_a/\bar{Y})_{\mathrm{N}}, \qquad (8.2.4)$$

with subscripts M and N denoting Mexico and the Netherlands respectively, $f_{a,\mathrm{M}}$ and $f_{a,\mathrm{N}}$ fractions of these countries' income recipients (excluding independent workers) belonging to age classes a (<25 through 65^+), and $(\bar{Y}_a/\bar{Y})_{\mathrm{N}}$ the ratios of mean income in age classes to overall mean income per income recipient in the Netherlands.

For the Netherlands, most of the figures required for applying (8.2.4) – i.e. with the exception of $f_{a,\mathrm{N}}$ and $(\bar{Y}_a/\bar{Y})_{\mathrm{N}}$ – could be taken from table 8.1. For Mexico, the corresponding figures together with $f_{a,\mathrm{M}}$, $f_{a,\mathrm{N}}$, $(\bar{Y}_a/\bar{Y})_{\mathrm{N}}$, and the resulting differences in age-specific and over-all savings ratios $\bar{s}^*_{a,\mathrm{M}} - \bar{s}_{a,\mathrm{N}}$ and $\bar{s}^*_{\mathrm{M}} - \bar{s}_{\mathrm{N}}$ are presented in table 8.2.

Evidently – as explained underneath table 8.2 – a number of approximations had to be applied, in order to bridge gaps in statistical information[3].

Table 8.2 shows – on the lines for $\bar{s}^*_{a,\mathrm{M}} - \bar{s}_{a,\mathrm{N}}$ and $\bar{s}^*_{\mathrm{M}} - \bar{s}_{\mathrm{N}}$ – that differences in life expectancies and in age distribution of the (income receiving) population may have considerable effects on savings rates.

The differencies between $\bar{s}^*_{a,\mathrm{M}}$ and $\bar{s}_{a,\mathrm{N}}$ *per age-class* are all due to mere discrepancies in life expectancy between Mexico and the Netherlands. These

---

1 Such a transformation has the additional advantage that the stipulated equality of economic variables between the two countries is less unrealistic with respect to *ratios* (such as wealth–income ratios and lifetime patterns of income) than with respect to absolute values (e.g. of income and personal wealth).

2 Presumably, the weights for males and females *per age class* will differ but slightly between the two countries in general, i.e. for most of the parameters and variables.

3 In particular, the authors were unable to obtain Mexican figures on age distribution of income recipients (exclusive of independent workers) corresponding to those adopted for the Netherlands. Therefore, two substitutes for income recipients were adopted for *both* countries, neither of them satisfactory, but erring to different sides, i.e.:

(A) 'employees', i.e. excluding pensioners and other people receiving non-labour income only, and

(B) 'all persons of 15 years and older', i.e. including people not receiving any income of their own, like a major part of married women and students.

TABLE 8.2.

Approximate hypothetical differences in savings rates between Mexico and the Netherlands due to the application of Mexican instead of Dutch age distributions and life expectancies to otherwise Dutch basic figures, around 1960

Variables and parameters				Age-classes with approx. mean age in yrs						Total
Symbol	Country	Meaning	Unit of measurement	<25	25–34	35–44	45–54	55–64	65+	
				20	30	40	50	60	75	
$\overline{L}_{a,\mathrm{M}}$	Mexico	mean life expectancy	year	48	39	32	24	17	9	
$\overline{\alpha}^*_{1,a\mathrm{M}}$	Mexico	mean current urgency to consume	10^3 year^{-1}	29.6	46.6	64.3	79.8	104.7	125.4	
$\overline{\mu}^*_{a\mathrm{M}}$	Mexico	mean income capitalization factor	year	63.2	24.3	17.1	12.2	9.5	7.6	
$\overline{v}_{a\mathrm{M}}$	Mexico	discount factor	1	0.147	0.210	0.278	0.383	0.507	0.698	
$f^e_{a\mathrm{M}}$	M	age-class shares of employees	%	37.9	23.6	15.7	10.6	7.1	5.1	100
$f^e_{a\mathrm{N}}$	N	age-class shares of employees	%	31.5	22.6	18.9	15.5	10.2	1.3	100
$f^p_{a\mathrm{M}}$	M	age-class shares of population 15 years and older	%	33.5	23.5	16.9	11.9	8.0	6.2	100
$f^p_{a\mathrm{N}}$	N	age-class shares of population 15 years and older	%	23.5	18.0	17.4	15.0	12.9	13.2	100
$(\overline{Y}_a/\overline{Y})_\mathrm{N}$	N	mean income ratios	1	0.31	0.96	1.22	1.29	1.22	1.10	
$\overline{s}^*_{a,\mathrm{M}} - \overline{s}_{a,\mathrm{N}}$	M, N	differences in savings rates between Mexico and the Netherlands, due to differences in life expectancies and in age distributions	%	−25.4	−14.6	−12.5	−9.7	−5.6	0	
$\overline{s}^*_\mathrm{M} - \overline{s}_\mathrm{N}$	M, N	differences in savings rates between Mexico and the Netherlands, due to differences in life expectancies and in age distributions	%	A. age distribution of employees						−14.5
$\overline{s}^*_\mathrm{M} - \overline{s}_\mathrm{N}$	M, N	differences in savings rates between Mexico and the Netherlands, due to differences in life expectancies and in age distributions	%	B. age distribution of population 15+ yrs						−7.4

Sources and ways of computation:

General: asterisks denote computed values

$\bar{L}_{a,\mathrm{M}}$ mean life expectancies of men and women in Mexico, according to U.N. [1963] table 26;

$\bar{\alpha}^*_{1,a\mathrm{M}} = \bar{\alpha}_{1,a\mathrm{N}} (\bar{L}_{a\mathrm{N}}/\bar{L}_{a\mathrm{M}})$;

$\bar{v}^*_{a,\mathrm{M}} = (1 + \bar{r}_\mathrm{N})^{-L_{a,\mathrm{M}}}$;

$$\bar{\mu}^*_{a,\mathrm{M}} = \sum_{l=1}^{L_{a,\mathrm{M}}} y_{al,\mathrm{M}} (1 + \bar{r}_\mathrm{N})^{1-l}$$

$$= \sum_{l=1}^{L_{a,\mathrm{N}}} y_{al,\mathrm{N}} (1 + \bar{r}_\mathrm{N})^{1-l} - \sum_{l=L_{a,\mathrm{M}}+1}^{L_{a,\mathrm{N}}} y_{al,\mathrm{N}} (1 + \bar{r}_\mathrm{N})^{1-l}$$

$$= \mu_{a,\mathrm{N}} - (1 + \bar{r}_\mathrm{N})^{-L_{a,\mathrm{M}}} \sum_{l=1}^{L_{a,\mathrm{N}}-L_{a,\mathrm{M}}} y_{a+L_{a,\mathrm{M}},l,\mathrm{N}} (1 + \bar{r}_\mathrm{N})^{1-l}$$

$$\approx \mu_{a,\mathrm{N}} - \bar{v}^*_{a,\mathrm{M}} \{1 + (L_{a,\mathrm{N}} - L_{a,\mathrm{M}}) \bar{r}_\mathrm{N}\},$$

assuming that $y_{a+L_{a,\mathrm{M}},l,\mathrm{N}} \approx 1$ for $1 \leq l \leq L_{a,\mathrm{N}} - L_{a,\mathrm{M}}$ and $L_{a,\mathrm{N}} - L_{a,\mathrm{M}}$ small (say, not more than 5 years);

$f^\mathrm{e}_{a\mathrm{M}}, f^\mathrm{e}_{a\mathrm{N}}$ derived from U.N. [1964] table 11;

$f^\mathrm{p}_{a\mathrm{M}}, f^\mathrm{p}_{a\mathrm{N}}$ derived from U.N. [1965] table 6;

$\bar{s}^*_{a,\mathrm{M}} - \bar{s}_{a,\mathrm{N}} \approx \bar{\alpha}_{a,\mathrm{N}} \{\bar{\mu}_{a,\mathrm{N}} + (1 + \bar{r}_\mathrm{N}) \bar{\kappa}_{a,\mathrm{N}} v_{a,\mathrm{N}}\} - \bar{\alpha}_{a,\mathrm{M}} \{\mu^*_{a,\mathrm{M}} + (1 + \bar{r}_\mathrm{N}) \bar{\kappa}_{a,\mathrm{N}} v_{a,\mathrm{M}}\}$

$\bar{s}^*_\mathrm{M} - \bar{s}_\mathrm{N}$ calculated according to formula (8.2.4).

---

figures are approximately equal to the values of Δs_1 in table 8.1 times the difference between Dutch and Mexican life expectancies[4]. With international convergence of life expectancies in progress, such differences in savings rates as represented by $\bar{s}^*_{a,\mathrm{M}} - \bar{s}_{a,\mathrm{N}}$ will tend to vanish. Anyhow, these differences are smaller at higher than at lower ages, since international as well as intertemporal differences in life expectancies diminish with increasing age.

All this is shown in graph 8.2. As in graph 8.1, the bases of the bars are proportional to the α's, for Mexico between the two uninterrupted lines, and for the Netherlands between the same left-hand uninterrupted line and the right-hand dashed line – per age-class. Again as in graph 8.1, the heights are composed of two parts, this time proportional to $\bar{\mu}^*_{a,\mathrm{M}}$ (for Mexico) or $\bar{\mu}_{a,\mathrm{N}}$

[4] Before rounding off to integer numbers of years!

(for the Netherlands), and to $(1 + \bar{r}_N) \bar{k}_{a,N}\bar{v}_{a,M}$ (for Mexico) and $(1 + \bar{r}_N) \times \bar{k}_{a,N}\bar{v}_{a,N}$ (for the Netherlands). As also appears from table 8.2, the values of these two vertical components differ so little between the two countries that graphically they are indistinguishable.

This means that the hypothetical savings differentials – i.e. insofar as they are due to mere differences in life expectancies – between the two countries

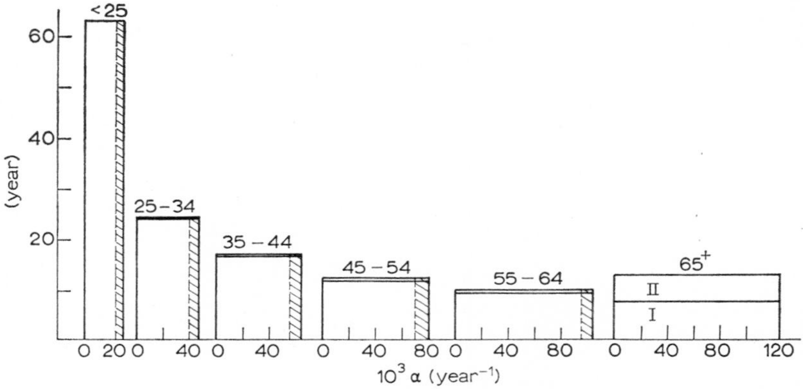

Graph 8.2. Differences between Mexican and Dutch savings rates per age class due to differences in age-specific life expectancies between Mexico and the Netherlands (but otherwise based on the same Dutch savings survey data for both countries – cf. tables 8.1 and 8.2). I: $\bar{\mu}^*_{a,M}$ or $\bar{\mu}_{a,N}$; II: $(1 + r_N) \bar{k}_{a,N}\bar{v}_{a,M}$; full lines: Mexico, dashed lines (if not coinciding with full lines): Netherlands.

are virtually equal to the products of $(\bar{\alpha}_{a,M} - \bar{\alpha}_{a,N})$ and the near-common heights of the bars; these products, of course, are the areas of the shaded parts of the bars.

With increasing age, the α-differentials tend to vanish (practically from 65 years of age onwards); the heights of the bars first diminish, but go up again around 65 years of age. Compared with graph 8.1, the heights of the bars in graph 8.2 change more slowly and reach a minimum at a higher age.

The figures for the overall (hypothetical) differences in savings rates $\bar{s}^*_M - \bar{s}_N$ show the joint effect of differences in age distribution and in life expectancies.

In order to split this joint effect into a life expectancy effect (I) and an age distribution effect (II), the following formulae were applied:

$$(\bar{s}^*_M - \bar{s}_N)_I = \sum_a f_a (\bar{s}^*_{a,M} - \bar{s}_{a,N}) (\bar{Y}_a/\bar{Y})_N, \tag{8.2.5}$$

with f_a alternatively denoting $f^{e}_{a,M}, f^{e}_{a,N}, f^{p}_{a,M}, f^{p}_{a,N}$, and

$$(\bar{s}^*_M - \bar{s}_N)_{II} = \sum_a (f_{a,M} - f_{a,N}) [1 - \bar{\alpha}_{a,N} \{\mu_{a,N} + (1 + \bar{r}_N) \bar{k}_{a,N}\nu_{a,N}\}] (\bar{Y}_a/\bar{Y})_N \tag{8.2.6}$$

with $f_{a,M} = f^{e}_{a,M}, f^{p}_{a,M}$ and $f_{a,N} = f^{e}_{a,N}, f^{p}_{a,N}$ respectively.

The numerical results of applying these formulae to the figures presented in table 8.1 and 8.2 are reproduced in table 8.3.

TABLE 8.3.

Hypothetical differences in savings rates between Mexico and the Netherlands, due to differences in life expectancy (I) and in age distribution (II), in per cents

	Weights			
	$f^{e}_{a,M}$	$f^{e}_{a,N}$	$f^{p}_{a,M}$	$f^{p}_{a,N}$
$(\bar{s}^*_M - \bar{s}_N)_I$	−10.5	−11.1	−10.5	−9.8
$(\bar{s}^*_M - \bar{s}_N)_{II}$	−4.2		+3.0	
$\bar{s}^*_M - \bar{s}_N$	−14.5		−7.4	

This table shows that the two kinds of effects add up to approximately the same as the total effect printed near the bottom of table 8.2.

Furthermore, the effects of differences in life expectancies are more important in an absolute sense than the effects of differences in age distribution between the relevant parts of the populations of Mexico and of the Netherlands.

For the 'life expectancy' effects it does not matter much whether the age-shares applied relate to employees or to all people aged 15 years and over; on the other hand, this choice happens to affect even the signs of the 'age distribution' effect. A major reason for the latter phenomenon is that in the highest age class Mexico has a relatively larger number of employees but a relatively smaller number of all (other) kinds of people, compared with the Netherlands. In part, of course, this reflects differences in life expectancies as well as in fertility rates between the two countries.

8.3. Summary and concluding remarks

Section 8.1 deals with the effects which an extension of life expectancies by one year would have had on savings rates in the Netherlands (cf. table 8.1); section 8.2 shows the gaps in savings rates resulting from differences both in life expectancies and in age distributions between Mexico and the Netherlands (in tables 8.2 and 8.3). All other things being equal, higher life expectancies appear to be conducive to savings, in accordance with the theoretical analysis presented in section 3.7.3.

The same models may be adopted for evaluating demographic effects on savings relating to other countries, at other (and particularly future) times. A prerequisite for such an application, however, is the availability of the required statistical data (about distribution of income and personal wealth by personal characteristics, survival rates, etc.), as well as ditto forecasts.

In principle, the simple savings model presented here may be further generalized and modified in various ways as set out in chapters 2 and 3; in view of the operational difficulties involved, however, such a course of action is recommended in the long run rather than for the near future.

CHAPTER 9

RETROSPECT AND PROSPECT

9.1. *How much rationality underlies the savings models?*

The micro-savings functions dealt with in chapters 2 through 4 may be objected to on the grounds that in reality people do not behave as rationally as seems to be assumed in the reasoning underlying those functions. For instance, one might hold the view that, in general, people do not look far ahead into the future, and/or that people do not have very definite ideas about prospective financial resources and needs, or even that people are not aware of any utility functions of future consumption. Below, we deal with these objections in two ways. First (in section 9.1.1) we plead the case for a certain minimum degree of rationality, in particular, with respect to theoretical but operationally meaningful savings functions; second (in section 9.1.2) we point out how generously *non*-rational (but not necessarily *ir*rational) behaviour is allowed for by the savings model in question.

9.1.1. IN DEFENSE OF RATIONALITY

The arguments in favour of founding consumption and savings functions on a (more or less) rational basis are aimed partly at economic relationships (of the behavioural kind) in general, and partly at savings functions in particular.

First, the rational foundation of behavioural relations is firmly established in economic theory[1], in the sense that it assumes economic units (persons or firms) to optimize, i.e. to maximize (or minimize) a certain economic variable or an objective function, possibly (and usually) subject to one or more constraints (e.g. utility maximization subject to a budget constraint). By and large this optimum principle underpins both neo-classical and modern economic theory.

---

[1] For an ample and thorough treatment of notions and discussions of rationality of economic behaviour up till World War II cf. Hennipman [1945].

On the other hand, the 'optimum principle' as a necessary basis of economic theory has been challenged (implicitly if not explicitly) by a number of economists. Some of them have even tried to replace the 'optimum principle' by something else; inter alia, by adopting 'satisficing' as an alleged rule of conduct. Such weaker postulates, however, cannot bring forth or support theories of the same degree of specificity as those based on the optimum principle. Hence, unless economists are able to adduce other premises at least as powerful as the optimum principle, the latter wins by default. Without the strong arm of a guiding principle, economic theory is left at the mercy of purely empiristic trial and error – an extremely inefficient and unsatisfactory way of carrying out research.

Second, with particular reference to savings behaviour, the assumptions underlying the savings models dealt with here are not as unrealistic as they might seem at first sight, especially in the eyes of practical people.

As regards the time-span of planning: since life-insurance companies apparently thrive on people's concern about the state of affairs *after* death, the notion of a savings plan extending *till* the expected time of decease seems modest in comparison.

Furthermore, expectations about income and needs may affect people's behaviour, inter alia, with respect to savings, even if they are not fully aware of those factors. By trial and error, the latter contributed to the shaping of traditional savings behaviour of the group to which income recipients belong, e.g. according to their socio-economic status. The importance of those factors for *reasonable* behaviour may be imparted to younger and older people by parents, teachers, preachers, vocational guidance advisers, employers, labour unions, tax inspectors and collectors, colleagues, neighbours, friends, relatives, newspaper, radio and television, and – last but not least – by the hard facts of life itself. Even traditions and common usage to which most people conform have at least some rational basis, although it may have been long since forgotten.

Those who do not conform to at least a semblance of rational behaviour, do not enter the savings scene, or disappear from it – temporarily if not permanently. Once again, we remind the reader that savings functions do not apply to all people, but only to a selection of them, viz. to income recipients, i.e. those who are able to save or to dissave in principle. No savings theory – neither our's nor others' – takes account of those losing the struggle for life by acting irrationally to such an extent that they became bankrupt, were placed under custody or guardianship because of dementia, feeble-mindedness or thriftlessness, were locked up in goal, landed on skid row or committed suicide; neither does it apply to minors (below a certain age, say, 15 years).

9.1.2. ALLOWANCE FOR NON-RATIONALITY

On the other hand, in order to allow for (possible) non-rationality, we are by no means obliged to drop the optimum principle: optimization is quite compatible with expectations, however unrealistic or unreasonable they may seem to be; provided, of course, that they are not inconsistent, e.g. if the target aimed at for personal wealth is so high that inequality (2.4.1.7) would be violated[2]. Unrealistic expectations may (and do) have real effects, as far as people's behaviour is based on them (as mentioned already in section 6.2.2.1); in this respect the 'degree of realism'[3] of expectations is irrelevant. For instance, healthy hypochondriacs in their early forties might fix their life expectancy at (say) 3 years – and plan their savings and other behaviour accordingly – although reasonably they might expect to live another 35 years. More generally, *any* value of L may be accepted without upsetting the theory set out above. This may be done by re-interpreting L as the savings-plan horizon, which need not (but may) coincide with the lifetime horizon. The excessively high values of the elasticities of income expectations ε, compatible with values of the empirical marginal propensity to consume, as discussed in section 4.2.3, may to some extent be due to such mental myopia (cf. Tinbergen [1933] and Strotz [1957]).

The same result, however, may be obtained by sticking to the former interpretation of L as life expectancy, viz. by assuming r_τ – in the varying-interest models of sections 2.8, 3.4 and 4.3.4 – to be infinite for $\tau > L'$, if L' ($\leq L$) is the length of the planning period, especially if K_L is independent of L (e.g. zero).

Contrariwise, people may be inclined to overestimate the time they still

---

[2] In the 'general basic' models of sections 2.4, 3.1 and 3.7 or the specific basic model of section 4.1, final personal wealth is a 'datum', like income expectations, although of a specifically intentional nature – in contradistinction to the models of sections 2.5 and 3.2, featuring final personal wealth as an instrument (for the pursuit of happiness).

[3] The 'degree of realism' of expectations is very difficult to assess a priori, being subject to wide differences of opinion. A posteriori, it may, of course, be evaluated by comparing expections with outcome. It is, however, possible that the outcome would have been considered as very unlikely, a priori.

have to live; this may be responsible (at least partly) for the fact that so many people still leave as much as they do.

Furthermore, the model allows people to have mutually differing appreciations of present and future needs (as represented by their α_τ-values).

Through the 'urgencies to consume' α_1, our specific savings model may even incorporate the effect of 'irrational' motives and considerations on current consumption and savings; examples are provided by alleged behavioural inertia such as 'past consumption' and 'maximum level of income reached before', and by 'social' (residential) effects, as suggested by Duesenberry [1949].

In this, as well as in other respects mentioned above, our generalized Modigliani-Brumberg model is much more flexible, hence more realistic than the simple, original.

Finally, income recipients may discount future money flows or assets differently for different time periods ahead, according to their individual outlooks.

Therefore, with such liberal interpretations, the savings model is by no means the straight-jacket it may seem to be, but rather represents a theory of 'non-rational rationality' – the counterpart of van Praag's 'theory of rational irrationality' [1968], based on people's mental limitations. Deviations between theoretical and empirical savings behaviour occur only if further specifications are imposed on the model for the sake of making it operational, e.g. by identifying L with life expectancy according to life-tables, basing income expectations on cross-sectional, synchronous age-specific income means per sex per occupational group (cf. section 6.2.2.1), and discounting at the current market rate of interest. Insofar as people's actual behaviour is based on assumptions and valuations other than the ones just mentioned, such deviations are not adequately accounted for by a deterministic model like the one developed in chapters 2 through 4; they call for the introduction of error terms, such as those entering the relationships trying to explain inter-individual differences in α_1-values.

In the macro-models too, error terms are introduced, albeit in order to take account of errors of measurement as well as mis-specifications of the savings functions.

Still, by definition or assumption, these error terms represent mere chance deviations; furthermore, systematic deviations may appear. Even in the latter case, however, "rational" or optimizing savings functions would make sense: in order to establish *whether* – and if so, to what *extent* – (savings) behaviour is (or is not) 'irrational', comparison with 'rational' behaviour as expressed by a 'rational' function (of savings behaviour) is in order.

Finally, we should bear in mind that savings plans – whatever their degree of "definiteness" – are not made up once and for all, but are subject to incessant revisions.

Summarizing, we conclude that the savings models developed in the theoretical part are sufficiently down-to-earth for justifying their application to empirical data – as borne out by the practical outcome.

9.1.3. IMPACT OF NON-ECONOMIC FACTORS ON SAVINGS AND CONSUMPTION

The latter conclusion, however, does not preclude the effect of non-economic factors – besides economic ones – on savings behaviour. On the contrary, the analysis of inter-individual α_1-values in chapter 6 bears witness to the importance of non-economic factors, in addition to economic factors incorporated in the financial resource variables R_1 – although in the latter ones too, psychological factors affecting expectations as well as bequest-motives play a rôle. In sections 2.10 and 3.6 even sociological considerations (keeping up – or down – with the Joneses) were assumed to possibly affect behaviour (cf. also Diagram 4.1).

On the other hand, we should beware of imputing savings variations between people at the same time, or for groups over time to psychological or sociological factors indiscriminately, whereas they may be ascribed more naturally to differences in economic factors. Cases in point are the attempts of economists such as Mendershausen [1940] to stress inter-racial differences in savings rates and by Duesenberry to support his savings theory of relative income, based on assumed effects of "surroundings" on individuals' savings behaviour.

The racial prejudice with respect to savings behaviour was debunked by Dorothy Brady and Rose Friedman [1947], while Tobin [1951] exposed the redundancy of the relative income hypothesis. Instead, the latter authors explained inter-racial differences in savings rates in terms of inter-racial differences in level and distribution of income, and attributed inter-city differences in savings rates to corresponding differences in cost of living. Klein and Mooney [1953], however, conclude that 'concerning the differences of opinion between Duesenberry and Tobin, our findings indicate that neither position is entirely correct' (l.c. p. 454/455); they seem to be inclined to re-assign a rôle to race (in connection with social status) as a means of explaining inter-group savings differences.

However, that may be, the moral of these discussions is that one should first look for explanations in economic terms, rather than turn immediately to psychological and sociological factors in an attempt to explain inter-group differences, perhaps in support of popular prejudices.

It does not detract, however, from the desirability of examining more thoroughly the impact of non-economic phenomena (such as religion) on savings behaviour than has been possible in the present study or has been done in previous studies.

Above all, our model – like its predecessor, viz. the one developed by Modigliani and Brumberg – highlights the paramount importance of biological and demographic factors for individual and collective savings behaviour – as illustrated in sections 8.1 and 8.2, respectively.

9.2. Comparisons between savings models[4]

9.2.1. MICRO-MODELS

9.2.1.1. Decision units. In purely analytical studies of total consumption and savings, the nature of the decision units to which the variables relate is often left undecided. A number of these studies suggest, and some of them even specify: 'individual persons'; others, however, allow for interpretation of decision units in terms of both 'households' and 'individuals'.

On the other hand, empirical savings studies – as well as the underlying savings surveys – generally centre around households as the reference units. An intermediate position is taken up in some recent studies introducing into the model variables relating to more than one member of the household, e.g. husband and wife (Ghez [1970], Gronau [1970]), or even supplemented by children (Lee-Gramm [1970]). This is akin to the inclusion of other people's consumption in the consumption function, as examined in sections 2.10 and 3.6 of the present book.

Otherwise, the latter considers individual income recipients as the relevant

[4] As before, we subsume consumption functions among savings functions, since consumption and savings are each other's complements with respect to income, and the latter variable always appears in both categories of functions.

decision units, provided they have reached a certain minimum age (viz. 15 years) – as explained in section 6.1.2. A special and promising way of reference to the household was introduced by Ben-Porath [1970], viz. by including the desired number of children among the arguments of the utility function, in addition to (would-be) parents' variables.

9.2.1.2. Contents

9.2.1.2.1. Savings. In various savings surveys, hence in savings analyses based thereon, 'savings' is defined in slightly different ways, depending, inter alia, on the social insurance systems prevailing in the countries concerned. Nevertheless, there is a notable tendency to conform to the United Nations standard definitions adopted for National Accounting.

In a few studies, the analysis of savings is restricted to parts of total savings, such as 'discretionary savings', or savings on deposit-book accounts (Hudec [1969]).

The basic idea underlying the present study, however, is that individuals 'plan' their savings 'in toto' (i.e. obligatory savings, e.g. in the form of social insurance premiums, together with discretionary savings). This means, inter alia, that the authors did not listen to the popular cry of 'saving for some purpose', which they consider to be somewhat overrated: just as the 'obligatory' nature of some kinds of savings seems exaggerated[5], motives as recorded in savings surveys happen to change or vanish overnight.

On the other hand, after deciding upon total savings an allocation of it to modes of saving (e.g. savings accounts, securities, land and buildings) may take place at a second stage, e.g. under the impact of net yields. For this purpose, an allocation model may render good services, as suggested by Korteweg [1971]. The present book, however, abstained from the latter more detailed kind of analysis.

---

[5] In particular, this applies to the so-called contractual savings, such as premium payments for life insurance. Apart from their initially voluntary nature, the ties of the savings contracts are seldom so tight that they cannot be loosened (e.g. by surrender of or borrowing on the policy, or converting it into a paid-up policy) – even if a certain loss is involved in such transactions. And though one may acknowledge the obligatory nature of part of the savings, one can safely keep to the 'comprehensive' savings theory advocated here: the fluidity and alternative disposability of money allow deficient or excessive obligatory savings to be made up by more or less voluntary savings, respectively, without a hitch (cf. Section 6.1.4).

9.2.1.2.2. Income. All micro-models known to the authors and pretending to explain (synchronous) differences in savings between reference units include *current* income (albeit of households more often than of individuals, such as heads of households, cf. section 9.2.1.1). What has been observed with respect to variations in definitions of savings, applies mutatis mutandis to income as well.

Expected income is a much more rare variable encountered in savings analyses. If included – as in the American studies by Klein c.s [1953], Mack [1958] a.o. – the expected income 'variable' is usually of a qualitative nature only, i.e. according to the trichotomy 'expected rise', 'approximate constancy' and 'expected decline' (sc. of income) – all within the next month, quarter or semester. Although the French type of 'Business Test' surveys would permit a more detailed classification according to degree of expected change by percentage intervals, it has not been used in Savings Surveys– unfortunately; the Savings Survey of the Netherlands was no exception.

Estimation of the present value of expected future income, as performed in our study, is pretty unique. We concede that the numerical elaboration of this principle is based on somewhat questionable assumptions (cf. section 6.2.2.), but at least it is not corrupted by such economic mysticism as gave rise to Friedman's phantom: 'permanent income'.

9.2.1.2.3. Personal wealth. A number of savings studies take account of personal wealth – e.g. Klein c.s. [1954], M. R. Fisher [1956] –, but most of them are restricted to only the liquid part of it, for the theoretical and practical reasons mentioned in section 1.3.2. In our study, the theoretical reason is rejected, i.e. savings are assumed to be affected by non-liquid assets in precisely the same manner and degree as by liquid assets: the former may be sold like the latter (albeit with somewhat more efforts and time involved), and anyhow it may serve as collateral for borrowing money. Fortunately, the high quality of the Savings Survey on which our analysis was based ensured that we did not have to restrict ourselves practically to the unsatisfactory 'pars pro toto', i.e., could operate with 'total personal wealth' – like Thore [1959] on the basis of data collected in a Swedish Savings Survey.

The 'personal wealth' meant above, however, merely relates to the beginning of the reference period. Intended final personal wealth did not enter empirical savings models except ours, presumably because the sponsors of savings surveys thought it immodest to ask people about their bequest intentions.

On the other hand, a number of theoretical savings models, e.g. by Friedman [1957], Spiro [1962][6], Yaari [1964], Hakansson [1969], feature final personal wealth as an argument of the individual's savings function, and even as an instrument of optimum savings and consumption policy. For reasons mentioned in section 6.1.4, however, the latter course has not been pursued in empirical savings studies, except in our own.

Another distinction between the former and the latter analyses is that personal wealth – as far as it is included in the analysis at all – is treated as a separate variable rather than combined with (current and expected future) income in the joint 'financial resources' variable.

9.2.1.2.4. Rate of interest. It is interesting to note how little interest economists generally take in the interest rate as a savings and consumption determinant – with the notable exception of a coriphaeus like the late Irving Fisher. That it is hardly ever taken into account in empirical, micro-economic savings analyses is explicable, because cross-sectionally rates of interest do not show sufficient variation to enable the estimation of their effects[7]; however, it is not entirely justifiable, because of the discounting effects of the rate of interest for converting future values to present values – as has been done in the present volume. On the other hand, the restriction most empirical savings studies impose upon themselves by disregarding all future income – unless haunted by the apparition of 'permanent income'[8] – may be interpreted as implicit infinite valuation of the rate of interest after the end of the reference period.

9.2.1.2.5. Personal characteristics. As in our own study, previous analyses took account of personal characteristics of members (mostly the head) of the household, insofar as the underlying savings surveys provided the information required.

---

[6] Spiro [1962] takes the view that there would exist (for the entire population) a 'desired ratio of wealth to consumption' – without argueing why. Furthermore, he is of the opinion that this principle should be 'extended from the aggregate to the individual'. It looks like a Barnum and Baily world to construct a micro-theory on the analogy of a macro-theory, whereas the proper way to proceed is building a macro-model on the basis of a micro ditto – as has been done in chapter 5 of this book.

[7] Even this statement may be challenged. The bonus savings plans, for instance, promise their participants higher overall rates of interest (viz. including the annual shares of the bonus within the contract term) than non-participants are able to obtain.

[8] The most conspicuous characteristic of 'permanent income' is its impermanence, due to its elusiveness.

For example, age is included in most analyses based on savings surveys, such as those carried out by Klein c.s. [1954], M.R. Fisher [1956], Watts [1958], Thore [1959] and Bannink a.o. [1967].

In addition, Morgan [1954] allows for the impact of residence (urban or rural) and extraordinary expenses on savings; furthermore, occupation was attended to in Klein's analysis, while education, marital status and size of household also entered Watt's extensive micro-economic, cross-sectional savings model. Finally, the effect of ownership (or mere tenancy) of dwellings on savings was studied both for Sweden (by Thore) and for the U.S.A (by Klein a.o.), while having a car was considered a savings determinant for Sweden (an exception), but not for the U.S.A. (the rule).

Comparing this set of variables with the list printed in section 6.1.4 under 1°, the two nearly coincide, with the notable exception of sex, incorporated in our analyses, but disregarded in most other studies on savings. The reason is that the latter relate to households as units rather than to separate members; and if personal characteristics are taken into account at all, they usually relate to the head of the household. And since this ruler is a male as a rule, there is no role assigned to sex in savings.

In addition, our study makes a distinction between participation and non-participation in bonus savings plans.

9.2.1.3. Form of the savings functions. Even where the other savings functions feature (approximately) the same variables as our's, they vary according to their form, i.e. according to the manner in which the variables are assumed to affect savings.

True, our own model too – derived in chapter 4 and applied in chapter 6 – is linear in income and wealth, but there the resemblance stops.

In some studies, like those by Klein c.s. [1954] and M.R. Fisher [1956], possible interaction between income and wealth with respect to savings is taken care of by means of the product of the former variables.

Occasionally, we encounter other non-linearities in micro-savings functions, such as squared income (in addition to income itself) for explaining savings as such (Klein and Morgan [1951]) and log-income for explaining savings rates (M.R. Fisher [1956]).

Since for such deviations from linearity no more reasons are given than for the adoption of linearity in general, one can surmise that the eventual choice of the form of the savings function is the result of trial and error rather than of thorough theorizing, as in our study; instead, we thought that matching income and wealth additively would be more appropriate for explaining savings and consumption.

9.2.1.4. Methods of quantifying the savings functions. With respect to the numerical specification of the parameters of the savings functions, the present analysis differs from previous ones.

Another difference is shown in the treatment (or non-treatment) of the rate of interest. This variable – not included (implicity) in other micro-savings models – affects savings through discount factors, themselves non-linear functions of the rate of interest, and applied to income and personal wealth.

Still more important is that personal characteristics too influence savings in an indirect manner, i.e. through the 'urgency to consume' as the multiplier of 'financial resources' R. On the other hand, variables representing the personal characteristics usually enter the equations for the savings rates (if not for the savings themselves) in a linear-additive way. This seems to be hardly justifiable – except from the point of view of computational convenience; however, it may well be the main reason why such unsatisfactory results were obtained for the estimated effects of personal characteristics on savings.

In particular, this applies to age. A number of economists engaged in savings research recognized the possibility, and even the plausibility of non-linearity of age effects on savings (rates).

Consequently, M.R.Fisher [1956] introduced age into the savings equation quadratically and non-monotonically, at least in an alternative version of his savings model; others – like Klein [1954] and Watts [1958] – included age-effects by means of dummy-variables for a categorical set of age-classes, thus leaving the (partial) relationship between savings and age unspecified analytically.

Theoretically, age affects savings in a complicated manner, i.e. both through R (financial resources) and through α_1 (urgency to consume).

Moreover, our relationship between consumption or savings, on the one hand, and income and wealth, on the other hand, is not only linear but also homogeneous; this means that there is no constant term, like in other models, but straight proportionality between current consumption and financial resources. In this respect, our model is simpler than the other ones, by combining variables, viz. incomes, personal wealth and the interest rate into the joint variable R, representing 'financial resources'. This, of course, reduces the number of parameters to be estimated a posteriori, partly because a number of them (among which the power of the discount factors) are assigned numerical values a priori.

In contradistinction, most empirical studies estimate the effects of (nearly) all variables on savings separately and a posteriori.

As explained in section 6.3.1 above, our procedure has the advantage that at the first stage of the analysis no parameter at all has to be (or even can be) estimated; on the contrary, the 'quasi-parameter' α_1 for 'urgency to consume' can only be calculated for each income recipient separately. It means that all economic variables (income, personal wealth, rate of interest) have already been taken care of. As a consequence, the analysis at the second stage can be confined to estimating effects of personal factors on savings through the urgency to consume.

In chapter 6 the latter analysis has been carried out by means of analysis of variance. As far as the estimation of the parameters is concerned, that method amounts to regression analysis by means of dummy variables. In this respect, our kind of analysis resembles other analyses such as those by Klein c.s. [1954] and Watts [1956], making a lavish use of dummy variables. The difference, however, is that the other studies include proper as well as improper (dummy) variables, whereas in our analysis merely the latter kind is represented. Moreover, the dummy variables in our analysis stand for characteristic–mixes of individuals rather than for characteristics separately, as in the other studies.

In this regard, the treatment of dummy variables parallels the way in which the proper (economic) variables are dealt with.

9.2.1.5. Signs and magnitudes of effects. Empirical savings functions differ with respect to contents, form and methods of numerical specification, as well as in delimitations of areas, groups of people and periods to which they refer. This forces us to keep our comparison of the numerical results, obtained by various methods, superficial, i.e. to restrict ourselves to signs and orders of magnitude of effects.

9.2.1.5.1. Income. According to chapter 4, α_1 and $1 - \alpha_1$ represent the 'net' marginal propensities to consume and to save, respectively. The results of our analysis, reproduced in tables 6.1 through 6.5, show that at least the group-averages of α_1 lie between 0 and 1; this means positive values for both the marginal propensities to consume and the marginal propensities to save. This agrees with the outcome of all other savings analyses known to the authors. On the other hand, the marginal propensities to save in the other studies tend to lie near the lower limit (0), whereas those resulting from our analysis are close to the upper limit 1. A possible exception may be made for entrepreneurs, whose marginal propensities to consume (and to save!) are occasionally found to be in the neighbourhood of $\frac{1}{2}$.

As explained in section 4.2.3 above, such conspicuous gaps in outcome are due to differences between the net and the gross concepts of the 'marginal propensities'. In the same sub-section an attempt has been made to reconcile both concepts by means of Hicks' 'elasticity of expectation'. There, the question was asked – and answered – what values should be assumed by those elasticities in order to yield 'gross' marginal propensities to consume near the empirical limits $\frac{1}{2}$ and 1 for selected ages (35 and 55 years); for this purpose, the α_1 – not yet known empirically – were provisionally equated to the reciprocals of the corresponding life expectancies. Thus, unreasonably high values were obtained for the elasticity of income expectation, viz. exceeding 1.

Here, the problem is reversed in the sense that gross marginal propensities to consume are calculated, starting from unit elasticities of income expectation applied to empirical α_1-values interpolated from table 6.1. This means that the gross marginal propensity to consume would equal $\alpha_1\mu$, with μ the income capitalization factor, introduced theoretically in section 6.2.2 and dealt with numerically in appendix C to chapter 6.

The outcome of this exercise is reproduced in table 9.1. This time, the resulting figures are, in general, nearly 1, but slightly higher occasionally; they do not seem altogether impossible. Confrontation of table 9.1 with 4.1 confirms the hunch expressed in section 4.2.3, viz. that α_1 is underestimated by equating it to L^{-1}, at least at ages 35 and 55.

That conclusion is supported by the observation that according to tables 6.1 through 6.5, $\overline{\alpha_1 L}$ is generally above 1.

Table 9.1 shows exceptionally high marginal propensities to consume – i.e. exceeding 1 – for company directors and teachers (especially at higher levels of education) and well as for the police force and military personnel. These differences are due partly to differences in income capitalization factors – as shown by table 6C.1 – and partly to differences in α-values between manual and non-manual workers, as will be obvious from table 6.1. Since the former inter-occupational differences disappear at the age of retirement, at age 70 at the latest, only two levels of marginal propensity to consume remain, viz. for the manual and the non-manual workers.

Table 9.1 does little to confirm the allegation – apparently supported by empirical evidence – that, compared with employees, entrepreneurs show lower gross marginal propensities to consume.

The underlying assumption of unit elasticity of income expectation, however, may be less realistic for independent workers, with their strongly

TABLE 9.1.

Values of $\bar{\alpha}_1\mu$ as approximations of gross marginal propensities to consume for married male heads of households in the Netherlands around 1960, according to the assumption of unit elasticity of income expectation

No.	Occupational group	Age in years				
		30	40	50	60	70
1.	Entrepreneurs	0.928	0.936	0.856	0.746	0.518
2.	Managing directors of limited companies	1.193	1.240	0.987	0.737	0.518
3.	Primary school teachers	1.131	1.079	0.932	0.817	0.518
4.	Teaching staff for secondary schools and higher education	1.266	1.125	0.973	0.835	0.518
5.	Civil servants	0.985	1.010	0.918	0.799	0.518
6.	Police officers and military staff	1.042	1.050	0.918	1.003	0.518
7.	Administrative staff	0.993	0.987	0.911	0.799	0.518
8.	Sales clerks	0.920	0.953	0.828	0.701	0.518
9.	Commercial travellers and insurance agents	0.887	0.924	0.842	0.693	0.518
10.	Other non-manual workers	0.961	0.964	0.869	0.728	0.518
11.	Factory workers	0.949	0.956	1.003	0.867	0.766
12.	Farm hands	1.045	0.956	0.995	0.857	0.766

Sources: $\bar{\alpha}_1$: mean urgencies to consume per age class from table 6.1, with distinction between manual workers (categories 11 and 12) and non-manual workers (categories 1 through 10);

μ: labour income capitalization factors per age class from table 6 C.1.

and accidentally variable income, than for employees, whose income is generally more predictable even if not entirely stable.

A lower elasticity of income expectation, say somewhere between $\frac{1}{2}$ and 1, would yield values of gross marginal propensities to consume that would agree better with those found for entrepreneurs in other empirical studies, not taking account of future expected income explicitly[9]; cf. also section 7.4.6.

For each occupational group separately, table 9.1 shows that with increasing age – at least after life has begun at 40 – the gross marginal propensities to consume tend to decline, hence that the gross marginal propensities to save tend to rise. The decline even seems to accelerate, especially between the ages of 60 and 70.

This phenomenon may be explained in several ways – not necessarily excluding each other. First, the assumed elasticity of income expectation – fixed at unity – may be over-estimated at lower ages, at which income expectations are still rather uncertain, at least more than at higher ages and particularly after the person in question has been pensioned off; then, both the fear of income reduction and the hope of income improvement have disappeared ('rien ne va plus').

On the other hand, this theory cannot apply to the lowest age-class; although at age 30 income prospects are less well predictable than at age 40, in-between propensities to consume tend to increase (albeit slightly) rather than to decrease.

Secondly, one may suspect that life expectancy tends to be overestimated, the more so according as people become older; by becoming used to life, they may even forget that they are mortal. This means that the α-values presented in tables 6.1 through 6.5 would be underestimated at higher ages rather than overestimated at lower ages. On the other hand, a possible underestimation of intended final personal wealth would give rise to an over-estimation of the α's; this would be relatively more important at higher ages than at lower ones, in view of the increase of the discount factor and the reduction of the time range of expected income.

For ages between 50 and 60 years, however, the gross marginal propensities to consume according to table 9.1 correspond roughly to those usually found in regression analyses of current consumption explained in terms of current income – to the exclusion of future income. Therefore, the relations between current and future income appear to be of paramount importance for savings. Unfortunately, however, they are elusive.

Presumably, they differ considerably between individuals, while for each

---

9 Another attempt at reducing artificially the apparent differences in (marginal) propensity to consume was made by Friedman [1957], viz. by confining the relation to that between 'permanent consumption' and 'permanent income'.

individual they vary over time, between the poles of pessimism and optimism (as suggested by Svennilson [1937]).

Anyhow, table 9.1 supports the hypothesis that a change in current income is generally accompanied by a change in expected future income in the same direction, if not to the same degree.

Although the effect of increases in expected future income on savings implied by our model was not evaluated in any other model, its negative sign was corroborated in those studies that featured dummy variables for the directions of changes in expected income: an expected increase or decrease in future income was found to depress and stimulate present savings, respectively (cf. e.g. Klein [1959]). Mack's [1958] surmise of asymmetry in income effects viz. that an increase in income would affect consumption and savings more strongly than a decrease in income of the same size is at variance with both our theory and empirical findings. Another hypothesis, viz. that 'permanent' and 'temporary' increases of income would decrease and increase current savings, respectively, could be neither accepted nor rejected (Klein [1951]). The latter outcome does not surprise us, since according to our model an increase of 'temporary' income must reduce savings, while an increase of 'permanent' income *might* likewise reduce savings, but need not do so actually: an increase in savings, albeit less than proportional, would be a more likely result.

9.2.1.5.2. Personal wealth. Our model implies that the effect of an increase in initial personal wealth on current consumption is negative, and numerically equal to the effect of the same increase in current income, multiplied by a discount factor (less than 1).

Both the negative sign and the small importance of the personal wealth effect – compared with the income effect – are confirmed by the vast majority of empirical savings analyses.

Occasionally, a positive effect of personal wealth on savings appears to result from regression analyses. Such apparent exceptions, however, may be attributed, at least partly, to high positive correlation between income and personal wealth. This means that a mixed income-and-wealth effect is mistaken for a pure wealth effect. Such contingencies can be precluded by a priori combination of incomes and wealth, together with interest rates, into one financial resources variable R – as adopted in our analysis.

Instead of looking upon a positive wealth effect on savings as merely a statistical deception, Duesenberry [1967] takes it seriously, viz. by interpreting the occurrence of relatively high or low values of both savings rates and personal wealth as possible signs of an abnormally high and low degree of thriftiness, respectively. Without rejecting such a possible explanation forthwith, one may point out that again the effect of one variable (viz. initial personal wealth) would be mistaken for the joint effect of a couple of variables (viz. the difference between initial and intended final personal wealth, the latter being conducive to or indicative of thriftiness). Operating with intended change in personal wealth – as in our study – instead of with initial personal wealth alone, would eliminate such confusion. But then, intended final personal wealth is 'hors concours'.

Tabular analysis applied to savings survey data for Sweden by Konjunkturinstitutet [1959] suggests a positive effect of personal wealth on the marginal rate of savings. Such an outcome, however, is not confirmed by American or British savings analyses.

Numerically, the equality between the ratio of the personal wealth effect to the income effect and the discount factor $(1 + r)^{-L}$ – as implied by our model – was not corroborated in other studies: differences between the net and the gross concepts of marginal propensity to consume adopted in the respective studies *depressed* the ratio of wealth-to-income effects below that discount factor – for people of average age. Since that discount factor rises towards 1 with increasing age, hence decreasing life expectancy, the initial personal wealth effect will also increase. However, this implication of our model did not strike a responsive chord in the established finger exercises on the 'savings, income and wealth' theme.

The use of liquid assets instead of personal wealth as an explanatory variable might (but need not) re-inforce the under-estimation of the apparent personal wealth effect: variations in the liquid part of personal savings may be larger than those in total personal wealth, not only in a relative, but also in an absolute sense.

9.2.1.5.3. Rate of interest. None of the other cross-sectional analyses gave any indication of the direction, let alone the order of magnitude, of the effect of the interest rate on savings. In the analysis presented in chapter 6, however, we found lower urgencies to consume for participants than for non-participants in bonus savings plans. This may be interpreted as a positive effect of the rate of interest on savings. We should be aware, however, of an alternative interpretation, viz. that people with a relatively low urgency to consume are more apt to participate in savings schemes (even without bonuses) than those feeling a more urgent need of present consumption. Unfortunately, the two interpretations are empirically inseparable.

9.2.1.5.4. Personal characteristics.

a. *Age*. Through L, age has a positive effect on α, whereas it depresses the income capitalization factor μ, as explained in appendix C to chapter 6. Furthermore, age has side-effects on α, inter alia, by moving people up through successive phases of life, characterized, for instance, by variations in the size and composition of the household, irrespective of the position which the person in question holds therein. As a consequence, the effect of age on the change-in-personal wealth component of R depends on age through its effect on past savings in a highly complicated, hardly traceable manner. Therefore, the overall effects of age on savings are virtually unpredictable. At least, this is implied by our model. For that reason, the occasional assumption that age affects savings monotonically (increasing or decreasing), let alone linearly, is too naive to be taken seriously. Hence, it need not surprise us that savings functions that are linear in age (if not in other variables) yield apparent age effects, now positive, now negative, but never statistically or otherwise significant (Klein [1951]). The presumption that age would have non-monotonic effects on savings seems to be supported by empirical evidence. The Swedish Savings Survey data, for example, suggest increase of savings rates till about the age of 55, followed by a decrease. On the other hand, Watts [1958], juggling with a host of dummy variables, inter alia, for age classes, found savings rates steadily increasing with age – after correction for other factors – up till and including the highest age class distinguished, viz. 55–64 years. This still allows for decreasing, and eventually negative savings rates from age 65 onwards. For people with positive personal wealth cumulated up till then, it is the rational thing to do, unless they would like to bequeath a still larger amount.

b. *Marital status*. Watts [1956] did not find any significant effect of marital status (likewise represented by dummy variables), and neither did we.

c. *Size (and composition) of family*. Klein c.s. [1954] and M. R. Fisher [1956] – introducing household size into the regression equations linearly – observed generally smaller savings (rates) according as the household is larger. Watts – again using dummies – came across non-monotonic effects[10]. In our analysis,

[10] Watts also refers to a link between savings planning and family planning. Although its existence should be certainly recognized in principle, it is hardly relevant to our

we found hardly any significant, let alone systematic effect of family size on the urgency to consume. In as far as the household is made up of children, the latter contribute children's allowance and tax deduction to the family's *disposable* income. This may give a slight upwards tilt to the regression line of household size effects on savings.

d. *Occupation.* In our model, occupation – like age – affects savings both through the urgency to consume α, and through the financial resources R. In our analysis, we found – ceteris paribus – higher α_1 for manual workers than for non-manual ones. Compared with the former, the latter may count on a steeper rise of labour income, hence on higher income capitalization factors μ over a wide range of ages. With respect to savings rates, these two sub-effects counteract each other, most likely in such a way that the scales are turned in favour of R over α_1. This means that – *ceteris paribus* – the savings rates of manual workers generally exceed those of non-manual workers.

In other studies, the caesura is made elsewhere, viz. between employees and entrepreneurs (only scantily represented in the savings survey on which we based our analysis). Klein c.s. [1954] and M.R. Fisher [1956] confirmed the common opinion that entrepreneurs' marginal savings rates exceed those of employees; they also conclude that the sign of this difference remains the same after correcting for the effects of other factors (such as income) associated with occupational dependence or independence. This means that, compared with employment, entrepreneurship would also have a *net* positive effect on savings.

A possible explanation of these findings – if true – has already been discussed in section 9.2.1.5.1. Therefore, we now confine ourselves to one aspect of the savings differentials not taken into account before, viz. that entrepreneurs, aiming at continuity of their business might assign higher values to final personal wealth than employees would have done. Therefore, the higher savings rates of entrepreneurs compared with employees might be attributed, at least partly, to a final personal wealth effect.

e. *Education.* This factor is related to occupation, since for performing particular kinds of jobs, certain minimum levels of education are required. Watts [1958] expected that higher education, by making future needs seem to be less pressing, would give rise to higher savings. Empirically, however, he

---

study, because of the generally conservative attitude of the population of the Netherlands around 1960 with regard to birth control: the Netherlands show the highest birth rate in North-Western Europe. However, we shall revert to this important relationship in section 9.3.

found that on the contrary a relatively high level of education (of employees) is generally accompanied by a relatively low level of savings. The latter result agrees with the conclusions reached above about savings differentials between manual and non-manual workers: the higher the education, the faster the growth of income to be expected, hence the less need to save, or the better opportunity to dissave (initially).

f. *Ownership of dwelling*. Klein c.s. [1954] found no significant differences in savings rates between owners and renters of dwellings – if all other savings determinants are equal for both groups. Our analysis, however, led to the conclusion of a net positive association between ownership of a dwelling and savings rate; the two-way causality, however, could not be disentangled.

9.2.2. MACRO-MODELS

9.2.2.1. Relationships and differences between macro- and micro-models in general. Theoretically, macro-functions are aggregated micro-functions, pure and simple. Our macro-savings model was deduced in this way in chapter 5.

Empirical macro-functions, however, are seldom derived from micro-functions, although they often display a superficial resemblance to each other: aggregate economic relationships tend to be explained in a manner suggesting that aggregates are units in their own right instead of mere collections of individual decision units.

The differences between the micro- and macro-relationships are largely due to practical considerations, in particular, regarding the use to which they are put. Micro-models – if not confined to the realm of pure theory – are usually designed for cross-section analysis, to be applied to survey data. Macro-models, on the other hand, are typically destined for use in time-series analyses, forecasting or planning. Evidently, these differences in aims and means between the two affect their contents, form and methods of numerical specification.

With respect to contents, i.e. nature and definition of the variables, the specification of the models is largely determined by whatever statistical or other information is available. In this respect, time-series analysis is generally more restricted than cross-section analysis of survey data: whereas time series data should be available for at least 15 years at a stretch, the reference period for survey data can be and usually is limited to one year or less. Besides, analytical purposes play a more important rôle in conducting occasional special surveys than in collecting routine general data. In so far as macro-relationships, such as consumption- and savings-functions, are part of larger, and in particular national models, they bear the traces of the general economic development of the country concerned. On the other hand, micro-relationships based on survey data appear to be less afflicted by national stigmata.

9.2.2.2. Contents

9.2.2.2.1. Savings (and consumption). Most macro-economic savings and consumption functions – like their micro-economic counter-parts – relate to the household sector rather than to the entire economy of a country; for other sectors, macro-models sometimes include separate relationships, such as retained profits for the business sector (Dobrovolsky [1951], Lintner [1953], Klein and Goldberger [1955], Mazumdar [1959] and G.R. Fisher [1971]) and Government consumption; the latter variable, however, is usually left unexplained, as an exogenous variable, and possibly an instrument of economic policy. This preference for single-sector analysis seems fully justified, both for theoretical reasons (cf. section 7.1.3) and in view of the empirical results obtained in our time-series analysis: those pertaining to the household sector alone (personal savings) are far superior to those pertaining to the entire economy (national savings); cf. section 7.4.3.

Some time-series analyses relate to a part or a particular mode of savings only (e.g. Tinbergen and van der Meer [1938]) with respect to savings through savings bank accounts). In our opinion, the analysis of fluctuations in such specialized savings could better be carried out in two stages, as suggested by Korteweg [1971] (cf. section 9.2.1.2.1).

9.2.2.2.2. Income. As in micro-savings analyses, (current) income is again the favourite variable for explaining variations in (aggregate) savings and consumption. Again, 'income' in this context means disposable income, i.e. net of taxes unless otherwise stated[11].

Time-series analysis permits the introduction of lagged variables, such as lagged income – in the wake of current income – into the regression equations. Intensive use – or rather abuse – is made of the latter possibility; if anything, it improves the 'fit', which is the first (and sometimes the only) consideration taken seriously by econometricians. The average retardations

---

[11] Such an exception is the study by Smith [1964], trying to explain savings in terms of national income and the rate of income tax separately.

implied by such distributed lag systems are not fixed a priori, for theoretical reasons, but merely a posteriori, opportunistically.

It looks anti-chronistic that economic model builders cling to the past, whereas savings behaviour is future-oriented. The reason, of course, is the lack of independent information about income expectations of entire populations. At least some surveys, on which synchronous cross-section analyses were based, doled out shreds of information about expected signs of changes (cf. Katona [1960]).

True, a number of studies paid homage to the concept of expected incomes, or even to its present value, merely by mentioning or symbolising it. When it comes to the point, however, they either adopt Friedman's operational definition of 'permanent' income as an x-year moving average of past incomes (cf. Brumberg [1956]), or approximate it by a linear combination of the average wage rate and an index of human wealth (Hamburger [1955]). Evidently, such short-cuts have little if anything to do with expectations proper.

Our macro-model neither ventures into the future nor retreats into the past, but keeps to the current period statically, according to a number of (admittedly questionable) assumptions.

Time-series analysis permits proponents of extremely retarded reaction to vent their feelings, for instance by introducing the highest level of consumption or income reached before (Duesenberry [1949], Brumberg [1956]) into the consumption function. In a continually upward moving consumptive society, such a variable drops out; in an increasingly economizing economy, the variable becomes a constant, hence it cannot be distinguished from the proper constant, otherwise known as the intercept. Only in the case of ups and downs, is there any fun in handling that variable; but then, econometricians thrive on ups and downs of economic life, just as physicians thrive on illness.

Apparently, our own macro-model has no chamber for such a ghost of the past; as observed in section 9.1.2, however, we might suppose that the urgency to consume (now) could receive a lift from previous higher levels of consumption. This means that peak-consumption would affect current savings and consumption only when joined to current income. This applies to the macro- as well as to the micro-savings and consumption function.

Furthermore, this 'nostalgia' variable still poses some tricky problems of aggregation, since it would be a miracle if everyone experienced the bliss of peak-consumption at the same time. Even apart from this 'far-fetched' variable, the derivation of macro-savings and -consumption function from micro ditto is riddled with aggregation problems.

First, introduction of non-linearities into the micro-functions requires the macro-functions to be adorned with special aggregates; e.g. income-squares in the micro-functions would entail income-variances in the macro-functions – provided the coefficients in the micro-functions are the same for all individuals. Generally, such refinements are omitted; the reason may be a justified fear of multicollinearity.

Occasionally, an indicator for the inequality of the income distribution, such as the α of Pareto, is included in the macro consumption function (Staehle [1937]); the erroneousness of such a slipshod procedure was, however, duly criticized by de Wolff [1939].

Sometimes, the strong assumption of equality of the coefficients in the micro-functions for all individuals is deemed inacceptable; then it may be replaced by the weaker assumption that the equality holds good within certain groups of people only. In particular, a distinction is made between entrepreneurs and employees, supposedly endowed with different marginal propensities to consume.

In practice, income received by entrepreneurs and employees is superseded by profits and labour remuneration respectively; evidently, such a silent shift is a mental error, since entrepreneurs may receive salaries (e.g. if moonlighting), while employees may receive capital income. In view of all the other defects of those analyses, however, disregarding such logical differences may not matter very much.

Treatment of income in consumption and savings functions in the manner outlined above, i.e. with distributed lags and distinction between wage and non-wage income, is established practice. One comes across it, inter alia, in the short-run models for the Netherlands (Central Planning Bureau [1970]) and the United Kingdom (Hilton and Crossfield [1970] and Surrey [1970]).

9.2.2.2.3. Personal wealth. Personal wealth is included in a fair number of macro-economic consumption and savings functions, studied separately or in the framework of complete annual models.

Usually, however, it is represented by liquid assets only. Examples are provided by Klein and Goldberger [1955] for the U.S.A., by the Central Planning Bureau [1970] for the Netherlands, and by Surrey [1970] for the United Kingdom; the latter's competitors, Hilton and Crossfield [1970] experimented with both net-worth and liquid-assets indicators of personal wealth. Liquid assets are also incorporated in separate consumption studies such as those carried out by Stone and Rowe [1956]. A rather peculiar 'measured wealth' variable, mainly consisting of debt, was used by Hamburger [1955]. On the other hand, Klein [1958] approximated national wealth by adding cumulated savings to a benchmark-value dating back to 1896; essentially the same method was adopted by us in chapter 7.

9.2.2.2.4. Rate of Interest. Consumption and savings functions comprise the rate (or rates) of interest less frequently than personal wealth. This may seem strange, considering that much more statistical information is available about the former type of variable than about the latter; on the other hand, the abundance of interest data may be the very reason that hampers the construction of one or more time-series of interest rates relevant to total consumption and savings, by 'embarras de choix'.

Among the few consumption functions including interest rates are those by Radice [1939] for Great Britain and by the Central Planning Bureau [1970] for the Netherlands.

9.2.2.2.5. Other variables. Among the other variables occasionally entering consumption and savings functions, the most conspicuous ones are lagged consumption, rate of change of the consumer price level and population size.

Allegedly, the introduction of lagged consumption in consumption functions rests on the assumption of an adjustment process à la Nerlove [1958]. Actually, however, the popularity of such linear first-order differential equations may rather be due to the high serial correlation of consumption over time[12], contributing considerably to the goodness of fit of the regression. With a view to avoiding multi-collinearity, lagged consumption appears to be an alternative and not a supplementary variable for explaining savings and consumption; cf. e.g. Klein and Goldberger [1955] for the U.S.A., and Ball and Drake [1964] as well as Hilton and Crossfield [1970] for the U.K.

On the other hand, neither our micro-model nor our macro-model leave space for adjustment processes. In our opinion, allocation of resources to consumption and savings is a matter of anticipation rather than adjustment; and insofar as adjustment – to unexpected changes, in (say) income – may be needed, we assume that it takes place instantaneously, at least with respect to total consumption.

---

[12] In turn, this phenomenon might be explained in terms of Nerlove's adjustment process.

The *rate of change in price level* presumably aims at introducing a speculative motive into the consumption and savings functions. The alternative versions of the basic model dealt with in sections 2.8, 3.4 and 4.3 also examined effects of changes in price levels; the essential difference, however, is that the latter represent expectations (for the future), whereas the former denote faits accomplis. The past is relevant only insofar as it affects the expectations, but such relationships are implied rather than explicated.

In our model, moreover, consumption and savings are influenced by the difference between the rate of interest and the change in prices (i.e. I. Fisher's 'real' rate of interest). True, the consumption function in the short-term model of the Central Planning Bureau for the Netherlands [1970] features both a change-in-price-level and an interest variable, but separately and in different forms, hence precluding any comparison.

Alternatively, price deflators have been applied to both consumption and explanatory variables such as income, for instance by Ball and Drake [1964] and by Hilton and Crossfield [1970] for the U.K.

Finally, a few models – such as Klein and Goldberger's [1955] – include population size as a separate explanatory variable in their consumption functions. This seems redundant, since population size is already implied in the aggregation of micro-relationships to macro-relationships. Deflating the variables by population size – as done by Hamburger [1955] – seems less objectionable; it may even help to improve the efficiency of parameter estimates (by O.L.S.). For this purpose, however, such a deflation is neither necessary nor sufficient; transformation of the savings functions into those for savings rates by using income as a deflator – or, equivalently, application of G.L.S. – is more appropriate.

9.2.2.3. Form of the relationships. Linearity is the rule in macro-relationships even more than in micro-relationships. For one thing, macro-variables show generally smaller coefficients of variation (over time) than micro-variables (between individuals); hence, there is less need for adopting fancy forms in time-series analyses than in cross-section studies, in order to allow for possible curvi-linearity. In systems of equations, non-linearity, at least with respect to endogenous variables and parameters, is still difficult to manage; consequently, consumption equations that form part of them are preferably kept linear.

The meaning of linearity of the relationships differs, however, according to the terms in which the variables are couched. For instance, the variables can be defined in absolute terms (as in most studies), or in terms of relative differences from year to year (as in the model of the Central Planning Bureau [1970]); the latter kind of specification is roughly equivalent to log-linearity.

Another aspect of the relationships is homogeneity (as in our model, with respect to income and wealth) or inhomogeneity (as in most other studies). Presence of a constant term in a relationship for savings as such means linear dependence of savings rates on the reciprocal of income. This implication is seldom welcomed enthusiastically, and occasionally rejected explicitly. In particular, this applies to those who believe that the macro-savings rates fluctuate around a horizontal trend. Since they cannot explain this secular constancy of savings rates theoretically, they attribute it to some mysterious Law of Nature. Adherents to this view, of whom Duesenberry is a prominent exponent, try to wriggle out of the consequences of trend-like increasing savings rates, with income increasing and the intercept negative; their favourite trick is to introduce into the savings and consumption functions escape variables (from the past), such as the previous highest level of consumption reached.

In savings functions that are linear in the link relatives of the variables, presence of a constant term implies exponential autonomous trends of savings.

The simplest way to avoid these unintended and awkward consequences of the constant term is to drop it – as has been done in our model[13].

The additional advantage is that deflating all variables by the same factor leaves the relationships essentially unchanged.

9.2.2.4. Estimation methods. The parameters of the separate savings and consumption equations have generally been estimated by means of ordinary least squares.

In so far as the consumption functions are part of complete national models, more sophisticated estimation methods, such as two-stage least squares or limited information maximum likelihood, tend to be adopted. However, these methods do not always improve the likelihood of the signs and orders of magnitude of the parameter estimates.

For our savings equation the 'Durbin least squares' method appeared to yield the most reliable results. Attempts at estimating the parameters in the

---

[13] This implies rejection of the alternative version of a micro-savings model with positive minimum levels of consumption subsumed in the utility function (cf. section 4.3.2).

savings relationship together with those of an aggregate production function in a three-equation model failed so far.

9.2.2.5. Results

9.2.2.5.1. Income. According to all macro-analyses of consumption and savings reviewed, the estimated marginal propensities to consume were always found to lie between 0 and 1.

This also applies to the cases in which income was introduced with distributed lags; then, the sums of the coefficients of the lagged and unlagged variables, considered as an approximation of the long-run marginal propensity to consume, were also less than 1. If lagged consumption is introduced into the consumption function, the coefficients of both variables (b_- and b) are always found to be positive and less than 1, together as well as separately; hence, the resulting 'equilibrium' marginal propensity to consume $b/(1 - b_-)$ also remains below 1.

The values of the marginal propensities to consume resulting from time-series analyses of consumption or savings generally exceed the values obtained in our analyses of both time-series and cross-section data.

The reason is, of course, the absence and presence of a personal wealth term, respectively; the latter absorbs at least part of the apparent effect of income on savings, especially in view of the fairly high correlation between income and personal wealth. The latter association is mainly due to the income-generating effect of capital accumulation; common 'scale' factors, such as population growth, play a secondary role.

Analyses incorporating wealth variables next to income effects (cf. Central Planning Bureau [1970]) yielded notably lower marginal propensities to consume than those disregarding personal wealth.

9.2.2.5.2. Personal wealth. Invariably, time-series analyses including wealth variables yield positive and negative effects of wealth on consumption and savings, respectively. This agrees with both the implications of our theory and the outcome of our own study of macro-savings functions – whether resulting from time-series analysis or based on the outcome of cross-section analyses.

On the other hand, the ratios of wealth-to-income effects in the other analyses tend to be even smaller than those resulting from our own efforts.

9.2.2.5.3. Rate of interest. In general, time-series analyses did not succeed in yielding significant effects of the rate of interest on savings (as already observed in section 9.2.2.2). A single one by Radice [1939] showed a positive value for that effect. This agrees with both our empirical results and theoretical expectations. The failure of other studies to show significant effects of the interest rate may be due, at least partly, to the unsatisfactory manner in which it used to be included in savings functions, to wit, separately and additively, instead of in multiplicative bonds, with income and personal wealth – as in our own analysis.

9.3. Research prospects

9.3.1. BRIDGING THEORY AND EMPIRICAL RESEARCH

At this final stage of our study we remind the reader of its main objective, viz. bridging the gap between theory and empirical research. What has been achieved so far is a rather narrow and provisional fly-over – with occasional pitfalls –, in need of extension and completion. As always, such bridging should be carried out from two sides – preferably simultaneously, so that theory and empirical analysis can meet half-way. The pertinent research program is outlined below.

9.3.2. EXTENSION AND ELABORATION OF SAVINGS THEORY

9.3.2.1. Micro-theory. Chapter 2 laid down rather heavy foundations for a general theory of savings. On that basis chapter 3 erected a slightly more articulate, intermediate structure, characterized by additive-separability of its utility functions. Chapter 4 extended it into a specific, addi-log linear micro-model.

It can be applied directly to cross-section data; furthermore, it allows a macro-model to be built on top of it, for application to time-series data.

These advantages, of course, are bought at the cost of over-simplification, lowering its degree of realism and limiting its scope of application. Chapter 4 offers a few suggestions for making the model more flexible, in particular, by considering future rates of interest and levels of consumer prices as variable rather than constant (section 4.3.4)[14]. This modification broadens the scope

[14] Another proposal, viz. to adopt survival rates instead of life expectancies, in order to approximate the present value of financial resources, has been put into practice in chapter 6.

of the model, inter alia, for assessing effects of inflation on savings. Hardly any theoretical difficulties are involved in such a generalization; the main problem, however, will be to underpin such extended models empirically.

A further step on the road towards realism would be to make a distinction between the lower rates of interest to be received from assets and the higher rates to be paid on loans. The abruptness of the transition from a higher to a lower rate of interest, or vice versa, following a change of sign in net worth, makes it difficult to handle this problem theoretically, let alone empirically (cf. Section 2.8.1.2). Provisionally, scanning the problem by means of simulation seems to be the best procedure.

This also applies to the related problem of the effect of a possible maximum debt on (optimal) savings behaviour. Preliminary exercises in this field (cf. appendix A to chapter 4) only just scratch the surface, where actually an in-depth study (on being in debt) seems indicated.

These refinements of the model of chapter 4, however, would still confine the model to consumption as the only kind of argument of the utility function. In order to break through this limitation, other versions of the savings model dealt with in chapters 2 and 3 should be made as specific as the basic model in chapter 4.

The simplest way to do so is to adopt the same, uniform type of utility function for the modified versions as for the basic model. Following the example set by Ghez [1970], we can specify the utility function (3.3.2.1) including hours of work as a completely addi-log linear function:

$$a_l(C_l) = \alpha_l \ln C_l \quad \text{with} \sum_{l=1}^{L} \alpha_l = 1 \quad \text{(as in (4.1.2.1))} \qquad (9.3.2.1.1)$$

and similarly

$$\beta_l(W_l) = \beta_l \ln (\bar{W}_l - W_l), \qquad (9.3.2.1.2)$$

with $\bar{W}_l$ the maximum number of hours (to be) available in periods $l = 1, \ldots, L$.

Then, the general solution (3.3.2.3) of the optimal consumption and working hours vector becomes:

$$C = \bar{R}_L \cdot d^{-1}\alpha; \qquad (9.3.2.1.3)$$

with $\bar{R}_L = -\Delta K + \bar{W}'U'd + \underline{Y}'d$, $\bar{W}$ being the vector of the maximum number of working hours, and

$$W = \bar{W} - \bar{R}_L \cdot (U'd)^{-1} \cdot \beta. \qquad (9.3.2.1.4)$$

Hence, the result is an additional separate set of work-hour equations, temporally corresponding to the consumption functions; practically, they are couched in the same terms, except that the marginal rates of remuneration comprised in the U-matrix enter the work-hours equations but not the consumption functions.

Therefore, specification of the more elaborate versions of the savings model in analogy to the basic model does not pose any theoretical difficulties[15]; this also holds good if the log-linear form is replaced by an equally well-manageable one, such as a quadric. Again the problems involved in imposing specifications such as (9.3.2.1.1) plus (9.3.2.1.2) on utility functions are more of an empirical nature, viz.:

(a) to test the appropriateness of such a specification (against alternatives), and

(b) to find methods for assigning numerical values to the parameters.

With respect to the contemporaneous values β_1 of the β's for different income recipients, the latter problem can be solved by calculating those individual values as:

$$\beta_1 = (\overline{W}_1 - W_1)/\{R_L\,(\dot{U}'d)_1^{-1}\}; \tag{9.3.2.1.5}$$

this presupposes, of course, that the elements of the U-matrix can be specified numerically, and that information about $\overline{W}_1$ and W_1 is available.

Such a model could be objected to on the grounds that as a rule working hours are fixed, or at least bound by minima and/or maxima; this would violate the assumption of free choice (with respect to the length of the working day or week) underlying the model implicitly.

Still, elaboration of this version of the model seems worthwhile. In view of the tendency to reduce the length of the working week, to extend the duration of annual leave, and to lower the age of retirement, the work-leisure dilemma gains in importance. Therefore, the difficulties resulting from incorporating working hours in the model have to be coped with anyhow.

On the other hand, inclusion of final personal wealth in the utility function seems too far-fetched to be taken seriously.

Furthermore, sociometric influences are not only ill-defined and elusive, but also too cumbersome to take into account at the moment.

Evaluation of the effect of uncertainty (such as relating to income expectations) on savings will be even more difficult, theoretically as well as practically; still, they are worth examining.

---

[15] Apart from the impact of income tax, cf. section 9.3.3.2.

The preceding suggestions intend to bring at least some of the versions of the savings model dealt with in chapters 2 and 3 to the stage of development reached by the basic model in chapter 4.

A more radical change in savings theory could be brought about by broadening its basis; by extending the scope of its utility function, it can develop into a comprehensive decision theory for the individual. Including hours of work in the model is already an important step towards that end. Such a theory, however, is still incomplete if not merged with a theory of family planning. In chapter 6, the size and composition of the household were treated as 'data', implying a passive attitude of people with respect to procreation once they are married. This may be a fair enough description of the situation in the Netherlands around 1960, the reference year of the Savings Survey. In the present and future 'pill'-era, however, such a premise seems to be untenable. This means that the utility functions should include, inter alia, household composition (and size) at various stages of the individual's life cycle, as proposed by Ben-Porath [1970]. Children may have been considered as providers for their parents' old age; however, the introduction and extension of old-age pension plans and the decline in children's willingness to care for their ageing parents at home, remove virtually all economic advantages of procreation. This transfers children from the category of indispensables to that of luxuries – as recognized by Becker [1960].

Therefore, a psychological approach to the problem of specifying the utility functions should supplement the economic approach. Since the usual a priori specifications of the utility function would fail in such a case, hardly any progress can be made in this field without quantitative, empirical and experimental research on human indifference functions.

In conclusion, we should like to point out that it does not make sense to push economic theory beyond the point where it stops to be operational due to lack of the statistical data to which it can be applied. Anyhow, this implies that economic theory should refrain from including elements that cannot be expressed in quantitative terms.

9.3.2.2. Macro-theory. The difficulties involved in extending micro-savings theory are amplified in attempts to build a macro-theory on top of it: the aggregation requirements are so exacting that they hardly allow the micro-model to become more sophisticated. At least, this applies to the form of the underlying utility function; separability is the pass-word here.

The consequences of the specification of the micro-model for the derivation of a macro-model are co-responsible for the simplicity of the micro-savings model of chapter 4. As set out in chapter 5, we already had to make use of an embarrassingly large number of assumptions and approximations in order to render aggregation at all possible[16].

Another limitation is of a practical nature: the macro-savings function has to be couched in terms of variables that can be assigned numerical values on the basis of statistical or a priori information. If the requisite data is available for the separate sex- and age-groups, we could leave the derivation of macro-savings functions at the first stage of aggregation (5.1.2.1); this would allow us a wider scope for refining the micro-savings function.

Furthermore, we would not have to confine the specification of the macro-savings function to totals or arithmetical averages, but could extend it to other aggregates such as variances and geometrical means, if pertinent information is at our disposal.

Meanwhile, one may experiment with alternative, more general macro-savings models, by dropping, relaxing or replacing one or more of the assumptions underlying the basic macro-model (5.1.3.13), or by introducing novel ones. For example:

(a) assumptions (5.1.3.4) and (5.1.3.9) about the constancies of the income and wealth shares of age–sex classes may be replaced by assumptions about trend-like movements of such shares, or by assumptions about constant ratios of mean income and/or wealth per income recipient between age–sex classes;
(b) assumptions (5.1.3.5) could be adjusted accordingly;
(c) in (5.1.3.8), the zeroes could give way to present values of paid-up life insurance premiums at the beginning of periods t.

9.3.3. APPLICATION

9.3.3.1. General. Abstract savings theory may have overtaken the practical possibilities of implementation; actually, chapters 2 and 3 may have contributed to that impression, even though we aspired to arrive at 'meaningful

---

[16] This applies to nearly all behavioural relationships in economics, but here even more than elsewhere. However, it does not come to the fore, since macro-relationships are usually posited without clarification instead of being derived from micro-functions. Therefore, the underlying assumptions and approximations cannot be subjected to a critical examination, which might expose them as incorrect.

theorems' in the Samuelsonian sense, as much as possible. What is needed now, above all, is **information**.

In principle, the kind of information required is dictated by theory[17]. The amount, frequency, and in particular the accuracy of the information to be obtained depends on the overall reliability of the outcome of the analysis aimed at, if not by the financial and political limitations of practicability.

9.3.3.2. Cross-section analysis. Most data needed for application of the micro-model in cross-sectional analysis will have to be collected in special

TABLE 9.2.

Additional information for analytical purposes

No.	Desiderata	Purposes
1	Extending savings surveys to all kinds of income recipients, in particular to entrepreneurs.	In order to avoid bias in the application of employees' 'urgencies to consume' to the entire population.
2	Repeating savings surveys.	In order to permit the estimation of changes in the 'urgencies to consume' of people classified by age, sex, occupational status and possible other characteristics.
3	Extracting (quantitative) information about the expectations regarding their future income, bequest intentions and discount rates.	In order to improve estimates of the present value of their expected 'financial resources'.
4	Gathering impressions of people's future need patterns, as well as indifference patterns with respect to children, leisure and consumption.	In order to render possible extensions of the savings model on the basis of more sophisticated utility functions.
5	Asking about people's religion.	In order to test Weber's theory of the impact of Protestantism on capitalism.

savings surveys. Table 9.2 lists the kind of information desired – approximately in order of decreasing priority – for the purposes mentioned.

---

[17] In contradistinction to that which occurs all too frequently, viz. that the theory is adjusted so as to accommodate the data that happen to be collected or published. It is also at variance with a common practice in sociology, viz. that unhampered by any theoretical attachment, a deluge of questions is poured over the poor interviewees according to the device 'one never can tell what may come out of it'.

With respect to this list, the following comments are in order:

Ad 1. The most serious omission in the 1960 Savings Survey of the Netherlands was that coverage was restricted to employees and pensioners, excluding entrepreneurs except in the rare cases in which members, other than heads of household, are independent[18]. True, some foreign surveys did include entrepreneurs; however, they hardly lend themselves to the kind of analysis applied to the Dutch survey data. In particular, it is hardly feasible to obtain savings and related data pertaining to individuals from those household-oriented surveys unless special arrangements for separate processing are made – as done in the Dutch case.

Ad 2. A new savings survey – already overdue – would be the ideal occasion to extend the survey coverage such that it becomes practically comprehensive, and to extend and rephrase the questionnaire, such as to include the questions posed under 3 through 5.

Ad 3. The drift of this proposal is to individualize the calculation of present values of financial resources rather than to carry it out on a collectivistic basis – as had to be done by us due to lack of private data. Indications of the order of magnitude (say, in five-percent intervals of expected changes in income within, say, the next five years) would already be an improvement, compared with the present state of ignorance; these data could be used to adjust the ready-made age-patterns of income for groups to individual peculiarities, giving them a more made-to-measure appearance. Mutatis mutandis, this also applies to private rates of discounting and the amount people would like to bequeath.

---

[18] We are fully aware of the reasons for provisionally excluding entrepreneurs from a Savings Survey – as mentioned in section 6.1.1 above and explained by the Central Bureau of Statistics [1963]. Independent workers are a much more difficult group of people to interview than employees, both for accounting and psychological reasons. First, the business sector and the private sector are often intermingled to such a degree that it is difficult to disentangle them; therefore, savings data of entrepreneurs is impaired by arbitrariness in both the drawing of a dividing line between the two sectors and the calculation of business profits and losses. Second, compared with employees, entrepreneurs are more reluctant to provide information about their financial affairs: for one thing, it is more difficult and time-consuming for the latter than for the former. Even apart from that, however, entrepreneurs resent being questioned about their state of affairs still more than other people. This may be interpreted, at least partly, as a sign of their independence: if they were as complaisant as employees are expected to be, they would probably be employees rather than entrepreneurs. This means that if entrepreneurs are covered by Savings Surveys, the pertinent data will generally be less reliable than data relating to other groups.

Taxation (of income) poses problems of its own. The income capitalization factors μ are calculated on the basis of ratios between gross incomes per group, although they are applied to net (disposable) income of individuals. This procedure would be correct only in the (merely hypothetical) case in which the average tax rates are constant. Contrariwise, the progressiveness of wage- and income-tax implies increasing and decreasing tax rates with income increasing and decreasing respectively – for people remaining in the same tax category. On the one hand, income tends to rise for the majority of people up to a certain age; on the other hand, by marrying and getting tax-deductible children, their tax rate falls if they would continue to earn the same amount of money. The latter phenomenon counteracts the former to a certain extent, although both the spouse and the children may contribute to the income imputed to the head of the household (children's allowance, if nothing else)[18a]. Most likely, the balance will generally be in favour of the tax-rate-increasing factors. This means that the income capitalization factors calculated for the cross-section analysis in chapter 6 may be over-estimated.

This bias might be reduced by multiplying mean typical income by the ratio of disposable to total income per sex-age-occupational group, regardless of the actual marital status and household composition of the person in question.

Taxation has even more penetrating effects in savings models taking account of possible substitution between income and leisure. The marginal rates of remuneration entering those models should be interpreted as *net of taxes*; however, the marginal tax rates corresponding to the marginal rates of *gross* remuneration depend, inter alia, on *total* income. The rather complicated, viz. elliptic relationships between Dutch marginal tax rates and income[18b] give rise to mathematical problems that defy analytical solutions, but are perhaps amenable to simulation.

Ad 4. Such supplementary information about people's subjective pay-offs is badly needed if the utility functions incorporate hours of work, and a fortiori household development variables. The authors are well aware of the difficulties involved; therefore, prior small-scale experimentation is in order.

[18a, b] The tax reform in the Netherlands, effective January 1, 1973, changed all this, by replacing the essentially elliptic tax-income function by a broken-linear function, and by taxing reparately the wife's and the husband's labour income.

Ad 5. Finally, it would be interesting to see whether there is any truth in Weber's [1934] theories about the effect of Protestantism on economic behaviour; and in particular, whether adherence to the Calvinistic principle of 'ora et labora' (pray and toil) results in (ceteris paribus) higher rates of savings by Protestants compared with Roman Catholics. It merely requires insertion of a question about religion in the questionnaire[19].

In order to avoid misunderstanding, we hasten to add that we are realistic enough to be fully aware of the cast-iron logic of the adage 'ask no questions and be told no lies'. For those who subscribe to the view that in regard to information 'nothing is better than anything wrong', the logical consequence of the latter consideration is not to start any empirical survey among human beings, or, if started, to discontinue it, and in no case to extend it. On the other hand, those endowed with the courage of despair are more inclined to gamble, according to the rule: 'any information, however defective, is better than no information at all'. In our opinion, both extremes should be shunned; as economists, we should proceed with collecting more detailed data by asking more probing questions till the decreasing marginal utility of this additional effort will be overtaken by its increasing marginal cost – heeding its decreasing reliability.

9.3.3.3. Time-series analysis. In order to improve time-series analysis, additional and better data on macro-economic variables is more important than refining methods of estimation[20]; this applies in particular if it enables us to deal with more detailed and sophisticated relationships, such as savings functions for separate age–sex classes, free of unrealistic assumptions and distorting approximations. Above all, this requires more information about personal wealth, especially below the property tax exemption limit; hitherto, the wealth variables are the weakest of all explanatory variables, even for all age–sex groups taken together.

---

[19] In the absence of a question on religion in the 1960 Savings Survey of the Netherlands, the modal religion in the interviewee's place of residence could be taken as a substitute for the person's real religion: because of the prevailing geographical concentration of religious groups, such a guess would be right in about 55 per cent of all cases provided the distinction according to religion is confined to the five major categories (Roman Catholics, Calvinist-Protestants, Dutch Reformed, other religion, no religion).

[20] All too frequently, one finds highly sophisticated estimation procedures applied to models that hardly deserve them, in view of their incorrect specification and/or unreliable statistical substratum.

On the basis of sounder estimates of the variables, one may try again to estimate the savings functions within the context of a system of equations, as suggested in section 7.3.4.

Still, the ideal solution would be to obviate estimation of macro-savings functions altogether, by basing their numerical specification on micro-data, collected in series of savings surveys. It is true that pertinent efforts reported in section 7.3.4. did not yet meet with complete success: the partial nature of the information at our disposal foiled such a tour de force. Thus, we complete the circle: progress in savings research requires that extension of our knowledge of the individuals' behaviour with respect to savings and related phenomena keeps pace with the development of savings theory; in turn, this theory prescribes the kind of information to be collected.

REFERENCES

ABRAHAMSE, A. P. J. [1969]. *The Powers of Some Tests in the General Linear Model.* Rotterdam, Rotterdam University Press.

ABRAHAMSE, A. P. J. and J. KOERTS [1969]. A Comparison between the Power of the Durbin-Watson Test and the Power of the BLUS Test. *Journal of the American Statistical Association*, Vol. 64, pp 938–948.

ANDO, A. and F. MODIGLIANI [1963]. The 'Life Cycle' Hypothesis of Saving: Aggregate Implications and Tests. *American Economic Review*, Vol. 53, pp. 55–84.

ARROW, K. J. and M. KURZ [1969]. Optimal Consumer Allocation over an Infinite Horizon. *Journal of Economic Theory*, Vol. 1, pp. 68–91.

BALL, R. J. and P. S. DRAKE [1964]. The Relationship between Aggregate Consumption and Wealth. *International Economic Review*, Vol. 5, pp. 63–81.

BANNINK, R. and W. H. SOMERMEYER [1966]. Determinanten van de individuele consumptiedrang; een econometrische analyse van de resultaten der C.B.S.-spaarenquête 1961. (Dutch, with Summary in English: Determinants of Income Recipients' Urgency to Consume; an Econometric Analysis of the 1960 Savings Survey in the Netherlands.) *Statistische en econometrische onderzoekingen*, issued by the Netherlands Central Bureau of Statistics, no. 7.

BARTEN, A. P. [1964]. Family Composition, Prices and Expenditure Patterns. *Colston Papers*, Vol. 16. Reprint Series no. 95 of the Econometric Institute, Netherlands School of Economics, Rotterdam.

BARTEN, A. P. [1966]. *Theorie en Empirie van een Volledig Stelsel van Vraagvergelijkingen.* The Hague.

BECKER, G. S. [1960]. An Economic Analysis of Fertility. *Demographic and Economic Changes in Developed Countries.* National Bureau of Economic Research, Washington.

BECKMANN, M. J. [1959]. A Dynamic Programming Model. *Cowles Foundation Discussion Paper*, no. 68. New Haven, Connecticut, U.S.A.

BEN-PORATH, Y. [1970]. Fertility, Education and Income – a Different Context. Paper presented at the Second World Congress of the Econometric Society, held in Cambridge, England.

BODKIN, R. G. [1970]. A Set of Additive Relationships Explaining Personal Savings and the Categories of Consumption Expenditures for the United States of America 1949–1963. Paper presented at the Second World Congress of the Econometric Society, held in Cambridge, England.

BRADY, DOROTHY S. [1946]. Expenditures, Savings and Incomes. *The Review of Economic Statistics*, Vol. 28, pp. 216–218.

BRADY, DOROTHY S. and R. D. FRIEDMAN [1947]. Savings and the Income Distributions. *Studies in Income and Wealth*, Vol. 10. National Bureau of Economic Research, New York.

BRUMBERG, R.E. [1956]. An Approximation to the Aggregate Saving Function. *The Economic Journal*, Vol. 116, pp. 66–72.

CENTRAL BUREAU OF STATISTICS, NETHERLANDS [1964]. *Inkomensverdeling 1959 en Vermogensverdeling 1960* (Distribution of Personal Income 1959 and Distribution of Personal Wealth 1960). Zeist, W. de Haan N.V.

CENTRAL BUREAU OF STATISTICS, NETHERLANDS [✱✱]. *Nationale Rekeningen*, diverse jaren (National Accounts, various years).

CENTRAL BUREAU OF STATISTICS, NETHERLANDS [1961]. *Maandstatistiek van het Financiewezen* (Monthly Bulletin of Financial Statistics), February 1961.

CENTRAL BUREAU OF STATISTICS, NETHERLANDS [1963, 1964]. *Spaaronderzoek 1960* (Savings Survey 1960).

Deel 1: *Methodologische inleiding* (Part 1: Methods and Definitions).

Deel 2: *Resultaten met specificatie per spaarvorm* (Part 2: Results and Specifications per Mode of Savings).

Deel 3: *Resultaten met specificatie per inkomensklasse* (Part 3: Results and Specifications per Income Bracket).

Zeist, W. de Haan N.V.

CENTRAL BUREAU OF STATISTICS, NETHERLANDS [1964a]. *XIIIe Volkstelling mei 1960* (13th Population Census of the Netherlands, May 1960).

Deel 4: *Geslacht, leeftijd en burgerlijke staat* (Part 4: Sex, Age and Marital Status).

Zeist, W. de Haan N.V.

CENTRAL BUREAU OF STATISTICS, NETHERLANDS [1967]. *Sterftetafels voor de Nederlandse Bevolking, 1961–1965* (Life Tables for the Dutch Population, 1961–1965). Zeist, W. de Haan N.V.

CENTRAL PLANNING BUREAU, NETHERLANDS [1970]. *Centraal Economisch Plan*. The Hague, Staatsuitgeverij.

DALMULDER, J.J.J. [1959]. *De Ontwikkeling van het Aantal Academici tot 1980. Aanbod en Behoefte*. Rapport van de Commissie voor Statistiek van het Interuniversitair Contactorgaan. Zeist, W. de Haan, N.V.

DE JONG, F.J., *see* JONG, F.J. DE.

DE WOLFF, P., *see* WOLFF, P. DE.

DOBROVOLSKY, S.P. [1951]. *Corporate Income Retention 1915–1943*. National Bureau of Economic Research, New York.

DUESENBERRY, J.S. [1949^1, 1967^2]. *Income, Savings and the Theory of Consumer Behaviour*. Cambridge, Mass. U.S.A., Harvard University Press.

DURBIN, J. [1960]. The Fitting of Time-Series Models. *Review of the International Statistical Institute*, Vol. 28, pp. 233–243.

EIZENGA, W. [1960]. *Demographic Factors and Savings*. Amsterdam, North-Holland Publishing Company.

ETTINGER, R.C.W. [1963]. *The Prospect of Immortality*. New York, Doubleday and Company.

FASE, M.M.G. [1969]. *An Econometric Model of Age–Income Profiles; An Analysis of Dutch Income Data 1958–1967*. Rotterdam, Rotterdam University Press.

FERBER, R. [1953]. *A Study of Aggregate Consumption Functions*. National Bureau of Economic Research, New York, Technical Paper no. 8.

FISHER, G.R. [1971]. Quarterly Dividend Behaviour. Ch. 6 of *The Econometric Study of the United Kingdom*, edited by K. Hilton and D. K. Heatherfield (Conference on Short-Run Econometric Models of the U.K. Economy). London, Macmillan and Company.

FISHER, I. [1930]. *The Theory of Interest, as Determined by Impatience to Spend and Opportunity to Invest it.* New York, F. Cass.

FISHER, M. R. [1956]. Exploration in Savings Behaviour. *Bulletin of the Oxford University Institute of Statistics*, Vol. 11, pp. 201–277.

FREY, B. and L. J. LAK [1968]. Towards a Mathematical Model of Government Behaviour. *Gesammelte Beiträge zur Konferenz: Mathematical Theory of Committees and Elections*, Band I, pp. 114–156. Wien, Institut für Wirtschaftsforschung.

FRIEDMAN, M. [1957]. *A Theory of the Consumption Function.* National Bureau of Economic Research, New York. Princeton, Princeton University Press.

FRISCH, R. [1933]. Monopole-Polypole, la Notion de Force dans l'Economie. *Nationaløkonomisk Tidskrift*, Vol. 72.

FRISCH, R. [1934]. *Statistical Confluence Analysis by Means of Complete Regression Systems.* Oslo, Universitetets Ökonomiske Institutt.

GHEZ, G. R. [1970]. *A Theory of Life Cycle Consumption.* Unpublished Ph. D. dissertation, Columbia University, New York.

GRAMM, WENDY LEE-, *see* LEE-GRAMM, WENDY.

GRILISCHES, Z. [1963]. Production Functions, Technical Change and All That. Report 6328 of the Econometric Institute, Netherlands School of Economics, Rotterdam.

GRONAU, R. [1970]. An Economic Approach to Marriage: the Intra-Family Allocation of Time. Paper presented at the Second World Congress of the Econometric Society, held in Cambridge, England.

GUPTA, Y. P. [1969]. A Note on the Durbin's Method of Fitting a Linear Regression Model with Autocorrelated Disturbances. Report 6907 of the Econometric Institute, Netherlands School of Economics, Rotterdam.

HAHN, F. H. [1970]. Savings and Uncertainty. *The Review of Economic Studies*, Vol. 37, pp. 21–24.

HAKANSSON, N. H. [1969]. Optimal Investment and Consumption Strategies under Risk, Uncertain Lifetime, and Insurance, *International Economic Review*, Vol. 10, pp. 443–466.

HAMBURGER, W. [1955]. The Relation of Consumption to Wealth and the Wage Rate. *Econometrica*, Vol. 23, pp. 1–17.

HENDERSON, J. M. and R. E. QUANDT [1958]. *Micro-Economic Theory.* New York, McGraw-Hill Book Company.

HENNIPMAN, P. [1945]. *Economisch Motief en Economisch Beginsel.* Amsterdam, Noord-Hollandsche Uitgevers Maatschappij.

HICKS, J. R. [1939[1], 1946[2]]. *Value and Capital.* Oxford, Clarendon Press.

HILTON, K. and D. H. CROSSFIELD [1970]. Short-Run Consumption Functions for the U.K., 1955–1966. Ch. 3 of *The Econometric Study of the United Kingdom*, edited by K. Hilton and D. K. Heatherfield (Conference on Short-Run Econometric Models of the U.K. Economy). London, Macmillan and Company.

HOUTHAKKER, H. S. [1959]. Education and Income, *The Review of Economics and Statistics*, Vol. 41, pp. 24–28.

HUDEC, Č. [1969]. Factors of Family Savings in a Socialist Economy. Paper contributed to the European Meeting of the Econometric Society held in Brussels.

INAGAKI, M. [1969]. Intertemporal National Optimality and Temporal Social Preferences. Institut International d'Economie Quantitative, Montreal.

INAGAKI, M. [1970]. *Optimal Growth: Finite Shifting versus Infinite Time Horizon.* Amsterdam, North-Holland Publishing Company.

JOCHEMS, D.B. [1962]. *Economische Weerberichten; Enige Empirische Onderzoekingen met Behulp van Conjunctuur-Testgegevens.* The Hague.

JONG, F.J. DE [1967]. *Dimensional Analysis for Economists.* Amsterdam, North-Holland Publishing Company.

KATONA, G. [1949]. Effect of Income Changes on the Rate of Saving. *The Review of Economics and Statistics*, Vol. 31, pp. 95–103.

KATONA, G. [1951]. *Psychological Analysis of Economic Behaviour.* New York, McGraw-Hill Book Company.

KATONA, G. [1960]. *The Powerful Consumer: Psychological Studies of the American Economy.* New York, McGraw-Hill Book Company.

KEYNES, J.M. [1936]. *The General Theory of Employment, Interest and Money.* London, MacMillan and Co.

KLEIN, L.R. [1951]. Estimating Patterns of Savings Behaviour, *Econometrica*, Vol. 19, pp. 438–454.

KLEIN, L.R. c.s. [1954]. *Contributions of Survey Methods to Economics*, by George Katona, L.R. Klein, J.B. Lansing a.o. New York, Columbia University Press.

KLEIN, L.R. and A.S. GOLDBERGER [1955]. *An Econometric Model of the United States, 1929–1952.* Amsterdam, North-Holland Publishing Company.

KLEIN, L.R. [1958]. The Friedman-Becker Illusion. *The Journal of Political Economy*, Vol. 66, pp. 539–545.

KLEIN, L.R. and J.N. MORGAN [1951]. Results of Alternative Statistical Treatment of Sample Survey Data. *Journal of the American Statistical Association*, Vol. 46, pp. 442–460.

KLEIN, L.R. and H.W. MOONEY [1953]. Negro-White Savings Differentials and the Consumption Function Problem. *Econometrica*, Vol. 21, pp. 425–456.

KOERTS, J. and A.P.J. ABRAHAMSE [1970]. The Correlation Coefficient in the General Linear Model. *European Economic Review*, Vol. 1, pp. 401–427.

KONJUNKTUR INSTITUT, SWEDEN [1959, 1963]. *Hushållens Sparande år 1957*, 2 Vols. Stockholm, Isaac Marcus Boktryckeri, A.B.

KOOPMANS, T. [1967]. Objectives, Constraints and Outcomes in Optimal Growth Models. *Econometrica*, Vol. 35, pp. 1–15.

KORTEWEG, P. [1971]. *De Monetaire Sector, het Aanbod van Geld en de Instrumenten van de Monetaire Politiek.* Leiden, Stenfert Kroese N.V.

KREININ, M.F., J.B. LANSING and J.N. MORGAN [1957]. Analysis of Life Insurance Premiums. *The Review of Economics and Statistics*, Vol. 39, pp. 46–54.

LANGE, H. and E. KAPTEIN [1958]. Prijsverwachtingen volgens Enquêtes onder Consumenten. *Statistica Neerlandica*, Vol. 12, pp. 243–253.

LEE-GRAMM, WENDY [1970]. A Model of Household Supply of Labour over the Life Cycle: the Labour Supply Decision of Married School Teachers. Paper presented at the Second World Congress of the Econometric Society, held in Cambridge, England.

LINTNER, J. [1953]. Determinants of Corporate Savings. Contribution to *Savings in the Modern Economy: a Symposium*, edited by W.W. Heller a.o. Minneapolis, University of Minneapolis Press.

LLUCH, C. [1970]. Systems of Demand Equations under Inter-Temporal Utility Maximization. Paper presented at the Second World Congress of the Econometric Society, held in Cambridge, England.

LYDALL, H.F. [1953]. *British Incomes and Savings.* Oxford Institute of Statistics Monograph no. 5.

MACK, RUTH P. [1958]. The Direction of Change in Income and the Consumption Function. *The Review of Economics and Statistics*, Vol. 40, pp. 239–258.

MAZUMDAR, H. [1959]. *Business Savings in India.* Groningen, Neth., J.B.Wolters N.V.

MENDERSHAUSEN, H. [1940]. Differences in Family Savings between Cities of Different Size and Location, Whites and Negroes. *The Review of Economic Statistics*, Vol. 22, pp. 122–135.

MODIGLIANI, F. and R. BRUMBERG [1955]. Utility Analysis and the Consumption Function: an Interpretation of Cross-Section Data. Chapter in *Post-Keynesian Economics*, edited by K.K.Kurihara, pp. 388–436. New Brunswick, N. J., U.S.A., Rutgers University Press.

MORGAN, J.N. [1954]. Analysis of Residuals from 'Normal' Regressions. Chapter 3 of *Contributions of Survey Methods to Economics*, by George Katona, L.R.Klein, L.B. Lansing a.o. New York, Columbia University Press.

NERLOVE, M. [1958]. *Distributed Lags and Demand Analysis for Agricultural and other Commodities.* National Bureau of Economic Research, Washington.

NETHERLANDS CENTRAL BUREAU OF STATISTICS, *see* CENTRAL BUREAU OF STATISTICS, NETHERLANDS.

OPHIR, T. [1961]. A Note on Samuelson's 'Exact' Consumption–Loan Model of Interest with or without the Social Contrivance of Money. *Metro-economica*, Vol. 13, pp. 32–35.

PEZEK, B.P. [1963]. Determinants of the Demand for Money. *The Review of Economics and Statistics*, Vol. 45, pp. 419–424.

PFOUTS, R.W. [1960]. Hours of Work, Savings and the Utility Function. Contribution to *Essays in Economics and Econometrics. A Volume in Honour of Harold Hotelling*, pp. 113–130. Chapel Hill, Cal., U.S.A.

PRAAG, B.M.S. VAN [1968]. *Individual Welfare Functions and Consumer Behaviour; a Theory of Rational Irrationality.* Amsterdam, North-Holland Publishing Company.

QAYUM, A. [1966]. *Numerical Models of Economic Development.* Rotterdam, Rotterdam University Press.

RADICE, E.A. [1939]. *Savings in Great-Britain; 1922–1935; an Analysis of the Causes of Variation in Savings.* Oxford, Oxford University Press.

RAMSEY, F.P. [1928]. A Mathematical Theory of Saving. *Economic Journal*, Vol. 38, pp. 543ff.

RAO, C.R. [1965]. *Linear Statistical Inference and its Applications.* New York, John Wiley and Sons, Inc.

REIK, TH. [1944]. *A Psychologist Looks at Love.* New York, Rinehart and Company, Inc.

REIK, TH. [1945]. *Psychology of Sex Relations.* New York, Rinehart and Company, Inc.

RICCI, U. [1926]. L'Offerta del Resparmio. *Giornale degli Economisti*, Vol. 66, pp. 73–101, 117–147 and Vol. 67, pp. 481–504.

SAMUELSON, P.A. [1958]. An Exact Consumption–Loan Model of Interest with or without the Social Contrivance of Money. *Journal of Political Economy*, Vol. 56, pp. 467–482.

SANDMO, A. [1970]. The Effect of Uncertainty on Savings Functions. *Review of Economic Studies*, Vol. 37, pp. 353–360.

SMITH, P.E. [1964]. Individual Income, Tax Rate Progression and the Savings Function. *The Quarterly Journal of Economics*, Vol. 78, pp. 299–306.

SOMERMEYER, W.H., J.G.M. HILHORST and J.W.W.A.WIT [1962]. A Method for Estimating Price and Income Elasticities from Time Series and its Applications to Consumers' Expenditures in the Netherlands, 1949–1959. *Statistical Studies*, issued by the Netherlands Central Bureau of Statistics, no. 13, pp. 30–53.

SOMERMEYER, W.H. [1960]. Een bijdrage tot de spaartheorie. (Dutch, with Summary in English: A Contribution to Savings Theory.) *Statistische en econometrische onderzoekingen*, issued by the Netherlands Central Bureau of Statistics, 1960, pp. 152–174.

SOMERMEYER, W.H. [1965]. Inkomensongelijkheid: een analyse van spreiding en scheefheid van inkomensverdelingen in Nederland. (Dutch, with Summary in English: Inequality of Incomes: an Analysis of Variance and Skewness of Income Distributions in the Netherlands.) *Statistische en econometrische onderzoekingen*, issued by the Netherlands Central Bureau of Statistics, no. 3.

SOMERMEYER, W.H. [1967]. An Analysis of Income Variance in the Netherlands. *Statistische Informationen*, issued by the European Economic Community, 1967, pp. 81–98.

SOMERMEYER, W.H. [1968]. On Timing and Locating Consumption and Residence, Considering Interregional Differences in Cost of Living. *Weltwirtschaftliches Archiv*, Vol.101, pp. 272–286.

SOMERMEYER, W.H. and K. VAN DE ROTTE [1969]. A Macro-Savings Function for the Netherlands, 1949–1966. Report 6912 of the Econometric Institute, Netherlands School of Economics, Rotterdam.

SPIRO, A. [1962]. Wealth and the Consumption Function. *The Journal of Political Economy*, Vol. 70, pp. 339ff.

SRINIVASSAN, T.N. and D.LEVHARI [1969]. Optimal Savings under Uncertainty. *Review of Economic Studies*, Vol. 36, pp. 153–163.

STACKELBERG, H. VON [1939]. Beitrag zur Theorie des Individuellen Sparens. *Zeitschrift für Nationalökonomie*, Vol. 9, pp. 167–200.

STAEHLE, H. [1937]. Short Period Variations in the Distribution of Incomes. *The Review of Economic Statistics*, Vol. 19, pp. 133–143.

STONE, R. [1954]. Linear Expenditure Systems and Demand Analysis: an Application to the Pattern of British Demand. *Economic Journal*, Vol. 114, pp. 511–527.

STONE, R. and D.A.ROWE [1956]. Aggregate Consumption and Investment Functions for the Household Sector, Considered in the Light of the British Experience. *National-Økonomisk Tidskrift*, Vol. 94, pp. 1–32.

STROTZ, R.H. [1957]. The Empirical Implications of a Utility Tree. *Econometrica*, Vol. 25, pp. 269–280.

SURREY, M.J.C. [1970]. Personal Income and Consumers' Expenditure. Chapter 4 in *The Econometric Study of the United Kingdom* (Proceedings of the Conference on Short-Run Econometric Models of the U.K. Economy, held in Southampton, 1969), pp. 99–109. London, Macmillan and Company.

SVENNILSON, I. [1937]. *Ekonomisk Planering*. Uppsala, Almquist and Wicksell's Boktryckeri, A.B.

TABARD, N. [1960]. L'Enquête Pilote de 1959; les relations entre le revenu, le patrimoine et l'épargne. En: L'épargne, numéro special de *Consommation*; *Annales du CREDOC*, 1960, pp. 65–81.

THEIL, H. [1961]. *Economic Forecasts and Policy*. Amsterdam, North-Holland Publishing Company.

THEIL, H. [1967]. *Economics and Information Theory*. Amsterdam, North-Holland Publishing Company.

THORE, S. [1959]. Ekonometriska metodstudier. In: *Hushållens sparande år 1955, en provundersökning*, Del II issued by KONJUNKTUR INSTITUT (Sweden). Stockholm, Almquist & Wicksell, Boktryckeri, A.B.

THORE, S. [1961]. *Household Saving and the Price Level*. Stockholm, Almquist & Wicksell, Boktryckeri, A.B.

TINBERGEN, J. [1933]. The Notions of Horizon and Expectancy in Dynamic Economics. *Econometrica*, Vol. 1, pp. 257–264.

TINBERGEN, J. [1942]. Professor Douglas' Production Functions. *Revue de l'Institut International de Statistique*, Vol. 10, pp. 37–48.

TINBERGEN, J. and B. VAN DER MEER [1938]. Verloop van het spaartegoed der spaarbanken. *De Nederlandsche Conjunctuur*, issued by the Netherlands Central Bureau of Statistics, 1938, pp. 128–140.

TOBIN, J. [1951]. Relative Income, Absolute Income and Saving. In: *Money, Trade and Economic Growth*, pp. 135–136. Cambridge, Mass., U.S.A.

UNITED NATIONS [✱✱]. *Demographic Yearbook*. New York.

VERDOORN, P.J., J.J.POST and S.S.GOSLINGA [1970]. The 1969 Re-estimation of the Annual Model (Model 69-C). Mimeographed Report of the Netherlands Central Planning Bureau, The Hague.

VON STACKELBERG, H., *see* STACKELBERG, H. VON.

WATTS, H.W. [1958]. Long-Run Income Expectations and Consumer Saving. In: *Studies in Household Economic Behaviour*, edited by Th.F.Dernburg a.o., Yale Studies in Economics, Vol. 9. New Haven, Connecticut, U.S.A., Yale University Press.

WEBER, M. [1934]. *Die protestantische Ethik und der Geist des Kapitalismus*. Tübingen, Mohr G.m.b.H.

WILKINSON, B.W. [1966]. Present Values of Lifetime Earnings for Different Occupations. *Journal of Political Economy*, Vol. 74, pp. 556–572.

WOLFF, P. DE [1939]. Consumption functions: a micro- and a macro-interpretation. *Economic Journal*, Vol. 49.

YAARI, M.E. [1964]. On the Existence of an Optimal Plan in a Continuous Time Allocation Process. *Econometrica*, Vol. 32, pp. 576–590.

YAARI, M.E. [1965]. Uncertain Lifetime, Life Insurance, and the Theory of the Consumer. *Review of Economic Studies*, Vol. 32, pp. 137–150.

AUTHOR INDEX

(fn = footnote)

SUBJECT INDEX

(Figures in italics refer to pages on which the concept is dealt with; a page number followed by *n* refers to a footnote)